Talleyrand
and his World

Talleyrand and his World

ROSALYND PFLAUM

afton press

FRONT COVER: Charles-Maurice de Talleyrand-Périgord, Prince de Bénévent, French politician and minister of foreign affairs under Napoleon and Louis XVIII, ca. 1790. Collection and Photographer: Hulton Archive. Getty Images.

FRONTISPIECE: Charles-Maurice de Talleyrand-Périgord (1754-1838). Artist: Pierre-Paul Prud'hon. Oil on canvas, 85 x 55 7/8 in. Purchase, Mrs. Charles Wrightsman, Gift in memory of Jacqueline Bouvier Kennedy Onassis, 1994. Image copyright © The Metropolitan Museum of Art / Art Resource, NY.

Copyright © 2010 by Rosalynd Pflaum
ALL RIGHTS RESERVED
First edition

No part of this book may be reproduced or transmitted in any form or by any means, electronic or mechanical, including photocopying, recording, or by any information storage and retrieval system, without permission in writing from the publisher.

Edited by Beth Williams
Designed by Mary Susan Oleson
Production assistance by Beth Williams
Printed by Pettit Network Inc., Afton, Minnesota

Library of Congress Cataloging-in-Publication Data

Pflaum, Rosalynd.
 Talleyrand and his world / by Rosalynd Pflaum.—1st ed.
     p. cm.
 Includes bibliographical references and index.
 ISBN 978-1-890434-81-6 (hardcover : alk. paper)
 1.Talleyrand-Périgord, Charles Maurice de, prince de Bénévent, 1754-1838. 2.Statesmen—France--Biography. 3.Diplomats—France--Biography. 4.France—Politics and government—1789- I. Title.
 DC255.T3P45 2010
 944.06092--dc22
 [B]
                                        2009052196

Printed in China

Patricia Condon McDonald
Publisher

Afton Press
P.O. Box 100, Afton, MN 55001
651-436-8443
aftonpress@aftonpress.com
www.aftonpress.com

To Bruce, Jason, Andrew, and Jeremy

Contents

Prologue 13

1. A Crippled Childhood 17
2. An Abbé à la Mode 47
3. The Bishop 69
4. The Deputy 91
5. The Exile 117
6. A Minister of the Directoire 147
7. A Co-Conspirator 177
8. Foreign Affairs Minister 203
9. Imperial Grand Chamberlain, 1804 229
10. Vice-Grand Elector 253
11. A Traitor or Loyal Opposition 281
12. President of the Provisional Government 305
13. L'Ambassadeur Extraordinaire 333
14. President of the First Ministry of the Second Restoration 363
15. Grand Chamberlain, 1815 387
16. Ambassador to England 411
17. Death of a Bishop 425

Bibliography 432
Quotes 435
Index 440

Illustrations

Following page 176

Louis XVI of France   i
Marie-Victoire-Eléonore de Damas d'Antigny   ii
Charles-Daniel de Périgord, the Comte de Talleyrand-Périgord   ii
Bishop Alexandre-Angélique de Talleyrand-Périgord   iii
Gabriel-Marie de Talleyrand, Comte de Périgord   iv
Adélaide de Filleul de Flahaut   v
Jacques Necker   vi
Mme de Staël, Germaine Necker   vi
Comte de Mirabeau, Honoré Gabriel de Riquetti   vii
The General Estates   viii
Storming of the Bastille   viii
Marie Antoinette in the Tuileries Palace   ix
Louis XVI says farewell to his family   x
Marie-Antoinette imprisoned in the Temple   xi
Joseph Fouché   xii
Catherine-Noël Worlée Grand de Talleyrand-Périgord   xiii
Emperor Napoleon Bonaparte   xiv
Josephine Bonaparte   xv
Napoleon's coronation   xvi

Following page 400

Château de Valençay   xvii
Princess de Courland, Duchess de Dino   xviii
Edmond de Talleyrand-Périgord   xix
Countess Marie-Thérèse Tyszkiewicz   xx
Count Charles-Robert Nesselrode   xx
Clemens-Lothar Wenzel, Chancellor Prince Metternich   xxi
Map of Central Europe in 1763   xxii
Map of Central Europe in 1812   xxiii
The Three Monarchs   xxiv
Tsar Alexander leads the Allied armies into Paris   xxv
Napoleon's abdication   xxvi
Alexander I of Russia   xxvii
Josephine Pauline de Talleyrand-Périgord   xxviii
Louis XVIII   xxix
Charles X   xxx
Louis-Philippe I   xxxi
Charles-Maurice de Talleyrand-Périgord   xxxii

Prologue

A FEW MONTHS AFTER HE WAS ORDAINED as a sub-deacon, on June 11, 1775, the festival day of the Holy Trinity, the twenty-one-year-old Charles-Maurice de Talleyrand-Périgord was present at the coronation of Louis XVI in the cathedral of Saint-Lazare in Reims, a year after the death of his grandfather, King Louis XV. The archaic religious ritual, which placed the indelible mark of legitimacy upon the French sovereign as king by divine right was always held in this cathedral and, for centuries, members of the Talleyrand-Périgord family had taken part. Today was no exception. His uncle, Monsignor Alexandre-Angélique de Talleyrand, participated prominently as coadjutor of the officiating Archbishop of Reims. And, as a singular sign of royal favor—in recognition of the fact that Charles-Maurice's father had been a *menin*, or gentleman, of Louis XVI's father, the dauphin, who died ten years before—Comte Charles-Daniel de Talleyrand-Périgord served in the coveted role of one of the four Hostages of the Holy Ampulla. According to hoary custom, this privileged quartet spent the previous night in the ancient Abbaye de Saint-Rémy, which had housed the sacred relic since the coronation of Clovis, the founder of the French monarchy in 496. Now the foursome, cloaked in cloth of gold, with great plumed black hats, their swords drawn and at the ready, escorted the golden canopy under which the Grand Prieur of the

Abbaye walked, carrying the Holy Ampulla in its elaborate case, through the tapestry-hung streets to the stirring music of drums, trumpets, and flutes.

Because Saint-Lazare was gothic, which was considered a barbaric style in the mid-eighteenth century, its famous old tapestries were used to disguise as much of the nave as possible. Its air redolent with incense, the odor of thousands of burning candles, and fresh evergreen boughs, the cavernous cathedral was already overflowing at 4:00 a.m., hours before the service began. The twenty-year-old queen, Marie-Antoinette, ablaze with jewels, was soon seated in the gallery gossiping with the Comtesse de Talleyrand, Charles-Maurice's mother, and the other brilliantly gowned ladies of her court, all adorned with the plumes that the fashion-conscious queen had lately adopted. The purple-robed bishops were in the choir, and the canyon-like nave was filled with magnificently attired dignitaries and other officers who were reconciled to standing six long hours for the privilege of attending.

At 7:30 a.m. military fanfares announced the arrival of His Majesty, preceded by the Archbishop of Reims and the constable of France, dressed in the long robe with silver lace in which, according to tradition, he had slept. Standing alone under a great baldaquin, Louis XVI followed the identical ritual, accompanied by the same interminable chanted prayers, that had been used at the coronation of Clovis. After the king lay full length on a square of violet velvet and the aged Archbishop of Reims did the same alongside, the litanies of the saints were said over them. Then the archbishop consecrated him, anointing him the required nine times with oil from the Holy Ampulla which, according to legend, had been supplied to King Clovis by a divinely dispatched dove for this purpose. Charles-Maurice's father and the other three hostages then returned the Ampulla to Saint-Rémy, and the coronation proper began. Six princes of the blood and six of the Church held the famous iron crown of Charlemagne, studded with rubies and emeralds, over Louis XVI's head. At its end, His Majesty was dressed in a great royal-blue robe and crowned. With Charlemagne's six-foot silver scepter in his right hand and Charlemagne's hand of justice in the left, he was solemnly led to the throne, high on a dais which was hung in violet velvet embossed with the fleur-de-lis, the emblem of French royalty ever since the time of Clovis. Saint-Lazare's great doors were thrown open and the populace surged in. White pigeons were released, and trumpets rang out, amid spontaneous shouts of "Long Live the King!" from the overwhelmed assembly. A *Te Deum*, followed by mass, completed the most splendid ceremony that had been seen in France for half a century. Afterwards, a long cortège, with Louis XVI at its head, crossed over a covered passageway to the archbishop's palace for the banquet tendered by the archbishop and attended by all of prominence that had come to Reims to participate, Charles-Maurice included.

This unforgettable event was the twenty-one-year-old neophyte's introduction into the great world where he was to play so prominent and prolonged a part and, if it was a moving experience for veteran courtiers, it should have been one, too, for Charles-Maurice. But the sole comment to be found about this momentous, activated medieval frieze in his voluminous, muchly reworked *Mémoires* consists of only a few lines. These are not philosophical comments such as one might expect from the man who shares with Metternich the distinction of being one of the two greatest statesmen in western Europe in the first half of the nineteenth century. Nor do they reflect his personal reactions to the religious, historic, or even political significance of this carbon-copy pageant from the distant past. Instead of the conventional wisdom such a moment might be reasonably expected to evoke, all that appears are the names of three "remarkable women" whom Charles-Maurice met that day "whose friendship never ceased to add enchantment to my life." [1]

What kind of self-portrait as a young man was the notoriously enigmatic Prince de Talleyrand-Périgord, one of the most fascinating, unscrupulous, ambitious men of all time, trying to limn for future generations? And why?

1

A Crippled Childhood

> *"I want people to talk about me for centuries, to discuss what I have been, what I thought and what I wanted."*—TALLEYRAND [1]

THE LIFE OF CHARLES-MAURICE de Talleyrand-Périgord, a "devil of a man," as Napoleon more than once referred to the controversial French statesman, is such a minefield of contradictions that anyone writing the story of his life can only point them out as part of his fascination and not attempt to explain each one. Motives are the realm of the novelist; a biographer deals in verifiable facts. To further complicate the latter's task of stripping away fantasy from the naked truth—legends and anecdotes included—Talleyrand's multi-volumed *Mémoires*, written when he was in his sixties and continuously reworked during the last twenty years of his life, are of little help. Their pages do not contain any of the expected revelations and only speak for his wonderfully selective, self-serving memory. They are at the beck and call of his repeatedly acknowledged obsession with his reputation in the eyes of future generations and must be accepted as such. So, whenever his personal account runs counter to thoroughly documented history, the latter must carry the day wherever possible. How much of the rest should be accepted at face value depends on educated assessments that make allowances for the known prejudices and predilections of the sources in question. Talleyrand also cannily instructed that his memoirs not be published until after his death—a not uncommon practice but which assured that few contemporaries might still be alive to gainsay him. And here fate lent a hand. He lived to be eighty-four and, through fortuitous circumstances, it was actually fifty-three years later, not simply his stipulated thirty, before the first volume appeared.

Despite his venality and the inconsistencies of his character, Talleyrand is a towering historical figure and one of the most fascinating men of all times. His life and career cut a wide swath across any study of France between 1780 and 1838, when he died, a time span which is all the more incredible because so many different regimes were involved. He played a significant role in every succeeding government of that entire period, a feat even more astounding because each new one was ushered in only after internal distress, bloodshed, and, generally, physical upheaval.

A bishop of the *ancien régime* and an elected member of the National Assembly at the start of the Revolution, his prominent participation in some of the most celebrated activities of that body, together with his work as the founder of the Constitutional Church, which caused the great religious schism in late-eighteenth-century France, are all telescoped into less than a page in his four-volume *Mémoires*. Someone perusing them for details concerning the Directoire, which followed the Revolutionary period in France and played a determining role in Talleyrand's entire future career, finds skimpy pickings. Fortunately, now, however, because of recent, painstaking, impartial research in contemporary documents, the true extent of Talleyrand's political complicity as foreign affairs minister and his resultant important influence in the two *coups d'état*—the *coup du 18 fructidor* and the *coup du 18 brumaire*—that accelerated Napoleon's rise to power are made abundantly clear. His relationship with the short Corsican general reads like a penny novel, ranging from his early, behind-the-scenes role that helped lead Napoleon to the imperial throne and, then, continuing on when he was Napoleon's collaborator and confidant during the early days of the empire. It ended, finally, with Talleyrand's betrayal of Napoleon and the emperor's ultimate exile almost two decades later.

Talleyrand's success in seizing and burning pertinent, incriminating parts of the all-important Tuileries archives, when the allies entered

Paris in 1814, destroyed most of the damaging written evidence therein concerning these portentous years, while his own carefully manicured work once again devotes only a scandalously few pages to them. As restorer of the former Bourbon dynasty under Louis XVIII, and His Majesty's foreign affairs minister, Talleyrand dominated the Congress of Vienna, which recreated Europe from the shards of the Napoleonic dream. A promoter of the new Orléans dynasty, he served, first, as counselor of Louis-Philippe and, finally, as peacemaker of the European crisis of 1830, which was dissipated by the London Conference that he directed.

Some historians say that Talleyrand's greatest talent lay in portraying his personal opportunism as cold, soulless calculation. In later life, he himself claimed to never have abandoned any regime until it had already abandoned itself. He argued that it was not the government that he served but always France, under whatever political form seemed to him to be wisest for the country's own good at that specific moment.

Was this man, the "Sphinx," as contemporaries came to call him and whom Germaine de Staël likened to one of those children's toys which, no matter how many times it was knocked over, always landed on its feet, a venal scoundrel, as his detractors claimed? Or was he a patriot, as he himself maintained?

Whatever else he was, Talleyrand was also Don Juan incarnate. Near the end of his long life the octogenarian, who was by then a living legend, was discussing current events with the rising political star, Adolph Thiers. The future president of the Third French Republic chided him: "Mon Prince, you are always talking to me about women. I would much prefer to talk politics."—"But what are politics, if not women?" [2] the older man retorted. Women were far more useful to him than he ever was to them. And Talleyrand did not hesitate to use them. Talleyrand might be in their arms or at their feet, but his devoted seraglio—as *tout Paris* referred, irreverently, to his discarded aristocratic mistresses who had banded together over the years through a mutual desire to be of service to their beloved "cher prince"—could reluctantly attest that Talleyrand was never in their hands.

As a young courtier, Talleyrand was presented to Louis XV in Mme du Barry's salon. He also received the visit of King Louis-Philippe on his deathbed—a signal honor for a mere mortal. Talleyrand was beloved by his intimates and his staff, and an abomination to others. He died covered with accolades, opprobrium, and slander.

In 1825, when Talleyrand had already been working on his *Mémoires* for a number of years, his reply to a remark of Metternich, the great Austrian chancellor—"I know what I owe to God and to mankind," [3]—indicates that he had begun to take seriously the obligation of a Talleyrand-Périgord for a seemly end. This, translated into the patrician code of ethics of a *grand seigneur* who had hitherto considered himself above the mores and criticism of lesser mortals, meant dying within the Church. But to do so the former Bishop d'Autun must furnish the Vatican with some plausible explanation for the several major aberrations of his life. His oft-repeated version of an unhappy, neglected childhood and subsequent forced entry into religious orders do just that.

Regrettably, although he was a prolific lifelong letter writer, the first one of Talleyrand's available for publication is dated July 16, 1782, when he was twenty-eight. So, aside from his *Mémoires*, the primary sources for his earliest years are, in general, secondhand reports of youthful reminiscences whenever, as an old man, he chose to regale friends about times past. Once they knew about his childhood, he emphasized, they would not be astonished at many things in his life. For Talleyrand to perpetuate the rumor that he had been dropped as a small youngster and his damaged foot not taken care of in time—leaving him crippled for life—helped his claim that he had been neglected in his early years.[1]

In pre-revolutionary France neither great wealth nor a distinguished career were as important as genealogy. To attain high office only two conditions need be met—the aspirant must belong to the nobility and enjoy royal favor. Judged by these standards, Talleyrand was over qualified. While some twentieth-century biographers and certain editions of the *Almanach de Gotha*, the bible of European blue bloods, may still debate the point, Talleyrand and his contemporaries, within and without France, never questioned his illustrious antecedents. As a descendant from the younger branch of the tenth century, sovereign counts of Périgord, he could boast of an extraction as old as that of the Capetians, a dynasty that preceded that of the Bourbon Louis XVI. Present-day Talleyrand-Périgords concur, claiming that this early connection was attested officially, in *lettres patentes royales* four centuries later and, again, in 1613. According to tradition, in 990 AD, when Hugues Capet, the Count of Paris and the first Capetian monarch, in a rage, angrily asked his insolent vassal, Adelbert de Périgord, "Who made you a count?" the latter haughtily retorted: "Who made you a king?" [4]—a famous reply of

---

[1] A recently discovered portrait by Carmontelle of Gabriel-Marie de Talleyrand, Comte de Périgord (1726–95), the older brother of Talleyrand's father, shows that Charles-Maurice was not the only club foot in the family. [Page 180, plate II, *Talleyrand, le Prince Immobile* by Emmanuel de Waresquiel, Librairie Arthème Fayard, 2003.]

questionable authenticity to everyone but Talleyrand. Together with a family motto blatantly declaring "Ré qué Diou"—["No king but God," i.e., "Beholden to no one but God"], the dominant trait handed down by the Périgords over the centuries was pride.

The name of Talleyrand itself supposedly derives from a distant Périgord who had been so nicknamed by his soldiers after they had seen him mow down whole rows of the enemy [taille-rang = to cut down], and most of Talleyrand's earliest ancestors were rugged feudal warriors. Later generations included two ministers of Louis XIV, the great Colbert and Chamillart, a number of distinguished prelates, and the Marquise de Montespan, who reigned over Versailles for twelve years as the favorite of Louis XIV, who sired eight of her children.

Talleyrand's father, Charles-Daniel de Périgord, the Comte de Talleyrand-Périgord, was an army officer. He was sixteen and his bride, Marie-Victoire-Eléonore de Damas d'Antigny, who was of equally distinguished Burgundian stock, was twenty-two, when they were married on January 12, 1751. Related as both were to the greatest houses in the realm, the young couple's marriage was naturally a prearranged one like that of their peers but, unlike the majority of similar unions, it was a happy one. Theirs was an exemplary *ménage* for that day of libertinage. After the nuptial service in Saint-Sulpice, the young couple moved nearby into their own apartment in the *hôtel particulier* of the groom's mother, in the aristocratic faubourg Saint-Honoré at 4, rue Garancière on the Left Bank. This mansion was empty most of the time—in earlier days fields of madder (*garance*), the source of the red dye so popular in medieval Paris, flowered here—because Madame la Marquise's duties as a *dame du palais* kept her at Versailles.

The ultimate glory for any aristocratic family in pre-revolutionary France was to be part of the royal entourage. Well before the time Louis XIV established Versailles as the permanent residence of the French monarchy, there had been Périgords in service at court. As the eldest in this ancient, blue-blooded family, which had produced generations of distinguished soldiers, Charles-Daniel had no alternative but a career in arms. To be poor like the Talleyrand-Périgords was no disaster, for an ancient, noble title was considered as more than an adequate substitute for wealth. Since Charles-Daniel lacked the wherewithal to buy his own regiment, let alone to incur the additional heavy expense of paying for his men's support—a necessity for one in his position—Charles-Daniel's future, like that of many of his impoverished peers, was entirely dependent on royal favor. This necessitated almost constant attendance at Versailles for the penniless young groom. His bride received a small stipend for her services as a lady-in-waiting in the household of the dauphine. However, their joint stipends were so inadequate that when the countess was carrying Charles-Maurice, their second son, she had to appeal to her mother for the bare necessities of her confinement. As was usual with someone of the countess's exalted rank, a responsible woman of the people was hired who moved into the rue Garancière before the infant was expected so that, immediately following its arrival, she could whisk the baby off to be cared for in her own home. In this convenient fashion—the gospel of nursing one's offspring had not yet been spread by Jean-Jacques Rousseau's *Émile*—the young mother could quickly resume her court duties as slender and effervescent as before.

Charles-Maurice was born on February 2, 1754, in his parents' Paris home. In keeping with contemporary religious customs and because of the current high infant mortality, he was christened that same afternoon at the neighboring Church of Saint-Sulpice. He was then promptly spirited off to an outlying neighborhood, which is generally thought to have been the nearby district of the faubourg Saint-Jacques.

Since patrician families in those days considered it a stigma to have malformed children, especially a son, his parents themselves may have helped perpetuate the tale that his deformity was the result of being left, at an early age, unattended on top of a commode from which he promptly fell off. Supposedly afraid she would be accused of carelessness and lose her lucrative charge, *la mère Rigaut*—as some authorities name her—said nothing. Talleyrand was doomed to life with a special shoe and a cane to help him drag around a cruel, heavy brace that has been preserved to this day—a block with a steel rod extending up the inner side of the leg to be tied with a loop below the knee to support the leg weakened by the malformed right foot. As he grew older, the foot itself atrophied until it was said to look like a horse's hoof with nails at the end resembling claws and the right leg became noticeably shorter.

For Comte de Talleyrand to have a son who was unfit to follow him into military service was a misfortune that may have resulted in a certain alienation of paternal affection for him. However, several letters from the countess to her mother, the Marquise d'Antigny, indicate that,

Talleyrand's *Mémoires* notwithstanding, she often thought about the small lad. When Talleyrand was four, his older brother, Alexander-François-Jacques, died leaving the younger one, Charles-Maurice, as the automatic future head of the family. In August of that same year, the countess advised her mother that Talleyrand was troubled with leg pains. Doctors were consulted and certain "appliances" unsuccessfully tried to improve his condition. Since she herself was also suffering—from a recent miscarriage—mother and son went to Forges-les-Eaux for a "thermal cure." There she whiled away the time for the small lad with stories of the rhinoceros she had seen at Versailles. Upon their return, she sent him off to spend the winter with his paternal great-grandmother although, she confided, "I am sorry to be so long without him." [5] But she knew that the fresh country air should be good for the delicate child, and he would also serve to keep the recently widowed, seventy-two-year-old Princess de Chalais company.

He was shipped off with Mlle Charlemagne, a trustworthy maid of her mother's, transformed into Charles-Maurice's governess to save money. The young woman proved to be an excellent substitute and he soon loved her dearly. To further economize, the pair did not travel in a *chaise de poste* as befit people of quality, but in the public Paris-Bordeaux coach, the cheapest way possible. Any discomfort this mode of transportation may have caused was more than compensated for by the excitement of the trip itself—the changing of horses at the many relay stations, the different places to stay each night, the ever-changing landscape as they got further south, and the succession of country inns. After bouncing around for seventeen days in this bare-bones conveyance, crowded with people from the lower walks of life with their packages and bundles, farm produce and an occasional rooster or rabbit, the pair were finally dropped off at the Princess de Chalais's château, some four hundred and eighty kilometers from Paris and very near the small community of Barbezieux. The exact amount of time spent here is hard to ascertain but, by Talleyrand's own account, it was the happiest of his formative years.

Talleyrand's great-grandmother's château had been rebuilt in the sixteenth century alongside the original *donjon* of an earlier day. In this region of France that was the birthplace of his father's family, the seigneurs de Chalais were still a force to reckon with. As befitting the granddaughter of Louis XIV's great Minister Colbert—who had become a princess through her second marriage—the old dowager had frequented the court of the Sun King and still maintained a way of life that had passed away elsewhere and contrasted rudely with that at la mère Rigaut's in the Paris suburbs. Here Talleyrand learned what it meant to be born a Talleyrand-Périgord. He would never forget who he was or let anyone else forget it. The manners and bearing of a *grand seigneur* that were to be his legendary trademark in Europe stem from the tremendous pride in race and in his patrician superiority that were nurtured by this time spent at Chalais surrounded by souvenirs of warriors, and distinguished churchmen and diplomats whose somber ancestral portraits crowded its walls. The old princess introduced him to the rites and traditions of the *ancien régime*, which were his by birth. She initiated him into the social graces required by his rank and demanded by the usages of the time.

The princess, in her Sunday best—a silk dress trimmed with lace, its sleeves a succession of ribbons and knots which changed with the seasons and ended in three-tiered, elaborately decorated cuffs—with an elaborate headdress tied underneath the chin, was regularly accompanied to the parish church each Sabbath by several of the noblemen from roundabouts. Being of inferior rank, they constituted her court, and the one who had the distinction of being a distant relation was singled out to carry the red velvet bag trimmed with gold tassels, which contained her missals. To remind those present that Mme de Chalais was no longer the only Talleyrand-Périgord in attendance, a little chair was drawn up alongside her *prie-dieu* for the frail child with the Périgords' delicately molded features—and a slightly turned up nose like one of Molière's insolent valets.

All the estate's sick that had come to request help were awaiting them outside the door of the château's apothecary when they returned. On its spotlessly clean shelves, alongside elixirs, syrups, and other medicaments were large jars emblazoned with the family's coat of arms. These were continuously being replenished from great tubs of various unguents and potions, carefully mixed, according to hoary Chalais recipes, once a year, by the village surgeon and the local priest. Here, in the "healing room," Talleyrand was once again at the princess's side, observing silently as the *grande dame*, sitting ramrod straight in a red velvet armchair before an old black lacquered table, regally distributed the weekly allotment of drugs.

By right of seniority, her oldest chambermaid was in charge at the door, summoning the patients in, singly. Two Sisters of Mercy interrogated each one and prescribed as they saw fit. Mme de Chalais pointed out the location of the remedy sought after and one of the gentlemen who were all still in attendance fetched it. Another brought a drawer from one of the armoires, which were along the walls and held a large supply of lint and rolls of fine old linen of different widths. Since it was time for her great-grandson to begin to learn his responsibilities toward lesser mortals, it was Talleyrand's job to remove the linen and hand it to the princess. She herself cut the bands and compresses that were needed. In addition, the tenant was also given some herbs to make a tisane, some wine, perhaps some medicinal drugs as well, but what was most welcome of all was the obvious interest the princess graciously took in the sufferings of such humble folk, as evinced by her kindly words of concern.

In retrospect, the time spent at Chalais would appear as the one bright spot in Talleyrand's early years. He remembered his great-grandmother with much warmth and affection and always "called her 'Grand'mère' . . . because I think this made me feel closer to her." [6] According to his *Mémoires*—which ignore contemporary family correspondence to the contrary—it was not his mother but Mme de Chalais who was the first woman in the family to show him what he interpreted as any signs of affection. He left her dissolved in tears.

Exactly how long Talleyrand stayed in Périgord is not clear. A letter of Mlle Charlemagne places her back in Paris by September 1, 1760, and she would never have left without her charge. On the other hand, Talleyrand speaks of returning at the age of eight—that is, in 1762. So there is approximately a two-year gap in the story of his early youth. For what he later termed "imperious reasons," neither parent was there to greet him when he descended from the Bordeaux coach.

Shortly after Talleyrand had gone to Chalais, his father, Comte de Talleyrand, either because of his own merits or because of the Versailles intrigues at which the countess had become an expert, was named one of the six *menin*, or gentlemen, attached to the thirty-year-old dauphin Louis, the son of Louis XV. This prestigious new appointment removed the count from further active military service but kept him in constant attendance on the heir to the throne. The count's new responsibilities, coupled with his wife's present obligations as lady-in-waiting to the dauphine, Marie-Josephe de Saxe, chained the pair even more tightly to Versailles, with only minimal shifts off duty. While such an arrangement was fine for the happily married pair, it made any family life virtually impossible for their offspring. On the other hand, it would have been unusual for the Talleyrands, and others in their milieu, to occupy themselves unduly over their children, let alone worry whether they met their returning, long-absent son or not—provided they sent someone to meet him. Furthermore, when Talleyrand was finally due to return, the countess, who was once again pregnant and anxious to have a normal baby, was not in good health.

Still, it is not hard to believe Talleyrand's bitter disappointment to find only an old family retainer awaiting him as he scrambled down from the coach at the station on the rue d'Enfer. What a cold reception, after the excited anticipation of a homecoming during the long, tiring journey north! And, by the time he wrote his *Mémoires* and complained about his neglected early years, he was addressing a sympathetic audience. They were not only conditioned by the upset wrought by the Revolution in the customs and mores of their class but, perhaps, even more so by Jean-Jacques Rousseau's iconoclastic theories about the upbringing of one's offspring and the need to show them tenderness. Such conduct would have been considered unseemly to an earlier generation and would have indicated a lack of manliness on the father's part.

The elderly footman immediately shuffled Talleyrand off to the Collège d'Harcourt. This year had just seen a great victory for secular education—and one that also strengthened Harcourt—when the *Parlement* was clamping down on the Jesuits and forbade them to continue teaching the young. Located near the Sorbonne, on the rue de la Harpe, one of the main thoroughfares on the Left Bank, it was one of the most distinguished and oldest elementary schools in Paris. Founded at the end of the thirteenth century, Harcourt was where most of the aristocracy sent their sons to receive their basic education and other prerequisite distinctions. Later rebuilt as the Lycée Saint-Louis, the school is still going strong today. Its inexpensive tuition was another attraction. In addition, Talleyrand's maternal uncle had spent eight long years here, while his own mother attended a similar boarding school for girls for an equally long stay.

Talleyrand arrived while the students were in the large refectory eating their midday meal. He was to share with his cousin, Chamillart de la Suze, an apartment and a private tutor, l'Abbé Hardi, who was instructed to take him to his family on the rue Garancière once a week, whenever they were in residence. Each time his father was present the count bade him farewell, afterwards, with the same admonition: "Do as the abbé tells you, my son." [7]

There is evidence from her correspondence that the Comtesse de Talleyrand paid more attention to her son—and followed his progress more closely—than it suited Talleyrand to later admit. When he came down with some sort of inflammation of the lungs and spent the summer with his cousins at the Château de la Suze in Maine, southwest of Paris, apparently his parents were there at least part of the time. And if Talleyrand complained more than once, later, that he had never spent a single week under the parental roof, he was in reality being raised little differently from most of his family and friends.

When he was eleven he got smallpox, one of the most dreaded and fatal diseases of the day that was felling people by the thousands. As a precautionary measure for the rest of the students, M. Lehoc, the Harcourt doctor, wisely and promptly quarantined him. Notified at once, Talleyrand's parents sent two servants with a sedan chair to take him to the nearby rue Saint-Jacques to the clinic of Mme Lerond, the nurse employed by the school. In keeping with contemporary treatment, which seemed designed more to prevent the spread of the malady than to help its suffering victim, he was kept in a small bed surrounded by double curtains. The windows of his room were closed tight and sealed so no air could go out—or come in. A blazing fire burned continuously on the hearth, and his high fever was stoked even higher with non-stop hot drinks. Although it suited Talleyrand to continue his gloomy family portrayal and accuse the Talleyrands of indifference toward their sick child, it would have been sheer folly to bring him home where there were now two small children—Archambaud and another little brother, Boson. However Talleyrand chose to categorize Mme Lerond's care, he recovered without any disfiguring pockmarks, unlike Mirabeau, Danton, Robespierre, and other future revolutionary notables.

As in most schools of the day, there was no mollycoddling of these young aristocrats. Punishment followed the crime, and Talleyrand had his share. Due for an accounting for some unacknowledged misdemeanor, "My pride as a nobleman revolted at such an indignity. I escaped from the college and I hoped that the intervention of my father would spare me this humiliation but on the contrary. He said, 'Monsieur, mon fils, one of our ancestors, Henri de Talleyrand, Comte de Chalais, became the favorite of Louis XIII because the king remembered that in his youth your ancestor had allowed himself to be whipped in his place'" [8]

Looking back at his years at Harcourt, Talleyrand's dominant recollection was one of unhappiness, coupled with a feeling of isolation and rejection. Although, as a cripple who could not move without some sort of cane or crutch and, therefore, was unable to participate in most of the rough-and-tumble play of his comrades, a number of them became his friends for life. But children can be cruel and thus set apart as different than the others, Talleyrand must have often suffered at their hands. In all likelihood it was in this school of hard knocks that he first learned the value of impassiveness—the need and ability to hide his emotions. This capacity, together with his inordinate pride as a Talleyrand-Périgord, which had been nurtured during his stay with his great-grandmother and made him so assured of his superiority, were two of his most salient traits throughout a long life. Both had their roots in these formative years.

Something else occurred during this period that was to have an even more crucial effect on his entire life. In the great French families of the *ancien régime*, only two careers were deemed desirable—in the army or in the Church, with the heir apparent usually slated for the former. Since the crippled Talleyrand was unable to so serve, the latter beckoned. But in the Church, vowed to eternal chastity, he would be unable to marry and fulfill his obligation as the head of the family to perpetuate the Talleyrand-Périgords. Fortunately, from the count and countess's point of view, there were now Archambaud and Boson, and the grave decision was taken to transfer Charles-Maurice's birthrights, with all that primogeniture entailed, to Archambaud. From a contemporary point of view this was the normal thing to do under the circumstances. Family feeling was strong but concerned the interests of the whole as a unit, not from the point of view of any particular one. An individual member, should the need arise, was expected to make sacrifices for the good of the rest—which, in this instance, meant to maintain and, if possible, augment the Talleyrand-Périgord wealth and honors. The notion that such an immolation on the altar of family constituted a grave injustice to their eldest child was a completely foreign concept. While many of the great bishops of the late eighteenth century assumed orders for lack of a better alternative as aristocrats, this did not prevent them from becoming outstanding prelates. Since it was normal for a family like theirs to decide their son's future, all that remained was to show Charles-Maurice the advantages that would be his as a Talleyrand-Périgord in the service of God. Exactly when Charles-Maurice learned what had been resolved is hard to determine.

In 1769—the same year Bonaparte was born at Ajaccio—Charles-Maurice's classes at Harcourt were finished. So the family sent him off on an extended visit with his father's brother, Monseigneur

Alexandre-Angélique de Talleyrand-Périgord, coadjutor and designated successor of the Archbishop of Reims, the number one ecclesiastic of France, whose see was accordingly the wealthiest and most prestigious in the country. His uncle was to orient him towards a career in the Church, and Charles-Maurice would experience at firsthand, amid the pomp and splendor of the Episcopal residence, what a glorious destiny was possible for a Talleyrand-Périgord in the service of God. Judging it unseemly for a close relative of the illustrious monseigneur to arrive by the public stagecoach, the protocol-conscious count and countess sent him directly from Harcourt in a *chaise de poste*, which made the trip in two days. Since Charles-Maurice admitted receiving a shock when he was asked to don a cassock upon arrival, it was probably not until now that he fully realized what his family had in mind for him.

The time Charles-Maurice spent with his uncle was divided between the archbishop's palace at Reims and at the nearby Benedictine Abbaye de Hautvilliers, 23 kilometers away. Here Monseigneur Alexandre-Angélique, the abbaye's titular head, often received Charles-Maurice's parents, and it would be nice to think that they continued to come now especially to see how well their son was adjusting to their plans for him. His mother writes in particular of a visit there with Charles-Maurice in August, en route to her tour of service at the court, which was then in residence at Compiègne.

Like more than one prince of the Church, the seventy-year-old Archbishop of Reims lived in a style that outshone that of many a prince of the blood. He denied himself nothing, not even a mistress—his beautiful young niece. And his time was spent, not in meditation and prayer or overseeing the vast responsibilities connected with the most important see in France, but shuttling between his different residences in a coach-and-eight with outriders, guards, and a numerous liveried retinue, hunting and arranging fêtes, concerts and plays to entertain his various guests.

When the coadjutor realized his nephew's lack of enthusiasm for an ecclesiastical career despite his exposure to these quasi-royal trappings, the monseigneur, to nurture his ambition, had Charles-Maurice read the biographies and memoirs of celebrated churchmen like Cardinals de Retz and Richelieu, who numbered among France's greatest statesmen. While his mother was far too religious to have forced her son into the Church had he categorically declined to do so, the count and countess were confident that he would end by accepting their decision. Like other noblemen's sons of lesser rank than a Talleyrand-Périgord, he could aspire to the Faculty of Law or to one of the many charges at court available for the aristocracy. But their benefits were nominal, the financial rewards negligible, and advancement slow. Talleyrand had already experienced the constraints of his parents' pinched finances and the vast discrepancy between their rank and their fortune. Only in the Church, where he was assured of powerful backing as the nephew of the coadjutor of Reims and as the son of the Comte and Comtesse de Talleyrand, who each held influential court positions, would he quickly have a lucrative post and a chance for rapid advancement. And it is questionable whether, at sixteen, such a career, pregnant with possibilities, was as repugnant to Talleyrand as he made out when, almost seventy years later, he so wrote the pope shortly before his death. More important, it was unthinkable for a Talleyrand-Périgord to say "No" to his father. To rebel would be unworthy of him. Charles-Maurice's situation as the oldest son, deprived of his birthright for something he had no control over, and its corollary, his reluctant entry into the Church, had a critical bearing on his entire life.

After spending almost a year in the gilded atmosphere at Reims—which he would later term "a year of exile"—Talleyrand obediently entered the seminary of Saint-Sulpice. Shortly afterwards on May 3, 1770, the countess wrote her mother: "My oldest son seems very happy, which pleases me." [9] At the end of the month, he was present, together with other black-cassocked seminarians, at the great festival and fireworks proffered by the city of Paris to celebrate the marriage of the dauphin and Marie-Louise in the Place Louis XV—today's Place de la Concorde. Such pains had been taken to assure the gala event's perfection that gallons of essence of bergamot had been poured on the Seine side of the Place itself lest the normally offensive odor there affect adversely the Austrian bride's delicate nose. While his fellow students were predominantly from the aristocracy, not everyone automatically entered the clergy when they finished, and the nine years of study required before being ordained a priest allowed Talleyrand ample time to change his mind.

The somber dull brown pile comprising the great quadrangular compound of the theological seminary of the archdiocese of Paris, which was even closer to his home than the Collège d'Harcourt, was only separated by a narrow open court from the imposing church of the same name, whose still unfinished towers loomed starkly overhead. Founded in the mid-sixteenth century, it consisted of some three hundred young men, housed in four separate units, connected by courts and gardens. The most important of these, where Talleyrand was naturally placed, was the Grand Seminary of Saint-Sulpice, also known as the "seminary of bishops." This was because so many of the scions of the great families of France who were enrolled here attained the purple. Constructed with suitable refinement for such an illustrious group, an entire forest had been purchased so that its paneled wainscots would be faultless and all match. The famed painter Charles Lebrun decorated its chapel ceiling with a magnificent *Adoration of the Virgin* and, over the altar, the *Descent of the Holy Ghost*.

Like his classmates', Talleyrand's day started at 5:00 a.m. and, after prayers and study, he went on foot with the group, three by three, to the nearby Sorbonne for theological studies. Most spare time, especially the hours when the others were involved in those recreational activities in which as a cripple he was unable to participate, were spent alone in the seminary's fine library, started by Cardinal Fleury. Taciturn and withdrawn, bitter that because he was handicapped he had had to yield his rights of primogeniture, Talleyrand read avidly and widely. He acquired an enormous storehouse of varied information that had little bearing on an ecclesiastical career but nourished his consuming ambition.

Life at Saint-Sulpice was without constraint. Seminarians were free to come and go as they wished and, with the passing of time, Talleyrand began to look elsewhere for distraction. The upper class's sole occupation was to enjoy itself. Duties and responsibilities were non-existent, and anything was permitted, provided it was veneered with the saving grace of elegance. Shedding his black cassock and nattily attired in short culottes and a small black silk coat, he was soon indulging in the number one pastime of the *ancien régime*, frequenting until the early hours the several public gambling establishments where it was acceptable to be seen. Or else he might visit the one or two fashionable homes where only the favorite game of the hostess was played—for high stakes—and a professional croupier was hired to preside over the tables. Talleyrand played every sort of game including faro and the Italian import, biri-biri and, as he got older, there was always at least one elaborately inlaid backgammon table permanently set up in a corner of his own salon. But his all-time favorite was whist, which had been imported from England in the reign of Louis XV and created a sensation in the salon of the king's mistress, Mme du Barry, where Talleyrand was first introduced to it.

There are numerous stories about Talleyrand's purported affairs with various women while still at Saint-Sulpice. The only authenticated one, which he himself details in his *Mémoires* involves, though not by name, Dorothée Dorinville, seven years his senior. Known as Dorothée Luzy, she was a popular soubrette at the Comédie-Française, which was already one of the three best theaters in the capital. Struck by her pretty face, one day, during the services in the chapel of Saint-Sulpice, he started attending more often, but he could not muster sufficient courage to speak to her. As relaxed as morals were during that period, even a Talleyrand-Périgord in a seminarian's cassock did not approach a strange young lady in a church without some pretext. A sudden shower unexpectedly came to his rescue as the two walked down the church's broad front steps afterwards. Talleyrand found the courage to offer Dorothée the shelter of his umbrella. Limping along beside her both their faces splashed with the wind-driven rain, he saw the young woman home, and she invited him in.

Most authorities place their meeting in 1772, a year after Dorothée had one of her greatest triumphs, as a substitute Aménaïde. She was pinch-hitting in Voltaire's *Tancrède*, opposite the playwright's favorite interpreter, the great actor Lekain. She lived very close by at 6, rue Férou, a little street that started at the end of the open court of Saint-Sulpice and which Talleyrand could see from the window of his seminarist's cubicle. Here Dorothée had a small upstairs apartment because it was within easy walking distance of the hall where the Comédie-Française was then playing. What Talleyrand fails to mention is that it was provided by her protector, M. Landry, a receiver-general of finances who had already sired the first of their several children—an offspring presumably already farmed out elsewhere. In short, this early idyll was hardly what Talleyrand chose to portray as a pastoral romance rather than a typical eighteenth century vignette of a gallant abbé and a comedienne.

Their ensuing liaison made his remaining years at the seminary bearable. With a total disregard for what anyone might say—a lifelong characteristic of Talleyrand's—they were always seen together everywhere in the neighborhood, so their affair could hardly have been a secret to seminary authorities. It only ended with Talleyrand's departure from Saint-Sulpice, and he would still speak of her with affection a half a century later. Under the influence of Dorothée, his melancholy yielded to a sprightly good humor and he blossomed into an accomplished young blade.

A scant two weeks after the death of Louis XV, Talleyrand was consecrated, on May 28, 1774, a *portier, lecteur, exorciste et acolyte* (gatekeeper, reader, exorcist and assistant)—the four minor orders which constituted the first rung of the French Catholic church's hierarchy. That September, after two years studying philosophy and almost three, theology, Talleyrand got the first of many special dispensations—this time because he was younger than was customary—and was allowed to present to the Sorbonne's Faculty of Theology his thesis for the degree of Bachelor of Sacred Theology. Written in Latin, of course, it was dedicated to the Holy Virgin and had as its theme: "Of what science are a priest's lips the guardians?"

In January of the following year, his uncle, the monseigneur, who was closely monitoring his nephew's progress, had Talleyrand, technically attached though he was to the diocese of Paris, nominated as chaplain in a parochial church in his own diocese of Reims. As with other benefices Talleyrand was to acquire, the apparent purpose of this appointment, a surprising one for anyone so young, was to confer income, his first. The post itself did not impose a single duty and any actual administrative work entailed was left to subordinates.

Shortly afterwards and just before his twenty-first birthday, for unknown reasons Talleyrand left the seminary of Saint-Sulpice. His departure ahead of schedule, with his remaining ecclesiastical studies at the Sorbonne not yet completed, was managed so discreetly that even today no one knows for sure exactly what brought matters to a head. But a remark of Talleyrand's some years later to one of the head Sulpiciens indicates he was asked to leave. His superior-general, M. Bourachot, had been unwilling, up until now, to discipline the offender, who was not only the nephew of the powerful coadjutor of Reims but, as a Talleyrand-Périgord, a potential high prelate himself, and had shut his eyes to any extracurricular activities. Talleyrand was not the first seminarian to have a mistress and even a large number of bishops and archbishops were guilty on the same score. A forced early departure from the seminary, however, would also explain why he was not with the rest of his class when they were invested at Saint-Sulpice. Instead, a special dispensation was again obtained, this time for "Carolus-Mauricius" to be ordained sooner than was customary.

The night before he took this decisive step into the Church, one of his *confrères* claimed to hear Talleyrand snarl: "They are forcing me to be a priest.... They'll be sorry." [10] He may still have been unreconciled with his fate but he had apparently accepted it. Reputed snatches of words, no matter how many times they are repeated down through the years, are no match for the cold statistics of dispensations frequently sought—and always granted—that bespeak Talleyrand's realistic acknowledgment of his situation. In solitary splendor, on Saturday, April 1, 1775, with the Bishop de Lomez presiding in the chapel of Saint-Nicolas-du-Chardonnet, a tonsured Talleyrand, clad in a long white alb, took the vows required by canon law, which bound him forever to God's service and to the virtues of chastity and obedience. He had already learned on the sidelines of the Harcourt playing field not to reveal his emotions, and his face was equally expressionless today as he was ordained a subdeacon, the first of the major orders in the Catholic church. For whatever reasons not a member of his family was present.

As a testimonial to his uncle, Monseigneur Alexandre-Angélique's benevolent prescience, Talleyrand, because he was now a subdeacon as well as a chaplain in a Reims church, qualified some two months later, for the much sought after privilege of attending, as a member of the clergy, the coronation of Louis XVI, who was his exact contemporary. For over a thousand years French sovereigns had been anointed in the cathedral at Reims in a religious spectacle that consecrated their rule by divine right, and Talleyrand's presence there on June 11, was at his father's specific bidding. Presumably the count was anxious for his oldest son to witness his distinguished family in action. Father and uncle both had featured roles in the day's pageant and hoped to further stimulate Talleyrand's ambition for the lofty future they envisaged for him.

The following morning Talleyrand participated in the "Laying-on-of-Hands" ceremony when Louis XVI, preceded by trumpets and followed by a cortège of mounted noblemen, came on his horse Vainqueur to the venerable Abbey de Saint-Rémy. Here in the park some two thousand poor souls afflicted with scrofula had gathered from every part of the kingdom in hopes of a miraculous cure from His Majesty, newly anointed by God's will. Surrounded by doctors and surgeons, and followed by the clergy—and Talleyrand—Louis XVI went the rounds, touching the sores of each one while pronouncing the traditional formula "God will cure you, the king is touching you." The Prince de Beauvau followed at his heels, repeating each time, "May God heal you, the king touches you." This and various other archaic ceremonies, which lasted five days, constituted Talleyrand's introduction into the great world where he was to play so prominent and prolonged a part.

The coronation forced the postponement until July 3 of the meeting of the General Assembly of the Clergy, which was traditionally held in May, every five years. The conclave's character was essentially financial, mainly to negotiate for the ensuing quinquennium the Church's so-called contribution—its taxes—to the king and also to allocate its own funds internally for the same period. The clerical contribution assumed greater importance than ever this year because France was getting ready to help the American War for Independence. France was willing to aid the colonists—George Washington was appointed their commander-in-chief that June 15—primarily because she wanted to see her old enemy England, on whom France herself was not yet ready to declare war, defeated. Since Monseigneur Alexandre-Angélique was automatically one of Reims's four allotted members, it was not hard to assure that another of the quartet should be Talleyrand who was now sufficiently accredited to attend.

Following the opening meeting in the abbatical palace of the Abbey of Saint-Germain-de-Pré in Paris, at which Alexandre-Angélique co-presided, the deputies reassembled in their usual place, at the convent of the Grands Augustins on the quai of the Seine, to elect officials for the forth-coming sessions. Here, again, nepotism played a role and Talleyrand was named as one of the two promoters. This was a delicate post, more administrative than religious, which was usually held by a full-fledged priest. It afforded the twenty-one-year-old abbé the opportunity to initiate himself in the affairs of the clergy, the most powerful body in the state. He was also appointed to one of the assembly's main committees. Indeed, in view of his uncle's continuous, behind-the-scenes efforts to make Talleyrand's entry into orders more palatable, it is hard to believe that had this career been as distasteful to the young man as he later wanted people to believe, and had he so confided to the monseigneur, the latter might not have helped him break the traditional pattern and do something else.

No business school could have served as a better initiation into the practical world of affairs than this stint as promoter. Perhaps because he had found something he really enjoyed doing, Talleyrand did an outstanding job. Since the role of promoter traditionally acted as a trial run for the key post of general agent for the interim period to follow the next quinquennial meeting—that is from 1780 to 1785—he was now virtually assured of this office, which was so coveted because it guaranteed a swift rise to a bishopric. There were only two promoters, selected by a complicated rotating system and named far in advance, but each must be an ordained priest—a requirement Talleyrand had ample intervening time to fulfill.

In September, Louis XVI conferred on him, earlier in his ecclesiastical career than was customary, a magnificent benefice, the venerable Abbaye de Saint-Denis in Reims. Not only did the abbey's substantial revenue assure him of a handsome yearly income—roughly four hundred and fifty francs in 1988—but, because of an immediate subsequent royal dispensation, no obligations of any sort were entailed. Talleyrand did not even have to live in the diocese of Reims. If etiquette so permitted, he would have had the opportunity to thank His Majesty personally when, three days before the assembly disbanded, Talleyrand and the other sixty delegates were ushered into the king's chamber at Versailles and presented to him individually. It is not known if this was Talleyrand's first presentation at court.

He received a good classical education and an unparalleled command of written and spoken French by the time he left Saint-Sulpice, but not even a Talleyrand-Périgord could advance further in the Church— and, hopefully, become a bishop—without first attaining the priesthood. This necessitated four more years of prescribed classes at the Sorbonne, including a mandatory second degree in theology, a two-year course available only for deacons. But Talleyrand was a young man in a hurry and since he was still a mere subdeacon, another special authorization waived any such requirements—as so often in the past. Unfortunately, there were no shortcuts to the long, tedious hours of study this class entailed in the Sorbonne's amazing sixty-thousand-volume theological library. Leaning on his cane and dragging slightly his right leg, Talleyrand daily crisscrossed the great inner court there, passing the somber chapel that Richelieu had built to house his tomb. As he hurried past, he had ample time to meditate on ways to emulate the great seventeenth century cardinal, the builder of a unified France. A career in the Church did not close the door to a career in statecraft or politics. There had already been several great French statesmen who started out as men of the cloth, and Talleyrand would later claim that his own education for the clergy was the best one possible for a future diplomat.

Talleyrand intended to enjoy life to the fullest and, in later years, he repeatedly remarked: "Anyone who has not lived in the years prior to

1789 cannot appreciate the sweetness of living." [11] It was accepted in that day for the clergy, especially those of the lower orders who, like Talleyrand, were addressed as "Monsieur l'abbé," to lead a frivolous and even gallant life, and he had no intention of letting his ecclesiastical vows hinder his pursuit of pleasure, especially now that he had an independent income. But first, interestingly enough, he paid off what his impecunious family still owed his tutors and the Collège d'Harcourt for his education, an illuminating expenditure which, like his passion for gambling, unconsciously emphasized why money—and what money could buy—would always be so essential for him. He had no intention of ever being what he termed "a poor devil."

Next, Talleyrand set up housekeeping in fitting style not far from the neighborhood of Saint-Sulpice. At 123, rue Saint-Dominique he rented from the nuns of Bellechasse an apartment on the top two floors of the small, three-story pavilion, flush on the street, which formed the entrance to their extensive convent enclave. The predominant sound was that of the steeple bells of the many similar religious establishments thereabouts. Most of the habitations of this sparsely populated district were *hôtels particuliers*, the private mansions of the *ancien régime* in which several generations of the same family lived, and Talleyrand's parents, brothers, and paternal grandmother had preceded him to number 63, a little further down on the same street. This Hôtel de Guerchy, like its prototypes, was a large residence sandwiched in between gardens on one side and, on the other, a great inner court. Leading off the latter were individual entrances to their personal apartments, and the whole was protected by high walls and a gatekeeper's lodge from the street proper.

It was a small but comfortable abode at number 123 furnished with the elegant good taste that would be Talleyrand's trademark and, like all his future establishments, smelt of ambergris, which he always kept burning somewhere. He ordered a porcelain table service with his family coat of arms—a red shield with three armed golden lions, tongued and crowned with azure blue—and, already a dedicated bibliophile, he immediately started to build a library. Shortly after he moved in his maternal grandmother, the Marquise d'Antigny, sent him several cases of wine to start a cellar. "If they're any good," wrote a family retainer, acknowledging their receipt, "they won't last long. M. l'Abbé is very generous and will want to treat all his friends." [12] These included Auguste de Choiseul-Gouffier from his Harcourt days—"the man I loved the most"—and the Comte de Narbonne. He was the godson of Louis XV's two old-maid daughters, who was reputed to be either the natural son of one of them or else, of Louis XV himself, a mysterious parentage that made him even more attractive to the opposite sex. Referred to as "the Triumvirate" by Marie-Antoinette, the three noble friends cut a wide swath through Paris's most scented boudoirs, sharing mistresses, including mothers and daughters, singers, dancers, and Comédie-Française stars, indiscriminately. Talleyrand's metamorphosis from a melancholy theological student to a man-about-town was complete.

As Talleyrand's interests broadened, anyone distinguished by birth or talent was equally welcome around 11:00 a.m. daily at Bellechasse for lively conversation over what Talleyrand himself termed a *repas tel quel*—an "indifferent meal." These meals consisted of cold meats, some sort of eggs, wine, and hot chocolate, a popular luxury imported from Spain. The small group was a heterogeneous mix, each one lured by the brilliance as well as the seriousness of the talk. The wide range of matters brought up ranged from the arts and letters to raucous tales of last night's gallantries, as well as to more serious matters overseas—the American Revolution and the recent Declaration of Independence there—and, at home, the treasury crisis and progressive politics. Filled with boundless hope, the guests were keenly aware that vast changes were in the air and that the future would differ greatly from the past.

Versailles had ceased to be the center of the universe as it had been under Louis XIV. It was no longer an isolated, self-contained community where art, fashion, and government were determined. The prestige that Louis XV had lost, Louis XVI would never recover. By now the aristocratic society of the *ancien régime* that constituted the ruling class and, to a large degree, those who held the responsible positions in government, was no longer a rigid entity, determined by birth alone. Genius and talent were recognized as on a par with blue blood and wealth, and to be admitted to one of the leading, contemporary Paris salons was as much sought after as had been admission to the court earlier.

Here, unlike in England, the sexes were mixed, and the hostesses of the more avant-garde drawing rooms had few snobbish prejudices, stirring together the most discordant elements. Poorly clad savants as well as men of letters mingled freely with red-heeled, bewigged aristocrats and a smattering of tonsured abbés with proper heraldic quarterings and frequently deplorable morals. France was at the pinnacle of the

Age of Enlightenment. Reason was king and freedom of thought and expression was the fashion of the moment, with no holds barred. This was the day of the *philosophes*, the freethinkers who were condemned by the Church and execrated by all respectable Christians, and the *encyclopédistes*, who had worked on Diderot and d'Alembert's vast encyclopedia—published between 1751 and 1772 and inspired by Chambers's similar English work—which had updated the progress of science and thought in all the disciplines. No subject was henceforth too sacred for feverish discussion; prejudice, convention, and tradition were all fair game. Elegant badinage was to be heard pro and con the issues of the day. When one talked about literature or philosophy, it was frequently not to be judicious or profound but to banter gloriously, to find the finest of the fine shades of meanings and to express the most exquisite refinements of what was considered good taste. As Talleyrand himself expressed it: "There are three kinds of knowledge: *le savoir*—knowledge itself; *le savoir vivre*—to know how to live (good breeding); and *le savoir faire*—to know what to do. And possession of the last two dispenses with any need for the first!" [13] In these exalted spheres word was never bruited about the bad harvests, one in '74, the epidemic of cattle murrain; and one in '75, the flour war and other disagreeable subjects. And the fad of the moment was to have different literary highlights read from their latest work or else to showcase—with a musicale featuring prominent musicians or singers from the opera—which side the hostess espoused in the bitter dispute between the partisans of the Italian composer, Niccolò Piccinni; and the German, Christoph Willibald Gluck, Marie-Antoinette's protégé.

His matchless pedigree automatically opened doors for the elegant Abbé de Périgord, supplying varied contacts that gave him a self-confidence and a maturity well beyond his years and a more worldly air than might be expected. His manner was distinction itself, the product of the finest breeding. In those places where such niceties alone did not suffice, his reputation as a man of wit and spirit—someone who could speak solemnly about nothing and superficially about weighty matters—was soon so widespread that Mme du Deffand demanded an introduction. Acceptance by this acknowledged oracle of the wittiest circles in the capital amounted to an open sesame to the most important Paris salons. Brought to her home, alongside the convent of Saint-Joseph, by a mutual friend one evening around 9:00 p.m., the conventional hour, Talleyrand described his presentation as one of the most emotional moments of his entire life. The blind woman, her head encased in a frilly bonnet which she always affected, even indoors—as did most women of quality—was sitting in a high-backed armchair, surrounded by a select circle of her chosen friends. After the footman announced him, the tall, good-looking young abbé, whose long golden hair made him conspicuous amid the powdered, bewigged guests, limped gracefully forward, his metal brace and obligatory cane transformed into an elegant accoutrement, tapping a characteristic obbligato on the parquet that people would always associate with him. Rather than move with a disgraceful hobble, Talleyrand, ever the *grand seigneur*, had by strenuous effort mastered a sort of undulating glide which added to his overall appearance the essence of distinction.

He had been forewarned that Mme du Deffand always ran her hands over the face of each newcomer to get some idea of his appearance and must have remembered how horrified she had been at Edward Gibbons's initial visit. The English historian's cheeks were so fat that Mme du Deffand had thought he was making fun of her and had turned his bare buttocks around for her inspection. After delicately tracing Talleyrand's slightly upturned nose and fingering his fine lawn neckwear—he rarely wore his full ecclesiastical garb when out in the world—his hostess commanded "Come, young man," and indicated the low stool beside her chair, which was reserved for whomever she wished to honor with a private conversation. Several of his *bon mots*—some impertinent and malicious, others profound, but always with a mixture of common sense and mockery—had already reached her ears, and she was anxious to pass judgment for herself. By his elegance of expression and his witty, lively conversation, which ranged easily over an extensive array of subjects, Talleyrand was quickly termed a kindred spirit and a worthy acquisition for her select circle.

In 1776, the young abbé resigned as chaplain in the Reims church, possibly because this post, which had made him eligible to serve in the General Assembly the preceding year, had now outlived its usefulness. Nevertheless, he spent considerable time in the environs of the cathedral city that fall at Saint-Thierry in his uncle's recently completed 130-room château on the site of the original abbey, while his mother was also in residence. Talleyrand as well as other members of his family would enjoy many subsequent vacations here, but whether all together at the same time is hard to determine. What is known, however, is that the following year, when his parents moved once more, this time to the rue Grenelle, they were still near him. As before, his parents and each of his two brothers had a special apartment in the same hotel, as did Monseigneur Alexandre-Angélique, who was helping out with the rent and desired an unofficial Paris *pied-à-terre*. In short, although house numbers in Paris of that day are deceptive because they corresponded to those of the lanterns in the street, the Talleyrand family remained in a close proximity which it is hard to lay at the door of a shortage of housing. And Talleyrand later recounts the pleasure he took in visiting his mother, a *"chef-d'oeuvre* of aristocratic civilisation," during those hours when he knew he would find her alone. "No one ever . . . possessed such fascinating conversation." [14]

In spite of his hectic pursuit of pleasure, Talleyrand was conscious of the necessity of becoming a priest as soon as possible, if he desired quick advancement in the Church. Special dispensations continued to be requested and granted to speed him on his way. And, the following March, he received his second mandatory degree in theology while still a subdeacon. He graduated sixth in his class but because first place was always reserved for the candidate with the oldest lineage, Talleyrand was automatically moved to the head of the group.

If one single person could be held responsible for the new freedom that made any subject, no matter how sacred, a fair topic for discussion, it was Voltaire. He was the bane of the Vatican which had placed all his writings on its Index of Forbidden Books—to their author's delight. The intellectual dictator of Europe, this man of letters had been in exile for twenty-eight years because of his unshakeable belief in human liberty, personal freedom of thought and toleration, and was now living at Ferney, just outside of Geneva. For many Parisians his great age—he was eighty-three—coupled with the distance of Ferney from the French capital—five days' travel—made him a legendary figure. So his return to Paris, the first week in February of 1778 for the premiere of his new play *Irène* at the Comédie-Française, created a sensation. He was fêted like the Messiah and accorded a reception the like of which had not been seen within living memory. *Tout Paris*—that is to say, all except the so-called respectable elements—flocked to see him where he was staying at the home of friends on the corner of the rue de Beaune and the Quai. The salon there was never empty. Blind old Mme du Deffand came. So, too, did Benjamin Franklin and his grandson. In Paris as one of the three American commissioners to negotiate an alliance with the French government for sorely needed help in the colonies' War for Independence, Franklin frequently walked from his house in Passy to the Auteuil home—always bursting with angora cats and flowers—of "Minette" Helvétius, the widow of the well-known philosopher Claude Adrien Helvétius, where Talleyrand made his acquaintance.

Within weeks of receiving his second theology degree, Talleyrand also came to Voltaire's house on the Quai to pay his respects although, even in Paris, where the clergy was noted for its worldliness, this visit of a man of the cloth to the most notorious scourge of the Church was deemed unseemly. But, then, it was not until the very end of his life that Talleyrand was ever concerned with the opinion of others. Conceivably the twenty-four-year-old abbé was drawn by curiosity, but it is far more likely that in Voltaire's cult of reason supported by common sense Talleyrand, who was already a confirmed sceptic, found a kindred soul. The old man's famed battle-cry, "Ecrasez l'infâme" (Crush the infamous), meaning the Church, epitomized the exact opposite of what Talleyrand had been taught at Harcourt, to obey and believe unquestioningly and at Saint-Sulpice, to respect authority.

On Talleyrand's first of two visits, he was received privately in Voltaire's bedroom, for Voltaire was anxious to meet young potential disciples. Perched on the edge of his bed in a darkened room and, squarely centered, by accident or purpose, in a shaft of daylight streaming dramatically through one-half of an otherwise shuttered window, the wicked old deist, a living skeleton, was the only thing clearly visible. Powdered curls cascaded down from a huge outmoded wig, framing his cracked, puckish face with its big nose and tiny, button-bright, eyes shining from sunken sockets. He was clad in a short, loose dressing gown from which his spindly legs and bony feet protruded and, because he was cold, he had thrown over his shoulders a red cloak lined with ermine sent him by Catherine the Great of Russia. A fervent admirer, the tsarina would, on his death, purchase his entire library of 6,210 books, and give his secretary Wagnière a pension to come to Saint Petersburg to arrange them on her shelves exactly the way they had been at Ferney. Scarcely visible in the gloom, his niece, Mme Denis, plump and no longer young, was in a corner making a pot of strong, imported Spanish chocolate, the odor of which permeated the room. Talleyrand stayed a good hour. Some accounts even have Talleyrand kneeling and receiving a benediction like young William Temple Franklin actually did, on another day. Whatever occurred and was said, Talleyrand never forgot meeting Voltaire, and his admiration for the patriarch was lifelong. That same night the famous apotheosis of the sage of Ferney occurred on stage at the Comédie-Française and, two months later to the day, Voltaire was dead.

Such unorthodox stirrings did not derail Talleyrand's uncle's plans for his future. He was still anxious to see his nephew become one of the next two general agents of the clergy, as had been promised, and the forthcoming quinquennial General Assembly was less than twenty-four months hence. This time, the rotating privilege of choosing the pair was the prerogative of the provinces of Aix and of Tours, and the Archbishop of Aix had already so designated his nephew. Since a general agent must also have some tie with the province proposing him Alexandre-Angélique, who had become the Archbishop of Reims on his predecessor's death the previous year, successfully prevailed upon the Archbishop of Tours not only to appoint Talleyrand as chaplain in a Tours church but also to name him as his candidate.

Meanwhile Talleyrand was having problems of a different nature with another high prelate. As titular head of the Sorbonne, the Bishop of Paris was too strict about the morals and discipline of the young subalterns in his Paris diocese to suit Talleyrand. In addition, Beaumont, whose quarrels with the *philosophes,* especially Jean-Jacques Rousseau, were famous, could not ignore Talleyrand's scandalous visits to Voltaire, the archenemy of the Church. The clergy was losing a lot of its public esteem under the hammer blows of the freethinkers, and Talleyrand's activities did not help its image. In pious rage, the worthy churchman summoned him in and administered a sharp reprimand. Anxious to escape his eagle eye, Talleyrand wangled special authorization—once again—to change from the diocese of Paris to that of Reims. On the same day that this was granted, September 17, 1779, he was finally ordained a deacon in his uncle's private chapel. But, like numerous other ecclesiastics, he had no intention of living in the provinces. Instead, he returned promptly to Paris on the pretext that he needed to be in the capital to cultivate people who could be helpful to him in his anticipated new job as general agent.

He had already fulfilled one essential qualification by his earlier stint as promoter in the clergy's previous General Assembly, but he could no longer postpone satisfying the second. In order to continue his rapid, dispensation-strewn progress to higher church dignities now that he was a deacon, he must take his final vows to be a priest. Normally this necessitated an obligatory six months delay. Thriving on the challenge of getting special favors, Talleyrand quickly cleared this final hurdle.

On December 17, 1779, the night before his ordination, after all his uncle's intriguing and maneuvering on his behalf—which he had accepted without hesitancy, so far as is known—at the very last moment Talleyrand was suddenly assailed by doubts. Unlike the rumored scene of regret when he was admitted to the ranks of subdeacon four years before, there is no reason to question the authenticity of the account of Choiseul-Gouffier, one of the carefree "Triumvirate." He tells of finding the candidate "in a sort of rage" that the time had come to sacrifice the joys of living that he had come to know. When his friend suggested that Talleyrand postpone taking the fatal step, he replied: "It's too late. There's no turning back now." [15]

To try and explain away this episode is almost impossible. It is true that for a confirmed non-believer with a questioning mind like his, the future as a man of the cloth was probably more repugnant than ever, entailing as it did blind respect for his superiors and blanket acceptance of their opinions. Still, it's hard to take seriously, so late in the game, any supposed second thoughts that Talleyrand might suddenly be experiencing about a clergyman's life. As one of only two general agents, at the head of the administrative and financial services of the Church in France, he would have one of the most prominent roles in the kingdom, in daily contact with the government and the court, and with additional money and honors to follow. How could ambitious Talleyrand, spurred on also, no doubt, by wounded pride at having been deprived of his birthright, balk at taking the unavoidable final step he had known about from the start? Conceivably, as one biographer suggests, the brilliant marriage to one of France's greatest heiresses earlier that year, of Archambaud, his favorite younger brother who had succeeded him as the head of the family—and whose wedding contract Louis XVI and Marie-Antoinette signed—may have given Talleyrand some pause. No one can say with any certainty. The happiness of Archambaud, who was always referred to in the faubourg Saint-Germain, as "archi-bête que beau" (as stupid as he is handsome), could have made him realize, as never before, what this ordination would mean in the way of personal sacrifices.

Talleyrand was well aware that in the circles in which he now traveled, vows were made to be broken. This knowledge, together with his first-hand, cold-blooded recognition that one could attain high ecclesiastic office not through merit but because of influence, intrigues, and family connections—at the beginning of the Revolution all but two of France's some one hundred bishops were blue blooded—must have further nourished the calculating young man's innate cynicism. In trying to sift fact from fiction and even making generous allowances for his prejudices and bias when he wrote his *Mémoires*, it is hard to accept Talleyrand's persistent, brazen claim that he was "a priest in spite of himself."

The following morning, in the chapel of the Episcopal palace at Reims, the officiating Bishop of Noyon, a suffragan of his uncle, pronounced the final words of the sacred ritual: "Tu est sacerdos in aeternum." (Thou art a priest forever.) Once more, for whatever reason—perhaps even at Talleyrand's request—not a single family member was present.

On the nineteenth, the newly tonsured priest, his alb covered with a sleeveless chasuble, celebrated his first mass and gave communion to his mother and father, who must have heaved a sigh of relief to see their oldest child safe in the arms of the Church at last.

2

An Abbé à la Mode

*"The Abbé de Périgord would sell his soul
for money; and he would be right for he would
be exchanging dung for gold."*—MIRABEAU [1]

ON TUESDAY, MAY 30, 1780, at the first working session of the new quinquennial General Assembly of the Clergy held in the convent of the Grands Augustins, the Abbés de Périgord and de Boisgelin—the nephew of the Archbishop of Aix—were officially acknowledged as general agents. Their term of office was to last through the five-year interval between the end of the current session and the beginning of the next. This constituted Talleyrand's initiation into administrative work and governance, as well as into the world of high finance.

If few were surprised at the appointment of clever, charming young Talleyrand, they soon were at the way the ambitious young abbé threw himself into his new duties. General agents usually got by without doing very much work. Such was the case with Talleyrand's colleague, the Abbé de Boisgelin, who was forced to retire briefly to a seminary after being found *in flagrante delicto* by the husband of his mistress. Since he was anxious to attract attention, Talleyrand did most of the work for the two of them. However, he was well paid and was assisted by a large staff of experienced specialists. Offices were in the same humid, shabby convent as the General Assembly meetings were, but Talleyrand rarely appeared there. Instead, his staff came to the rue de Bellechasse, where he personally oversaw the correspondence with the French clergy and, of the two-thousand-plus letters sent out during his five-year stint, most were signed by Talleyrand.

As liaison between the Church and the state, the general agents were charged with the defense of the clergy's privileges. In the temporal domain there was countless litigation of all sorts. In religious matters more complicated problems arose daily. Because the Church was responsible for the registers for baptism, marriage, and death it also assumed practically single-handed the monumental task of welfare—the hospitals and poor houses—throughout France. Whenever ecclesiastical matters were under discussion or the rights of the Church were threatened, the general agents were authorized by Louis XVI to participate at the Royal Council. As a gauge of their importance, two armchairs were drawn up for the pair just to the right of the presiding official.

The well-organized church with its huge annual budget enjoyed complete exemption from taxes on its enormous holdings. Its general agents were charged with the administration of its funds—both its income and expenditures—and dealt officially with the king's ministers, especially those connected with finance. Nothing in this field was beneath Talleyrand's attention, and he even tried to help the humble parish priests with their pittance of a salary keep abreast of the current sky-high inflation. Perhaps to belie his still youthful appearance, he adopted a cold manner and reserve, which gave him a haughty air and would become second nature to him.

Determined to leave nothing undone that might hasten his advancement, Talleyrand cultivated his contacts in these various new, influential milieus, where he got unique on-the-job training simply by keeping his eyes and ears open. To successfully discharge this new office he needed backing not only at the court—which he was already guaranteed by his parents' position—but he also needed support in the world of finance. Here his reputation as an up-and-coming, capable administrator with a solid grasp of the huge portfolio of information relating to church matters was helped by a number of constructive reforms he proposed, even if they never came up for a vote. Talleyrand preferred the advice and counsel of practical men of affairs rather than that of theoreticians, the latter of whom flourished in abundance at the moment. The Genevan financier Isaac Panchaud and Radix de Sainte-Foy were two Bellechasse regulars and it would be difficult to say which one had more influence on their host. It was the former who initiated him into all the intricacies of the Bourse, the French stock exchange, which had had a peripatetic existence over a long period of time and was presently located on the rue Vivienne and open from noon to 1:00 p.m. five days a week. Unfortunately, as more than one authority on this period has pointed out, an important part of Talleyrand's financial dealings prior to the French Revolution will never be fully known, and certainly not in detail, until Panchaud's personal papers are available.

Sainte-Foy, eighteen years Talleyrand's senior, remained an intimate colleague—and his right-hand, financially speaking, the one man from whom he had practically no secrets—until his death two decades later. Completely amoral, the epitome of elegance and good taste and almost his equal intellectually, this roué—Mme du Barry, among countless others, had been his mistress before she became Louis XV's—had a profound influence on the young abbé. Consciously or subconsciously Sainte-Foy, with the finest cook in the kingdom, a wine cellar without peer, a magnificent townhouse as well as a luxurious country house on the Seine, both furnished with matchless collections of paintings, books, and *objets d'art*, became his role model. It was Sainte-Foy who made the rounds of the gambling houses with him. Sainte-Foy, as the finance man for the Comte d'Artois, the king's brother, was a true insider and not hesitant about taking advantage of his position in the entourage of the royal family. He initiated the younger man into the practical aspects of stock jobbing and the influence of money on politics. Sainte-Foy's enormously successful operations—under and above the counter—have become far better known than any of Talleyrand's, at least his early ones. With the passage of the years, he would handle most of the many questionable financial deals Talleyrand was involved in, including those with the two leading international banking houses of the day—Baring in London and Hope in Amsterdam. Around Sainte-Foy revolved a whole group of bankers and speculators with whom Talleyrand now became friendly.

As a young man slated for advancement who was beginning to attract attention as a serious man of affairs, Talleyrand's social activities now assumed an important functional role. Throughout this period an irresponsible society both at Versailles and, increasingly, in Paris, meddled more and more in government affairs. Talleyrand needed the backing of the leading salons of the capital where a new power, opinion, the uncrowned ruler of the day, was being formulated. The salons dared to criticize openly the court, including heretofore sacrosanct Marie-Antoinette and Louis XVI, and young women, when they were not debating the perpetual financial woes, might argue *ad nauseum* whether tobacco from Virginia should be taxed, or about similar abstruse matters. In these gilded chambers attempts to influence ministerial decisions and appointments became the norm after the triumphal campaign recently waged by Mme Necker to hoist her husband, Jacques, into the office of General Director of Finances in 1777, although he had three strikes against him, as a foreigner—he was a Genevan—as a business man, one of Europe's wealthiest, and as a Protestant. She had helped to ensure her success by craftily selecting Friday as her day at home—thereby garnering the *philosophes* who much preferred meat to fish—and spent several hours each morning at a little *bonheur de jour*, polishing her phrases and then manipulating that evening's conversation so she might shine with these supposedly spontaneous *bon mots*.

With the influence of salons an acknowledged ingredient for success, it was equally important to build a reputation for discrimination and know which invitations to refuse. Talleyrand had long since discovered that the secret of pleasing in society was to "let oneself learn the things he already knows from those people who do not know it." [2] Nightly, he would make the rounds of certain drawing rooms specifically to keep abreast of what was happening. Next, he would stop at those where to be seen was tantamount to recognition as one of the more distinguished men of the day. He might even visit the studio of Mme Vigée-Le Brun, Marie-Antoinette's favorite portrait artist, who remembered Talleyrand for his "supreme elegance despite his limp." Sometimes he met intimates, by arrangement or by chance, in the loge of some private box at the Opéra or at one of the other two theaters so popular with people of quality—the Comédie-Française or les Italiens. He then continued on with them to the home of one of the actresses or ballet dancers for a night of revelry and, perhaps, high-stakes gambling.

Noontime conversation at the rue Bellechasse ranged far and wide. Any remaining satisfaction over the fact that the aid granted by Louis XVI in the victorious American War for Independence—where Talleyrand's youngest brother, Boson, was presently fighting—had helped avenge French defeats at British hands during the earlier Seven Years War, was proving expensive. Even though a series of loans, engineered by Necker, accounted for most of this extensive assistance, the Treasury's shortfall persisted. The appearance in 1781 of the minister's famous *Compte Rendu*, the first state budget ever made available for wide publication, had unexpected and disastrous consequences. Although the amounts required for the maintenance of Versailles and for other royal expenses equaled actually only about one-half of the amount that the British budget allocated to its monarchy, public indignation soared, and mounting street *mêlées* caused His Majesty to demand the Genevan's resignation, this same year. Discussion around the table in a more ribald vein surely followed the appearance that same fall of the long awaited dauphin. He was the second child conceived after His Majesty listened to the advice of his visiting brother-in-law, Emperor Joseph II of Austria and, following an operation for phimosis—a kind of minor anatomical retouching—was finally able to consummate his seven-year-old marriage.

In the fall of 1783 Talleyrand again spent an extended, six-week vacation at his uncle's, the archbishop, at the Abbey de Saint-Thierry, and part of this time, one, or both, of his parents was there. There is no way of knowing whether he was at Versailles when drums rolled and Etienne Montgolfier's sixty-foot-high, blue taffeta balloon, named, of course, *Montauciel* (literally "climb into the sky") wobbled into the air for its epochal eight-minute flight with, as captive passengers in its suspended basket, a duck, a rooster, and a sheep. But he was certainly keeping an eagle eye on the château where the peace was signed with England ending the American War for Independence. This document simultaneously put an end to certain speculations he and Panchaud shared, as well as to his partnership with Auguste de Choiseul-Gouffier, one of the "Triumvirate," in the arming of a privateer equipped to chase cargo ships with the hope of reaping a handsome profit, as their friend, Beaumarchais, the author of *The Barber of Seville*, was doing so successfully.

Once more there was a serious financial crisis and, this time, Talleyrand in his role as general agent was automatically involved because a lot of the clergy's money was affected. He and Panchaud sat on the commission set up to examine the situation and, as general agent, he was subsequently chosen to give its report. This, Talleyrand noted in his *Mémoires*, marked his "official debut in the world of business."

With the nomination of Calonne as General Controller of Finances, a wave of optimism swept over the country. Women had their own schemes about how to reform finances and, overnight, banished from their wardrobes the latest style hats, which were called "à la Caisse d'Escompte" because, like the Caisse d'Escompte—a large discount bank founded by Panchaud which was now facing ruin—they, too, were minus a bottom. Calonne and Talleyrand both traveled in the same influential circles and were close neighbors, as well as distant cousins, but it is not known exactly when he first met the suave, smiling Calonne, twenty years his senior. Talleyrand cultivated Calonne because he had power and Calonne, Talleyrand, because he had demonstrated his acumen as general agent. The young abbé might have proven his ability in financial matters, but in other spheres there was room for doubt, especially after one evening when Talleyrand arrived at Calonne's with a vial, tucked in his vest pocket, containing some miraculous water that Cagliostro, the charlatan *à la mode*, had given him as a remedy for headaches. Unfortunately, this cure-all did not help when another guest unexpectedly came down with a migraine.

Feverish speculation and stock jobbing swept Paris, as the Bourse surged, manipulated by rumors. A born gambler like Talleyrand was better situated than most to participate advantageously because of advanced inside information of events that were capable of producing fluctuating values on the market place and which he also gleaned through a reprehensible abuse of his friendship with Calonne and especially with Panchaud who now, together with Dupont de Nemours, served as Calonne's consultants. But Talleyrand was never overly burdened with scruples; he was only concerned with the net result. As he once remarked: "Society is divided into two classes: the shearers and the shorn. One must always be with the former against the latter." [3] Talleyrand also joined forces with a shadowy Paris canon, l'Abbé Espagnac, who was Calonne's principal agent for any dealings on the Bourse, in a speculative scheme resulting from a Calonne reform to call in and melt down, then reissue, certain types of French specie. Whenever the two ran out of money they could call on another Genevan compatriot of Panchaud, Frédéric Perregaux, who had recently opened his own bank in Paris, and on the latter's international clientele in the great banking centers of Amsterdam, Frankfurt, and London. Perregaux's strong English connections, especially with the great Baring Bank, would prove invaluable to Talleyrand over the years. No doubt Talleyrand also trafficked in influence, a popular sideline of the day, which he later, as a diplomat, elevated to a fine art. In order not to interfere with what he hoped would be a quick rise in the Church hierarchy, Talleyrand did such a good job of concealing his multiple transactions that there are still, today, a great number of dead ends.

Although an old saying claims that "one only loans to a rich man," it took some doing in that day and age for Talleyrand to acquire notoriety even before he acquired fame. What might, with generosity, have been considered the follies of a young aristocrat could not, in his case, be ignored any longer. Despite the fact that he never neglected his work as general agent, his life was considered scandalous. Talleyrand was even seen in the company of singers and ballerinas from the Opéra during Holy Week. His reputation as a gay lothario meant that every woman wanted the cachet of being his mistress. Talleyrand may have subconsciously felt set apart as if disgraced, because he was a cripple, a handicap which had already cost him his birthright, and strove to redeem himself—at least in his own mind—by bettering *Don Giovanni's* "mille et tre."

Talleyrand had passing, simultaneous affairs with any number of *grandes dames*, and others. Of varying ages, they were frequently older than he was and, more than once, he switched from mother to daughter or daughter-in-law and then back again. One never appeared to be jealous of another, possibly because each was playing the same game with other lovers and had her share of illegitimate offspring by them. Long-lived Talleyrand remained an intimate friend whose career these women continued to foster long after they no longer shared his bed. Many belonged to families who were influential at court. Others, as hostesses of prestigious salons, were a power in their own right; adding the satisfaction of playing a role to that of devotion to Talleyrand, they became indispensable allies whose backing was often significant. And he had what was needed to please them—his distinguished lineage, his wit, his renown as a Don Juan and, most important of all, his growing reputation as a man too competent to be ignored. Nor was Talleyrand wasting his time. In a letter dated August 20, 1784, the Junoesque Comtesse de Brionne, one of the most intelligent women of the day, and old enough to be his mother, successfully persuaded her friend, Gustave III of Sweden—a Lutheran but very close to Pius VI—to try and get a cardinal's hat for Talleyrand. His Majesty did not succeed.

There is no consensus as to how Adélaide de Filleul de Flahaut and Talleyrand first met, although by the early 1780s, she had ready access to the same circles he frequented. Some say it was at Versailles; others, through a mutual friend, the lowly born Marmontel, a popular writer and philosopher, who had known her since she was tiny, and was a regular at Bellechasse. Twenty-year-old Adèle, as she was known to friends, was almost seven years younger than Talleyrand. Of bourgeois antecedents, she was left an orphan in a convent when her mother, a reputed former inmate of Louis XV's famed royal brothel, *Le Parc aux Cerfs* (The Deer Park), a small villa in the town of Versailles itself, died. Following the marriage of her older sister, Julie, one of the loveliest-looking women of the day, to the Marquis de Marigny, the brother of Mme de Pompadour, Louis XV's celebrated mistress, Adèle lived with her. Possessed of a pleasing figure with just a hint of plumpness, she had an oval-shaped face, too thin lips, luxurious chestnut hair curling under the powder, and big brown eyes that the well-known painter, Mme Vigée-Le Brun, an authority in such matters, termed "the wittiest in the world." In 1779 Adèle made a surprisingly good marriage for an eighteen-year-old bourgeois with no dowry. The Comte de Flahaut de la Billarderie was a respected army officer from impoverished but well connected country aristocracy, and their age difference, he was fifty-four, was perfectly acceptable in a society which did not expect the lively young bride to be faithful to him. As befitting Flahaut, the younger brother of the Comte d'Angiviller—the director of the Royal Buildings, as well as of the Academies of Painting and Sculpture—and Adèle, the sister-in-law of the Marquis de Marigny, who was superintendent of the Beaux-Arts, the fashionable newlyweds were given several cavernous "grace-and-favor" rooms perched on the top floor of the Louvre. Built originally as a massive tower protecting Paris against Norman invaders, this royal residence had been turned into a free caravansary after Louis XIV moved the court to Versailles. Now it was as packed as a rabbits' warren with impoverished court parasites, for whom there was not even a garret available in the château out there. One duke installed a stable in part of the ground-floor rooms allocated to him. Linen hung out of some tenants' windows to dry. One or two even kept chickens and rabbits on their landings. And a number of sculptors and artists, including Greuze and Fragonard, had their studios here.

As in the case of others similarly honored, Adèle and her husband had placed at their disposal a team of contractors and architects to construct an apartment to suit their needs, building a wall here, lowering a ceiling there, with no regard for their neighbors or for hygiene.

The elderly count had certain military duties that kept him away a great deal and, when he was home, he spent most of his time in his study, which was on the floor below. This granted Adèle full rein to establish a salon—the most important piece of business for a young bride of quality. Through a childhood friend who was now her rich sister-in-law, the Comtesse d'Angiviller, and who had one of the better known salons of the day in her own Louvre apartments, clever, vivacious Adèle met the best Versailles society not to mention the artistic and literary elite who owed much to the patronage and support of d'Angiviller and Marigny in their official capacities.

Perhaps, in the beginning, Talleyrand's reputation as seduction personified excited Adèle's curiosity. Perhaps, from her point of view, to snare the gallant abbé would be a triumph on a par with the recent romantic escapade of her sister Julie. She had captured the effeminate libertine cardinal, the Prince de Rohan, and deserted her husband to tour the country at his side, disguised as a young priest, before their affair finally terminated. Talleyrand's liaison with Adèle would last a decade, but there is only one mention of her in his *Mémoires*. Soon the new *mènage à trois*—with an elderly husband who only rarely demanded his marital rights hovering discreetly in the background—was so universally accepted that it ceased to be a matter of gossip. Although Talleyrand was never Adèle's exclusively, and he never demanded fidelity from any of his mistresses, Adèle called their affair a "marriage of the heart." While Talleyrand continued to go the rounds, one could always be sure of finding him, now, at some time during the evening at Adèle's, where his presence added greatly to the prestige of her gatherings. Although Adèle had sufficient wit to say nothing commonplace and was extremely intelligent, politics was never the most important matter under discussion here. Neither were the more practical aspects of the day—the misery in the countryside and the famine stalking different parts of the land. But the talk sparkled, ideas flowed and, due in part to the apartment's small size, an unusual note of intimacy prevailed which added an unexpected sensation of warmth to the gathering. Because, like Talleyrand, Adèle loved gambling, there were always several tables of trictrac (backgammon); perhaps one of biribiri, a lotto-like game; and whist, Talleyrand's preference.

A son, Adèle's only child, was born on April 21, 1785, with Talleyrand's blue-grey eyes. Her complaisant husband, like a true gentleman, promptly accepted the boy as his. Indeed, the count's world would have been surprised had he done otherwise, and the delighted parents had plenty of excuse to name the infant Charles, for there were already three Charles de Flahauts in the cuckolded husband's family. To round out the fiction—knowingly or unknowingly—one brother of the count served as godfather, while the godmother was Adèle's lifelong friend, the Comtesse d'Angiviller, the wife of another.

At the first working session of the next quinquennial General Assembly of the Clergy, held in Paris that May, Talleyrand's five-year stint as general agent terminated. By then, Talleyrand was conceded to be more than just another charming, dissolute "salon abbé." He had acquired the reputation of an ambitious, capable thirty-one-year-old on the way up. In recognition of his fine performance, he was chosen to serve as one of the assembly's two secretaries for the present series of meetings—a significant post. Barely halfway through its session, Prince Louis de Rohan, Cardinal Archbishop of Strasbourg and grand almoner of France—the erstwhile lover of Adèle's sister, Julie—was arrested in Versailles's great Hall of Mirrors, in the presence of the entire court, as he was about to celebrate the service of the Assumption. And the famous scandal of Marie-Antoinette's diamond necklace burst upon an unsuspecting public. This bizarre swindle that has never to this day been satisfactorily resolved—except to vindicate the queen—centered around a pretentious bauble, consisting of 647 diamonds weighing 2,800 carats, that was the lifework of the jeweler to the Court of France and had been designed by him originally for Mme du Barry, the mistress of Louis XV. The complex plot had been masterminded by a scheming adventuress, Mme de la Motte, who persuaded the dissolute, gullible Cardinal de Rohan, who was trying to win Marie-Antoinette's favor, to purchase it to present to the queen; then Mme de la Motte intended to cheat him out of it. At this point, the necklace itself disappeared, never to be seen again, and, with it, Marie-Antoinette's reputation. An orgy of rumor and accusation ensued that was followed by an avid public from Moscow to London, and that transformed the queen, an innocent bystander, into the "Austrian strumpet," irretrievably tarnishing her in the eyes of the man in the street and making the dynasty the ultimate victim. Since Rohan, because of his position, could only be judged by his peers, the remaining sessions of the clergy's General Assembly were adjourned for a year in an effort to limit the damage.

So it was not until July 17, 1786, that the mandatory accounting of their five-year stewardship as general agents was presented by Talleyrand

and Boisgelin. Talleyrand followed up, the next day, with his personal, in-depth report on public education, which he had undertaken because he felt the need for its reform. The assembly was so delighted with their efficient work that the pair received not only the customary remuneration but, in addition, a generous bonus. The two also had the unusual distinction of being recommended by the conclave to the king for higher office, even though, as Talleyrand noted wryly in his *Mémoires*, he had done the bulk of the work for the both of them.

Frequently general agents were named bishops even before the end of their five-year tenure, and a number of recent vacancies should have ensured that Talleyrand be similarly rewarded. Unfortunately Louis XVI who, like French kings since the time of François I, had the right to fill vacant sees, was genuinely pious and harbored the absurd notion that a man of the purple should lead a virtuous life; Marie-Antoinette was equally prejudiced—for a variety of different reasons. Some current princes of the Church did have irreproachable virtues, and the king was not anxious to nominate as a bishop someone for whom, as His Majesty pointed out, "le Saint Esprit serait seulement l'esprit tout court." [4] For a priest of the Talleyrand-Périgord family, whose "talent and zeal" had just been publicly acknowledged by the highest clerics in the land, not to immediately receive a bishopric speaks volumes. As his letters show, Talleyrand was disappointed because the episcopate was the antichambre of power and the higher his position in the Church the better his chances of access to the highest functions of government.

At the gatherings in Bellechasse now one of the main topics of discussion was the commercial treaty with England signed this same fall that established something like free trade between the two countries. Talleyrand already favored the establishment of strong political and economic ties between the two sides of the Channel as a basis for European peace, a stance he would never alter as long as he lived. But Louis XVI's ministers were also looking in the opposite direction and wondering what was going to happen in Prussia when the ailing Frederick the Great died. Following Talleyrand's suggestion, a well-qualified acquaintance and distant cousin five years his senior, whom he met originally through Panchaud and who was in need of a job, was sent to Potsdam at the expense of Calonne, the finance minister. Comte de Mirabeau, a brilliant, renegade noble, whose prodigious memory made him a walking encyclopedia, had the secret mission of also evaluating the disposition of the failing monarch's heir, Friedrich-Wilhelm II, and was to warn Calonne the moment the Prussian king was no more. Mirabeau, whose ugliness, augmented by badly pitted scars—the result of his mother's misguided trust in a quack's guaranteed remedy for smallpox sores—never curtailed his success with the opposite sex, was as eager for power, fortune, and a place in the sun as Talleyrand. The pair shared a cynical contempt for mankind and a similar indifference to the means required to achieve one's ends. They frequently fought bitterly and Mirabeau once remarked: "The Abbé de Périgord would sell his soul for money; and he would be right for he would be exchanging dung for gold." [5] But they were always reconciled. Talleyrand, who was designated to receive Mirabeau's reports and edit them for Calonne and Louis XVI, seized the opportunity to have Mirabeau also analyze—for Talleyrand's personal use alone—the feasibility of possible future speculations in Berlin for Talleyrand and their mutual friend, Panchaud. Talleyrand had an innate ability to juggle values and commodities between foreign capitals while Panchaud, according to Mirabeau, who was certainly in no position to talk, was "the only man who knew how to make the chicken with the golden eggs lay eggs without gutting it." [6]

As the archbishoprics of Bourges, then Nancy, and, finally Lyon, became available and were awarded, one by one, to others, Talleyrand became more discreet, but no less active, in his financial dealings so as not to jeopardize further his chances for the desired appointment. His increasing interest in the political scene, which he looked at realistically as a path to riches, more than filled any void in his life left by the termination of his duties as general agent.

The distress of the Treasury reached such proportions that the king was obliged to convoke the Assembly of Notables who represented the privileged in the land and had not met in more than a century and a half. Financial rescue of the state hinged upon political change to reform the way the Crown got its income. His Majesty looked to the Notables not only to resolve this matter but also to redress other related problems facing France, where the social inequities were based on prerogatives, and the privileged class would not tolerate change.

Because Calonne fell seriously ill, the assembly was postponed once, and it was not until February 14, 1787, eight days before its rescheduled opening, that the General Controller of Finances asked Talleyrand with his hardheaded business sense and political know-how for help.

Such an invitation was too flattering to be turned down, especially for someone envisaging the possibility of a future ministerial portfolio. Unfortunately, only a handful of days were available for a job that needed a minimum of five to six months of work, plus additional time to print up its recommendations. Talleyrand spent a week at Versailles, where the main offices of the Finance Ministry were located on the rue de la Surintendance, working with Dupont de Nemours, Panchaud, Mirabeau, and Calonne, among others, preparing memoranda to be presented to the Notables for action. He was in the gallery when the one-hundred-and-forty-odd delegates first convened, on a bitterly cold, rainy winter day, at the Salle des Menus Plaisirs—the storehouse where the king's minor playthings were kept: his tennis rackets, musical instruments, theater sets, and the like. It was conveniently located on the Avenue de Paris, the direct road to the capital, and only a scant ten-minute walk from the château proper. Unfortunately, His Majesty's hand was forced by a cabal of the Notables who were unwilling to yield an inch where changes affecting themselves were concerned. Calonne, who had expected his proposals to be imposed, not merely proposed, was dismissed, and the Notables, who had no alternate solution ready, were soon dissolved.

Public agitation, that was to lead to a head-on collision between the backers of the king's authority and those of Parliament's, appeared as censorship weakened and people, even in the provinces, started criticizing both the government and the monarchy. Public opinion—that of the man-in-the-streets, as well as that of the salons—was now beginning to count. *Lèse majesté* was the rule of the day. Rabble-rousing pamphleteers hawked their wares, decrying the extravagances of the court along the recently completed, shop-lined public arcades surrounding the gardens of the Palais Royal. This business venture, transforming the grounds of Cardinal Richelieu's former palace, which was presently the home of the heavily indebted Duc d'Orléans, prompted His Majesty to remark to the duke cynically: "Mon cousin, now that you are going to become a shopkeeper, (I suppose) we will only see you at Versailles on Sundays." [7] Since Orléans, the next in line for the throne after the king's own children and brothers, forbade the police to enter *chez lui*, the Orléans compound enjoyed more freedom than any place else in Paris. So it furnished a mixed audience from all levels of society for anyone desirous of airing revolutionary theories and inclined to criticize the government.

Parisian authorities were having trouble preserving order. As befitting a king who came to the throne wanting to be loved, Louis XVI kept changing ministers in an effort to conjure up the necessary changes that must be simultaneously politically liberal and also restore fiscal balance. After serious troubles in Grenoble and elsewhere in the provinces, His Majesty recalled Necker, whose pompous self-assurance was reassuring and whom the public considered a wizard capable of pulling money out of a hat. Then, shortly afterwards, the king took the momentous step of summoning the General Estates to meet on May 1 of the following year, 1789.

His announcement was greeted with widespread approval because this body, which had not met since 1614, represented the whole populace and, unlike the Notables, had the authority to give France the badly needed reforms. As in the past, its deputies were to be chosen by the three Estates—the clergy, the nobles, and the commons. For someone ambitious like Talleyrand, whose political activities had hitherto been confined to working behind the scenes or through the powerful salons, the chance to be elected a deputy represented a new, direct route to open political power. And he intended to take advantage of it.

Despite the Church's thundering disapproval and the Sorbonne's fulminations, the secret order of Freemasons, which had neither a religious or a political character as such, had spread from England throughout most of western Europe and even to Vienna, where Mozart's opera, *The Magic Flute* that borrowed freely from its ritual, would be premiered in 1791. Freemasonry was now at the height of its popularity in France and was permeated by the rationalism and liberal, republican ideals so in vogue. To join was *à la mode*. Even Voltaire had become a member when he was in Paris. Benjamin Franklin was one of its highest local dignitaries, as was the Duc d'Orléans, but authorities are not in agreement as to whether Talleyrand did likewise at this time. Other clubs and groups for discussion of France's problems sprang up everywhere, cutting across all sections of society.

Talleyrand was extremely active in the "Société des 30," later called the Constitutional Club, where Mirabeau, Lafayette, Dupont de Nemours, and Panchaud discussed the paramount issues to be addressed by the forthcoming General Estates. The idea for a constitutional monarchy was in the air. They debated the essential rights of man and even the possible nationalization of the Church properties, the immunity of which, although taken for granted, had been under increasing fire for several decades. And why not? The Throne was always short of money and the Church had so much. The political maneuvers necessary for the success of these various projects were also studied. Much time was spent evaluating the precedent-shattering innovation recently undertaken in the provincial assembly in the Dauphiné—a new form of representation by individuals, not by the Estates as three separate entities, the clergy, the nobles, and the commons. The heady ferment of political upheaval was in the air.

From his contemporaries' point of view Talleyrand was a man of order, compromise, and moderation. He was considered a liberal yet, for him, like for many late eighteenth century aristocrats, the proletariat was non-existent and society was divided into three classes, of which the third constituted the bourgeoisie. In his eyes, the Third Estate had a right to liberty, prosperity, and protection from oppression, but it was the prerogative of the aristocracy to recognize and implement these rights, not that of the Third Estate to claim them unilaterally. Because he favored—then and always—an English-style, constitutional monarchy with control exercised by responsible ministers, Talleyrand became a charter member of the Club des Valois, a circle for like-minded gentlemen, organized and presided over by the Duc d'Orléans who housed it in his Palais Royal compound. The Orléans faction espoused government reform in which it should hold power behind the scenes, a change to be effected by a "kid gloves" revolution—without recourse to the bloodshed intrinsic in any more radical upheaval—and Talleyrand anticipated an important post with it.

This same fall of 1788, the bishopric of Autun became available. Meanwhile Talleyrand's father, now a brigadier-general decorated with the exclusive Order of the Holy Ghost, the most sought after decoration of the *ancien régime*, lay mortally ill. From his sickbed the count, who may honestly have still hoped that more ecclesiastical responsibility might reform his eldest son and who was undoubtedly more concerned about protecting Talleyrand-Périgord interests than the welfare of the Church, petitioned Louis XVI to grant this seat to his oldest son. No doubt because His Majesty remembered how close the count once was to his own father, compassionate, pious Louis XVI reluctantly shut his eyes to Talleyrand's shortcomings and, on November 2, 1788, named him to the vacant bishopric. On November 3, the huge, elaborate funeral convoy for the late Maréchal de Biron had to be rerouted so its mournful chants would not disturb the dying count. He passed away the next day at fifty-four.

In the church of the day, most bishops' incomes were double those publicly avowed. Since the bishopric of Autun, while one of the most important in the kingdom, with three times as many parishes as most, had revenues deemed scanty in comparison with those of other dioceses, His Majesty awarded Talleyrand another benefice, the Abbey de Celles-en-Poitou—where Talleyrand would never once set foot—even before confirmation of his new office arrived from the Holy See. This meant that he received, tax free, a total equivalent of approximately three million 1991 French francs solely from his various church-related functions and benefices.

For whatever reason, Talleyrand was not ordained in his uncle's cathedral at Reims, as might have been expected. He spent the last week prior to his consecration taking the traditional retreat in a cell a few leagues from the capital, at the Solitude d'Issy, the former home of Marguerite de Valois, the first wife of Henry IV, which was now a dependency of Saint-Sulpice. It was so cold that Talleyrand took sick and spent most of his time in bed, interspersing long conversations with the director of the Solitude with visits of friends bringing the latest news from Paris. A few weeks before his thirty-fifth birthday, Talleyrand was ordained privately by the same Monseigneur Grimaldi, the Bishop of Noyon, who had presided when he became a priest. In the midst of the long, tiring ceremony, which was held in the tiny adjacent chapel of the Saint-Saveur, where a stove had been lighted to ward off the unseasonable chill, he had a brief fainting spell, but quickly recovered. Fatigue or emotion, who knows? Neither his mother nor his two brothers were present. Their failure to appear could be interpreted as a public disavowal of the late Comte de Talleyrand's dying wish and the king's decision to grant it but, for aristocrats like the Talleyrand-Périgords, this is unlikely. More probably Talleyrand wanted to keep the ceremony as low keyed as possible—for whatever reason—and did not want them present. By his solemn consecration as a bishop, a post ardently solicited rather than one he might have been forced to accept as the inexorable workings of fate, Talleyrand placed himself in a situation vis-à-vis the Church from which withdrawal was almost inconceivable.

The following day, Monseigneur Charles-Maurice de Talleyrand-Périgord received from the Archbishop of Paris the pallium, which high prelates are entitled to wear. The one placed around his shoulders was a sacred heirloom handed down, from one Bishop d'Autun to another, since the days of the seventh century saint, Syagrius and it had been woven at Rome from the wool of blessed sheep grazing in the pastures of the first Christians, at the convent of Sainte-Agnes-hors-les-Murs. Then the newly consecrated Monseigneur de Talleyrand went to the Louvre to sup with his mistress.

Making Talleyrand the Bishop d'Autun may have filled his religious mother with mixed emotions—as a native from there she was reputedly shocked to see her sacrilegious son so elevated—but his appointment was not indefensible in a day when a bishop's job was largely administrative. And Talleyrand had proved himself to be a good administrator. But he was in no immediate hurry to leave Paris and discontinue active participation in his many affairs, nor would he be the first bishop of the day to administer his diocese from a distance. Instead, he moved into a mansion near his former Bellechasse abode, that was also near the home his widowed mother, aided by his uncle, the archbishop, had recently purchased. From this abode, the Hôtel de Sarin at 17, rue de l'Université, at the corner of the rue de Beaune, which was more befitting his new status, he dictated splendid pastoral letters, full of his "burning desire" to join his flock. These were subsequently read from the pulpits in his diocese. He also dispatched there a new vicar-general, the trusted Abbé Desrenaudes, who had already worked with Talleyrand when he was general agent and would stay with him until he died.

If the last General Estates of 1614 had been a stepping-stone for the great Bishop of Luçon—Richelieu—to become a cardinal and then the powerful head of the king's council, there was no reason why the General Estates of 1789 should not do as much for ambitious Talleyrand. With his sights now fixed on a political post, preferably at the head of Finances, which he considered the most important branch of the government, he must next be chosen the Autun clerics' delegate to the forthcoming General Estates. The minute these election dates were announced, Talleyrand departed, snugly tucked into his new coach, a splendid affair with velvet upholstery and cushions and uniformed lackeys hanging on outside by means of long worsted straps. With his coachman smartly cracking the whip, because he was anxious to waste no time en route, he traveled at a fast clip over rutted, icy, roads through a countryside largely paralyzed by the unusually extreme cold that made provisioning of those areas most in need of help more difficult than usual. While facilitating his coach's passage, the frozen rivers prevented making bread from what little grain was available after a poorer than usual harvest.

The central Burgundian town of Autun about three hundred kilometers southeast of Paris had been created, as its name indicates—Autun is a shortened form of *Augustodonum* (the place given by Augustus)—to replace the earlier fortress of Bibracte nearby. Perched on the hillside known as Mount Montjeu, its appearance was still very much that of a Roman imperial town except for the towering cathedral of Saint-Lazare, which had been originally planned as a Byzantine basilica and was made of native Burgundian sandstone, the favorite building fabric of the French Middle Ages. On Thursday, March 12, lookouts signaled Talleyrand's approach and church bells tolled a welcome when his coach crossed the Arroux River and passed through one of the two Roman portals that were still supported by its remaining medieval walls.

Similar to any religious event in a small community, Talleyrand's investiture, the following Sunday, was celebrated like a popular fête. As the steeple clocks chimed midday, most of the ten thousand Autunois, anxious to catch a glimpse of their new bishop, swarmed through the narrow, slanting streets following the procession of canons as they carried the traditional cross and holy water up to the bishopric's seventeenth-century palace at the top. Here, in his purple and lace finery, surrounded by his grand vicars, Talleyrand awaited to pronounce his first oath of office—in Latin. He was then conducted, surrounded by chanting priests, to take formal possession of his Episcopal seat. Talleyrand's second oath was administered on Saint-Lazare's vast twelfth-century porch with its celebrated carved columns. One of the most imposing porches in Europe, it was so large that it dwarfed Talleyrand and the other participants. This extension had been originally intended as an exterior church where the poorer victims of illness or disease could perform their devotions without entering inside—a precaution dictated by the prevalence of contagious diseases in an earlier day. At the end of the service, which followed in the cathedral proper, Monseigneur the Bishop d'Autun, intoned the *Te Deum* and, with a large theatrical gesture, solemnly blessed the worshipers. By one of those coincidences dear to the heart of historians, one of Autun's vicars who greeted Talleyrand that day, was a Corsican abbé who, not quite ten years before, had arrived there from his half-savage

Mediterranean isle to deposit his two young Bonaparte cousins, Napoleon and Joseph, at the diocese's college. As children of the island's local aristocracy, they had to learn French before the former, whose name would be indelibly linked with Talleyrand's in French history, could proceed to the Royal Military College of Brionne to be educated at royal expense.

Once these essential religious formalities were dispensed with, Talleyrand had only one thought—to be chosen deputy by his clergy. Combining the motions of being a good bishop—though he was little concerned with the saving of souls—with the demands of campaigning for the diocese's votes, he hobbled with his cane to the great Sulpicien seminary to exhort the young students to work hard. He also visited parish churches and preached at the Oratorian College. Annunciation Sunday, Talleyrand could not refuse when his flock begged him to officiate. This was a grave mistake. For it was quickly evident to his consternated acolytes that their Monseigneur was out of practice. But Talleyrand, ever the *grand seigneur* with his courtly manners, had little trouble charming the Burgundian ministry who were flattered to be invited to a series of elegant epicurean dinners featuring, among other choice dishes, "raie au beurre noir"—skate in black butter—that became legendary and were even more welcome now that the price of flour—and wood—was climbing astronomically in the provinces as well as in Paris. During Lent, fasting was strictly enforced throughout France by police supervision of local butcher shops, and fresh fish was hard to come by in Burgundy, especially this severely cold winter when ice extended far out from the Channel shores. So, Talleyrand arranged by royal authority to have the mail coaches, which serviced the Paris-Lyon line, rerouted to pass by Autun and leave a daily supply at the local market.

Throughout France, in every bailiwick and district, people were gathering at His Majesty's bidding to compose *cahiers*, or notebooks, of their local complaints and also of their hopes, for presentation at the forthcoming General Estates. At the same time they were to elect their representatives for each of the three separate bodies of that assemblage—the clergy, the First Estate; the nobility, the Second; and commons, the Third. Not everyone was entitled to vote. To participate in this, the first national electoral campaign since 1614, a citizen must be a taxpayer. This qualification differed from locale to locale and resulted in the disenfranchisement of about one fourth of the disgruntled Parisian populace. Over two hundred clerics from his Autun diocese gathered, as bid, in one of the seminary halls close to the cathedral and Talleyrand who, as bishop was their honorary president, never missed a session. He explained in such detail the principal problems to be at issue in the General Estates that his highly practical views were incorporated almost verbatim in the Autun *cahiers*. There were only four candidates, Talleyrand and three priests, and the issue was never in doubt. On April 2, Talleyrand was elected by a very large majority.

His goal accomplished, Talleyrand had no further need to stay buried in the provinces. Instead of leaving immediately which might, with just cause, be deemed unseemly, he waited a few days. Then, for some inexplicable reason, he chose to leave early on Sunday the twelfth. On Easter morning, of all days—without officiating at a single sacred office on one of the holiest days in the Christian calendar—Talleyrand was assisted into his elaborate carriage and whisked back to Paris. Perhaps, as some scandalized contemporaries intimated, he was afraid of a fiasco like that on Annunciation Sunday. He departed in so great a hurry that, in 1900, a latter-day successor found in a corner of the palace, still unpacked, crates of a crystal table service of two carafes and sixty-seven glasses. This gift was offered to Talleyrand on his installation as bishop by Creusot, a neighboring manufacturer of fine crystal for Marie-Antoinette. These remained on view in a local museum until the World War II bombardment of the Creusot foundries shattered the building. He never came back to Autun, except to pass through as a minister of the First Consul.

Talleyrand returned to the capital no longer just another of the many worldly abbés to be found in society and, as such, to be dismissed lightly, but a highly placed, powerful prelate. Life for the "Bishop," as even his friends now addressed him—some, certainly, with tongue in cheek—resumed its previous frenetic schedule. He must have been blessed with an iron-clad constitution for, sometimes, it seemed that all he required was an hour of sleep and a bath. Then he was off on his rounds once more, watching and waiting to see what was going to happen in Paris, which was already in a feverish state of excitement over the forthcoming General Estates.

Talleyrand first met Gouverneur Morris at Adèle's, shortly after the American statesman's arrival in France, sometime that spring of 1789. Unbeknown to Thomas Jefferson, who had succeeded Benjamin Franklin as the American minister in Paris, Morris was there on a secret, fact-finding mission for President George Washington—with the ostensible cover that he had come on semi-official business involving tobacco, grains, real estate, and the American debt to France. He needed contacts not only with people in political circles but also with the upper crust of opinion-making society and the financial world, and *entrée* to an established salon like the Comtesse de Flahaut's was invaluable. In addition, the convent-educated young woman spoke excellent English and his French, at first, left a lot to be desired. It is thought that Morris met her at the Versailles home of a mutual friend, the banker Cabarrus, whose daughter Thérèse was destined to win fame as "Notre Dame de Thermidor," the wife of the revolutionary leader Tallien, and who would play an important, albeit minor, role in Talleyrand's subsequent life.

A bachelor, well over six feet tall, with a strong, athletic figure, the American's bearing was so imposing that the sculptor Houdon would ask him to pose for the statue of George Washington on which he was currently working. Morris also came equipped with a formidable reputation as a lady killer, plus a wooden leg—a novelty for even the most sophisticated French and which was acquired, *tout Paris* whispered, erroneously, when he jumped out of an open window to escape a cuckolded husband.[1] Morris found Adèle "a pleasing woman . . . not a sworn enemy to intrigue." And the phrase "Nous verrons" [sic]—"We shall see"—soon optimistically peppered the American's assiduously kept, candid diary which is the only source for some of Talleyrand's daily activities during the first three years of the French Revolution.

Initially, the bishop did not make a good impression on the newcomer, two years his senior, who found him "sly, cunning, ambitious, malicious." An opinion no doubt colored by the philandering Morris's obvious desire to share Adèle's bed. Fortunately for all concerned, the Comte de Flahaut was more absent than ever. The renown naturalist Buffon had recently died and Flahaut, thanks to his brother's intervention, was appointed his successor as head of the Royal Garden—today's *Jardin des Plantes*—a magnificent and honorable sinecure that entailed a most welcome addition to the strained Flahaut finances as well as frequent, on-the-site inspections. But, in Adèle's set it was the fashion for the mistress of a drawing room to be at home alone, surrounded by a group of admirers, and to have snared as one of her coterie the attractive, cosmopolitan foreigner whom everyone was clamoring to meet was considered a real coup.

[1] The leg was lost in an attempt to drive a pair of wild horses in a phaeton.

Morris wasted no time adjusting to the free and easy ways of the *ancien régime*. He was soon ushered in even though Adèle was dressing—while she was still in a shift, having her hair powdered by one chambermaid, her hands manicured by a second, and raising one leg to be taken care of by a third, so she was only free to greet him with a nod of her head. Some days she was still in bed, not too worried about hiding little of what he might see; others, she was enjoying the luxury of a bath—in water generously laced with milk to render it opaque. For, unlike most other well-bred Parisians, who used almost no soap, Adèle considered bathing as something other than a curative measure and, Morris noted approvingly, she was "sweet-smelling" and even "washed under her armpits with Hungary Water."

3

The Bishop

"People are always saying either too many good or too many bad things about me. I enjoy the honors of exaggeration."—TALLEYRAND [1]

THE GENERAL ESTATES WAS SCHEDULED to open in Versailles, in the same Salle des Menus Plaisirs where the Notables had met previously. Far too many expectations rested on the heads of the deputies assembling there from all over France. Everyone expected a miracle. At midday, on Friday, May 1, 1789, a brace of superbly mounted heralds, in violet coats enriched with golden fleurs-de-lys, passed through the streets preceded by a company of hussars and trumpeters. At every intersection the trumpets ceased, and the heralds proclaimed the opening of the Estates "De Par Le Roi!"—("By the King's orders!")

At 11:00 a.m., on Saturday, May 2, the official presentation of the individual deputies to His Majesty began in the château's Salon d'Hercule. Because tradition was meticulously observed, when Talleyrand and the other representatives of the clergy, the First Estate, entered the Salon d'Hercule, the double-paneled doors were flung wide; they remained that way for the group from the Second Estate, the nobles. In the late afternoon, after His Majesty had lunched and napped, the royal bedchamber was deemed adequate for those from the lowly Third Estate, and only one panel was opened—to show the bourgeoisie its place. The next day the Sabbath was observed.

Monday, the fourth, steeple bells started chiming at dawn and an air of anticipation rustled through the good-natured crowds already jostling and shoving for a good vantage point for the spectacular show. Talleyrand was to participate in the short parade of the three orders from the Church of Notre Dame, just outside the royal compound, to the nearby Church of Saint-Louis to celebrate the mass of the Holy Ghost and get God's blessing on the Estates' work. The town's normal population of some sixty thousand tripled as a host of Parisians and others from the surrounding countryside, and further away, poured in to witness the magnificent spectacle, which was destined to be the monarchy's last. For two gold louis, a goodly sum, Adèle rented a window overlooking the procession's route and invited Gouverneur Morris to accompany her there. Others were not so fortunate, while the more agile felt themselves lucky to get a perch on some crowded rooftop. It was a mild spring day, the sun was shining, and everyone was in a holiday mood. The tapestries and pennants, which hung out from the mansions lining the way, formed a canyon of color, at the bottom of which stood, musket to musket, a double row of soldiers in dress uniform, alternating with the *Cent Gardes*—Louis XVI's fabled Swiss mercenaries—in their magnificent Renaissance coats, paneled with lozenges of red and gold.

Marching music of trumpets, drums, and clarinets filled the spring air, and the pageant began. The deputies, some twelve hundred of them, appeared in the prescribed costumes and time-honored order. The Third Estate—lawyers, petty officials, and professional men largely from the urban bourgeoisie—wore the required black, which they hated, from head to toe—black hose, short black mantles, three-cornered black hats, completely unadorned. Adèle spotted Mirabeau, Talleyrand's friend from Aix-en-Provence, striding among them and pointed him out to Morris. To ensure his election as the champion of the people, he had dropped his inherited title of "Count" and, tossing his unruly mane in an attention-getting gesture, he was easily identifiable by his badly disfigured face and massive frame, bedecked with a myriad of outsized glittering buckles and buttons. Then came more music. What a contrast when the deputies representing the nobles, the Second Estate, hoved into view, attired in gorgeous, many-hued costumes with lace jabots falling from the neckbands around their throats, gold-trimmed capes, white-plumed hats, turned up à la Henry IV, and ceremonial swords. Amid their ranks the king's troublemaking cousin, the Duc d'Orléans, stood out like a crow among peacocks in his black commoner's garb. A great favorite among the populace for his liberalism, he, too, had successfully maneuvered to be elected as a Third Estate representative. However, earlier this morning when the procession was being formed and the grandstand-playing Orléans took his place in line with the other bourgeois deputies, to the crowd's enthusiastic applause, the Royal Master of Ceremonies hurried over and demanded that he move back with the princes of the blood where he belonged, at His Majesty's explicit order. Next came the First Estate, the cardinals in their eye-catching scarlet velvet vestments and the bishops with white cassocks over their purple ones. At their own insistence, the higher prelates were separated by a hastily rearranged group of royal musicians, from the lower clergy in their modest black cassocks, enormous capes, and square hats. As the great gold cross on Talleyrand's chest reflected the sun's rays, someone recognized him limping along in a black cassock—he was still in mourning for his father—and shouted out his name. Because he held his head high, with his blond hair pulled back under his miter, Talleyrand, who had a sturdy frame and was tall for his day—his passport said "5 ft., 5 inches"—appeared even taller. Morris noted that his bad right foot was barely visible under his long robe, until he got tired, near the end, then he dragged it and relied more heavily on his crosier. Following the Archbishop of Paris, who carried the Holy Sacrament under a sheltering baldaquin, was Louis XVI, resplendent in a cloth-of-gold mantle, his open carriage drawn by four pairs of matched black steeds. As Marie-Antoinette passed beneath the terrace of the Small Stables, she lifted sad eyes to a sickly-faced, eight-year-old reclining on a mound of cushions. The tuberculosis-wracked, dying dauphin, who had been brought from his sick bed to watch the show, smiled back. Pages and equerries came after, and His Majesty's falconers, the only participants not to carry a lighted taper. The hooded bird riding on each one's wrist, a carry-over from medieval times, betrayed the monarch's love of the chase, a passion which had dictated the location of the General Estates at Versailles rather than in Paris in order to interfere less with the king's daily hunt. Thirty-six richly caparisoned coaches containing the queen's ladies-in-waiting and the courtiers, their diamonds ablaze in the noonday sun, brought up the rear. Still more musicians followed.

Tuesday, the fifth, the General Estates' official opening ceremony was held in the Salle des Menus Plaisirs, which had just been converted to accommodate this far larger group. Unfortunately, sanitation, never the best even at the château—which stank horribly—included makeshift outdoor latrines, in rank contrast with the vast 120-foot-long hall with its majestic row of columns, decorative frieze, and elaborate cornices. Here, tradition again prevailed and, as might be expected, everything was arranged visually to emphasize the respective ranking of the three Orders.

Talleyrand was seated on an upholstered chair with the rest of the clergy and nobles to the left of the king's throne, which was generously swathed in violet velvet swags embroidered with golden fleurs-de-lys. A smaller one for the queen, directly below it, was similarly adorned. To the right were the dignitaries and officials of the court and the princes of the blood, on stools, chairs, armchairs, according to their station. In the semi-circle opposite the throne, on hard uncomfortable benches with neither cushions nor backs and crowded closely together, sat the lowly Third Estate. Louis XVI opened the proceedings with a short address which His Majesty had twice rewritten.

Then the pompous Necker, his absurd wig, with one sausage-like roll of hair parallel to and above each ear, slightly askew, strode to the podium. Instead of the expected political tirade, succeeded by a plan of proposed reform, the finance minister droned on and on, figure by figure, depicting the exchequer's burgeoning deficit in so much tedious detail that the king had trouble suppressing more than one royal yawn. The Genevan's thick accent did not help the situation. Matters did not improve when the meticulous Necker—who had taken the precaution of rehearsing there, the night before, to be sure he could be heard in every nook and cranny—lost his voice after half an hour. His secretary had to substitute for him, droning on for another two and a half hours.

Given the gravity of France's financial situation Thomas Jefferson, who was present, was shocked to see the General Estates' inauguration transpire in what he termed "an operatic décor." But Gouverneur Morris was so fascinated by the whole performance that he got up at 4:00 a.m. the following morning to allow ample time for the two-hour ride out—plus a likely tie-up at one of the farmer-generals' fifty-four unpopular tollhouses ringing Paris—and still insure a good seat for the 10:00 a.m. session. Chaos greeted him. To attend to the preliminary piece of business, the verification of each delegate's powers,

Talleyrand and the rest of the clergy retired, as was customary, to the First Estate's own smaller chamber; the Second, to theirs. But no similar alternative place had been provided for the Third Estate which remained in the great Salle des Menus Plaisirs. Its members were determined that the General Estates no longer meet in three separate assemblies, as in the past, but together for this formality and insisted that the others rejoin them there to do the verifications in common. This was a canny innovation which implied that the delegates should not be segregated in any future sessions. Instead of voting thereafter by separate estates, as heretofore, which meant one vote per group, they would remain together and vote by heads—as had been done recently in the province of the Dauphiné. This would assure the domination of the Third Estate, which was larger than the other two combined. The whole future of the assembly depended on a response to this question but, unfortunately, neither Louis XVI nor his shortsighted ministers had foreseen that this problem might arise and did not come provided with a ready answer. So this paramount issue was foolishly left to be decided on the floor.

The nobility, the Second Estate, presented an almost solid front against this radical new approach and any other new reforms, the only hold-outs being some fifty of its younger members, many of whom had gone to America to fight with Lafayette. The First Estate did not. Its Achilles' heel proved to be the country priests who, with their hard lot and long list of grievances, had more in common with the Third Estate than with their own hierarchy. The bitter struggle over where to sit—and how to deliberate—lasted weeks. The First and Second Orders were unable to reach any consensus, and the stentorian voice of Mirabeau, who is generally credited with being the *deus ex machina* of the crisis, could be heard bellowing above the babble of the Third, urging them not to concede. It was a hopeless deadlock.

Finally, in mid-June, following a motion proposed by the Abbé Sieyès, the Third Estate arrogated the title of "National Assembly," sent an ultimatum to the other two orders to join it, and proceeded to the long delayed verification of its own deputies' powers. The First Estate voted by a narrow margin to remain separated but, as the roll call of the Third proceeded in the great Salle, several poor country priests had second thoughts and daringly slipped in to join them. Following their example, more than two hundred of the lowly parish curates—out of the two hundred and ninety-one ecclesiasts—trickled over during the ensuing days.

Louis XVI was in deepest mourning for the little dauphin who had died two weeks before. He was at his country seat at nearby Marly where Louis XIV had built the cumbersome, creaking machine to raise the waters of the Seine and send it by aqueduct to the unquenchable fountains of Versailles. He might have trouble making up his mind about most things, but he was adamant that the three orders must maintain their time-honored separation. So his advisors urged that His Majesty meet this unexpected challenge by once again addressing the entire General Estates. When the Third Estate and its new recruits gathered the next morning, the Salle des Menus Plaisirs was locked. They could hear workmen pounding inside preparing for the forthcoming royal séance. The deputies stubbornly refused to disband but were undecided what to do next, and milling around outside in an unexpected downpour did not help their dispositions. Suddenly one of them, Dr. Guillotin—whose name has gone down in French history for another, macabre reason—remembered an unused tennis court close by that belonged to a friend. Following him, some six hundred soggy, angry deputies trooped over to the rue du Vieux Versailles, getting madder by the minute, with Mirabeau in a sedan chair surrounded by his gesticulating cronies and followed by an ever larger, curious crowd. The empty court echoed starkly. Jumping on a simple pine table requisitioned from a neighboring tradesman, their president, Sylvain Bailly—an astronomer whose only previous claim to fame was the discovery of Jupiter's moons—called the group to order. Then, with one hand outstretched, the other on his heart, he led them in taking an oath never to be separated until "we have formed a solid and equitable constitution as our constituents have asked us to do." [2]

Continued maneuvering won over certain of the highest born nobles, but only a handful of prelates changed sides. Talleyrand's situation was a delicate one. Never an idealist but a reformer and, above all, a practical man, he realized that, by remaining with the First Estate where he belonged, he risked compromising his future standing with the new majority coalescing in the upcoming assembly. So, on June 26 he, too, took his place in the Salle des Menus Plaisirs and none too soon, if he was to reap credit with the left. The following day, the king, overwhelmed at the continued rebelliousness of the recalcitrant deputies, backed down, handing the Third Estate an important victory. There was now legally and officially a National Constituent Assembly in which each delegate had an individual vote. In celebration that night, all sorts of firecrackers—

squids, rockets, serpents—were available at cut-rate prices, craftily subsidized by the Orléans faction. They exploded in the Paris skies until well past midnight with bright colors and attention-getting noise, while the heavens at Versailles remained prophetically pitch black.

Talleyrand commuted incessantly to Paris. To feel the capital's pulse, it was essential to know what was being said in its salons and mushrooming political clubs, especially in the Duc d'Orléans's hyperactive Palais Royal Gardens, where rabble-rousing agitators working overtime, harangued the crowds around the clock. Unfortunately, the only satisfactory means of daily communication was either by a round of personal calls or by dispatching a footman with handwritten notes hither and yon and then awaiting a response. But Talleyrand had plenty of stamina and was not slowed down by the heavy brace he dragged around, although his daily schedule was a backbreaking one. The number of places he sometimes visited in one evening—or the number of times in one day he dragged himself up the one hundred and sixty musty, steep stairs and, then, down from Adèle's aerie—defies enumeration. Luckily he did not seem to require much sleep.

After a grueling day in the hot boisterous assembly at Versailles and a tedious ride in to Paris, jiggling around over the uneven cobbled stones, trying to read in his book-lined carriage, followed by the evening's usual heavy calendar, Adèle's small elegant salon, high in the Louvre, was a welcome haven. Talleyrand rarely missed a night there when he was in town. The bishop soon grew accustomed to seeing the attractive American bachelor rather than another man, or the maid, singled out to star in a recently imported custom considered chic in Adèle's circle—personally preparing and serving the midnight tea, an expensive luxury. Relations between Talleyrand and Adèle had by now evolved from a passionate to a tender, enduring attachment, a pattern that would repeat itself over and over again with the many mistresses in his life. With a roving eye like that of many another contemporary prelate, Talleyrand could not refrain from playing the field any more than Adèle could restrain her coquetry—and her ever-fluttering fan. And he did not expect faithfulness in a mistress.

Her soirées did not begin until after nine and lasted until after midnight. When no one remained at the whist and tric-trac tables and the other guests had also departed, Adèle and her two lame admirers conversed for several hours about the day's events in the small, partially screened off, intimate nook of the salon where Adèle kept her harpsichord, her harp, and a little table on which to indulge her hobby as a writer. The flickering light from the guttering candles in the wall sconces and on the small tables threw into relief Talleyrand's slightly turned-up nose. This gave his face a somewhat effeminate cast as he sat, his bad right leg stretched stiffly out, taking frequent pinches of snuff from a delicately chased gold *tabatière* which he drew from a deep, ample pocket. The soft glow dealt kindly with the burly Morris's big head, handsome masculine features—and wooden leg. Adèle was in the shadow sitting, as Morris's diary describes her, in her usual place between her harpsichord and writing table, her little stool tucked under her feet, listening carefully. It was a tribute to her perceptiveness that she was able to keep these two brilliant cripples so closely attached to her—and so congenial with each other. From Talleyrand's point of view, Morris was a mine of invaluable, first-hand information. For he had been a delegate from Pennsylvania to both the American Continental Congress and, subsequently, to the Constitutional Convention, where he served with distinction in the drafting of that document's final version.

This main work of the deputies at Versailles was being conducted by a small elite of proven ability, working largely in caucuses, and the reform of the French constitution now took precedence over the country's financial debacle. On the morning of Tuesday, July 14, Talleyrand, who had given his maiden speech only the week before, was the second person to be nominated to the crucial, forty-eight-man committee that was to draft this new charter. His relationship with Morris would be put to good use and may, conceivably, have even been a factor in his selection. Because of the press of business, the assembly was opening daily at 6:00 a.m., and Talleyrand had already put in a long day when, suddenly, there was a commotion outside in the street, and a dusty courier, who had ridden out posthaste, burst into the hall with electrifying news: Paris was up in arms and besieging the Bastille.

The reports of turmoil in Lyons, France's second largest city, the threat of national bankruptcy, and the highest bread prices in history had increased the general malaise, acerbated by the onslaught of hot weather, until the discontent of hungry, frustrated Parisians was palpable. Little was needed for it to explode. Worried by the mounting tide of violence, the king had lately increased the garrisons around Versailles in case force might be needed to safeguard order. On the eleventh, three days earlier, Louis XVI, perturbed by Necker's inability to resolve the exchequer's problems, abruptly dismissed the bourgeois Genevan—and other liberal ministers—sending him and his wife into immediate exile straight from their dinner table, with nothing but the clothes on their backs. En route to Coppet, his home, he stopped in Brussels long enough to personally guarantee the millions of francs required to pay for a shipment of desperately needed wheat that was on its way to the French capital. Necker might no longer be thought competent in financial circles, while the court held him accountable for the catastrophic opening of the General Estates. But the Parisians still considered him capable of achieving miracles. Outraged that Necker had just been sent packing, worried by rumors that the augmented royal troops were being mustered to march on the city, nurtured by desperation, Paris erupted in open revolt.

Crowds roamed the city all Monday, exhorted by patriots carrying plaster busts of Necker, their hero, whose return to office they demanded. Egged on by fire-breathing extremists and manipulated behind the scenes by Machiavellian radicals with their own agenda, they wandered through the streets, unhitching horses and pulling frightened people from their coaches, breaking into storefronts. Early Tuesday, demagogues learned that the gunpowder desperately needed, if people were to use any of the thirty thousand muskets that they had just commandeered from les Invalides, could be found at the Bastille. Because of the narrow, crooked streets it did not require a huge number to constitute a sizeable and effective mob as Parisians streamed towards the hated state prison at 132, rue Saint-Antoine, a symbol of despotic power in the popular mind, where anyone might be imprisoned at royal whim.

Talleyrand and the other deputies were still hard at work in the long summer twilight when the news they dreaded arrived. The Bastille had fallen and its prisoners released—a paltry seven in all: two lunatics, four forgers, and a blue-blooded delinquent—while the head of its governor, de Launay, was being proudly paraded on a pike throughout the streets. The remainder of the night the deputies spent in feverish conferences both in the Salle des Menus Plaisirs and at the château.

The following morning, Louis XVI and his two brothers, attired in unadorned morning coats, walked over unescorted. Gone was the customary panoply of majesty. The king announced he was recalling Necker and, in addition, as a measure of good faith, the immediate withdrawal of most of the regiments whose presence had caused so much alarm. The same afternoon, the assembly sent to Paris a deputation of thirteen deputies to help establish calm there, including Talleyrand, his uncle the archbishop, and Lafayette, who had just been appointed commander-in-chief of the National Guard which had been hastily created at the Hôtel de Ville the day before.

Talleyrand correctly interpreted Paris's turn to violence and the king's yielding to the mobs as a prescription for impending disaster. The dissolution of royal power left wide the door to every possible excess. Whether Talleyrand was alone or accompanied when he went to warn Louis XVI, whether others also went to Marly with similar ideas, the night of the sixteenth and seventeenth or the seventeenth and eighteenth, is not clear. Talleyrand's trip was facilitated by his intimate, Sainte-Foy, who was the comptroller of finances for the king's brother, the Comte d'Artois. Delegated by the sovereign, Artois arose from slumber to receive him. For two hours Talleyrand pled that the monarchy's last hope lay in the temporary dissolution of the assembly—by force if necessary. Then, he argued, it should be reconvened at some future date, with a new slate of deputies who must be elected in a different manner. Thoroughly alarmed by what Talleyrand was saying, the count dressed at once and obtained an immediate audience with Louis XVI. Unfortunately, His Majesty's ministers were in disagreement on how to proceed and the king was strongly opposed to any move that might shed one drop of French blood. Artois reported this to the waiting Talleyrand and, the next day, Artois left the country.

There was nothing more Talleyrand could do for Louis XVI. Now he must decide whether to follow the king's brother into exile or remain behind and try to do something for his country—and himself. He elected to stay. If any one thing in his *Mémoires* is to be taken at face value, it is evident that Talleyrand throughout his long life considered himself a patriot whose prime concern was France. And, of course, he was always happiest when this coincided with what was best for Talleyrand. Already his views regarding many of the inequities in the financial and educational systems were on record in the program he submitted earlier, when Autun's candidate for deputy. He was hopeful that he and his liberal friends might institute reforms, which could still save the throne and guide the incipient Revolution to a constitutional monarchy, thereby ensuring the creation of a more dynamic, powerful France—as well as a splendid future for himself.

On the seventeenth, when the king came to town to repeat to the Parisians the same hopefully reassuring announcement at the Hôtel de

Ville that he had earlier made to the assembly, Adèle again managed to rent a window along his route to see the spectacle. Because all traffic was forbidden in Paris that day, she and Morris had to proceed there on foot but, for once, it was possible to do so without fear of being run over by competing carriages. Sidewalks, a novelty recently imported from England, were still not greatly in evidence, although the ever-present pickpockets were, as Morris, stumping along, discovered to his chagrin. The royal arrival was hardly worth their five-hour wait. Gone was the elaborate pageantry that heralded the opening of the General Estates, a scant two months before, and Morris characterized the cortège of deputies straggling along in the rear as "disorderly." At the last moment, Talleyrand changed his mind—for unknown reasons—and was not among them.

The riots and the fall of the Bastille may have shaken Parisians in general, but high society chose to believe that these were only minor disturbances. Paris had its usual summer attractions: the theaters were open, Franconi's circus with its trained stag played to packed audiences, and the streets teemed with visiting English tourists. Since a tour of the Bastille ruins was *le dernier cri* among Adèle's set, and Talleyrand was too busy to take her, Morris secured a pass through Lafayette whom he knew from the marquis' American days. A demolition crew was already at work and, scrambling everywhere amid the overwhelming stench, enterprising entrepreneurs were salvaging what they could to make into brooches, pins, and paperweights to hawk to gawking patriots.

Gallantry leavened with politics might be the supreme diversion of women in most French salons of the day, but Adèle was only interested in public affairs to the extent that her circle was. She still regarded what was transpiring outside her Louvre windows objectively, as scenes from another planet, not as something that might conceivably have relevance for herself. Her world might be fast polarizing between her husband, his conservative family and friends, and Talleyrand and his reform-minded, liberal coterie, although, for Adèle, the revolution was still little more than a game in which the farsighted men attracted to her puzzled over state finances and budgets, and studied proposals and motions, however, throughout his long life Talleyrand was never adverse to using the opposite sex, some of whom would serve him with great distinction. As Morris had already discovered, "France is the land of women," and his diary documents the extent to which Adèle was Talleyrand's almost daily confidante—and associate—during this crucial period. Because the bishop respected her common sense and tact, he used Adèle as a sounding board as well as a go-between to facilitate contacts and even to garner powerful, highly placed support for himself with her friend Montmorin the foreign minister and others. When there was talk later that Lafayette was to be asked to head up a new cabinet and that Talleyrand was under consideration for one of the posts, it was Adèle who asked Morris to arrange a series of meetings between the bishop and Lafayette, whom Talleyrand scarcely knew. Largely because of his American experiences, the thirty-two-year-old general carried so much weight that he was considered an essential component for the success of any proposed slate, even though he was a political novice. As a selling point, to assure that Talleyrand would receive a portfolio Morris, who was anxious to please Adèle—each was playing his own game at the moment—reminded Lafayette that with the bishop "you also get Mirabeau." It was Adèle who conferred with Vicq d'Azyr, Marie-Antoinette's physician, and "set him to work to remove some of Her Majesty's prejudices" for such an appointment, because the queen did not like Talleyrand. Adèle also helped Morris—whose command of French she once remarked, was good but was it French?—correcting his memorandum that was to be read to Louis XVI and translating his letters to Lafayette.

The American learned, like the bishop, to appreciate her fine mind. However, he was a vain, practiced seducer and, when he pushed his suit with her, Adèle spoke of "a marriage of the heart," clasping her hands together and looking heavenward, without mentioning anyone specific. Morris uttered the bishop's name and she nodded, saying she "[could not] commit an infidelity to him." However, the word "platonic" was not a staple of her vocabulary and Adèle, who would end up as one of the two women to play a leading role in Morris's life, succumbed some time in midsummer. As numerous pages in Morris's journal attest, Adèle and the American frequently performed "the genial act" more than once a day, here, there, and everywhere except in bed. These included in his carriage with "the coachman staring straight ahead;" in the small salon, while Adèle's nearsighted cousin played the pianoforte close at hand; even on a dirty landing in the Louvre's dark halls, fetid with the collected treasures of the ages. Given the circumstances of their mating and the elaborate costumes of the day—granted street clothes were simpler than evening dress—how they were able to "join in [their] devotions to the Cyprian queen" to either's satisfaction taxes the imagination. How Adèle avoided numerous pregnancies poses another practical question although she still suffered from the ministrations of an incompetent midwife four years after her son Charles's birth. If Adèle and Morris's mutual physical desire was insatiable, nothing is known of the intensity of Talleyrand and Adèle's passion. Although Adèle, in an unguarded moment, let slip that the bishop "deployed more skill than vigor." [3] "No wonder," remarked one cynical French biographer, so many of Talleyrand's mistresses were slightly fatigued, older women!

Talleyrand may or may not have been taken aback by this change in the American's relationship—a short time later Adèle claimed he was jealous—but he was a practical man of the world. Morris's timely advice, garnered from their midnight chats *à trois*, furnished Talleyrand with invaluable insights, which he then went home to mull over and frequently incorporated into the final draft of the morrow's speech that he had just discussed with them. The two men understood each other well and Morris, who was as much of a snob, intellectually and socially, as Talleyrand, remarked later on the charms of conversation with the bishop rather than with "one of those halfway minds which see just far enough to bewilder themselves." [4] The American warned, from his own recent firsthand experience, that successful constitutions represent the art of compromise. He had important suggestions for the drafting of a document that would be favorable to the French people themselves as well as to the monarchy. So Talleyrand invited Morris to the National Assembly to confer with those colleagues who sat with him on its all-important Constitutional Committee. When Talleyrand read this group's first report in a subsequent general session, Adèle and Morris got up at 5:00 a.m. and hurried out to hear him. The Marquis de Lafayette was the first to propose that the deputies draft a "Declaration of the Rights of Man" as a preamble to their new constitution, and he worked on one with Thomas Jefferson, a friend from his American stay, until the diplomat was recalled. Each word, each phrase was hotly debated not only in the Salle des Menus Plaisirs, but on the streets of Versailles and in the Paris salons. On August 4 the deputies took up the preliminary recommendations for this revolutionary measure, which the Constitutional Committee had already worked out in exhaustive detail. In the midst of a tempestuous, all night session, Lafayette's brother-in-law, the young Vicomte de Noailles, a scion of one of France's oldest, most aristocratic families, who was nicknamed "Jean sans Terre" (Landless John) for obvious reasons, jumped to his feet and, in a sudden outburst of patriotism, impetuously abandoned his numerous inherited titles and privileges. Others, including fellow veterans from the American War of Independence, followed suit with similar sacrifices. By the time dawn streaked the eastern skies, the last vestiges of the French feudal structure were swept away. Talleyrand subsequently proposed and drafted the celebrated sixth article of the declaration's final twenty-two, which claimed the right of all citizens to be equal, and "to be so treated." Reading this article makes one wonder to what extent—at least in the beginning—Talleyrand's revolt against the social order of his day stemmed subconsciously from a feeling that he himself was one of its victims when he had to relinquish his birthright.

Although the finished product incorporated some of the most radical ideas of the day, a decided whiff of aristocratic condescension permeates it. The right to vote was extended to all French males over twenty-five—with certain other specific qualifications thrown in—and created an electorate of four million, making this the largest experiment in representative government in Europe. But women and black slaves were still disfranchised. By the end of August, the document was unanimously adopted and accepted by the king, with disastrous results for the moribund *ancien régime*. Because the liberties it enshrined included the protection of freedom of speech, publication and assembly, together with the removal of censorship and prosecution for the same, a vast, broad new audience was opened up, literally overnight, for political discussions. Transportation-wise, the latest Paris news was already able to reach the entire countryside within three to four days and, now, within the next three years, the press jumped from the sixty-plus newspapers of substance that were currently blanketing France to around five hundred in Paris alone.

A boiling cauldron of new ideas, the National Constituent Assembly was made-to-order for an ambitious thirty-five year old. Talleyrand's feverish activity there covered a wide range but centered, primarily, on questions of finance, a field in which he was emerging as an authority. Unfortunately, his well-known fondness for gambling for high stakes—a weakness shared by many contemporaries, including Adèle—and his reputation for unscrupulous use of inside information in his speculations on the Bourse and for his manipulations in government funds damaged his public image. But, as a Talleyrand-Périgord, he considered himself above criticism and commented in a letter this fall: "People are always saying either too many good or too many bad things about me. I enjoy the honors of exaggeration." [5] When Morris and Adèle accompanied Talleyrand to supper at a friend's, the fuss the assembled guests made over the bishop indicated that those present expected him to soon hold a post of great power.

Famine stalked the countryside. Unrest in the provinces was on the rise and the deficit in the exchequer skyrocketed out of sight. The people could not support another tax and the best remedy Necker could offer was one short term loan after another, at ever higher rates, with ever smaller results. For more than a century, the enormous wealth of the Church, composed of gifts given down through the ages by the faithful to guarantee their salvation, had tempted needy statesmen and, by the late Enlightenment, practicality began to color their vision. Louis XIV had cast envious eyes upon these assets, and Frederick of Prussia wrote Voltaire, more than a decade earlier, "In France when all other expedients have been exhausted . . . they will be forced to secularize the convents and abbeys." [6] The Vatican aborted such an attempt by Marie-Antoinette's brother, Emperor Joseph II of Austria. As France's largest landowner, the Church possessed one fifth of all the land in the country. Early that summer, Buzot, a deputy not further identified, launched the suggestion that the Church's worldly possessions were not its inalienable property but belonged to the nation. A similar thought was voiced in the Salle des Menus Plaisirs, a few days later, by a deputy from the bailiwick of Charolles. And soon, thereafter, two colleagues of Talleyrand, actually proposed this takeover, but their motion provoked such a storm that it was quickly tabled. But only temporarily. The seed was planted and germinated tantalizingly in fertile soil. Hungry people greedily eyed the farms and forests, the lush meadows and well-stocked streams of the monasteries and bishoprics and, soon, the deputy Treilhard was appointed by the assembly to study the matter in depth and make a report.

Talleyrand was already thinking along the same lines. As Morris's journal indicates, there had hardly been a day this past month when the possibility of a ministerial post for the bishop had not been discussed in the Louvre. France's predicament afforded him an excellent opportunity to demonstrate his financial acumen and thereby insure his elevation to this coveted rank which he considered the open sesame to great wealth and power. What the Genevan Protestant dare not broach he, a Catholic bishop of irreproachable lineage, could. One fall night, Talleyrand again discussed nationalization of the Church's vast real estate holdings as a last desperate measure. Morris felt his proposed motion was well done. Since it was imperative to realize the maximum value possible from these ecclesiastical properties in the shortest time feasible, Morris outlined a technical plan for their sale which greatly impressed Talleyrand. The American noted in his journal: "He is bigoted to [his plan] . . . attached to [it] . . . as an author, which is not a good symptom for a man of business. However, our friend [Adèle] insists with him so earnestly that she makes him give up one point. She has infinite good sense." When Talleyrand leaves the Louvre, the last item of the day's business is duly recorded: "[We] close as lovers what we had commenced as politicians."

The afternoon of the next day—Tuesday, October 5—Talleyrand was in the Salle des Menus Plaisirs when a disheveled, bedraggled host of market women burst in, shouting for bread. A gust of hatred was blowing over France. Starving Parisians, acerbated by the rising high cost of bread—when there was any—and lack of jobs, were getting restless and out of hand, inflamed by torrents of vicious pamphlets against the monarchy. The tocsin, that centuries-old signal of alarm, reverberated ominously from the Church of Sainte-Marguerite throughout Monday night. In the early dawn, led by a man beating a drum, the women commandeered two cannons and walked all the way out to Versailles, braving the mounting wind and rain. Their anger increased—as did wine and recruits—during the six hour march. After haranguing the frightened deputies for several hours, the motley crew insisted on speaking to the king in person. Louis XVI was finally located, out hunting as usual and, after the disorderly horde overpowered the security, killing two royal bodyguards, and burst, shrieking, into the château, His Majesty acquiesced to their demands. Several hours later, under a cloudless sky, with scarcely a breath of air stirring the trees, the royal family set off for Paris, virtual prisoners of the victorious mob. Talleyrand was designated as part of the official escort of deputies accompanying their humiliating return. Singing that they were bringing back "the baker, the baker's wife, and the baker's lad," the hiccupping, dirty crew marched alongside carrying on the end of their pikes loaves of His Majesty's bread, while others took turns parading around, brandishing on high the heads of their two victims. A train of wagons and carts filled with flour from the royal pantries followed. When the dramatic procession finally reached the Tuileries, after more than an eternity of five hours en route, Talleyrand went directly to the Louvre to discuss the latest happenings. But Adèle and Morris were out shopping—at Sèvres for porcelains, and elsewhere for mirrors and other items on a long list just received from President Washington. A scant seventy-two hours later, almost at the end of the morning session, Talleyrand requested permission to address the assembly. Because he rarely did so, silence fell as he slowly made his way between the green, baize-covered tables and up the steps of the podium. At his best in intimate groups, he was not a good speaker in crowded halls despite his grave, deep voice; the impact of his speeches derived more from their content than from any oratorical skills. But Mirabeau and others with whom he was in intensive consultation felt Talleyrand was the logical person to bring up the controversial proposal he was about to set before the house. Having served as general agent for five years he was in a better position than anyone to know the full extent of the Church's vast holdings, while, as a high ranking member of the clergy, he would carry more weight and lend the proposal the appearance of being in the best interests of the Church itself. Transforming what might be considered a sacrifice into a gift, the bishop wasted no time. Extraordinary situations demanded extraordinary resolutions; since the state had no money it must take it from those who had. This was a measure whose time had come. By counseling the clergy to accept it rather than to submit to it, Talleyrand revealed his lifetime *modus vivendi* as a politician—to sacrifice what he took for granted was already as good as lost. But he was not recommending all give and no take. In return, because the clergy had a specific social role, the state must assure the Church's maintenance and guarantee all its members a living wage. This was a clever ploy for support for the measure within the hierarchy itself, where the humbler priests had as much of a struggle to eke out a living as their lowly parishioners. Pandemonium erupted even before Talleyrand finished.

Talleyrand resumed his customary impassivity. Maintaining, in a letter to an intimate "if reason refuses to accept the means which I propose, necessity will do so," [7] he never again discussed his epochal motion in the chamber itself. Instead, Mirabeau took over to guarantee its passage. He and Talleyrand shared many of the same views on domestic and foreign affairs. While Talleyrand neither admitted nor denied their collusion in the present instance, intimates who knew both men were anxious for a change of ministry—Mirabeau, too, desired a portfolio—suspected that the pair were agreed in advance on the best way to proceed. They had worked in this fashion before. Mirabeau was by nature a fighter and approached life as a combat arena. For Talleyrand it was a chessboard and he, a player, full of give and take. From the initial reactions, Mirabeau quickly realized that Talleyrand's motion, as stated, was too complicated for the average Frenchman and risked being lost in insurmountable difficulties. So, two days later, he substituted his own stripped-down version. One of the best, most fiery orators of the period, his rage boiled over at his colleagues' incomprehension. Shaking his unruly mane, only partially restrained in a black taffeta bag at the nape of his neck, his head tilted defiantly forward over the podium, the mountainous Mirabeau stormed at his colleagues.

The deputies were anxious to remain at the center of the action and decided to follow His Majesty into the capital. This proved to be a fatal error because their move placed the assembly at the mercy of the volatile city mobs. But what a relief it was for Talleyrand, who no longer needed to commute to and fro between Versailles and Paris, traveling by the back roads to save time and taking his chances with the thieves and gypsies abounding in the wild Bois de Boulogne.

Exactly one year after his long-sought elevation to the bishopric, on November 2, the fiercely fought debate over the despoliation of the Church calmed sufficiently to allow a vote. A noisy intimidating crowd packed the galleries, while outside hundreds more, reportedly subsidized by revolutionary agitators, were excitedly awaiting the results. The roll call—568, some say 510, for; 346 against, with 40 abstentions—was held, ironically, in the palace of the Archbishop of Paris where the National Constituent Assembly was temporarily housed.

Few other propositions would so profoundly modify the basic structure of pre-revolutionary France. Talleyrand's role in the confiscation of the Church's wealth was not only one of his most significant acts as a deputy but also one of the most controversial of his entire career. It is interesting—and revelatory—that he does not mention it anywhere in his *Mémoires*. Overnight Talleyrand, the man of the *ancien régime* who for so long attempted to act as a moderator between the liberals and conservatives, was transformed into a man of the Revolution. Ripped asunder were his carefully cultivated ties with the court. His horrified mother and his uncle, the Archbishop of Reims, considered what he had done a betrayal of his vows to God and the Church. He became known as *le diable boiteux*—the lame devil—and rightist cartons portrayed him as a double-faced Janus, whose moderation was labeled duplicity. But the aristocratic bishop was no longer suspect in circles that now mattered and amid the myriad rumors afloat about the composition of a probable new ministry his name—and Mirabeau's—surfaced most frequently.

Since the Treasury could not realize the confiscated real estate's true worth if it was dumped on the market all at once, Mirabeau proposed anticipating its value and issuing special paper money, *assignats*, that could be used to purchase these nationalized properties or else be redeemed at the *assignats'* face value by those who desired land. Talleyrand worked on the legislation creating this famous tender, the unexpected abuse of which was to prove so catastrophic that within six months he would try to curb its issuance. If, as contemporary scandal mongers claimed, Talleyrand and Mirabeau made a killing by procuring masses of these *assignats* when they depreciated through fear of the state's bankruptcy, then soared sky high when the market realized that they were actually based on something tangible, there is little trace—yet. Morris, in whose esteem the bishop had risen greatly on further acquaintance, discounted such reports. But it is only natural to wonder to what extent Talleyrand, who had lost the income from all his abbeys and their dependencies when they were seized along with the other ecclesiastic holdings, was able to recoup by taking judicious advantage of the resultant fire sale. Current research is proceeding apace in this fertile but still shadowy field of investigation.

With the advent of cold weather, the boisterous legislators were finally established in their permanent home—the remodeled Manège. This was an oval-shaped, former riding academy and covered ring, which had been built to teach Louis XV to ride as a child, and which extended the length of the North Terrace of the Tuileries where the rue de Rivoli is today. On the surface, His Majesty's government remained in control. In the assembly Talleyrand and the liberals still thought there was a chance to consolidate what gains had been accomplished to date towards a constitutional monarchy on the English model, and they hoped to stop a further slide towards anarchy. But, in reality, actual authority was already passing to the radical political clubs and the revolutionary elements whose influence was on the rise, fed by the deteriorating economy and resultant distress. In an endeavor to reinforce their growing presence in the circles of power, the latter managed to sideline the most seasoned politicians, who were mainly the conservatives, by manipulating the deputies into passing a resolution that the incumbent legislators were ineligible to accept office. This was not as crushing a blow as it ought to have been to Talleyrand, who well knew that in those volatile times any decree could be overturned, and he and Mirabeau started working behind scenes at once for its reversal. One day when Mirabeau was again enumerating the qualifications he considered essential for any ministerial candidate—and drawing an excellent self-portrait—Talleyrand interrupted his badly disfigured colleague: "Should you not add that such a man should be strongly marked by the smallpox?" [8]

Little actually changed as far as Talleyrand's personal life was concerned. One of his two brothers emigrated, and some of the great townhouses of friends in the aristocratic faubourg Saint-Germain were boarded up because their owners had fled, but most of his intimates remained. Any excuse still served the Parisians to gather and talk politics, and Talleyrand continued to go the rounds nightly to keep up to date. Occasionally the food shortages that were devastating the average households intruded. One midnight when the bishop stopped by Adèle's hospitable Louvre apartment, which was as welcoming as usual with its heavy silk curtains pulled against the season's chill and a blazing fire on the hearth, he found her for the first time inconvenienced by the market's shortcomings and forced to substitute a certain type of cheese for cream with the midnight tea. He lay down his hat and cane and, as the observant Morris remarked, took "a chair in the manner of a man determined to stay, and I think with the intention to perform the part allotted to me." Soon afterwards, the American left and, "considering the state of expectation to which . . . [Adèle] was raised," he thought "the chances were greatly in the bishop's favor."

Adèle became frantic when she heard the rumor that every tenant in the Louvre was to be expelled. She was already beside herself because Talleyrand was turning more and more to Germaine Necker, the Baroness de Staël, the wife of the Swedish ambassador. As hostess of one of the most important political salons in the capital, where the liberal aristocracy flocked, Germaine was in an unassailable position to help any aspirant to power. The ascendancy of Jacques Necker's star ever since his triumphant return to France after the fall of the Bastille, made Germaine, his spoilt only child, far more influential—and hence more interesting—to Talleyrand who hoped she might be able to help him. So he dissimulated his very mediocre opinion of Necker as a pretentious financier. It was as if two talkers had seduced each other.

Germaine's powerful intellectual grasp and lively, scintillating talk mesmerized the bishop, while she was heard to remark: "If [his] conversation could be purchased, I would gladly go into bankruptcy." [9] Morris, who compared her to a chambermaid in looks, felt that he, personally, was not up to the brilliance of the conversation there and likened the embassy on the rue du Bac to a temple of Apollo. "The few observations [sic] I make have more of justice than splendor and therefore cannot amuse."

The twenty-three-year-old Swedish ambassadress was not pretty with a swarthy complexion, superb big eyes, thick lips, and heavy black hair, which she would soon hide underneath a trademark turban. Germaine dressed in notoriously bad taste and never hesitated to display what she considered her best features—chunky arms always exposed and a generous bosom forever draped in a décolleté gown even when traveling. Moderation and restraint were foreign to her. Colossal self-assurance, inherited from her father, was a dominant characteristic; a craving for love and politics, her motivating forces. Nevertheless, few men could resist her fascination and domineering impetuousness and, by early winter, Talleyrand was, reputedly, one of her lovers, although he later was heard to exclaim "She violated me!"

With Germaine one can never be sure about these personal matters. She would always maintain that Comte de Narbonne, one of Talleyrand's "Triumvirate," was only a platonic friend, whereas her posthumous letters unequivocally establish him as one of the "three great loves" of her life—the second was Talleyrand—and the father of her two sons. Narbonne was understandably disturbed at Talleyrand's invasion of his territory and, within Morris's earshot, proposed to Adèle, in a half-serious, half-bantering manner, a pleasant, *quid pro quo*, revenge.

Germaine managed to sit next to Morris one night when he dined at the Swedish Embassy to discuss the American debt with Necker and, as their conversation grew animated, she suggested that they talk in English, a language her husband did not understand. Later Morris confided that she gave him what Sir John Falstaff calls "the leer of invitation." In all human probability a few interviews would stimulate her curiosity to the experiment of what can be effected by the Native of the New World who has left one of his legs behind him.

Talleyrand rarely shelved a mistress and throughout a long life he remained on excellent terms with most of them. Adèle was still his *maîtresse en titre* (mistress in title), and his visits continued unabated down the Louvre's long, poorly lit corridors and up the one hundred and sixty tortuous, steep steps to the top floor. A carping critic might imagine that the American, with his firsthand legislative and financial experience, was now more of a drawing card there than comely Adèle. To this Morris's journal gives the lie, making abundantly clear the extent to which Talleyrand continued to rely on Adèle's help—as well as on his own.

When Adèle brought the four-and-a-half-year-old Charles de Flahaut in from the countryside where he was being raised, Talleyrand often requested to have dinner with mother and son. This holiday season was no exception for a get-together which Morris, the only contemporary to ever authenticate—twice—Talleyrand's paternity, termed "a real family affair." The bishop never officially claimed Charles, or any suspected subsequent offspring, but he was fond of children and never failed to look out for his only son's welfare.

4

The Deputy

"Laissez-passer Maurice Talleyrand, allant à Londres par nos ordres."—DANTON [1]

ALL THE LITTLE KIOSKS THAT HAD SPROUTED along the boulevards selling *marrons glacés* (candied chestnuts and almonds) and other suitable gifts for New Year's—the traditional day of the Christmas season for adults to exchange presents—were dismantled. Paris turned bleak. It was so cold and icy that horses kept slipping and tumbling down and had to be destroyed, but inside the Manège heated, angry disputes kept the legislators of the National Assembly warm. The scene swarmed with agents from abroad, each prowling to see what might transpire to his own country's advantage. William Pitt, the English prime minister, kept an up-to-date list of debt-ridden French lawmakers and paid off many of their obligations in an on-going effort to destabilize England's great rival. On the home front, the best indication of the climate in French power circles was the number of motions brought to the floor of the Manège—but tabled—requiring that deputies declare their financial status and its evolution since their election to office. This spring, in return for His Majesty's wiping out Mirabeau's mountainous debts, and in addition to a handsome regular stipend, the ambitious and ugly deputy would become the secret counselor of Louis XVI. Unfortunately, the king did not pay much attention to Mirabeau's sound advice.

When Morris learned that the assembly had abolished all pensions, he hurried to the Louvre to console Adèle. He was earlier than usual and found her ailing on the divan, moaning that she could no longer afford to live in the capital and would have to move to the country—a fate worse than death. Hovering around was one of her maids, red-eyed from weeping and offering to live on bread and water for the next few months, if that would help; another could be heard pouring water into a basin for a foot bath to comfort her. Catching a glimpse, through a half open door of Talleyrand taking the chill off her bed with a warming pan of hot coals—an animated Fragonard—the American confided to his journal: "It is rather curious to see a reverend Church Father performing such an operation."

Adèle accompanied Morris to order a tablecloth for President Washington—at a cost approximately equal to two-thirds of the Flahauts' remaining income. To take her mind off her shrinking pocketbook, the young woman frequented the Variétés, the Opéra, and the Comédie-Française, often continuing on to some gathering at friends' where gaiety ruled and "Blind Man's Bluff" was the amusement of the moment. Talleyrand remained attached, if not faithful. While he continued to come and discuss various political strategems, the bulk of his time away from the Manège was spent on the Left Bank at the Swedish Embassy on the rue du Bac. The formidable ambassadress, Germaine, was already pregnant with her first child—Narbonne's son—but no one would have guessed it from her behavior. One guest there, the well-known English woman, Miss Berry, sniffed indignantly that her hostess was so occupied with "the bishop" that she did not even know Miss Berry was in the salon.

When the deputies decided to give an accounting to the public of their activities to date, they designated Talleyrand to do so. Pleased with his glowing report, which they ordered printed up and sent into the provinces, the flattered lawmakers elected him, in mid-February, their president for the customary fortnight term, a nice compliment. His importance was growing in the Manège and he was on all the important committees—the one drafting the new constitution as well as those on education and finance. Talleyrand appropriated as his own the novel idea, first broached by the celebrated, late French economist, Turgot, that nothing could be more helpful to the still woefully ailing economy than the establishment of a uniform standard of weights and measures throughout the country. He then went one step further and recommended that a similar standard be implemented simultaneously in England. His report, which was tabled, would, a decade later, become the basis for the present day metric system and marks the first official expression of Talleyrand's lifelong desire for an entente and alliance with the Court of Saint James.

The nationalization of the ecclesiastical possessions necessitated a complete overhaul of the Church's finances, so the deputies decided to reform its structure from the ground up. Brought out of committee in April, their proposal did not affect the dogma or liturgy, but substituted democratic state control for that of Rome, even tailoring the boundaries of bishoprics to be identical with the existing French departmental ones. Because church dignitaries were now to be equated with justices of the peace and other state officials, they were to be chosen by the same local electoral colleges, as vacancies occurred. They did not need to be confirmed by the pope who was to be notified of the election results purely as a courtesy. Weeks of bitter debate ensued with the diehard radicals, who were not in a conciliatory mood, carrying the day as the new Civil Constitution of the Clergy was hammered out in the Manège.

After being accepted on July 12, the bill that was to plunge the French church into a devastating schism then went to Louis XVI, whose sanction was required to make it legal. Ironically, only the general euphoria permeating the land, as delegations from the local national guards from all over the country marched into Paris to participate in the great *Fête de la Fédération*, can explain how anyone expected the Vatican to accept this document, which would split the country asunder.

Everyone of any importance was to attend this splendid spectacle that was to be held two days later and was intended to symbolize the bright future awaiting France. Propaganda on a gigantic scale, the fête had the two-fold purpose of commemorating the first anniversary of the fall of the Bastille and of symbolizing the unanimous approval of the whole country for the new order which was no longer dependent on the will of a king but on that of free citizens. The swearing of fealty to the unity of the French nation and to the brotherhood of man was to be solemnized on July 14, by a mass, as was customary on similar occasions of great importance in Catholic countries.

The vast Champ de Mars, which was in front of the École Militaire and was used by the cadets for parades and drills, was the chosen locale because it was situated within the city's walls and could easily accommodate the one hundred and sixty thousand expected. Unfortunately, final arrangements were not approved by the assembly, which was responsible for the affair, until June 21, leaving far too short a time for the huge task of preparing for anything on this scale. When it was clear, by the beginning of July, that nothing would be ready on time, several thousand people from every walk of life, pitched in, turning the esplanade into a pulsing ant hill. Their patriotic enthusiasm was contagious. Members of the court, *grandes dames* with liberal leanings, and shopkeepers, worked feverishly, side by side, with shovels, brooms, and pickaxes, round the clock. This was done to the tune of *Ça Ira*, which became the theme song of the day, and was blared forth nonstop by military bands as the esplanade was transformed into a vast amphitheater with forty rows of seats on an encircling belt of graded slopes. Rocks had to be removed before the ground could be leveled and then excavated to a depth of four feet to support the pyramid of dirt required to prop up the altar. Huge amounts of sand and gravel were also required to give the surface firmness to withstand the pressures of the surging crowds. Anticipating a crushing throng, placards were posted everywhere with rules and instructions for the great day. Wearing a tricolor was mandatory and women who wished to be present were instructed not to wear hats, in order that "everyone might see."

As the great day neared, one item of major importance remained. Only a bishop could officiate and, unfortunately for Louis XVI, he had few to choose from. Talleyrand was one of the handful of liberal prelates supporting the new constitution of the Church left in the assembly, and he was by far the most popular. The fact that His Majesty waited until the last minute to name him indicates his dilemma, and it was not until July 13 that M. de Saint-Priest, the minister of the king's household, formally notified Talleyrand that he had been picked. Even had he wanted to, he dared not refuse the king or offend the assembly, let alone the Parisians who were looking forward to a great spectacle. Overnight the Bishop d'Autun was transformed from Parisian notoriety to a nationwide celebrity.

Talleyrand must have known he would have to be selected. No one could have better appreciated the irony of the situation. Several delicious legends exist, dwelling on his lack of practice for conducting this ritual. One in particular describes a dress rehearsal in the home of friends, before a makeshift altar, with Mirabeau in a snuff-bespattered jacket as his acolyte and Talleyrand's little dog, Piramé, excitedly yapping and snapping at his master whom he did not recognize in such strange attire. However, the bishop had already gotten a bona fide run through when he participated in a civic fête, two days earlier—on July 11—at Versailles, and presided at a mass set up on the grounds of the château.

By dawn on the fourteenth the rain had already begun. By the time the fifty thousand national guards—with Lafayette, their commander-in-chief, and his general staff cantering alongside—together with the visiting delegations and the entire assembly were lined up in the heart of Paris and marched eight abreast to the Champ de Mars, it had turned into a downpour. Once they were seated in their allotted places on the slopes surrounding the esplanade, the doors of the Military Academy at its end opened. Three hundred priests and the children's choir, both in white with tri-colored belts, appeared, followed by grenadiers carrying the sacred objects of the Mass. Bringing up the rear, leaning on his cross came Talleyrand, in his pontifical vestments. As he passed Lafayette on his white charger at the foot of the elaborately decorated, open-air Altar of the Fatherland elevated in the middle of the Champ de Mars, Talleyrand is supposed to have whispered, "Don't make me laugh." Given the circumstances, this widely repeated anecdote is in such uncharacteristically poor taste that it appears to be just that—anecdotal— although Lafayette himself is the source. With water dripping down onto his face from his gold miter, Talleyrand hobbled up the twenty steps. Salvoes of artillery announced the arrival of the royal family and Louis XVI, who no longer sat in regal isolation but democratically shared twin chairs on the dais with the president of the assembly.

Personifying the reconciliation of the *ancien régime* with the new revolutionary society, Talleyrand in his sodden robes, swung the silver censor of holy water over the assembled multitude, and conducted the Mass. A rolling of drums heralded the end of the service, and every few minutes the skies would clear as Talleyrand next proceeded with large sweeping gestures to bless the royal family and the banners of each of the eighty-three departments' national guards.

Then came the climax. With piety attended to, patriotism now took over, and Lafayette took center stage as the embodiment of the citizen-soldier. With swirling winds sweeping across the altar, he administered a solemn oath of allegiance to the nation, the new constitution, and the king. The assembled representatives of the national guards from the different municipalities thundered "I so swear." Louis XVI and the royal family did likewise. To the accompaniment of twelve hundred musicians, the Reverend Bishop Talleyrand intoned the *Te Deum,* which the vast assemblage chorused and, by the time he had finished, the rain had finally stopped and the sun reappeared.

While Parisians embraced one another and danced on the muddy ground in the fervor of the moment, Talleyrand peeled off his soaking bishop's attire, which by now weighed a ton, and relieved his tension by hurrying to one of the two gambling houses popular with men about town in the Palais Royal compound. He promptly broke the bank and, with franc notes stuffed everywhere, even in the rim of his hat, he proceeded to supper at the Vicomtesse de Laval's. Later he returned to the same tables, broke the bank a second time and returned once more to the vicomtesse's to empty his bulging pockets onto her floor in a shower of golden louis. One of the three "remarkable women" whom Talleyrand had first met at his debut into society, at the coronation of Lous XVI years before, Mme de Laval like the other two, the Duchess de Luynes and the Duchess de Fitzjames, would remain the core of Talleyrand's seraglio down through the years, always faithful, always ready to help and presumably still sharing his bed—intermittently. He could always use his winnings for, although costs were skyrocketing, he still lived extravagantly and owed everyone. Perhaps, now, he might even pay his carriage maker who, as was customary in the aristocratic faubourg Saint-Germain, was denied entry even into the bishop's courtyard. Anxious to settle his bill, the poor man had been lying in wait for him for days, just outside the impressive entry at 17, rue de l'Université. When liveried footmen swung the massive doors open one day, and Talleyrand, on his way out, deigned to enquire what he was still doing there, the desperate tradesman, bowing low, humbly reminded the prelate that he had owed him a large sum of money for a long time. "Why so I do, so I do," Talleyrand declared breezily and motioned the coachman on his way. Paying bills was a bourgeois custom but, as befitting a *grand seigneur,* he gladly paid the debts of his friends.

If the clergy had been shocked by the previous nationalization of the Church's properties, they were outraged by the new legislation to create a state church, which forced the issue of allegiance to Rome and officially became law at the end of August, when His Majesty at last reluctantly approved it. So sure were they that it would be condemned by the Vatican that most of them considered it null and void. The pope did reject it, and angry debates—in which Talleyrand did not participate—swirled around the Manège about how to end the disorder spawned everywhere by the clerical resistance. To stop its spread, disgruntled radicals rammed through a motion at the end of November that, since the clergy were no longer different from any other government functionaries, each member must swear a similar oath of allegiance to uphold their new Civil Constitution—which His Majesty had only recently sanctioned—or be replaced. On December 26, when Louis XVI, after a month-long struggle with his conscience, gave his approval, the decree became law, and the deputies from the clergy had one week in which to conform.

Talleyrand was not in the Manège the next day when some sixty of them trooped in to become constitutional priests. Of course, a bishop never mingled with his subordinates so it was not until the following morning that Talleyrand chose to comply. Because calculating Talleyrand, who was normally a late riser, rarely did anything without a reason, one can only speculate why he chose to appear so extremely early, when only a handful of lawmakers were ever there, shuffling papers and talking over that day's agenda in small groups. He took the required oath—and then disappeared. Some contemporaries commented that he was paler than usual. As a Talleyrand-Périgord, Talleyrand always considered himself above any need for explanations to mere mortals. If the king went along with the assembly's latest decree as being in the country's best interests, surely it was not up to Talleyrand to do otherwise. Unlike the Bishop d'Autun, the vast majority of the clergy did not fall into line, while his horrified mother and his scandalized uncle, the Archbishop of Reims, emigrated together, shortly afterwards.

Talleyrand had been gradually eliminating more and more of anything Episcopal from his attire. Although his friends persisted in calling him "the bishop"—with a grin—he had long since replaced the customary ecclesiastical neckware with a jabot; now the pectoral cross, which he had been wearing more concealed than in evidence, disappeared completely. And this winter of 1790-91 the famous artist Greuze painted him in a light blue suit with a white vest and chamois culottes, with his neck wrapped high in fine batiste.

Germaine de Staël was temporarily absent, her salon shuttered and closed. Her father, Necker, had resigned that fall and she followed her parents to Coppet, their home on Lake Geneva, as soon as possible after the birth of her first child, Narbonne's son, in August. When Morris returned from an extended trip through the Low Countries with a Newfoundland puppy—an exotic new breed—as a suitable gift for the lovely young British Ambassadress, Lady Sutherland, and a magnificent set of buttons for Adèle, he was chagrined to find his place at the Louvre as "the friend of the family" pre-empted by handsome blond Lord Wycombe, a titled Englishman already much in demand by *tout Paris*. Several years Adèle's junior and the oldest son of the Marquis of Lansdowne, a former prime minister, Wycombe had come abroad to finish his education, as was the custom among his peers. He was presently enthroned in the place of honor by Adèle's side at the theater, at her suppers, and in her boudoir. What Talleyrand thought of this new addition is not known—nor if, and when, Adèle succumbed to her new admirer's blandishments. But Morris was convinced she had, and he was profoundly jealous. Given the loose morals of the day and the custom of adolescent, arranged marriages often between virtual strangers, it is amazing that the French countryside was not overpopulated by blue-blooded bastards. But Adèle, like many another of her circle, still suffered from certain ill effects of her accouchement when Charles was born and never produced another child—presumably because of a clumsy midwife's ministrations.

In the process of redefining some of the government's functions, the assembly created a new administration for the Department of Paris. This was an important post whose thirty-six well-paid members were to be chosen, as with similar committees, by the city's electoral board. Talleyrand confided to Morris that this was the only "door open for him" and declared himself a candidate, but he was not an automatic choice. Maneuvering was required, as well as his resignation from the see of Autun; if elected, his residency in Paris was obligatory. It was not until the third round of voting five days later that he was picked, on January 18, along with Mirabeau and several other well-known liberal constitutionalists from the assembly.

If Talleyrand did not yet deserve the dubious distinction of being one of the founding fathers of the Constitutional Church, as virulent critics were already referring to him for his role in the cataclysmic financial changes in its structure, he soon would. For he became solely responsible for establishing the hierarchy of a rival to Rome by his consecration of the first "constitutional" bishops. The deadline for members of the clergy to take the mandatory new oath to the state came and went with shockingly few compliances. The vast majority refused to submit and had to resign, leaving the new state church in France decapitated. For it to function properly, it must establish a hierarchy, starting with a bishop in every department. Several were quickly selected from competing priests by the designated nominating committees but, according to the law of apostolic succession that the Civil Constitution had preempted intact from the Holy See, two indispensable requirements still remained before the new prelates could assume office: their ecclesiastical confirmation and their consecration. Both prerequisites must be satisfied within a month of their selection and could only be executed by a properly qualified bishop—one who had himself been anointed in the Church of Rome. Like a chain reaction, without qualified prelates to ordain other new colleagues to ordain still others, the new ecclesiastical organization would collapse. Of the one-hundred-plus French Roman Catholic bishops, only the bishops of Viviers and of Orléans, the Archbishop of Sens, and Talleyrand had taken the required new oath of allegiance to the Civil Constitution of the Clergy and were accordingly qualified to perform this sacred ceremony. When the first three backed out—with acceptable excuses—Talleyrand was left. Elthough he had just resigned from the see of Autun, once a bishop, always a bishop, in the eyes of the Vatican, even one without a bishopric, and Talleyrand retained the valid power, until the Holy Father withdrew it, to formalize the nominees in their new status.

  Talleyrand's acquiescence is one of the most indefensible acts of his life. An ambitious man, who became famous for his uncanny ability to accurately predict future results of present actions, he should have foreseen that France would end up with two Catholic churches, a Roman one and a state one. His claim, in the briefest of words in his *Mémoires*, that he was motivated by a desire to save France from the clutches of Protestantism—God forbid!—or deism, cannot be taken at its face value because it was not substantiated. And he gives the lie to his often repeated assertion, in the years to come, that he was always happiest when what was best for France was also best for Talleyrand. A schism in the Church did not benefit the former, while it did help Talleyrand shore up his influence within the surging radical ranks.

  He knew that if he consecrated any of these elected bishops he would be excommunicated, and possibly this was the reason he was willing to do so—to ensure his escape from the Church where he had never wanted to be. Perhaps Talleyrand considered his participation as integral to his prior decision to follow the lead of Louis XVI and uphold the Civil Constitution. Because the request for the ordination of the newly chosen constitutional bishops came from the civil administrators of their respective sees, he may have chosen to regard the whole affair as a political issue rather than a religious one. As such, it behooved Talleyrand who, in his capacity as an official in the Department of Paris was anxious to strengthen his position in revolutionary circles, to cooperate with his counterparts elsewhere.

Promptly at 10:00 a.m., on February 22, with a copy of the register from Finistère, where he had been elected, tucked under his arm and in his pocket a request from the director of that· department that Talleyrand confirm him officially as bishop before two clerics, as required, the Abbé Expilly appeared at the doorstep of the rue de l'Université where Talleyrand lived. At 11:00 a.m., the Abbé de Marolles, bishop-elect of Aisne, appeared with similar documents, but from the head of the department of Aisne.

Exactly what Talleyrand did the next thirty-six hours is not known, except that he made out a will with Adèle his heir, presumably to protect the future of their son, Charles, and left instructions that it was to be delivered that same evening. He intended to take it back if he lived through the morrow. Adèle was frantic when she returned, late at night and found it. Remembering a recent conversation, she was convinced that Talleyrand was determined to commit suicide and, in tears, she aroused their good friend, Radix de Sainte-Foy, at 4:00 a.m., to search for him. He was unsuccessful, and it has since been determined that Talleyrand and his two assistants, as well as the two bishops who were to be consecrated, spent the night with the Oratorian fathers—secular priests—in whose church the services were to be held. All five had received anonymous threatening letters and Talleyrand, who was no coward, was purportedly carrying a small pistol.

By early morning Lafayette, who had been notified ahead of time, already had members of the National Guard on hand in case of trouble. Although there had been no notice of the special service to be held at the Oratorian Church, a large crowd of curious Parisians was slowly gathering, attracted by the military band. At 8:00 a.m. Talleyrand appeared in his pontifical robes. The father superior of Saint-Sulpice, where Talleyrand had once been a seminarian, did not deign to appear in person but sent, instead, two qualified observers hoping, no doubt, to find some deviation from the prescribed liturgy. There was none and, at the end, the two new bishops were escorted home with great pomp, on foot, surrounded by a detachment of the National Guards, complete with band and, at their head, Lafayette on his favorite white charger. The mayor of Paris and a sizeable number of fellow citizens followed. Talleyrand did not.

Pius VI's anticipated condemnation of the principles of the Revolution and of the Civil Constitution of the Clergy was not long in coming and served Talleyrand well. The threat of excommunication cast him in the public's eye as a victim of unwarranted persecution for helping to implement the assembly's laws. To further ingratiate himself with the more radical elements, Talleyrand continued to confirm additional civil bishops; recent scholarship says fifteen. But he did not consecrate any more after the first two; in his *Mémoires* he claims only one.

After confirming his last one on March 31, Talleyrand hastened to join Mirabeau, who had just gone on the payroll of an agent of Catherine the Great, and several friends for dinner at one of the many eating establishments located in the Palais Royal arcades. Here, *chez Robert*, currently the number-one restaurant in the capital, Mirabeau, ever excessive in all things, consumed a hearty meal, washed it down with bottles of Talleyrand's favorite Chambertin, and took violently ill. Forty-eight hours later, with Talleyrand at his bedside, the man who towered over the political scene died. Talleyrand delivered his funeral oration at Saint-Eustache.

Following the same strategy he and Mirabeau had jointly espoused, Talleyrand was still trying, along with other moderates, to shore up the monarchy and the new constitution in an effort to keep the revolution from sliding into anarchy. Violence smoldered underneath the surface, but the time was not yet ripe for a republic. Louis XVI was having trouble with his conscience over the decree inaugurating the constitutional clergy and preferred not to attend Easter services presided over by one of them. On April 18, the Monday after Palm Sunday, when His Majesty and his family tried to go to the royal château at Saint-Cloud to celebrate with the Roman Catholic prelate there, an excited Parisian mob prevented them from leaving, afraid they might flee to Rome as Louis XVI's two old-maid aunts already had. Two days later, whether motivated by personal ambitions or by unadulterated patriotism Talleyrand, who was anxious to replace Mirabeau as secret counselor to the beleaguered king, a financially attractive position of great power, wrote to Louis XVI offering his services.

On May 1, Pius VI's long-awaited brief was published in the *Moniteur*, suspending Talleyrand from all ecclesiastical functions and, as anticipated, threatening him with excommunication if he did not recant within forty days. Of course, he did not and continued life unperturbed. When he dined at the Louvre or with Morris it was still on delicacies from afar—oysters from Colchester, trout or carp from the Rhine, and partridge from Querci. More friends emigrated but the exuberant Germaine de Staël, claiming that she missed " the gutter in the middle of the rue du Bac," returned from Coppet and resumed her place in the front row of the diplomats' box at the Manège. Here she kept her footmen busy ferrying a constant stream of congratulations, advice, and invitations to the speakers on the floor below. Her reopened salon in the Swedish Embassy was once again a rallying center for the moderates, with many of whom she was working to try and persuade His Majesty to flee his capital. Salvoes of cannon alerted Talleyrand and all Paris of the Royal Family's detection and detention at Varennes in mid-June when they finally did try to escape. In a quandary what to do with him, the deputies at the Manège declared His Majesty's role in the government temporarily suspended, and he became a virtual prisoner in the Tuileries. Marie-Antoinette's hair turned white overnight, while the more moderate politicians' faith in a viable constitutional monarchy was further undermined.

Gouverneur Morris and Adèle went often to the Manège. It was one of the things to do and because the capital was so full of English sightseers, seats in the visitors' gallery were harder to get than places at the Opéra. The American, who had just returned from a month's stay in London, discerned a new "note in the roar of the city's streets" but crossing the Seine, at night, on one of the few old bridges built with houses on them that remained from an earlier day, he was struck anew by the city's serene "indescribable beauty.... A fine moonshine, a dead Silence and the river descending gently thro the various bridges between lofty Houses all illuminated ... and on the other side the Woods and distant Hills." [2]

A sense of foreboding was slowly pervading the atmosphere as antimonarchist sentiment continued to grow, fed by hunger, poverty, lack of work, and anticlericalism. Mirabeau's death had not only deprived the throne of one of its stalwarts, but it had created a power vacuum in the

Manège which was being filled by Danton, the leader of the Cordelier club, and Maximilien Robespierre, the head of the Jacobeans. These two and their increasingly radical clubs—each bearing the name of the religious order in whose deserted establishment it was housed, the first in an ancient monastery, the second in a former convent—were agitating for a republic. On September 2, the long-awaited constitution, which embodied the ideals of liberty and equality while preserving the monarchy, was signed by Talleyrand and the other twelve who had been working on it these past months and voted in. He was selected as one of a sixty-deputy escort of honor to present it to Louis XVI for His Majesty's acceptance.

One matter of business remained—the completed survey of the education committee, which Talleyrand now gave. Schools in France were as badly in need of reform as everything else; formerly the Church's responsibility and staffed by priests, they lost most of their teachers when the recalcitrant clergy refused to take the civil oath. A vast problem that Talleyrand had been interested in since his days as a general agent and which he now tackled as a labor of love and, for once, completely devoid of any ulterior motives, education was what Morris referred to as "the bishop's ... hobbyhorse." Aided by a team of experts in the field and reworking his text off and on over the past summer with Adèle—although she complained tearfully to Morris of the bishop's neglect of her and was consoling herself with Lord Wycombe, her young English swain—the report he prepared took three days simply to read aloud. To Talleyrand's exasperation, his exhausted audience voted to turn the whole matter over to the new House. With its insistence that education must be available to all, regardless of age or sex—an unheard of idea for the day—it would serve as a point of departure for the great reforms in French education in the nineteenth century.

At the end of the month, after decreeing in a self-righteous mood of abnegation that its present members were ineligible to serve in the Legislative Assembly, which would follow, the Constituent Assembly, its job done, passed out of existence. However, Talleyrand was hardly sidelined. The capital was still the source of political change throughout France, and he had recently wangled his elevation to the Executive Committee of the Department of Paris housed in Mirabeau's former place.

While the government summoned to office by Louis XVI under the new constitution was composed of moderates interested in seeing a constitutional monarchy succeed, the new deputies of the Legislative Assembly were splintered as to their own ultimate aims, with even the extremists divided among themselves. Each group reacted differently to the sabre-rattling of a minuscule but determined army of counter-revoltionary émigrés who were massing in the Rhenish-Palatinate along France's northeastern borders under His Majesty's brother, Artois; and Condé, the royal cousin, and threatening invasion. Even the populace was alarmed at their belligerence. The people were already disturbed by the Declaration of Pillnitz which had been signed, a short time before, by the Austrian emperor and the Prussian king, and they took at face value its vague menace, "calling on European sovereigns to strengthen the monarchy in France," [3] as another military threat. Public opinion was belaboring such external interference in French internal affairs, which Parisians termed a humiliating insult, and blamed it on Marie-Antoinette's efforts to get her brother Leopold II of Austria to come to the sovereigns' rescue. Not surprisingly, war became a domestic political calculation—and a distinct possibility—in the jockeying for power. Whoever controlled the French military would be in a position to control France.

The latest cabinet, formed in accordance with the new constitution, was itself divided on the course to follow. Narbonne, the father of her year-old son, whom Germaine de Staël had just succeeded in making war minister, realized that the royal couple looked upon war as their last hope. If the assembly succeeded in taking France into war, Their Majesties felt confident that all the European powers would become involved, and that the French army would then rally loyally behind the king and queen and deliver them from their own people. On the other hand Narbonne, who knew the badly disorganized and demoralized state of the French military—woefully understaffed by the desertion of a good proportion of its predominantly aristocratic officers—hoped to avoid as much of a confrontation as possible and reasoned that Leopold II would be stalemated in advance if France could come to terms with England and Prussia. The foreign affairs minister concurred. Before the year was out a suitable negotiator was dispatched to Berlin. Now someone must be found to go to England where the French had not had an ambassador or representative since the preceding fall. Germaine's salon had a candidate—willing and ready.

With Narbonne holding a portfolio as war minister, Talleyrand, who had been impatiently marking time on the sidelines, was once again confident of resuming a prominent role. It is hard to tell to what extent his insistence that the war minister look more closely across the Channel for help—either by an alliance or at least by a promise of neutrality—was the decisive nudge Narbonne needed to do so. As Talleyrand had already demonstrated in his earlier endeavor to coordinate a common weights-and-measures policy with England, one of the few consistencies in a long life would be his ceaseless search for ever closer ties with that country. Talleyrand was never a warmonger, and he would remain convinced until he died that the best hope for an enduring peace was the closest possible association between England and France, a country whose population, almost three times larger than England's, was the fourth largest on the continent.

Whether he was presently counseling this course of action largely because he himself coveted the appointment is hard to ascertain for, as might be expected with Talleyrand, there was already, or soon would be, a lucrative personal angle. One of the bargaining chips the negotiator was authorized to offer England was possible restitution of the French island of Tobago. Just as indemnification for the famous Jecker bonds almost a century later figured prominently in France's establishment of a Mexican empire with Maximilian and Carlotta on that cactus throne, at stake now was suitable indemnification for foreign investments made in the West Indies isle before it had been given back to France almost a decade earlier. And, unbeknown to the authorities, the Swiss and English planters who were involved promised a secret, generous compensation for Talleyrand's special services on their behalf. The post seemed tailor-made for him, and he claimed, as a trump, his earlier acquaintance with Pitt, the incumbent English prime minister. The latter's subsequent disclaimer of any such prior meeting when the pair, as teenagers—Pitt was five years Talleyrand's junior—were briefly in residence, at the same time, in the Archbishop of Reims' palatial residence is equally plausible, given that edifice's vast size.

It is ironic that Talleyrand, who would share with Metternich the distinction of being the outstanding European diplomat of the first half of the nineteenth century, should start his new career with an unofficial assignment. But, as a member of the recent Constituent Assembly, Talleyrand was ineligible to accept office under the crown. However, as in the past, he excelled at circumventing what he considered bureaucratic red tape. To camouflage the nature of Talleyrand's trip, Narbonne obligingly dispatched a mutual intimate, Lauzun, the future Duc de Biron, to buy four thousand horses for the army. Given his service overseas in the American War for Independence, the dashing, handsome Lauzun, would seem an impolitic choice, but the one-time lover of Catherine the Great spoke excellent English, which Talleyrand did not, and through frequent trips to London he had many friends in influential circles there. From the casual onlooker's point of view, Talleyrand was simply accompanying him.

Two more aristocratic representatives of a revolutionary government than "citizen Lauzun" and "citizen Talleyrand" could hardly be imagined. They arrived, via Dover, and stayed at the Golden Square in London. On January 28, 1792, Talleyrand, armed with a letter of introduction calculated to assure him of a hearing, presented himself to Pitt, who received him as stiffly as only Pitt could, and informed him that since he was there on an unofficial mission, he must deal with Grenville. Talleyrand never saw Pitt again, and the young foreign secretary, who wanted to keep his hands free, diplomatically speaking, was hardly more cordial. Good conservative Tories, both were suspicious of anything that lacked proper authorization, let alone of anyone with credentials from a tottering government. The next day Talleyrand attended the opening of Parliament and when, later, he was presented at the Court of Saint James, his reception was no better than at the Foreign Office. The assistance that the French had given England's American colonies in their successful fight for freedom still rankled George III. He did not think highly of any supporter of any revolution, let alone the present one in France, while the queen, to show her displeasure with a constitutional bishop who was under threat of excommunication, turned her back—literally. Talleyrand reported back to Lauzun: "This was the right thing to do, because she is ugly." In accordance with Their Majesties' lead, Talleyrand was automatically excluded from official circles as well as from that part of society, that slavishly followed the court's dictates. Matters were not advanced when Lauzun was arrested, that same week, and hauled off to debtors' prison for unpaid debts, presumably from a previous visit. Talleyrand claimed it was a frame-up and had such a hard time getting him released that, once he was free, Lazun lost no time in returning to Paris.

Not only was London already the largest city in Europe—Paris was second—it was also one of the centers of French emigration, within which were numerous cliques. Their misfortunes exacerbated their rancor, adding another impediment to Talleyrand's chances of success. For the first wave of émigrés, the diehard royalists, who were derogatorily dismissed as the "aristocrats" by refugees who arrived later, virulently hated the "men of '89" as the latecomers, the constitutional monarchists like Talleyrand, were called. The former considered the latter as traitors because of their hope to save the throne by a directed revolution. Since they also held Talleyrand as one of those most responsible for their own misfortunes and those of Louis XVI, the "aristocrats" launched a bitter campaign, full of lurid tales about his many mistresses and financial speculations, in the local press.

Londoners who encountered him in large groups were as distrustful of a cold, reserved Frenchman as a Frenchman was of a talkative Englishman. Luckily for Talleyrand, who was always at his best in small groups and never more seductive than in his own social milieu, influential members of the Loyal Opposition welcomed him warmly and he spent the rest of his time in their congenial, brilliant company—another cardinal sin in predominantly Tory England. Lord Lansdowne, a former prime minister and one of the Whig leaders whom he knew from Paris, frequently invited him out to his great home, Bowood, in Wiltshire—where Talleyrand and Adèle's granddaughter, Emilie de Flahaut, would one day preside as the wife of the Lansdowne heir. The father of Lord Wycombe, Adèle's friend, Lansdowne also introduced him to Charles James Fox, the Whig son of Lord Holland and England's finest speaker, and to Sheridan, the famed playwright turned politician.

Ordered home for consultations with the French foreign minister, Talleyrand's carriage was stopped by a friend, on March 9, as he entered Paris, with the news that Narbonne had just lost his portfolio. During Talleyrand's absence, in-fighting between the different factions had intensified, and Louis XVI turned to the Girondists—as the group of deputies from the Gironde were called—to form a new cabinet. They, too, wanted war which they saw as the only way to restore order at home but, instead of a limited war against the émigrés' army massed along the border, the Girondists wanted to strike directly against Austria, France's ancient enemy and the staunch opponent of revolution everywhere. So Louis XVI, anxious to avoid the charge of collusion with any forces outside France, agreed to a declaration of war against his wife's brother, Leopold II.

Negotiations with England assumed more importance than ever and Talleyrand was ordered back to London at once to complete his task, this time under the Marquis de Chauvelin, the twenty-five-year-old Keeper of His Majesty's Wardrobe, who was Talleyrand's handpicked choice as a successor to Lauzun. Shortly before he left, Talleyrand's friend, Sainte-Foy, sold him several pieces of choice real estate from the former royal nursery on the Champs Elysées, which was still a country road where cows grazed in the summer. This purchase, together with his personally annotated, detailed blueprints for the construction and decoration of an extravagant *hôtel particulier* to be built there for himself, as soon as possible, indicates that Talleyrand was anticipating a windfall of some sort.

On the eve of his return to England, Talleyrand sent a footman to Adèle with a note asking if there were any capitalist friends whom she wanted to oblige. "I will shortly be able to place their money most advantageously." [4] But he must know at once. His departure was imminent, and he was so busy that he could only see her for a few hours that evening. Small wonder. It is a fitting testimonial to Talleyrand's capacity for intrigue, as much as to his ability to inspire confidence, that he was setting forth, this time, with three lucrative, sometimes conflicting, missions—the original charge, from Louis XVI's government to maintain English neutrality, and two other secret ones. The first came from his friend, the writer Choderlos de Laclos of *Les Liasons Dangereuses* fame, and involved lobbying with the Prince of Wales's clique on behalf of the traitorous Duc d'Orléans who was aspiring to supplant his royal cousin, Louis XVI. The second came from the mayor of Paris and entailed a huge three million pound credit, payable from the Legislative Assembly's Finance Committee. This was to be used to further the sacred cause of the Revolution and assist subversive English patriots by subsidizing pro-revolutionary agents and buying arms, as well as newspapers, the latter of which were to be distributed free to the lower classes.

On the last Sunday of April Talleyrand was back in London preceded by the news that a French crusade "for universal liberty" had been declared and that French troops were already pouring across France's northern borders to establish a republic in Austria's Belgian provinces. Because of a variety of complications—fiscal reform at home and continuing troubles ranging from Ireland to the Far East and Tipu Sahib, the sultan of Mysore and a French ally—neither Pitt nor Lord Grenville, was any more anxious for war than before. However, the threat now menacing the great Channel ports of Antwerp and Ostende forced Grenville to reconsider and George III, on May 25, officially declared

English neutrality. This was not the formal alliance Talleyrand was seeking, but it was better than nothing, and he received a congratulatory letter from the French foreign minister. The fighting on the continent turned the man-in-the-street openly hostile to the French. One afternoon, when Talleyrand and some of the legation went out to the public gardens at Ranelagh for a stroll, they were shunned as if they had leprosy, and a large quarantine-like space was conspicuously established—and maintained—between the Londoners present and his group.

In Paris matters were coming to a head. At the beginning of July 1792, the radical clubs who wanted the war to continue, not so much to spread the Revolution abroad—as the Girondists initially desired—but rather to establish a dictatorship at home and kill off the monarchy, pushed the assembly to declare the fatherland in danger, and to assume emergency powers. An urgent appeal from the president of the Executive Committee of the Department of the Seine who wanted to discuss the explosive Paris situation with him brought Talleyrand hurrying home again. Shortly afterwards this official together with Talleyrand and the majority of the department's administration resigned. Conditions were deteriorating so fast that the constitutional monarchists had at least seven different plans afoot to spirit the royal family out of the capital. Talleyrand, like the rest of the Swedish Ambassadress's coterie, favored Germaine's proposal of a flight to Dieppe, but it was rejected, like the other schemes, by both Louis XVI and Marie-Antoinette.

On the whole, Parisians made do as best they could with a certain semblance of normalcy. All twenty theaters in Paris remained open and were full nightly. Gouverneur Morris, who had recently been appointed American minister to replace the departed Thomas Jefferson, continued to shop, with Adèle's help, for necessities for his new official home on the rue Planche, around the corner from the Swedish Embassy—livery with lace for his staff, porcelain for the table, mirrors. Because the court ceremonial as practiced at Versailles continued uninterrupted at the Tuileries without the slightest concession to the changed state of affairs, the snobbish, protocol-conscious American never missed one of Louis XVI's *levées*, often stopping en route to visit his sick dog in a neighboring hospital.

At the end of July, a contingent from Marseille marched into Paris, singing their favorite marching song that would soon reverberate ominously throughout the continent. Part of a detachment of national forces called in from throughout France to help defend the capital in case of invasion, they spread throughout the city, rampaging in the streets, smashing storefronts, pulling terrified people from their carriages. Almost simultaneously, the blunt manifesto that was issued by the Duke of Brunswick, the commander-in-chief of the Austrian armies, and his new ally, the Prussian king, which menaced Paris with destruction should anything happen to Louis XVI and Marie-Antoinette, galvanized the Parisians. Forgotten was their own invasion of the Low Countries, which was going badly at the moment for the ill-equipped, mutinous French troops. Brunswick's inept threat was termed an insulting intrusion into domestic affairs and turned the war overnight into an affair of honor that must be avenged.

The cool weather ended and it was oppressively hot. On August 6, Talleyrand dined at Morris's new American legation with Adèle and her husband. Paris was turning into an armed camp and, two days later, the mayor announced that he could no longer guarantee the safety of the Tuileries. Frightened for the safety of his family but unwilling to be responsible for bloodshed, the king closed the gates to the château's great park, which was normally kept open for popular enjoyment. The tense city was ominously quiet.

On the night of the ninth the tocsin never stopped clanging and the radical insurrectionists—the Commune—assumed the legal government of the Department of Paris. In anticipation of a rumored assault on the Tuileries and hoping to find security with the deputies, the king and the royal family walked over to the Manège, early in the morning. "Fall is coming early this year," His Majesty remarked matter-of-factly, kicking at the dead leaves on the ground in his path. The attack on the palace, spearheaded by the Marseillais, only lasted about an hour-and-a-half and began around 9:30 a.m. Peering from his Louvre windows and seeing the mob rushing in, the elderly Comte de Flahaut hastened over to be of service. Around noon, Adèle dressed seven-year-old Charles as inconspicuously as possible and sent him with a trusted maid across the Seine to the American Legation for safety, and she followed him there before dusk. Where Talleyrand spent the day is not known but he spent the night at the home of a political colleague, M. de Sémonville.

The sack of the Tuileries and the slaughter of its defenders, the famed Swiss Guards, by an angry mob provoked a showdown between the assembly which, by and large, still favored some form of a constitutional monarchy, and the Commune. Crowded into the tiny reporters' box behind the rostrum in the Manège for three stifling days—without even a change of clothes except for a suit of her own son's which the British ambassadress smuggled in for the dauphin—the royal family agonized while the fate of the monarchy was debated. Finally the deputies, besieged by the crowds, menaced by those Parisians who had participated in the Tuileries assault, voted the suspension of royal power and dispatched the royal family to the donjon of the Temple, an ancient fortified Templar monastery in the heart of Paris. With actual power now in the hands of the Commune who controlled the city, the Legislative Assembly was no longer consulted except for form—if at all—and a new Executive Council of six assumed Louis XVI's duties and responsibilities. Its dominant figure, Danton, whom Talleyrand knew as a former Orléanist and who had served with him in the Administration of the Department of Paris, was the minister of justice, although he did not measure up to even the Tammany definition of an honest man—someone who, having taken a bribe, stays bribed.

Just as the August 10 insurrection sounded the knell of the constitutional throne and of the new constitution itself, so it also doomed Talleyrand's political ambitions. He had been following events, hour by hour, in the corridors of the assembly and at the Hotel de Ville, to both of which his former functions still gave him *entrée*. The militant press and the radical clubs now lumped together the rich and the aristocracy, the court and the traditional clergy, as the sources of their troubles. The prisons filled to overflowing, and convents and monasteries were appropriated to house these enemies of the people as more than a thousand Parisians were swept into custody on the flimsiest of excuses.

Seeing which way the wind was blowing, Talleyrand kept a low profile, and little is known with certainty of his activities during the following days. He did what he could for those constitutional friends who were already either in the Abbaye prison or in hiding. Stories abound, some unquestionably fictitious, about how he lurched daily over the cobblestones in an open cabriolet, hiding in its trunk first one colleague, then another. After Germaine courageously faced down a patrol of overly zealous citizens demanding a house search while Narbonne crouched precariously underneath the altar in the embassy chapel, Talleyrand helped the redoubtable ambassadress disguise her lover as a governess and smuggle him out of town.

Nor was Germaine the only woman of Talleyrand's acquaintance who rose to unexpected heights of bravery in those harrowing days. When Comte de Flahaut was put on the wanted list for his participation in the ill-fated defense of the Tuileries and had to go into hiding, he needed a passport to leave Paris. Adèle proved her mettle by going directly to the source. She bearded Méhée de la Touche, the head commissioner in charge of issuing these *laissez-passer* at home, while he was being shaved. After rejecting her impassioned plea, the gruff official, engaging in a game that two can play, walked into an adjoining room, temptingly leaving a pile of the permits on a nearby table in plain sight—and the door ajar. As anticipated, Adèle seized one, the man returned to catch her in the act and . . . some time later Adèle walked out with the desired prize.

Like with other controversial events in Talleyrand's life, certain facts are well established but the surrounding circumstances remain unknown—whether deliberately hidden or not—and contradictory interpretations are inevitable. Some claim that when the Executive Council, anxious to calm Europe, felt the need for recognition of the new status quo and for acceptance of its legitimacy, Danton called on Talleyrand because he was the most qualified person available to prepare such a document. Others aver that Talleyrand, who was a survivor in every sense of the word, had already volunteered his services wherever they might be needed because he wanted reappointment to Chauvelin's mission as an excuse to recross the Channel.

Be that as it may, on August 18, Talleyrand wrote an apologia for the bloody Tuileries' sacking and the deposition of France's legitimate sovereign that the Executive Council immediately approved and dispatched to the various European courts that same day. In this document, an outstanding example of sophistry, honed by his long apprenticeship in the classrooms of Saint-Sulpice and the Sorbonne, Talleyrand claimed that the rights of the French nation—and, hence, the legitimacy of its new republic—must always prevail. He audaciously laid the blame for the fall of the monarchy on Louis XVI because His Majesty "visibly encourage[d] internal dissension" by his persistence in continuing to surround himself "with enemies of liberty" and remained "unmoved by remonstrances" urging the imperative need to get rid of them. Finally the assembly, whose only concern was the welfare of the people had no alternative but to seize power and suspend all the monarch's functions "as much for the people's own good as for His Majesty's personal security." [5] This document is a major blot on Talleyrand's memory. One of the few pieces found in any archives to date that is entirely handwritten by Talleyrand—for whatever reason—he could never, later, disclaim authorship, because it also appeared in innumerable European presses of the period. One can only wonder how Talleyrand could bring himself to so accuse, before the world, the monarchy to which his family for centuries and he, himself, owed so much. For it is inconceivable that he believed his own justification.

Since no change was contemplated in the thrust of French foreign policy concerning England, Talleyrand had every reason to be disagreeably startled when a friend of Danton's, Jean-François Noel, was sent to London in his stead. This alarming evidence that the council lacked confidence in him, coupled with the discomforting insistence of many to continue to address him as "Monseigneur d'Autun" or "the bishop," finally convinced Talleyrand that the time had come for him to depart. His dogged determination not to flee illegally, like the rest of his friends, but to depart with his credentials in order, so that he might experience no difficulty in returning some day, indicates that farsighted Talleyrand already envisaged such a future possibility. Unfortunately, the latest requirements for these precious documents necessitated the screening of any Parisian seeking them by a specially appointed Commune committee. This was something that Talleyrand dared not do, for fear of arousing the suspicions of these rabidly antimonarchist patriots.

Throughout the last week of the month he knew, like most of Paris, that different sections of the Commune were discussing a massacre of everyone arrested since August 10. So when, on August 28, the stringent passport regulations were amended to enable the harried foreign affairs minister to extract a *laissez-passer* when needed for any of his agents—provided all six members of the council approved and signed each individual request—Talleyrand swung into action. In his *Mémoires* he claims that he solicited, directly from the council itself, a temporary mission to London to do further work on the details of his earlier proposal of a joint English-French system of weights and measures. A document in the Foreign Affairs archives merely states that he made his request on the grounds that he had urgent business to attend to in England which would require several days to wind up and that had been left unfinished at the time, because he originally expected to be back in London shortly.

Meanwhile, on August 19 the Prussians had crossed the French frontier and a few days later the important defenses at Longwy crumbled, exposing to siege Verdun, which lay astride the road through the Marne Valley to Paris. On Saturday, September 1, surrender there was imminent when Talleyrand was encountered, shortly after midnight, in Danton's salon at the Ministry of Justice on the Place Vendôme, booted and spurred and ready for travel with his hair done up in a little pigtail and wearing leather culottes, a short coat and a round hat. After an hour's wait, Danton appeared with the disappointing word that the Executive Council refused him any mission to England. They did not trust him.

When news of Verdun's fall to the Duke of Brunswick reached Paris the next morning, the Commune posted placards everywhere, prematurely announcing that the enemy was at the gates and calling the citizens to arms. As part of a well-orchestrated plan to complete its seizure of power, the tocsin was soon heard and the city gates were locked and bolted. Clubs and pikes were distributed to the citizens, and the assembly voted to sit in permanence. Three cannon blasts, the agreed signal, reverberated and, by 4:00 p.m., Paris mobs were attacking the bulging prisons of l'Abbaye, des Carmes, and de la Force, where most of those rounded up since the fall of the Tuileries were incarcerated. Claiming that the prisoners herded in there constituted a potential Trojan Horse because they were planning to escape and attack honest citizens from the rear, should the enemy succeed in breaching the city's defenses, the crowds slaughtered some fourteen hundred men, women, and children—approximately half the total prison population of the capital. The radical phase of the revolution had begun.

Even for Talleyrand life was now a matter of staying alive from hour to hour, as the people turned from slaughtering prisoners to attacking suspected enemies of the revolution on the streets, often even dragging them from their homes. Many of Talleyrand's friends had been killed; others disappeared. The late summer days were so hot that perch, which had been alive in the morning, were spoiled by dinner. "So rapid a state of putrefaction I never saw," commented Gouverneur Morris. General tension was evident everywhere, and nerves triumphed over manners even at the British Embassy where the burly American had just dined: "I laughed a little too much . . . and [the Ambassador] gets a little too much in a passion [with one of the guests]," he noted in his diary. One of the few foreign diplomats still in Paris, due to the time lag of overseas communications, Morris was not ordered to leave his post like the others until almost the bitter end. He had a harrowing experience on the boulevards, one twilight, when he was surrounded by an angry, drunken mob, shouting "A la lanterne!" "A la lanterne!" as they shoved him towards one of the streetlights whose long cords had served as a makeshift gallows for more than one luckless citizen. He only escaped being hanged on the spot by quick-wittedly removing his wooden leg and brandishing it in the air, a replacement, he shouted disingenuously, for the real one lost in the American War for Independence.

Just as it is only in very recent years that rigorously pursued research has succeeded in lifting the veil and ferreting out, in detail, how capital a role Talleyrand actually played during 1789 and 1792, so only the latest, exhaustive perusal of primary sources has finally clarified the manner in which he ultimately got the desired exit authorization. As Adèle could attest, Talleyrand had never been and would never be adverse to using women and, as usual, a woman now served as his intermediary. Mme de Valence, a tiny heavyset brunette with a pretty face, either had been or would be one of his many mistresses. A member of the Orléanist coterie from a happier day and the daughter of Talleyrand's former Bellechasse neighbor, the Comtesse de Genlis, little else is known about the dumpy but pretty brunette—or her husband, the Général de Valence—except that she had recently managed to obtain the release of the imprisoned Charles de Lameth, a deputy in the Legislative Assembly. So Théodore de Lameth, who had also been a legislator and like his brother, Charles, knew Talleyrand not only through Orléanist circles but also as a familiar at the Swedish Embassy, felt obligated to her. Knowing that Danton owed his life to both brothers for services rendered the previous year, Mme de Valence entreated Théodore to intervene. He did and he, himself, has left an account of his successful interview with Danton.

When Talleyrand saw Morris on the eighth he showed him his passport, received at 1:00 a.m., September 7, from Danton in person: "Laissez-passer Maurice Talleyrand, allant à Londres par nos ordres..." It was signed by Danton and the other five members of the Executive Council whom Danton had persuaded to do likewise. Danton insisted that Talleyrand must not depart as a fugitive. He must travel by post and soldiers would escort him through the gates. Suspicious that the Legislative Assembly at the Manège was itself considering flight, the Commune unexpectedly shut the city barriers, and this may be why Talleyrand did not set out for Boulogne until the tenth.

It is hard to believe that he and Morris, who was with him four out of his last ten days in Paris, did not discuss the safety of Adèle and seven-year-old Charles de Flahaut. Given the perilous times, the American who normally recorded everything of even the most intimate nature in his journal, may have felt it imprudent to commit any detailed plans to paper. But, in love with Adèle as he was, Morris would surely have commented therein if Talleyrand, who had already taken the precaution of shipping out his valuable library, had not expressed normal concern for mother and son. Under the present circumstances, it was no doubt wisest to entrust their flight to the American minister and the young Englishman, Lord Wycombe, who were both so interested in her—and better qualified, perhaps, than any native—to get the pair out safely.

5

The Exile

"America has thirty-two religions and a single entrée."—TALLEYRAND [1]

HELD UP BY CLUTTERED ROADS and inns bulging with refugees all fleeing west, it took Talleyrand eight days to reach the Channel. No aristocrat of the day would dream of ever traveling anywhere without a minimum of one maid or valet, and Talleyrand was no exception. Faithful Courtiade, a few years his senior, expected to devote his entire life to his master, and the only concession he had made to the recent convulsions was to replace the black culotte and long fitted coat conforming to his dignity as the servant of a high church official for that of a gentleman's gentleman. Bad weather detained the pair another eight days at Boulogne, and the crossing was rough.

Talleyrand reached London at almost the same time as the news that the day following its opening session, on September 20, the National Convention, the successor to the Legislative Assembly and destined to be the longest-lived of the revolutionary assemblies, formally declared the Republic. He rented a small house on Woodstock Street in one of the prettiest parts of London, where he settled down with his library and resumed a liaison with a former mistress, the Comtesse de la Châtre, who set up housekeeping for him. Meanwhile, François de Jaucourt, the countess's erstwhile lover and father of her six-year-old son, was snatched from the guillotine by Germaine de Staël and also fled to London. Talleyrand and the countess naturally invited him into the household, which became a temporary *mènage à trois*.

Talleyrand found it hard to adjust to life in London under his present circumstances. But every day brought more constitutional friends trickling over, forming a congenial buffer against the rest of the French refugees, whose continued incivility towards him was only matched by their contempt. Such an adversarial condition sharpened Talleyrand's wit. "I can pardon . . . [them] for not sharing my opinions but I cannot pardon them for theirs" [2] was his sole comment. Details of the September massacres filtering over intensified the royalists' feelings towards this renegade bishop in their midst—even though he had never wanted a revolution, only a constitutional monarchy—and heightened the horrified reactions of the English to the entire French colony. However, Talleyrand remained as welcome as ever in the small Whig inner circle. And, unlike Lafayette, who was imprisoned the minute he crossed the border into Austria, Talleyrand was free. One of his first acts—he called it a matter of courtesy—was to contact Lord Grenville, the foreign secretary, to advise him of his arrival and to emphasize that he no longer had any, even semi-official, government appointment. When he encountered Théodore de Lameth with some mutual friends around this time, Talleyrand acknowledged Lameth's help in getting his passport: "Il me manquera toujours quelque chose de nécessaire tant que je ne vous aurai point prouvé ma reconnaissance" (I shall always lack something essential until I am able to prove to you my gratitude). [3] He also wrote to thank one of the Executive Council in Paris for signing his *laissez-passer*.

How and when Adèle and young Charles, accompanied by her devoted Polly, arrived and settled down at 27 Half Moon Street is not known. Talleyrand claimed he was unable to assist her financially because of substantial losses of his own, but Wycombe is presumed to have paid her rent, and one of his young English comrades helped with Charles's schooling. Friends and acquaintances, bearing some of the most illustrious hereditary titles in France, learned to do various sorts of work to survive, one designing artificial flowers, another assuming the post of a school headmistress. Adèle became a milliner, making the straw hats that were currently the rage and were copied from the portraits of the celebrated

Mme Vigée-Le Brun, one of Marie-Antoinette's favorite artists. Unfortunately, there is no counterpart for Gouverneur Morris's invaluable, day-to-day Paris journal to help document Talleyrand's English stay. But, as is so often the case with a long-standing liaison like Talleyrand and Adèle's, habit figures largely and the drifting apart is gradual. The cataclysmic upheaval both had been through undoubtedly played a role.

The French men had a harder time adopting a trade than the women and worked at anything they could find. Little is known about any possible financial transactions of Talleyrand at this time, nor is there anything to indicate whether he continued his previous secret projects for the mayor of Paris or the Orléanist clique. His was now a humdrum existence and, without a carriage, which he could no longer afford, his bad leg made it hard for him to get around. He occasionally visited Maria Cosway, the wife of the painter and Thomas Jefferson's reputed heart interest. Present day historians now are convinced that his path must also have crossed that of Catherine Grand, a glamorous courtesan of the day and his own future wife. It would be even stranger had they not met. He also saw the Comtesse de Genlis, whose daughter had been so instrumental in obtaining his passport. A former mistress of the Duc d'Orléans and the governess of his children, she lived in a humble dwelling, close by, with two of her charges, the sixteen-year-old Princess Adelaide d'Orléans, sister of the future king, Louis-Philippe, and one of the duke's natural daughters. They, too, were confecting hats to help eke out their meager existence. The evening was the brightest part of the day, when Talleyrand and one or two others, all in equally straitened circumstances would appear there, each with his own sugar and some small offering towards supper. Gently vaunting the extreme frugality of his hostess—of whom he once remarked that "in order to avoid the scandal of coquetry, she always yielded easily" [4]—Talleyrand arrived, once in a while, with a small bunch of flowers, or he might gallantly produce a candle from his pocket, which he gaily lit and placed on the tiny mantle. But his main contribution—and the principal fare—was his own lively conversation. On a rare occasion when Mme de Genlis was able to produce a sumptuous feast and invited over a considerable group from the Orléanist faction Talleyrand, upon his arrival, was heard to whisper mischievously in her ear, "I promise not to look too surprised." [5]

Like other compatriots, Talleyrand closely followed events across the Channel where Dumouriez's victory at Jemmapes in early November marked the transition of the war from a French defense action into a "crusade for universal liberty," granting help to all those groaning under the yoke of despotism who wished to recover their liberty as sister republics. Prompted by this turn of events was an unsolicited memorandum that was found among Danton's papers on his death and that was dated November 25 and signed by Talleyrand, suggesting that France's future foreign relations should be impregnated with moderation. This document is a remarkable example of Talleyrand's clairvoyance and a foretaste of his future diplomatic acuity and basic philosophy. With his insistence that France should abandon its age-old ambition to expand and become the greatest power in Europe and that the new Republic should, instead, remain within its own boundaries and develop its own wealth and resources, Talleyrand is already foreshadowing a policy which suggests why, as Napoleon's foreign affairs minister, Talleyrand and the emperor would never, in the long run, see eye to eye.

Just when his pocketbook dictated a move to a smaller house, in Kensington Square, and when his morale must have been, accordingly, at a low ebb, Talleyrand learned that, on December 5, the National Convention in Paris had placed him on the dreaded list of proscribed citizens. A terrified Versailles locksmith, Gamain, had revealed to the Minister of the Interior the existence of a small safe hidden in the wall of a dark Tuileries corridor. This was a simple hole that he helped dig out, a year-and-a-half before, dumping the rubbish secretly into the Seine. His Majesty, an amateur blacksmith, and Gamain's pupil had made an iron door while the royal valet, Derey, held a candle and, then, Gamain added a lock and hinges. Among the six hundred odd documents discovered inside were two from M. de LaPorte, the Intendant of His Majesty's civil list, disclosing Talleyrand's offer of assistance to the Crown following Mirabeau's death. Although Talleyrand's actual communication was never found, these explanatory letters were sufficient evidence for the National Convention, which was becoming more bloodthirsty with each passing day, to take action. Although he hurriedly issued a public disclaimer which appeared in the Paris *Moniteur*, Talleyrand's civil rights, like those of others similarly listed, were forfeited, seals were put on his property, and an order was issued for his arrest, which was tantamount to a death sentence if he ever again set foot in France.

The one other spot exuding charm and gaiety for Talleyrand during this drab period was Juniper Hall, near Mickleham in the Surrey

Downs, some sixteen miles southwest of London, on the road between Leatherhead and Dorking. Rented by the generous Germaine de Staël as a haven for her lover Narbonne and any other liberal friends who needed asylum, Juniper Hall was not a great Georgian house but it was spacious, and its decorations in the Adams style—graceful garlands on the walls and ceilings, and finely sculptured fireplaces—lent it an air of luxury. Mme de la Châtre and Jaucourt soon moved there, and Talleyrand frequently came down on the post coach to join them. At the devastating news that Louis XVI was being brought to trial, charged with crimes against the French people, consternation and gloom prevailed there. As their anguished thoughts focused on His Majesty, Narbonne, who had only recently arrived in Surrey, gallantly rushed up to London to try and wangle a safe-conduct to cross the Channel and testify in the king's behalf. Hardheaded, realistic Talleyrand did no such quixotic thing, while Germaine, writing from Coppet, where she had given birth only weeks before to Narbonne's second son, threatened suicide, should he do anything so rash. Worried about her hold over him, intrepid Germaine ignored her parents, left her newborn in a wet nurse's arms and sneaked across danger-fraught France. She managed to join Narbonne in England about January 21, 1793, the day Louis XVI, clad in white, the color for royal mourning, walked unassisted to the guillotine. Although the only European precedent for such an ignoble act had been the beheading of the English king, Charles I, it was England that now manifested the most indignation. Theaters closed, the Court and Parliament spontaneously went into mourning, and every man who had a black coat or could procure one, put it on. As did Talleyrand.

With Germaine in residence, Talleyrand was more often in Surrey than in London. Adèle, who felt no more at ease here than she had in the Swedish Embassy in Paris, rarely if ever accompanied him, and Talleyrand must have been well aware of hidden tension between the two women. Fascinated at having almost next door the notorious bishop and these other charming, highborn foreigners, some of whom had even played a role in the strange, dangerous events overseas which constituted the main topic of conversation in London, the cultured Locks of adjacent Norbury Park, saw them often. Another neighbor from the postcard-pretty, nearby village of Mickleham, Mrs. Susanna Phillips, invited down her sister Fanny Burney, a lady-in-waiting to Queen Charlotte and whose novel *Evelina* had won her acclaim as a writer, to meet this remarkable group. Through their father, the well-known musicologist, Dr. Charles Burney, the two women traveled in elite social and intellectual circles, yet the forty-one-year-old Fanny quickly decided that nobody she had ever met was more fascinating than the "Juniperians." Although their thoughts were monopolized by what was happening in France, they managed to jest, argue, and play games, seemingly oblivious to their present circumstances and uncertain future, as if they were still in their Paris salons. Fanny wrote her father that before she had met these French people, she had no idea "what conversation was"—no faint praise from someone who had often been with Dr. Samuel Johnson and won his approval. Nor was she ever completely clear about the fluctuating relationships among those in residence although their number was somewhat reduced in the wake of the convention's latest decree, declaring all émigrés' property subject to immediate forfeiture, if the owners did not return to France at once. As the chaste English woman, with her six petticoats and old-fashioned corset, explained naively to Dr. Burney, everyone lived together "as brethren." But for a forty-one-year-old spinster, who may even have still believed that the stork brought babies, Fanny learned in a hurry. She married one of the few unattached men present—General d'Arblay, who had served under Lafayette in the National Guard—with Narbonne serving as best man.

She had been prejudiced in advance about Talleyrand because of his scandalous reputation. But, as was so often the case with that wicked charmer, when he set out to bewitch, Fanny was quickly disarmed. Not so much by his seductive smile and the witty twinkle in his blue eyes, as by his delicate yet pointed wit and by the infinite pains—familiar, caressing, attentive—he took to please and amuse her. Of course, he succeeded. Fanny wrote London that he was "one of the finest members and one of the most charming of this exquisite set.... His powers of entertainment are astonishing, both in information and in raillery ..." [6]

The daytime was spent in making and returning calls, and driving around the picturesque, peaceful Surrey countryside at the foot of the North Downs for hours on end. Their only conveyance was a dilapidated, two-seated cabriolet with Germaine always riding in state in the covered part, twisting a piece of paper between her fingers—a new habit that would last a lifetime; the ambassadress got up with such a wand and went to bed with one. This arrangement, with either Talleyrand or Narbonne daily relegated to the dickey—that seat at the back where a servant usually sat—turned conversation, a necessity of life for those concerned, into a contortionist's trick for anyone uncomfortably perched outside, even after Talleyrand impatiently knocked out the glass partition separating the front from the back. He also learned to enjoy angling, one sport, which, like horseback, he could participate in despite his crippled foot. In the evening Germaine, who was turning increasingly to writing, read aloud the beginning of her first really original work, *On the Influence of Passions on the Happiness of Individuals and of Nations*, as fast as she finished each chapter. Talleyrand declared that he had never heard anything better reasoned, nor better written, but he made fun of her monotonous, singsong delivery, and Germaine responded in like fashion. "Mme de Staël was very gay and M. de Talleyrand very *comique*," Susanna Phillips reported.

It seemed as if everyone was writing and, another night, when one of the guests was to read his tragedy, *The Death of Strafford*, General d'Arblay unexpectedly disappeared. After he was sent for several times and still did not appear, Germaine impatiently decided the author should start without him. "Oh, but he will be unhappy to miss anything," [7] Talleyrand replied, limping out of the room to fetch him and returning, a few minutes later with the other in tow. One distinguished historian amusingly postulates that Talleyrand, who could be mischievous when he chose, was not, perhaps, motivated by kindness but determined that if he had to sit through a boring evening, so should his friend.

Dr. Burney, ever watchful of his brood, looked on askance at his prim and proper daughters, whom one authority aptly refers to as "two little figures straight out of the sedate drawing rooms of *Sense and Sensibility* who had wandered into the elegantly disordered alcoves of *Dangerous Liaisons*." [8] When Fanny dutifully referred to him Germaine's invitation to spend several weeks at Juniper Hall, her father neither forbid nor encouraged her acceptance. Instead he pointed out certain facts of life regarding the Germaine-Narbonne ménage, which sublimely innocent Fanny, shocked at the mere intimation of such indecorum, indignantly refuted. "She seems equally attached to M. de Talleyrand . . . all this little colony lives together like brothers and sisters. Indeed, I think you could not spend a day with them and not see that their commerce is that of pure but exalted and most elegant friendship . . ." [9] Nonetheless, her father's admonishing finger broke the spell and, fearful she might forfeit her pension from the queen, a chastened Fanny returned to London.

Since February, England was officially at war with France because the French had incorporated Belgium into their own country and—to quote Napoleon, later—held Antwerp "like a pistol at the head of England." By late spring, Germaine realized that her own and her friends' position there was untenable. Fear and suspicion of the French émigrés living in their midst were reaching hysterical heights, and the English made every effort to limit any possibility of the revolutionary contagion spreading across the Channel. Parliamentary committees, acting as if they possessed a job description of Talleyrand's secret missions on his second trip to London, were tracking down suspected agents from the French government. They were also investigating emissaries from the radical Paris clubs who were known to be prowling the land, preaching upheaval to the Irish revolutionary committees and offering assistance to subversive democratic societies of Scotland and England. An Alien Bill was in preparation. Germaine de Staël's husband and her father, Jacques Necker, who controlled the purse strings, were pressuring her to return to the family home at Coppet, in Switzerland. At last that young woman tearfully agreed— "after four months snatched from life's wreckage" [10]—provided that Narbonne and Talleyrand each gave a solemn promise to follow her as soon as she could make suitable arrangements for them with the local authorities. In Talleyrand's case this would prove easier said than done.

Talleyrand's reduced circumstances must have been a difficult cross for such a proud man to bear, and he finally put up his last remaining possession of any value, his extensive collection of books, for auction, in nine lots, a real sacrifice in more ways than one. The sale realized a ridiculously low figure, nowhere near its worth, in large part because of a new, malicious campaign waged by the vindictive royalists. One of Talleyrand's first extravagances had been building a library and he would always love books, not only for the companionship of their content, but for the physical feel of each volume itself, an appreciation of the materials used, the print and binding. He could spend hours by himself with them and, as one intimate remarked, the only way to truly know Talleyrand was to spend time alone with him in his library.

For someone accustomed to playing an important role on center stage, these inactive months must have been very trying. After Philippe-Egalité, the Duc d'Orléans, perished on the guillotine, Talleyrand started to write a life of Orléans. This was never published separately, but appeared revised, years later, as an insert in his *Mémoires*. Adèle, who had likewise been forced to move for lack of funds and had lately learned that her husband had been guillotined, pulled out an unfinished manuscript from her days as a lady of leisure and she, too, began writing—full time. With Talleyrand's encouragement and Lord Wycombe's help, she got the book *Adèle de Sénange* heavily subscribed to, in advance, by his aristocratic friends and now was working round the clock to finish it, developing the original story into a lightly disguised autobiography. Because she did not have the wherewithal for a copyist, she was performing this menial task herself, while Talleyrand served as proofreader at night. Full of sentimental effusions and passionate transports, Adèle's writing furnished the reading public with a welcome contrast to the somber, dramatic novels of Ann Radcliffe which were then so in vogue. And it took off. The book's successful appearance that fall in England and on the continent, where it was translated into several languages, earned Adéle considerable income and launched her on a successful career as a novelist.

Adèle de Sénange and the *Duc d'Orléans* were not the only manuscripts Talleyrand was busy with that fall. He helped Germaine find a London publisher for her *Reflexions on the Trial of the Queen, by a Woman*, a pamphlet, which she dashed off at white heat when Marie-Antoinette went to the guillotine. Then he corrected the galleys and, worried about its sale, he even wrote several anonymous reviews of it for the English press. As their continued correspondence bears witness, Germaine was getting nowhere in her efforts to find a haven for Talleyrand, who would have followed her to Coppet except that the local authorities would have none of him.

Without any prior warning, around 5:00 p.m. one foggy night in late January in 1794, two staccato knocks on his door roused Talleyrand, bundled in his fur-lined housecoat, from his study. There stood two men, clad all in black, with scowling faces to match. Messengers of State, their dispatch was equally somber: Talleyrand must leave England within five days. The current Alien Bill did not require them to give any reasons. Nor did they, though he later learned that he, a Belgian, and two other unidentified persons were the only people ever prosecuted under this law, and the four received their walking papers at the same time. It is hard to believe that Talleyrand was taken completely by surprise for, in addition to Germaine's efforts to find him asylum near Coppet, he had already been exploring his possible welcome elsewhere on the continent and learned that Florence, his second choice, did not want him either.

The dignified protest he sent to Pitt and to the foreign secretary claiming his innocence was to be expected and is simply one more example of his frequent attempts to obfuscate an issue. Whether he had actually been continuing to pursue either of the occult missions with which he had been earlier entrusted—which seems unlikely—beggars the point. A victim of his own reputation for guile, there was no foreigner in all of England to whom the Alien Bill could more aptly apply. It is only surprising that the English government let Talleyrand stay as long as it did, even if he had led as blameless a life, since his arrival as an émigré, as he maintained.

Neither Pitt nor Grenville deigned to reply but Talleyrand was granted a short respite. Upon ascertaining that the only countries open to him were Denmark and the United States, he chose the fledgling republic, of which he had heard so much from Gouverneur Morris and also from his own brother Boson, who had served there during the American War for Independence. The United States was only ten years old and this budding experiment in democracy interested him. He also hoped to remake his fortune in the New World and, once he booked passage on the first ship leaving for Philadelphia, Talleyrand spent the next fortnight visiting various English banking and shipping firms to offer his services as their overseas representative. His prominence and his background in financial affairs in France sufficed them to overlook his political background and advance him a letter of credit for more than eight thousand dollars in American money. Several of his French friends loaned him what little they could spare, while Narbonne, to help out, got a loan on his properties in Saint-Domingue (Haiti). Talleyrand wrote Germaine that he would return the instant she found him a haven. "See that we are not apart for more than a year. Adieu, *chère amie*, I love you with all my heart." [11] Then, with Adèle serving as one letter-drop, and a London business correspondent as another, on February 15, Talleyrand boarded the American vessel, the *William Penn* moored in the Thames in Greenwich and due to set sail momentarily. One of the heads of the constitutional party, who was intimate enough to *tutoyer* him and almost his age, Baron Albert Briois de Beaumetz, accompanied him.

Leaving on such short notice posed no problem for Talleyrand, but he was afraid it would for his valet who might not want to leave his wife and family without saying goodbye before setting off on such a long journey and for an indefinite period of time. So Talleyrand, who all his life was considerate of his servants—and they, in turn, were devoted to him—suggested that Courtiade follow on the next available packet.

—"No, no. No! You cannot go alone and unattended. I will go with you but just give me until tomorrow evening."

—"That is impossible."

—"Bah! It's not a question of my wife," cried Courtiade, bursting into tears. "It's that accursed laundress who has all your fine shirts and your mousseline cravats. Without them, *mon cher maître*, what kind of a figure will you be able to cut in a foreign country?" [12]

The ship had barely weighed anchor and entered the Solent when a violent tempest arose with heavy winds and high seas. Still in sight of land, Talleyrand faced the disastrous possibility of being washed up on the French shore but, luckily, the *William Penn* rode it out, and fishermen from Falmouth towed her into port for repairs on her torn sails. They did not sight another vessel the rest of the trip, which was fortunate. For the English ships they might meet, especially near the Banks of Newfoundland, were known to be stopping American ones and impounding them. The French, who could be encountered anywhere, would take and pillage them, while the Barbary Pirates, if they laid hands on the *Penn*, would sell everything and everybody on board. Talleyrand was seasick the first few days but the rest of the trip was uneventful. The thirty-eight days at sea gave him ample time to reflect on the present sorry state of his affairs—forty-years-old, poorer than he had ever been since he was a seminarian, an exile from his fatherland with a tarnished reputation and nothing to hope for from either the victorious radicals or the defeated Bourbons. Evidently, his enthusiasm for the United States did not increase en route because when they encountered a schooner setting sail for India, as they were entering the Delaware River with a pilot boat, Talleyrand would have switched vessels then and there and gone to the Far East. He had always evinced an interest in this exotic country from his days of intimacy with Calonne and Panchaud, when he had attempted to establish a French-Indian bank, but there was no room for him on board, so he continued on to his original destination.

Philadelphia, which had recently superseded New York as the national capital, lacked the grandeur Europeans expected to characterize such a city. The government buildings, Independence Hall, and the foreign embassies were all modest but, as anticipated, the residence occupied by

President Washington, the "President's Palace," was the most imposing one there. The City of Brotherly Love was essentially a community of homes, constructed largely of reddish pink and white brick, with white trim. Unlike in Paris, the streets were not only laid out at right angles and very clean, but they had wide sidewalks, mostly paved with bricks, which proved a blessing to a cripple like Talleyrand. While its main business was government, Philadelphia's true life was to be found in its wooden docks piled high with cargo and shops stuffed with European luxuries. To Talleyrand's Old World eyes, the bustling throngs on busy thoroughfares must have seemed exotic—adult Quakers in their sober grey costumes topped with broad-brimmed hats, young Quakeresses in white with close muslin caps, merchants, blacks. Talleyrand wrote Germaine that he experienced more kindness from total strangers such as these than he had received from anyone anywhere in a long time.

The first person he looked up was the Dutchman, Théophile Cazenove, by now a naturalized American, whom he had known in Paris, some ten years earlier, as one of the entourage of the Genevan banker, Panchaud, a Bellechasse intimate. Cazenove had been in Philadelphia for four years, representing land operations for the "Six Houses of Amsterdam" for whom he had created the "Holland Land Company." His affairs were flourishing and, since he had a fine French chef, Cazenove generously invited Talleyrand and Beaumetz to stay with him until the pair got settled. With his help, they soon moved into a small bedroom above a German baker, on the corner of Spruce and Second Street, in what Talleyrand described as "a miserable house . . . at the end of a wretched cul-de-sac," but they continued, for an indefinite time to eat their main meal with Cazenove—a substantial saving for the two impoverished newcomers. Not only was living high, but the gourmet Talleyrand never grew accustomed to American cooking and bemoaned that "America has thirty-two religions and a single entrée." [13] He never elucidated further.

He came armed with numerous letters of introduction and was anxious to meet those Americans most responsible for the successful establishment of a workable liberal constitution—that goal which had eluded Talleyrand and the other French liberals. One of the very first he saw was the brilliant Secretary of the Treasury, Alexander Hamilton, to whom Lord Lansdowne had sent a warm recommendation, claiming that Talleyrand had acted with "perfect rectitude" while he was in England.

Make of it what one will, this is a surprising statement from the former prominent Whig, considering what has now been brought to light about Talleyrand's secret missions to that country. It is an excellent example of the pitfalls confronting any effort to shed light on exactly what Talleyrand did—and when. Either Lansdowne is referring only to the period when Talleyrand was there as an émigré, or else the English lord was woefully ignorant of all that he had been up to during his earlier visits to London. Hamilton and Talleyrand were two kindred souls—and womanizers— with many of the same interests in governmental and financial areas and would become good friends. Only three years older than Talleyrand, the American also spoke excellent French, having learned it from his Huguenot mother, so language was no handicap.

When Hamilton, George Washington's right-hand man, offered to personally give to the president, who had just been re-elected to a second term of office, Lansdowne's impressive letter of introduction on the visitor's behalf, Talleyrand had every reason to expect a prompt invitation to the President's Palace. Talleyrand did, indeed, get a quick reply. Washington refused to see him. News of his arrival had greatly disturbed Citizen Joseph Fauchet, the newly arrived French minister, who was confident that his government would look with great displeasure on any sort of official recognition for a man whose name appeared on France's official list of proscribed émigrés. Convinced that Talleyrand and Beaumetz were there to conspire against the incumbent French regime, he hastened to the State Department—which consisted of six people, including the secretary of state—where he created a terrible scene and demanded that President Washington must chose between an émigré and himself. If Talleyrand was received in the President's Palace, Fauchet would never set foot inside there again. Washington had no alternative. Non-intervention in European affairs was one of the basics of American foreign policy, a principle the president, as the head of a neutral state, was especially anxious to reaffirm in the present European conflict that set France against England and the rest of Europe. Furthermore, how could he possibly receive a man who had been expelled from England when, at this very moment, John Jay was in London tackling delicate reparation negotiations with the British that Washington was anxious not to upset? So Washington assured Fauchet in writing that he would never receive Talleyrand "either in public or in private" while, later, he expressed to Lansdowne his regrets at being unable to receive his friend, "for political reasons."

After this unexpected rebuff from the head of a young country, barely independent, which must have been like a slap in the face to a man of Talleyrand's former political importance and the bearer of one of the oldest names in one of the most aristocratic European societies, Talleyrand wasted no time in conforming to another New World custom. He swore before the mayor of Philadelphia to "be faithful and have a loyal allegiance to the Republic of Pennsylvania and the United States of America." As in London, once the king refused to receive Talleyrand, the court circle followed suit so, now, the small group of power and influence rotating around the president did likewise. As did Mrs. William Bingham, the doyen of local society, and her set. However, foreigners from across the ocean, let alone a titled one with a scandalous reputation, always afforded a welcome diversion and other prominent people made a great fuss over him. Talleyrand did not lack for invitations and a game of his favorite whist. He was invited to join the prestigious American Philosophical Society, founded by Benjamin Franklin, although his poor command of English made it difficult for him to participate in some of its distinguished members' more heated discussions.

Talleyrand also discovered here a number of his former colleagues from the Constituent Assembly as well as several friends who had served as officers under Lafayette. One of the former, Moreau de Saint-Méry, who had been a deputy from Martinique, had a small, modest book and stationery store at 84 First Street. In the back office of the store some ten to twelve of the French refugees, all liberals, although from differing backgrounds, gathered nightly to discuss and dissect any news that might have been received from home. Talleyrand was soon an intimate here—still teasingly referred to by several as "Monseigneur"—and liked nothing better than to linger over a glass of a good Madeira, "warranted to have passed the Cape," after savoring a tasty late meal, to which each one contributed and which Mme Moreau de Saint-Méry prepared. Sometimes the group was so boisterous, their voices so loud, that staid neighbors complained. More than once when they got ready to retire Talleyrand, anxious to finish a conversation, followed the couple to their apartment upstairs, and Mme Moreau de Saint-Méry had to remind him that her husband had to get up early to go to work, even if Talleyrand did not. He rose, instead, around 10:00 a.m., ate a light breakfast and devoted the rest of the day to correspondence, walks, visits, gallantries, business affairs, until he and Beaumetz went to Cazenove's—or elsewhere—to dine.

With his education, background, and inherent indolence, Talleyrand never really adapted to the hustle and bustle of American life. But he was by nature and inclination a gambler, and he was well qualified, by past experience, to attempt to rebuild his fortune by speculative means. He arrived at a propitious time when European capital was looking abroad for a safe haven in which to invest. The rapid development of the American economy and the stability and wisdom of its government, together with the healthy state of its public finances and reestablished credit under Hamilton, the high interest rates available, all acted as a magnet. In Philadelphia land speculation was at its peak with American capitalists outbidding each other, buying up large parcels of the back lands to sell for development. Most acquired much more than they could pay for, even on time, so their ultimate success depended on the European market where, sooner or later, they were forced to try and unload part of their holdings. Lafayette's brother-in-law, the Vicomte de Noailles, and Omer Talon, a nephew of Talleyrand's long-standing mentor, Radix de Sainte-Foy, were deeply engaged in selling, in France, shares in a large land development, "The Asylum," in the region of the Susquehanna River, in Pennsylvania, and regaled the regulars, gathered nightly in the little bookstore, with details. There were also other ways to make money along the same lines, bringing together overseas banking and shipping firms and American opportunities, then managing and sharing in the results on a commission basis. But, to take the best advantage of any of them, Talleyrand needed adequate backing, and this required patience because of the appreciable time lag in correspondence, to and fro, from the continent. More than one essential contract disappeared en route, jettisoned when the ship it was on was menaced with capture.

Talleyrand had barely arrived and studied the situation at firsthand before he wrote Germaine seeking to represent her in the United States. However, although, at one point, both she and her father, whose fortune remained one of the continent's greatest, would have a sizeable investment in real estate in America—largely in Pennsylvania, Connecticut, and New York state—when it came to this kind of transaction, she preferred to deal with her father's agent, as it was her father's money and he held the purse strings. But Talleyrand was nothing if not persistent and, taking a different tack, he was not bashful in reminding the Swedish ambassadress that "if some of the friends of Monsieur, your father, would send ships to America or if some Swedish people send over merchandise to be sold either to New York or for Philadelphia, I am in a position to do good business [for them]." [14] "See what you can do" was a constant theme in his extensive correspondence with Germaine during this period. Meanwhile, he sought and secured the best American connections without a single questionable character or stockjobber among his contacts on either side of the ocean.

To avoid the annual onslaught of contagious fevers in Philadelphia, which came with the warmer weather and thrived on the effluents from the port's narrow, crowded harbor, and the cemeteries within the city's limits, Talleyrand, who preferred the cooler, damper summers of France, decided to take advantage of a trip into the northern wilderness that was being organized by his friend Cazenove for another Dutch colleague, Harm Jan Huidecoper, an agent of the counting house of Hope and Company of Amsterdam and, also, Alexander de Beauharnais—the first husband of the future Empress Josephine—wanted to investigate lands there. Judging from letters that Talleyrand wrote during this period, it is debatable whether he himself was yet ready, or in a position, to do anything more serious than that. Most likely curiosity to see at firsthand what he might some day be offering for sale motivated this luxury-loving, sophisticated Frenchman rather than any urge for adventure of the primitive sort on which he was now embarking. While Talleyrand was never lacking in physical courage, one wonders if he had any real idea what such a foray into the American hinterland entailed in the way of hardship, especially for a cripple. Cazenove gave Talleyrand a detailed questionnaire concerning what to look for and what he would need to know, should Talleyrand decide to invest in land, and which Talleyrand scrupulously filled out later on location. He and Beaumetz were especially interested in seeing a vast tract of virgin territory that was being offered for sale by one of the largest American landowners of the day, General Henry Knox, who was serving his final year as secretary of war. This acreage was still available cheap because it lay in northern Maine, near the disputed Canadian border, and was outside of any populated regions.

They set forth, on June 24, on the daily 6:00 a.m. stagecoach lumbering north. Though it came as a surprise to discover that the frontier began in Philadelphia's back yard—"less than fifty leagues from the nation's capital I no longer saw the hand of man" [15]—Talleyrand confessed his delight with the undertaking from the beginning. They took the long route by way of Trenton and Princeton, where they passed

Nassau Hall, then the largest academic building in the land and, after a long, two-day trip over bumpy, rough roads, reached Newark. There a sailboat took them across the great mouth of the Hudson River to New York.

The principal commercial city of the New World with its picturesque gabled houses, a reminder of its early Dutch settlers, presented a startling contrast to Philadelphia. One of Talleyrand's first impressions was that of numerous chained slaves, along with pigs and cows—and dead rats—on its streets, many of which were so narrow that sidewalks were forbidden. He was present for its Fourth of July celebration and parade, which he watched from a house on Broadway opposite Governor Clinton's mansion. It would be interesting to know how he felt it compared with the French equivalent, the Fête de la Fédération, in which he himself had starred, four years before. Ten days later, they departed for Boston, en route visiting Yale University where they were received by its president, Ezra Stiles. Talleyrand preferred Boston, the intellectual center of the United States, to either New York or Philadelphia, finding it more European in its culture and ways of thinking. Here, Talleyrand introduced himself to Stephen Higginson, one of the principal businessmen of the community, with whom he expected to do business; then he and his friends were outfitted for their expedition. For the time being, Courtiade would not have to worry about the state of his master's mousseline cravats and fine baptiste shirts, for Talleyrand was donning the sturdy gear of a hardy pioneer.

Wherever there was an option, the party traveled by water, out of deference to Talleyrand's bad foot and, about the middle of August, the party took a boat as far north as they could, to Machias in the province of Maine—it was not yet a state. Then on by land to the bay of Passamoquoddy alongside the still ill-defined Canadian border which John Jay was at that moment trying to establish, among other matters, in London. From here they proceeded inland, hacking their way through primeval forests inhabited only by wolves and bears. Often they traveled on horseback, taking care to get an easy-gaited old mare for Talleyrand. Then, again, they jounced along in rattletrap coaches over roads made so impassable by rain that they often had to get out and continue on foot. They paddled up some rivers in canoes, were ferried across others on crude rafts, slept in pioneers' log cabins in the backcountry, and suffered from swarms of mosquitoes and large flies. But Talleyrand's good humor and sense of the ridiculous never left him, even at his own expense. One evening, towards dusk, the party got separated and not seeing or hearing anyone or anything, Talleyrand called out in concern: "Courtiade, are you there?" Close at hand, but invisible in a nearby thicket, the faithful valet replied mournfully, "Alas, yes, Monseigneur, I am." [16] At his lugubrious voice and at the incongruity of his form of address under the circumstances—probably both were equally unshaven and dirty, maybe even in tatters—Talleyrand burst into laughter, in which Courtiade, quickly realizing the absurdity of the situation, joined in.

Nothing is more telling about Talleyrand, the man, than the way he summarized his impressions of this trip. Another famous contemporary, the French writer and diplomat, Chateaubriand, filtered the experiences of a similar but longer excursion—in 1791—through the lens of his romantic imagination, and saw deep forests with lush foliage, silent and mysterious, and the Indian as a noble savage. Practical minded Talleyrand rarely permitted himself to succumb to the beauties of nature. He considered the prairies and meadows, the landlocked bays along the New England coast, the untouched rivers, in terms of land to develop and domesticate and regarded the Indian as a "work-horse," smelly and filthy beyond words.

The foursome finally embarked at Portland, and they were back in New York by the end of September. Because it was very hot and the pest was still raging in Philadelphia, Talleyrand decided to round out his education in American land values and availability by visiting a region already in full development, situated between Albany and the Great Lakes. This would also give him a chance to see some other sites that had been offered to him, on Wood Creek and the Mohawk Rivers, by Colonel W. S. Smith. Huidecoper dropped out and they were joined instead by a young widower, Thomas Law. He was a big, blond Englishman with a melancholy face, who had recently arrived from London and would wed Martha Curtis, President Washington's granddaughter.

Although to go by coach would have been cheaper, out of consideration for Talleyrand the travelers took the twenty-six-hour boat trip up the Hudson to Albany, the outpost for the Northwest Territory. Upon arrival, Talleyrand located Monsieur and Madame de la Tour du Pin, long-standing friends from France. They had been unable to await his arrival earlier in Boston and were living temporarily in Troy, a small nearby community, until their own house, which they had recently bought, was ready for them. Twenty-four-year-old Mme de la Tour du Pin's excellent command of English had helped her adjust well to her new situation. She was already earning money selling little pats of homemade butter with her family crest impressed on each one. Lucy was just about to roast meat for their evening meal over an outdoor fire when she heard a deep masculine voice exclaim: "It is impossible to thrust a spit through a leg of mutton with a greater air of majesty." [17] And Talleyrand bent to kiss her hand.

Talleyrand and the others were staying with General Schuyler, the father-in-law of Alexander Hamilton, where Lucy and her husband were invited to dine the next day. Talleyrand was not aware—until then— that both the young couple's fathers, whom he had known well—Count Arthur Dillon was another veteran of the American War for Independence—had been guillotined. Because Talleyrand had known her since childhood, he assumed "a sort of paternal and gracious attitude which was full of charm." As she confided in her journal: "One cannot help regretting in secret that there are so many reasons for not esteeming him, for it was impossible to remember his vices once one had spent an hour in his company." When the travelers returned to Troy to taste Lucy's lamb, she again fell under his spell: "An exquisite sense of what is proper manners prevents him from telling me things that would displease me and if, as occasionally happens, he forgets . . . he immediately catches himself, saying, 'Ah! It is true. You don't like that.' " As the little party trotted back once more to Albany, they saw the general waving a fistful of papers excitedly at them from the veranda.

The post had just arrived from France and, with it, several gazettes full of unbelievable news. The French armies were winning abroad, while the internal situation was worsening. Out of necessity, the convention had tolerated the dictatorship of the Committee of Public Safety and of its dominant figure, Robespierre. Then, that spring of 1794, he succeeded in sending Danton to the guillotine and became the uncontested master of France. Robespierre inaugurated the Reign of Terror. The pace of executions mounted and food shortages and rising bread prices caused further unrest. July 27—the nineth of Thermidor by the new revolutionary calendar—Robespierre and his associates were, in turn, overthrown by a conspiracy mounted by the more moderate elements of the government and, the following day, they, too, were guillotined. The Terror might be broken, but the little group at the Schuylers, passing the journals to and fro, avidly reading and re-reading every astounding word, realized that relief would not come overnight. How this unexpected event—which heralded in the final phase of the revolution—would translate into personal terms must have been uppermost in Talleyrand's mind, as he checked the lists of those carted off in the last tumbrils, just hours before Robespierre's arrest, and discovered the name of his sister-in-law, Archambaud's wife, the pregnant mother of three young children. For, as his correspondence with Germaine ceaselessly echoed, "If I have to stay here a year, I shall die." [18]

When the quartet left Albany to do a little sightseeing, the young couple de la Tour du Pin joined them for the six days needed each way to Fort Niagara to see the falls. On their return, by way of Lake Ontario and Lake Oswego, they were in a hurry to reach Albany before the advent of the rainy season and snowstorms. There was plenty of time for talk on a trip of this nature and Talleyrand and Law, who had spent fourteen years in India as the governor of Patna for the British East India Company, concocted an elaborate money-making venture with that distant land, which still so intrigued Talleyrand. The pair's aim, to sell American land to the wealthy officials of the British East India Company, would have the added attraction, for English colonials, of bypassing scrutiny and the taxes they normally incurred when remitting payments home to London. Upon his return, Talleyrand was delighted to find Alexander Hamilton in Albany and, during the time that their stays overlapped in the Schuyler household, their intimacy ripened. Of all the people whom Talleyrand met in the United States, Alexander Hamilton impressed him the most.

By mid-November Talleyrand was back in Philadelphia, his head full of other, equally lucrative schemes and, of course, with one eye cocked across the Atlantic to see what kind of reaction was setting in. He took pleasure in spoiling Lucy from afar, sending her unexpected gifts, godsends that were always the envy of her neighbors—one time, a well matured, sweating Stilton cheese, another, a handsome lady's sidesaddle and saddlecloth. When he learned, through the émigré grapevine, that she was bedded down with malaria, a box of quinine tablets appeared. Writing about Lucy to Germaine, he confided that "she slept every night with her husband, which is very commendable here. They only have one bedroom. Warn . . . Narbonne about that and be sure to emphasize that this is an essential if one wants a good reputation over here." [19] Talleyrand would never adjust to the heavy atmosphere of Puritanism in Pennsylvania, founded, as it was, by the austere William Penn; he thought

American women too restrained and their conversation dull. Instead, he took a handsome black woman, identified only as Doudou, for his mistress. Still a rule unto himself where public opinion was concerned, Talleyrand paraded Doudou up and down Philadelphia's main street daily, a small pet tagging behind his every faltering step, to be greeted by the pursed lips and whispers of shocked surprise of staid natives and Quakers alike who could never get over the public spectacle of an ex-Catholic bishop arm-in-arm with his black mistress. For, although the capital of the new country, Philadelphia was still a small provincial town in many respects, and Talleyrand was well-known by sight. Talleyrand's well-trained dog innocently added to the scandal. Whenever he wanted to come in, he scratched at the door. If neither his master or Courtiade opened it, and he could not find Talleyrand anywhere nearby, he could be seen running to Doudou's. He had quickly mastered how to raise her door latch with his paw and, if no one was there, either, to let him in, he pushed the door open and stretched out on her bed to await the couple's return. This liaison lasted, apparently, until the end of Talleyrand's American stay.

In late April, Talleyrand and Beaumetz returned to New York where the climate was more to his liking at this time of year. Early in June, he made a quick trip back to Philadelphia to meet the new French minister, Adet, and learn at an official level about conditions in Paris. When he discovered that moderation was the order of the day there and that a number of constitutional friends had already been released from prison while others were slowly coming out of hiding, his eventual return became a distinct possibility. Adet, who was cordiality itself, as opposed to his predecessor, emphasized that the first step was for Talleyrand to get his name removed from the official list of émigrés whose lives were still in danger if they ever set foot in France. Since Talleyrand had been so classified by the convention, it was up to that assembly to abrogate its own decree, and the pair discussed the best way to go about this.

Dated June 16, 1795, Talleyrand's petition to the National Convention for permission to return and place himself at the service of the Republic was entirely in his own hand, which made it a rarity and was indicative of the importance he attached to the document. Heretofore, Talleyrand had never denied he was an émigré. Now, he found it expedient to point out that it was unjust that he be so regarded because he possessed a valid passport signed by Danton and the other five members of the Executive Council which proved he had gone to London on official business. He did not mention that he had worn mourning for Louis XVI while in London. Talleyrand's plea was dispatched, together with instructions to submit it at an opportune moment, in triplicate, each copy on a different ship to ensure arrival. One went to Germaine at Coppet; one pro forma, to Barras, an influential deputy; and the third was addressed to Desrenaudes who was, and would remain until his death, as loyal to Talleyrand in the handling of confidential matters and ghostwriting as Courtiade was in a different capacity. Starting out as Talleyrand's vicar-general in Autun, then assisting him as deacon at the first Fête de la Fédération, Martial-Borye Desrenaudes had since left the Church and was now entrusted with the delicate task of rallying sufficient votes to assure success when Talleyrand's request was brought to the convention floor.

The questions of timing and of who should—and would—speak out on his behalf were equally important and impossible to orchestrate from thousands of miles away. By the end of July Talleyrand learned that Germaine was back in Paris. Convinced that the only feasible political course was to rally behind the Republic, the ambassadress reopened her salon and again had the ear of most of the men in power. Talleyrand knew he could count on her. As he would comment, years later, when he was an octogenarian, "What are politics if not women?" [20]

Weeks went by, then a month and, as still no word came from across the sea, he deluged Germaine with letters. Small wonder that Talleyrand, whose morale and feelings about the United States fluctuated with the state of his personal affairs, should be increasingly disenchanted with certain American customs. A lifelong dog-lover, he noted sourly: "Don't speak to me about a country where I have not found anyone who was not ready to sell me his dog." [21] For someone who had continuously maneuvered for a portfolio as the open sesame to riches and power, the Frenchman found it incomprehensible that Alexander Hamilton, whom he enjoyed seeing frequently—and with whom he would correspond until Hamilton's death a decade later—should have to resign as secretary of the treasury and revert to his law practice in order to support his family. One of the differences between the two cultures that astounded Talleyrand the most was the Americans' exaggerated reverence for money. As he wrote Lord Lansdowne: "Money is the one universal cult. The amount of money that one possesses is more important than any other distinction." Whereas, for Talleyrand money—up to now—was only the means to enable him to live the way he wanted to.

Because of the housing shortage in New York, Talleyrand and Beaumetz had been reduced to living in cramped quarters in a tiny house on Stone Street. But life improved when they finally moved in with some French friends, the banker M. Olive and his wife, on Bloomingdale Road. The la Tour du Pin couple came into town to see the pair, and many an enjoyable evening was passed together at Law's splendid mansion, sitting out on the terrace under the stars, while Talleyrand and Law worked on preliminaries for their joint Indian venture. Another friend, Count Antoine de la Forest, the French general councilor in New York, who had already done very well for himself in land investments, was a new business associate. Talleyrand was also acquainted with the well-known political figure, Aaron Burr, who had recently defeated General Schuyler for the Senate, and he was a frequent guest at Burr's beautiful home, Richmond Hill, just outside the city. However, Talleyrand could not, as some claim, have "discreetly courted" Burr's daughter, because Theodosia was then only twelve. Years later, after the famous duel in which he killed Hamilton, Burr was in Paris and left a card upon Talleyrand. With fine sensibility, Talleyrand instructed his major-domo to inform Mr. Burr, upon his return call, that Hamilton's portrait—which Talleyrand had requested that Mrs. Hamilton give him—hung in his bedroom.

He made a quick trip to Boston, about which very little is known and when, on his return, he found Beaumetz seriously ill. He moved with him to a more commodious lodging in Brooklyn where Talleyrand could take better care of him and watch for the incoming packets from France. As impatient as Talleyrand was for news, his lack of it did not mean that his allies overseas were neglecting him. The moment his petition reached Paris in the beginning of August, Desrenaudes set to work corralling the support of Talleyrand's friends and former associates. Fortuitously, on August 11, a brochure appeared, written by a well-known politician, entitled *French Fugitives and Émigrés*, in which the author suggested that the moment had come to make distinctions between fugitives from the revolutionary atrocities and those craven souls who had deserted their country by fleeing earlier. Among several prominent examples cited were citizens Talleyrand and Beaumetz, as well as a prominent general.

The scene was now set and, a scant two weeks later, Desrenaudes presented Talleyrand's petition to the convention. Three days later, thanks to Germaine's friendship with Thérèse Tallien, her husband, Jean Lambert Tallien—one of the leading architects of Robespierre's overthrow and a current chief in the post-Thermidorian reaction—publicly endorsed the pamphlet's point of view, declaring that "justice has not been done to Talleyrand-Périgord." Another four days passed and the deputies ordered the official paper, *Le Moniteur Universel* to carry *in toto* Talleyrand's formal request, together with his accompanying notes, which Desrenaudes then had made into a broadsheet and distributed to each legislator. This reprint's existence, which Talleyrand conveniently chose to forget in later years, would give the lie to his oft-repeated assertion, as an old man, that he had never personally solicited permission for his return. In the meantime, Germaine found the right person—someone who carried sufficient authority and was a good orator—to act as Talleyrand's spokesman and plead his cause to the National Convention. Marie-José Chenier, the brother of the guillotined poet, André Chenier, and one of the most eloquent speakers of the day, did not know Talleyrand personally. But his mistress, Eugénie, the Comtesse de la Bouchardie—who, like several other indigent aristocrats, ran a small elite gambling establishment in her salon that was popular with diplomats and the military—was a friend of both Thérèse Tallien and Germaine. These two cleverly intimated to Eugénie that, as a test of the powerful speaker's love for her, she should persuade Chenier to champion the absent Talleyrand. How the vain young woman, proud of her hold on Chenier, succeeded, pestering him at every turn, accompanying herself on the harp as she sang Chenier's own melancholy poems about the sorrows of exile, which she set to music, is the stuff of legends—if true. The entire evening of September 3, Germaine spent with Chenier and the countess planning strategy and arguments. On the morrow, he gave an impassioned plea on the floor, and a motion was passed without a dissenting voice to expunge Talleyrand's name from the list in question. He was free to return legally to France at any time. When Napoleon, years later, asked Talleyrand whether it was true that Mme de Staël was given to intrigue, he replied: "To such an extent that if it were not for her intrigues, I should not be here now." [22]

At the beginning of November, Talleyrand received the welcome news, and he wrote to thank Germaine: ". . . the rest of my life I will spend wherever you are. Will M. de Staël give me a small room?" [23] But there was not any question of an immediate return. No one in his right mind ventured across the Atlantic until the equinoctial gales were over, if it could be avoided. Furthermore, he wanted an official copy of the convention's decree in his favor and a regular passport in good order before setting forth, and he also had a number of half-finished business deals he wanted to terminate. Prudently awaiting the end of an epidemic of yellow fever, he did not go back to Philadelphia until early in December, where he found the latest journals from abroad with word of another fundamental change in France.

After placing an unknown general, Napoleon Bonaparte, the son of a family of dubious nobility from Corsica, a remote, savage Mediterranean island known only for its bandits and poverty, in charge of its troops to forcefully put down an insurrection in the streets of Paris, the convention had voted itself out of existence and been replaced by the Directoire. The country's recovery from the last tumultuous years was slow. The third and final partition of Poland had destroyed the European balance of power. And France had now reached its natural boundaries—the Alps, the Rhine, the Pyrénées—in its successful crusade to impose the Rights of Man and of the Citizen on its "enslaved" neighbors, who were forced to pay steep indemnities in return. Although the government had no money to pay its troops, or buy the material needed, the present aim of her victorious armies was to surround France with vassal states. They did this by creating new republics under the guise of supposedly snatching territories away from the other "tyrants" of Europe. While the main thrust of the French military was being pursued in Germany, the following March of 1796 General Napoleon Buonparte was dispatched to start the Italian campaign, which was envisioned as a diversionary maneuver, immediately following his wedding to the widowed Josephine, the Comtesse de Beauharnais. While legend has it that the young Corsican was chosen because he was taking Josephine, the former mistress of Barras—the principal member of the Directoire government—off that official's hands, the fact that the young Corsican was one of the generals who had most studied the question of possible operations in Piedmont undoubtedly weighed more heavily in his selection.

Talleyrand's fascination with the Far East and the fabulous profits to be made there continued unabated but had by now assumed a different form. Exactly when he decided that the earlier scheme of selling American land to wealthy English colonials in India was impractical and switched to a two-way trading expedition between Calcutta and Philadelphia is not known. Such an enterprise had been tried, for the first time, shortly after his arrival in Philadelphia, and the profits were reputed to have been more than five hundred percent over and above the costs entailed. Now, with American backing, Talleyrand and Beaumetz outfitted a similar ship and began to load it with cargo. Beaumetz and his bride, the sister-in-law of General Knox, were to go along to oversee the other end of the project on the spot. Talleyrand was likewise engaged in the preliminaries necessary to assemble a cargo of sugar, coffee, and spices for a ship on which he himself hoped to return to Europe. Boats were not easy to locate. For a variety of reasons he needed a neutral vessel, bound for a neutral port. To complicate his problem, seamen were superstitious and fearful of the Lord's anger, and several of the captains he approached warned that, in a storm, more than one crew had been known to throw overboard a defrocked priest to appease Him.

After rounds of farewells, both in New York and Philadelphia, and a quick visit to see the site on the Potomac of the new American capital to be built from scratch by a compatriot, Pierre L'Enfant, Talleyrand was off. He sailed on the Dutch brig *Den Nye Proeve* (The New Ordeal), on June 13, 1796, for Hamburg, the great neutral port for north and central Europe. Tucked in his pocket was a contract for his conditional purchase of one hundred thousand acres of Pennsylvania land, with a proviso giving him fifteen months in which to sell it abroad. If Talleyrand had not been very happy in America, he had learned a lot. His years of exile had permitted him to experience at first hand democracy in action and broadened his point of view regarding France and her role with other nations. Heretofore, he had seen the world through the eyes of the *ancien régime* for whom Paris was the center of the world; in America he encountered a new nation oriented towards the future. His point of view regarding money also changed. Much as he might have denigrated the American obsession with amassing money for itself alone, Talleyrand, too, became similarly imbued. Now to acquire a fortune became an end in itself. He would unscrupulously accumulate an enormous one and take great personal satisfaction in managing it meticulously.

It rained a little each of the forty days he was at sea, but the company was congenial, and no ships bothered them en route. As the brig was slowly coming up the Elbe, M. de Ricci, a member of Adèle's former Paris salon, clambered up its ladder to deliver to Talleyrand her astonishing entreaty that he not land but return at once to America. Once he got over the shock of this amazing greeting Talleyrand, who knew Adèle so well, should have realized how desperate she must be to even broach such an absurd request. Unfortunately, he was not the man to modify his plans from simple complaisance, especially when the reasons given were no concern of his. And probably the thought of spending another forty days at sea was more than he could contemplate. So he disembarked. Perhaps because of this reception—as hard as that is to believe—the only time Talleyrand ever mentioned Adèle in his entire *Mémoires* is in a passage, written decades afterwards, which deals with the shipboard incident: "Madame de Flahaut['s] . . . reason for doing so was that people were saying she had been on rather intimate terms with me and she feared that my presence should be an obstacle to her marriage . . . I thought I could without any impropriety take no notice of the extraordinary reasons alleged . . ." How much better for Talleyrand never to have mentioned Adèle rather than only in this disparaging fashion which reflects so badly on the author.

If their relationship had finally been reduced to a limited one before Talleyrand was obliged to leave England, time and distance had since emphasized this change. Interestingly, for someone who became known for maintaining warm, affectionate ties with his former mistresses—identified, in later years by *tout Paris* as Talleyrand's seraglio because of the way they banded together and furthered his best interests—Adèle became the one exception. She had returned to the continent, late the same year that Talleyrand had gone to the states, and joined other refugee friends, including Mme de Genlis and Princess Adelaide, in Bremgarten. Shortly afterwards, the princess's twenty-two-year-old brother, the future king, Louis-Philippe, arrived, traveling under a pseudonym and anxious to go to America, but lacking a passport and funds. So Adèle, who had never lost contact with Gouverneur Morris, even after he was no longer the American minister in Paris, contacted him for help. A hundred gold louis was at once forthcoming and, at the very last moment, she decided to accompany the young prince to Hamburg to see him safely off. Traveling incognito and mostly at night because of his deadly fear of recognition, the pair, with Adèle's faithful Polly, an equerry and one other Orléans servant, set forth in mid-March of 1795 in a six-horse traveling coach and a three-horse cabriolet. By the end of the month Adèle was in Altona, only a long, treelined *allée* away from Hamburg. Here she saw Morris, whom she had not seen since Paris. He helped her get settled in a small house of her own before taking off, shortly afterwards, on a trip to London where his first guest was young Charles de Flahaut, no doubt so Morris could send Adèle an up-to-date account of her son whom she had left behind in an English academy.

Because she still needed to earn a living, indestructible Adèle resumed making hats, while starting another novel, *Eugénie and Mathilde*, full of autobiographical echoes of her most recent wanderings. The next winter was dreadful for her, and she was stricken with snow blindness. Tired of fending for herself, not only as an émigré but also as a widow, Adèle was extremely anxious to get married, but this was farthest from Morris's thoughts. So she turned to newly arrived Lord Wycombe who—like a cad—confided to Morris that he was happy to have an affair with her but he was not interested in matrimony. Then, providentially, the Portuguese minister to Denmark, José Maria de Souza-Botelho Mourâo e Vascocellos, a man of letters and from a distinguished, wealthy family, descended from Vasco da Gama's lieutenant, visited Hamburg. De Souza, two years older than Adèle, had enjoyed reading *Adèle de Senanges* and, when he learned that its author was residing in nearby Altona, he asked to meet her. The pair was soon inseparable. A true measure of normally resilient Adèle's subsequent despair over the lack of any marriage proposal, even from de Souza, was her desperate, unrealistic plea delivered to Talleyrand dockside. Although he ignored her request that he return to the States at once, he gave the pair a wide berth when he reached Hamburg. But it was another six years before the frail Portuguese finally proposed and, in the interim, Talleyrand's relationship with Adèle, while unfailingly courteous, was never again an intimate one.

Talleyrand, whose face was already hardening into the impassive mask which would become second nature to him, arrived with a fever and spent most of his first two weeks in bed at an inn, the "Roman Emperor." A goodly portion of the *ancien régime* had preceded him here, including many personal friends, not to mention numerous Orléanists who congregated around Mme de Genlis and her Orléans charges. With as tart a tongue as ever and still a trim figure, the countess had lost none of her gaiety and charm, and the pleasure of her company more than compensated for the contretemps with Adèle. The tricolor republican cockade was flowering prominently among the thousands of refugees, not only from France but also from northern Europe, and Talleyrand adopted it in order to distinguish himself from other aristocratic émigrés. Because Hamburg at the moment replaced London as the bank of Europe, far-sighted Talleyrand had come with useful letters of introduction from American friends. These helped him not only to establish invaluable connections with some of the Hanseatic League's most prominent bankers and businessmen, but also to sell the commodities that he had brought over with him on the brig, luxuries to add variety to the Spartan diet enjoyed by so many of the French in recent years. He prudently banked here, as a hedge in case of future internal problems in France, his not inconsiderable American earnings—probably around one hundred thousand dollars which he had received, that spring, as a commission for the successful sale of a large piece of land for Robert Morris, a relative of Gouverneur Morris—and Talleyrand planned to borrow money in Paris as needed.

For anyone anxious to be brought abreast of the latest continental developments, Hamburg, the customary halting spot for both couriers and travelers, was the place to be, the crossroads where news from Paris, Berlin, London, and Vienna converged. It was an added stroke of good fortune for Talleyrand to find that the Wurtembourgeois Count Charles-Frederick Reinhard, a career diplomat who had been part of his entourage during Talleyrand's first trip to London, was presently the French minister to the Hanseatic League. Like Talleyrand he, too, wanted to see the political gains of the revolution conserved and its excesses stripped away, and he was well qualified to give Talleyrand an in-depth, up-to-date briefing about the situation in Paris. The Directoire was stabilizing, while coping with the Jacobins and the extreme Left; its Italian army under General Bonaparte was sweeping all before it; and financial affairs were picking up.

In the beginning of September, Talleyrand set off with another passport, made out to "citizen Talleyrand," which he had taken the precaution of getting from the neutral Hanseatic League. With "his cow"— his large leather suitcase—and a small trunk, stowed away in a stagecoach with room inside for six below and a place outside for three poor souls riding on top, Talleyrand traversed the Batavian Republic, as the Low Countries were renamed following their capture by the French the year before. When he stopped in Amsterdam, its capital, presumably for business reasons since it was the home base of Cazenove, certain difficulties arose, about which not a great deal is yet known. Whatever the problem was, it detained him there almost two weeks and greatly alarmed Germaine, who was afraid he might delay his return to Paris. Talleyrand had been far too important a political figure for the Directoire police not to have been alerted to his arrival on the continent and not to have been suspicious of his Orléanist sympathies because of his constant attendance on Mme de Genlis in Hamburg. After frequent stops in inns famed as the worst in all Europe, Talleyrand reached Brussels, which a victorious republican army had snatched from imperial Austria—with whom republican France was still in conflict—and which had been transformed into the principal city of a French administrative department. Jouncing along the notoriously ill-kept roads, exhausted by the heat and dust, he pushed on until, finally, three long days later, he saw in the distance—Paris! He had been gone four years. Now forty-two, he was home at last.

6

A Minister of the Directoire

"He has all the vices of the ancien régime as well as those of the new one. He will always keep a foot in both camps."—Mme de Staël [1]

IT WAS LATE SEPTEMBER, with just a hint of autumn in the clear air, and the chestnut trees along the boulevards were beginning to shed a few leaves. Returning graver and more ambitious than ever, Talleyrand considered it strategic to move in with an old friend, Mme de Boufflers, in the village of Auteuil, on the outskirts of Paris rather than in the capital itself, to take soundings. Forced to build his life anew, he must try to recover his possessions, find some sort of congenial activity and acquire the wherewithal to live as he felt it his due.

Talleyrand hardly recognized his native city. It resembled a junk shop. On the Left Bank, where he had lived all his life, the beautiful gardens, which surrounded the lovely old mansions and convents lay abandoned and overgrown. Friends' family homes had been converted into warehouses. Wine and vegetable shops masked their sculptured facades, and portraits of ancestors stared out from shop windows loaded with the loot of palaces. There were still very few sidewalks and, when it rained, it was impossible to cross the streams rushing down the middle of most streets until planks were thrown across them as bridges. Exaggerated fashions on passersby epitomized the extravagant passion for amusement. After the Terror's orgy of bloodletting and the nightmare of the recent past, the French, although facing an uncertain future, were rediscovering the joy of being alive and could at last breathe in comparative freedom. Public balls, spectacles, and fireworks had replaced prisons and revolutionary committees. The wives of the newly rich took the place of the former ladies of the court of Louis XVI and Marie-Antoinette.

The Directoire, which presently governed France, was a bizarre regime that was probably the most corrupt, inefficient one which that country had ever known. It had been conceived to maintain in power a moderate bourgeoisie who had drawn from the Revolution all possible advantages and intended to enjoy them. The new Constitution of the Year III—according to the revolutionary calendar—established a bicameral legislature with a total of seven hundred and fifty members divided, according to age, into the Council of Ancients, a body of two hundred and fifty, and the Council of Five Hundred. One third of these deputies were elected every year by a restricted suffrage, based on certain financial qualifications. Executive power was vested in a directorate, composed of five all-powerful directors, popularly known as "The Five," one of whom rotated off each year, and whose sole qualification for office was to have voted the death penalty for the late Louis XVI.

As usual, after most social upheavals or wars of long duration, the new republic was dominated by unscrupulous, immoral parvenus who had made a fortune fast, with no questions asked: profiteers, men who cornered the primary market of necessities, munition makers, suppliers to the armies, and their attendant swarms of parasites. Their vulgar luxury barely hid the hunger and misery of most Parisians who were compelled to form pre-dawn queues at butcher shops and bakeries in order to make purchases before the meager supplies available ran out. Coal and wood for heating lacked, as did butter and sugar. Candles, indispensable for lighting, soap and tobacco could only be bought on the black market.

Although there was no money to pay its armies or buy the matériel they required—the troops were forced to live off the inhabitants wherever they were stationed—war was the sole resource of the bankrupt government. It was an industry of prime importance, as long as France continued triumphant, guaranteeing the Directoire's security by keeping its victorious generals away from home and also filling its empty exchequer with loot from the conquered countries more successfully than any forced domestic loans could. Once the Austrians, whom the French republicans considered the worst tyrants in Europe, had been chased out of Belgium, one of their vast empire's far-flung possessions, they could only be reached in Germany, which The Five, equally interested in enlarging upon France's natural borders, now envisaged as the main field of French military operations. The role of Bonaparte's army had been considered as a secondary, diversionary one, to strike at the Austrians in their Italian possessions and immobilize a part of their forces there. The young Corsican general's southern successes that previous spring of 1796, culminating with his entry into Milan, compensated for the recent failures in the north of the two larger republican armies. The second part of his Italian campaign had already opened with the start of the siege of Mantua in June. By the time Talleyrand returned, all Paris was shouting "Vive General Bonaparte!" until it was hoarse. Each victory bulletin from the southern front was accompanied back to the capital by another score of conquered regimental flags and convoys of booty for the Treasury.

Talleyrand took care, for the moment, to remain aloof from the various political factions, preferring to watch and wait, before declaring himself. Although he had previously addressed to Barras a copy of his request for removal from the dreaded proscribed list, he did not yet know the number-one director personally. The Gascon vicomte, whose greed was proverbial, was the soul of the Directoire and, when not debauching or gambling, he was filling his pockets with both hands. The other four were typical representatives of the revolutionary bourgeoisie, hostile to Jacobin terrorism as well as to any clerical or royalist reaction. All of them mistrusted Talleyrand not only because of his aristocratic ancestry but also because of his often equivocal role in the past. The one thing that he shared with them was his lack of scruples, something not one of them was in any position to hold against him.

Talleyrand's mother and two brothers had not yet returned and only a handful of his friends were yet back. So, to add further to the briefing he had received in Hamburg and be brought up-to-the-minute, Talleyrand decided to attend a session of the Institut de France, of which he had been made a member the previous fall while still in America, one of the few appointments for which he never had to angle. Established by law the previous year and divided into four classes, comprising the country's outstanding men of science, arts, and letters, membership here was considered a great honor and, in Talleyrand's case it was not undeserved. For in his *Report on Public Education* delivered to the Constituent Assembly five years previously, he had proposed its creation to replace the Royal Academies of the monarchy, which no longer existed. The Institut as such was not a new idea but, because it was developed in such detail in his report, Talleyrand was given full credit as its creator. It had been considered only proper at the time to elect "citizen Talleyrand" to be one of its first members as a tribute to his talent and work as an economist and a sociologist. Talleyrand was warmly welcomed by this select gathering; by chance, at this, his first meeting, his section was renewing its volunteer staff and, as a sign of welcome, he was offered, and accepted, the honorary post of secretary. He was also asked to prepare two papers to be read at one of its four great annual meetings the following year, which were open to the public.

Before he did anything else, Talleyrand also wanted to thank the people who had been instrumental in arranging his return. Unfortunately, Germaine de Staël, who had spearheaded his campaign, was in exile at the Necker family residence at Coppet, on the shores of Lake Geneva with the current love of her life, the pamphleteer and politician Benjamin Constant. She was threatened with arrest by the Directoire for her political intriguing against it if she ever again set foot on French soil. However, he did see Marie-Joseph Chenier and his mistress, Eugénie de la Bouchardie. And of course, he also saw Germaine's friend, Thérèse Tallien. She was nicknamed by the Paris press "Notre Dame de Thermidor" for her part in her husband's participation in the overthrow of the tyrant Robespierre, on the ninth of Thermidor, two years before. Thérèse's present role as one of the ambidextrous Barras's mistresses and also his official hostess gave her an enviable position in Directoire society, even higher than the one she had previously held as the wife of Jean Lambert Tallien, the third member of Thérèse's current ménage.

Driving through Paris in her claret-colored carriage or parading through the packed, disorderly salons during the nightly receptions in the Luxembourg Palace—the former home of Marie de Médicis, the wife of Henry IV, where all five directors lived—with Barras's arm around her slender waist, Thérèse was Paris's style setter. "On ne pouvait pas etre plus richement deshabillée!" [2] Talleyrand exclaimed when he first glimpsed the fair Thérèse, clothed in the classic style of the ancients—made popular by the continuing excavations at Herculaneum—with a gossamer tunic and loosened bodice, her arms, legs, and feet bare with jewels on her toes. Talleyrand considered the gatherings at Barras's receptions as barely a notch above those of an undistinguished gambling house and preferred the ones at Thérèse's own home, "La Chaumière." At the end of the Allée des Veuves, which led from the Champs Elysées to the Seine, this was the place to be seen, and Talleyrand was soon a *habitué* there. In this parvenu world demimondaines and, sometimes, interlopers even lower, held sway, and it did not take Talleyrand long to discover that the influence of women was as important for success as before the fall of the Tuileries.

At La Chaumière Talleyrand renewed contact with Comte Casimir de Montrond. His young mistress, a smoky-colored Creole from Saint-Domingue, Fortunée Hamelin, one of the wittiest women of the day, shared a leading role there with Josephine, Madame la Générale Bonaparte—who was away at the moment with her husband and his army in Italy. The friendship between Talleyrand and the handsome blond Montrond, which dated from their London days of exile, quickly developed into an all-encompassing intimacy. Although Montrond always wore a glove on his left hand because his little finger was deformed and continued down to the wrist, he was a former cavalry officer renown for his duels. Two kindred souls, Montrond shared with Talleyrand the same cynicism and contempt for humanity and would be his lifelong confidential man for the most delicate affairs—around the gambling tables as well as in financial transactions and speculations, even in those involving political activities and secret diplomacy. Because he was such a reckless, compulsive gambler with enormous debts, Talleyrand nicknamed him "The Infant Jesus from Hell." A famous Beau Brummel of the day with his wigs, his silver bidet, and his irresistible charm for women, Montrond might have stepped straight from the pages of *Les Liaisons Dangereuses*. His sole redeeming virtue was his absolute loyalty to Talleyrand and his discretion regarding the latter's affairs. When Talleyrand remarked one day to Fortunée that he liked Montrond because he was not overburdened with scruples, Montrond replied that he liked Talleyrand because he had none.

At Montrond's Talleyrand resumed ties with his old friend, Radix de Sainte-Foy and, through Radix, with the banker Frédéric Perregaux and other survivors of the financial milieu he knew so well before the Revolution. Hard-pressed for funds, Talleyrand gambled daily, fortunately winning more than he lost. Cheating was beneath him. In America he may not have had a lot of money but he had never known real poverty, and he did not want to now. Although he was not in actual need, he could not remain long without employ.

For a financier as skillful as Radix de Sainte-Foy, money was easy to make, especially in speculations on the grain market and as a purveyor to the armed forces. This last was one type of investment Talleyrand never seems to have participated in, and it would be nice to think he did not because of his hatred for war. One of the first affairs he was now involved in with Sainte-Foy; Perregaux; and Michel Simons, a Belgian newcomer, was a complex deal converting foreign currency, gold, and silver into French species. Barras's approval was required but, rather than compromise himself, farsighted Talleyrand, adroitly persuaded Sainte-Foy to be the contact man. If nothing else, Talleyrand must have received a commission, while waiting for his position to improve so he could participate on a larger scale.

Probably for more freedom of movement, by the first of the year 1797, Talleyrand moved from Auteuil to nearby Passy where he rented several rooms in the Château de la Tuilerie, so-called, like the royal palace in Paris, because of its location on a former tile *(tuile)* factory. A beautiful property that had formerly belonged to the guillotined father-in-law of young Lucy de la Tour du Pin, whom he had seen the previous year in America, La Tuilerie was a proper Auteuil address from an *ancien régime* point of view.

Each of the gambling houses that the Directoire authorized to open had its own clientele, and most furnished, as an added service, not only girls, when so desired, but even rooms where their patrons from the two legislative chambers might confer together privately. While politics in general no longer interested any but the politicians and the diehard royalists whose Bourbon counter-revolution was making formidable progress, many decrees were written and many a political intrigue hatched in these discreet upstairs parlors. Talleyrand's favorite was centrally located on the Place Vendôme and was backed by Radix de Sainte-Foy and Michel Simons. Whether he frequented there solely for the gambling—especially craps, recently imported from England—or the plotting and scheming, or both, is hard to say. Only one thing was certain. Given the confused situation in the two legislative councils—the Five Hundred and the Ancients—the financial disorder, the general insecurity, the permanent state of war, the impotent, discredited Directoire was far from stable and could not last indefinitely in its present form. It behooved a prudent man like Talleyrand to establish a strategy for the future, despite his openly avowed intention, upon his return, not to take an active role in public affairs.

He might write Germaine de Staël at Coppet that he was spending his time attending to business matters that he had begun in America and Hamburg. On the other hand, an English diplomat who dined with Talleyrand at the banker Perregaux's home at the end of January, reported that "the former Bishop d'Autun . . . is moving heaven and earth to be employed by the Directoire." [3] At this point, ambitious Talleyrand, conscious of his own superiority, experience, and capabilities as compared with the mediocrity and poor caliber of the incumbent Five, was aiming sky-high and considering his chances to become a director when one must automatically rotate off, later that year. Or, as second choice, he might be appointed to a cabinet post, preferably the Foreign Affairs portfolio rather than the Finance one he had previously coveted. In addition to being one of the ex-leaders of the Constituent Assembly, his new claim for consideration was his long stay in America, where fifteen states each had its own constitution and where he was able to witness, at first hand, liberty in action.

On February 20, at a critical moment in the pre-election maneuvers for the first mandatory renewal of one third of the seats in each of the two chambers, Talleyrand shed his pose of impartiality. After the votes were counted it would be too late to expect any reward for his support. In a letter published in reply to several journalists' venomous charges accusing him of being an Orléanist, Talleyrand declared he had no political affiliations and was only interested in "the well-being and glory of the French Republic." [4] This blanket denouncement of the opposition was not lost on The Five, and Talleyrand could reasonably expect to be rewarded by them at some future date.

As part of his campaign, the time was ripe to give the first of two promised lectures to fellow members of the Institut because the prestige attached by contemporaries to all learned societies assured the wide dissemination of whatever he had to say. On April 4, in one of its four annual open meetings, Talleyrand read his *Memoir on Commercial Relations of the United States with England*, a thirty-minute talk in the three-hour program which began at 5:00 p.m. These sessions in the Louvre's great Hall of the Caryatides were always well attended but interest was heightened, today, because Talleyrand was considered someone to watch—and to hear. Most of the diplomatic corps attended in their special tribune, while the general public happily availed itself of the privilege of being wedged tightly onto banquettes in a space that normally seated only twelve hundred. The acoustics were terrible, even for Talleyrand's deep, resonant voice, and the heat was stifling. The members of the Institut themselves sat around a double, horseshoe-shaped table in the center, and Talleyrand appeared first. More than one echo of his many têtes-à-têtes with Alexander Hamilton about economic theories was easily discernible and, as he had intended, his audience left convinced of his obvious ability as an up-and-coming statesman.

As Talleyrand pointed out to the astute Madame de Staël, such a favorable impression was important for his revived and growing importance. That redoubtable female had finally browbeaten her way into getting permission to return to France, provided she remain at least eight leagues—about twenty miles—away from Paris. Furtively crossing the capital on Christmas day, the formidable ambassadress was now ensconced with Benjamin Constant at Hérivaux in an ancient small abbey, which he had bought with a loan from her father and was now furnishing. Talleyrand wrote her frequently and often came out to see her. Since he could not afford a carriage of his own and had become accustomed to public transportation, his bad leg notwithstanding, during his years of exile, he took the 10:00 a.m. daily coach from the Lion d'Or in the faubourg Saint-Denis. He generally brought along some other guests to help amuse the proscribed woman, including dumpy Mme de Valence, who had been so instrumental in getting Talleyrand his passport to leave the country years before. Talleyrand's finances were at a low ebb and Germaine, who was never so happy as when her friends were in distress and she could help them out, loaned him some money, because he would not, or could not, borrow from his banker friends.

She was back in the Swedish Embassy on the rue du Bac some time late that spring, having cajoled the Directoire into letting her return there for the imminent birth of Constant's child. Germaine, naturally, gave birth in public like a queen, with never less than fifteen people chattering around her when Albertine, a redhead like her father, appeared. The March elections had seen the royalist deputies soundly trounce the republicans and, when the presidencies of the two new chambers as well as one directorial replacement were voted on, in mid May, Talleyrand still inspired too much distrust among The Five to even be considered for the latter position. However, it did not hurt to see his name publicly discussed as a potential candidate. By now The Five, who were fighting among themselves as well as against the opposition deputies, needed all the support they could get. Since she was anxious to once more play a prominent role on the Parisian scene and also to gratify the political ambitions of both Talleyrand and Constant, Germaine resumed her role as an influential political hostess to the nation's leaders, just as she had been in her salon's halcyon pre-revolutionary days. She re-established her former warm contacts with Barras and, because she could be useful to him, Barras reciprocated.

Stimulated by the two recent elections, public opinion was now bubbling. Talleyrand was greatly disturbed by the resurgence of the moderates in the legislature because the Church, which was his irreconcilable enemy for his role in the schism, had played an important role in their success. Nor was he any happier about the inroads of the Bourbon supporters who promised draconian reprisals against anyone who had aided the overthrow of the monarchy. Many royalists sauntering along the boulevards flaunted eighteen buttons on their tight, form-fitting coats—for Louis XVIII, the guillotined king's brother and heir—to show where their sympathies lay, and political clubs were suddenly *à la mode*. To counteract the propaganda of the reactionary Club de Clichy a new club, whose name, the Cercle Constitutionel, indicated its allegiance to the principles of 1789—and to the Republic—was formed in June and installed in the former Montmorency townhouse on the rue de Lille in the faubourg Saint-Germain. With Talleyrand, the Abbé Sieyès, another friend from the Constituent Assembly, and Constant prominent among its founders, the Cercle got off to a fast start and soon boasted some six hundred moderate liberals as members. It also got control of a journal and established a delivery service, by cabriolet, to expedite the sheet's diffusion throughout Belgium and the northern part of France. By the end of June, Talleyrand was chosen as one of its board of commissioners and, never a man to miss an opportunity, he led an official delegation from the Cercle to call on Barras to place this new group "at my disposal and even at my feet, for me to do with as I wished," [5] Barras noted in his memoirs.

The Five realized that the hatred Talleyrand engendered among both the resurgent clergy and the royalists was the best guarantee of the ex-Bishop d'Autun's loyalty to the incumbent regime. And, gradually, by dint of hard work Talleyrand was modifying their individual attitudes in his regard. Not one of them looked on Talleyrand with any great favor, although none was as outspoken as the coarse, wall-eyed Jean-François Rewbell, who had the shape and voice of a butcher and was suspicious of anything that Talleyrand was involved with. But Talleyrand still had no more than a nodding acquaintance with Barras, their acknowledged leader. And once more, as had been and would be the case throughout his long life, it was a woman who came to his rescue.

While it has long been accepted that it was Germaine de Staël who first brought the pair together for a private conversation, as both Talleyrand and Barras would maintain—for unknown reasons of their own—this has lately been disproven. Towards the end of June the Duchess de Brancas, a close relative of Barras, brought Talleyrand to Suresnes, the director's splendid country home that he had luxuriantly furnished with liberated treasures from the former royal storehouses at Versailles. There, according to the Comte d'Allonville, who was present at the same soirée, and whose memoirs were published the year Talleyrand died, in 1838, Talleyrand analyzed the situation in Paris as he saw it and urged Barras to take action. Later, when the guests sat down to gamble and Talleyrand took a hand at *bouillotte*—something he could not have avoided doing, had he wanted to, since five players were required—he discreetly borrowed ten louis from Allonville. Although a skillful, lucky player, Talleyrand deliberately managed to lose tonight to put his host in a good humor, a favorite strategy of his.

Financial necessity made Talleyrand an eager opportunist, and two prestigious appointments were soon available, either one of which he coveted. The first appointment was that of plenipotentiary to the Anglo-French peace negotiations due to open at Lille. After the successful conclusion, that February of 1797, of the seven-month siege of Mantua, Bonaparte had started a new offensive. By spring the route to Vienna was open and, after destroying five armies each larger than his own and beaten its best generals, exhausted Austria sued for peace. When William Pitt the Younger, who was already deep in the midst of serious domestic problems, realized that England was now alone in the field against republican France, the English prime minister decided that the time had come to attempt to negotiate an English-French accord. Talleyrand's campaign for some government post had reached the point where Barras claimed that he would not be sorry to send him to Lille—which had been chosen as the site of the parlays because it was midway between the two countries' capitals—to rid Paris of his intrigues. Lille would be an ideal showcase for his purported diplomatic talents but, to his great disappointment, Talleyrand received only one out of the five directors' votes for the job.

But an opening also loomed in the Foreign Office where the resignation of its present minister, Charles Delacroix, was pending because of his ill health. Contemporary gossip delightedly named the philandering Talleyrand as the father of the child the charming Mme Delacroix was carrying—the future famous Romantic painter, Eugène Delacroix who would bear a certain facial resemblance to Talleyrand. However, modern medicine has decisively scotched that long-lasting rumor in the art world by claiming that the unfortunate minister's cyst did not preclude impregnating his own wife. Be that as it may, citizen-Delacroix's forthcoming operation meant that the ministry on the rue du Bac would soon be vacant. Since he had failed to get the Lille appointment, Talleyrand felt that the rue du Bac one must surely be his. And he had no intention of letting it slip away.

When a new journal, *The Conservateur*—that is to say, the "guardian of the incumbent regime"—was founded, Talleyrand assumed charge of its foreign policy section as an excellent showcase for his own ideas on the subject. His years of exile in the United States had greatly widened his perspective, and he no longer approached the matter from a parochial point of view but on a worldwide basis. This presupposed a necessary balance of power for which peace was essential—two interdependent prerequisites that would dominate his thinking and underlie his actions for the rest of his life, and on which would rest Talleyrand's principle claim to fame as a precursor to the diplomats of modern France.

Anxious to keep his name before the public as much as possible, Talleyrand had still another chance to call attention to himself and limn what his program might be as foreign affairs minister when he gave the second of his two promised talks before the Institut on July 3. This time the Louvre's great hall was even more crowded than for his first address. People were still pushing and shoving to enter as he slowly navigated the steps of the podium. "On the advantages of new colonies under the present circumstances" stressed the nation's desire for peace. France had now reached her natural boundaries, which were far enough from the heart of the country to ensure its protection. If the government still felt the need to expand, it should be overseas. The whole colonial question had already been much debated prior to the Revolution, and an earlier foreign minister, the Duc de Choiseul, whom Talleyrand had known, had already begun negotiating for cotton-rich Egypt. Why not continue along these lines?

At this particular moment, when the twenty-four hours in a day were insufficient for everything Talleyrand was trying to accomplish, a distraction of an entirely different nature appeared—Catherine-Noël Worlée Grand, his future wife. Contemporaries took it for granted that the two had met previously, though there is no agreement on which side of the Channel, or when, this occurred. Indeed, it would have been stranger had their paths not crossed, since the circles they traveled in often intersected. Fouché, the well-informed future minister of police, always maintained this was the case. In one purported letter to the minister Lebrun, as early as January of 1793, Talleyrand speaks of Madame Grand whose "friendship" he says he possesses.

This is the only instance where he is known to have bestowed a nickname on his Dulcinea; it makes Talleyrand seem warmer and helps somewhat to explain his hold on the opposite sex, all of whom, young and old, always adored him. But one wonders whether "Kelly"—as he supposedly called her—is not an early misreading of "Kitty," in some document or letter of the period, an error that has been perpetuated ever since. The latter is much more in keeping with a *grand seigneur* who, to quote his young friend, Lucy de la Tour du Pin, "was never guilty of poor taste." While Talleyrand played the field, even during Adèle's heyday, his many, often simultaneous, liaisons of any duration were always with the most intelligent and influential women around. They would remain faithful members of his seraglio—as outsiders referred to them—as long as he lived. Normally more than beauty was required to attract him. Catherine, eight years younger than the forty-three-year-old Talleyrand, was the one exception. No doubt her hold on him was predominantly sexual. Certainly pride of possession also played a role, for Catherine was an international beauty who would be an ornament in any household.

Always referred to as "l'Indienne" in the scandal sheets, Catherine was born in Tranquebar, a Danish commercial port in India, of French parents. The statuesque blonde adventuress was wed at fifteen, then involved in a celebrated lawsuit brought by her husband against her first lover, a prominent Englishman seated on the king's Supreme Council of Bengal and, next, heard of in London in 1782. Her slim, supple waist, flawless figure and languorous, seductive walk, so often noted in women from that part of the world, did not go unnoticed. Local chroniclers titillated the English public with the prominence of Catherine's lovers, her jewels, her carriages, and lifestyle, including one delightful episode when she dined, clothed only in her long golden tresses, with one of the more dashing young men-about-town. Eventually she crossed to Paris, where she was soon the mistress of Valdec de Lessart, who was then foreign minister and, because it was chic at the moment to be well educated, she hired a master of handwriting. Commissioned to paint the exotic stranger, Mme Vigée-Le Brun produced an ornamental likeness that today hangs in The Metropolitan Museum of Art in New York and is the epitome of eighteenth century sentimentality. Using a pose the artist employed whenever she found a sitter too vacuous, she depicted Catherine, with her blue eyes, accented by her dark eyebrows, gazing skyward, and did full justice to a tip-tilted nose amazingly like Talleyrand's.

Chased by the Revolution back to London, the high-priced courtesan now reappeared in Paris, early in the summer of 1797, when Talleyrand was doing his utmost to get the Foreign Affairs portfolio. This time she was accompanying the Marquis Cristofero Spinola, the London representative of the Republic of Genoa and a friend of the diplomat James Harris, Lord Malmesbury. Spinola had come, presumably, to quietly coordinate an English press and political attack against Bonaparte who had just occupied Venice and was now eyeing Genoa. Because Spinola's mission was so successful and the two Directoire Councils, the Five Hundred and the Ancients, were violently attacking the Italian policy of the Citizen-General, Spinola and Catherine Grand were placed under strict police surveillance. Nothing daunted, the pair multiplied their contacts. Spinola and the dashing Catherine, who did not know the meaning of the word inconspicuous, next appeared at a gala official ceremony, celebrating the arrival of more conquered Austrian regimental flags, at the Luxembourg Palace. Three days later, on July 1, they were ordered expelled from France. Catherine managed to stay on to serve, to all appearances, as an informer and letter-drop for Spinola and Malmesbury who, as head of the English delegation to the French-English peace negotiations, was presently at Lille. Her association with Spinola was so well established that her continued presence in France must have posed a problem for the authorities, but who intervened in her behalf is not known. Did she contact Talleyrand?

Whatever the prior relationship between the pair, Catherine was now thirty-six and had aroused the attention of the police. Talleyrand may not have been rich enough nor important enough for her to pay any attention to him before. But now he seemed on the verge of attaining high office, and it was time for calculating, cold-blooded Catherine to settle down. There would never be any indication of affection on her part for Talleyrand whereas he, as a connoisseur of women, claimed that Catherine had all that was needed to charm and to please: a soft, transparent skin whose delicacy was already proverbial, unwavering good humor, and a sweet breathe—because of her fine teeth. This last was a sufficient rarity for him to emphasize it and meant that, unlike Josephine, General Bonaparte's wife, and other belles of the day, Catherine did not have to keep a handkerchief forever over her mouth. When someone pointed out that she lacked wit, Mme Vigée-Le Brun countered that M. de Talleyrand had enough for two, and Mme Grand may have seemed like a refreshing whiff of fresh air in comparison with the overpowering Germaine de Staël. Indeed, the ways of the flesh do not lend themselves to analysis. Although the ministry on the rue du Bac seemed almost within Talleyrand's grasp, at a moment which seemed to dictate more prudence than usual—even for him—he set Catherine up in a small establishment on the outskirts of Paris, near Meudon, where he was driven whenever he could snatch a few free hours.

Unfortunately, though the Constitution of the Year III was stuffed with checks and balances, it contained no provision for arbitrage in any dispute between the executive branch, backed as it now was by the republican army and those who had been getting rich under the Directoire, and the predominantly moderate legislative branch, backed by a large part of public opinion. When the opposition started to repeal a number of laws emasculating The Five's powers, Barras was convinced a movement was under way to oust them. No longer able to govern with the Five Hundred and the Ancients, the directors must knuckle under or conspire to strengthen their own hand, if they did not want to perish. A majority of them—Barras, Rewbell, and the frightful hunchback, La Réveillière—opted for action and carried the day. To prepare a coup d'état, competent, reliable officials with experience and proven ability must control five of the seven cabinet portfolios—the key ministries of the Police, the Army, the

Navy, the Interior, and Foreign Affairs. But the pool of such talent was steadily shrinking. The émigrés were not to be considered, the military with four armies in the field was bereft of talent, and the deputies of all parties were constitutionally forbidden to hold office. To compound the selection of a new Foreign Office head, the government was negotiating for peace on two fronts, both at Lille with the English and in Italy, where final talks were resuming with the Austrians. And Talleyrand had already proven his ability as a skillful negotiator.

Barras needed Talleyrand. His nomination was a political nomination and politically motivated. In addition to his capability, another factor that must have weighed heavily enough in Barras's eyes for him to back a candidacy which constituted such a bone of contention, was Talleyrand's value as a sufficient token presence—as an aristocrat and an émigré—to assuage some of the moderates in the troubled days ahead. Nobody summed up this unique qualification better than Germaine de Staël whom Barras himself quotes as singing Talleyrand's praises: "[M. de Talleyrand] has all the vices of the *ancien régime* as well as those of the new one. He will always keep a foot in both camps. You can never find anyone more useful." [6] And Talleyrand, faithful to his lifelong tenet, "in important circumstances, one should put women to work," [7] was stepping up his visits to the rue du Bac. At this critical juncture Radix de Sainte-Foy was also extremely helpful because he frequently acted as Barras's intermediary in political matters as well as in his personal financial speculations.

The precise scenario for the days immediately preceding the prerequisite cabinet changes, in the middle of July, is the picture of confusion. Each director stumped for his own slate, and the official report of their final sessions for the reshufflement are all too brief relative to the Foreign Affairs portfolio. Talleyrand himself and Barras give different, highly subjective accounts of the steps taken to assure the former's victory, each version emphasizing—or de-emphasizing—its author's own participation. Taking into account their prejudices and predilections, these accounts, written years afterwards are, not surprisingly, at loggerheads, and have evolved into legends, heavily encrusted with contradictions. Barras, a notorious liar, has Germaine throwing herself into his arms, bosom heaving and almost escaping its tight bodice, offering to sacrifice herself à la Iphigenia, on dear Talleyrand's behalf, a scene which, given that emotional woman's potential, has somewhat the ring of truth.

Talleyrand's *Mémoires*, in which he picks and chooses at will, with only a dash of truth tossed in, to concoct posterity's version of his career, are patently absurd concerning the circumstances of his appointment and portray his contempt for the intelligence of future readers.

When the Directoire finally voted, four of the new officials to be selected were from the Cercle Constitutionel, including Talleyrand. Barras immediately dispatched Germaine's paramour, Benjamin Constant, to the theater where Talleyrand was absentmindedly watching the stage with one eye and the door to his loge with the other, anxiously awaiting the results. Rushing to the Luxembourg to thank his sponsor, he kept clutching Constant's knee in the carriage and repeating over and over, "We must make an immense fortune! An immense fortune!"—if that gentleman can be believed. His goal achieved, it is nice to picture Talleyrand, whom some were beginning to call the "sphinx," giving public vent to his emotions. If true, this incident, together with his bestowal of a nickname on Catherine, makes him seem more human.

Talleyrand already knew the former Hôtel Galliffet on the rue du Bac, not far from the Swedish Embassy at number 102, that housed the official residence and ministry of Foreign Affairs. Set between a pair of entry pavilions—today replaced by two buildings at numbers 90 and 92—which in turn opened onto a first and, then, a second courtyard, the magnificent townhouse, designed by Jacques-Guillaume Legrand, with ten meters high, Doric columns on two facades, had been completed just before the Revolution. The Marquis de Galliffet and his wife fled without ever having lived there, and it was appropriated, and furnished, by the government just three years ago. With an enormous garden on the far side, magnificent salons whose hand-carved wainscots were the envy of all, and a superb double staircase, crowned with a cupola to let the daylight in, the Galliffet was one of the most beautiful dwellings in the entire faubourg Saint-Germain. It conveyed an aura of immense grandeur of which even a Talleyrand-Périgord could be proud and it came equipped with a swarm of unpaid servants presided over by Joris, a stolid Swiss major-domo. Payment was still due on several new carriages belonging to the household, and the meals were cooked in an exquisite Sèvres porcelain service for fifty because there was no money to buy the customary earthenware. Starting with such a base, Talleyrand quickly established a dazzling lifestyle—even for Paris of the Directoire—which indicated he expected to fully avail himself of the many financial advantages of his new position, over and above his handsome ministerial salary and expense account, as the various foreign chancelleries quickly learned.

He had barely assumed office when Portugal's impending peace treaty with the French Republic was signed, with both Barras and Talleyrand benefiting handsomely. It may have been a questionable practice but it was a widely established, acceptable European tradition for high government officials to expect to be remunerated for the advantages which their talents secured for the interested parties and the states they served. There was no implication that these men sold their consciences, and Talleyrand never did. He was too patriotic for that—and not that stupid—although he would never hesitate to turn his public position to his private profit, a practice he developed into a fine art. The recent and continuing, successful campaigns of French arms, not to mention the organization of new satellite republics, involved laborious negotiations, in which the foreign affairs minister would be the inevitable intermediary and they represented a bottomless gold mine. He might lack the power of final decision, but Talleyrand was now in the enviable position of being in the driver's seat, and it is hard to imagine that a foreign government would be niggardly when it came to paying for an intervention that might reduce the sacrifices demanded of it. Foreign ambassadors who had to deal with him might complain but they acquiesced. They had no choice. And the price came higher, should it be necessary to buy votes of the citizen-directors, two, three, or four of whom might sometimes end up sharing what had been intended for all five. Talleyrand's new, ringside view of international affairs as an insider also placed him in a better position than ever before to play the Bourse in London, Amsterdam, and Hamburg.

The administrative experience Talleyrand had acquired, years before, as general agent of the clergy stood him in good stead, and he inherited a competent, adequate staff from his predecessor. Talleyrand might adopt the *ancien régime* assumption that as an aristocrat he was not bound by any task nor preoccupied by any cares—an affectation of indolence that was typical of pre-revolutionary blue bloods and best summed up by his maxim—never to do anything himself that he could delegate to someone else. But, while his method of work did seem to bear out his reputation for laziness and he spent relatively little time in his office, the finished form and substance of any document or letter bearing his signature was his alone. And he would exclaim, after detailed editing and numerous drafts, "Yes, it is indeed that." He also brought in several of his own trusted collaborators who would remain with him until the end. The faithful Desrenaudes, who had stage-managed his campaign for reinstatement in France, handled mainly work of a personal nature. Jean-Baptiste de Gouy de la Besnardière, a minor diplomat; and Alexandre Blanc de la Nautte d'Hauterive, a recent French consul in New York—both of whom Talleyrand had seen in America—oversaw his diplomatic work. All three were accorded the privilege of little private rooms under the eaves. Desrenaudes had ready access to him at any hour, as did Montrond and Radix de Sainte-Foy, who were primarily concerned with Talleyrand's extensive, personal financial affairs and, on occasion, negotiated, furtively, on his behalf with emissaries from abroad posted to Paris. This inner circle, together with the corps of secret agents, which was *de rigueur* in any similar chancellery, kept Talleyrand so well informed with what was transpiring in a wide range of circles, both inside and outside France, that he was generally better informed and more equipped to evaluate events than most of The Five, with the exception of Barras.

As Chateaubriand, the diplomat and author, who did not like him, took pains to point out: "[Talleyrand] signed events; he did not make them happen." [8] Unfortunately, most other critics of Talleyrand as a statesman forget that he did not have a free hand at the Hôtel Galliffet under the Directoire—nor would he under the Consulate or the empire—and was personally opposed to many of the policies his ambition forced him to serve. At the moment, all he had to do was to put the official state signature at the bottom of the conventions that the Republic's generals had already sealed with their brilliant successes in the field. His joint interest in finance and economics as well as in foreign policy—a rare combination for the day—helped account for his pacifism. For Talleyrand, the sole goal worthy of a foreign affairs minister was to obtain and maintain peace. Once France was assured of her security—when her natural boundaries were protected—the nation must concentrate on the development of its economy.

Under the Directoire, the ministers did not work as a cabinet with The Five and, when asked to assist at one of their council meetings, they were not allowed to speak. At the first such meeting which Talleyrand was privileged to attend, almost a month to the day after assuming office, Lazare Carnot accused Barras of having suppressed a letter that should have been submitted to each one of them. A quarrel broke out and both men jumped excitedly to their feet. Carnot raised his hand defiantly:

—"I swear on my word of honor that is not true."
—"Don't raise your hand," countered Barras. "It will drip blood all over." [9]

Talleyrand's comment, in his *Mémoires*, "These are the men who ruled France," indicates his contempt for some of the vulgar, violent personnel he was working with.

He entered the Hôtel Galliffet at a decisive moment. A showdown was imminent between the republican Five and the two councils. Street clashes were on the rise. The time had come, Barras realized, for the army, which was a bastion of republicanism, to play the decisive role. The triumphant military, reaping the rewards of victory—lucrative foreign occupations and pillage—would never tolerate the reestablishment of a monarchy. Although it was unconstitutional to bring more than a certain number of troops within a specified distance of the capital, once the necessary ministerial changes had been made, Barras then appealed to the army to send in units to be available should the need arise. When his first choice, General Hoche, whose command, the Army of the Sambre and Meuse, was reasonably close at hand, unexpectedly took sick and died, he turned to Bonaparte.

In Italy a variety of circumstances had transformed Bonaparte from a simple army general into a negotiator and plenipotentiary as well. Without consulting The Five, and ignoring their formal orders to the contrary, crucial, on-the-spot decisions had been made, that April, as Bonaparte hashed out the details of the armistice with defeated Archduke Charles at Eggenwald, near Leoben deep in the heart of Austria. Ordinarily, such insubordination should have been inadmissible on the part of the Citizen-General, who was now ruling over northern Italy from the castle Mombello, outside Milan, where he was established with his general staff—and Josephine—amid all the regal trappings of a court. On the other hand nothing was more welcome than the war indemnities that he was demanding from the subjugated Italian states, together with the rumbling wagonloads of booty that he was rapidly funneling into Paris, bulging with pictures and objets d'art from their various museums—only part of which he retained for himself and his officers. Luckily, the Directoire, determined as it was to retain power, had held its tongue, because now Bonaparte's help was needed and, on June 15, the day preceding Talleyrand's nomination to the Galliffet, the general promised his support to defend the republic. Two days later, however, Bonaparte had second thoughts and, anxious to keep his options open because he knew that he held a trump card—the great desire of the French people for peace—he cautiously sent off a personal aide, General Augereau, rather than appear in person.

No one watched with more interest than Talleyrand this increasing influence in the French capital of the distant Citizen-General. To an astute observer of human nature like Talleyrand, it was obvious that anyone as aspiring as Bonaparte would not long be satisfied with executing, compliantly, orders from a distant government. How far into the future Talleyrand gazed at the moment, it is impossible to say, but he did not have to be a seer to grasp France's urgent need for a strong leader who could reconcile or at least dominate all the factions, someone with the army behind him. As a high official now in a weak government that he must know was already doomed, Talleyrand owed it to himself to think about the future. In the long haul Barras was not the answer. Was the young general?

Talleyrand was not in office more than a week, when he wrote his first letter to Citizen-General Bonaparte. To do so was not inappropriate for an incoming foreign affairs minister, but it would be interesting to know whether he also wrote the generals who headed the other three army divisions. This letter, as flattering and insinuating as anything Voltaire ever wrote to his patron, Frederick the Great of Prussia, at the height of their honeymoon, announced his appointment to the Galliffet, and is a prime example of Talleyrand's great gift for making himself understood by what he left unsaid. In a guarded but calculated appeal to Bonaparte's ambitions—"I gain confidence from the knowledge that your glory cannot fail to facilitate any negotiations that I may be required to undertake . . ." [10]—he was counting on the general's need for an ally in Paris, especially one high up in the administration.

Talleyrand himself could not have dictated a more satisfactory reply, prudent and guarded, than the one he received on August 5—"I will be flattered to exchange letters with you often so as to keep you fully informed . . ." [11]—which showed that his message had been clearly understood. Similar vaulting ambitions and an equal lack of political scruples allied the pair with Comte Miot de Melito, the French minister in Turin who was, of necessity, in constant communication with the Galliffet and would act as a conduit, transmitting confidential information on the preparations for the anticipated coup and on the political situation in Paris. Because the pair were anxious to keep their complicity hidden, only a few traces remain to point to a double correspondence directly between Bonaparte and Talleyrand, one official, the other secret.

From the outset, Talleyrand made it clear that he intended to reestablish the forgotten etiquette of his *ancien régime* predecessors at the Galliffet. He had barely assumed office when two ambassadors appeared, one from Rome and the other from the Ottoman Porte—the government of the Ottoman empire. Attired for the first time in the overly elaborate, blue and poppy-colored outfit designed for Directoire officialdom by the celebrated painter, David, and that came complete with a dashing, beplumed hat and ceremonial sword—an occupational hazard for anyone with a leg brace—Talleyrand presided at their separate, formal presentations at the Luxembourg.

Upon his arrival at Marseille, Esseid Ali Effendi had to suffer the indignity of being put, together with his vast staff, including his "donne-la-pipe" [pipe-bearer] and his "donne-le-café" [coffee-bearer] and all his belongings, even his letter of accreditation, in the quarantine station at Pomègue, to be disinfected like the lowliest traveler. Not until six weeks later was he able to continue on to Paris, in a fittingly foul mood. Because of its proximity to both the Austrian and the Russian empires and its nominal suzerainty over Egypt—a country of which Talleyrand had spoken as a possible French colony in his recent Institut speech—this picturesque delegation represented a power with whom France was anxious to strengthen its ties. So Talleyrand treated Esseid accordingly, and honored him with a formal ceremonial dinner that same evening at the Galliffet to which he invited the loveliest women of Paris. When asked to select his own dinner partner Esseid, a great ladies' man, chose—to Talleyrand's amusement—the beautiful young Lucy de la Tour du Pin, just back from America, who was undoubtedly the most modest and virtuous of the entire female contingent present. Although he refused to speak French, which he understood perfectly well, the Turkish plenipotentiary would never be seen in public without a bevy of pretty Parisians making a great fuss over him. To each he presented gifts evocative of the exotic mysteries of the harem—sweet-tasting lozenges, essence of roses and sachets blessed by the mufti. When one young lady complained of the Turkish custom which allowed each man four wives, Esseid gallantly replied: "That's because it takes four Turkish women to equal one French one." [12]

Equally gallant, Talleyrand continued to see the glamorous Catherine Grand whenever possible and, in August, he took her to meet the international financier Perregaux, whose name, like that of Radix de Sainte-Foy, appears so often with Talleyrand's in many questionable financial affairs of this period. This may have been a social occasion, pure and simple, but, with the chances for peace seesawing at Lille and, in the light of Catherine's previous role with Spinola and her later involvement in certain shakedowns of foreign emissaries, it is tempting to wonder at the nature and extent of her participation with Talleyrand in any skullduggery now. Even today the Lille peace negotiations are hidden in a cloud, crisscrossed by intrigue at the highest level. Colonies like the Cape of Good Hope—possession of which controlled the commerce of the Indian Ocean—Cochin and Ceylon were reputedly available there for a price. A memorandum of English Prime Minister Pitt, who kept a list of heavily indebted French legislators whose votes might be bought, mentions a million-pound fund approved by George III for influence-buying among the directors themselves. Incriminating documents found recently among the papers of several of The Five, including Barras, who was likewise involved, confirms that suspicions regarding Talleyrand's personal dealings across the Channel at this time were justified.

Talleyrand had only been in office a few weeks when Barras, who now considered him as his principal civilian supporter—a role which Talleyrand accepted, anxious to retain his portfolio, but which he would later play down in his *Mémoires*—assigned him to recruit supporters for the Directoire's fragile minority in the Ancients and the Five Hundred. Germaine once more placed her salon at Talleyrand's disposal to hammer home The Five's determination to resist a royalist return to power. Dinners succeeded one another nightly at the Galliffet where the usual mix included generals from the Army of Italy, a number of borderline monarchists whom Talleyrand was ardently wooing, and the mandatory handful of beautiful women. Afterwards he would single out a few to follow him for a more intimate discussion in his private office unadorned, at the moment, except for a large portrait of Bonaparte on the wall and the usual silver receptacles of burning ambergris always associated with Talleyrand.

On September 2, Catherine made her first recorded appearance at the Foreign Affairs Ministry at one of these sit-down, five o'clock dinners for thirty. Because of the remarkable freshness of her beauty she more than held her own with Thérèse Tallien, another guest, and it was apparent to all present that if she did not yet hold the role of mistress of the house, she held the key to the minister's heart. As word of his infatuation spread, Adèle de Flahaut, just back in Paris with young Charles—due, in all likelihood, to Talleyrand's intervention with the proper authorities who could, otherwise, prove difficult—rashly commented that Talleyrand had been captured by the "Danish colonies." This disparaging reference to Catherine's birthplace, Tranquebar, placed Adèle once again in Talleyrand's black book, although he would always keep a fond eye on their son, and oversee his education and welfare from afar.

When Barras learned that royalist conspirators were about to mount a coup of their own, the Directoire went into action. At midnight, on September 3, Augereau's troops entered the sleeping capital, their gun carriages bumping noisily over the cobblestones as they encircled the Tuileries, the seat of the two councils. Booming cannon, around 3:00 a.m., awoke the city as sign posters rushed everywhere, plastering up declarations that Paris was under martial law because of the discovery of an Anglo-royalist plot to overthrow the Republic. Talleyrand, whose only concern was to be on the right side of the broom, spent most of the afternoon and evening at the Galliffet, playing whist in his private apartments. When messengers arrived every couple of hours from Barras and Augereau, he smiled but said nothing—the principal advantage of being seated at a card-table, which he always exploited whenever possible during crucial moments in his life.

There was little public reaction. That night the theaters along the boulevards were filled as usual and by noon, on the fifth, the government was in complete control. Talleyrand accepted without a murmur the results of the *coup du 18 fructidor*—so-called because France was still using the revolutionary calendar—which he had helped bring about: the annulment of the recent election results which had produced a royalist majority in the two houses; the arrest of one of the two dissenting Five—the other fled the country—the removal from office of the presidents of both councils and the deportation of some one hundred and sixty-three opposition lawmakers in iron cages to Guiana; and the confiscation of more than thirty independent newspapers. And, just as Talleyrand had, earlier, justified to the rest of Europe the storming of the Tuileries and the imprisonment of the royal family, so he did now with this attack on France's parliamentary democracy, which successfully postponed a monarchic restoration. But the coup did not give the Directoire a new life. Only a reprieve.

Ten days later Bonaparte received a letter from Talleyrand complimenting him on his aide, Augereau's, impeccable behavior. "The operation succeeded without any bloodshed. . . . We had to ignore the Constitution for just one second, but never again, I hope." [13] The *coup du 18 fructidor* had immediate repercussions on the discussions which Bonaparte was negotiating, near Udine at the foot of the Venetian Alps, as a follow-up to the earlier, Leoben armistice, and they greatly strengthened his hand. For the Austrians realized that they could no longer hope for a royalist revolution in France, and approaching winter made further military maneuvers impossible. However, if Bonaparte thought that his support of the recent coup entitled him to a free hand now, he was sadly mistaken. The general did not wish to give priority to The Five's desire to bolster France's natural frontiers along the Rhine over his own determination to organize his Italian conquests into independent republics allied to France. Matters were at loggerheads and, at one point, Bonaparte threatened to resign his command.

If Talleyrand ever had any questions about what little authority he actually possessed as a minister, they were completely dissipated when he was not invited to The Five's deliberations about the treaty directives to be sent to Bonaparte. He was not even consulted. His bitterness at such treatment permeates his letter of October 26, addressing his "heartfelt" compliments to the general on the signing of the Campo Formio treaty— as it came to be known—which, in its final form, flouted the Directoire's specific, detailed orders. Even with allowances for the epistolary style of the period, Talleyrand's ending—"Adieu, General. Adieu. Friendship, admiration, respect, gratitude; I could continue indefinitely . . ." [14]—may seem excessive but its message was clear; Talleyrand did not share the views of the Directoire and did not hesitate to accept Bonaparte's. Already aware, after the Leoben preliminaries, that the general was not a man to follow the dictates of a distant government, Talleyrand adopted a stratagem that would become second nature, attempting to limit Bonaparte's actions while sustaining them, instead of confining himself to bolstering the government's instructions as a proper minister should.

He urged the Directoire to accept the treaty as a *fait accompli*. Because The Five knew how anxious the French people were for peace, once again they did not reprimand Bonaparte for disobeying orders and went along.

Shortly before the finalizing of the Campo Formio treaty, an American delegation arrived in an attempt to resolve mutual problems on the high seas. Because England and France were at war, the French Republic had been seizing American boats charged with merchandise destined for London, and the trio had come to negotiate just indemnities. When they met briefly with Talleyrand, L'Aurore ironically hoped that tall, handsome, Brigadier-General John Marshall, the future chief justice, had brought along a grammar book because he could not speak French; nor could large, heavyset Charles Pinckney, a former aide-de-camp of George Washington. The third member, elfish Elbridge Gerry, an erstwhile congressman, who had known Talleyrand briefly in Boston was the sole one who did and, of course, Talleyrand, whose English had always been minimal, spoke only French as befit his position. Had the plenipotentiaries naively nourished any illusions that they might be accorded a special welcome in view of the foreign affairs minister's many months of hospitable exile on American soil, the trio was sadly disillusioned. Instead, their mission developed into an unsuspected, ticking time bomb for Talleyrand and was destined to be one of the rare times when he got his comeuppance.

Rather than a date now being set for the formal reception required by protocol—after which the actual negotiations could begin—Talleyrand's agents informed the Americans that to proceed further they must make a substantial gift of cash to the foreign affairs minister. They must do likewise to Barras—Talleyrand had discovered that to pander to Barras's avarice was the surest way of strengthening his own position—while a proportionate sum was necessary to appease the rest of The Five, who were "exceedingly irritated" at a recent address of President Adams to Congress about the French-American situation. In addition, the trio must agree to a substantial loan to the French government. Although the Americans were aware of the European custom of diplomatic extortion, they were shocked at the totally new idea of having to pay, first, just to be received and properly accredited. Furthermore, a loan was out of the question since they had specific instructions to do nothing to compromise American neutrality in the on-going British-French war. So desperate was the Directoire for funds to pay the troops brought into Paris for the recent coup and to continue the war against England that Talleyrand's intermediaries next suggested, as a way around the difficulty, a complicated transaction involving Dutch bonds in the French Treasury. Talleyrand himself had earlier tried to place these securities with Malmesbury at Lille and, later, did persuade the senate of the free city of Hamburg to so subscribe in a futile effort to prevent a French takeover there.

Days passed into weeks as a steady stream of visitors came and went—unofficial, as well as secret, agents—exerting pressure on the three Americans to acquiesce. In mid-November Gerry and Marshall moved, for reasons of economy, to a suite of rooms in the elegant hôtel of the Marquise Reine-Philibert de Villette, at 54, rue de Vaugirard, facing the Luxembourg Gardens. It was a veritable Voltaire museum, including a Houdon bust of the great man under which incense burned round-the-clock and, alongside, his heart was preserved in a silver case. The charming marquise took an immediate liking to the pair; there are even intimations that her relationship with Marshall may have exceeded the customary bounds of renter and landlady. One of the most engaging women in Paris she, consciously or unconsciously, joined the fray. All his life Talleyrand was never at a loss to find members of the opposite sex willing to help him out, and the famous "Belle et Bonne" [literally "Beautiful and Good"]—Voltaire's nickname for her when she was young and lived with him as his adopted daughter at Ferney—more than once gently reminded the pair of France's financial assistance during the American Revolution. At one point—never verified—Catherine Grand's name was also bruited about as serving in a similar capacity with the foreigners.

The American affair dragged on, one of many dossiers piling up on Talleyrand's desk while official plans were being made for Bonaparte's triumphant return to Paris to celebrate the Austrian peace. As staff officers of the Army of Italy circulated to and fro between army headquarters and the capital, the foreign affairs minister entertained them, together with Lucien Bonaparte—six years his brother's senior—encouraging them to talk about Napoleon to help Talleyrand round out his knowledge and understanding of the twenty-eight-year-old man of the hour.

At 5:00 p.m., in the wintry twilight of December 5, the Citizen-General arrived and went straight to his home on the rue de Chantereine—which would shortly be most appropriately renamed the rue de la Victoire. Although Talleyrand claims in his *Mémoires* that it was Bonaparte who sought their first interview, as soon as the foreign affairs minister heard Bonaparte was in Paris, Talleyrand sent an aide to see if he might call. Barras had already come and gone and the general, who was too tired to see anyone else, proposed that he himself come by the following morning before he went to call on the other directors.

Among the handful of intimates honored with a hurried invitation to be present was Germaine de Staël who already saw herself as the Egeria of France's new idol. Although consistently late, she was so eager to greet the young hero that she appeared in the great state salons on the Galliffet's second floor a full hour ahead of time. At 11:00 a.m. sharp, Bonaparte was announced and Talleyrand, his body rigid, as always, to disguise the fact that he was a cripple, undulated forward to meet him. Carefully attired in a silk suit with knee breeches, white stockings and diamond-buckled shoes, a costume that had been *à la mode* prior to the Revolution, his milky pale, clean-shaven face topped by his abundant, powdered hair, peering over the fine white linen which Courtiade had carefully wrapped high around his throat, the foreign affairs minister epitomized the *ancien régime*. A *grand seigneur*, his distinction revealed in voice, manner, and gesture, Talleyrand belonged to a species which Bonaparte had only caught glimpses of before—and which held an endless fascination for him all his life. In striking contrast, Napoleon Bonaparte—he had dropped the hard-to-pronounce, Corsican spelling of his name as sounding too foreign—fifteen years Talleyrand's junior, seemed the personification of energy and force. His thinness, his nervousness with its sometimes bizarre manifestations, the disturbing feverishness of his glance, together with an aquiline nose and tightly pressed lips, hollow, olive-cast cheeks and thin black hair falling limply to his coat collar—all reinforced the initial impression of Bonaparte that so charmed the older man. He appeared to Talleyrand as "Destiny's choice. . . . Twenty victories are so becoming to a pale young hero with fine eyes and a look of exhaustion . . ." [15]

As the pair slowly made their way through the small group of guests, pausing for an occasional word here and there, Talleyrand introduced him to the impatient Germaine. The general regretted that he had just passed through Switzerland without seeing her father and, for a moment, that formidable female was, by her own admission, speechless with emotion—as hard as that is to believe. Standing alongside was the celebrated navigator, Bougainville, whose around-the-world journey in 1766 to 1769 on board *La Boudeuse* interested Bonaparte more. Then the pair disappeared into the foreign affairs minister's private office.

Bonaparte insisted, in his faint, lingering Corsican accent, on what a pleasure it was to correspond with a foreign affairs minister who was of a different stripe than The Five. Aware that Talleyrand was the nephew of the number one ecclesiastic of France he took pains to point out that, he, too, had an uncle high in the church, the Archdeacon Fesch, adding ingenuously: "In Corsica, you know, an archdeacon is the same as a bishop in France." But, as became clear with the passage of time, while both men shared a similar lack of moral and political scruples, there was a basic misreading between them. For Talleyrand, who lived for pleasure—the pleasures that power could bring and, or, money buy—power was nothing more than a tool; for Bonaparte, power and glory were an end in themselves.

Talleyrand then accompanied Bonaparte to the Luxembourg to pay his respects and discuss his new appointment as commander-in-chief for a proposed invasion of England. All efforts to reopen the stalled peace negotiations at Lille had failed because the *coup du 18 fructidor* had replaced the peace party and most of the moderate factions in the two councils by diehard republicans and the war party. The Five were also preoccupied with Bonaparte's official welcome, and Barras assigned Talleyrand, as foreign affairs minister, to arrange the celebration rather than the war minister who should normally have done so. It was the citizen who had negotiated the peace who was to be honored, not the general whose victories and caravans of plunder were keeping the Directoire in power.

At noon on the following Saturday, a brisk, clear December day, thundering artillery announced the opening of the fête as Talleyrand escorted the general in an open carriage over the Seine, through streets lined with cheering Parisians. To reassure them—and the government—about any future ambitions he might nourish, Bonaparte appeared in a simple uniform without braid or decorations. What a contrast between the slight Citizen-General, in his modest republican attire, and the other dignitaries as the official cortège marched into the great court of the Luxembourg, rimmed, for the event, with the finest boxed orange trees from its greenhouses, to open the ceremonies. The star of the day led the way, at his heels the war minister, Scherer, and Talleyrand, limping along in his tricolored ceremonial best. A brilliant escort fanned out behind, like a peacock's tail, headed by The Five, all of whom, with the exception of Barras, looking exceedingly ridiculous in their elaborate costumes. When

Bonaparte reached the foot of the flower-bedecked Altar of the Fatherland, festooned with captured enemy flags, he placed the actual Campo Formio treaty upon it. Talleyrand was the first to speak, introducing and welcoming the general. Great salvoes of artillery kept interrupting the succeeding speakers, lest someone forget that the guest of honor was a military man; bands played favorite republican tunes and, at the end, pupils from the conservatory sang. Only after the dinner that followed were the dignitaries able to remove their hats. Parisians had been asked to illuminate their homes that evening. The public squares and monuments were also a blaze of light, and the entire populace was in the streets, despite the crisp air, to admire the superb fireworks.

Bonaparte avoided public appearances and, on the rare occasions when he left the small, unpretentious house that had belonged to Julie Talma, the great actor's wife, which Josephine had been renting and which he now bought, he was always attired, unassumingly, in unadorned grey, as at the fête. Since the general was reputed to have already confided, while still in Italy, that the sole career he now aspired to was membership in the Institut de France, there was no reason to question his apparent sincerity. But, as in the matter of Bonaparte's personal attire, it is impossible not to wonder how much of the general's public persona at this point in his career might not have been, to some degree, subtly inspired by Talleyrand, a consummate politician when it came to gauging public moods. Nothing was easier for Talleyrand to arrange than Bonaparte's Institut nomination, and Talleyrand commented, in his introductory speech of the new member of the Mathematics Section: ". . . what we should fear is his ambition . . . that we may be unable to tear him away from a studious life in retreat." [16]

But another Talleyrand remark concerning Bonaparte's disinterestedness that was currently making the rounds was capable of a different interpretation. When someone, who was dissecting the general's talk at the Luxembourg, repeated Bonaparte's final words there—"When the happiness of the French is based on better organic laws, all Europe will become free" [17]—and wondered what he meant: another coup d'état? Talleyrand countered, "Only time will tell."

Louis XVI of France (1754–93) ruled as king of France and Navarre from 1774 until 1791, and then as king of the French from 1791 to 1792. He was arrested during the Insurrection of August 10, 1792, and tried by the National Convention. He was found guilty of treason and executed by guillotine on January 21, 1793. He was the only king of France to be executed. Artist: Antoine-François Callet (1741–1823).

Charles-Maurice de Talleyrand's parents Marie-Victoire-Eléonore de Damas d'Antigny and Charles-Daniel de Périgord, the Comte de Talleyrand-Périgord. They were married on January 12, 1751. Artist: Joseph Chabord.

OPPOSITE PAGE: Bishop Alexandre-Angélique de Talleyrand-Périgord (1736–1820) was a French churchman as well as a politician. This painting was commissioned by the bishop's nephew Charles-Maurice de Talleyrand in 1822. Artist: Joseph Chabod.

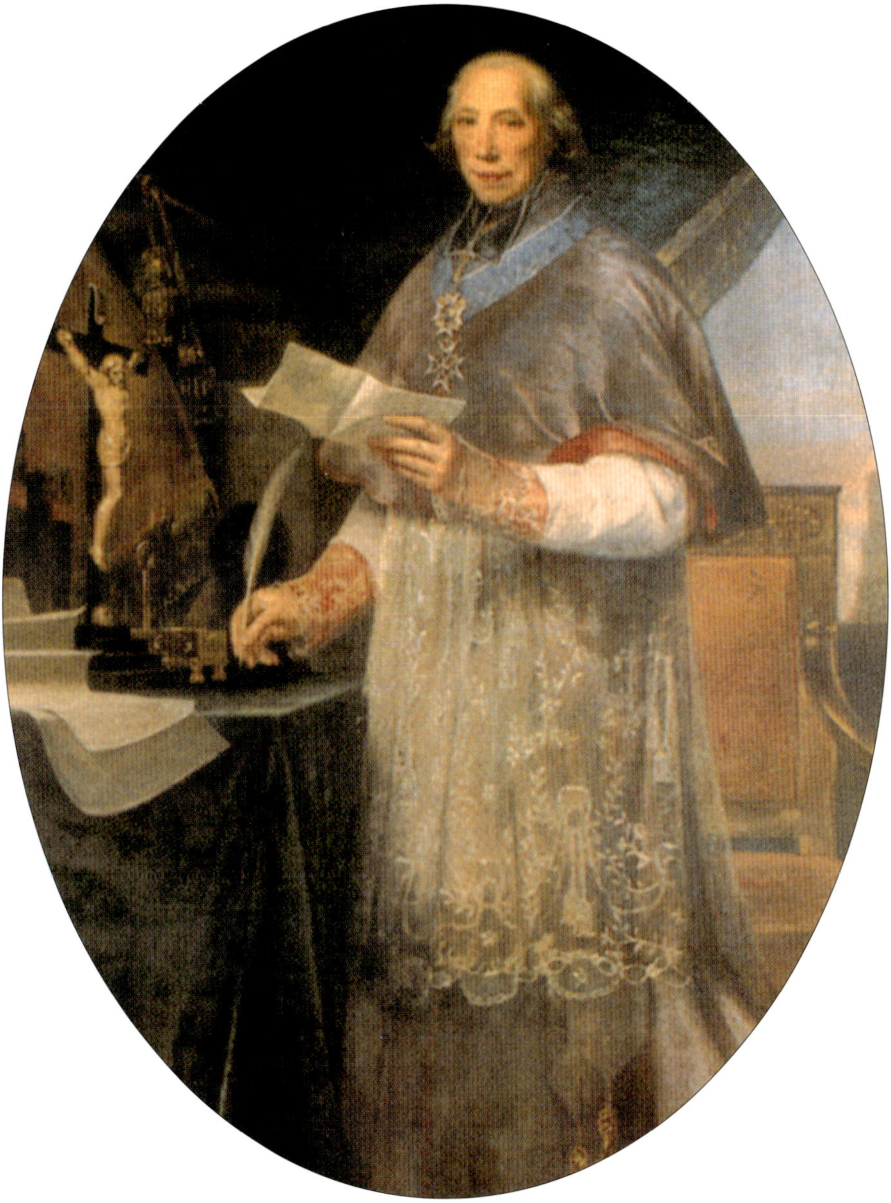

Gabriel-Marie de Talleyrand, Comte de Périgord (1726–95). This drawing of Talleyrand's uncle reveals his clubfoot, which implies that Charles-Maurice de Talleyrand also had a clubfoot and that the condition was hereditary. Artist: Carmontelle.

Adélaide de Filleul de Flahaut, Talleyrand's mistress and mother of his son, Charles, who was born on April 21, 1785. She was married to Comte de Flahaut de la Billarderie, a respected army officer. He was thirty-six years her senior.

TOP RIGHT: Jacques Necker (1732–1804) was the minister of finance to Louis XVI. He was also a banker, statesman, and economist. His economic reforms could not prevent the Revolution of 1789. Artist: Joseph-Siffred Duplessis. Location: Château, Coppet, Switzerland. Photo Credit: Erich Lessing / Art Resource, NY.

BOTTOM RIGHT: Mme de Staël, Germaine Necker (1766–1817) was the wife of the Swedish ambassador Baron Erik Magnus Staël von Holstein, and the only child of Jacques Necker. She was the hostess of one of the most important political salons in the capital, where the liberal aristocracy flocked. She became an author and a leader of the Romantic Movement. Artist: François Gérard (1770–1837). Oil on canvas. Location: Château, Coppet, Switzerland. Photo Credit: Erich Lessing / Art Resource, NY.

OPPOSITE PAGE: Comte de Mirabeau, Honoré Gabriel de Riquetti (1749–91) was a French revolutionary, a writer, diplomat, freemason, journalist, and French politician. He was also a famous orator and statesman. During the French Revolution, he joined the Third Estate as a member of the Constituent Assembly of 1789. Artist: Joseph Boze (1744–1826). Musée de la Ville de Paris, Musée Carnavalet, Paris, France. Photo Credit: Erich Lessing / Art Resource, NY.

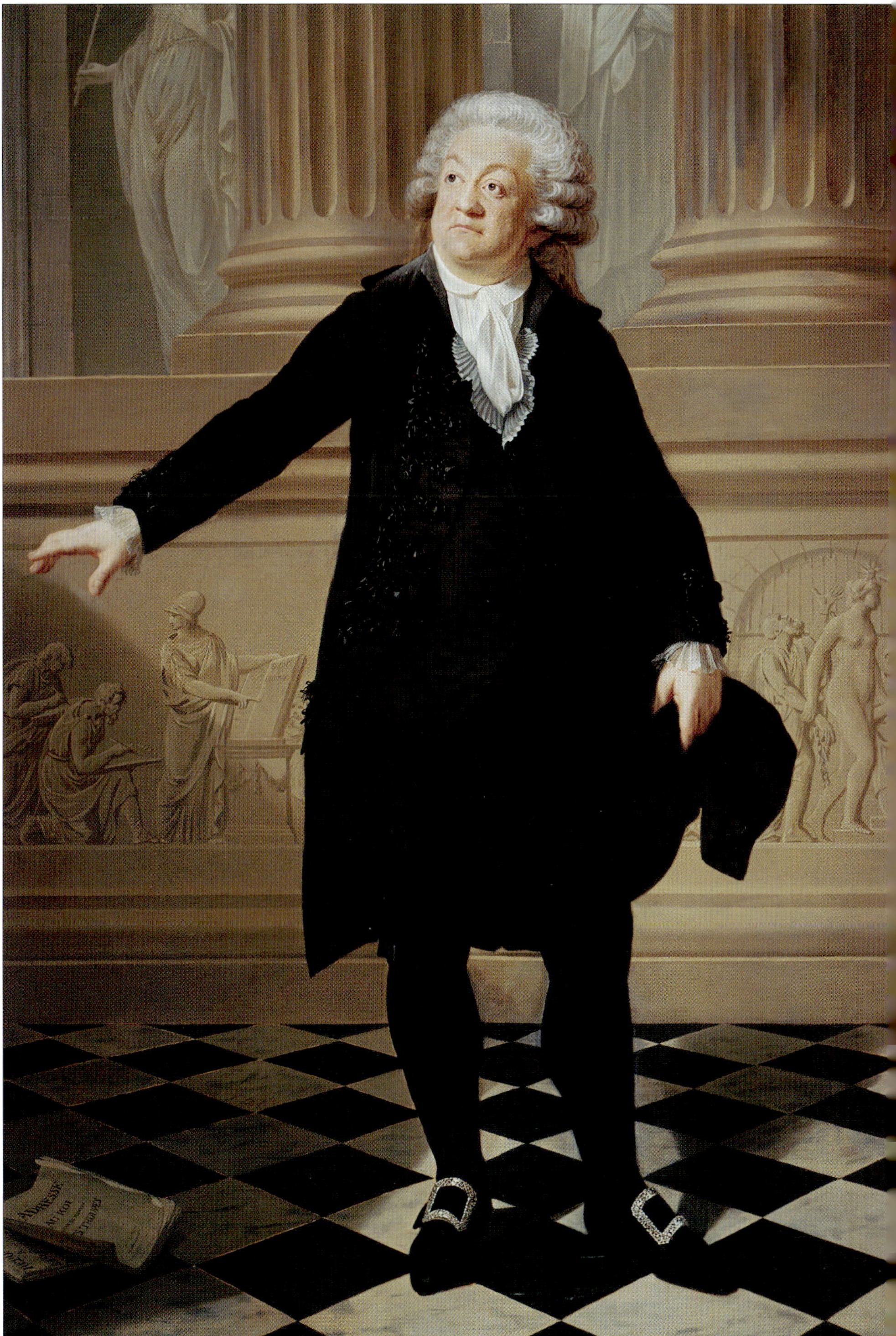

The General Estates, which opened on May 5, 1789, consisted of three separate bodies representing the French estates of the realm: First Estate, the clergy; Second, the nobility; and Third, commons. Artist: Louis-Charles Auguste Couder. Painted 1839. Photo: Gerard Blot. Location: Châteaux de Versailles et de Trianon, Versailles, France. Photo Credit: Réunion des Musées Nationaux / Art Resource, NY.

Storming of the Bastille and the arrest of Governor de Launay took place on July 14, 1789. Artist: Unknown. Oil on canvas, 28.7 x 22.8 in. Musée national du Château de Versailles, Versailles, France.

On June 20, 1792, an angry mob broke into the Tuileries Palace to confront Marie Antoinette. Artist: W. Alfred Elmore (1815–81), ca. 1860. Oil on canvas. 13.8 x 14.6 in. Photo: Michèle Bellot. Musée de la Révolution Française, Vizille, France.

X

Marie-Antoinette was imprisoned in the Temple. She was tried, convicted of treason, and executed by guillotine on October 16, 1793, nine months after her husband's death by guillotine. Artist: Unknown, eighteenth century. Location: Musée de la Ville de Paris, Musee Carnavalet, Paris, France. Photo Credit: Scala / Art Resource, NY.

OPPOSITE PAGE: Louis XVI says farewell to his family. On Monday, January 21, 1793, he was guillotined in front of a cheering crowd in the Place de la Révolution, which is now known as the Place de la Concorde. Artist: Jean Jacques Hauer (1751-1829). Location: Musée de la Ville de Paris, Musée Carnavalet, Paris, France. Photo Credit: Scala / Art Resource, NY.

Joseph Fouché (1759–1820) was a French statesman and minister of police under Napoleon Bonaparte. He was very much in favor of Louis XVI's execution and criticized those who wavered. Collection: Hulton Archive. Getty Images.

OPPOSITE PAGE: Catherine-Noël Worlée Grand de Talleyrand-Périgord, Princess de Bénévent (1762–1835) was the mistress and later the wife of Talleyrand. She was known for her striking Nordic beauty, as well as her candid public comments. 1783. Oil on canvas. Oval, 36.25 x 28.25 in. Artist: Louise Elizabeth Vigee-Le Brun. Bequest of Edward S. Harkness, 1940. Location: The Metropolitan Museum of Art, New York, NY, U.S.A. Image copyright © The Metropolitan Museum of Art / Art Resource, NY.

xiii

Emperor Napoleon Bonaparte (1769–1821) was the military and political leader of France and emperor of the French as Napoleon I. His actions shaped European politics in the early nineteenth century. Collection: Hulton Archive. Photographer: Imagno. Getty Images.

Josephine Bonaparte (1763–1814) was the first wife of Napoleon. Since she was unable to bear Napoleon any children, they were divorced in 1810 leaving Napoleon free to marry Marie-Louise of Austria even though he was still very much in love with Josephine. Artist: François Gérard (1770–1837). Hermitage, St. Petersburg, Russia.

Napoleon's coronation as emperor to the French took place on December 2, 1804, in Notre Dame by Pope Pius VII. Artist: Jacques Louis David (1748–1825). Painted 1806–07. Oil on canvas. Location: Louvre, Paris, France. Photo Credit: Erich Lessing / Art Resource, NY.

7

A Co-Conspirator

"One must put women to work."—Talleyrand [1]

DETERMINED TO REINFORCE HIS POSITION with the man of the moment, Talleyrand had recourse to his own maxim, "One must put women to work." [2] He knew how much Bonaparte was in love with Josephine and decided to honor her with a ball. This would flatter and please both husband and wife, and it could not be interpreted as a political gesture by the directors but simply as an affair of gallantry. Originally scheduled for Josephine's return from her husband's army headquarters in northern Italy, it had to be postponed twice while she dallied en route—unbeknown to the general—with her current lover, Captain Hippolyte Charles, nine years her junior. Wine, food, and guests had to be rescheduled; trees and shrubs removed and brought back each time.

A tremendous success, the affair exemplified the good taste and tact to be expected of a Talleyrand-Périgord and was in such contrast with the vulgar entertainments of The Five that Bonaparte would evoke it, years later, when he was in exile on Saint Helena. Because of the surprising eclecticism of the guest list of five hundred, uniting both the pre-revolutionary aristocracy and the Directoire, two of the directors refused to appear. The other three, including Barras, showed up in civilian attire and riding hats to demonstrate their displeasure.

Carriages were already backed up all the way to the Seine as a light snow fell, early that January evening. The celebrated architect Bellanger was in charge of the overall effects and, in the first courtyard, he had reproduced a bivouac scene complete with a campfire and martial music to recall the general's glorious successes with the Army of Italy. In the second, a small temple had been built to house a bronze bust of Brutus that had been brought back from Rome by the victorious soldiers. Standing at the main entrance, the figure of Joris, the formidable Swiss major-domo, was illuminated by the pre-revolutionary clusters of candles spread lavishly in wall sconces and in the great crystal chandeliers inside. An army of uniformed footmen were lined up, one to each rung of the twin, curved staircases, lavishly decorated with potted flowering shrubs, whose fragrance mingled with the pervasive ambergris, burning in silver vessels everywhere, that was always associated with the host.

Talleyrand was at the center top, attired in a minister's formal dress—a plumed hat on his head and a sword at his side—leaning on a gold-handled ebony cane, to greet his guests as they slowly edged their way towards him. Just as when he carved a roast at dinner, he had his own scale of affability. Those he wished to honor most received a warm handshake; some, two fingers; the rest, a touch of the wrist. The women, who had been requested for patriotic reasons not to wear fabric manufactured in England, were mostly attired à la Flora and à la Diana, in sheer muslin and transparent voile of rose or silver from Mme Germon, the couturière of the moment. Accordingly, most of the fireplaces, as well as additional braziers had been lit to keep them warm. Their hair, already worn short, to reflect the bobbed hair of the guillotine's victims, was now styled à la Titus.

Talleyrand went down to the door at 10:30 p.m. when the guests of honor arrived, accompanied by Hortense de Beauharnais, Josephine's fifteen-year-old daughter by her late husband, who was already a favorite of the general. Bonaparte was not in military attire but in a severe black redingote, buttoned up to the neck, and Josephine wore a plain yellow tunic, bordered in black. Her sole jewel was a simple diadem of antique cameos, a gift from her husband, worn atop a small cap of gold cloth, rather than any of the magnificent jewels bestowed on her by various Italian rulers.

The orchestras playing in the great second-floor salons stopped and the chattering groups fell silent when the trio entered, but the well-wishers quickly surrounding them opened out as Germaine de Staël approached. Like a greedy Venus flytrap, the crowd then closed around them again in order not to miss a word of their encounter. Brash Germaine, who was already convinced that it was her duty to become the helpmate of the hero of the day, did not waste a moment:

—"Who in your opinion is the greatest woman alive or dead?"
—"She who has produced the most children." [3]

This was certainly not the reply the chunky ambassadress anticipated but, said with a smile, as Bonaparte did, before turning abruptly on his heel and walking away, his remark was only malicious, not grossly rude as certain eavesdroppers hastened to report.

A half-hour later, supper was announced, and everyone proceeded into the banquet hall to the sound of military music. After proposing the first toast of the evening—to the Republic—Talleyrand took his place, standing behind Josephine to serve her from the sumptuous meal prepared by his head chef, Riquette. Only the women were seated, as had been customary at similar affairs in the past. The other men followed suit, each standing behind the woman of his choice. Another small but significant indication of changes yet to come occurred when the dancers who had been part of the evening's earlier entertainment expected to be seated with the guests for their own meal. Their request was ignored, none of the Jacobins present spoke up on their behalf, and they were ushered into the servants' quarters to be fed.

De rigueur fireworks followed in the garden. Paris had not seen such an evening in more than a decade, and Josephine was suitably dazzled, as Talleyrand had intended. Although the honored guests left at 1:00 a.m., dancing continued to some of the first waltzes ever heard in Paris, and a new quadrille, "the Bonaparte," was also introduced. But the host, whose increasing pallor was generally attributed to his very late hours—he never retired much before dawn and always slept late in the morning—had long since disappeared with a few intimates for several rounds of whist in his private quarters.

Since the Directoire now considered England as France's chief enemy, Bonaparte set off with Josephine, early in February, on a tour of inspection of the Channel embarkation sites being established between

Calais and Ostend. He returned convinced of the impracticability of such a project, at least at this time, although he knew that his own road to power and to the Luxembourg—the Directors' Palace—lay through new victories. As a Mediterranean, the adventurous soldier had always been attracted by the Orient. General Desaix, in his report on a mission to the headquarters of the Army of Italy, that previous summer, mentions various conversations which Bonaparte had with him about the land of the pharaohs. The latter, himself, in a dispatch to the Directoire soon afterwards talked of a possible occupation there to preserve French commerce in the Levant. Ever since, the question of Egypt kept cropping up in his correspondence with the foreign affairs minister.

Whether, in the beginning, Bonaparte realized it or not, he was preaching to the converted. For Talleyrand, in his second lecture at the Institut, upon his return from America, had preempted an idea of one of his famous predecessors, Choiseul, and named Egypt as the ideal choice for a lucrative, new French colony. As the birthplace of an ancient civilization, it would be a distinguished acquisition. It was also rich in cotton and occupied a strategic position on the direct road to India, while still being sufficiently isolated so that its fate would be of slight concern to the other great powers. More recently, the foreign minister's interest in the land of the pharaohs had mounted as communication from Magallon, the French consul in Alexandria for the past thirty-five years, kept reaching the Galliffet recounting the recurrent difficulties that French businessmen were encountering there. Furthermore, in view of the present crumbling state of the Ottoman empire, which exercised suzerainty over most of the eastern Mediterranean shoreline, Talleyrand was worried lest the Porte's real estate become the prey of Russia or Austria. Accordingly, shortly before the Bonapartes' return to Paris, the minister presented to the Directoire an unsolicited, voluminous Foreign Office evaluation of the entire situation and recommended that France dispatch an expedition to seize those parts of most value to France, especially Egypt.

Once back in the capital, Bonaparte conferred with Talleyrand at length about substituting for the Directoire's proposed Channel crossing the establishment of Egypt as a strategic base of operations from which to forge a Suez route to threaten England's vital Indian empire. Next the general met alone with the directors to discuss this further. There followed a number of agitated meetings of The Five without Bonaparte but including the foreign minister. During one of them,

Talleyrand quarreled with Rewbell, his *bête noire*. Rewbell hurled an inkwell at him, shouting, "Vile émigré! Thy reasoning is as distorted as thy foot!" [4] A short time later, when the cross-eyed director questioned him about the status of another matter, Talleyrand patronizingly refused to tutoyer him in return.

In a subsequent conversation with Wilhelm Sandoz-Rollin, the Prussian minister, to whom Talleyrand often talked when he wanted something repeated to the Prussian court, he maintained that the time had come to halt France's crusading efforts to impose the Rights of Man and of the citizen upon the entire continent. Might not an overseas foray reduce tension and reassure Europe as to where France might strike next? Taken at its face value and given how little power Talleyrand really had as foreign minister, it is hard to assess how seriously this statesman-like approach to French foreign policy weighed in Talleyrand's thinking at this point. And historians are still debating to what extent he must share blame for the subsequent ill-fated Egyptian undertaking.

Suddenly, in the midst of the directors' continuing Egyptian deliberations, word was received of the death from a malign fever of the French ambassador in Istanbul. Although Turkey had ceased to exercise any real power in Egypt, where its representative, the pasha of Cairo, was no more than a puppet in the hands of the Mameluke beys who were the country's actual rulers, nonetheless, the attitude of the Sublime Porte was of prime consideration. Since it was paramount for the venture's success that the Ottoman government understand that Turkish inability—or disinterest—in punishing the beys for their infamous conduct towards French citizens justified French intervention, Talleyrand immediately volunteered to take the late diplomat's place.

His surprising offer to depart eastward as soon as the military expedition got under way testified to his confidence in the success of the proposed Egyptian campaign. Whether Talleyrand actually expected to go, this gesture not only emphasized the importance he attached to the undertaking, but affirmed his desire to prove his indispensability to the man of the hour. The holder of high office in a weak government that was threatened by conspiracies on every side, and an opportunist adept at flairing the wind, Talleyrand's priority was, naturally, to think about himself. As Chateaubriand, Talleyrand's sharp-tongued critic, was to comment, years later, "When M. de Talleyrand is not plotting, he's trafficking." [5] And vice versa, as now.

The Five were only too willing to let themselves be convinced. They viewed Bonaparte's growing aura of fame with increasing uneasiness and were happy at the thought of having the ambitious general and his equally dangerous Jacobin veterans far from Paris. Furthermore, the returns from this new venture promised to far surpass Bonaparte's loot from liberated Italy, which had greatly helped the government avoid bankruptcy. Early in March of 1798 the "kings for a day," as Bonaparte disparagingly referred to The Five, formally approved the plan.

Scarcely two weeks later, Talleyrand's private life suddenly took a very public turn. Love and, or, sex acts in its own mysterious ways. Hard as it is to imagine such a roué being so smitten—although it makes him more human—Catherine Grand's hold on Talleyrand had sufficiently tightened for him to continue to overlook her shady past and promiscuity, which was on a par with that of Thérèse Tallien and Josephine Bonaparte, not to mention the existence of a husband somewhere who might cause trouble. And now the police had gotten their hands on a letter of hers to an émigré in London. The affair is murky at best but, apparently, Catherine, despite her previous run-in with the police, was indulging in a risky cross-Channel correspondence, which she thoughtlessly entrusted to anonymous couriers because she had no confidence in the regular post. A copy of what was in the purported epistle—"Piedcourt [Short-Foot] importunes me from morning til evening . . . he speaks to me of marriage . . . I promise and I am profiting" [6] was promptly on Barras's desk. Concerned only with getting Catherine released, the haughty, cynical ex-bishop, in turn, disregarded caution. For almost the only time on record, Talleyrand publicly exposed himself to the mercy of another man and wrote Citizen Barras:

—". . . Mme Grand has just been arrested as a conspirator. No one in the whole world could be more removed from—or more incapable of being involved in—any such an affair. She is a very lazy *Indienne,* the most idle woman I have ever met . . . I love her and I swear to you, as man to man, that she is innocent." [7]

The director did not wish to assume personal responsibility in this matter, knowing that Talleyrand's presence at the Galliffet remained a bone of contention with his colleagues. Instead, he took malign pleasure in sending a copy of the foreign minister's communication to each one, declaring that the issue could only be resolved at the regular council meeting, the following day. The next morning, when it became evident that the others were determined to use Catherine's predicament to even their scores with Talleyrand, Barras put an end to the acrimonious dispute by turning the matter over to the minister of police who at once cleared and released the frightened woman. Interestingly, at some later date her dossier in the Archives Nationales appears to have been carefully expurgated. Catherine was now linked indelibly with Talleyrand in the public eye. Although she had been married according to both Catholic and Protestant rites, revolutionary laws granted dissolution of a marriage on the flimsiest grounds, and she moved swiftly to get her divorce from George François Grand, who had not shown any signs of life for the past five years.

Meanwhile, the intransigent American commissioners Marshall, Pinckney, and Gerry were still in limbo. Because of the time lag in communications with the distant United States, Marshall had gotten in touch with Rufus King, the American minister in London, and learned that Talleyrand had just offered, on behalf of the Directoire, to make peace with England for a bribe of one million pounds sterling. This was to be split among The Five, with the foreign minister getting one hundred thousand pounds, but the deal fell through, according to King, because the English lacked confidence in the agents presenting it.

Early that spring, Talleyrand's dealings with the still unofficially accredited Americans reached a boiling point. After scheduling a meeting alone on three separate occasions with Gerry, the single French-speaking member, then, for unknown reasons, unapologetically canceling each one, Talleyrand managed to have several fruitless discussions with him. When he finally did meet informally with the trio, to avoid language problems he confirmed his agents' proposals, including the loan to France, which was an absolute precondition for doing business there, by writing them down on a slip of paper, which he showed to them, then promptly burned. Finally, with the matter still unresolved, the Americans demanded their passports—to Talleyrand's utter amazement. An uproar greeted the three when they returned to the states empty-handed, and one of the many toasts at a banquet in Marshall's honor in Philadelphia would reverberate down through American history and be repeated by every patriotic schoolboy: "Millions for defense but not one cent for tribute!" The reports which the commissioners had sent home from France were made public in President Adams's report to Congress on the whole sorry episode—with Talleyrand's three principal agents, Hottinguer, Bellamy, and Hauteval rechristened "X, Y and Z." Echoes of the resultant uproar against the Directoire and its high-handed foreign minister ricocheted across the Atlantic when the American government refused to receive Victor Dupont as the new French consul in New York. After *The London Gazette* crowed over the story, Talleyrand took to the official *Moniteur* to proclaim his innocence. Instead of retaining his usual icy indifference in the face of an adverse press, he haughtily disavowed his subordinates, although they were well-known members of his immediate entourage. Even the impetuous Germaine de Staël, who still took liberties with Talleyrand that no one else dared, stormed into the Foreign Ministry demanding that he clear himself of the heinous American charges. Having heard her through, he left the room without saying a word and did not return.

Although in a very sorry state internally, with highwaymen operating only a few kilometers from Paris, France's frontiers were now largely protected by a long line of vassal states, hiding under the name of sister republics, which extended from the Zuder Zee south. Alarmed at her improved continental situation, England and Russia formed a new coalition. With Italy also in an uproar and with troubles threatening on every side, the Directoire, on the theory that offense is the best defense, declared war on Austria. Nonetheless, as already agreed upon, Bonaparte, together with forty thousand veteran troops and some of the Republic's best generals, set sail from Toulon on May 19. His recently enlarged goal now included driving the English from all their Levant possessions before piercing the Isthmus of Suez where he was to join forces with French naval warships and invade India—a wild dream, in retrospect, but on a par with his future accomplishments. Secrecy was so complete that few of those on the four-hundred-plus vessels in the various convoys, setting sail from five different ports, had any true idea of their destination. Stimulated by Parisian interest in the recent excavations at Herculaneum, Bonaparte had also enlisted some one hundred scholars who were aboard to collect the treasures of the pharaohs and especially of the Ptolemies.

Contrary to Bonaparte's expectations, Talleyrand never left to present his credentials as ambassador to the Sublime Porte. Perhaps he had never intended to go. Two profoundly complicated men, both Talleyrand and Bonaparte would give differing accounts of their original understanding. Although Talleyrand could never be completely faithful to any one woman, conceivably his feelings for Catherine weighed in at this point, and he did not want to leave her. Furthermore, even had Talleyrand desired to go to the Levant, he was not a free agent but a servant of the Directoire. After the naval disaster inflicted by Admiral Nelson at Aboukir on August 1, Bonaparte's army was the prisoner of the desert, cut off from its home base. When word of this disaster seeped slowly into France—one of the first pieces of real news concerning the French expedition that the English deliberately let slip into the country—the Directoire may have wanted their foreign minister to stay put.

For Parisians, Bonaparte still could do no wrong. Distance and misfortune only added to his halo, and he was considered the innocent victim of political intrigue. On the other hand, Talleyrand's scandalous private life and sharp financial practices, not to mention his recent mishandling of the "XYZ" affair, which had been widely publicized on two continents, was an automatic target for a disgruntled citizenry looking for a scapegoat. So, naturally, he received the bulk of the blame for the general's misfortunes. One by one, the most important diplomatic matters began to bypass the Galliffet, and his appearances at the daily meetings of The Five became limited to every other day. However, he managed to keep his portfolio because he still adroitly retained the friendship of both Bonaparte and Barras.

When the name of the director who must automatically retire was drawn, by lot, at the annual spring elections of 1799, Barras, who was still the leading figure among The Five, once again directed the hand of chance. With Talleyrand's behind-the-scenes assistance, a mutual colleague, the Abbé Emmanuel Sieyès, the acting ambassador in Berlin, was the replacement. This plump former Jesuit had a hobby of drafting constitutions, and returned home with a new one, guaranteed to end the present sorry state of the Republic, crammed in his bulging pocket. Like Talleyrand, who introduced him to Bonaparte's two brothers, Lucien and Joseph, he favored a restored monarchy of sorts.

Talleyrand decided the time was approaching for a strategic retreat from a government on the verge of collapse. He rented a friend's small furnished house on the rue Taitbout as a temporary private residence, his passport was ready, and his fortune which, after two years at the Galliffet was now sizeable, was divided between banks in London and elsewhere abroad. He also arranged for Count Reinhard, who had been so helpful earlier in Hamburg, to succeed him, knowing that the count would serve as an effective interim minister—until Talleyrand returned—

and loyally follow his off-stage instructions. His first letter of resignation was rejected but, in late July, Talleyrand's second one was accepted, almost two years to the day after he first entered the Galliffet, leaving Barras and Sieyès as the only two men of any stature in the government. Simultaneously, and largely on Talleyrand's explicit recommendation, a minor functionary in the Foreign Office, the former Jacobin deputy and regicide Joseph Fouché, ill-dressed, ill-washed, and foul-mouthed, took over as minister of police on the Quai Malaquais. Described by Chateaubriand as a "hyena in human clothes" Fouché, although the faithful husband of an ugly wife, had a reputation for ruthlessness, earned by his grim suppression of royalist uprisings in the Vendée and at Lyon, which would be invaluable in any power struggle. Of even more immediate importance, anything of consequence that happened in France would at once reach the ears of Sieyès—and of Talleyrand.

Then, as now, any Parisian worth his salt had some sort of country retreat especially for the summer months. But no two contemporary accounts agree as to where exactly Talleyrand, his bitch Jonquille, who must have been a golden retriever—a jonquil is a daffodil—and Catherine spent this late summer and early fall, except that he remained in the environs of Paris. Catherine did not. Her exact whereabouts are cloaked in mystery. According to rumor she had already, at the beginning of their liaison, presented her lover with one unexpected gift—some form of venereal disease—for which both required treatment by Marie-Antoinette's famous German doctor, M. André Seiffert. So there is nothing so unusual about her now giving him another, far more welcome, present. The evidence strongly indicates that Talleyrand's unofficial family was growing and that Catherine gave birth this fall to his child. Talleyrand, himself, in an 1813 letter noted "Charlotte will be fourteen in October," [8] and her subsequent marriage contract pinpointed October 4.

Talleyrand was inordinately fond of children and, about this time, he placed young Charles de Flahaut, his son by Adèle, on whom he was keeping a watchful eye, as a probationer in the Depot Général in the Ministry of the Marine, a titular post which permitted the lad to continue his studies. While the air still held the remains of summer light, Talleyrand and Catherine returned to Paris where Talleyrand resumed his pre-Galliffet schedule, arising around noon to make the rounds of the salons to keep abreast of the situation, listening and recruiting future support.

More than once, that spring, The Five had discussed whether they should recall Bonaparte who was presently fighting, with mixed success, on the land route to Constantinople. They had not heard from him in months, but he seemed the only person capable of saving France from both impending invasion and civil disorder. Finally, on May 26, Admiral Bruix was given a letter to take to the Citizen-General ordering him to return, leaving part of his forces in Egypt if necessary. Whether Bonaparte actually received the directors' formal orders or deserted his men is a moot point. Slipping away on a stormy night when the patrolling English ships had gone to Cyprus to revitalize, he arrived, on October 9, after a forty-day crossing, at Fréjus, at a small port in Provence, with a handful of trusted officers. Lining his route as he churned north Paris-bound, the natives, who had never been interested in the Egyptian campaign from the start, thought the country was saved and greeted their hero, with his hair much shorter and his olive complexion more sallow, enthusiastically.

After a bitter quarrel with Josephine over her numerous infidelities—and who desperately summoned her two Beauharnais children to intervene—a night of reconciliation ensued. Then Bonaparte gave an accounting of himself in a two-and-a-half hour session with the directors. The Five found it hard to punish an officer who, conceivably on his own initiative, had done what the Directoire had commanded him to do in a written order, which he may never have received. Bonaparte was the essential pivot, at the right time and in the right place, and it was paramount to have him on their side.

The fact that Talleyrand did not attempt to see the general, but waited to be summoned seems to indicate that Talleyrand was concerned about Bonaparte's reaction to his failure to go to Constantinople as promised. But while the Citizen-General had military fame, he also had political aspirations and, for these, he needed Talleyrand's experience, skill, and knowledge of the world. How much calculation was mixed with genuine admiration in the Citizen-Minister's relationship with the Citizen-General at this point is impossible to determine. But one of the few core beliefs of Talleyrand—as a former monarchist—was the need for a strong, one-man government. He saw in Bonaparte the soldier who could impose order as well as regenerate and re-establish France, the country Talleyrand loved, as a dominant player in the European family of nations. Bonaparte was interested in power; because Talleyrand was not, he could never consider the officer as a rival. He only cared about enjoying life as he saw fit, with the wherewithal this entailed, and this presupposed a high official position.

When Talleyrand presented himself, he took the precaution of having two intimates, Admiral Bruix and Pierre-Louis Roederer, a political colleague of long-standing, accompany him to hopefully avoid, or shorten, any unpleasant scenes. But Bonaparte was too concerned about the future to waste time about the past. Mutual interests allowed little time for recriminations. Both men hated the Jacobins and were opposed to a return of the Bourbons, Talleyrand because his past made reconciliation with them most unlikely, the general, because they barred his road to the top. The pair agreed that a return to peace and security in the Republic required the elimination of the Jacobins and the successful passage of certain constitutional amendments. Since Bonaparte was under forty, he was too young to be legally nominated a director, so a coup was required. Because The Five were split over the need for changes in the existing government; with Barras undecided, Talleyrand emphasized the need for his neutrality, if not his acquiescence. Since an adroit accomplice among the directors was equally mandatory Sieyès, the constitution drafter, seemed the logical choice. In his latest proposed charter the five directors were to be reduced to Sieyès himself and two others, who were to be known as consuls. The word "director" was now anathema.

Bonaparte's younger brother Lucien, who was already in frequent contact with the abbé, knew he was looking for some general to assure the prerequisite military support of the staunchly republican army. Bonaparte had met Sieyès once, the year before, but mutual distrust now kept them apart. Although time was all-important to circumvent the many royalist and Jacobin plots reportedly being hatched, the pair kept wangling unbelievably, like old women, over who should first call upon whom. Bonaparte complained that the drums had not been beaten upon his arrival at the Luxembourg; Sieyès felt he had been kept waiting too long. Talleyrand, tapping his brace with his cane, lounged nonchalantly on one of Josephine's little camp chairs in the rue de la Victoire salon—a frame of fashionable elegance filled with the Pompeian style furniture then in vogue and that she had redecorated with a military touch including, upstairs, her bed in the shape of a tent. Arguments swirled about. Bonaparte agreed to participate, provided he, too, was named a consul and, finally, Talleyrand got the two together. Clandestine, nocturnal meetings to arrange the details followed. These were enormously complicated because the abbé, like the other four directors, lived in the Luxembourg Palace—where he slept, in deadly fear of assassination, in a locked closet off his bedroom. More than once, when Talleyrand was accompanying an important recruit to meet him there, the latter had to remain hidden in the darkened carriage while Talleyrand dragged himself up the stairs to ascertain whether the director was alone and not expecting anyone.

Although Bonaparte had the army behind him, the coup was a civilian one, coordinated by Talleyrand. Sieyès, Fouché (the police minister), and Lucien Bonaparte, assumed active roles in the days ahead, while every strand of the web they were weaving at the rue de la Victoire and at Sieyès's passed through Talleyrand's hands at the rue Taitbout. In characteristic fashion, he performed no specific function himself, but set numerous intimates to work, while his personal Paris bankers, the Perregaux, served as contacts with his other banks, Hope in Amsterdam and Baring in London. Talleyrand also undertook the ticklish task of converting Barras to the idea of a reform in the regime—one which the Citizen-Director was led to believe would be minor and not affect his personal rank.

The plot began to materialize on October 25, sixteen days after Bonaparte's return to France when, through skillful manipulation, Lucien Bonaparte who, the year before, had been elected a deputy from Corsica, assumed the leadership of the Five Hundred. An unusual post for a twenty-four-year-old, Lucien as president would be able to keep control of that body should any opposition manifest itself there. Since Sieyès could already count on the votes of a majority in the other legislative body, the Ancients, substituting a new constitution became relatively easy.

In the evening, five days afterwards, Talleyrand was so anxious about the outcome of a meeting between Bonaparte and Barras that he went with Fouché, Admiral Bruix, and another, to the rue de la Victoire to await the general's return. Because the dialogue had not gone well, Barras no longer figured in the picture. When it was decided, forty-eight hours later, at Lucien's—on November 1—to substitute an entirely new regime, Sieyès agreed to answer for the parliamentarians' support, Bonaparte for the army's. Because the pair's every movement was being closely monitored, it was hard for them to work out details; therefore Talleyrand continued to act as liaison.

Well past midnight the next night, after dining at Rose's, one of the minister's favorite restaurants, he and Bonaparte were working alone together at the rue Taitbout, when they were startled to hear a detachment of cavalry halt on the opposite side of the street and horses whinnying. Puzzled and afraid they were about to be arrested, Talleyrand quickly blew out the candles. Stealing stealthily down the long hall to a front window, the two conspirators peered anxiously into the misty November night. As Talleyrand noted in his *Mémoires*, the two burst into relieved laughter when they discovered that a carriage had broken down just outside and was being hastily repaired by its accompanying escort. The gambling rooms in the Palais Royal arcades nearby had just closed and, because of the fear of robbery in the dangerous streets, mounted guards nightly escorted the cashier with the day's proceeds to the banker, who lived nearby.

To allay suspicions, on November 7, Josephine entertained at a large family dinner for thirty—including Talleyrand—and the police, overwhelmed with whispers about various schemes to overthrow the Republic, were reassured. Surely no woman would entertain on the eve of her husband's coup. Afterwards, Talleyrand returned home. He was playing whist in a corner of his crowded salon, silent, as usual, except to call out the cards, when a trusted messenger from Bonaparte suddenly appeared. Was something wrong? An intimate, in the know, cast the newcomer an enquiring glance. The latter with a sign of his head silently replied "No." The former so indicated to Talleyrand, whose only reaction was to take another pinch of snuff. The card players continued their game in silence; the women kept on laughing and gossiping, with Catherine in silent attendance, in a distant corner. Later Talleyrand learned that the action scheduled for the morrow was to be postponed. More preparation was needed. Although speed is the fundamental ingredient in any power-grab, this one deliberately required two days.

The next day, Friday, Josephine threw up the smoke screen of still another party. Meanwhile, Lucien as head of the Five Hundred convoked some twenty deputies on whom he could rely to a meeting. Once they were convinced themselves, each one present agreed to persuade twelve colleagues apiece of the need to transport the two councils, exposed as they were to the rumor-laden air and fickle crowds of the capital, to the safety of the royal château, across the Seine in the countryside at nearby Saint-Cloud.

At 5:00 a.m. on Saturday, November 9—the "18 brumaire" according to the revolutionary calendar—notices were delivered to this handpicked group, convoking a rare 7:00 a.m. session in the Tuileries, at which this unprecedented, but constitutionally permissible, transfer of both the Ancients and the Five Hundred was pushed through. Bonaparte was also appointed to the command of all the troops in the Paris area with the charge of saving the state from purported Jacobin conspirators. Because Fouché deliberately did not relay this surprising turn of events to the directors, Barras, who was blissfully unaware his own ouster had been decided upon, along with that of the other four, remained confident that the plotters would keep him abreast of the rapidly developing situation.

That morning Talleyrand was up about the hour he usually retired and already being dressed by the ever-faithful Courtiade when Roederer and his son, Antoine, arrived. The pair had already been at work for hours, supervising the plastering throughout the capital of the various pamphlets, posters, and documents required for launching today's action, which Talleyrand and the father had written jointly and which had then been printed up by the son, under the pretence of becoming a printer's apprentice at an establishment on the rue Christine. While Courtiade added some finishing touches, Talleyrand and the elder Roederer drafted a paper for Barras's resignation before setting off for the rue de la Victoire.

There they found Bonaparte's courtyard filled with high-ranking, bronzed officers in formal attire, their cocked hats decorated with tricolored plumage, astride champing horses. Other scarred, booted veterans were being ushered in, singly, their heavy swords and spurs clanking on Joséphine's highly polished parquet floors, to swear to Bonaparte on a crucifix not to reveal anything about what was going to happen. After a last minute conference with the general, Talleyrand, who had assumed the vital job of ousting Barras definitively from the scene, picked up in the study three million francs as persuasive tender—if such should be needed—and proceeded with Admiral Bruix to the Luxembourg Palace.

By now the military had fanned out, taking up its positions throughout the city, including around the Luxembourg, where Sieyès was having his daily riding lesson. Determined to caracole at the head of the troops with Bonaparte and the others in an anticipated victory parade, the rotund abbé, bouncing up and down like a rubber ball, presented such a ludicrous spectacle that Barras had taken to watching him from the balcony of his apartment. This morning, Barras was still there, laughing until his sides ached, when the soldiers invested the gardens; at Talleyrand's express request, Sieyès had prolonged his lesson to make sure that Barras, who had been alerted that today the Rubicon was to be crossed, could see for himself that the palace was already surrounded.

Talleyrand and the admiral arrived to find a somber Barras seated with a single guest at a table set for thirty of the usual sycophants and job seekers, who had been scared away today by the commotion-filled streets. The pair lead the director back to the French doors overlooking the gardens to show him the soldiers fraternizing now with a growing, restless crowd. Drums could be heard and bugles, punctuated by angry clamors that made Barras distinctly uneasy. Talleyrand would never indicate if he was surprised at the ease with which he persuaded the obviously startled Barras to resign, but he had come prepared. Perhaps Barras realized that it was in his own best future interest to avoid any appearance of opposition to Bonaparte, the hero of the day. The former director was off, at once, into gilded exile at his country estate with an escort of dragoons—to make sure he did not change his mind. And Talleyrand, three million francs richer, spent the evening in the rue Taitbout's packed salon, silently playing cards, his face impenetrable as messengers came and went. The Directoire had collapsed and all legal authority now lay in the hands of the two councils. So far everything had gone as anticipated.

A soft rain fell during the night but, early Sunday morning, a long procession of carriages of every description, carrying the deputies, as well as curious Parisians, mingled with men on horseback and troops on the foggy road to Saint-Cloud. Talleyrand arrived shortly before midday to take over a small house adjacent to the palace that had been rented expressly for him by Collot, one of Bonaparte's financial backers, who had made a fortune purveying to the Army of Italy. A traveling coach with six harnessed horses stood at the ready in front of the door—in case a hurried exit was called for. At Bonaparte's request, he was accompanied by a handful of intimates—Desrenaudes from his office staff, Montrond, Roederer, and others—who were to infiltrate the two councils, all eyes and ears, and report back to Talleyrand. He, in turn, was to make a running digest of their reports, together with any personal recommendations, which was then to be sent to the general by a stream of special staff members brought out for this purpose.

At noon, as the pale sun finally broke through the overcast the meetings in both houses were scheduled to start, but workmen were still nailing tapestries over broken windows. For the royal château, which had been built by Monsieur, Louis XIV's brother, had not been inhabited since Louis XVI and his family were here almost a decade before. This delay was unfortunate because it gave the deputies, many of whom were stunned by the rush of events, time to gather in heated discussions about what to do. While Talleyrand impassively stoked the fire in his little rented house and his host, Collot, jingled the louis in his pocket, Bonaparte, mounted on a splendid black Spanish horse belonging to Admiral Bruix, clawed nervously at his face until it was bloody and rode around exhorting his troops.

It was illegal for the military to enter into the sanctuary of any assembly, and the general blundered badly, once they were in session, when he impatiently ventured into the vast gallery of Apollo, with its Mignard ceiling, to address the Ancients on the need for immediate action. Amid booing and hissing he beat a hasty retreat. Alerted to the unexpected hostility, Talleyrand could be clearly seen from the royal terrace when he ventured out to appraise the situation firsthand. Although not a man for this type of action, Talleyrand never lost his sangfroid. Bonaparte fared even more poorly in the Orangerie in the château's opposite wing where Lucien was now presiding over the Council of Five Hundred. Angry legislators crowded around, gesticulating and shoving, and he had to be pulled outside by his own grenadiers. Quickly recovering, Bonaparte sent in Murat and a column of his men, ostensibly to rescue Lucien—and, then, to clear the hall. At the sound of the rolling drums beating a charge, and the soldiers shouting "You are dissolved!" terrified deputies fled panic-stricken in every direction, red ceremonial togas flapping as most jumped or clambered through the open windows into the night's deepening shadows.

"I can pardon people for not being of the same opinion as I am, but what I can not pardon them for is to hold the one they do," [9] Talleyrand commented succinctly at the news. "It's time to dine." Regardless of circumstances, Talleyrand would never fail to make provision for an excellent meal—with friends. And he set off with Montrond and one or two others to the house of the Belgian banker, Michel Simons, who was expecting them for supper in nearby Meudon. Both Catherine and Fortunée Hamelin, Montrond's creole mistress, were already there. Meanwhile a handful of badly shaken lawmakers were rounded up among the shrubbery and here and there on the grounds of Saint-Cloud. In a rump session they docilely voted approval of a decree that Talleyrand had secretly helped draft earlier, creating a temporary executive committee composed of Sieyès, Roger Ducos—two of the outgoing five directors—and General Bonaparte, who were to be known as consuls of the Republic. A suitable flurry of trumpets then announced the trio's entry, and they took their oath of office.

Although their hopes now reposed on a thirty-year-old soldier of fortune whose sickly aspect aroused some doubts about his physical resistance, most of the French enthusiastically applauded the coup of the 18 brumaire. They interpreted this victory of force over legality as a return to domestic order and peace abroad. When the three provisional consuls held their first meeting early the next morning in the Luxembourg, Bonaparte, because of his control over the army, at once assumed command and made it evident that he did not expect to be pigeonholed in military affairs. Talleyrand was not immediately returned to the Galliffet because of continuing, anti-Talleyrand public opinion. However, one of Bonaparte's first official acts was to thank him, with Roederer and one other "in the name of the fatherland" in a private meeting on the following Thursday. Before the week was over, two commissions of twenty-five each, from the Five Hundred and the Ancients, set to work around a huge, magnificent tea table in Josephine's new Luxembourg apartments reworking and adapting Sieyès's latest constitution—with Talleyrand in the wings. This one virtually established the constitutional monarchy he had been hoping for, ever since 1789, but with an elective ruler, rather than an hereditary one.

A little more than a week later, Bonaparte handed the green morocco portfolio of foreign affairs minister back to Talleyrand, declaring: "He possesses a lot of what is necessary for negotiations, familiarity with the ways of the world, knowledge of the courts of Europe, finesse not to say too much, an immobility in his features that nothing can alter and, finally, a great name." [10] This last was an attribute on which the parvenu Bonaparte always laid great store. He also admired Talleyrand's ability to elude an indiscreet question. When Bonaparte asked how he had already gotten so wealthy, Talleyrand deftly riposted: "That is very simple. I bought government bonds on the 17 brumaire"—the day before the coup—"and I sold them three days later," [11] an adroit reference to the almost miraculous confidence that the new regime inspired throughout the land overnight.

As a further indication of Talleyrand's high standing in the general's esteem, when Bonaparte made one of his rare exits from the Luxembourg and went to Malmaison, Talleyrand was one of a handful to accompany him. Located across the Seine, some eight miles west of Paris, this dilapidated seventeenth century abode, known as *malo maison* (the evil house) ever since pirates lived thereabouts at the time of the eleventh- century Norman invasion, had been bought by Josephine, the previous spring. No expense would be spared as she gradually transformed it into a suitable residence, including a miniature park with vast greenhouses in which to grow the exotic flowers she loved and remembered as a girl growing up in Martinique. Here Bonaparte would relax as much as he ever could, even indulging in "Prisoners' Base" and other games with the young friends of his stepchildren, Hortense and Eugène de Beauharnais.

No doubt because of his recent sorry experience working with the five directors, Talleyrand, at his first meeting with Bonaparte in his capacity as foreign affairs minister—and, therefore, automatically the key member of his cabinet—claimed the privilege of working and corresponding directly with him. Probably no other man was ever so close to Bonaparte, an intimacy that gave him an unequalled preeminence among contemporaries at home and abroad and which he would do everything possible to preserve—at least in appearance. Talleyrand was the only person included when Bonaparte consulted the other two provisional consuls about the first list of new prefects. Whether any of his recommendations for these jobs were followed is unimportant but, as an indication of his formidable influence and power, Talleyrand's appearance at this official consultation clearly spells out where he stood in the hierarchy of the new regime. He was the only one of all Bonaparte's ministers and advisors to have a countless number of private conversations with him each week. Because these were invariably lengthy, the great problems of the day in various other fields besides foreign affairs must surely have surfaced, and here Talleyrand's experience was without peer. He was in a position to exercise a wide range of influence, the importance of which is indisputable but impossible to gauge because, unfortunately, little is known about their discussions since no one else was ever present. Any pertinent notes and reports which might incriminate or help establish Talleyrand's responsibility in various paramount decisions were carefully destroyed when the victorious allies entered Paris in April of 1814.

Talleyrand at once set to work to attain the peace which he and France so ardently desired and, for the moment, his concepts and interests coincided with those of the general. But if he nourished any illusions about what freedom of action Bonaparte would permit him in the exercise of his functions, he was quickly disillusioned. Nor was he free to name his diplomatic personnel. Not only did the First Consul expect to have the final say about all matters under discussion, he also demanded to be filled in with everything there was to know about them. Since Bonaparte could not tolerate criticism and took advice poorly, Talleyrand soon learned to limit himself to carrying out the First Consul's instructions to the Foreign Office, and rendering an account of their execution. Their intimate collaboration enabled him to take Bonaparte's full measure and to get to know him better. More than once Talleyrand's good sense checked Bonaparte's imagination. If one cynical motto, borrowed from the Duc de Praslin, another predecessor at the Galliffet—"Never follow your instinct; it might be good"—might not be applicable, another, which he had long ago drilled into his subordinates, "Above all, not too much zeal!" would save the head of state from many hasty decisions. Talleyrand's lifelong reliance on time as a trustworthy ally in even the most troublesome circumstances allowed the frequently impetuous general leeway to change his mind and cancel his actions.

On December 12 with their work finished, Bonaparte convened the fifty commissioners to ratify the legal instrument on which they had been working so feverishly and to replace the three provisional consuls, with three officially elected ones. Warming himself in front of the fire, he illegally supervised and, from time to time, interfered to be sure he retained the number one spot. Within twenty-four hours he relegated judiciary and administrative matters to the new number two consul, Jean-Jacques de Cambacérès, one of the country's leading jurists, and to Charles-François Lebrun, number three, both of whom would have little to do except supply the First Consul with information and advice. Talleyrand, the coup's *eminence grise*, always referred to them by the latin "Hic, Haec, and Hoc" ["This one, that one, and the other one"]—the masculine form for Bonaparte; the feminine for the effeminate jurisprudent, and the neuter, for the pale Lebrun.

Shortly after the first of the year, Talleyrand purchased from Richard Codman, a Bostonian, the first home he ever owned, at 35, d'Anjou-Saint-Honoré, a fashionable neighborhood on the Right Bank.

Built in the eighteenth century by the Marquis de Créqui, it had subsequently been confiscated as the property of an émigré, so he was able to get a lot of its original furnishings. Although there was an enormous garden in the rear, it had only one drawing room that he enlarged by adding a combined hothouse and gallery. In this elegant setting, which he furnished with his customary good taste, its air perfumed with the ever-present burning ambergris, Talleyrand spent his evenings and nights, with politics momentarily forgotten. A handful of his old friends, including several from his seraglio, who lived nearby, always remained after the late, 2:00 a.m. supper—a popular *ancien régime* custom that their host had revived because it was so conducive to the intimate conversation he preferred and in which he shown. Evoking past memories and recounting anecdotes punctuated with his usual sparkling wit, Talleyrand took infinite pains to please and amuse his enraptured guests who politely ignored Catherine, treating her almost like an intruder. She disliked these late hours. Wrapping herself in one of the rare Kashmir shawls Bonaparte had brought back from Egypt, woven from the down of Kughize goats, warmer than wool yet so soft it could be drawn through a ring—a supreme luxury until finally copied by a Scot in Paisley—she invariably complained of a headache, early on, hoping, unsuccessfully, to persuade the faithful few to leave.

Catherine now presided over a small menagerie—her several small pug dogs; Talleyrand's own bitch, Jonquille; and a new edition, Simia, a tiny monkey. This was a popular pet for fashionables of the day, and was a gift from Baron Denon, the famed archaeologist who had been with Bonaparte in Egypt and would become famous as the first director of the Louvre. Quickly relegated to the Ministry's offices, the little creature proved adept at stealing letters and became such a holy terror that he was joyfully dispatched to Malmaison when Josephine was so amused by his antics, one day, that she requested him for a gift. As befit her new role of official hostess at the Galliffet, Catherine was taking lessons in appropriate carriage and bearing from Despreaux, Marie-Antoinette's former teacher. The glamorous "Indienne" more than held her own with the other prominent beauties of the day, for Parisian society remained that of a demi-monde with all standards abolished, and anyone, who needed to approach the foreign affairs minister or required his intercession and good will, quickly learned to court her. When someone questioned her about her nationality, her reply "Je suis dinde"—which could be interpreted as an unwitting pun ("dinde" = a stupid woman; also "d'Inde" = an ungrammatical way of saying "des Indes" = from India)—quickly circulated through *tout Paris*. It was so delicious to have the most intelligent man in France married to a silly goose. Whether she was actually as stupid as some claimed, or whether anecdotes, which made her ridiculous, were circulated to snipe at the foreign affairs minister, is hard to ascertain. Some absurdities from an earlier day and even another country, were recycled and attributed to her, as was the case with a famous Horace Walpole story about mistaken identities which originated at his home, Strawberry Hill, some thirty years before.

Ever since the unexpected failure of the XYZ affair, a flood of private correspondence bears witness to Talleyrand's efforts for a reconciliation with America. Since the present quarrel could only help the English, Bonaparte was equally anxious to resolve the matter. Whether it was the First Consul's idea, or Talleyrand's, George Washington's death created an opportunity to flatter American pride and, simultaneously, touch French sensibility with the kind of public ceremony at which the First Consul excelled. Decreeing that France should render fitting homage to the first American president, he ordered a ten-day mourning period for the army, with crepe attached to all of its flags, and held a moving funeral eulogy at the Invalides. Ten days later, another spectacle of a different nature pandered to the populace when the Bonapartes moved with all their chattels and paraphernalia into the Tuileries, the home of France's former rulers, escorted by several military bands, the general staff in full dress, the council of state, and all the ministers. Bonaparte's installation was completed by the end of the month when the paved court of the Tuileries was separated from that of the carrousel by a grillwork with pilasters surmounted by Gallic roosters. Their outstretched wings caused Parisian malcontents to comment: "They want to fly away because the fox is inside."

The military situation was critical. As much as France wanted peace, the country did not want it at the expense of its natural frontiers, and the people and the army were prepared to fight to save them. Even Talleyrand reluctantly realized that the only way to change the attitude of those powers hostile to France was by fresh victories. Paris succumbed to a wave of patriotism, as Bonaparte prepared to go to the Eastern front. With the drums of recruiters on every street corner beating in his ears Talleyrand's son, fifteen-year-old Charles, swept away, like so many of his generation, by the thirty-one-year-old Bonaparte's rapid rise to power, wrote a letter to him, volunteering and asking to be one of his aides-de-camp. "Be assured that I will be killed or else I will justify your choice." [12] It is highly unlikely that the lad would have received any reply, had not his father intervened, just as he had on his behalf the year before. Charles did not get the post requested but, four weeks later, he was assigned to the elite Corps des Hussards Volontaires. Nicknamed "the Canaries" because of their handsome, bright yellow dolmans, this unit had been formed to act as Bonaparte's escort in future campaigns. Preferring active service, he soon wangled a transfer and got his baptism of fire at Marengo. Here, on a hot June day, after a miraculous crossing of the Alps through the famed Saint-Gothard Pass, ten of whose forty leagues of mountain roads were deemed impassable for wagons—three hundred of which were required to transport essential French artillery and munitions—the fate of Italy was decided. Bonaparte's victory over the Austrians consecrated the new regime, strengthening the First Consul's hold on France.

The *Te Deum* sung a few days later, in Milan's great cathedral, to celebrate this success furnished Bonaparte with an excellent opportunity to reveal his intentions to make peace with the Vatican. He realized such a reconciliation was of prime importance for any new government anxious to maintain power and essential for a complete reconstruction of predominantly Catholic France. If he could unite and marshal the support of the entire French clergy, including the constitutional one, he would also remove the extreme royalists' most reliable allies for a possible Bourbon return. Bonaparte learned that Pius VII, newly elected in Venice, was also anxious to resolve the French schism and, before leaving Italy, he instructed Cardinal Martiniana, the papal envoy, to advise His Holiness that he, too, was ready to explore the possibilities of an accord.

Upon his return to Paris Bonaparte, flush with Italian real estate as a bargaining chip, charged his foreign affairs minister to reopen the issue of a possible return of Louisiana to French hands. Talleyrand, still colony-minded despite the Egyptian fiasco, had already been putting out feelers concerning this former French possession. One of France's most prosperous overseas settlements, Louisiana had been lost to Spain since the disastrous Seven Years War, some forty years before. But now, fortunately for France, the Spanish queen, Maria-Luisa, the sister of the Duke of Parma, expressed an interest in acquiring a piece of Italy for her daughter, newly wed to her own nephew, a son of the aforesaid grand duke; in her next breath, Her Majesty likewise wanted some Paris frocks. Talleyrand was happy to oblige and satisfy both royal whims, for the consulate was already at work reestablishing the hegemony of French fashion on the continent, an industry which had formerly constituted one of France's most important sources of exports. Before the end of the year Mlle Minette, the current high priestess of style, would be off for Madrid, in person, to assure that Bonaparte's gift of ball gowns arrived in good condition. A preliminary treaty restoring Louisiana to France was also signed but remained secret for the moment because of the fear that England, the mistress of the high seas with whom France remained at war, might grab it.

The cold brisk days of approaching winter heralded in a busy work schedule at the Galliffet. After months of difficult negotiations, not to mention the arrival of a new American commission in Paris and General Marshall's appointment as President John Adams's secretary of state, a treaty restoring peaceful relations on both sides of the Atlantic was signed. Meanwhile on the continent, ever since the Austrian defeat at Marengo, an armistice had prevailed and terms establishing the perimeters of the peace negotiations which were due to be held in Lunéville, a central location for those concerned, were being hammered out. Because their military strength was nearly exhausted, the Austrians kept stalling for time in order to raise fresh troops. Furious at the delay and well aware of their intention to drag the situation out until snow and ice made campaigning impossible, the First Consul was, nevertheless, so anxious to secure peace that he sent word to Vienna that he wanted to consult about an overall European settlement that should also involve England.

One hour after Count Louis de Cobenzl arrived, Talleyrand took the wily Austrian diplomat to the Tuileries for a long session with Bonaparte, who promptly nicknamed him, behind his back, the "northern bear" because the cross-eyed, globular count was so ugly. This was a great handicap in the Paris *haut monde* where it was essential to please the eye in order to be assured of an audience for one's wit. To exert further pressure, Talleyrand insisted that Cobenzl, who was a former classmate at the collège d'Harcourt and spoke excellent French, stay with him at the rue d'Anjou. Hard bargaining sessions at the Tuileries did not prevent Talleyrand from doing the rounds of Paris with his guest. In addition to attendance at a meeting of the Institut, the pair went to the Opéra and the Comédie-Française, and heard Mme Grassini, the pretty, well-known

Italian diva whom Bonaparte had imported from Italy—for more reasons than one—sing duets with Garat from the Gluck repertoire for which he was so famous. They saw the great Vestris and Gardel dance. They even managed to squeeze in part of the hit show at l'Ambigu-Comique—Aude's *Mme Angot in the Harem at Constantinople.* They were also invited out to Malmaison where, after dinner, Bonaparte dragged the pair into his study for further talks that got nowhere.

Talleyrand, like Choiseul before him, believed in an entente with Austria, the hereditary enemy, and felt that stability among European states, and peace, depended on an old-fashioned balance of power. France should side with England and Austria, old established countries, and unite against—or, at least, try to curb—Prussia and Russia, whom Talleyrand considered parvenus on the scene. On the other hand Bonaparte, for whom war was the indispensable means to bring his enemies to their knees before bargaining began, was convinced that another Austrian defeat was necessary to get Vienna to negotiate on his terms. The fundamental difference between this approach to foreign policy and Talleyrand's—that war was a means to be employed reluctantly, when all else failed—had not yet surfaced. Talleyrand might not always approve of the decisions Bonaparte would take but, whether he had the ability, like another famous statesman, Cardinal Richelieu, Marie de Medici's legendary advisor, to conceive a policy and adhere to it while trying to dominate events, instead of following and ratifying results produced by a victorious sword, remained to be seen.

Bonaparte notified his armies that hostilities were to resume the day the armistice expired. Eleven days after it had run its course, the decisive French victory at Hohenlinden, in Bavaria, on December 3, combined with the Austrians' earlier disaster at Marengo, left Vienna no choice but the bargaining table at Lunéville. There, in that frontier town southeast of Nancy, near Strasbourg, the ancient palace of the dukes de Lorraine was being put in order with furnishings sent out from Paris. Joseph Bonaparte, one year older than his brother, the First Consul, was designated minister plenipotentiary to conduct on-the-spot negotiations, just as he had with the Americans a few months earlier.

On the home front Bonaparte, who had an abiding respect for convention, was clamping down on some of the more flagrant abuses of decency in the capital where a number of women were dying from the "muslin disease"—probably pneumonia. The ancient Greek styles then so popular were far more suited to a Mediterranean climate than a cold, damp Parisian winter, especially since those wearing the slim, revealing gowns persisted in dampening the sheer, clinging material to do full justice to their figures. When Thérèse Tallien appeared in a loge at the Opéra clad only in a leopard skin, her arms and legs smothered in jewels, she was informed that such nude attire was no longer acceptable. But the poor state of public mores was only the surface manifestation of a deeper malaise. Profoundly concerned with the need to remedy this and also restore domestic order, the First Consul knew that the best approach was to mend the schism in the French church, as he had intimated earlier.

Despite the obviously difficult position in which such a detente would place him personally, as one of the principal architects of the original rupture between state and church, Talleyrand's attitude was characteristic. Once it was evident that there was nothing he might say or do to get Bonaparte to change course, practical-minded Talleyrand determined to make the best of the potentially disastrous situation which menaced both his career and his private life. By November, when Monseigneur Spina arrived, at the First Consul's invitation, there was no more outwardly enthusiastic partisan of the benefits to be expected from the projected reconciliation than the foreign affairs minister, and he was intimately involved—as he had intended—in the long secret discussions, which followed. Many contemporaries, especially from the Vatican, would later maintain that Talleyrand, while pretending to serve Bonaparte's religious policy, was perfidiously sapping the negotiations—like Ulysses's wife, Penelope, who undid at night what she had been laboriously weaving during the daytime. But this is hard to believe for Talleyrand knew how set the First Consul was on this rapprochement.

8

Foreign Affairs Minister

"Any miscalculation can be denied."—TALLEYRAND [1]

In the midst of these ongoing talks, on Christmas Eve in 1800, en route to a special command performance of Haydn's *Creation* at the Opéra, Bonaparte and Josephine miraculously escaped unharmed when an infernal machine, a large cask filled with gun powder and shrapnel, which had been placed on a horse-drawn cart tied up to block their passage, exploded prematurely. Twenty-two passers-by—and the horse—were killed and another fifty-six wounded. Although Bonaparte thought the bomb was of Jacobin origin, both Talleyrand and police minister Fouché disagreed. Their suspicions were justified when, after three weeks of intensive investigation, the latter's agents proved conclusively that the plot had been conceived, financed, and directed by French royalists based in England. The cabinet there, worried that Vienna might buckle to stiff French demands at the Lunéville conference table, had obligingly turned a blind eye, hoping to stiffen the Austrians' backbone with the tantalizing prospect of the imminent disappearance of Bonaparte.

The foreign affairs minister considered this a good opportunity to prove to a nervous Europe that the First Consul was the liquidator, not the continuer, of the French Revolution. Since swift punitive action was called for, it was also a chance to dispose of any remaining dissenters to the Consulate, and to do away with the last semblance of parliamentary government. "What good is a senate if it is never used?" [2] Talleyrand demanded. To forestall any negative discussion in the Legislative Corps, the opposition's refuge, the proposed rigorous new measures completely bypassed the legislators and were placed, instead, before the complaisant Senate. That body, composed of the Consulate's staunchest defenders, immediately sentenced one hundred and thirty Jacobins to deportation and condemned twelve others to death. A precedent was established, and the arbitrary *senatus-consulte*, suggested by Talleyrand, represented a long step down the road to absolute power and was, henceforth, frequently resorted to, illegally superseding the legislative body while preserving the fiction of constitutionality.

When Tsar Paul I got the news of the bombing, he immediately banished Louis XVIII, who had been living, together with a small entourage, which still included Talleyrand's uncle, the archbishop, as his guests in the Courland ducal palace at Mittau. Before heading west, Louis XVIII addressed a letter to Bonaparte congratulating him on his fortunate escape and containing overtures about a possible return to France. The First Consul—in concert with his foreign affairs minister—made a courteous but negative reply. Whereupon, Talleyrand, a firm believer, as always, in being prepared to tack, given some unanticipated future emergency, arranged to meet the Abbé de Montesquiou, who had delivered Louis XVIII's message, at the salon of one of Talleyrand's devoted seraglio. There he managed a private conversation *à trois*; as an unnecessary indication of their personal relationship, Catherine was included as a silent witness. And the abbé left Paris with the distinct impression—which Talleyrand wanted him to have—that the foreign affairs minister would be the ideal intermediary should anything ever develop between Bonaparte and Louis XVIII.

The complications entailed in the final dealings at Lunéville proved to be a bonanza for the foreign affairs minister's habitual financial legerdemain. Rumors concerning when the treaty would be a *fait accompli*—even, at one point, actually withholding news about it—were skillfully circulated by Montrond and other of his agents in London, Paris, and Amsterdam to make the Bourse rise or fall as best suited

Talleyrand's own speculations of the moment. The foreign affairs minister also ensured the insertion of a special article stipulating that some fifty-three million florins worth of bonds owed to the Austrian emperor and whose value had shrunken to almost nothing because the war had lasted so long, must be reimbursed one hundred percent. Talleyrand then borrowed the sum required and, together with Simons, the Belgian financier, bought them at the bargain rate of eighteen million. After Lunéville, they soared to their former value, netting the foreign affairs minister another tidy windfall.

The peace agreed upon at Lunéville on February 9 was a triumph for France the equal of—if not greater than—her victories in the field, with Talleyrand, whose policies still broadly coincided with Bonaparte's, playing the principle diplomatic role. It was an unmitigated disaster for Austria and the Holy Roman Empire, whose origins could be traced back to Charlemagne and which, as Voltaire once pointed out, was neither Holy, Roman, nor an empire. It was presently composed of three hundred and sixty separate states, mainly outside of German territory but including most of German-speaking Europe, and now lost outright its Low Countries. Germany did not exist as a political entity but was made up of sovereign states, and the lands of the Germanic princes on the Rhine's left bank were ceded to France to help finish off its natural frontiers which that country had been striving to obtain since Richelieu's time. The principle that the dispossessed rulers were to be compensated for their preempted territories by being awarded land on the right bank, was clearly spelled out but, unfortunately, its implementation was not. Cannily, Talleyrand included a clause giving to France—a euphemism for the foreign affairs minister—the right to participate in resolving these claims, an authorization that was to provide a staggering lode of additional wealth to be mined by Talleyrand, for thousands of square miles, tens of thousands of souls, millions in revenues were at stake. The transfers of sovereignty involved would mutilate the German territory of the Holy Roman empire and foreshadowed its break-up, while sowing the first seeds of future European wars.

A scramble for power was inevitable, with the biggest indemnities due the King of Prussia and the elector Palatinate of Bavaria. It was quickly evident that all relevant decisions would be made, not at the Imperial Diet in Ratisbonne, as originally intended, but in Paris where Talleyrand personally oversaw the operations. Durand de Mareuil was his alter ego at the scene itself, together with the Prince de Nassau-Seigen and one or two others, including the Baron de Gagern. While the ultimate financial take involved in these territorial readjustments would stretch out for a number of years because of the many ramifications, it is conservatively estimated that the foreign affairs minister's ultimate reward was between thirty and forty million francs. By comparison, in 1803, Mme de Recamier's private residence, long considered one of the finest properties in all Paris, sold for three hundred and sixty thousand francs. Small wonder that Germaine, whose father was earlier reputed to be the richest private individual in Europe, should soon write Dupont de Nemours that Talleyrand now was.

The Invalides' cannon announcing the welcome official news of the war's end added to the post-Lenten gaiety. Masked, costumed Parisians were everywhere in the snow-encumbered streets that day— on foot, in carriages and cabriolets, even perched on top of coaches— celebrating, for the first time since the Revolution, with their famous Lenten parade. Not unexpectedly Talleyrand seized the occasion for another of his sumptuous fêtes to assist the gradual integration of French society, which was Bonaparte's aim. This was held at Neuilly, a former home of his intimate, Sainte-Foy, to the west of Paris on the Seine, which he was renting because it was almost equidistant from Paris and Malmaison, where he had to go so often. This magnificent property consisted of a series of one-story pavilions and had been extensively rebuilt a half a century ago. Talleyrand's guest list included, as befit a gentleman of the old school who would never be able to accustom himself to the male-dominated society Bonaparte was now ushering in, some three hundred women, mostly young and pretty, bearing the most celebrated names in French history. He was such a superb host that the elite of Paris gladly accepted, persuading themselves that they were going to a private affair at Talleyrand's, not showing their adhesion to the Consulate. Although Bonaparte was not fond of such entertainments, given the guest list, his presence was assured. Accordingly, Germaine de Staël, whom Talleyrand had been seeing less and less, requested an invitation in the name of their long-standing friendship.

The Swedish ambassadress's path had not crossed that of the First Consul all that winter, and she did not want to miss this opportunity. So she stationed herself prominently in the first of the thronged salons. Passing through, Bonaparte stopped in front of her. Scrutinizing her customary decolletage as if, one guest reported, he were inspecting the battle scars of a grenadier, the First Consul commented brusquely, "No doubt, Madame, you have nursed your children yourself?" [3] The usually voluble Germaine was tongue-tied. Before she could recover—the First Consul always had this effect upon her—Bonaparte wheeled and was gone, and she would never again see him face-to-face. The impetuous Germaine could not comprehend that, by thrusting herself on Bonaparte in this fashion, she was placing Talleyrand in the position of having to choose between her and the First Consul who clearly did not care for her. It is a devastating commentary on Talleyrand as a man that, rather than disturb his own relationship with the First Consul, he henceforth prudently put increasing distance between himself and his erstwhile, long-standing benefactress whom he now considered so unpredictable as to be dangerous. As a lame excuse for such behavior, Talleyrand later maintained that the services Germaine bestowed on others were motivated by selfishness—to satisfy her own thirst for authority and desire for power.

Once matters were satisfactorily concluded with Austria, Bonaparte was free to concentrate on his other *bête noire*, England, when two disparate events abroad greatly strengthened England's hand and made him reconsider any such military thrust. First, a rapid courier, traveling from Moscow in a record-breaking fortnight, brought word that Tsar Paul I had been killed in a palace revolt, and his successor—and son—Alexander I, was determined to improve Russian-English relations. Secondly, Admiral Nelson's victory over the Danish fleet at Copenhagen confirmed British rule in the Baltic. Consequently, the First Consul did an abrupt about-face and instructed his foreign affairs minister to send out peace feelers to London instead. Pro-British Talleyrand was already one jump ahead of him. So anxious was Talleyrand to improve the French-British picture that he had already, several months earlier, dispatched Montrond, with his impeccable London connections, across the Channel for accurate firsthand information on King George III's recurring bouts of madness and on the stability of the incumbent cabinet. Shortly afterwards, Pitt's resignation, after seventeen years as prime minister, paved the way for a successor, Henry Addington Sidmouth, who was less uncompromising about French relations.

Meanwhile, ever since the end of the year, secret, in-depth conferences with Monseigneur Spina about a concordat had been barely inching along until the exasperated First Consul threatened the papal representative, in front of Talleyrand, at Malmaison, to have the French forces, which were still occupying a large part of Italy, invest the Vatican states as well, if they could not reach an accord. So yet another draft was taken to Rome accompanied, this time, by a special gift for His Holiness, the celebrated Madonna of Loreto, a relic, which had been liberated earlier—along with other church spoil—by the victorious French. The log jam was broken. Pius VII accepted as a *fait accompli* the 1789 seizure of the Church's vast properties, Bonaparte acknowledged Catholicism as the state religion, and the papal secretary of state was dispatched to Paris to resolve the remaining litigious questions.

He arrived, late one night in mid-June, and was high-handedly summoned to appear "in full regalia," at the Tuileries, at precisely 2:00 p.m. the next afternoon. The hour specified was that of the recently inaugurated parade-past of the consular troops in their distinctive new uniforms, attendance at which was mandatory for the three consuls and the other great officials and functionaries of the state. A pulse-stirring event, this trooping of the colors, held every two weeks, became so famous that visitors from all over Europe would flock to see it. Whether or not his attendance at this display of military might was intended as a veiled threat, the doughty cardinal, Hector Consalvi, rose to the occasion. Ignoring the imperious directive, he was determined to establish the ground rules before he even met the First Consul. When Talleyrand arrived to conduct him to the Tuileries, he appeared in his everyday attire—black with red stockings, cap and collar—not *la grande pourpre,* the special purple attire cardinals wore only in the presence of the pope or, sometimes, at the court of a monarch whose subject they had originally been. Immediately after the ceremony, Talleyrand led the monseigneur to the First Consul. Bonaparte barked that Consalvi had exactly five days in which to wind up any loose ends or he would establish a state religion. No other words were exchanged, the audience was over, and Talleyrand escorted the prelate out.

One of the thorniest problems, not only for Rome but also from the point of view of Bonaparte, who was so intent on restoring order and decorum to the scene, was the situation of great numbers of the secular clergy. Some ten thousand, according to contemporary estimates, had forsaken their vows and today had wives and, often, a family. An easy answer was the inclusion, now, of a clause that permitted the lower church orders so affected to resume the standing of ordinary citizens, which meant marriage was acceptable for them. Unfortunately, this decision could not apply to those who had taken religious vows; a bishop, like Talleyrand, would be committing bigamy because he was "sacerdos in aeternum." The disgruntled foreign affairs minister claimed this solution inadequate since it was in the best interests of France—read, of Talleyrand—to include even this last group. He had never wanted to enter the Church, and this seemed a God-given opportunity to regain his civilian status and even wed Catherine—should he so desire. For Bonaparte was starting at the top of the Parisian scene and pressuring his official family to set a good example by no longer flaunting their mistresses publicly.

Realizing that the moment was not auspicious for pressing the matter further, Talleyrand decided on a strategic retreat, claiming an attack of rheumatism—*une cure diplomatique*, his friend, the Austrian minister Cobenzl, commented wryly. Just before taking off, he wrote the First Consul, with the unbelievable sycophancy of an eighteenth century courtier: ". . . my forthcoming absence will create for me the most painful of privations . . . I am distraught at going . . . my devotion will only end with my life." [4] Then he and Catherine, escorted by the usual entourage, including another woman to keep Catherine company, and a princely retinue, set out southwards, far earlier than was his wont, for Bourbon-l'Archambault, a spa in the department of the Allier, where Mme de Sévigné, the famed seventeenth-century woman of letters, and her husband used to come. Couriers sped to and fro, daily, and the ever-watchful Talleyrand dictated a number of last minute changes in the proposed Vatican document, while soaking in thermal waters. Bonaparte was in the usual hurry, this time because he wanted the signed covenant to bear the date of July 14 and to be announced at the great state dinner, that same evening, commemorating the fall of the Bastille. But it was not until the night of July 15, 1801, that the final version of the Concordat was off to the Holy See.

Talleyrand, however, was not resigned to failure, and the question of his marriage to Catherine assumed the importance of an affair of state when the pope's new nuncio arrived. Bonaparte had specified Monseigneur Caprara, doubtless because the First Consul hoped this very elderly eminence would prove easier to deal with. He brought with him a specific papal refusal to consider the question of a married bishop. Talleyrand did not want to give up Catherine. "La Questa Donna," as the pope would always refer to her, was not willing to go of her own accord, let alone quietly, and Bonaparte did not want to give up his foreign affairs minister whose personal life he wanted brought into line. The First Consul was not pleased by the indignant complaints of foreign diplomats' wives who found it titillating to be received at the Galliffet by the notorious ex-Bishop d'Autun, but considered it a totally different matter to be expected to pay their respects to his courtesan mistress. Bonaparte's subsequent offer to solicit Rome for a red *birretta*—which so many kings' ministers had worn in the past—to compensate for the loss of the voluptuous blonde "Indienne" indicated how little Bonaparte knew his man, who promptly rejected his proposal.

Talleyrand's reasons for now wanting to regularize his scandalous relationship, despite the Church's injunction to the contrary, can only be surmised. Catherine was one of those women men do not marry, and nothing was more shocking to a Frenchman, for whom the importance of family was paramount, than a misalliance. The explanation he gave shortly before his death, at the end of a long life, is, perhaps, as valid as any, epitomizing, as it does, the ambiance of his day: "It was a time of general disorder.... Nothing was of any real importance." [5]

Such was not Bonaparte's point-of-view. He was deadly serious about cleaning up public morals and was already quarreling with his younger brother, Lucien, of whose choice of a bride he disapproved. Practical Talleyrand had no intention of forfeiting his high office and his intimacy with the First Consul, solely because of his relationship with Mme Grand. Amused gossips whispered about nightly scenes with the distraught woman who, at one point, allegedly rushed to beg her friend Josephine to intercede with the First Consul on her behalf. Peace and quiet at home and no change in his established routine were important to a man like Talleyrand who, as his seraglio could attest, had still never broken ties with many of his former faubourg Saint-Honoré mistresses. Inbred Talleyrand-Périgord arrogance and resentment at interference in his private affairs may have played a part. So, too, might have pride of possession. Catherine also knew too much about some of his financial affairs. A bill of sale, dated late this fall, shows that the pair borrowed jointly to purchase an immense forest near the Belgian frontier at Pont-de-Sains with their friend Michel Simons, who supplied the wood for the construction of the French navy's ships.

The probability that Catherine was the mother of Charlotte, now almost two, who was being raised, hidden far away, and that the child was

Talleyrand's could be another determining factor. By a strange quirk in the marriage and divorce laws of the day, this small girl might legally be considered a Grand offspring; on the other hand, from the point of view of social acceptance, there was nothing to stop Talleyrand, especially once he was wed, from going to court to be named her guardian. And this he would eventually do. Although he would never lose his roving eye, there was also indisputable evidence that his ties with Catherine had greatly strengthened. The previous year, he had appeared before a notary public to secure her financial future, giving her the household furnishings, silverware, tableware, linens from the rue d'Anjou, together with all the jewelry and diamonds then in her coffers. In short, Talleyrand still loved Catherine.

Josephine's daughter, Hortense de Beauharnais, who was by now engaged to marry Louis Bonaparte, another still younger sibling of the First Consul, was accustomed to seeing the lame foreign affairs minister sitting with a bored, non-committal expression, toying with his cane and taking snuff, night after night, in her mother's salon at Malmaison, whenever Bonaparte was out there. Consequently, she never forgot the sudden look of pained astonishment etched fleetingly on that pale, sphinx-like face when, one fall night, the booming of the distant Invalides cannon could be heard while they were seated at dinner. Earlier that afternoon a telegraphic message from London had been brought to Malmaison, where Bonaparte was working with the other two consuls, to announce that preliminaries to hold peace talks had been signed with the English, after months of fruitless efforts and ten years of war. Overjoyed, the First Consul had immediately ordered the artillery to announce the good news to the capital but neglected to so advise Talleyrand, whose annoyance at not being alerted first was, for one brief, telltale second, clearly visible. Throughout the rest of the meal, the observant Hortense noted with amusement her laughing stepfather's marked efforts to make amends to his ill-humored minister.

Amiens, a convenient halfway point between the two capitals, was selected as the meeting site, and the same procedure prevailed as at Lunéville and would hold true for major diplomatic negotiations for the next five years. Talleyrand outlined a number of objectives, whose orientation the First Consul subsequently refined to correspond to the preliminary accords already signed, frequently on the battlefields. Then it was up to the foreign affairs minister to issue precise instructions to the

French plenipotentiary pro tem—a role Talleyrand himself would frequently assume—and he would closely supervise to assure their faithful execution. From start to finish, it was his show. He pulled the strings vis-à-vis his foreign counterpart, in this instance Lord Charles Cornwallis. One of England's best generals, Cornwallis, who had capitulated at Yorktown during the American Revolution and then gone on to a distinguished career as the governor-general of Bengal, was magnificently received when he arrived in Paris, in early December, to consult with Talleyrand and Bonaparte. With his grave demeanor and his impressive figure, decked out in a scarlet uniform bristling with decorations, he looked every inch the part as he strolled, towering over the small First Consul at his side, out onto the Tuileries balcony to see the brilliant show of fireworks in his honor.

With defeated Austria deprived of the support of her English ally, Bonaparte was determined to take advantage of this moment to assure French domination in northern Italy. Most of that region was still occupied by Murat's army, and Europe had been aghast when the First Consul, instead of returning Piedmont to its rightful owner, the King of Sardinia, annexed it. Since this latest acquisition did not correspond to the requirements of the defense of France's natural boundaries, the continent wondered uneasily whether Bonaparte's move presaged another conquering Caesar. Their fears were not allayed when five hundred of the most prominent cisalpine citizens were invited to attend a special assembly to be convoked in Lyon to establish the region's new government, and Talleyrand was sent to woo them.

The foreign affairs minister, who did not care for travel but was destined to do more and more of it, set forth on the four-day trip south shortly before the end of the year. His route took him through Autun, the seat of his bishopric in which he had never set foot since his hasty departure that Easter morning of 1789. As his coachman started up Mont Monjeu, on which the old Burgundian town was perched, one of the many potholes strewing the route damaged Talleyrand's carriage so badly that an immediate halt was necessary. While the broken axletree was being repaired on the main square, in the looming shadow of the cathedral of Saint-Lazare, the cold forced the foreign affairs minister to retreat inside an adjacent tavern. As luck would have it an old-timer, imbibing his daily ration of wine, recognized him. Soon the smoke-filled room was filled with curious, gawking Autunians, those with long memories hissing and hurling epithets at their impassive former bishop until he was able to resume his journey.

With Bonaparte delayed by unrest in Paris, Talleyrand spent his nights at Lyon's Hôtel de l'Europe, wining, dining, and cajoling never less than eighty of the many delegates assembled there. A short time later these same men, well coached by Talleyrand—in accordance with the First Consul's instructions—elected the latter president of the new Italian Republic, which was intended to act as an effective buffer between France and Austria.

Concurrently, the last minute details of the English-French treaty negotiations were still being haggled over at Amiens with Cornwallis. In late March, Talleyrand went to the Tuileries, his portfolio stuffed, as usual, with papers to be gone over with the First Consul. When he was all through, he stood up and, solemnly withdrawing the last remaining document, handed it to Bonaparte. It was the eagerly awaited, finally signed treaty from Amiens.

Why had not Talleyrand given it to him, first thing, Bonaparte demanded. "Because, if I had, we would never have been able to get anything else accomplished. When you are happy, you can think of nothing else." [6]

What a tactful tit-for-tat from his minister who was, obviously, still smarting from the First Consul's negligence, the previous fall, in failing to inform him the second that the preliminaries of the same treaty had been finalized. Talleyrand was never intimidated by Bonaparte. Conversely, the First Consul would never tolerate from anyone else Talleyrand's respectful impertinence, which spoke volumes for their personal relationship until the end.

The Amiens settlement, following that of Lunéville, granted France the general peace which Talleyrand had wanted for so long. France, enlarged now to thirty million people and possessing land from the left bank of the Rhine, to the sea, was a formidable continental presence, as great as in the halcyon days of Louis XIV. The double achievement of peace abroad and peace at home—the formal Concordat, initialed by Pius VII, had just been approved by the consulate's two legislative bodies—presented a golden opportunity for one of those pulse-stirring ceremonies which never failed to strike a responsive chord of national pride. At 6:00 a.m. on Easter Sunday of 1802 Parisians were noisily awakened by thirty salvoes of the Invalides' cannon, to be followed by ten additional salutes hourly until noon. Ringing out for the first time in ten years, "deep-voiced Emmanuel"—as Notre Dame's famous bell was fondly referred to by Parisians and which had been one of the lucky ones not melted down for ammunition during the Revolution—joined in to herald the *Te Deum* to be held there in celebration. It was still tolling when Bonaparte, resplendent in his First Consul's uniform, with the famous Regent diamond glistening on the hand-guard of the Egyptian scimitar which served in lieu of a sword, arrived at the great west portal. He was escorted by turbaned members of the army's picturesque Mameluke corps, composed of the bravest of his defeated Egyptian foes, who had returned to France with him. Throughout the service, most of his military staff, who were present only under duress, repeatedly complained of hunger, then crunched loudly on chocolates that their aides surreptitiously purchased for them from vendors hawking their wares outside. Forty four-horse carriages were required to convey, to and fro, the consulate's official family, and, later, after the irony of kneeling on a prie-dieu for a good part of the three-hour service, Talleyrand entertained the entire diplomatic corps at dinner at Neuilly.

Throughout the past winter the question of Talleyrand's marriage had seemingly remained dormant, but he made sure that Catherine was seated next to the nuncio at every state function or dinner. She plied the monseigneur with attention, begging him to be her advocate with the Holy Father. The cardinal stuffed her little pugs with bonbons whenever he visited Neuilly, smiled—and promised nothing. After exhaustive research through eighteen centuries of papal history uncovered several earlier bishops who supposedly had married, Talleyrand personally wrote the Holy Father not once but twice, citing these examples and requesting that he, too, be relieved of his vows so he might do likewise. But the Vatican archivist, Monseigneur Marini, succeeded in finding a flaw in each instance. The First Consul found the domestic situation of the number-one official in his cabinet—his foreign affairs minister, whose signature followed his own on the Concordat—increasingly intolerable. Bonaparte had returned hundreds of thousands of French souls to Rome's fold, yet the Holy Father still refused to grant his wish concerning a single individual. When Bonaparte, at Talleyrand's urging, now sent a letter stating that "the request for secularization by Citizen Talleyrand is personally agreeable to me," [7] and advised François Cacault, his plenipotentiary to the Vatican, to take the affair in hand, Pius VII was placed in an embarrassing situation. In a brief of reconciliation, a measure of exceptional clemency, His Holiness went so far as to withdraw the ban of excommunication on "Autun," as Talleyrand was known at the Vatican. But this did not address legitimizing a union with Mme Grand. Nor did still another brief, dated June 29, which went one step further and granted Talleyrand secularization.

Neither Talleyrand nor Bonaparte were disposed to be thwarted any longer. By the terms of the recent Concordat, every papal action affecting France had to be ratified by that country in order to become effective there. Accordingly, acting on Bonaparte's express instructions, the Minister of the Cult, Portalis, read aloud, at the next council meeting, only carefully culled excerpts from this latest papal document. Because it was, naturally, in Latin, one embarrassed counselor admitted that he had not used that language since singing vespers as a schoolboy and vainly requested a translation. Although raised hands, questioning looks, and stifled laughs indicated that other colleagues were in the same predicament, Cambacérès, the second consul, rammed through approval, and the brief appeared, the next day, in the *Bulletin des Lois*. Because it was not published in its entirety, as was customary, some perspicacious souls wondered if there might not be something in the Vatican message that the interested parties did not want disclosed but, to the general public, its publication in the official paper meant that Rome had capitulated completely. Talleyrand himself knew otherwise. Now he must act quickly—and quietly—before Rome was aware of his plans.

The marriage contract, which gave continuing, generous financial proof of Talleyrand's attachment to Catherine, was signed at Neuilly, three weeks later, on the night of September 9 by Napoleon and Josephine; the second and third consuls; Talleyrand's two brothers; and Maret, the secretary of state. The document indicated that both his parents were dead. Charles-Daniel, the Comte de Talleyrand, had, indeed, passed away years before, but the countess was very much alive and still living as a guest of the Duke of Brunswick, in Wolfenbuttel where she had been ever since going into exile. Why her son chose to so list her is open to conjecture.

The civil ceremony was performed the next day, by Adrien Duquesnoy, the mayor of Paris's tenth arrondissement, where the bridegroom lived, but it did not occur at the mayor's office, as most long thought. Talleyrand's friend, Roederer, who now held an important post in the Council of State, received a note from his son, Antoine, asking him, at Talleyrand's request, to stop by the Galliffet at 4:00 p.m. that afternoon. There Roederer learned that he and the other witnesses, Admiral Bruix, Radix de Sainte-Foy, the Prince de Nassau-Siegen—one of the groom's principal agents in the remaking of the North German map—and another, must instead be, at 7:00 p.m., at the mayor's home at Mousseaux (Monceau), a small village just outside the capital—presumably to ensure privacy—and he so scribbled on the back of his son's note.

The bride and groom spent that night at Admiral Bruix's country place, and the traditional religious ceremony took place the following morning. Parisians refused to believe that the "bishop," as Talleyrand's friends continued to call him, was able to find any priest willing to give the nuptial blessing and were amused that he was enough of a conformist in such matters to want to bother. It is only fairly recently that records have been found substantiating that Father Pourez of Epinoy-sur-Seine obliged, no doubt because Catherine was one of his parishioners, having spent a number of summers in a small, rented house near his church. The delicate problem of how to announce their marriage was resolved when Sainte-Foy suggested that Catherine invite a large group to dinner. "I will arrive late, after your guests are seated, so everyone will look around to see who is causing so much commotion. Then, when I have their attention, I will come up to you and say, in a loud voice, 'Ah, Mme de Talleyrand, I am so sorry . . .'" [8]

As the news filtered out, the scandalized faubourg Saint-Germain and all the *feuilletons* were filled with gossip about this mismated union between the defrocked, forty-eight-year-old bishop and a divorced adventuress of forty. But, as one cynic commented: "If you're in mud up to your neck, what difference does it make if you have it over your head?" [9] Probably the most delightful tidbit was attributed to his valet, Courtiade, who always said "us" when speaking of his master's variegated intimate life: "To think that we have come to this, after having enjoyed the favors of . . ." [10]—and he would proceed to list all the *grandes dames* in Talleyrand's seraglio. Of course, the Vatican which, up to now, had observed the most complete secrecy about the entire proceedings, was wild, and Cardinal Consalvi, in a special missive, called the attention of the nuncios in the various European courts to the distorted fashion in which the Council of State had chosen to interpret the papal document.

Ever since the Amiens treaty, the capital was bulging with foreigners who excited much curiosity because so few had been seen there in so long—Germans, Russians, Austrians, but mostly English, who always arrived in their own traveling coaches. A ghost from Catherine's past came too. George François Grand, her former husband, now grown very fat, knew a good thing when he heard it and was there for blackmail, claiming that Catherine was still his wife. The couple had been married under English law which did not recognize the divorce she had gotten in France during the Terror. A distraught Catherine, with Talleyrand's help, wrote M. Van der Goes, the minister of foreign affairs of the Republic of Batavia, who eventually found him a lucrative post in the distant Dutch colony of the Cape of Good Hope.

Run down though Paris might still be, the city was ablaze with lights at night. The best restaurants with their large, snowy-white napkins and silver place settings were still to be found in the Palais Royal compound, which remained the center of entertainment. Eating habits were changing; it was becoming fashionable to dine later, so something more substantial—lunch—was called for. But, to anyone of distinction passing through the capital, the place to see and be seen was at the Galliffet. As one titled British lady, noted for her snobbism, reported home, "Power and marriage make so great a difference here that not paying a visit [there] . . . would be reckoned a ridicule." [11] Tolerating Catherine's pretentiousness was a small price to pay to enjoy the company of the fascinating foreign affairs minister.

Catherine took her new role as his wife very seriously and insisted on displaying herself at a weekly reception there. Amid liveried servants passing trays of Egyptian coffee, chocolate, and Spanish wines, *tout Paris* jostled its way between two long rows of straight-backed, gold chairs, which ran the entire length of the great salon and were crowded with chattering guests, up to where the lady of the house was receiving, in a high-backed, tapestry-covered armchair. Impressed with her own importance, Catherine sat bolt upright in a magnificent embroidered gown, ecru-colored—the stylish shade of the moment for an elegant woman— her fabled blond locks entwined with flowers, her neck and arms glittering with diamonds the likes of which had not been seen for more than a decade and were beginning to reappear. As usual, she spoke little but she did not always utter the gaffes attributed to her. At her first formal appearance at the Tuileries after the wedding, the First Consul expressed the hope that the "good conduct of the citizeness Talleyrand would make everyone forget the past indiscretions of Mme Grand." Catherine's disarmingly flattering reply, "I only have to be inspired by the example of Mme Bonaparte" [12] proved that she was not as stupid as claimed, for her friend's private life continued to leave a lot to be desired.

After years of political turmoil, the majority of the French knew a good thing when they saw it. Little back stage maneuvering was needed to rewrite the constitution and extend Bonaparte's term of office, first, for ten years, then, to Consul for Life. Unfortunately, royalists and republicans alike saw themselves betrayed by the man on whom they had so recently pinned their hopes. Among those fervently opposed to France's falling under Bonaparte's dictatorship was Germaine de Staël whose salon, which was now one of the more prominent opposition ones, she referred to as a "hospital for defeated parties." From here emanated such outspoken criticism of Bonaparte that the few fraying threads of friendship remaining between the Swedish ambassadress and Talleyrand wafted away. Her next book, *Delphine*, was the ancestor of the political novel. Containing a preface that was an undisguised insult to Bonaparte, it was an instant success in France, England, and Germany, with Germaine herself portrayed as Delphine, the heroine, and Talleyrand as the villain, Mme de Vernon. Bonaparte ordered a digest made of the book, read it and, turning literary critic, damned it. There is no record whether Talleyrand ever actually read *Delphine* but, when someone asked him what he thought about the novel, he praised it to the skies, raving about the author's tremendous talent. "She has disguised both herself and me as women." [13]

Because the peace of Lunéville, followed by that obtained at Amiens condemned young Charles de Flahaut to idleness, he was authorized, as a young lieutenant on the rise and, probably, due to Talleyrand, to transfer to General Murat's staff. Murat, the most brilliant cavalryman of the day, was slated to become the military governor of Paris. His home was the most animated—and the least virtuous—in the capital. For his wife, Caroline, a sister of Bonaparte, considered her husband's dashing aides-de-camp, who included the richest, most aristocratic and handsomest men in the capital as her personal *cavaliers servants*. Occasionally Charles, who had grown into a tall, handsome good-looking young officer with the easy, innate grace of a Talleyrand-Périgord and who was already a most accomplished lady's man, put in an appearance at Neuilly, although never officially acknowledged by his father. Talleyrand's intimates often took advantage of good weather to come out here in mid-afternoon to stroll around the extensive grounds, whose terraces swept gently down to the Seine, play billiards—a special favorite of the ladies—or, perhaps, gather about the great round table in the main salon to leaf through the volumes of their host's etchings, one of the largest contemporary collections of its kind. Talleyrand would appear in time for dinner, then go, perhaps, to Malmaison, to confer with Bonaparte, return to scan late dispatches, and again join the group for whist and supper. Charles had developed a fine baritone voice and, if he was in the mood, he might sing. Or another, equally talented, guest would play the harp.

Amiens only provided a breathing spell between hostilities. By spring, France's relations abroad were once more deteriorating and England kept complaining that certain stipulations in their recent treaty were being violated. On Sunday, March 13, 1803, there was a reception for the diplomatic corps at the Tuileries. Upon entering, flanked as usual with palace prefects shorter than himself, Bonaparte immediately strode up to Sir Charles Whitworth, the English Ambassador. In one of those dramatic scenes that became his trademark, the First Consul angrily attacked the diplomat claiming, in a voice purposely raised so all the other guests might hear, that England wanted war. From this day on, the positions in both countries hardened on the several issues which once more divided them. In the following weeks, Talleyrand met frequently with the English ambassador, trying to affix the blame for what had gone wrong, and Whitworth acknowledged to London the French foreign affairs minister's efforts to delay the inevitable rupture.

About this time James Monroe, President Jefferson's special envoy, arrived to wind up the infamous XYZ imbroglio and to conclude talks, which had been quietly proceeding, about the purchase of Louisiana. Not all the ministers—nor all the French—were pleased with this arbitrary sale, which Bonaparte regretfully referred to as his "Louisianicide," but he needed the money for his upcoming war with England. By coincidence, the very day in May that the sale was secretly completed, Whitworth demanded and received his passports and left. Talleyrand persuaded him to travel slowly so that negotiations to resolve the break might continue, but the final propositions that reached the English ambassador, at Breteuil, en route, were unacceptable. Four days later, France formally declared war and England, without any official notification on her part, recommenced hostilities, seizing French vessels on the high seas.

Bonaparte was gradually transforming himself into emperor and Talleyrand, who had been the First Consul's accomplice, was soon to be reduced to his subject. As moderation began to abandon Bonaparte, his ever-expanding, poorly disguised ambitions about restructuring the map of Europe made him increasingly difficult to work with because he would brook no opposition. He was so unreceptive to Talleyrand's counsels of moderation and efforts to prevent another rupture with England that one may wonder why peace-loving Talleyrand, who had every reason to be proud of the situation in which France now found herself abroad, did not turn in his portfolio. A more highly principled man might have done so—although no useful purpose would have been served—despite his fondness for the younger man whom he genuinely admired. On the other hand, the terror, which the First Consul was beginning to inspire on the continent, was a great source of income for him because all the European powers wanted to stay in Bonaparte's good graces and attributed far more influence to the foreign affairs minister than he actually had.

Talleyrand, resplendent in red velvet, heavily embroidered with gold passementerie, figured prominently at the first official celebration of Bonaparte's birthday on August 15. This was also the Fête of the Assumption of the Virgin that had been commemorated for centuries in every Catholic country including France, and the day's elevation to the status of a national holiday was but another sign of the handwriting on the wall. So, too, was Bonaparte's decision to make Saint-Cloud his principal summer residence now that his staff had outgrown their quarters at Malmaison. Just as its Lantern Monument was lit to indicate when he was in residence—as, previously, for Louis XVI—so, too, life became more circumscribed for those in his entourage. With hierarchy assuming increasing importance, Bonaparte separated his table from that of the other officers at meal times, and etiquette was correspondingly more rigid.

The annual visit of Talleyrand and Catherine's to Bourbon-l'Archambault that fall, to partake of the hot sulfur baths and drink their daily quotient of its curative waters, presented an ideal opportunity, away from the capital's prying eyes, for the couple to quietly augment their family circle. Over the years Talleyrand would give various explanations for the sudden appearance there now of young Élisa Alix Sara, superficially maintaining—among other explanations—that she was the orphaned child of friends. Blonde, like Catherine and Talleyrand, with a name so reminiscent of Talleyrand's own—she was always known as "la petite Charlotte"—the little girl also had their same delicate complexion. She assumed an important role in their ménage, and the solicitude and doting affection with which both he and Catherine would always smother her ought to have erased the doubts of even the most cynical regarding her actual parentage. Convinced, while at the spa, that this wonder child was old enough to learn to read and anxious for her to begin, Talleyrand, who would personally supervise her education from start to finish, decided, to everyone's astonishment, to undertake this important elementary task himself. Whenever he scolded the youngster for not paying sufficient attention—which was often, given her tender years—the four-year-old threw a tantrum and Catherine, who was capable of more tears than Niobe at the death of her last offspring, was wracked with loud sobs.

On their way back to Paris, the couple made a short, twenty-five league detour through nearby Berry to inspect Valençay in the department of l'Indre, Talleyrand's latest acquisition, which he had purchased sight unseen. As the pomp and ceremony of the late monarchy was slowly reappearing, Bonaparte mandated that the private establishments of high government officials do justice to their roles. Aware that the sumptuous receptions held at Chanteloup, the country home of the late statesman, the Duc de Choiseul, had added immeasurably to the prestige and glory of France, he wanted Talleyrand to possess a residence not too far from the capital where he could entertain distinguished foreigners in similar fashion. An invitation to visit here should constitute a reward for the ambassadors of those sovereigns with whom Bonaparte was pleased. This was advice the foreign affairs minister was happy to accept, especially since the First Consul assumed responsibility for the loan Talleyrand took out for its purchase; even very wealthy men never possess enough money. About two hundred and sixty-five kilometers from Paris, Valençay was one of the few princely estates to have survived, intact, the ravages of the Revolution. The imposing Renaissance château with its deep moats, flanked by massive towers, capped with slate roofs and with a sixteenth century donjon forming its entrance, was enclosed in a carefully maintained three hundred and fifty-acre park and was of royal proportions with twenty-five master suites. The domain itself included roughly forty thousand acres of forests and fields, not to mention twenty-three villages, over which

Talleyrand would rule in almost feudal fashion. They were here barely three days before Bonaparte recalled him. This was not nearly sufficient time to visit his vast new possession, but it was sufficiently long for Catherine to play at being "Madame la patronnesse" and to establish a school for poor, deserving peasant girls of the neighborhood. "She's a second Mme de Maintenon!" the irrepressible Germaine de Staël quipped at the news, comparing her to Louis XIV's morganatic wife who was famous for a similar institution she set up at Saint-Cyr. Henceforth the pair would visit Valençay each year, following their cure.

Talleyrand's mother, the Comtesse de Talleyrand, who had finally decided to return, was in Paris by now. Scotching any rumors that they were not on good terms, Talleyrand found an apartment for her in a private hotel at 36, rue d'Anjou-Saint-Honoré, near his own home. His younger brother Boson who had come back two years before, would also live here.

As with the Directoire before it, the leitmotif of the Consulate remained the see-sawing dangers threatening the regime from the Left and, even more, from the Right. Although ruthlessly crushed by republican forces ten years before, diehard Breton royalists in the Vendée, in western France—known as Chouans because the hoot of this little owl was their secret rallying signal—had engineered uprisings ever since. Early in February 1804, one of them, Bouvier de Lauzier, was picked up in Paris and confessed to the renewal of plotting against the First Consul. Two days later, General Moreau was arrested on charges of high treason. The turncoat victor of Hohenlinden and a known dissenter, he had been secretly meeting with Georges Cadoudal, the principal Chouan leader, who had been hiding in the capital for the past five months and had recently been named the supreme commander of the royalist troops in the East. As the most formidable conspiracy to date unraveled, Bonaparte realized he had underestimated the strength of lingering royalist sentiment. No matter how many of the faubourg Saint-Germain returned from exile and gave him lip service, he would never be, for them or the Chouans, anything but a usurper. Complaining that "the air is full of daggers," Fouché, the minister of police, ordered a sweep to locate another troublemaker, Pichegru, the former conqueror of Holland, who was known to be in the pay of the Bourbons and also rumored to be hiding thereabouts. A fortnight later he was found.

Then, on March 9, Cadoudal himself was picked up in the Latin Quarter, not far from Saint-Germain-des-Prés, and revealed that ships from the English Navy were at his command to ferry royalist arms and men across the Channel. Just as four years before, London was once more lending a hand, apprehensive about French invasion plans—and Bonaparte's intentions in general—and hopeful that these might be aborted if the First Consul were dead. However, it was stipulated that Cadoudal's plans not be triggered until the arrival of an undesignated prince who was to coordinate final arrangements. He had not yet appeared, and Cadoudal never revealed who he was; perhaps he himself had not yet been told.

Almost concurrently, a report was rushed to jittery Paris that still another renegade, General Dumoriez, the victor at Valma and Jemmapes, who was living in the neighborhood of Strasbourg, in the duchy of Baden, had been reputedly sighted on the French border. It was quickly ascertained that the Bourbon Duc d'Enghien, the grandson of the Prince de Condé, the leader of the émigrés, was also dwelling thereabouts, in nearby Ettenheim. The last of the Condés, the thirty-two-year-old Enghien, who had fought against the republican armies on the Rhine in 1800, was suspected by the local authorities of being involved in royalist agitation in the neighborhood and had been spotted, on more than one occasion, slipping secretly across the Rhine into France—for romantic trysts, it was later ascertained. Meanwhile Bonaparte—influenced or not by Talleyrand, whose role in the Enghien debacle is murky at best—jumped to the conclusion that this young man was the unknown Bourbon that Cadoudal had been instructed to await.

The capital was at the mercy of every rumor. Authorities were on edge, and Talleyrand knew that, if a terrorist struck down Bonaparte, it would probably be the end of his career as a high official. The First Consul was exasperated. Since Louis XVIII had made it abundantly clear that he had no intentions of renouncing his claims to the throne, could the menace of a royalist restoration ever be removed? To further color his thinking, Bonaparte was well aware that his gradual assumption of supreme power had not passed unobserved by diehard Jacobins, not to mention the many regicides in the assembly and administration whose support was essential, lukewarm though it was. To be kept in line, these republicans needed reassurances that Bonaparte was not severing connections with his own revolutionary past and would not, one day, turn against them.

On March 10, the First Consul hurriedly consulted General Murat, who was by now the governor of Paris, and Talleyrand. Claiming that the safety of the state was at issue, Bonaparte demanded: Was it against international law to seize Louis XVIII's cousin as an enemy of the French Republic, even if he was presently living on neutral foreign soil?

Bonaparte immediately issued a command to capture the duke and bring him back posthaste to Paris, while Talleyrand dispatched a terse note—without a word of explanation or excuse, without any demand for authorization—to advise Baron Edelsheim, the foreign minister of the Elector of Baden, that Bonaparte had ordered two small detachments across the frontier to get Enghien. In so doing, Talleyrand was well aware that, despite his lifelong aversion to bloodshed, he was signing the young Bourbon's death warrant as a suspected traitor.

Four nights later the duke was picked up by a French raiding party led by General Ordener and his men. While he was en route to the capital, Bonaparte received word that Dumouriez was not, as previously reported, anywhere in the vicinity of Ettenheim. A Badois mispronunciation of the name "de Thumery"—an intimate of the prince—had been mistaken by the French police for "Dumouriez." But the die was cast. On March 20, Enghien was at the château of Vincennes, on the edge of Paris. Because Bonaparte specified that the issue must be resolved that same night—two hours earlier, his grave had already been dug—he was at once led before a specially convoked military court where he was accused of having borne arms against the Republic, of being in the pay of the English, and of having participated in Cadoudal's British-sponsored conspiracy against France. No time was wasted. On the basis of the flimsiest evidence, with hardly the pretence of a hearing, and without any lawyer, Enghien was found guilty. Taken into the château's dried-up moat, the duke courageously refused a blindfold, a portable light was pinned on his shoulder to indicate the location of his heart, and he was shot before dawn. Talleyrand, as foreign affairs minister, defended this political execution to French ambassadors abroad in a memorandum, which was intended to counteract any criticism in the various European courts of such a blatant violation of international law.

Throughout his life, Bonaparte would keep repeating to confidants that Talleyrand had been the first to draw his attention to Enghien and had urged him to be harsh. Nonetheless, in a document dictated less than two weeks before he died, he assumed full responsibility for the deed, maintaining that Talleyrand had only done what was necessary for the good of the state.

It is almost impossible to assess Talleyrand's precise role in this, one of the most reprehensible crimes of the Napoleonic era. In his own, unreliable *Mémoires* which were written near the end of his long life, Talleyrand claimed that the First Consul's real motive was a long-standing determination to bind himself irrevocably to the republicans and that this was the first opportunity to present itself. However, his enemies lost no time maintaining he composed the entire scenario, from start to finish. Two of them, Chateaubriand and Méneval, a future secretary of Bonaparte, later claimed to have seen a letter Talleyrand wrote to the First Consul recommending the arrest of Enghien and the need to stop once and for all these recurrent conspiracies, regardless of whom was involved. Such a letter, if it ever did exist, was never found. Most likely it was burned during the minister's *auto-da-fé* of his personal archives in 1814— to prove what Talleyrand always maintained: "Any miscalculation can be denied."

Frenchmen in every walk of life were horrified and correctly convinced that Enghien was innocent; it later developed that it was Armand de Polignac whom the royalists in Paris had been awaiting. The whole episode was an unpardonable outrage that even the staunchest Bonapartists found difficult to stomach, prompting Boulay de la Meurthe, a member of the Council of State, to exclaim: "It was worse than a crime; it was a blunder." [14] On the morning after the execution, one shocked colleague commented: "What a horrible event!"

—"Come, come," Talleyrand calmly replied. "Are you mad? What is there to make such a fuss about? A conspirator is captured near the frontier, he is brought to Paris and shot. What is so extraordinary about that?" [15] And, when a friend counseled him to resign, he responded: "If, as you say, Bonaparte has been guilty of committing a crime, that is no reason for me to do something foolish." [16]

From the point of view of practical politics, the prince's fate accomplished what it was intended to do, effectively discouraging any further plotting against Bonaparte and eliminating the possibility for any regicide to switch sides and participate in any proposed Bourbon restoration. Three days later, Talleyrand held a great ball, which his friend Lucchesini, the Prussian minister, informed his government he had been ordered to give to create the impression that nothing unusual had transpired. The entire diplomatic court was present, as protocol demanded, but hardly smiling. Catherine, of course, presided although, interestingly, she had had sufficient sensibility to refuse to attend a gala that Cobenzl, the Austrian ambassador, had given, two months previously, because it was the anniversary of the death of Louis XVI.

The Austrian emperor, François II, accepted at face value Talleyrand's circular giving the consular government's rationale for arresting Enghien on neutral Baden soil. Alexander I did not and ordered the entire Russian court into mourning. Despite the scandalous, highhanded manner in which the affair was handled, Bonaparte's popularity was not dampened. For those who stopped to think about it, once the step had been taken from Consul for Ten Years to Consul for Life, it was evident that the ambitious man would only be satisfied with the establishment of some monarchic form of government. On the other hand the nation, tired of so many political convulsions, craved the stability offered by a fixed regime. The Cadoudal conspiracy further prepared opinion for such a change, which was now touted as essential for the safety and good of France, and there was much talk about what the title of a new head of state should be.

Talleyrand favored "emperor," which was not tainted like the word "king" in republican eyes. Furthermore, it was most appropriate for a military man such as Bonaparte, especially one who had always been fascinated by imperial Rome. There was also much talk about the need for heredity to assure the glory and prosperity of France, for the existence of a solitary head of state would always constitute a temptation for conspirators. Nothing is known about a meeting the First Consul called to discuss these related questions with a few trusted advisors, nor what role, if any, Talleyrand took there. As an aftermath, on May 18, a new constitution was unanimously approved in the Senate. Then, while salvoes of cannon announced this *senatus-consulte* to Parisians, the lawmakers themselves proceeded in a body to Saint-Cloud to offer the imperial crown to Bonaparte, to be handed down from male to male. Talleyrand arrived soon afterwards and was among the first to congratulate the new emperor as "Your Majesty."

When Napoleon—as Bonaparte would henceforth be known—published his first list of honors, the highly lucrative, honorary post of arch-chancellor went, not to Talleyrand, as everyone, including that gentleman himself, expected, but to Cambacérès, the erstwhile second consul. There is no way of knowing whether Talleyrand was provoked or not. But, in addition to retaining his post at the Galliffet, he now assumed the role of grand chamberlain. As one of the six grand officers of the new Imperial Household, this position officially attached him in a very personal way to the head of state because of his henceforth obligatory presence in innumerable, largely ceremonial, circumstances. As holder of one of these highly sought-after sinecures copied from the old Bourbon court, Talleyrand was henceforth addressed as "His Excellency" and, naturally, he received an additional handsome annual stipend, not to mention an elaborate set of different costumes for various occasions.

9

Imperial Grand Chamberlain, 1804

"You are one of the principal interests of my life and when I say that, I am reducing them to two or three. ... I embrace you and press you to my heart."
—TALLEYRAND TO HIS SON, CHARLES DE FLAHAUT [1]

NAPOLEON WAS DETERMINED not to be consecrated like his royal predecessors by a mere Archbishop of Reims, but by a pope, like Charlemagne, the emperor of the West, in 800 AD. Such an induction would give the ceremony an international aspect, a political as well as a religious one, and would legitimize Napoleon in the eyes not only of France but of all Europe. Accordingly Talleyrand who, in his new capacity as the grand chamberlain was charged with nominally overseeing all imperial ceremonies, must also, as foreign affairs minister, negotiate for Pius VII's presence. Given the pontiff's advanced age and poor health, Talleyrand started what promised to be a difficult assignment by meeting with Cardinal Caprara at the end of June. The time had come for Napoleon to resume his fight against England and, shortly afterwards, he left with Josephine to inspect the military installations on the Channel. The unexpected death of Admiral Latouche-Tréville, charged with bringing the

Mediterranean fleet into the Atlantic, forced the postponement of embarkation plans, so Napoleon decided to visit the recently annexed northern provinces and the garrisons on the banks of the Rhine. When the imperial entourage stopped at Aix-la-Chapelle—Aachen, Charlemagne's ancient capital—on the frontier, the crowned heads of the many small German states thereabouts either came in person or sent their ambassadors to pay their respects. For wherever Napoleon was, there was the seat of the French government. Talleyrand, following his annual cure at Bourbon-l'Archambault, joined Napoleon here. Because he had left an ailing Charlotte at home, he awaited the arrival of each courier with such obvious anxiety that the foreign dignitaries assembled there were consumed with curiosity. Conjectures of every sort ran wild. One day, Talleyrand abruptly interrupted a serious conversation with Monsieur d'Azara, the Spanish ambassador, to read the post just handed to him for the latest word about the small girl. A short time later, that bewildered dignitary asked Mme Duroc, one of the ladies-in-waiting, in a low voice: "Madame, could you tell me what a charlotte is?" Unaware of the reason for his question, the startled duchess replied with the first meaning of the word that came to mind: "Why, Monsieur, it's the name of a dessert made with apples!" [2]

When Napoleon continued on east, Talleyrand followed him only part way before hastening back to Paris to attend to various delicate details concerning the forthcoming papal visit. He also reminded the Vatican to be sure that the Holy Father came well supplied with rosaries; the ladies at court loved that sort of thing. He may even have had his own wife in mind but, unfortunately, Catherine's name appeared high on the list, which was forwarded from Rome, of those individuals who must not be presented to His Holiness. The Holy See still considered "questa donna"—as the Church would always refer to her—as the concubine of the ex-Bishop d'Autun because the latter had never officially received permission to marry. What a humiliation for the haughty Talleyrand!

Although the advent of the head of Christendom to officiate was a tremendous coup, protocol-conscious Napoleon was unwilling to take second place to Pius VII, even if the Holy Father was his guest. Accordingly, on the day of his arrival, the emperor arranged to meet His Holiness, as if by accident, in the large forest which surrounded the magnificent royal château at Fontainebleau and which was still dripping, that morning, from a recent downpour. Clad in a simple green hunting costume, Napoleon dismounted to greet the elderly pontiff. Though travel weary after a difficult passage over the snow-covered Alps, the pope likewise courteously descended—in his white robe and silken shoes. After mutual greetings in a sea of mud, an imperial carriage appeared, as if by magic and, superseding the papal one, was skillfully maneuvered between the two men, separating them. Each might thus enter the vehicle by his own door. In this fashion the French emperor arranged to step in from the right side, thereby gaining the place of honor. Once the precedent was set, it was simple to maintain this seating arrangement throughout the papal visit.

Talleyrand officially greeted the head of Christendom to France in the Oval Court at the foot of the château's famed horseshoe-shaped staircase and, together with other appropriate imperial officials, conducted him to his apartments. Several days later, the papal party proceeded to Paris where an elaborate suite had been prepared for His Holiness in the Pavillon de Flore, overlooking the Seine. An additional fifty-six rooms were reserved for his large entourage directly above. Whatever Talleyrand's exact feelings at the refusal of the pope to acknowledge the existence of Catherine, they must have been magnified when he was suddenly summoned to be one of the witnesses as another irregular marriage was hurriedly rectified. A horrified Pius VII had just discovered that only a civil ceremony united Napoleon and Josephine eight years before and issued a thundering ultimatum. If His Holiness was to participate in the coronation the next day, their vows must be immediately regularized in Catholic eyes.

Notre Dame required much repairing, both inside and out, to make the setting worthy of the occasion, because the massive, twelfth- and thirteenth-century stone structure had suffered from neglect during the Revolution. In the hands of the artists Jean-Baptiste Isabey and Jacques-Louis David, the vast interior was redesigned as if for a theatrical spectacle, and any remaining bare stone, once they were finished, was hurriedly covered with tapestries, flags or velvet hangings. The exterior was boxed in with painted cardboard; thirty-six statues representing the principal towns of France were designed and placed on a huge, four-arched gothic porch of painted wood constructed to hide the badly dilapidated front portal. Centuries-old houses, which previously nestled up close to the cathedral, were demolished to make adequate space for the triumphant arrival of the imperial couple and their huge retinue. Adjacent streets and quais were swept and sanded. Although on Sunday, December 2, it was bitterly cold with traces of white on the icy streets, Parisians already lined the route when a papal assistant, astride a humble mule and carrying a large wooden cross, opened the procession from the Tuileries in traditional fashion. Pius VII, who would have a chilly, two-hour wait near the high altar, came next. Talleyrand followed close on the heels of the imperial pair, in one of the eleven carriages designated for the great officers of the empire and the ministers of state. His new costume, like those of the other dignitaries, was by Isabey and David, in the style of the Renaissance sovereign, François I. Although somewhat overdone, it created a different effect than the previous *opéra bouffe* creations of the Directoire and, around his neck, was hung the traditional key of office which indicated that the bearer had unlimited access to the ruler at all times. Talleyrand had witnessed the coronation of Louis XVI at Reims, while his father participated. Today he himself was slated for a role. However, when His Holiness learned that the grand chamberlain was designated by court custom to ritually dry the emperor, after the sacred unction had been applied to his head and hands, the scandalized pope pointed out that this would constitute a sacrilege. So Talleyrand relinquished this specific part of his functions to the grand chaplain.

After changing into their coronation robes in the adjacent Archbishop of Paris's palace, tiny Josephine, beaming with joy, was the cynosure of all eyes as she was ceremoniously escorted into the icy cathedral. The newly created Bonaparte princesses, covered with diamonds and sulking at their brother's order to hold up their detested sister-in-law's massive train, grimly did so, scowling. Next Napoleon appeared in solitary splendor in an ankle-length, sashed, satin gown reminiscent of classical Rome, over which he wore a purple velvet, ermine-lined mantle, lavishly strewn with golden bees. The ceremonial handling of this cloak became the grand chamberlain's responsibility, after the *Veni Creator*, when Their Imperial Majesties' insignias of power were placed on the high altar to be consecrated. In accordance with certain deviations from the proscribed ritual that Talleyrand had previously worked out with the Vatican, the emperor, rather than the pontiff, crowned both himself and, then, his consort, to indicate that, as a triumphant finale to a most ambitious political operation, he was not beholden to Rome for their investitures.

Amid the roar of hundreds of cannon on both sides of the Seine and the pealing of church bells throughout the city, hundreds of torch-bearing footmen and pages, both mounted and on foot, illuminated the return to the Tuileries. Because it was already getting dark by 3:00 p.m., at that time of the year, lighted chandeliers were strung between the columns of the Gabriel buildings lining one side of the Place de la Concorde. The Tuileries gardens and palace already sparkled with thousands of colored lamps hung from the tree branches. Wine flowed freely amid fireworks and dancing in the streets. The next morning, the emperor distributed eagles for the regimental flags, and public festivities continued another ten days. Because the court calendar was even fuller, the imperial ladies-in-waiting, who must never wear the same gown twice at the Tuileries, were each granted ten thousand francs to help defray—but barely—their additional expenses.

The papal visit permeated everyone's thoughts and colored all conversation, especially Catherine's—perhaps because she remained *persona non grata* in the Holy Father's presence. At one state dinner she admired a costly necklace the British ambassadress was wearing. "The price was not exorbitant," the diplomat's wife replied, "and certainly not so high that M. de Talleyrand could not easily afford to purchase one just like it for you." There happened to be a lull in the conversation, so Catherine's astonishing reply—"Mon Dieu, Madame, how mistaken you are! Do you think I married the pope?" [3]—carried far, well above the clatter of glassware and silver.

While the emperor dreamt of a Europe united by French military might, his foreign affairs minister dreamt of one united by French diplomacy. Though still a counselor who was always consulted, Talleyrand was heeded less and less, and he ruefully admitted that the most difficult person he had to negotiate with was Napoleon himself. Even though no one else enjoyed the same freedom of speech with His Imperial Majesty, whether Talleyrand still thought he had a chance to act as intermediary between his master and Europe, or to temper and direct imperial policy, is open to speculation. Incipient conflict was sprouting between the pair for, as the rupture of the peace of Amiens and the resumption of war with England indicated, it was increasingly evident that Napoleon's objectives and the true interests of the country were diverging.

The Revolution's armies had claimed to have a worldwide mission to protect the oppressed and establish justice everywhere but, now, the newly crowned emperor was primarily concerned with assuring the permanency of his own system. The first step was to bind northern Italy more tightly to him by changing its status from satellite to that of annex, despite Talleyrand's unsuccessful efforts to dissuade him. He foresaw that such a step would provide England with the allies she lacked. For Italy as a nation did not yet exist and, since several of the political entities in that peninsula still belonged to Austria, Vienna considered this region as its proper sphere and could not calmly support French extension here. Nonetheless, shortly after the first of the year, Talleyrand was instructed to prepare for the takeover of the Italian Republic which had been voted into existence several years before—with Napoleon its elected president—and which was now to be transformed into a kingdom.

After an arduous crossing of the Mont Cenis pass on a mule-supported litter in unexpectedly wintry weather for April, Talleyrand once more assumed his coronation duties as grand chamberlain. In Milan's gleaming white cathedral Napoleon again crowned himself, this time with the ancient Iron Crown of the Lombards, the same one that Charlemagne had worn that was reputedly composed of the nails which pierced the feet and hands of Jesus. The announcement of the impending coronation had startled Europe, causing Russia to sign an alliance with England. The menace it conveyed was further heightened when the French emperor, instead of assuming the plausible title of King of the Lombards, opted for the more threatening one of King of Italy.

Talleyrand recuperated from these arduous past weeks at Bourbon-l'Archambault, where Catherine and Charlotte waited. At the same time Napoleon proceeded to the Channel coast to boost the morale of his troops, who were bored to death with inactivity and momentarily expecting the French fleet, which was to ferry them across the Channel for the descent on England. While in Boulogne His Imperial Majesty received word that, as the foreign affairs minister anticipated, Austria had joined the new Russian-English coalition and delivered an ultimatum that France renounce the kingdom of Italy. Shortly afterwards a large Austrian army poured across the River Inn to invade Bavaria, a French ally, and Napoleon wheeled his men for a lightning attack. Imperial headquarters were established at Strasbourg, where the Grande Armée was soon crossing the Rhine, so Talleyrand and the other ministers and high officials converged there. All foreign diplomats accredited to the French government followed, as did Josephine and a large portion of the imperial court.

Just prior to leaving for the frontlines, Napoleon dined with his foreign affairs minister and François-Marie-Charles de Remusat, his first chamberlain and, afterwards, the three proceeded into his bedroom. Suddenly, Napoleon only had time to tell Talleyrand to shut the door before he was seized with convulsions and fell to the floor. Talleyrand quickly limped over to him and, with Remusat's help, loosened his neckwear because the moaning, slobbering man appeared to be choking. While the horrified chamberlain tried to give him some water, Talleyrand doused His Imperial Majesty with *eau de cologne*. Some fifteen minutes later, Napoleon revived, and they were able to hoist him into a chair. Before the two witnesses had time to recover from their initial shock, the emperor began to speak. He redressed himself, swore the pair to secrecy and within a half-hour was in the saddle and off.

Talleyrand remained behind ready to catch up with Napoleon the moment French cannon determined the hour of negotiations with Austria. Although he had heard previous rumors of Napoleon's attacks of epilepsy—which dated from his childhood and which Josephine had always managed to quickly hush up—he had never witnessed one, and those few moments made a vivid, indelible impression on him. For a man unusually gifted with the ability to see clearly into the future, as his past history had proven, he had ample time at Strasbourg to ponder on the empire's fragility and future, in the light of Napoleon's frightening spell. The emperor's sickness was of a nature to greatly augment the risks entailed by his far-flung ambitions. An emperor who is not a general can be an epileptic, but not an emperor who doubles as his own commander-in-chief. If he fell unconscious during the decisive half hour of a battle, the empire might not survive. Where would that leave France? And Talleyrand? The thought of Napoleon's death also brought to the surface his submerged personal feelings of affection for the younger man and, in phrases that might seem overdone to modern ears, he wrote the emperor daily, assuring him of his devotion and of his concern for his well-being.

Of all the catalogued letters from Talleyrand to the emperor between 1800 and 1809 the one written on October 17, 1805, the day word came that Austrian field marshal Karl Mack was negotiating to surrender the heavily garrisoned city of Ulm, on the Danube, is the only one where he sketches an overall foreign program. With Napoleon once again victorious, it took courage to send this famous memorandum in which he disregarded the tenet, "Word has been given man to disguise his thoughts"—which he long ago appropriated as his own—and spoke out. For what he had to say ran counter to Napoleon's philosophy. Talleyrand's thesis was the *ancien régime* concept that peace could only be established and endured in Europe by a balance of power. His proposed, moderate program was the same as it had always been: France must have a solid alliance with at least one of the great European powers—with which country might vary, depending on the circumstances—to make any future war impossible. Therefore, it was in the emperor's interest not to crush or enfeeble Austria but to reconcile her to France by a temperate treaty and make her an ally. Unfortunately, actualities—current French defeats on the high seas as well as French triumphs in central Europe—were momentarily conspiring against Talleyrand's long-range concept. Admiral Horatio Nelson's sweeping English victory over the French fleet at Trafalgar, on October 21, was, from his point of view, especially disastrous at this particular moment. For it would make London more intractable at the bargaining table. Conversely, it only stiffened the emperor's resolve, in the light of England's reaffirmed, undisputed mastery on the high seas, to strengthen the imperial grip on the continent itself. However, this might prove easier said than done, even for Napoleon, because the tsar, who had already ordered his troops west, arrived in Potsdam and signed an alliance with the wavering Friedrich-Wilhelm III, which meant that France now had pitted against her Austria, Russia, England—and Prussia.

Meanwhile, the capitulation of Ulm opened the gateway to Vienna. Since Talleyrand's route to the Austrian capital took him through Linz, where a one-time mistress, the Comtesse de Brionne, who had once tried to get him a cardinal's hat, was living ever since she emigrated in 1799, he wrote requesting permission to call. In reply, the countess precipitously departed, leaving an envelope addressed to him. On the outside, underlined, and in capitals, were his various titles since Napoleon's advent and, inside, his unopened note. Talleyrand's reactions to her elegant disavowal of their former relationship are not known.

The emperor was already pushing on east in the whirling snow to face some one hundred thousand advancing Austrians and Russians before Talleyrand reached Vienna. The incredible speed whereby the Grande Armée engaged the enemy in the tiny Moravian village of Austerlitz, has few equals in the annals of war. Here, on December 2, his soldiers presented Napoleon with a fitting present to commemorate his coronation, one year ago to the day. The French triumph at what came to be known in German as "the Battle of the Three Emperors" was so crushing that the Hapsburg Francis II came in person to solicit an armistice and the Romanoff Alexander I who, at one moment barely escaped capture, left his allies in the lurch and retreated into Poland with his personal guard.

The moment of victory always tests a statesman. Three days after word of this latest military success reached Talleyrand, he dared address a second plea similar to the one he had earlier sent from Strasbourg, urging magnanimous treatment of the fallen foe. Unfortunately, his reiterated words of caution only displeased Napoleon, who was impatiently awaiting him to oversee the peace treaty negotiations. Since the Danube was only half frozen over, Talleyrand's carriages and staff had to wait, stranded, on one side's snow-encrusted banks, while the minister wrapped like a mummy, from head to toe, in luxurious furs—and clutching his ever-present, green morocco portfolio—was ferried across alone in a tiny rowboat. It was a difficult, dangerous crossing and even the two stout natives who manned the craft, one rowing, the other using his oar to fend off the swirling ice chunks, admitted relief, once they safely deposited their distinguished passenger on the opposite shore.

French General Headquarters, at Brunn, the Moravian capital, a short distance from Austerlitz, was a bustling shambles. An unending stream of captured Austrian battalion flags and Russian regimental standards jostled with prisoners bearing some of the greatest names of the Austrian empire. Nearby one hundred and eighty pieces of enemy artillery were being dismantled for transmission to Paris, later to be transformed into a national monument in the Place Vendôme. Talleyrand had scarcely put in an appearance before Marshal Lannes insisted on taking him out on a two-hour tour of the battlefield to proudly show him where "swords had honed diplomacy's pens." The only time on record when he ever set foot on the actual scene of action, let alone when it was still littered with the dying, as well as the dead—whose bodies were already being pillaged by the usual scavengers—must surely have been a sobering, provocative experience. So, too, was living in Brunn itself. Most of those injured in the recent fighting were transported here, turning the city into a vast hospital, "a horrible place with some four thousand wounded . . . dying in quantities each day." [4] It smelt like one, too, Talleyrand noted, when he wrote his valet Courtiade, still in Munich, to send some Malaga wine, "very dry and as little sweet as possible."

He did not intend to sacrifice his post for the sake of his opinions, and dutifully executed imperial instructions. When he succeeded in getting a last-minute, ten percent reduction in the astronomical reparations that Napoleon was demanding, contemporaries strongly suspected that a good portion of this saving found its way from the Austrian treasury into his own deep pockets instead. At the formal signing ceremony Talleyrand, together with the other participating plenipotentiaries, also received the customary gold box, liberally studded with huge diamonds—his were the largest of all—from Francis II. Napoleon might proudly inform Josephine that the "battle of Austerlitz is the finest I have ever fought," but like Cadmus, he had sown here the seeds of his ultimate downfall. The Hapsburgs' thousand-year-old Holy Roman empire composed of more than three hundred principalities, duchies, landgraviates and the like, lost nearly three million subjects and ceased to exist for all practical purposes but, in making an example of the futility of rebellion against all-powerful France, a dangerous fallen foe was created. Nor could the French emperor relinquish the satisfaction of humiliating Europe's oldest and proudest dynasty by dating his decrees from the Imperial Palace—he had preempted the Austrian empress's personal suite—where Talleyrand was also installed. The pair could frequently be seen in the long galleries of Schönbrun, the tall, older man hobbling alongside the fast walking, fast talking emperor, working over the latter's plans for the reorganization of the German-speaking parts of Europe.

More than one historian feels that the emperor's disdainful dismissal of Talleyrand's reiterated, sound advice and plea for moderation regarding Austrian-French relations marks a turning point in his relationship with Napoleon. While both men desired peace and order in Europe, there was an irreconcilable difference between them regarding the means to achieve this. For Talleyrand, whose keen sense of what was politically feasible had already been proven in the Directoire, peace could only be obtained by diplomacy supplemented, as a last resort, by armed might. For the emperor, who now considered himself Caesar's successor, the desired ends must be imposed, if need be, by force. Since Talleyrand knew that Europe would never consent to this, once he abandoned all hope of ever persuading the emperor to pursue a reasonably moderate foreign course, a breach between the pair was inevitable.

Meanwhile, the domestic scene was badly in need of Napoleon's personal attention. The financial situation of the government and the country as a whole was critical, and the French were no longer blind to the astronomical expenses of the Grande Armée's continuing victories. The Bank of France was almost bankrupt, because the emperor had been stripping its coffers for his military endeavors; money was becoming scarce and business was paralyzed. The constant hostility of the English, untouchable on their island, was manifested by innumerable continental diversions subsidized by the English cabinet, and Parisians were unhappy and complaining out loud because of the never-ending conscriptions of their young. The cannon from the Invalides barked whenever there was good news but the accompanying bulletins, which were read from the stage in the theaters, were received without applause.

Hastening home from Vienna the emperor, who had decided to adopt Mazarin's matrimonial policy for Louis XIV and attach the proud House of Bavaria to his cause, stopped in Munich, its capital. The hand of the eldest Bavarian princess was a cheap price for that country's ruler to pay for the Pressburg treaty's elevation of Bavaria from a duchy to a kingdom. To inform Eugène de Beauharnais, Josephine's unsuspecting son, who was now Viceroy of Italy, that he had found that young man a suitable bride, the emperor sent off from Munich a cup painted with a glorified likeness of the teenaged Princess Augusta. A scant two weeks later they were wed—a union that proved to be surprisingly happy—and the emperor continued on his way.

In line with the same agenda, and imitating early day popes who consecrated cardinals from their own family ranks, the emperor soon gave the throne of Holland to his brother Louis and that of Naples to his brother Joseph. He would, in similar fashion, reward his closest collaborators, thereby binding them ever more closely to his empire's fortunes. This creation of a new aristocracy of fief holders, personally attached to the imperial throne, was a scheme to which the Italian peninsula, already geographically divided into parcels, readily lent itself. The first week in June Napoleon, as King of Italy, imperiously annexed two small Neapolitan enclaves that the Church had held for some eight hundred years and, as a mark of great imperial favor, gave one to General Bernadotte, Joseph's brother-in-law, creating him the Prince of Ponte Corvo. The other Lilliputian property, Bénévento, he presented to Talleyrand, sending him, in characteristic fashion, an advance copy of the morrow's *Moniteur* together with an accompanying note: "You can see for yourself what I have just done for you." [5] He could not help but be pleased at such a public indication of his imperial standing.

Drawing aside the curtains around his master's bed to let the noon sun stream in, the following morning, the snobbish Courtiade queried: "How shall I address Your Excellency now? Will His Serene Highness wear the same suit His Excellency wore yesterday?" [6] The new Prince de Bénévent directed the stream of visitors and friends flocking to the rue du Bac at the news to proceed to Catherine's suite. "She's the one to congratulate. Women are always charmed to be princesses." [7] *Tout Paris* might titter at how fast Catherine started signing herself "the Reigning Princess of Talleyrand," but a perspicacious few quickly spotted the appropriate crown her husband wasted no time in adding to his family coat of arms. A word from the new sovereign, granted during a chance encounter, was considered like a blessing, and the slightest courtesy, a favor. Perhaps, because the revenue Bénévent produced was minimal—roughly one fifth of that from Valençay—Bénévent's new "Ruling Prince," a title transmissible to his male children, never visited its one small town that housed almost half of its some forty thousand natives.

Once again Talleyrand was a disapproving participant in events which he seemed to direct. The empire of the Hapsburgs was now no more than a phantom, and Napoleon was in a position to reconstruct central Europe. The remaining mosaic of small western and southern German-speaking states could no longer count on defeated Austria for assistance and, because many were desirous of avoiding Prussian domination, it was only natural that they should look to Napoleon for the security that the defeated Austrians had previously provided. Consequently, they were anxious for the proposed new Confederation of the Rhine, which Napoleon now offered as a substitute for the thousand-year-old Holy Roman empire and which was intended to serve as a solid buffer to protect the French empire. The tiny, young Baron Emmerich de Dalberg, a scion of a most distinguished Rhineland family, who had been recently appointed the Baden minister at Paris, won his spurs as a new recruit to Talleyrand's inner circle—he was of the same stripe—by adroitly maneuvering the German princes into line. His uncle, the Archbishop Charles de Dalberg, provided an invaluable assist and, following Talleyrand's canny suggestion, chose Cardinal Fesch, Napoleon's uncle, as his coadjutor.

Since every chancellery in Europe now knew the French foreign affairs minister's *modus operandi*, envoys of the principalities, duchies, landgraviates involved, who came and went at the rue du Bac, were amply supplied with gold. But it is generally agreed that the sums Talleyrand realized this time were nowhere near as huge as those in the past. He received each diplomat separately and, frequently, at dinner while, in an alcove at the end of the long gallery on one side, several musicians played excerpts from Mozart's *The Magic Flute*. So no one knew the terms of the others' agreements, which had already been worked out by Talleyrand's discreet agents. The resultant treaty forming the Confederation of the Rhine was signed at the ministry in mid-July. Each member of this offensive-defensive alliance with France was to be represented at a new diet to be convened periodically at Frankfurt under the presidency of Archbishop Dalberg who was now elevated to Prince-Primate. Of the numerous Germanic states remaining after the famous Recès, three years before, which had cleared the left bank of the Rhine for French occupancy, ultimately sixteen joined this new group, thereby placing all southern Germany under French protection. In recognition of these mind-boggling events, one month later, the Hapsburg Francis II, had no choice but to officially dissolve the archaic Holy Roman empire of which he was the head and which had never, even in its heyday, possessed a lot of German-speaking lands, and become simply Francis I, emperor of Austria.

Although Napoleon authorized the construction, under Jean-François Chalgrin, of not one, but two "arcs de triomphe"—the more famous of which still stands—celebrating the triumphs of the Grande Armée, not all France was unanimously in support of His Imperial Majesty's plans. Metternich, the new Austrian ambassador, who arrived in Paris the following month, soon advised his government that there was no longer a single party in France but two. One was composed of the military and those whose fortunes were shackled to Napoleon's dream of a Europe ruled by France. The other comprised those who foresaw that Napoleon's ambition would ultimately ruin France and included Talleyrand who, the Viennese chancellery learned, was commencing "to oppose with all his strength and influence, the destructive projects of the Emperor." [8]

The formation of the Confederation of the Rhine hardly improved French relations with Prussia, which had signed a treaty with

Russia some time before Austerlitz and, in mid-September, after many disquieting rumors, Prussian troops invaded Saxony. In short order Napoleon left Saint-Cloud for the East. Talleyrand arrived at Mainz three days after the emperor had already moved ahead, but Josephine and part of the imperial court were already established here on the Rhine. So was her daughter Hortense who, as queen of Holland, had been sent there to avoid possible English capture. As the cold, wet days of October slipped past and November's frosty breath foretold the advent of a northern European winter, Hortense saw the celebrated foreign affairs minister in a different light than she had as a girl at Malmaison: "The attentions of a man who rarely confers them are always effective. . . . When . . . [Talleyrand] unbends to the extent of speaking to you, he seems utterly charming. And if he goes so far as to enquire about your health, you are prepared to love him forever." [9]

In the days to come, Talleyrand, who kept busy scouring the city's famous book dealers for rare volumes for his library, did not hide from the two Dalbergs—uncle and nephew—his disapproval of this new war. While he was substituting a cure at nearby Wiesbaden for a visit to Bourbon-l'Archambault, the French overwhelmed the Prussians at Iéna and Auerstadt, taking more than two hundred and fifty regimental flags and capturing more than one hundred thousand Prussians. Because of the breakneck speed of the Grande Armée's advance, the amplitude of the Prussian disaster and the extent of the combat zone, news of the French successes against the fabled German forces, still basking in their former reputation for invincibility under the late Frederick the Great, took ten days to reach Talleyrand. Meanwhile, Murat's heroic cavalry continued on and cleared the road to Berlin where he soon checked into the appropriated Unter den Linden mansion of the Prussian minister of state.

Prussia had been conquered in less than a month, and Napoleon was convinced that he could quickly finish off the Russian armies, which were pouring westward. That left England as the only other enemy now facing France. During the past spring and summer, serious attempts at reconciliation with London, when Fox became the Foreign Secretary after Prime Minister Pitt's death, came to naught with the former's own untimely end. With Fox passed the last hope of peace between the two. Finally realizing that, despite his enormous land-based power, he could never prevail militarily because of England's geographic position, Napoleon decided to accomplish the same ends by utilizing his great war machine to sever its commercial lifeline and starve it into submission. His famous Continental Blockade became the fulcrum of his entire future course of action, a draconian measure, which forbade any commerce with that country and the confiscation of all products made there. Correspondence across the Channel was prohibited and English citizens were subject to French internment as prisoners of war. Called upon to furnish historical and legal precedents to justify so unwise a measure, Talleyrand did so in a long position paper, dated November 20. Because his memorandum was copied, almost verbatim, into the official imperial embargo, which was promulgated the following day, some authorities unrealistically hold him largely responsible for the thinking behind this disastrous edict. In order to be effective, as Talleyrand well knew—and Napoleon should have—no leakage from any port on the continent was possible, and the blockade could only be successful with the cooperation of every European country allied with France or occupied by French forces. Russia and the neutral nations of Europe must also yield or face invasion by the Grande Armée and be forced to comply—a tyrannical submission which could only breed further wars.

But this was not the only possible *causus belli* on the horizon to concern Talleyrand. For Napoleon had discovered in the royal palace at Potsdam a recent letter from Madrid, which the Prussian king had accidently left behind when he fled his capital. In this Spain, although France's ally for the past six years, treacherously agreed to attack the French in the rear while Napoleon was engaged beyond the Rhine. Shortly afterwards, when word was received that the Spanish army was mobilizing, the emperor angrily confided to Talleyrand that he would destroy the Spanish branch of the Bourbons. This undoubtedly dispersed any remaining illusions Talleyrand might have nourished that he still could temper Napoleon's actions. For once there seems to be no reason not to take him at his word, when he wrote in his *Mémoires*, years later—albeit with the advantage of self-serving hindsight—"I then swore to myself that I would cease to be his minister as soon as we returned to France."

Shortly before Napoleon pressed on to meet the Russian regiments now advancing to their ally's assistance, Talleyrand was at his side to receive a deputation of influential Polish leaders from the Prussian-held section of Poland. They regarded the emperor as their fatherland's long-awaited savior and came begging for help. For generations, Paris had been a great magnet for the Polish aristocracy, most of whose education had been by French preceptors at home, or in the French capital, where so many of them went to acquire a sheen. They spoke the language fluently, and their love affair with all things French went back for at least two centuries when the Poles had elected a son of Catherine de Medici, Prince Henri d'Orléans, their king. The recent Prussian debacle at French hands renewed their hope for a restoration of their homeland, which had been divided three times in the last thirteen years—1772, 1793, 1795—between its rapacious neighbors, Russia, Austria, and Prussia, and now no longer existed as an independent entity. Like most of his diplomatic contemporaries, Talleyrand considered Russia, whom he distrusted and whose tsar was unwilling to make peace, an eastern rather than a European power. Theoretically, a strong and independent Poland, separating Prussia and Russia geographically, like a wedge, as it did, should serve as a barrier against Russian aggression in the west. So the emperor instructed him to appear in Warsaw as soon as it was successfully occupied, with all threat of danger past, in order to evaluate the situation on the spot and offer advice concerning that country's future.

Considering the rigors of his last trip in the Grande Armée's wake, Talleyrand could not have been too happy at the prospect of spending further time still farther away from the pleasures and comforts of Paris, with the predominantly crude, tough, military high command for daily companions, instead of the select few with whom he customarily preferred to spend his soirées. His lameness made it difficult to get in and out of a carriage without assistance and his fastidiousness made the abominable roads and lack of amenities intolerable. Since the inns along the way were in the poorest of conditions, filthy and full of repugnant bugs, he often continued to travel through the night, for his traveling berlin was well equipped and complete, naturally, with a *chaise percée*. When his marching orders came, he set forth with the usual entourage—Courtiade, a cook, and four other servants—following in separate coaches. He was also accompanied by a translator and certain members from the different sections of the rue du Bac ministry, whom he authorized to appear booted at meals, regardless of who else might be present, because it was impossible for each to travel with the customary, prerequisite wardrobe. Because the route across the eastern marshlands was a river of mud, which was now freezing, accidents were numerous. At one point his own coach tipped over but, luckily, he himself was not hurt.

Since there was not sufficient help along that deserted stretch to right it immediately, and not even a military one-horse chaise—which he had already been forced to resort to, more than once—Talleyrand spent the night in his mud-caked carriage where it lay on its side in the half-frozen ditch. Help arrived with the dawn, but it took a good half of a day before the minister could continue.

The ashen, pinched faces of the peasants he spotted along the way spoke volumes about the country's deplorable poverty. But they did not prepare Talleyrand for the scabby, maimed beggars, both young and old, whom he saw on both sides as he entered Warsaw, scrambling like maggots over refuse, fighting for the few edible morsels that could be salvaged from the piles of garbage which were a fixture even in the palace courtyards. Winter had already laid a heavy hand on the somber city along the Vistula, reducing it to a drab study in black and white. More Asiatic in appearance than European, Warsaw's several fine avenues with numerous squares surrounded by handsome buildings compared favorably with those in other European capitals except for their almost total lack of illumination, a severe handicap during the long nights at this season. Talleyrand was assigned a splendid mansion on the Avenue Miodowa, which had been built by Tepper, a rich banker who had been assassinated some years before—and boasted the one bed with side curtains in all Warsaw. An additional advantage was that its chimneys did not smoke, unlike those in a similar large establishment made available for the flamboyant Joachim Murat and his officers.

Napoleon's advance guard had galloped into Warsaw several weeks before, led by Murat, the most spectacular cavalry general of the age, as gaudily attired with flying plumes and much gold braid as if he were leading one of his famed—and feared—battle charges. Prominent among those aides-de-camp who never left his side in the recent blistering campaign was Charles de Flahaut whom Talleyrand had personally arranged to have transferred to the general's staff, several years earlier. A son to be proud of, Charles's bravery had singled him out for mention in a number of Grande Armée dispatches. And here, far from Paris, where animosity between Adèle and Catherine tended to keep father and son apart, the pair had a chance to become reacquainted. But not for long.

Unfortunately relations, which were already strained between Murat and Flahaut, the reputed lover of his wife, Caroline Bonaparte, were not helped when the general, on a whim, decided his immediate staff must don uniforms of the same color as his livery—amaranthe, white, and gold. When Charles indignantly refused, claiming he was a soldier not a footman, an incensed Murat demanded his transfer. Napoleon, who had just returned from an inspection tour of various advance locations, and never took kindly to his sister's many paramours, was happy to oblige. Claiming pettily that he could never see what women saw in that young man—"with his never-ending legs"—the five-foot two emperor who, nevertheless, knew how to reward indisputable merit, promoted the twenty-two-year-old to captain, then ordered him to the Thirteenth Light Cavalry nearer the front.

Because Poland's terrain, like the weather conditions, was vastly different from that in which his soldiers were accustomed to fighting, the emperor felt the need for more time in order to strengthen his supply lines and raise a large army of Polish volunteers. With fighting thus temporarily out of the question and the Carnival season just beginning, His Imperial Majesty declared amusement to be the order of the moment, regardless of the short dreary days and overcast skies. Although intoxicated with joy and hope, the aristocracy had trouble organizing fêtes because their "liberators"—as they hopefully referred to the French—were occupying the only suitable palaces, reducing the rightful tenants to a few small back rooms where it was impossible to entertain properly.

After much hurried discussion it was decided that the first great ball should take place at Talleyrand's. Because, even there, the available space necessitated limiting the invitations, only fifty women were included, each one waiting with bated breath for a glimpse of the man who was making all Europe tremble. Suddenly, the doors into the great hall opened noisily and Talleyrand appeared to announce in his deep voice the magic words "The Emperor!" Dragging his bad leg, he slowly preceded Napoleon around the room to introduce him to the assembled guests. Among those present was the Countess Marie de Walewska, the dainty, fair-haired, eighteen-year-old whom the emperor's roving eye had already singled out. Disguised as a peasant, Marie had been among those offering him bouquets when he stopped to change horses at the post station Bronie, before entering the city's gates for the first time. But what role, if any, Talleyrand played in the emperor's successful, whirlwind courtship of this patriotic young Iphigenia, whose seventy-year-old husband had been convinced by the city fathers that the future of Poland depended on her captivating Napoleon, is not clear.

That same evening, the Warsaw magnates, who had previously presented to Talleyrand—through the intermediary of Baron Emmerich de Dalberg—a sizeable sum to assure his backing for martyred Poland's cause, were in for a shock. Unaware that, in his capacity as grand chamberlain, he was also little more than a glorified maître d'hôtel with some belittling obligations in the imperial household, those dignitaries may have had second thoughts about their lobbyist's vaunted effectiveness. For, whenever Napoleon announced he was thirsty, it was Talleyrand, a fine damask napkin over his arm, a vermeil tray in his hand, who presented a gold goblet filled with lemonade—that had been pretested for poison, as with everything Napoleon either ate or drank—to His Imperial Majesty. However, as one of the titled guests observed admiringly: "His aristocratic hauteur never leaves him, whatever he does." [10]

Once the fighting resumed on the lower Vistula, news of the two-day battle at Eylau, one of the bloodiest in history and fought in a blinding blizzard, slowly trickled back. Talleyrand did not find his son's name among the never-ending lists of casualties and wasted no time requesting that Murat return Flahaut to his Warsaw staff. When Talleyrand wrote Murat a second time, as a follow-up, his letter so advising Charles was of such surprising tenderness that Flahaut forwarded it to his mother, Adèle, who treasured it the rest of her life:

> "Today I have written to [Murat] . . . to repeat my request that he recall you to his side. I was as insistent as if this were something personal—and it is. . . . Whenever you find a scrap of paper, write me how you are, what you are doing, and what you would like. You are one of the principal interests of my life and when I say that, I am reducing them to two or three . . . I embrace you and press you to my heart." [11]

Charles was not his only young offspring on Talleyrand's mind. Far away though he was from Paris, he expected to be kept fully posted on seven-year-old Charlotte and, when he did not hear, sizzling dispatches home demanded: "Why have I given you a writing master if he does not send me your news?" [12] Other family matters were of equal concern.

Louis de Talleyrand-Périgord, the elder of his brother Archambaud's two sons, and presently an aide-de-camp of General Berthier, was in and out of Warsaw frequently with dispatches from Berlin. Talleyrand's legitimate heir, he had recently come of age, which meant that it was his uncle's obligation, as head of the Talleyrand-Périgord branch, to find him an appropriate—a euphemism for rich and aristocratic—bride. Talk frequently revolved around this search when Talleyrand sat late in front of the roaring, crackling fireplace in his high-ceilinged, book-lined study with Count Alexander Batowski, the official liaison officer of the *pro tem* Warsaw Government with French General Headquarters. Batowski, who was the son-in-law of a Parisian banker friend of Talleyrand's, Vicomte Edouard de Walkiers, had not realized that the French emperor was reserving any suitable, unmarried French heiresses for his own officers, as part of a calculated program to build up a Napoleonic aristocracy. In an effort to be helpful, since Talleyrand was now hunting abroad for such a gem, Batowski repeatedly mentioned the fourteen-year-old Princess Dorothea de Courland, the youngest daughter of one of the wealthiest families in Europe—"She is a Peruvian gold mine." [13] This nugget Talleyrand carefully stored away with other pertinent information, although Batowski failed to disclose that Dorothea was also his own natural daughter.

With Eylau indecisive and the Russians still to be beaten, Napoleon remained in the field to oversee regimental regroupments. Both the climate and the Russians were inexorable; never before had he encountered such difficulties. In the emperor's absence, Talleyrand assumed the role of acting governor of French-occupied Warsaw with all the additional administrative activities this entailed. Since Napoleon also instructed him to keep his finger on the local pulse, he had never less than twenty for dinner nightly, including natives as well as some of the foreign ambassadors and functionaries who had long since caught up with Napoleon's base.

He also doubled as a military intendant, purveying all the needs of the Grande Armée, which was suffering greatly because of the unusually severe winter. The men were short of everything, and the poverty-stricken countryside had already been stripped bare by the previous passage of Russian troops. Greatly concerned, the emperor sent orders to close Warsaw's gates and seize, for his soldiers, the food brought in daily to feed its citizens. After Talleyrand and General Berthier courageously pointed out that to do so ran the risk of provoking a rebellion of the local populace, Napoleon was forced to look elsewhere.

Talleyrand's new responsibilities included visiting hospitals to comfort the wounded veterans and distributing gratifications—medals and money. And, as so often throughout his life, a woman was at hand to help him—Countess Marie-Thérèse Tyszkiewicz, the niece of Stanislaus-Augustus, the last King of Poland. Talleyrand's mistress from day one of his arrival, Marie-Thérèse, the middle-aged wife of a fat, enormously wealthy homosexual, was not particularly attractive physically, with one inadequately camouflaged glass eye which, gossip averred, she had received, years before, escaping discovery during a midnight tryst with a lover. Although she was not happy at the minister's dalliance with the ballerinas and stars of the Comédie-Française whom Napoleon had ordered to Warsaw to entertain while he was in residence, the resourceful countess turned her salon into an annex of Talleyrand's headquarters and enlisted the help of her brother, Prince Josef Poniatowski. A future marshal of the Grande Armée, the prince was invaluable in the enlistment of the newly formed elite Volunteer Polish Corps, and Talleyrand and his entire staff attended the blessing of its regimental flags at a brilliant ceremony on the Place de Saxe before it left for the front.

When Napoleon settled down at the great fortified schloss of Finkenstein to await the spring thaws, the Countess Walewska joined him, and Talleyrand did likewise. It was a lonely life at best, in the midst of the endless eastern marches, with no other women around and, one evening, he surprised the emperor's brother-in-law, Prince Borghese, bored to distraction, dancing a *contredanse* with a chair for his partner while fellow officers hummed an improvised tune. Napoleon worked long hours governing his vast European empire from this remote bastion, driving his officers and overworked staff hard. Even Talleyrand, used to late hours though he was, sometimes found it difficult to keep awake. One night, while the wind howled outside and still another spring storm unexpectedly blew down from the north, depositing yet more snow, the foreign affairs minister caught His Imperial Majesty dozing off in the midst of a conference the pair were having. Protocol notwithstanding, Talleyrand gathered an armful of cushions and stretched out also. Napoleon was the first to awaken. Furious at such *lèse majesté* on the part of a subordinate, he rudely shook his minister awake: "Scoundrel! How dare you sleep in the presence of the Emperor!" [14]

Napoleon rejoined his divisions shortly before the Russians' crushing defeat at Friedland, where Flahaut again covered himself with glory and, as one of only fifteen survivors from the entire Thirteenth Light Cavalry, was once more promoted. When Talleyrand wrote to congratulate the emperor from Dantzig, the recently capitulated, key fortress of the Baltic, he courageously included a word of warning, as he had after Austerlitz—a brave thing to do, knowing the imperial frame of mind. Talleyrand hoped that Friedland was the last battle the emperor would wage, let alone participate in personally, as he had at Eylau, and now, "exposing himself to new perils, even though I know how much Your Majesty disdains them." [15] The past months on the Grande Armée's trail had vividly underscored what unnecessary risks Napoleon's aggressive policies were posing not only for the emperor personally but also—and even more importantly—for the fragile new empire which rested almost solely on the imperial shoulders. Talleyrand did not dissimulate to Dalberg and other intimates his concern. As the frightening revelation of Napoleon's epilepsy had earlier emphasized, the same unanswered question loomed ever larger: What might happen should Napoleon be killed? The dreary bogs, the monotonous plains, and vast spaces only contributed further to such disturbing thoughts.

Talleyrand was not the only one close to Napoleon thinking along similar lines. A series of letters he received from General Caulaincourt who, as Master of the Horse, was also a member of the imperial entourage, shows that, while there was still strong enthusiasm for war and all its attendant honors among the military, Caulaincourt and certain others were battle weary; they were anxious to shore up their personal situations through a peaceful consolidation of the empire—by means of a withdrawal to France's natural frontiers and an assurance of the imperial succession. The same fatigue with war was echoed in Paris, where the bells of Notre Dame were forever tolling for yet another *Te Deum* to commemorate still more dead.

Alexander's surprising request for an armistice, following the disorderly retreat of his troops straggling eastward after Friedland, necessitated the foreign affairs minister's presence at the Tilsit treaty table. Upon his arrival combative General Savary arrogantly informed him "If peace is not concluded within a fortnight, Napoleon will cross the Niemen."—"And what, pray tell, will he be doing on the other side?" [16] Talleyrand coolly queried. The ironic courteousness of his reply—a form of humor in which he excelled—was unquestionably lost on the gruff soldier. A small barge had been constructed with two richly decorated tents and anchored in a suitable spot in the river separating their respective armies, to enable the two emperors—the tall blond, thirty-year-old

Romanoff and the tiny dark, thirty-eight-year-old Corsican—to be rowed out and meet on neutral ground in the middle.

That first day, defeated, humiliated, and uninvited, Friedrich-Wilhelm III sat astride his horse on the muddy right bank, in the drizzle, his eyes glued on the floating trysting place, awaiting the return of his ally, the tsar, who held in his hand the fate of the Prussian king and of his kingdom. To Talleyrand's embarrassment—and unlike in the past—he neither participated in any of the rulers' discussions, nor did he share the emperor's ear. Napoleon knew that Talleyrand no longer saw eye-to-eye with him on his plans for Europe, so his duties were confined to a strictly secondary level, limited to executing the details and signing the treaties with his Russian and Prussian counterparts. Yet, at Tilsit, major decisions were made. By a *tour de force*, Napoleon persuaded Alexander to desert Prussia and, instead, to form an alliance with France to bring England, France's one remaining enemy, to her knees. Napoleon was as pitiless towards Prussia as he had been with Austria, stripping the former of more than a third of its territory and of some five million inhabitants. However, Talleyrand did concur in the decision not to return Poland to its people. After six months on the scene, he now deemed this impossible; the Poles were too divided among themselves. Uncharacteristically and for the first time on record, he returned money, which he already had in his pocket, but he could not help the dejected Warsaw citizens who had hoped to have him intervene successfully on their behalf.

During their two weeks at Tilsit, both on the barge and during their long daily horseback rides together, Napoleon and Alexander became friends and tried to outdo each other in sumptuous exchanges of gifts; the French emperor would wear the sable-lined coat he received on all future winter campaigns. Early in July, 1807, the French, anxious to return home, broke camp. As the emperor hurried west, Talleyrand, who found travel so increasingly disagreeable, traveled more slowly.

10

Vice-Grand Elector

"The only vice he lacks."—Fouché [1]

TALLEYRAND'S HEALTH HAD SUFFERED greatly from these past months of breakneck travel at the emperor's beck and call and, now, as he proceeded leisurely westward, there was ample time to consider his own future in the light of recent events. Certainly no one could accuse him of deserting Napoleon when imperial fortunes were on the wane. Expert as he had proven at foreseeing the future and, given his serious misgivings about Napoleon's present course of action, which he seemed increasingly unable to temper, he was more than ever convinced that peace was in the best interests not only of France but also of Europe. So there is every reason to believe that by the time he reached Paris, Talleyrand's mind was made up to leave the Galliffet. Insiders quoted Talleyrand as saying "I do not want to become the executioner of Europe" [2] and his self-serving *Mémoires* state "I left the ministry as I wished." While Paris was unable to decide whether he exited by the door or by the window, the lack of unbiased contemporary accounts declaring that Talleyrand was ousted is the best possible indication that his resignation was mutually acceptable. Those in a good position to know, like the haughty Austrian ambassador, Count Klemens von Metternich—for whom mankind only began with a count and whose affair as one of the many lovers of the emperor's sister, Caroline, assured him of a direct imperial pipeline—were caught unawares and frankly astonished at the news.

While there is no specific evidence how the pair actually came to terms, and to bargain with His Imperial Highness was unimaginable, Talleyrand must have been delighted with the outcome. Ten days later he was sworn in, at Saint-Cloud, as the imperial vice-grand elector—"the only vice he lacks," [3] jeered Fouché, the jealous police minister. Since Napoleon's older brother, Joseph, who held the lifetime post of grand elector, was now King of Naples and no longer lived in Paris, Napoleon created this post especially for Talleyrand. His new dignity was accompanied by a greatly augmented stipend, a different, equally elaborate, red velvet uniform—a jacket and cloak trimmed with still more gold, to be worn over his white culottes; lace sleeves embroidered from cuff to shoulder in gold; a magnificent black felt hat, bound with gold braid and topped by a flowing bouquet of white feathers—and a new coat of arms. As vice-grand elector he ranked immediately after the Imperial Family and the former second and third consuls: the arch-chancellor, Cambacérès; and Lebrun, the arch-treasurer. His Carolingian title, like theirs, originated in Charlemagne's court, and he could now be seated alongside them to hear *Te Deum* at Notre Dame, rather than be relegated to the row behind. This glorified post was devoid of any real functions, relieving Talleyrand of daily routine, as well as of public responsibility for the implementation of policies of which he highly disapproved. Talleyrand did not forfeit his privilege to enter the imperial apartments at any time, and the emperor could still seek his advice whenever he wished, without having to contend daily with the constant opposition of such an independent, strong-willed official.

The official celebration that August of Napoleon's birthday heralded in several weeks of almost Oriental splendor and magnificence at the Tuileries. Concerts, ballets, and fireworks succeeded each other nightly. Elegantly attired Parisians, the women aglitter with diamonds, the men ablaze with decorations, jostled with ambassadors and the greatest European seigneurs; present, too, were new heads of state from the recently realigned Germanic countries who owed their present titles to Napoleon, and numerous petty royalty, anxiously currying favor. Nineteen-year-old Catherine de Wurtemberg also arrived for her wedding in the Tuileries chapel to Napoleon's brother Jérôme, whose new kingdom, Westphalia, had been created at Tilsit; theirs was to be one of the few happy, dynastic marriages arranged by the French emperor. Already on the plump side, it was hoped that Catherine would never assume the grotesque proportions of her father, the Wurtemburg monarch, who escorted her there and who was so obese that he was accompanied by a special table constructed to accommodate his enormous girth whenever he sat down at a meal.

That fall, a completely refurbished Fontainebleau was opened for six weeks, from late September to mid-November, and Napoleon ordered the imperial court, his cabinet as well as other dignitaries—some twelve hundred in all—to appear for the entire autumn hunting season. To create the desired ambiance—and bolster the French fashion industry and commerce in general—prescribed formal attire was required for each occasion and, where the ladies were concerned, no gown could be worn twice. As in the days of Louis XIV and Louis XV, a regular schedule was set up: Napoleon received once weekly in his apartments; on specified days there were receptions, followed by cards and gambling, in the empress's suites. Twice a week, the Comédie-Française would come out and perform, and a rotating schedule was established whereby different members of the emperor's family, his immediate entourage, and the various cabinet ministers were assigned certain evenings to entertain the more prominent guests and visiting plenipotentiaries at still more dinners and balls. The hunt, which was very popular, was held on fixed days, weather not withstanding, but only those designated in advance might attend—whether on horseback or in one of the imperial stables' elegant calèches. As in pre-revolutionary days, specified attire for the men was mandatory, but now Napoleon decided that the women must do likewise. Their hunting costumes were designed by LeRoi, the couturier *à la mode*, with each princesses' household assigned a different color. However, affairs of state were not neglected, and the emperor maintained a heavy workload.

For whatever reasons—recent investigations indicate he was being blackmailed by a mysterious Mme Beaugeard who had played some role at the time of Charlotte's birth—Talleyrand felt the time had arrived to become the legal guardian of the eight-year-old. But, aside from the brief appearance this entailed before a Paris first arrondissement justice of the peace, he remained at Fontainebleau for the entire season. Each evening Napoleon withdrew early and summoned Talleyrand almost nightly for long private talks during which they also discussed the secret treaty that was being hammered out with Spain. Portugal, because of its close ties with England, had been flagrantly ignoring the Continental Blockade, and the surest way to stanch this hemorrhaging was to seize the possessions of its reigning House of Braganza. To do so, French troops must pass through northern Spain, and the present negotiations, which were intended to facilitate their passage, were soon enlarged to spell out a joint Spanish-French expedition to seize and apportion Portugal between themselves.

At some point another factor imperceptibly crept in. Napoleon had had his eye on the whole Iberian Peninsula, presumably, at least, ever since the year before when he learned, in Berlin, that his supposed Spanish ally had treacherously agreed to attack him in the rear when least expected. And, by now, that country resembled a well-ripened pear ready to be plucked. For the Spanish Bourbons were locked in a bitter, three-way power struggle between the adherents of King Charles IV, who was in the last stages of senility, and the ugly queen, Maria-Louisa—both portrayed so vividly for posterity by Goya—with the followers of their oldest son and heir, Ferdinand, the Prince of Asturias, as well as with those of the omnipotent Godoy, the Spanish prime minister. What easier way to establish French domination over the entire land below the Pyrénées than by this joint expedition which would, like the entry of the famous Wooden Horse on the plains of Troy, ensure the unopposed, peaceful penetration of French troops into Spain? As with his earlier involvement in the Directoire's ill-fated Egyptian episode, Talleyrand's exact responsibility, if any, for this change of emphasis is not known. This is unfortunate. For nothing, with the possible exception of his involvement in the tragic death of the Duc d'Enghien, is more damaging for his reputation as a statesman than his precise role in this adventure which would prove so disastrous because it ultimately drained the military strength of the empire when it was most needed for the defense of the Rhine.

Admittedly obsessed with what future generations might think of him, Talleyrand would devote an entire separate section of his *Mémoires* to exculpate himself in this sorry episode. Fortunately, from his point of view, his longevity permitted him to continuously rework this chapter, which did not appear until long after most of those contemporaries who might have contradicted him passed away. Had there really been a letter confirming his involvement across the Pyrénées that Chateaubriand, ever one of Talleyrand's more acrimonious detractors, claimed to have seen? If any such incriminating evidence did exist regarding his purported role in the Peninsular War—and, possibly, other equivocal matters—it was destroyed in the famous *auto-da-fé* of state documents that he hurriedly conducted in the Tuileries before the victorious allies entered Paris, in 1814.

On the face of it, for a man who attempted to temper the emperor's ambitions and limit France's liabilities after Austerlitz and, again, at Tilsit, to have favored, at the outset, this march southward seems highly unlikely. And those current reminiscences of the day, which held him to be one of the prime supporters of the emperor's Iberian policy, were, for the most part, written by colleagues who were already biased against Talleyrand. On the other hand, the attractive young Comtesse Claire de Remusat, a lady-in-waiting who, with her husband, was a prominent member of the imperial court and a favorite of Talleyrand, saw him almost daily at Fontainebleau, and her diary, written without *parti pris*, presents a more objective perspective on his life during this period. According to "Klari," Talleyrand was against the use of a firm hand in Portugal and strongly opposed the Spanish-French accord from the beginning; he did offer advice, and complained that it was not taken. Napoleon would always maintain the contrary and that Talleyrand was not as innocent as he would have liked posterity to believe. The truth probably lies somewhere in between for Talleyrand, an experienced courtier, was adept at pandering and telling the emperor what His Imperial Majesty wanted to hear and, more than once, followed through on imperial policies which were diametrically opposed to his own.

On October 15, in front of Talleyrand and the entire court Napoleon lashed out at the Portuguese minister in one of those carefully arranged public scenes in which His Imperial Majesty excelled. "I will not permit a single English envoy in Europe! If Portugal does not do what I wish, within two months the House of Braganza will no longer reign in Europe!" [4] A formal declaration of war against that country soon followed.

While Catherine, Her Most Serene Highness, the Princess de Talleyrand, was busy assuming extravagant new airs, more in keeping, she felt, with the dignity of the wife of the number three dignitary in the land, Talleyrand resumed his busy, pre-Galliffet life of daily rounds of visits to keep abreast of the news. He attended the popular lectures being given by Dr. F. J. Gall at the Athenaeum explaining phrenology, that learned man's new study purporting to prove that the conformation of the skull was indicative of mental faculties and character. And his nightly whist parties with his cronies recommenced. He was also pulling strings to get his son, Flahaut, assigned to Berthier's General Staff, the ultimate training pool for the emperor's personal aides-de-camp. Talleyrand likewise performed other new, largely ceremonial, duties. He was required to sign the birth certificate of the future Napoleon III. Queen Hortense of Holland, the wife of Napoleon's brother, Louis, nearly fainted from the overpowering ambergris odor of his heavily powdered hair—still his own—when Talleyrand dragged himself up to her bed, afterwards, to compliment her. Meanwhile, his home on the rue d'Anjou was a mecca for those innumerable foreign ambassadors and dignitaries, not to mention Parisians, who considered him the sole voice for peace in the empire as France and Europe watched with mounting alarm the latest manifestations of Napoleon's burning determination—ever since the rupture of the peace of Amiens—to conquer England.

Almost simultaneously with the entry of Junot's men into Lisbon, the emperor, intent on expanding and consolidating his power in Italy and sequestering its entire coastline, reached Milan after a difficult crossing of Mont Cenis. Already possessing the northern and southern parts of the Italian boot, he now wanted the middle and, soon, the entire papal administration would be in French hands and the successor of Saint Peter, Pope Pius VII, shut up in the Quirinal. Despite the lateness of the hour, when Napoleon returned to Paris, a month later, he immediately sent for Talleyrand and had the first of several, long, five-hour discussions with him about the latest developments. Once occupation of Portugal was a *fait accompli*, French troops proceeded to take possession of the most strategic positions in Spain. Slowly the bickering Spanish royal family realized Napoleon's treachery and, at Godoy's advice, they fled Madrid. The French emperor, who had headed south to be able to direct events closer to the scene—and was presently gamboling with Josephine on the beach south of Bordeaux—benevolently offered to meet them to help resolve their problems. These were now further complicated because Charles IV abdicated in favor of his not overly bright, oldest son, Ferdinand of Asturias and, then, retracted. Once together on French soil, at Bayonne, Napoleon brutally tricked father, mother, and heir into surrendering all claims as the ruling house of Spain, before graciously permitting the old king and queen to depart. He next persuaded a small clique of Spanish grandees to legally elevate his oldest Bonaparte brother to the now vacant throne as "don José Primero"—by switching Joseph from Naples and replacing him there with his brother-in-law, Caroline's husband, Joachim Murat. This was still another European scepter in the family—with Louis ruling in Holland; Jérôme, the King of Westphalia; and Josephine's son, Eugène de Beauharnais, Viceroy of Italy—and the French empire now extended from Gibraltar to Hamburg.

Little did Talleyrand realize, when he penned the prerequisite courtier's letter congratulating His Imperial Majesty on acquiring his latest crown jewel—and urging him not to expose himself needlessly by crossing the Pyrénées—that the very next morning Napoleon would send word that his vice-grand elector was to receive the former heir to the Spanish throne and his brother at his magnificent estate at Valençay. The imperial orders were detailed and explicit. Talleyrand himself must be there to welcome such distinguished guests and do all possible to amuse them; Mme de Talleyrand was also to be present, with four or five other ladies. "If the prince . . . should become attached to some pretty woman—preferably one whose loyalty to France was assured—so much the better as this would be the surest way to keep an eye on him." [5] The emperor might point out that it was a privilege and an honor to be designated the host of the royal pair, but Talleyrand was not fooled. He knew that Valençay had been deliberately chosen as their gilded prison to indelibly implicate him in the Spanish usurpation and to discredit him in the eyes of Europe as the custodian of the young *infantes* who had lost their heritage through deception. His reply, thanking Napoleon for the "honorable mission His Imperial Majesty deigned to give him," also gave no indication that he perceived the cynical innuendo—an unheard-of affront—regarding the role Napoleon indicated Catherine might play to make their guests feel at home.

Talleyrand and his wife, surrounded by their servants, decked out in red and yellow livery to match the Spanish flag flying from the central tower, were at Valençay's great portal to greet the twenty-four-year-old prince, the future Ferdinand VII; his younger brother; and their uncle. Accompanied by a large retinue as well as staff, some fifty in all, they drove up in clumsy, old-fashioned royal coaches, dating from the days of Philip V. The magnificence of their reception masked their true status as prisoners—they were to be here until

1814—and, from the start, they were treated with the same ceremony and etiquette as at the Escurial. No one was admitted to their presence without their permission, and anyone who approached them must be in court attire. On the other hand, they had far more freedom than in Madrid, where they could never go out together without their father's written permission. To be free to come and go as often as they desired was an unheard-of pleasure. Talleyrand also hired an old former guard of the Prince de Condé, who had taught the Duc de Bourbon, to show them how to shoot. Foucault, who had worked from childhood in the French royal stables, gave them riding lessons. Talleyrand's chef even learned how to cook the horrible Spanish ragouts they demanded. The terrace in front of the château was transformed into a ballroom for dancing the bolero and fandango, and guitarists, including the famous Castro, were stationed throughout the garden.

With matters going from bad to worse, Spain appealed to London for assistance and, three weeks after the initial English landing, Junot was chased from Portugal, surrendering his entire army of some twenty-six thousand to Wellesley, the future Duke of Wellington. By now, almost all of Spain was up in arms against the French army of occupation in what threatened to be a long-lasting guerilla war. With hope concurrently rising in subjugated Europe, Napoleon hastened north. He must call up reinforcements from the Grande Armée stationed as far away as the Rhine and the Vistula in order to stabilize the fast eroding Spanish situation and put Joseph, who had fled Madrid after only eleven harrowing days, back on his new throne. He wanted assurance that his ally, the tsar, would guarantee him a free hand below the border by keeping Austria, which was silently starting to rearm, a servile neutral. At Tilsit it had been understood that there would be a follow-up meeting with Alexander at Erfurt, a small, sleepy town in the middle of the Saxon duchies, roughly midway between their two countries, and the sooner this was held the better. In the treaty he now intended to extract from the tsar, the emperor had no intention of committing himself about any other joint future plans, even regarding the Levant. Since no one in the imperial entourage, including the present foreign affairs minister, was as well prepared to accomplish this as Talleyrand who, as a Talleyrand-Périgord, was never intimidated by even the greatest crowned head, the emperor summoned him to Nantes for a consultation en route.

The emperor's unfeigned delight in the success of his Bayonne coup aggravated Talleyrand's displeasure at his own unsolicited role as jail keeper, and he averred that His Imperial Majesty—who failed to appreciate the difference between his *coup d'état de brumaire* and this recent one—had lost more than he had gained by his swindle.

—"What do you mean?"

—"Mon Dieu! It's very simple and I will give you an example. If a gentleman commits a folly, treats his wife badly, even if he gravely wrongs his friends, he will, no doubt, be blamed. But, if he is rich, powerful, resourceful, society will treat him with indulgence. However, should that same man cheat at cards, he will immediately become *persona non grata* and never forgiven." [6]

Talleyrand claimed that the emperor turned pale, became embarrassed, and did not address another word to him that day. So it seems surprising that His Imperial Majesty, knowing of Talleyrand's disapproval of the Bayonne episode, should, nevertheless, have entrusted him with this delicate mission. Unlike the perspicacious Austrian Ambassador Metternich, who compared Talleyrand to a sword honed to a sharp point and knew that it was dangerous to toy with such a man, His Imperial Majesty evidently did not believe that anyone could—or would—gainsay him.

Leaving behind his wife and her ladies at Valençay—with her over-ripe charms, Catherine had interpreted her role as hostess literally, grasping at one last, autumnal fling as the mistress of the Duc de San Carlos, Ferdinand's chamberlain, who was ten years her junior— Talleyrand followed Napoleon to Paris. He just missed his son Charles de Flahaut, who was already in the Bayonne area and finally attached to General Berthier's staff. But often, on his way to a Tuileries conference concerning his own new eastern assignment, his carriage was forced to detour around the great Cour du Carrousel because still another division of the Guards was marching in review—only the Grande Armée was provided with transportation—before setting forth for the Pyrénées.

Heeding Napoleon's injunction that there was no negotiation that a sufficient spectacle of power would not facilitate, Talleyrand generated such excitement over the forthcoming meeting that every prince and sovereign worthy of the name considered it mandatory to appear there in homage to the French emperor. The same day that Talleyrand arrived at

Erfurt, September 24, Metternich wrote from Paris: "Talleyrand does not yet betray; he criticizes and wants to direct."

The little Saxon town on the river Gére was abuzz with activity when Talleyrand got there, almost a week ahead of Napoleon, to oversee that all was in readiness for its prestigious guests, and the first person he sought out was his friend, Caulaincourt, who was already there. Not only their mutual desire for peace had kept them in close touch since Tilsit, but also personal reasons. As French ambassador to Russia, Caulaincourt had placed Talleyrand's nephews, who were both in the military—his heir, Louis, who had died of typhoid some weeks before; and Edmond de Talleyrand-Périgord, his younger brother, who succeeded him as heir-presumptive—on the embassy staff in Saint Petersburg. Talleyrand was trying to get the emperor to waive the interdiction against any divorced woman serving in the Imperial household, so the disconsolate Caulaincourt could marry the beautiful Comtesse Adrienne de Canisy, one of Josephine's ladies-in-waiting, whose grandmother, the Comtesse de Brionne, had been, long ago, one of Talleyrand's dearly beloved mistresses. Caulaincourt desired an end to hostilities as much as he did and, in his last letter to him, before setting forth, Talleyrand voiced the hope that "not plans for war but overtures for peace would result from the forthcoming meeting."

Talleyrand had done his job well. Erfurt, which was still occupied by French troops since their victory at nearby Iéna, two years before, was Tilsit on an even more elaborate scale, rivaling François I and Henry VIII's famous "Field of the Cloth of Gold" encounter. The emperor, who was installed in the palace of the former prince-bishop, which was now smothered in purple hangings and golden bees, had ordered a *mis-en-scène* and display of unparalleled magnificence. So the Imperial storerooms and the state-owned Gobelin and Sèvres establishments obliged with a profusion of furniture, tapestries, and bibelots. As the focal point for the next two weeks, His Imperial Majesty was surrounded by an imposing cortège of marshals and generals, with a backdrop of subservient crowned heads, including his own brother, the new King of Westphalia with his plump, adoring bride, and the Bade heir apparent—who was the brother-in-law of Alexander I and had just wed Josephine's niece, a pretty blonde. For the kings of Bavaria, Wurtemburg, and Saxe, as well as the Grand Duchess of Bade, not to mention the numerous princes of the Confederation of the Rhine—each accompanied by their highest dignitaries—an appearance was equally mandatory. While the French emperor had refused to permit any official Austrian representative to be present, Baron de Vincent was allowed to be there as an observer, thanks to Talleyrand. He informed Vincent that he would do everything possible to assure that nothing transpired that would be destructive of Austrian interests and turned him over to his ubiquitous henchman, Baron Dalberg, the ever helpful Bade minister, to see that he was kept well abreast of all proceedings.

As much of a showman as the French emperor, Alexander tarried at Weimar to be sure not to arrive until after Napoleon. When the tsar did appear, surrounded by his Imperial Guard, Napoleon rode outside Erfurt's medieval walls to meet him, informally, and the pair returned to the accompaniment of martial music and a deafening twenty-one-gun salute apiece. Talleyrand presided at Alexander's ceremonial, courtesy visit to the French emperor, which followed. That evening, the Princess de Tour-et-Taxis, the Prussian queen's sister and a cousin of Alexander, sent over a footman to announce that she had just arrived, and Talleyrand hurried over to greet her. He barely set foot inside her salon when the autocrat of the north appeared unannounced and accompanied by Caulaincourt. Alexander promptly demanded a cup of tea and shortly afterwards disappeared into an alcove with Talleyrand. This was the way Talleyrand liked to do business—surrounded by beautiful women and a select company regaling each other with good conversation. So, apparently, did the tsar for, when he left, Alexander declared he would come back nightly, after each evening's official entertainment, for another cup of tea—to Talleyrand's delight. What easier way to obey Napoleon's injunction to see Alexander often to keep him in a cooperative frame of mind?

Contrary to his evasiveness regarding his involvement in the Enghien and Spanish affairs Talleyrand, in later years, never denied his betrayal of Napoleon at Erfurt. But what actually passed between Talleyrand and Alexander can never be unequivocally known—since there was no one else present—even though, upon his return home, he discussed these meetings with Metternich, who at once reported them to Vienna. While an analytical perusal of the cold historical facts does assign to Talleyrand an important role in the results obtained at Erfurt, it is not the supremely significant one he managed to stake out for himself in the eyes of the world as the savior of France and of Europe. His own version of what transpired at Erfurt, one of the best known episodes in his long life, is a prime example of Talleyrand's "Myth-Making" at its best, one which he proudly repeated to numerous colleagues over the years. They, in turn, accepted his account unquestioningly and reported it in their own memoirs, just as Talleyrand, concerned, as always, about his reputation with posterity, no doubt intended that they should.

In one of their earliest rendezvous Talleyrand, convinced that Alexander was the instrument to break the Napoleonic stranglehold on the continent, claims he went straight to the point, proposing not the French-Russian alliance which Napoleon wanted, in order to keep Vienna in tow, but a Russian-Austrian alliance against Napoleon.

> "Sire, it is for you to save Europe and you can only do so by standing up to Napoleon. . . . The French people are civilized. Their sovereign is not. . . . Therefore it is up to the sovereign of Russia to be the ally of the French people. The Rhine, the Alps, the Pyrénées, are the conquests of France. The other acquisitions are the conquests of Napoleon. France has no wish to keep them." [7]

Talleyrand arranged to have this identical point of view—that Napoleon was sacrificing France to his empire—also reach Alexander from different sources there, in order to convince him that it represented the thinking of all conscientious French citizens.

Each subsequent midnight, in the mundane setting of the Princess's fashionable apartments, the tsar revealed to Talleyrand the progress of that day's negotiations with Napoleon. Drinking tea with the women, then sitting apart, often three hours at a stretch, Talleyrand repeated the same themes, evening after evening while reviewing, pro and con, the proposals that the two sovereigns had just been discussing that day. Whenever Talleyrand suggested additions and deletions to be brought up the following morning, Alexander took down notes. Talleyrand was engaged in a great game for vast stakes, playing off against each other the two rulers on whom the fate of the continent depended. Some might claim that his admitted actions constituted treason to France and treachery to Napoleon, but Talleyrand knew treason's price. Ever the gambler, he was risking his own life to achieve an objective, which was neither personal nor petty.

The rapport between the two rulers was as good as at Tilsit and, bypassing their foreign ministers, they dealt one on one during those daytime meetings, which revolved around affairs of state. At night it was a different matter. In a setting straight out of the *Arabian Nights*, state dinners and balls succeeded each other in neighboring castles. A full troupe of thirty-two was brought from the Comédie-Française—including its greatest star Talma, as well as its newest ones, Mlle Duchesnois and Raucourt, and the captivating Mlle Bourgoin, "the goddess of joy and pleasure," who at once caught Alexander's roving eye—to present a repertoire chosen by Napoleon himself.

After discovering, on opening night, that the lavishly bedecked imperial loge with its celebrated "parterre of kings" was too far from the stage for his partially deaf guest of honor, who was also having trouble seeing but was too vain to wear glasses in public, his host ordered the orchestra pit covered over and two chairs placed upon it, one for himself and one for Alexander. During a production of Voltaire's *Oedipe*, at the famous line, "The friendship of a great man is a blessing of the gods," Alexander reached over and gripped Napoleon's hand emotionally, to the enthusiastic delight of the audience who interpreted his gesture to indicate that all was going well between the pair. Corneille's masterpiece, the tragedy *Cinna*, was produced, a few nights later, and one can only wonder whether Talleyrand who was seated, as grand chamberlain, in his accustomed place behind the emperor, concurred when the heroine, Emilie, declaimed, "Perfidy is noble when tyranny is involved."

Midway through the Erfurt schedule, a two-day excursion was planned, starting with a wild boar hunt in the nearby forest of Ettersbourg. Napoleon and the tsar made their base at Weimar, a small fortified town in the heart of the Thuringian mountains, which the Dowager Duchess Anna-Amalie, a niece of Frederick the Great, had made into an important cultural center. Here the two greatest living German men of letters, Wieland and Goethe, still resided. That night, at a dinner tendered in his honor by the reigning Grand Duke Charles-Augustus, the French emperor flaunted his humble beginnings—"When I was a lieutenant in the French artillery" [8]—before the startled other guests, mostly the proud hereditary heads of hoary dynasties now truckling to this *parvenu's* beck and call. Goethe, who was also present, was horrified by Talleyrand's appearance—his partially closed eyes, expressionless face and enigmatic smile. "One can conceive of his having such a face. One cannot conceive of how he can keep it." [9] En route home, the next day, the group visited the battlefield of Iéna and, with maps in hand, were given a step-by-step explanation of the Prussian defeat there.

One night both Alexander and Talleyrand appeared at the Princess de Tour-et-Taxis' earlier than usual, and the tsar asked their hostess not to receive any other guests that evening. Then he drew from his pocket a draft of the convention on which the two rulers were presently working, a document which, unbeknown to Alexander, had, in essence, been originally drawn up by Talleyrand himself before leaving Paris and which the tsar now wanted to go over with him. The French emperor had given the document—with a few personal additions—to the tsar to study with the express understanding that Alexander was not to show it to a soul.

Napoleon pressed Talleyrand to persuade the tsar to sign this projected agreement. Instead, he nightly urged Alexander, "Don't yield" and, in his *Mémoires*, he would proudly trumpet, "At Erfurt I saved Europe." Talleyrand, who had come to Erfurt determined to safeguard peace, had reason to feel that his nightly sessions with Alexander were successful for, when the final agreement was initialed by the respective foreign ministers, Napoleon did not get the outright assurance of assistance he wanted against Austria. Since the mercurial, weak tsar had already undergone a change of heart regarding French-Russian relations before his arrival, it is hard to evaluate exactly what weight Talleyrand's counseling carried, because many other factors also came into play. Perhaps, without his intervention, fickle Alexander might have acceded; but he had never been sincere with Napoleon and wrote his mother, "He who laughs last, gets the best laugh." [10] He also sent François II a personally written note—a rare courtesy—to assure Vienna not to be concerned about any measures taken at this meeting.

One last item remained on Napoleon's agenda. He had no heir and, because of the need to found a dynasty, the possibility of a divorce was already being openly discussed in Paris. Since one of Alexander's sisters, the Grand Duchess Catherine, was of an age to be considered a logical choice for a successor to Josephine, Talleyrand was entrusted with the delicate task of discreetly sounding out the tsar. The emperor would get his reply, three months later, when Catherine, whose mother referred to Napoleon in public as that "Corsican parvenu!" was engaged to the Prince d'Oldenburg. Napoleon might come away from Erfurt empty handed, matrimonially speaking; Talleyrand was more successful. Never one to waste an opportunity, he did not consider it *lèse majesté* to follow up his talks with Alexander about a potential French empress with a discussion of his own difficulty in finding a suitable—meaning "very wealthy"—bride for his sole remaining nephew and heir, Comte Edmond de Talleyrand-Périgord.

Adept at squirreling away nuggets of financial information for future reference and use, Talleyrand had never forgotten, in a similar conversation in Warsaw, over a year before, Count Batowski's description of an eligible Courland princess whose family was so rich that the Prussian government, embarrassingly short of cash, borrowed from it to pay for the late king's state funeral. Brazenly mixing personal with official business, Talleyrand now asked for her hand, since Princess Dorothea had become a Russian subject when her stepfather, Grand Duke Peter, sold Courland with its deep water Baltic ports to Catherine the Great. Her grandfather, plain Ernest Bührein, had received that country as a gift from Tsarina Anna, whose life-long paramour he had been. No other imperial favorite in Russian history, with the exception of Potemkin, ever wielded as much influence as the lusty Ernest. The ten years when Anna sat on the Russian throne are still known as the Age of Biron [as he later spelled his name]—Bironovishtchina.

No matter how posterity might question or attempt to diminish the exact value of Talleyrand's nocturnal conversations with Alexander, the tsar obviously felt he owed Talleyrand a debt of gratitude if only for his exposure of important stresses and strains within the emperor's own entourage. Sensing a way to pay his obligations to the notoriously mercenary Talleyrand, ruble-pinching Alexander, who was as tight with money as his lowliest serf, graciously gave his consent. To do so cost him nothing and assured him not only of Talleyrand's gratitude but of his continued valued services, and the tsar was anxious to keep his lines of communication open with him. In fact, Alexander was sufficiently pleased to render him an additional favor—a subtle attention which the latter accepted as such—re-routing his homeward journey by way of Löbikau, the Courland schloss in Saxony, in order to tell the grand duchess himself, as her liege lord, of his plans for her youngest child. It was not much of a detour, and it would be a pleasure to see the delectable Anna-Dorothea again. Their presumed affair had earlier titillated European court circles when Her Serene Highness came to Saint Petersburg to settle—as sovereign to sovereign—financial details regarding her late husband's estate. For all her vaunted femininity, the grand duchess could have outwitted

Attila the Hun and ridden roughshod over Genghis Khan had either one crossed her. And, in a matter of weeks, she negotiated the matter, which her emissaries had been unsuccessfully attempting to do for more than two years.

When the tsar left Erfurt, Caulaincourt, who had promised Talleyrand to act as intermediary in the affair—as well as to locate skins to bind books for his library, which Talleyrand had been having a hard time buying elsewhere—and the unsuspecting Comte Edmond de Talleyrand-Périgord, who had come west as part of his staff, accordingly joined Alexander's suite for the stop-off at Löbikau. Upon leaving the Courland estate, Caulaincourt continued on in Alexander's coach as far as Leipzig. From there he sent to Paris a glowing report concerning the Courland family, together with the tsar's encouraging account of the grand duchess's initial reception of the marriage proposal.

As soon as he received word that the grand duchess looked with favor on Edmond as a prospective bridegroom, Talleyrand wasted no time and, thirty-six hours later, Archambaud, Edmond's father, was on his way to Löbikau. Since Archambaud lacked his older brother's finesse and financial acumen—he still retained his youthful epithet, *aussi beau que bête* [as handsome as he is stupid]—Talleyrand asked Batowski to accompany him because of his former intimacy with Her Serene Highness. The count had been largely responsible for Anna-Dorothea's success when she courageously made three trips to Warsaw, in the middle of winter, to garner support in the Polish parliament for her ongoing struggle as ruling grand duchess with the rebellious Cour nobles. He was to handle the financial stipulations that were necessarily complex, considering the size of the fortunes involved. As head of the family, Talleyrand also sent along the customary letter formally asking the grand duchess for her daughter's hand, in which, with characteristic shrewdness, he flatteringly stressed his nephew's good luck at the prospect of gaining so congenial a mother-in-law. He then arranged for Edmond to have a three-months leave of absence to go to Löbikau for the wedding.

Because Napoleon expected him to entertain in a style befitting his ranking in the empire, Talleyrand was only too happy to oblige. Accordingly, that spring, he had switched residences with a Scottish entrepreneur, Quentin Crauford, with whom Montrond frequently did business on Talleyrand's behalf in some of the latter's more obscure transactions. A certain amount of money was also involved, some of it promised from the imperial privy purse as had been the case with Valençay. With the purchase of the Hôtel Matignon[1], at 57, rue de Varenne, not far from his former ministry, Talleyrand moved back to the Left Bank, which was now considered "the provinces" by certain snobbish members of the *haut monde* who preferred the right side of the Seine. The Matignon with its forty-plus rooms was considered the magnificent equal of the Galliffet and located between the court and the gardens in the classic French manner, with the separate buildings housing the servants' quarters, stables, kitchens, and carriage house attached on either side and hidden behind a single-story facade. Its new proprietor promptly set to work on the time-consuming task of restoring and refurnishing it, including, as embellishment, such touches as extravagant bouquets of porcelain flowers, copies of those Louis XV had ordered for his country houses from the royal porcelain factories at Vincennes. These overflowed squat, ormolu-decorated tubs fitted between the tall doors and were surmounted by matching gilt mirrors to reflect the eternal beauty of their pale petals. He also added a built-in bathtub—the latest luxury, which only a few great Parisian mansions possessed. For variety, he decorated several of the bedrooms in the modern style, with straight-limbed mahogany lines and a glittering ormolu decoration which had come into vogue after Napoleon's Egyptian expedition. But, as might be expected, the master apartments represented the ultimate in traditional French interior decorating—splendor without vulgarity—with superb examples of the famed eighteenth century cabinetmakers' signed *chefs-d'oeuvre*. He enlarged the already enormous, four-acre park by buying the adjacent pavilion, opening onto the rue de Babylon in the rear. He then added a different dining room and music salon so guests might better enjoy concerts under the auspices of his new music director, Sigismund von Neukomm. The pudgy Salzburg composer and musician was assisted by a violinist and harpist who were likewise in residence, and he also gave piano lessons to Charlotte.

    Without his former, high-pressured schedule, Talleyrand devoted more time to his table, although he himself ate virtually only one meal a day—at dinner. Food was not intended to be eaten in one gulp, or vintage wine in one swallow, as Napoleon was want to do, but to be savored and commented on, often in a general discussion. One English guest, Lady Shelley, noted that their host would analyze the meal with as much interest and seriousness as if discussing some political question of importance.

[1] The Hôtel Matignon, was destined to be the twentieth-century residence of the French prime minister.

At the Matignon—as at Valençay—he had a staff of forty and now spent a leisurely hour each morning discussing the day's menus with his chef. Thanks to Antoine Carême, who made his reputation as the number one chef in *tout Paris* during the twelve years he remained in Talleyrand's service, the Matignon set the finest table in the capital, and an invitation to dine there was as eagerly sought after as that of any potentate. Each morning, when this "pastry architect," as Carême preferred to call himself because of his incredible spun-sugar table decorations, appeared, all in white, with a large butcher knife stuck coquettishly in his belt, Talleyrand was subjected to the same bitter tirade about how the shortage of sugar caused by the Continental Blockade was spoiling his handiwork.

Following what he labeled the "insignificant routine" of a high dignitary, Talleyrand leisurely inspected the massive building program being carried out by Baron Vivant Denon, as part of Napoleon's determination to remake the dark, walled medieval city into the most beautiful modern capital in the world. While the narrow, unpaved rue de Varenne, like most of the streets on the Left Bank, was perpetually muddy from the open sewer in its middle, the Pont Neuf, the prototype of the newer bridges across the Seine, was no longer crowded with four- and five-story buildings and shops on both sides of its span. There were so many slabs of sandstone lying in the middle of the boulevards that his coachman had to slow the horses to a walk and pick his way carefully around them as he visited the major construction sites in the rue de Rivoli just outside the Tuileries gates. He frequented the studios of numerous artists, including that of an old acquaintance, the well-known portraitist, Mme Vigée-Le Brun, for advice from her husband, a dealer, on the authenticity and price of numerous purchases for the gallery he was building—as a speculative investment as well as for his pleasure. He also sat several times for François Gérard, the official government portrait painter.

In order to supplement the French troops pouring across France into the Iberian Peninsula and to finish "that devilish business," Napoleon ordered the largest draft of young men since attaining power. But, as other recent call-ups already indicated, the hundreds of fleeing prospective draftees were on the increase. So, before His Imperial Majesty left, at the end of October, to join his troops, Napoleon ordered Talleyrand and several other highly placed members of the government to give four suppers weekly apiece, each one for thirty-six guests to be chosen from among the legislators, ministers, and councilors of state. There could be no more efficient way for the imperial secret police to keep tabs on what Parisians were saying and thinking during his absence, a traditional time for malcontents to have a field day. This was perhaps an ironic request—or a veiled threat—where the Matignon was concerned. For no one was as outspoken in his criticism of Napoleon's continued aggressiveness as Talleyrand.

Unfortunately an autocracy offers no outlet for legitimate opposition, but salons, which had been in eclipse since the Revolution, were making a comeback, especially now that the official *Moniteur* was the only available source of information. They had constituted Talleyrand's lifeblood at an earlier age as the rendezvous of criticism—and wit—and once again he put them to use, embarking on a conspicuous campaign for peace in the small intimate drawing rooms where he was the oracle. With barbed shafts of disapproval about how the King of Spain had been hoodwinked out of his Bourbon inheritance, Talleyrand emphasized his desire to force the imperial regime to moderate its ambitions. Given his exalted position, he was well aware of the weight carried by his words—which were simply an extension of his conversations with Alexander—just as he knew that every one of them was repeated to the emperor. But it would be wrong to attribute to him and his proselytizing efforts a preponderant role in events of the next few years.

The day following his return from Erfurt, Talleyrand, who was determined, by keeping Vienna and Saint Petersburg fully informed, to further the policy he jump-started there for a united effort against Napoleon's war mania, met with Metternich. In the weeks ahead he remained in close contact with "the Blafard [the Pale One]," as he would always refer to the very blond Austrian and, early in December, that shrewd diplomat made a quick trip to Vienna to impress upon François II and Count Stadion, the foreign minister, that "two parties exist in France. . . . At the head of one is the Emperor and the military. . . . At the head of the other M. de Talleyrand . . . and all those who have fortunes to preserve." The general opinion, he emphasized, was that the second group was not working for the overthrow of the emperor but for the consolidation of his regime through the establishment of peace and the founding of a dynasty.

Meanwhile, d'Hauteville, one of Talleyrand's long-standing, trusted aides, knew that Fouché who, as head of the General Police, was the most powerful man in France whenever the emperor was abroad, shared the same nightmare as Talleyrand: what would happen should a Spanish sharpshooter or an assassin's knife fell Napoleon? Equally possessed of an unscrupulous ambition, Talleyrand and Fouché enjoyed a well-known, love-hate relationship that was as fixed in the political picture as high tide follows low, for they were too alike in careers, temperaments, and abilities to be anything but rivals and enemies over the years. But, as d'Hauteville knew, the former was never one to let his personal feelings of antipathy stand in the way of his own best interests. While Fouché, unlike Talleyrand, could not have cared less what happened to Europe, he, too, was equally concerned about the dangers ahead for his country and anxious for peace in order to protect his personal status quo. So d'Hauteville was able to quietly reconcile the pair at a country home of his near Bagneux.

Presumably to smoke out any other like-thinking, peace-loving Frenchmen, the two crafty schemers carefully choreographed an elaborate scene to announce that they had combined forces. On the evening of December 20, late enough at a gala reception at the Matignon to be sure that *tout Paris*, as well as the diplomatic and financial world, and high imperial dignitaries had all arrived, Talleyrand's major-domo announced Fouché's appearance in a stentorian voice. An unexpected hush fell over the crowded, flower-bedecked rooms. There was an audible gulp of universal astonishment as word spread, and everyone peered over each other's shoulders as if to witness the Second Coming. Filthy as usual and as badly dressed as ever in the soiled finery of his high imperial post, with his neck cramped into a stiff, gold-embroidered collar, the powerful minister who was making his initial appearance there, remained poised at the great double doors—like an actor awaiting his entrance cue—to give his host ample time to hobble across the beeswaxed floors and ostentatiously greet him. Their arms warmly linked, the pair strolled slowly through each high-ceilinged, candlelit salon to make sure they caught everyone's eye and, only then, settled down in a prominent alcove where they could be seen but not heard, engrossed in intimate conversation for the rest of the soirée. Their congeniality was tantamount to a political manifesto, and word of it spread quickly in every direction. Talleyrand was deservedly known as the "sphinx" and, since he could have met Fouché many times without anyone being the wiser, why were they making such a public spectacle of their unexpected reconciliation?

Their conspicuously public encounter was not the act of men secretly conspiring for a coup while their lord and master was away. Did the pair hope to serve notice that they were a rallying point for other grumbling Frenchmen?

The next night Madame Mére encountered the two at the home of Talleyrand's good friend, the Princess de Vaudémont. Well aware of their mutual dislike, she could hardly believe her eyes when she saw them huddled together, so the large, heavyset woman, weighted down with sufficient jewels, feathers, brocade, and lace for two, sidled up closer. Although unable to hear very much, it was sufficient to gather that they were talking about her "Nabulio." Convinced they were up to no good, she made a hasty, undignified exit to hurry home and pen a brief warning to him.

In Talleyrand's eyes the empire was the equivalent of the strong monarchy he had always advocated, even in his revolutionary days. Since both the apostate bishop and the Jacobin regicide of the Convention had every reason to fear a restoration of the Bourbons but were agreed upon the need, under the present circumstances, to have a successor on tap, should misfortune strike, they settled on Joachim Murat, the famous soldier who was wed to Napoleon's sister Caroline. Both he and his wife were very ambitious, and they considered themselves exiled when they did not receive the Spanish throne—which went to her brother Joseph—and, instead, were crowned the king and queen of the kingdom of Naples. When Lavalette, the Imperial Director-General of the Post, which opened all the mail, learned that Talleyrand and Fouché had written advising Murat to hold himself in readiness to hasten to Paris at their first signal, he immediately notified Eugène de Beauharnais. As Viceroy of Italy, Josephine's son had the courier carrying the incriminating letter seized and forwarded the document posthaste to Napoleon, who got it about the same time he heard from Madame Mère. Until now, His Imperial Majesty had chosen to ignore whatever reports he received about Talleyrand's remarks, secure in the efficiency of his imperial establishment and full of contempt for "mere mortals." But a plot to undermine the imperial regime was something else. Still it took two to have a conspiracy and, until now, he had found security in the well-known bad feelings between Talleyrand and the police minister.

Napoleon set off northward at once, traveling the first part of the way from Valladolid to Burgos on horseback to save time, before switching to a *post chaise*. Talleyrand hastened to alert Metternich, whom he had seen several times since his return from Vienna, that the emperor was en route home and, early on January 23, the guns on Mont Valérien barked out the customary notice to Parisians that the emperor was again in residence. Once back, Napoleon wished to verify the various alerts before taking action and, to the best of anyone's knowledge, His Imperial Majesty never did learn the true nature of Talleyrand's many rendezvous with the tsar at Erfurt. But intrigues at the Imperial Court were more numerous than generally acknowledged, and Napoleon wanted to make an example to keep the reins of authority strong. So he resumed the usual imperial calendar—granting audiences, inspecting the various public works in progress, and going to the Opéra with Josephine. Only five days were required to confirm everything. A past master at creating scenes in public, he called a special meeting of his Privy Council at which the grand dignitaries of the empire, including Talleyrand, were present, as well as several ministers, and Fouché, whom he had already dressed down in private, the night before. The emperor could not afford to have such an integral part of his administration as the General Police be disorganized when continuous news trickling in from Central Europe, where Austria was secretly rearming, meant that the emperor would soon have to turn eastward once again.

Beginning with a few general remarks, Napoleon reminded his audience that as high government officials they had no right to even think for themselves, much less give their thoughts expression in public. Gradually whipping himself up into a fury, marching to and fro, his hands behind his back, clenching and unclenching his fists, he launched into a monologue directed at Talleyrand. Angry words spewed forth in an uninterrupted stream. Hardly a term of abuse was not applied. Stupefied—and frightened—by the solid half hour of invectives, no one else uttered a word. The picture of nonchalance, Talleyrand leaned characteristically—to support his bad leg—on the edge of a small table near the fire. Not the flicker of an eyelash, not the raising of an eyebrow betrayed whether he knew he was being addressed. All seemed to wash off him. His haughty silence and his impassive expression struck the emperor like a slap across the face. Stopping in front of his prey, His Imperial Majesty barked, "You deserve to be broken like a glass. I have the power to do so, but you're not worth the trouble." Imperial dignity forgotten, losing all control and barely taking a breath, the little Corsican reverted to a soldier's language.

"You would sell your own father if you found it profitable . . ." "You're just common shit in a silk stocking." [11] Exhausted emotionally and physically, Napoleon was unfit for further business, and the meeting was about to break up. In search of a still more mortifying taunt the emperor, as he turned to leave, hurled "You did not tell me that the Duc de San Carlos was your wife's lover." As Talleyrand left, he confided to his stunned colleagues, "What a pity that such a great man should have such bad manners," [12] adroitly reducing the whole episode from a matter of treason to a question of poor manners.

Those at work in the adjacent chambers were accustomed to an increase in decibels whenever the emperor indulged in one of his many tantrums and scarcely looked up as Talleyrand passed through. A friend, Comte de Ségur, asked why the session had lasted so long. Talleyrand clasped one of his hands and murmured "There are some things one can never pardon." [13] Words that in another time and place might have provoked a mortal duel were simply to be considered in terms of imperial protocol—as those of a master to a servant. But Talleyrand would neither forget nor forgive this rebuke in front of his colleagues. His feelings toward the emperor were forever altered.

Upon his return to the Matignon, Talleyrand found an official memorandum requesting the return of his grand chamberlain's key but not notification of his immediate banishment into exile, as he had had every reason to expect.

The next morning the *Moniteur* presented this change as a purely administrative measure to update a prior order which was intended to prevent any one official from accumulating several imperial functions simultaneously.

Late in the day the usual Sunday reception was held at which Napoleon expected all his ministers to put in an appearance. Following the code of an experienced courtier in an absolute monarchy, Talleyrand swallowed his disgrace and was the first to appear. Anxious to obtain a good place in the Throne Room where he could be easily seen, he arrived even before the footmen lowered the great chandeliers to light their candles and dispel the twilight gloom. As customary Napoleon, sniffing great pinches of snuff from a large gold and diamond box, passed before the guests, arranged in a circle, addressing a word to each one. When he came to Talleyrand, His Imperial Majesty looked the other way. The following Sunday, the same scene repeated itself. This time, Napoleon stopped to ask the mand next to him some administrative question. When that worthy could not reply Talleyrand, in complete violation of court etiquette, supplied the answer—as if he and the emperor were on the best of terms—then bowed and kissed the imperial hand. If Napoleon had not spoken to him, he had at least spoken to the emperor. The ice was broken and gradually their relations returned to normal, although the old intimacy was gone.

Meanwhile, Talleyrand had offered his services to Metternich, "in behalf of the common cause." His inference that he needed money because of the outrageous cost of continuing to board the Spanish princes, in addition to buying the Hôtel Matignon, has been attested by dispatches exchanged between the Austrian ambassador and his foreign minister, who quickly gave the diplomat *carte blanche* for any sums necessary. These reports, describing the pair's almost daily meetings—with Talleyrand always referred to as "X"—and dating between the end of January and the debut of hostilities with Austria in April when Metternich had to leave Paris, cannot be gainsaid.[2]

Intelligence rather than character was the main attribute of Talleyrand, whose name was to become a byword for lack of principle in an unprincipled age. Moral integrity was hardly his long suit and, if he thought about it at all, neither was gratitude, whereas the old saw that the end justifies the means was tailor-made for this complex man. The timing of Talleyrand's offer makes it hard to believe that the dramatic dressing-down in front of his peers did not play a role in his present decision. Something new entered the equation. It is difficult to know if Talleyrand's latent hostility towards the emperor from this time on resulted from bitterness or was simply his abandonment of a cause he judged lost. The two seem inextricably intertwined. It was one thing as a high imperial official to betray Napoleon, alleging altruistic, patriotic concerns but another, once money enters into the picture.

Anxious as Talleyrand had been, since Erfurt, not to interrupt his lines of communication with Vienna and Saint Petersburg, the tsar was equally desirous to retain his personal contacts with him. While the eccentric Prince Kourakin remained his official ambassador in Paris, Count Charles-Robert Nesselrode now appeared, ostensibly as Kourakin's counselor. The red-headed young diplomat, who had been brought up by his cousin, Baron Karl-Theodor Dalberg, the Prince-Primate, wasted no time in presenting himself at the Matignon, declaring that he was responsible for maintaining a private correspondence with the tsar and

---

[2] These reports were discovered in the mid-1930s in the government archives on the Ballhausplatz in Vienna. Full of details about the sums to be paid and how they could be best channeled to escape detection, presumably through Frankfurt where the family of Baron Emmerich de Dalberg pulled most of the strings. They cannot be gainsaid and the whole episode is a shabby one.

had a letter for Talleyrand from him. As Alexander intended, Talleyrand henceforth had his private Russian pipeline, through Nesselrode's coded correspondence, in which "Henri" became his *nom de plume*.

He was closely monitoring the progress of his nephew Edmond's anticipated engagement to Princess Dorothea, which the tsar had brokered and which was encountering unanticipated difficulties. When Batowski finally sent him a draft of the dowry arrangements, he enclosed the grand duchess's formal acquiescence to Talleyrand's official request for her daughter's hand. But, the mother emphasized, Dorothea's consent had yet to be won. While it was as unusual for a girl in her circumstances in Eastern Europe—as in the West—to have a say in such matters, everything about the sixteen-year-old princess was extraordinary, not least the fact that, since her three older half-sisters were all unhappily wed, her mother had promised her love-child she might choose her own mate. Brought up as befitted an enormously wealthy *wunderkind*, Dorothea's personal palace on Berlin's famed *Unter den Linden* was so immense that the French commandant of the occupied capital had preempted it for his personal use. There the princess had had her own distinguished salon of intellectuals established by her governess to polish her charge's social graces. She had the spoiled, insufferable Prussian Crown Prince as a playmate, and the late Polish King Stanislaus-Augustus's former secretary as her preceptor. Not surprisingly, Dorothea was accustomed to having every wish granted and, now, she considered herself engaged to the elderly Prince Adam Czartoryski, the famous Polish patriot and Stanislaus-Augustus's first cousin, who was until recently the foreign minister of Tsar Alexander. Reading between the lines, Talleyrand decided that additional pressure was needed. So he advised Batowski to stay put in Löbikau. Then he wrote Caulaincourt requesting that Edmond return there for the grand duchess's birthday in February and bring with him a letter from the tsar—Talleyrand knew he had a friend in Alexander—pushing his nephew's suit. Talleyrand had also discovered that Czartoryski's mother did not favor Dorothea as a potential daughter-in-law and was proving to be an obstacle, so he cannily advised the grand duchess that he had received his own eighty-year-old mother's blessing of the proposed marriage.

Although Edmond knew that as heir of the great house of Talleyrand he would have nothing to say about the choice of his bride, the dashing count could not have been pleased with his uncle's selection. Ten years Dorothea's senior and already a confirmed boulevardier with a love of the military, Edmond would have been better off, and probably a lot happier, never married, let alone to the studious Princess Dorothea. Nonetheless, he appeared, as commanded, at Löbikau, the day before the birthday celebration, with the tsar's requested letter, totally unaware of the turmoil which his appearance sparked. For his purported fiancée still obstinately considered herself engaged to the elderly Pole, and it is questionable whether either uncle or nephew ever did learn the true story of how the Courland princess was finally maneuvered into becoming a most reluctant bride.

That afternoon, the grand duchess handed her daughter His Imperial Majesty's communication, importantly encrusted with massive red and black seals and worded like an ukase. Then she gave her the one from Talleyrand, which was designed to reduce any further opposition at Löbikau to the marriage. Dorothea read them both carefully. In her memoirs, in which she captured with almost total recall how her mother tricked her into marriage, she commented, "I do not think M. de Talleyrand ever drafted the most important diplomatic note with greater care than he gave this letter." [14] When the girl still refused to go along, the grand duchess lashed out furiously in a terrible scene that Dorothea never forgot. But she stuck obstinately to her point. She considered herself engaged to Czartoryski.

The grand duchess was so distressed that her birthday celebration fizzled out dismally, and she did not sleep that night, trying to resolve her dilemma. She discussed the impasse with Batowski the next morning, and he reminded her of recurrent rumors of bad blood between Czartoryski and Alexander since Poland had been wiped off the map. There was no need to elaborate. Anna-Dorothea understood. In the light of the two men's present hostility, it would be one thing if Dorothea flouted the tsar's desire by flatly refusing to wed Edmond, but to do so expressly to run off with Prince Czartoryski could easily prove the grand duchess's undoing. And independent Dorothea might do exactly that. So Anna-Dorothea and Batowski dreamt up a scenario to thwart her.

That evening, a scene written and directed by the latter—the girl's natural father—was performed when the schloss's great bronze dinner gong sounded. The courier had come shortly before and, as was customary, each member of the household brought to the table the most recent tidings from abroad. An elderly Polish countess, who was a pensioner of the grand duchess, arose from a sickbed to be coached in her lines. The last to assemble, she rushed in, clutching a handful of mail. "Excuse me! Excuse me! I had so many letters I could not get through them quickly. *Ma chère*," she turned wide-eyed to Anna-Dorothea. "Prince Czartoryski is finally engaged! I have every detail!" To emphasize her scoop, she raised an envelope triumphantly in her shaky hand. Bitterly indignant at the prince's defection, Dorothea pushed back her chair so abruptly it toppled over with a crash. "M-M-maman! . . . I will marry whom you wish."

Because imperial authorization was mandatory in all similar matters affecting the families of members of the Imperial Household, when Edmond and his father returned to Paris with this welcome news Talleyrand, who was still in disfavor, did not wish to risk a denial, so he had Archambaud make the necessary request. Shortly afterwards, father and son made one more trip East. Nothing but a Lutheran ceremony was possible at Löbikau. Since Edmond was a Catholic and religion was no issue with Dorothea, Talleyrand arranged for the wedding service to be held at Frankfurt, on the route west. After the April 22 ceremony, the Prince-Primate, Baron Karl-Theodor Dalberg, who had blessed the marriage, gave Dorothea a wondrously wrought little bird that chirped and beat its wings inside a golden cage, an appropriate gift for the woebegone bride. The guns were barking once more and, that very day, Napoleon won an important victory over the Austrians at Eckmühl. Forty-eight hours later the groom, who was only a pawn in his uncle's chess game, left to join the Grande Armée. And Dorothea continued on west with Fraulein Hoffman, her governess—and Anna-Dorothea.

11

A Traitor or Loyal Opposition

"[Talleyrand was] in their arms and at their feet but never in their hands."—LE COMTE DE SAINT-AULAIRE [1]

AS TALLEYRAND CHATTED WITH MOTHER and daughter in the family salon about their trip that first evening following their arrival, his gold-handled cane slowly outlined a pink Aubusson rose at his feet, while his connoisseur's eye appreciatively appraised his visitors. He was disappointed in the young Slav princess whom he had gone to such lengths to procure for his nephew. Dorothea was still an underdeveloped, sallow prune with overly dark eyes in a small pinched face, and he had no taste for unripe fruit. But Anna-Dorothea was another matter. She might have the slightly too long, aquiline nose of all her Medem family, but she still boasted the delicate skin and ivory complexion so prized in northern women. Her graceful beauty, which was only slightly faded at forty-eight—successive attempts to hide the increasing number of grey strands had turned her auburn hair black—appealed to his discriminating palate. So did her sovereign airs and seven hundred years of blue blood, even if her ancestors had been crude Teutonic Knights in the savage hinterlands when his were already riding at the French kings' right hand. Time and distance had magnified her career and achievements, transforming her into a glamorous political personality on terms of intimacy with everyone worth knowing in Central and Eastern Europe, and Talleyrand quickly pronounced the petite, vivacious grand duchess "delightful," the greatest compliment in his vocabulary.

Since tonight was family night, Catherine de Talleyrand made an appearance, as well as Edmond's sister, Melanie, and his father, Archambaud. In the center of the table reposed Carême's special greeting to M. Edmond's bride and her mother—a welcome arch modeled after the plans for the Arc de Triomphe which was being built to crown the slight hill at the end of the Champs Elysées. As usual Carême presided over the serving of the meal with as much aplomb as Napoleon watched a cavalry charge led by one of his swashbuckling marshals. Because the guests were late sitting down, his sauces were in danger of curdling; his eyes were glowering and his cap quivering, two telltale signs. Moving quickly to avert a drama of potentially earth-shaking magnitude, Talleyrand beckoned his temperamental chef to his side and deftly smoothed his ego. An array of soups was ladled out and served by the footmen standing behind each chair; fresh fish which had been rushed, packed in ice, from the Rhine followed. Next, small pâtés, melon, and roast meat in pastries. Then the host, with the prerogative of a great seigneur but contrary to custom, selected a succulent rack of lamb *pré salé* to carve himself. Starting with the grand duchess, he offered the slices around the table in the order of the guests' importance, ending with Dorothea because she was the youngest.

At the end of the meal Carême, with a great flourish removed the *pièce de resistance* from the middle of the table and began to slice up his masterpiece. Anna took only a taste of this mouth-watering concoction of nougat, biscuit, spun sugar, and whipped cream. "It's delicious. But it's so rich, it would be a sin to take more," she remarked with a dazzling smile that showed her still perfect teeth, a great plus in that day and age. —"Surely, my dear Duchess, you know that every sin is negotiable, eh?" Talleyrand's overly long eyelids opened for the briefest of seconds and that rarest of phenomena, the glimpse of a twinkle, was discernable.

When Charlotte put in her usual appearance, peeking tonight from behind an immense agate and silver receptacle in which burned the customary ambergris, Talleyrand dotingly made her the star attraction. Thoroughly spoiled and not pretty, with protruding buck teeth, she was accepted by everyone as an object of curiosity—and an integral part of an evening at the Matignon. Spoiled and petted like an old man's darling, she promptly dove below the table to pinch beneath his skirts the hairy legs of the papal delegate, who smiled like a martyr; his limbs were already sore because Josephine's two prize carlins had earlier made mincemeat of them. Later, when she reappeared, attired in a Spanish costume, and danced a tarantella, Talleyrand led his guests with as much applause as if the child were Mlle Elssler, the premiere ballerina at the Opéra.

It was up to Talleyrand, as the head of the family, to look after Dorothea, since Edmond was off with the Grande Armée, and to arrange that she saw everything worthwhile in the French capital. It was equally important for him to look after the captivating grand duchess with her important political connections. The days whirled past like leaves in the breeze that came soughing through the Bois de Boulogne, the half wild royal hunting preserve out near the Abbaye de Longchamps where Talleyrand frequently took his guests for an afternoon drive. People were sitting in the Tuileries's gardens enjoying the flowering chestnuts and the late spring, reading rented newspapers affixed to long poles—individual papers were too expensive to buy. The quartet of famous Venetian bronze horses that was perched atop the Arc de Carrousel in the Tuileries's great courtyard was hitched to a huge, still empty chariot which was awaiting, as occupant, a golden statute of the emperor. Irreverent Parisians gawked below and punned, *"Le char l'attend"* (literally, "The chariot awaits him," but phonetically, *"le charlatan,"* some people's name for Napoleon.) Jugglers and acrobats, dancing bears and goats climbing ladders performed in the streets. At Franconi's popular circus, a trained stag starred and, at many corners, donkeys carried baskets of flowers for sale. For Dorothea's sake, they even went to the café Garchy on the rue de la Loi, near the boulevards, to savor *biscuits aux amandes* and divine apricot ice surrounded with fresh peaches, and bought barley sugar in the popular candy shop, Le Fidèle Berger (The Faithful Shepherd), on the rue des Lombards. It is questionable who was the most exhausted, Talleyrand, mother or daughter by the time he delivered them to the rosy brick château, Rosny, a maternal inheritance of Edmond's which had been built by Henry IV's famous minister Sully, where the young bride was to stay until her husband returned from the battlefront.

Then Talleyrand proceeded south to Bourbon-l'Archambault for his annual cure, only to be called back to Paris by his eighty-year-old mother's death. He had been supporting her and now took charge of her funeral, which was held in the Church of the Assumption in late June.

Because he wanted to see the grand duchess again—and no one who was anyone would be seen in the capital in mid-summer—he invited her to join him at Pont-de-Sains, one of his properties in the north, near the Belgian frontier, not far from Avesnes. This property had been bought largely as an investment because of its one thousand hectares of trees in the immense forest that had formerly belonged to the Duc d'Orléans and which were in demand for the navy's building program. Relatively isolated, quiet and peaceful, the establishment, with its working forge, was more like a big farm than a seignorial residence, and both the grounds and house were in the midst of a large-scale development program. This included the dredging of a big new lagoon with a ridge at one end which could only be reached by boat and where Talleyrand intended to place a small *"Temple d'Amour,"* supported by four columns of red marble which had formerly been bought by Louis XIV for Versailles. During Anna-Dorothea's stay, he had this popular conceit constructed as an exact copy of one Josephine recently had erected at Malmaison. To celebrate her visit, it was then dedicated to his glamorous guest at a rustic fête in her honor.

For once, Napoleon missed Talleyrand when the final details of still another Austrian peace treaty were being haggled over in Vienna after the Grande Armée's victory at Wagram. Caustically, Napoleon upbraided his present foreign affairs minister, Champagny: "You have stipulated one hundred million francs as indemnity for France, every sou of which will go to the Treasury, I know. When Talleyrand was foreign affairs minister, perhaps we might have ended up with only sixty thousand francs, and he would have pocketed forty thousand. But ten days ago everything would have been wound up. Settle this affair at once." [2]

The emperor returned to his capital to find public opinion less reassured by his continuing imperial victories and more concerned with his insatiable taste for war. The empire was already the double of Charlemagne's; its very heterogeneity would prove the source of its fragility. The situation in Spain was far from reassuring and slowly consuming the cream of the Grande Armée. Relations with the Vatican had reached the point of no return. Because of papal refusal to acquiesce to certain French demands, including cooperation with the Continental Blockade, the aged pontiff had been arbitrarily stripped of his secular power, kidnapped at bayonet point, and whisked from the Vatican. Saint Peter's successor was a prisoner of state,

Napoleon was excommunicated, and devout Catholics were in an understandable uproar. And all the while England, Napoleon's principal target, stoked from afar these various, smoldering fires.

Presumably to distract attention from such unpleasant realities, the forthcoming winter season was scheduled to be a particularly brilliant one at the Tuileries. Talleyrand had had ample time to learn that the grand duchess, who had grown up in the French-oriented culture of most of the eastern European aristocracy, was a great admirer of Napoleon. Indeed, it is more than likely that Anna-Dorothea, being Anna-Dorothea, had come west harboring some thought of adding the French emperor's scalp to those of other prominent rulers which reputedly were already dangling from the belt encircling her dainty waist. However, imperial protocol could not be waived even for the former reigning grand duchess of Courland. So he arranged for her mandatory official presentation to the imperial couple at the earliest possible moment, to ensure that her name should appear on the guest list for all Tuileries functions. Anna-Dorothea was gratified not only to be received alone, an exceptional honor and almost unheard of for a woman, but also to observe that the hussars, standing at attention with their halberds before the entrance to the Throne Room, threw open not one but both doors as they announced her, a courtesy normally extended only to reigning sovereigns. Napoleon greeted her amicably. "We are honored, Madame, to welcome an intimate friend of our dear cousin and ally, Tsar Alexander. We shall do everything to make your stay a pleasant and a long one." [3]

Inadvertently, perhaps, the emperor did more in this respect than he realized. In a day when relaxed morals and uncompromising manners were taken for granted, Catherine de Talleyrand had committed the unforgivable sin of brazenly continuing to flaunt her liaison with the handsome young Spanish Duc de San Carlos, the equerry of the captive Spanish Prince of Asturias. As a result Napoleon had recently forbidden her to set foot inside the Tuileries. Then rumor reached the imperial ear that Catherine had been peddling influence, offering ready access to her husband "for worthy causes." Fingering a six-strand pearl necklace—a "gift from a deserving Westphalian official"—twisting a large Siberian sapphire on her index finger—a "present from the Polish ambassador"—she reputedly was doing very well for herself until an indignant Helvetian delegation refused to go along and complained directly to Napoleon. Lashing out angrily, the emperor ordered the Duc de San Carlos into exile in the sleepy little town of Bourg-en-Bresse, and Catherine was dispatched to one of Talleyrand's outlying properties.

Talleyrand had at last found a woman who was worthy of him. Anna-Dorothea was everything that Catherine was not, and she seized her opportunity, as much the pursuer as the pursued. With her command of five languages—most educated French women spoke only French—and her regal airs, the grand duchess was a worthy companion for a man who, throughout his life, loved to bed down beautiful women, preferably clever ones with whom he might discuss sensibly his favorite topics—the affairs of the world and books—afterwards. Jealous of Anna-Dorothea's magnetic appeal, his seraglio was not inclined to be generous in her regard. So nicknamed by salon society's fashionables, this handful of Talleyrand's former mistresses from the cream of the French aristocracy faithfully rallied around him. The fragrance of their former passion preserved by the potpourri of memory, vicariously reliving their gilded youth and the vanished world of yesteryear, they were determined to keep "dear Charles-Maurice" amused and be of service during these trying days. Because it was of paramount importance that Talleyrand remain as well informed as possible and create the impression that he was still at the emperor's right hand and not reduced, as he actually was, to limited appearances at court and rare contact with Napoleon, he never missed Sunday mass in the château's chapel. For the Tuileries was one of the best places to pick up the latest rumors, but nothing equaled the seraglio as a news-gathering agency—without arousing the suspicion of the imperial secret police.

Only the previous year, after a long careful inspection, this coterie had reluctantly accepted another newcomer, the Countess Marie-Thérèse Tyszkiewicz, Talleyrand's erstwhile Polish mistress, when she moved to Paris, afraid he would forget her and grateful for any crumbs of affection he might still toss her way. At least Marie-Thérèse, as the niece of the last King of Poland, had proven invaluable to their beloved when he was acting governor of Poland and her extensive, impressive family connections in Austria as well as in Poland provided a made-to-order continental listening service. Now the seraglio was aghast at the thought of opening their ranks once more. And for another foreigner who was the celebrity of the season, conjuring up as she did, for insular Parisians, the spell of barbaric, far away places. The words stuck in their throats to address as "Your Highness" this fascinating Slav with jewels fit for a king, simply because she had once ruled some pinpoint of a duchy they had trouble locating on any map.

Talleyrand's relations with the grand duchess settled into a happy pattern when Anna-Dorothea moved into her own spacious apartment in a mansion at 103, rue Saint-Dominique, not far from him. Carefully orchestrated by the faithful Courtiade, one of the Matignon footmen appeared every morning with a note in Talleyrand's tiny, illegible scrawl outlining, with a touching tenderness and in the full-blown, flowery style of his generation, plans for his *chère ange's* day. Fortunately, Talleyrand's stalwart valet was better organized than the Countess Tyszkiewicz's majordomo. The latter recently made the countess the laughing stock of *tout Paris* when he mistakenly sent Talleyrand at supper one of her notes, written well in advance and intended for delivery the following morning, in which Marie-Thérèse related how she had lain awake all night, unable to sleep because she was thinking of him.

Late that fall, Talleyrand was already playing whist at one of the Countess Tyszkiewicz's packed, weekly soirées when Anna-Dorothea arrived, pausing at the door after she was announced to be sure that everyone saw her in her latest Leroy creation. Then she swept in, ever the gracious sovereign, nodding here, smiling there, reveling in the sudden lull she caused as she threaded her way amid the guests throwing dice and gambling for the usual high stakes, past the professional croupiers required by law to keep the banks, around the tables of tric trac, écarté, and biribi to where Talleyrand sat. "I never saw anyone take more pleasure in showing off a gown," one of the seraglio whispered, consumed with envy at the open adoration on Talleyrand's notoriously impassive countenance. "The grand duchess requires adulation as a sick man wants leeches." "She lives on it," another drily replied.

When Talleyrand and Anna-Dorothea got up to leave, their hostess accompanied them to the door. Once she was out of earshot of the others she reported with an air of great importance—and in a conspiratorial whisper—that she had just received word from her most reliable Warsaw sources that Marie Walewska, Napoleon's young Polish mistress, was carrying an imperial bastard. This irrefutable proof that the emperor was not sterile but that Josephine had become barren was invaluable grist for Talleyrand's mill, coming as it did at this particular time. For Talleyrand knew that the empire could endure no longer than Napoleon himself until his succession was settled and, in the recent campaign, during an attack on the town of Ratisbon, Napoleon had been slightly wounded in his big toe. Although the emperor was back in the saddle and off to show himself to his alarmed troops before the army surgeon had finished his work, this slight mishap, the first to befall Napoleon on the battlefield, had far-reaching consequences. Not only did subjugated Europe suddenly realize that the great man was not immortal, but it highlighted for the emperor, as never before, the fragility of the entire imperial structure and his need for legitimate heirs to carry on and establish a dynasty.

Napoleon procrastinated another month, following his return west, before he informed the empress, whom he still loved, that she must depart. Because the emperor was first contemplating marriage to a Romanoff, this was his "Be Kind to Russians" period, and Anna-Dorothea was the recipient of exceptional imperial cordiality which Talleyrand encouraged her to accept. Fruit and flowers from the imperial greenhouses, invitations to sit at Napoleon's table at dinner, were all flatteringly proffered on a family basis, as from one member of the European family of rulers to another. "It is your due because the tsar took a personal hand in the marriage of your daughter to one of my subjects," the emperor explained. From Talleyrand's point of view, an extra pair of ears at the château was invaluable under the present circumstances. Anna-Dorothea was delighted to have found a way to be helpful to him and alerted friends at the Saint Petersburg court to keep her up-to-date by special courier.

The imperial crisis hurtled to a climax. Two weeks before Christmas, Talleyrand and the grand duchess were in the small Tuileries theater to see Corneille's *Nicomède*, but the drama offstage took the spotlight from the great Talma who was playing the lead. Josephine, her eyes red from weeping, was not in her usual seat but in a box to one side, alone except for a single lady-in-waiting standing behind her. Just before the curtain went up, Napoleon appeared in the imperial loge which faced her. Afterwards, the court assembled in one of the galleries and, this time, the emperor and empress entered together. Followed by their respective suites, they slowly made their way around, engaging some guests in conversation, making others miserable by ignoring them. Josephine did not try to hide her unhappiness. She started to cry and hurriedly left the room before she reached Talleyrand and Anna-Dorothea. Napoleon swiftly followed. Both their households did likewise, and the great hall emptied unexpectedly early.

The Bonaparte clan had already been ordered to Paris, and Talleyrand's morning *billet*, on December 14, cryptically informed the grand duchess that he must appear at the château that evening along with the rest of the court. It was well past midnight before he arrived in the rue Saint Dominique, still in his red velvet, gold-encrusted vice-grand elector's uniform, dress sword at his side, to describe the painful Throne Room scene in which Napoleon divorced Josephine. The emperor was now free to find another consort and, at a subsequent masquerade at the arch-chancellor's, Anna-Dorothea heard Napoleon comment, in his peculiarly flat voice, that he did not care whom he wed. "I am only marrying a womb."

There had already been indications that Talleyrand was once more on the road back to imperial favor. When the Saxon king, Frederick Augustus I, came to Paris on a visit, as a courtesy, Napoleon sent his vice-grand elector to greet him at Meaux and escort him in to the capital. Not surprisingly, a newly arrived Austrian attaché reported to the Ballhausplatz that Talleyrand "has his foot in the stirrup but he is not yet in the saddle." Once an Austrian archduchess became a prime possibility, no one was better qualified than Talleyrand to explore the possible ramifications such a candidacy might pose on the European dynastic chessboard. Soon the vice-grand elector again enjoyed unlimited, unannounced access to the emperor at all times, and the pair had long daily conferences together.

When Napoleon unexpectedly convoked a high-level meeting of his grand dignitaries and ministers to decide between the three available matrimonial prospects—a sister of the tsar, a daughter of the king of Saxony, and a Hapsburg archduchess—Talleyrand favored the Austrian candidate. Marriage with Marie-Louise, so-named after her godparents, her aunt Marie-Antoinette and Louis XVI, would not only enable France to re-enter the family of reigning dynasties; such a union would also expiate the heinous crimes of the Revolution and the guillotining of Marie-Antoinette in the eyes of legitimist Europe, and reconcile it to the empire. In short, Talleyrand was pleading once again—albeit indirectly, through the conservation of Austria—for the balance of power as the only way that continental peace could be established and endured. Whether or not Talleyrand's arguments carried the day—as usual he made his point with a minimum of words and did not enter into any discussion—that same evening, Napoleon sent a courier to Vienna.

By early February the deafening boom of the cannon at the Invalides announced Napoleon's engagement. To Parisians, the news that their emperor—General Bonaparte—was to bed down a descendant of the Holy Roman Emperor Charles V seemed a more incredible achievement than any of his victories in the field. They hoped it forecast the start of a different foreign policy.

The tsar was not the only one worried about what the forthcoming, new imperial marriage forecast. In the hopes of ferreting out enough accurate information to plan Austria's future continental role, an anxious Metternich, who had recently become the Austrian chancellor, courageously turned over the reins of power and accompanied the young bride-to-be to France on the pretext of guiding her first steps there.

On All Fools' Day, April 1, Talleyrand participated in the civil ceremony at Saint-Cloud uniting Napoleon and Marie-Louise. The following day, he was in the glittering official *cortège* with its handsome military escort and blaring bands, which accompanied the imperial couple's spectacular noon entry into their capital. To witness the pageantry and pomp at first hand he procured tickets for Anna-Dorothea and the Princess Tyszkiewicz on the temporary platform constructed for prominent government figures at the top of the Champs Elysées, alongside the skillfully camouflaged, and as yet far from finished, Arc de Triomphe. Napoleon insisted that the formalities of his marriage follow in every detail those of the dauphin with Marie-Louise's aunt, Marie-Antoinette, and the religious ceremony transpired in a temporary chapel installed in the Louvre. Because thirteen of the twenty-eight cardinals present in Paris still balked at participating on the grounds that Napoleon's marriage to Josephine was not truly dissolved, the emperor was forced at the last minute to order their seating rearranged so that their reduced number was less evident. For a young girl who had never owned more than a braided-hair bracelet and a single coral necklace, Marie-Louise was aglitter with diamonds. Her Imperial Majesty looked pale—and tired. But who would not be after being bedded down two nights running by an impatient husband-to-be, anxious to prove his insatiable virility, although he was twice her age. What a shock that must have been for the young Austrian archduchess who had been so carefully reared that she had never been allowed anything but female pets.

At first, Marie-Louise was not permitted to hold any big receptions because "Nana"—or "Popo," as his bride soon took to calling him—was convinced that women conceived more readily when they did not exert themselves, that is to say, "outside the four walls of the imperial bedchamber." However, Napoleon could not keep Marie-Louise to himself forever, and distinguished visitors crowded into Paris for the spectacular festivities given by the Senate, the Imperial Guard, and the Hotel de Ville—Paris's Town Hall—in honor of the newlyweds. In fact, there were so many that the bride was soon bored and was discovered by the horrified Austrian ambassador rearranging her bouquet rather than observing the spectacular fireworks representing her ancestral home, Vienna's Schönborn palace, at an extremely lavish affair tendered by the groom's sister, Princess Pauline.

When Talleyrand returned from a late May meeting at the Tuileries, he disclosed that Napoleon was convinced that the empress was pregnant. Some court wit lost no time punning that Her Imperial Majesty's looks would be improved once she had a *nouveau né* (literally, a newborn infant, but, phonetically, a *nouveau nez*, a new nose). However, this proved to be wishful imperial thinking. Marie-Louise had developed a passion for French cooking, especially French pastry, and her stomach upsets were caused by overindulgence.

After a final visit to Malmaison for the grand duchess to bid farewell to Josephine before returning east to spend the summer at her estate, Löbikau, with her other three daughters, Talleyrand headed south to Bourbon-l'Archambault for his annual cure. Here, in this tiny town of some three thousand inhabitants, locked in a pleasant hollow between rolling hills in the department of the Allier, Talleyrand invented the word "vacation." Few crowned heads traveled with a more impressive retinue although accommodations at the spa were simple, and he did not always reside in the same place. He benefited so greatly from these visits that he extended his stay to a minimum of three weeks, and they became a sacrosanct part of his calendar.

At Bourbon-l'Archambault the fastidious Talleyrand's train of life was far simpler than his Paris friends would ever have believed possible. Daily at what was, for him, the ungodly hour of 10:00 a.m., two husky local porters transported His Excellency, well swaddled in a white wool burnoose, down the steep incline in a sedan chair to the "Bain du Prince," the largest of the thermal pools which, as a signal honor, was reserved exclusively for his use when he was in residence. Here he spent the better part of each day, soaking in the hot sulfur baths and drinking the six prescribed glasses of the foul-smelling warm water, as every self-respecting Frenchman did, once a year, to restore his liver. He did not mingle with the others who were taking the cure. When dignitaries from nearby districts came to pay their respects or request his help in some government affair, Talleyrand greeted them while playing whist in the evening, a ploy which automatically reduced conversation to a minimum. But he did mingle freely with the townspeople and was more talkative in this retreat than any place else. Although accompanied by the valet who always shaved him, Talleyrand preferred the local *figaro* who never failed to regale him—in his coarse Bourbonnais accent—with the latest village gossip. Likewise, he opted for the services of the official doctor in residence rather than use his own man. The pedantic Dr. Faye was straight out of Molière, pompously sprinkling inappropriate, garbled Latin quotations throughout his conversation, that made any ladies present blush—although they did not understand a word of what he was saying—and Talleyrand maliciously refused to translate them, claiming he did not want to scandalize the fair sex.

Napoleon's marriage to an unsophisticated bride transformed the atmosphere of his parvenu court, and the château assumed the air of sober respectability befitting a ruler whose father-in-law was the venerable Austrian emperor. This change was reflected in the choice of the twelve contemporaries His Imperial Majesty selected for Marie-Louise's newly enlarged household. The inclusion of Dorothea in this exalted list, Talleyrand wrote the grand duchess, was in recognition of his support of the Austrian marriage. When the court made its annual move to Fontainebleau the grand master of ceremonies inducted the young women into office at an elaborate ceremonial and, then, Talleyrand officially presented them to Their Imperial Majesties. After commenting wickedly on one extremely skinny inductee whose *décolleté* Anna-Dorothea would have to see to believe—"Indeed it would have been impossible to bare more and show less!" [4]—he reported to the absent grand duchess that her daughter was "suitably dazzling." Her pregnancy was artfully disguised by clouds of silver tulle, embroidered with cornflowers and made adjustable by a row of cleverly arranged diamond safety pins. She was on her initial, three months tour of duty and, because Talleyrand was included in the imperial party and quartered in the same palace wing, he and his niece finally had a chance to get acquainted. He was enchanted. Like her mother, the girl talked and listened well—and he soon decided that there was not another soul there with whom he could enjoy so much good conversation. At one point, he suggested they send the grand duchess a copy of the verse making the palace rounds: "The sex of the infant, the hope of the fatherland, even for the emperor is still a secret. For the first time in his life he doesn't know what he did." "Of course, the emperor is positive the baby will be a boy," Dorothea retorted, and they both chuckled.

Talleyrand's relationship with Napoleon during this period resembles a roller coaster ride—down one minute, up the next. His activities now are more discernible through the memoirs and diaries of strangers of note and private individuals than from a perusal of official documents, for the Matignon was the one place in the capital where the continental aristocracy felt at home. Talleyrand always preferred to conduct business and discuss foreign policy over the tinkle of glass. His lavish weekly receptions served the practical purpose of enabling him to speak with and, hopefully, influence, the many prominent European statesmen who would not consider a Paris visit complete without calling on him. His many outspoken criticisms, here, there, and everywhere, about the imperial regime were automatically reported to Napoleon as Talleyrand anticipated. The emperor would comment on them to his aides and then dismiss the matter, convinced that as long as he knew what Talleyrand was saying—and doing—Talleyrand could do him no harm. His Imperial Majesty never suspected that the vice-grand elector purposely avowed his disapproval openly—to lull Napoleon and persuade him that he knew all there was to know about his third-ranking official's activities. In similar fashion, the *cabinet noir* only discovered in his personal correspondence what he wanted them to find there. Years later, when asked why he did not take stronger measures regarding Talleyrand before it was too late, Napoleon replied that he underestimated his power to harm him. His Imperial Majesty must also have had some lingering affection for the individual who shared with him responsibility for the corpse of the Directoire on which the Napoleonic empire was founded.

Talleyrand was having pressing financial problems which, like those of most of France and the rest of the continent, were greatly exacerbated, if not caused, by the Continental Blockade. Not only was he saddled with the draining expenses of the Spanish royalty still imprisoned at Valençay, but his own princely lifestyle at the Matignon continued, as did his appetite for high-stake gambling. And now his friend Michel

Simons's Brussels bank, in which he kept substantial funds, failed. Where money was concerned, Talleyrand was an inexplicable world unto himself, governed by a single principle, expressed early in his youth: "Never be a poor devil." His conduct with money was hard to justify. As earlier he had no qualms about accepting Austrian remuneration for his services, so—deplorably—in mid-September, he did not hesitate to write asking the tsar for a million and a half francs, even detailing how to send the money which, he brazenly specified, he needed by November. With marvelous irony, the equal of Talleyrand's own, Alexander justified his refusal on the grounds that he was acting in Talleyrand's own best interest; nor did the tsar burn the former's incriminating letter as requested.

Unfortunately, this was not the end of the vice-grand elector's monetary difficulties. Earlier in the year, the apprehensive city fathers of the port of Hamburg had paid Talleyrand handsomely for his protection in an effort to escape anticipated French annexation as the emperor endeavored to seal any remaining fissures in the Continental Blockade. To no avail. When a December decree united the Hanseatic cities with the empire and Talleyrand refused to give a refund, a deputation from the indignant Hamburg senate complained directly to Napoleon who, outraged, demanded that they be reimbursed at once. As a temporary stopgap Talleyrand was reduced to selling his beloved library, as he had when under duress years earlier. Hard pressed, he had the audacity to rewrite Alexander for help—with no better luck than before, although he continued to send information to him through Nesselrode.

Talleyrand was seeing an increasing amount of his son this winter. Flahaut, who had been seriously wounded in the fighting around Vienna the previous year, was still recuperating, wrapped in flannels from head to toe and losing his hair, in a fine new apartment in his mother, Adèle's, home on the Grande Rue Verte. Since Talleyrand stopped by almost nightly, he usually visited Adèle too—she was even seen occasionally at the Matignon—especially as she was acquiring a small but fine collection of paintings, including a Titian that Josephine had given her and which he greatly admired. Charles was by now the paramour of Queen Hortense de Beauharnais, Josephine's daughter and the wife of Napoleon's brother, King Louis of Holland. Theirs was a protracted, tumultuous affair in which Adèle played an important supportive role. Missing Charles when he was far away, Hortense had sent him many small gifts—a seal, a cross, a romantic ballad of her own composition full of her longing for him. Published anonymously, "Partant pour la Syrie" (Leaving for Syria) became one of the most popular songs of the day, hummed by everyone with an absent beloved. Charles was having difficulty finding a suitable gift in return—something rare and precious. "Why not a lock of your hair?" Talleyrand suggested.

By the time the grand duchess returned from the East, her feelings regarding the emperor had undergone a profound change. One of his greatest admirers before she even set foot in Paris, once His Imperial Majesty began to consider a Russian bride, Anna-Dorothea with her Romanov connections envisioned herself playing an important role in the projected new imperial household. However, with Marie-Louise as his consort, Napoleon's attentiveness to the grand duchess underwent a marked decline which that spoiled woman resented. Going to and coming from Löbikau, the conditions of the countries she passed through and the increasing hardships of the natives there who were coming under French rule, together with the shocking, first-hand experiences of numerous friends and relatives thoroughly disillusioned her. She no longer thought of the French emperor as the savior of mankind. She also sensed a change in the tsar's attitude towards him. The spell of imperial achievements had worn thin. She disliked Napoleon's dictatorial methods and recoiled with disgust at the latest examples of mounting imperial pettiness—the exile, albeit brief, of Montrond, Talleyrand's close friend, for speaking out against the government's current neglect of the vice-grand elector. Subjected to the latter's clear and concise reasoning, it required little effort for him to turn her into the emperor's implacable enemy. Anna-Dorothea became the vice-grand elector's conduit to her vast network of important central European friends who were already against French imperialism. She was invaluable as Talleyrand's eye, ear, and voice and henceforth took orders from him.

Talleyrand was delighted when the imperial couple agreed to act as godparents for Napoléon-Louis, Dorothea's first child, but they were unable to appear at the christening because of their own imminent blessed event. Seven days later, while he was dining with the grand duchess, Talleyrand received the message all France was expecting: "Marie-Louise is in labor." He rushed home, donned full court regalia and proceeded to the Tuileries to await the imperial offspring with other dignitaries whom protocol convoked there.

The next morning the official salvoes commenced. "One, two, three . . . nineteen, twenty . . ." There was a dramatic pause after the twenty-first boom, and Paris held its breath. "It's only a girl!" someone cried. Was Josephine's sacrifice in vain? But the gunner at the Invalides had a sense of humor—or of history. For the cannon soon resumed and continued the one hundred and one rounds specified for a boy. While the big bell of Notre Dame tolled, the news was likewise broadcast to the prefect of every department, to every military governor of Napoleon's vast empire, and to every foreign capital, aided by the Chappe system of military wireless. Simultaneously Madame Blanchard set out from the École Militaire in a balloon to carry the glad tidings through all the towns and villages she passed over.

Two months later François Charles Joseph Bonaparte—*l'Aiglon* (the Eaglet)—was baptized at Notre Dame in a ceremony that the emperor decreed should be the greatest of his reign and was intended to solidify the empire. Not only Talleyrand but Dorothea participated—the former limping alongside the other grand officers of the empire, the latter with the imperial ladies-in-waiting following Marie-Louise, who was literally covered with diamonds; even the sleeves and border of her robe were made of diamond vermicelli.

Recalled from his post in Saint Petersburg for the solemn occasion, Caulaincourt came out frequently for long talks with Talleyrand at the Château Neuf, formerly Henry IV's hunting box, at nearby Saint-Germain-en-Laye, which Anna-Dorothea had purchased and restored for summer use. Both men were distressed at France's perceptible drift toward a rupture with Russia and hoped that the Eaglet's advent might induce Napoleon to settle down and consolidate his gains for his son's sake, although the emperor had already ordered War Minister Clarke to increase arms manufacture.

On August 15 Talleyrand went to the Tuileries to pay his respects at the annual dual festivities celebrating the Fête of the Assumption and His Imperial Majesty's birthday. There Napoleon dressed down the Russian ambassador before the entire diplomatic corps, catching him completely by surprise and leaving him beet red. The next day, following a ministerial conference in which he outlined his intended campaign against the tsar, the emperor's absorption with Russia—and, possibly, his pent-up annoyance at Talleyrand's continuing disapproval of his continental policies—triggered a second recorded public scene. At the sight of

Dorothea, Alexander's subject, innocently attending the empress, Napoleon peevishly berated her for Edmond's latest folly.

—"Madame, how could your husband spend ten thousand francs for cameos?"

—"S-s-sire, Your Majesty has been ill informed. M-my husband has not been that foolish." The young woman's stammer betrayed her agitation.

—Ignoring her, His Imperial Majesty turned to his chief-of-staff, who was standing alongside. "You ought not to tolerate these things by one of your aides-de-camp. . . . At any rate, as you well know, I haven't paid any attention to these poor Périgords for some time."

Talleyrand soon had more direct evidence of continued imperial displeasure. He was sitting in the library at the Château Neuf helping Charlotte with her history lesson, while Anna-Dorothea was finishing a needlework billfold for him. The early fall sun, red as a cider apple, had sunk in the west and darkness pressed down like a thick wet sack when a footman appeared to say that an officer from the minister of police was at the door. The captain, hat tucked respectfully under one arm, was promptly ushered in, bowed ceremoniously and handed the vice-grand elector a dispatch dripping with seals. Talleyrand, his pale face as sphinx-like as ever, read the contents. Catherine had seen the Duc de San Carlos again, ignoring Napoleon's express command to the contrary. Despite an imperial injunction forbidding their correspondence, she had managed to remain in touch with her paramour. When she was passing through Ain, which was near Bourg-en-Bresse, where the Spanish duke was residing, still in banishment because of their liaison, the forty-nine-year-old woman disguised herself in the clothes of one of her male attendants and visited her lover. As a result she had been exiled still further from the capital, and the minister warned that the emperor threatened to send Talleyrand there also, if he could not control his wife. His admonition revealed the extent of the emperor's irritation, and Talleyrand dared not ignore the message, although why he should have been blamed for this meeting of the two middle-aged lovers is not clear. Faced with the possibility of exile too, Talleyrand told the captain to wait outside for a reply and dragged himself over to the cylindrical marquetry desk. Rolling back the top, he sat down and started to write. Several hours and innumerable drafts later—after reading aloud and reworking each line with Anna-Dorothea—he had a response that satisfied him. He had already eaten supper, his one significant meal of the day so, after a catnap, he let Courtiade shave and dress him and, at 5:00 a.m., he was off in his carriage, bound for Paris and the police minister's levée, where the affair was quickly settled to his satisfaction. In keeping with the dignity of the family name, Catherine was permitted to return to the Hôtel Matignon with the understanding that she live there in semi-retirement, and nothing further was said about any punishment for Talleyrand.

The grand duchess was the real winner. For Talleyrand profited from Catherine's escapade to live increasingly apart with Anna-Dorothea. On the surface the pattern of their life at Saint-Germain-en-Laye was a quiet one. He spent a lot of time outdoors. Astride a small chestnut mare, he rode daily with Charlotte under the tall oaks of the nearby forest, swinging his crop, now fast, now slow, as he concentrated on European problems. Talleyrand's musician-in-residence was on hand for the girl's piano lessons and entertained in the evening by playing personal compositions or improvising. While Talleyrand still drank very few spirits, with the exception of a good madeira, he was partial to coffee which he liked to savour in silence. So Carême sent out his special blend fresh daily from the Matignon and showed the grand duchess how to prepare the superb mocha which the fastidious Talleyrand insisted must be: "Black as the devil, Hot as hell, Pure as an angel, Sweet like love." [5]

The only discordant note was the Comtesse Kielmannsegge, a Saxon friend of the grand duchess whom she had invited to visit her. The countess who came west a fervent Bonapartist did not, unlike her hostess, lose any of this original enthusiasm. She saw the Château Neuf for the nest of anti-Napoleonic intrigue it was and, in her diary, she noted her highly uncomplimentary, first impression of Talleyrand "with his limping gait, his heavy body, his flashing eyes, his snake-like mouth and jaw, his paralyzing smile, and his affected flatteries." [6] In short order, she became the mistress of Savary, the Duc de Rovigo, who had replaced Fouché as minister of police and for whom she was soon an effective spy, reporting on the suspicious increase in the grand duchess's letters to the tsar. All of these were now dictated by Talleyrand, then written out by his devoted seraglio friend, the Vicomtesse de Laval, and sent to Saint Petersburg over Anna-Dorothea's signature. He kept reiterating the need for a close understanding with Austria and emphasized that for Russia to get the necessary European backing, Napoleon must bear the odium of beginning the war that Talleyrand hoped was to put an end to the Napoleonic passion for conquest.

When the Russian attaché, Count Nesselrode, was suspected by the imperial police of espionage and recalled, he was replaced by an intelligence officer from the Russian Imperial Guard. This new young colonel, Tchernychev, like his predecessor, was secretly accredited to Talleyrand by a holograph from Alexander, and was as welcome at Saint-Germain-en-Laye as Nesselrode had been. Meanwhile the police minister was stepping up the tempo of arrests and not solely because His Imperial Majesty had become overly sensitive to criticism. There were other reasons for this accelerated activity. When Tchernychev was due to leave Paris on one of his periodic trips to Saint Petersburg, he stopped at the Château Neuf to say farewell and collect some of the grand duchess's mail for the tsar. A few hours later, one of his colleagues was at the door demanding to see M. de Talleyrand at once. The colonel's secretary had just been arrested but his terrified cohort had managed to slip out the back door while the agents were still searching the colonel's bedroom. "No," the frightened man replied to Talleyrand's questioning, nervously twisting his hat by the brim, he did not think he had been followed to Saint-Germain-en-Laye. And "Yes," the colonel had gotten off safely. This was a relief. What if the true nature of Anna-Dorothea's present correspondence with Alexander came to light? Sufficient evidence of Tchernychev's spying was unearthed to justify official disregard for diplomatic immunity, and some of the Russian embassy servants were jailed. The trail did not stop there. The clerk in the war ministry who had been feeding the colonel army secrets was tracked down, summarily sentenced and speedily executed.

When the sale of the Matignon became financially imperative, painful as this was for Talleyrand, it was the emperor who came to the rescue. Not only did the state purchase his hotel but also his charming pavilion, La Muette, on the heights of Passy and, in addition, paid him an indemnity—of sorts—for boarding the Spanish princes still at Valençay. While Napoleon was in the habit of granting similar largesse— "[Marshals] Ney, Oudinot, and so many others never began or finished a battle without demanding such gifts from me" [7]—still it was surprising, under the circumstances, for Talleyrand to be receiving such imperial bounty. Thanks to this windfall, he was able to straighten out his affairs, as well as purchase the Paris townhouse of the Marquis d'Hervas, at 2, rue Saint-Florentin. Across from the Tuileries gardens, his new mansion was the magnificent equal of his former residence, but on the opposite—the Right—Bank of the Seine and lacked a park. He also acquired as his *de rigueur* summer abode, the château at Saint-Brice-la-Forêt, to the north of the capital.

The emperor did not hesitate to use Talleyrand whenever he considered him indispensable and, with war looming ever nearer, Napoleon called him to the château and asked him to undertake a crucial confidential mission. He was to be posted to Warsaw for the duration of the forthcoming conflict with the same functions he had held there earlier—to stimulate the Polish war effort and to supervise the victualing of the Grande Armée. Only Talleyrand possessed the requisite experience—as well as the highly placed Polish friends—to assure this. The vice-grand elector agreed to go but, because the designation of such a high government official for this task would dissipate any lingering doubts concerning an approaching opening of hostilities, silence about his new appointment was required.

When word of his upcoming assignment trickled out, Napoleon jumped to the conclusion that Talleyrand was responsible and was so furious that he immediately dispatched another in his place. Matters were not helped when, twenty-four hours later, the imperial censor discovered that Talleyrand had recently drawn a large draft on a bank in Vienna. The emperor summoned him to the Tuileries and thundered: "Is Austria trying to bribe you?" Talleyrand truthfully replied that he had been preparing for his forthcoming Polish post by getting the foreign currency he would need there. Napoleon ordered the leak traced. When the trail led to the salon of the Vicomtesse de Laval, he was positive his original supposition was correct. Talleyrand must be the culprit. As a warning to him and to teach society busybodies and newsmongers in general a lesson, Napoleon ordered the hostess in question into temporary exile. When the secret police finally exposed the wife of the incumbent foreign affairs minister, the Duchess de Bassano, as the responsible party, Napoleon rescinded the innocent vicomtesse's sentence and ordered the culprit to apologize.

Every day now, during the spring of 1812, the boulevards of Paris were streaming with marching soldiers. The rat-a-tat-tat of enlistment drums on every corner, and the rumble of military wagons over cobblestones filled the air as camions and cannons rumbled east.

Although Napoleon, when he left to join the Grande Armée, forbad Marie-Louise to invite him to her weekly whist night, Talleyrand fulfilled his duty and donned full court attire to pay a visit to the infant Roi de Rome—l'Aiglon.

The first units of the French army crossed the Niemen, five days after the American declaration of hostilities against England. Ironically, by interrupting traffic on the high seas, the War of 1812 virtually put an end to all contraband, thereby rendering partly useless the present French war effort. Talleyrand's seraglio was already scattering to avoid the Paris heat. Talleyrand so orchestrated their departures that every afternoon for almost a week, he arrived at a different hotel, solicitously stowed a hamper stuffed with the famous pâté of red pheasant and truffles from his Périgord estates into the waiting carriage, and escorted another of his *chères amies* part way on her trip. The Countess Tyszkiewicz left for Warsaw to follow more closely the fate of her beloved Poland. The "sultana"—as the seraglio members huffily referred to Anna-Dorothea behind her back—was the last to leave, anxious to personally oversee the protection of her eastern properties from the ravages of war. Talleyrand and Dorothea accompanied her as far as the first relay post where her great traveling berlin must change horses.

With Edmond, her husband, already headed east to join his regiment, Dorothea divided her time between the two new residences of *l'oncle's*, concentrating especially on his country seat. For Saint-Brice was in the forest of Montmorency, near Écouen, and close enough to Saint-Cloud to enable her to commute for her tour of duty when the court moved there. At nineteen, the last traces of the immature, underdeveloped child bride had vanished. However, Dorothea's appearance—with her haughty features and enormous eyes—was still too unusual for her to be called pretty. She had adopted the court vogue of heavy makeup, but the rouged circles painted on her pale cheeks, like on a doll's, did not detract from the velvety softness of her face. Dorothea's well-trained, eager mind, far more questioning and independent than her mother's, delighted Talleyrand as much as her improved looks. She had a surprising maturity of judgment, coupled with a refreshing absence of preconceptions and prejudices—although she never forgot her due as a princess. The deference she accorded *l'oncle* and her genuine interest in his ideas and convictions beguiled the cynical, hardened statesman, and he was challenged by the opportunity to shape his young niece's thinking.

He was also enjoying the daily history lesson, which he gave to Charlotte and his brother Boson's eleven-year-old daughter, Georgine who, with her parents, was spending the early fall with them. Just as Talleyrand spread out on a big table a huge map for the girls to locate with pins and follow the approximate whereabouts of the Grande Armée in the unknown vastness of Russia, so did most Parisians, each of whom had some beloved one with Napoleon. Talleyrand and Dorothea participated with the rest of officialdom in a victorious *Te Deum* in packed Notre Dame to celebrate the bloody, hard fought battle of Borodino on the Moskova River and, that evening, all the government buildings were illuminated.

Once Talleyrand moved back into town, the Marquise Aimée de Coigny, Montrond's former wife, was doubly welcome—especially with Anna-Dorothea and the Countess Tyszkiewicz still absent—when she made it a point, each morning, after doing her daily errands, to stop by the rue Saint-Florentin for a long chat. Enlisted by her present lover, Count Bruno de Boisgelin, an ardent royalist agent, to work for the Bourbon cause, she agreed that the present political situation could not last. Meditating with her about the *dénouement* which he saw approaching, Talleyrand, after enumerating Napoleon's faults and the harm which he was inflicting on France, concluded that he must be destroyed, "no matter how."

Gloomy rumors spread like pea soup fog over the capital, fueled by the intermittent official communiqués. After capturing the frontier fortress of Smolensk, called from its site the "Key of Russia"—just as Wellington and the British marched victoriously into far off Madrid—Napoleon set off eastward, virtually unopposed. Lured on by the elusive, retreating Russians, the emperor was anxious to finish off Alexander's forces and to winter in Moscow. After a fierce battle at the small town of Borodino on the snaking Kalatsha River, just west of Russia's Holy City, he entered the religious capital of the country. In spite of Russian-instigated fires, which started in Moscow's Chinese quarter that same evening and quickly spread, destroying part of the city, Napoleon remained there for a little more than a month. Failing to receive Alexander's anticipated offer of peace, the emperor finally decided on the retreat that a prematurely icy season would turn into a disaster. The Grande Armée was still deep in enemy territory when the tsar's dreaded ally, winter, struck. The first snow began to fall and the temperature dropped below freezing.

The famous *Bulletin XXIX* exploded like a bomb across the pages of the *Moniteur* on December 16, 1812, spreading the news of the French rout and Napoleon's narrow escape at the crossing of the Bérézina River. The next day, when Talleyrand started forth on his daily round of the various salons, his coachman had to slow down frequently to avoid the crowds gathered wherever *Bulletin XXIX* was posted. Everyone was listening carefully, anxious to catch some particle of hope they might have missed, while the few who could read the dramatic communiqué did so out loud, over and over, for the benefit of latecomers. Slowly, bit by bit, reality in all its horror sank in. Of the four hundred thousand men who proudly crossed the Niemen going east, only some twenty to thirty thousand straggled over it westward bound. Thousands died from exposure; other thousands were slaughtered by the peasants or ambushed and killed by the relentlessly pursuing Cossacks. Hundreds were prisoners. One question was on every Frenchman's lips: Where was the emperor?

Two days later, there was a loud pounding—instead of the customary scratching—on the door of the empress's Tuileries suite at the unheard-of hour of midnight, just as Dorothea finished her tour of duty and was getting ready to go home. Seconds later, two unshaven men bundled in furs thrust open the paneled doors and hurtled in. It was the emperor! And Talleyrand's good friend, Caulaincourt, the former ambassador to Russia! As the horses of the bottle-green court carriage, with its coachman and footman in livery to match, trotted her home, Dorothea wondered what *l'oncle* would make of Napoleon's unexpected reappearance. But she was unable to find out for, when she was deposited between the two marble lions at the great front door of the Hôtel Saint-Florentin, the lackey there informed her that "Monsieur" was still out. So Dorothea hastily scribbled a few lines relating what had occurred and rang for the trusted Courtiade to give them to Talleyrand before he retired.

12

President of the Provisional Government

"Even his civilities are usurious investments which must be paid for before the day's end."
—Pozzo di Borgo [1]

ALERTED BY QUICK-WITTED DOROTHEA, Talleyrand was one of the first to welcome the emperor home, hurrying to the château even before the canon of the Invalides barked out the dramatic news to still sleeping Parisians. If commerce and industry were in a critical state at home, the situation was equally gloomy abroad. There was growing fermentation in the German-speaking states and increasing disaster in Spain and, now, Talleyrand learned that the emperor had lost his entire cavalry, not to mention some one thousand artillery pieces, in his ill-fated Russian adventure. The army would have to be rebuilt; even more important, a difficult diplomatic campaign must be waged to strengthen existing alliances. For there was a very real danger that Napoleon's so-called "allies"—who were bound to him by gunpoint—would suddenly realize that the French emperor was no longer invulnerable and bolt. As might be expected, the emperor reverted to his usual panacea in similar situations in the past, for he was convinced that only a military victory could redress the worsening situation. Talleyrand, on the other hand, was more convinced than ever that the present situation called for peace, not more fighting.

Talleyrand's letters eastward to the grand duchess continued to be circumspect and non-committal, with no mention of public affairs, as if they were written solely for the benefit of the *cabinet noir*. Ever anxious to give himself as many options for the future as possible, Talleyrand seized the holiday season to send a New Year's greeting to his uncle, the Archbishop of Reims, his first communication since Alexandre-Angélique had gone into exile almost a decade before. This worthy, who was currently serving as the royal chaplain at the tiny, cheerless Bourbon court in Hartwell, England, wasted no time in showing the innocuous epistle to the guillotined Louis XVI's brother—the future Louis XVIII—as his nephew had hoped he would. Accepting it as the potential harbinger of better fortune, that stout, gout-ridden gentleman, who had a strong sense of humor, replied bitingly, "God be praised, Monseigneur l'Archévêque! Bonaparte must be near his end, for I wager that when the Directoire was on its last legs, your nephew wrote in the same way to him as the conqueror of Italy. If you answer him, tell him that I accept the augury of his good memory." [2]

At a council meeting, the first week in January, called after word was received of the defection of the Prussian army—and just prior to the news that the Prussian king had allied with the tsar—Napoleon went around the table asking for advice. Greatly troubled, as in the past, by the emperor's predilection for military action as the cure-all, Talleyrand certainly wished no good to the emperor's present policy. However, professional pride undoubtedly entered in when asked to deliver an opinion on such a question and, rather than say what he knew Napoleon wanted to hear, he said what he himself believed, as in his famous memorandum from Strasbourg years before. Courageously, Talleyrand urged him to negotiate. "Today you still have some chips with which to bargain that could be sacrificed without really affecting your imperial power. If Your Majesty waits and loses them, you can no longer come to terms." [3]

If Napoleon did not want to follow Talleyrand's advice, he did want to take advantage of the latter's international prestige and ability. While diverging in detail, accounts of high government colleagues agree that, during the next few days, Talleyrand was ordered back to the château several times and, with his good friend Caulaincourt acting as intermediary, offered the return of the green Foreign Ministry portfolio. These contemporary memoirs unanimously speak of various strings attached to the imperial proposal, but they disagree as to what these conditions were. Did Napoleon insist that Talleyrand first relinquish his official position as vice-grand elector? Did he require that Catherine de Talleyrand and certain other females be banned from the rue du Bac? Napoleon had already branded her as a troublemaker to Caulaincourt, when the tiny handful of imperial intimates was rushing home with the emperor on the long, melancholy sleigh ride from Russia. Napoleon must have known that anyone as proud and independent as Talleyrand would not tolerate interference in his private life. Whatever the actual stipulations, Talleyrand had a plausible excuse for his refusal. He had been out of office and banished from the imperial confidence. How could he be expected to pick up the maze of the emperor's thinking on a moment's notice? In his desire to curb Napoleon at Erfurt, Talleyrand betrayed the man as an individual but, in denying the emperor his services now, was Talleyrand also betraying France? Presciently terming the Russian debacle "the beginning of the end," Talleyrand must have felt there was no point in dwelling on the past. As he loved to say: "The good Lord has put our eyes in our foreheads so we can look ahead, never behind." Following his third refusal to serve, the exasperated emperor's burst of anger reverberated in his ears as His Imperial Majesty stomped out. "The emperor is charming this morning," Talleyrand remarked as he limped through the courtiers clustered, eavesdropping as usual, in the adjacent chamber.

With the emperor once more in residence criticism sank to a muted whisper but, so strongly had public reaction set in against further bloodshed that it was increasingly difficult to round up conscripts for the badly needed troops. To bolster public morale and present a brave front for the man in the street, weekly balls were renewed at the Tuileries, despite the fact that all Paris was wearing black for missing beloved ones, and many appeared at these affairs minus an arm or a leg. For gallantry in the recent fighting on the distant eastern steppes, young Flahaut was elevated to the coveted post of imperial aide-de-camp, which carried with it membership in the imperial household. And, when Napoleon went out to the small Trianon château at Versailles for a brief respite from the capital's somber atmosphere with only Marie-Louise, Queen Hortense, and three aides-de-camp, one of them was Flahaut, whose unacknowledged, eighteen-month-old son by the Dutch queen, was being secretly raised in the countryside with a trusted family servant of Adèle de Flahaut. Despite the rigors of the recent campaign Charles, unlike most of his comrades had, surprisingly, now put on weight and Talleyrand commented—paternal pride showing through—that he had obviously just returned from Cocayne—a fabled medieval land of luxury and idleness.

Recent events in the east rekindled royalists' hopes, and they increased their efforts to ferret out potential supporters, especially in imperial circles. Since Aimée felt it no longer prudent to appear so regularly at the Hôtel Saint-Florentin, she maintained contact with Talleyrand less conspicuously in his seraglio's salons. When Napoleon returned to the German battlefields in the spring of 1813 she resumed her visits to the Saint-Florentin. Talleyrand mentioned increasingly the possibility of a regency for Napoleon's son, the little King of Rome, or even a national monarchy under the Duc d'Orléans, a collateral Bourbon cousin. Aware the royalist pretender stood no chance to aspire to the throne unless he could get the support of a powerful section of imperialists who would follow Talleyrand's lead, and anxious to know more exactly where the vice-grand elector stood, one day Aimée mentioned a letter she and her lover Boisgelin were composing to Hartwell. This explained the present situation in France and insisted on the importance of wooing Talleyrand to the royalist cause. After getting up and hobbling to the door to be sure no one was listening outside, he closed it tightly and came back to Aimée, shrugging his shoulders. "Mme de Coigny, I wish the king well, but . . ." his voice dragged off. How could he be sure of Louis XVIII's reactions to many items in his own revolutionary past? Could a married priest ever be tolerated at the court of the Most Christian King? What about his participation in the Enghien affair? Or his role as jailer of the captive Spanish princes? He then explained that he did not personally know the legitimate heir to the Bourbon throne and requested to see a draft of their letter. "I confess that I have no wish to expose myself to forgiveness instead of gratitude, or to have to defend myself." [4] The next day when she returned with their letter he read it aloud and encouraged her to carry on this correspondence, saying that the pair should keep him posted. He then pushed aside the fan-shaped, bronze fire screen. Twisting the letter, he lit it from a candle, threw it in flames into the fireplace and crossed the shovel and tongs on top so as to prevent any ashes from flying up the chimney. As a statesman he knew how to destroy a secret secretly, Aimée observed in her memoirs, where she takes credit for bringing the vice-grand elector into the fold, ". . . I easily excited his bile against the emperor"—as if Talleyrand's anti-Napoleonic bile needed any stimulation.

Meanwhile the emperor, who was resolved to strike fast and dispose of Russia and Prussia before Austria was ready to join the fray, set forth with an entirely new army and, in less than a month, impressive French victories chased them behind the Oder River. Unfortunately, by pushing so far so fast, the emperor found himself overextended, and any further course of action was hindered by poor supply lines. Since Austria was still not ready to join the fray and Napoleon, too, was in need of time to beef up his army and cavalry, the emperor agreed to Metternich's suggestion of an armistice. This opened under the Austrian's presidency in Prague in mid-summer, but talks soon broke off when it became evident that the French emperor was not negotiating in good faith but only stalling for time. At midnight, on August 11, as the door of the famous Gothic clock on Prague's Town Hall sprang open and out stepped the wooden figures of the Twelve Apostles to bow and retreat, one by one, with each stroke of the clapper, the chancellor signed the Austrian declaration of war on France. The order was immediately given to light the mammoth signal bonfires on the crest of the hill high above the city to relay across Bohemia their message of impending bloodshed and carnage. The Russian-Prussian-Austrian coalition vowed not to lay down arms until Napoleon was so tamed that he could no longer cause any more trouble, and the Austrian field marshal, Prince Schwarzenberg, was named commander-in-chief.

This summer, like the previous one, Talleyrand spent in the country at Saint-Brice, riding horseback in the morning with Charlotte and, in the afternoon, reworking his notes of conversations with Napoleon. His only court duty was a twice-weekly visit to Saint-Cloud to pay his respects to the empress—and, incidentally, pick up the latest news. Never one to anticipate or hasten things along, he was patiently monitoring the developing scene, while trying to make the *cabinet noir* forget about his existence. One day he asked the Comtesse Kielmannsegge: "What opinion do you think posterity will have of me? People always talk too ill or too well of me. I enjoy the honors of exaggeration. *Eh bien*! I want people, for centuries to come, to discuss what I have been, what I have thought, and what I wanted." [5] Around him and under his influence there was a slowly burgeoning number of doubters in the highest official circles, including in the Senate, as each individual commenced to think of himself. Audacious premises were discussed by Talleyrand and his intimates and, with an absent emperor, no one any longer feared to share these thoughts with others—in whispers.

Talleyrand's nephew, Edmond, had been in and out of Paris intermittently, on leave, and Dorothea, who was again *enceinte* and feeling poorly, spent a good part of each afternoon languishing on a couch. However, one late fall day she bundled up in a greatcoat she had had lined with remnants from bundles of sables the tsar had given her as a wedding gift and watched from a Hôtel Saint-Florentin balcony, as *l'oncle* officially participated when the Imperial Chief of Staff presented Marie-Louise with twenty recently captured enemy flags. The crowds were exultant at this stirring, military pageant in the great, festively decorated square below. Through his private underground, Talleyrand knew that the victories being celebrated had already been superseded by a major catastrophe at Leipzig in mid-October. Overwhelmed by sheer numbers, the French barely escaped, hacking their way through a bloody hole to beat a full retreat across the Rhine. Who knew what these same cheering masses would do when they learned that France itself was now on the verge of invasion? And, hard on the fleeing French heels, the allied general headquarters followed their swift-moving, westbound armies, flaring out like a vast peacock's tail, swollen by the surplus baggage wagons necessary to accommodate the needs of a king, an emperor, and a tsar in the field. The closer the allies' campaign, with England as paymaster, came to a finale, the nearer to the surface surged the power struggle between the Austrian chancellor and Alexander for control of the war's last stages. One day the pair almost came to blows over the route the armies should take. Then, the next, a temperamental tsar received Metternich, the latter reported, "like a mistress after a bad case of the sulks," and embraced him affectionately.

Early in November Madame de la Tour du Pin, with whom Talleyrand had remained in contact ever since the couple had come back from America, visited him before returning home, so she might bring her husband, who was now prefect at Amiens, the latest news. Talleyrand suggested she delay her departure another twenty-four hours. Napoleon was due back momentarily, and he promised to stop by after he attended the imperial levée at Saint-Cloud. Spotting the vice-grand elector in his bedchamber the next morning, the emperor lashed out: "What are you doing here? You claim to be in an opposition party . . . and you imagine that if I were to fail . . . you would be the head of a Regency Council? Take care,"

His Imperial Majesty barked. "Nothing is gained by fighting against my power. I assure you that if I were dangerously ill, you would be dead before I was." Ever the consummate courtier Talleyrand, who was never at a loss for words, suavely replied, as if he had just received a new sign of imperial favor. "Sire, I had no need for such a warning for me to fervently pray to heaven for the conservation of your Majesty!"

Lucy was anxious to start her homeward journey, but it was after 11:00 p.m. before Talleyrand arrived. Ignoring her obvious impatience for information, and to tease her, he took up a candelabrum and started leisurely examining the pictures on the wall. Unable to control herself, the young woman impatiently blurted out, "You have seen the emperor?"

Talleyrand tossed a log onto the fire and settled down in a comfortable chair, drawing another over to prop up his bad right leg. Finally, fumbling in his pocket, Talleyrand drew out a crumbled newspaper clipping, which he had lately received through his personal pipeline in the censor's office, and handed it to her. "Here, you know English. Read this article." It described a London dinner given recently by the Prince Regent in honor of the Duchess d'Angoulême, the daughter of Louis XVI. The dining room was draped in sky-blue satin, with bouquets of lilies-of-the-valley all around and an *epérgne de table* was decorated with the same flowers; there was also a *service de Sévres* showing different scenes of Paris. Stupefied, Lucy handed the paper back to Talleyrand. With that exquisite sly smile only he possessed, he folded it slowly and stuffed it back into his pocket. Then he rang and told the footman to call her carriage because she insisted upon driving back to Amiens that night.

His Imperial Majesty apparently received convincing proof that Talleyrand was in communication with his enemies, but he still hesitated to accuse him of treason. This was not the moment to roil the simmering domestic scene by attacking him on such a charge.

In mid-December the allies, from their Frankfurt headquarters, offered a peace proposal which was promptly rejected. So their armies, three hundred thousand strong, with the three sovereigns riding at their head, set forth westward. Throughout France fatigue, exhaustion, discouragement, disgust, the need for rest predominated, together with an overwhelming desire for a return to family life and regular work. In the two principal salons where official society gathered, word of this invasion into French territory produced diametrically different reactions. At the foreign secretary's, an imperial miracle was anticipated; at the Hôtel

Saint-Florentin, peace was demanded at any price and one discreetly murmured—with no small satisfaction—about the possible fall of the empire. An expert navigator, the crafty Talleyrand was not yet sure what the wave of the future might wash ashore, and he was cautiously keeping his options open, awaiting the course of events. As one member of his seraglio commented cryptically, "Whatever course Charles-Maurice chooses to follow, nothing he does would surprise me—except an error of taste."

Upon his return from the obligatory appearance at the Tuileries' New Year's Day reception, Talleyrand managed a courtesy call, together with the grand duchess, on Josephine out in the country at Malmaison. Some ten days later, as a council meeting was breaking up, the emperor, whose mistrust of Talleyrand was being nourished anew by continuing rumors, unexpectedly raised his voice, claiming he was surrounded by traitors. In a replay of earlier scenes, though he had nothing new or more specific to accuse him of, His Imperial Majesty turned to face Talleyrand, spewing forth a stream of harsh, offensive words. That gentleman, who was standing near the fireplace, shifted to lean against the mantel and gazed over his master's head into the distance, as if totally oblivious to all the commotion. The imperial anger spent, the emperor exited, slamming the door. Calmly accepting the proffered arm of another councilor, Talleyrand then left too, proceeding downstairs without once opening his mouth. What principle of honor could keep him attached to the service of any man who so belabored him? His horrified colleagues expected an immediate order to conduct him to the donjon at Vincennes. This time, Talleyrand, too, must have thought his time had come because, when he got home, he had a vast quantity of possibly compromising papers destroyed.

On Sunday, January 23, following mass, Talleyrand was an impassive witness when the emperor received the officers of the National Guard in the great Hall of the Marshals and, in a dramatic, emotional scene, presented to them his three-year-old son, l'Aiglon—the Eaglet—and Marie-Louise. This was the last time Talleyrand would ever again see Napoleon who left for the front at dawn, forty-eight hours later. The main line of battle now shifted and lay between Paris and the frontier. The campaign Napoleon was to fight on French soil, outmanned and outgunned, would be the most brilliant of his career, with sixteen-year-old boys dying bravely alongside exhausted veterans; while masses of allied troops converged on all sides of the enemy, he was compelled to operate on the flanks and rear rather than in front.

With Napoleon away and news scarce in Paris, the Tuileries remained the best source of information. So, punctually at 5:00 p.m., Talleyrand dined nightly with Anna-Dorothea before hastening there to play whist, usually at Marie-Louise's table. There was also the customary facade of official entertainment, including a lavish fête given by the visiting queen of Naples, Napoleon's sister, Caroline. None of the several thousand guests present that evening seemed aware that three enemy armies were marching towards the city, alternating fighting with attempted peace negotiations.

Talleyrand, who was inordinately fond of children, made a point of stopping regularly to check on the newest family addition, Alexander-Edmond, named after his godfather, the tsar. Dorothea's older boy, Napoléon-Louis, was the French emperor's godchild. There was no longer fresh milk for little Dorothea, not quite two, and for her brothers, and no more cream for the adults because the army had impounded *l'oncle's* cows at Saint-Brice. Horses had also been requisitioned but, fortunately, Talleyrand, as a member of the Regency Council, was permitted to keep a pair, for it was impossible for him to walk any distance. He warned that conditions would get worse before they got better, but there was nothing to be uneasy about—yet. Nonetheless one should be prepared for any eventuality, "so as not to commit any imprudences."

Four days after Caulaincourt undertook the renewal of peace negotiations, which had moved from Frankfurt to Châtillon-sur-Seine, Talleyrand sent the grand duchess a charming miniature of the Virgin with instructions to "place [this] above your bed to protect you from danger wherever you are. I love you with all my soul—in harsh times as well as gentler ones." [6]

And she was off, accompanied by a trunkful of Talleyrand's clothes—in case he was caught short and had to quit the capital in a hurry—to join Dorothea, who had already left with her youngsters and a battery of nurses and maids, for Rosny, Edmond's inherited, rosy brick château overlooking the Seine, sixty kilometers northwest of Paris. Urging the grand duchess to believe only what he himself wrote, Talleyrand's daily letters remained calm, with just a rare recorded cry of anguish at the humiliation of seeing France at the mercy of invaders. "One would have to be without an ounce of French blood not to suffer horribly from all the evils and all the humiliation our unhappy country is experiencing." [7]

When Mâcon fell, the irrepressible French, who would pun until Judgment Day, claimed that they did not know how to respond when they were attacked by twenty-four bore cannons because they only had cannons *du vin* (cannons of twenty bore).[1] The wildest rumors were the order of the day. This lack of accurate information so disturbed Talleyrand that he arranged a private code with Caulaincourt to remain abreast of the negotiations the latter was conducting at Châtillon and was willing to keep Talleyrand secretly posted in the hope that the latter could help force Napoleon to accept peace. Suddenly, the emperor, although outnumbered five to one, wheeled and defeated several allied detachments. When one of his aides tried to moderate his elation Napoleon, drunk with hope, replied in his best barracks-room argot, "The lion isn't dead yet. It's too early to piss on him." [8] His Imperial Majesty, a shrewd gambler, promptly raised the ante for Caulaincourt's peace mission, and the Big Four—England, Austria, Russia, Prussia—concluded that it was impossible to negotiate with the emperor. They had no alternative but to rid Europe of him once and for all.

Even from the battlefield Napoleon kept an eye on Talleyrand. When the police minister, walking past, unusually late one evening, noticed several carriages parked in the entry of his hotel, he decided to pay an unannounced call, hoping to catch him conspiring. Eluding footmen and servants, the heavyset Rovigo managed to creep up the great front staircase unnoticed—no small feat—and burst open the library doors only to find the master of the house playing cards—whist, presumably—with several of his regular cronies. As soon as the grand duchess heard of this she rushed back to town to be with him. Talleyrand was overjoyed and touched that she wanted to share these perilous days at his side. "Ah, *ma Chère*," his billets now echoed, "I can bear everything when I am near you. . . . In times of anxiety, one needs to be near those one loves and you . . . are the first and tenderest interest of my love." [9]

Time dragged by with no further news. The orders His Imperial Majesty sent to Paris were no longer carried out unhesitantly but questioned. His officers had fought almost without respite since 1789, so long as war meant glory and conquest, and they were engaged outside France. This was something else again. Imperial personnel, especially the military, was discouraged, not because of daily dangers but because there

---
[1] i.e. vin = wine or vingt (20).

was no foreseeable end to them. Now they, too, wanted peace; the whole country wanted peace.

Because of his reputation for shrewdness, all Paris visited Talleyrand to know his thinking. He alone, they thought, could find a way out of the current impasse. Since he never revealed his secret thoughts, it is debatable if his own mind was yet made up which way to go. To maintain his reputation as the best informed man in the capital was hard work. Since he was still privileged to read all official reports, his handsome coach and horses, with their liveried attendants, could be seen daily making the rounds. A stop at the Postmaster-General's, on the rue Jean-Jacques Rousseau, was a must because this was the headquarters for couriers carrying dispatches between the army and the government. Talleyrand was next deposited at the Prefect of the Paris police where he was shown the day's summary of events with its crucial particulars on the worsening public moral. Equally rewarding was a visit to the Luxembourg Palace, the Paris residence of Joseph Bonaparte, whom Napoleon had named lieutenant-general during his absence, and where he often picked up nuggets of value.

He also touched base, as often as it was prudent, with Aimée de Coigny, as well as with his adoring seraglio, whose aristocratic faubourg Saint-Germain roots made them a built-in claque, should their "dear Charles-Maurice" opt definitely in favor of a Bourbon restoration. For these women could persuade royalist doubters to overcome their natural distaste for a renegade like Talleyrand and convince them that for France to be won over to the cause of Louis XVIII his help was essential. Everywhere, everyone was preoccupied with the same thought: Everything is coming to an end. What comes next?

The off-again, on-again peace negotiations at Châtillon, which had opened in early February, were especially disturbing to Talleyrand who considered an allied military victory as the best way to dispose of Napoleon and was worried that the emperor might come to terms with the allies at the conference table. For he was convinced that a change of government was the only way to get the country back on its feet and reverse the imperial course of war—and still more war. If the allies won—which seemed almost certain—they would be the real masters of France. They must not treat with Napoleon, thereby propping up his floundering regime. But would they leave the country free to choose its own institutions or deliver it up to an anarchy of which it was impossible to foresee the results? Opinion in the city was divided. With whom would the allies treat? Was there any chance of a Bourbon Restoration? Or did Metternich prefer a regency for Napoleon's son, l'Aiglon? Since Francis I was l'Aiglon's grandfather, such a solution would place the Austrian emperor and his chancellor in a dominant position. But l'Aiglon was only a child. His regime would never survive the unrest and disorder that must necessarily follow France's defeat. And what did the tsar want? Even the grand duchess did not have a clue. The last letters that had succeeded in reaching her from influential eastern European sources only mentioned that before departing to command his army, Alexander had taken to reading the Bible daily and was increasingly leaving important meetings to consult it for guidance.

The best way to parry the danger of the disastrous continuation of the empire was to alert the allies to the exact situation in Paris and to the increasing interest there in a Bourbon restoration. Here Talleyrand's whist crony, the Badenois Baron Emmerich de Dalberg, once more proved his resourcefulness. But heads would roll should his scheme miscarry, and nervous tics crisscrossed the wiry diplomat's birdlike face as he outlined his plan. It was one thing to talk treason, another to enter into active communication with the emperor's enemies. Nonetheless, an acquaintance, Baron de Vitrolles, a confirmed, starry-eyed royalist, was anxious to brief the Comte d'Artois, Louis XVIII's brother, who was presently at Nancy, with news about the growing Parisian enthusiasm for the Bourbons. And he was willing to undertake the perilous mission of penetrating the enemy lines to reach allied headquarters. As credentials Dalberg intended to supply Vitrolles with the names of two Viennese sisters whose favors he had once shared with Metternich's predecessor at the Viennese Ballhausplatz. The women's names were to be written on a piece of paper small enough to slip into Vitrolles's watchcase and in invisible ink that would only appear when the scrap was held over a candle. Dalberg would also furnish the emissary with the carnelian seal engraved with his family coat of arms that was presently dangling from the watch chain stretched taut across his vividly embroidered vest. These two items would clearly identify the royalist to the former Austrian foreign minister as having come from the Badenois.

So far so good. But how did Dalberg intend to accredit Vitrolles to the Russians, Talleyrand demanded. He shrugged. This should not prove a problem either, since the present Russian foreign minister was his cousin, the same red-headed Count Nesselrode who had been a frequent visitor at the grand duchess's summer home at Saint-Germain-en-Laye when he was stationed in Paris some years before. Since Nesselrode was familiar with his cousin, Dalberg's, handwriting, Talleyrand suggested the latter send him a note and rang for a footman to bring some writing materials. Clearing a space on an adjacent, ormolu-decorated, Reisener desk, and half leaning, characteristically, against it, he dictated while the Baden minister wrote, on a small square of notched stationery bordered in gray: "The person I am sending to you is completely trustworthy. Listen to him and be grateful to me. You are walking on crutches when you can make use of your legs to greater advantage." [10] The meaning was clear. To put an end to useless fighting—and a probable military occupation of France—Talleyrand was willing to give the enemy the signal to take Paris. However, like the monkey in the fable who would not risk singeing his paw to get the chestnut, but let the cat do it for him, Talleyrand was too cautious even to meet Vitrolles. So, on the face of it, only the Baden minister accredited Vitrolles to the Austrian and Russian officials. If, at the outset, Dalberg should encounter hesitancy convincing Vitrolles of Talleyrand's support for his mission, the grand duchess would readily do so. She had become acquainted with the intrepid royalist when he lived in an émigré colony near her country seat, Löbikau, during the Revolution.

 The end of the first week in March, Vitrolles set off on a Lyon-bound coach on a trip that would have done the intrepid three Musketeers proud. Talleyrand must have found the ensuing silence deafening for, conceivably, his own neck might now be at risk, but there is nothing to indicate his state of mind as time passed with no word from Vitrolles and no noticeable allied reaction. Then word reached Paris that Wellington, who was marching north, sweeping all before him, had taken Bordeaux and that, several days later—on March 12—its jubilant inhabitants had hoisted the royal standard on its highest tower. The following week, thanks to Caulaincourt and their private code, Talleyrand was again the first in Paris to learn that the negotiations at Châtillon had definitively broken off. Following hard upon word of the Bordeaux proclamation, this was welcome news to those anxious to supplant the emperor, and probably decisive for Talleyrand.

 As the news from Bordeaux seemed to indicate, there was a ground swell for the Bourbons. The return of the former ruling house would seem to be the best way to get the French ship of state afloat again. But would it be the best way for Talleyrand to save himself and all his baggage? This was the essential determinant for him. Whatever the new regime, Talleyrand wanted a major role in it equal to the one he now enjoyed, and he intended to realize all possible advantages for himself while limiting further catastrophes for France. This personal agenda determined his public actions and, from this point of view, treason became the most sacred of duties. As he would say, in later life: "It was neither betraying Napoleon nor conspiring against him. I have never conspired in my life except at those times when I had the majority of the French for accomplices and we searched together for our country's salvation." To what extent revenge played a role is hard to determine. If wounded pride was a sufficiently strong factor for a man to risk, or lose, his life in a duel over a real or imagined insult, what can one say about the proud, aristocratic Talleyrand's reactions to the repeated, scurrilous epithets the emperor hurled at him.

Difficult as it is to pinpoint when Talleyrand finally decided that Louis XVIII was the answer—both for himself and for France—these two events occurring at this particular time presumably crystallized his thinking and put an end to his indecision. Up until now events had not imposed the necessity for Talleyrand to choose between what he considered the only two feasible alternatives to the Napoleonic empire—a Bourbon restoration or the regency of Marie-Louise. And he had successfully avoided committing himself irrevocably either way, playing whist with the empress without breaking contact with Aimée and the Bourbons.

Dorothea's next tour of duty as imperial-lady-in-waiting was due shortly. But *l'oncle* was so concerned about her safety that he forbade her to leave Rosny and started spreading rumors of her illness in order to manufacture an acceptable alibi for her impending absence from court. He also advised Anna-Dorothea that there was still no need to be on edge. But his own nerves clearly showed through when he complained bitterly to her about the allies' continued lack of response to Vitrolles's presumably successful mission. "All that faces him [Prince Schwarzenberg] is the corps of Marmont . . . which can't possibly put up any resistance, and still he doesn't move. It's unbelievable. The proverbial Austrian slowness never deserved its reputation more." [11]

Nesselrode would preserve in his personal archives the small square of paper that Vitrolles had given him, pinned together with the notation that it had determined the allied march on Paris. Its obscure message had been taken seriously because Vitrolles was accepted as accredited by Talleyrand, and it was well known that the wily statesman never associated with any venture unless it had a good chance of success. This was the first indication the allies had, since entering France, that he might cooperate and left the distinct impression, as was intended, that there were people in Paris who would guide and help them. However, the allied command had a healthy respect for Napoleon as a military strategist who had bounced back successfully after severe defeats in the past. Undecided among themselves about the proposed march to the French capital, they kept postponing a decision. Then, on the night of March 24, Cossacks intercepted an imperial courier. Among his dispatches were a series of reports from the minister of police, and other officials, warning Napoleon that public opinion was so opposed to resistance that it would be almost impossible to defend the city if the enemy approached because the populace wanted peace at any price. Whatever the ultimate determining factor the tsar, no longer hesitant, gave the order to continue on to the French capital the next morning, and the allies soon had two hundred thousand men concentrated between the Marne and the Seine.

Paris had been without news of Napoleon for some time but restaurants, cafés, even the Franconi circus, were packed. Parisians were restless, curious, seeking and passing on the latest rumors. Carriage loads drove out to Meaux to see the cannon protecting the capital, and the Louvre had a rush of visits from people who feared its treasures would soon be carted off by the allies as Napoleon had done earlier in their respective countries. Would the Russians also sack Paris like the French had Moscow? As the conviction mounted that the emperor with the sixty-thousand-plus troops still with him would not arrive in time to rescue his capital, Parisians debated whether the city should resist at all, and the menace of invasion hung in the air.

On Sunday, the twenty-seventh, Talleyrand's morning billet to Anna-Dorothea tersely commented: "The empire is crumbling." However, he found the château in excellent spirits that evening. Marie-Louise gave the order to cut the envelope holding the cards, and he had an early game of whist with Her Imperial Majesty. Nonetheless, friends who came to the small salon attached to Talleyrand's loge at the Comédie-Française later to enjoy an ice during the *entr'acte* of Beaumarchais's *The Barber of*

Seville, had been delayed by the throngs of peasants driving their livestock before them into the comparative safety of the city's outskirts.

The next day the allies clashed in the suburbs with the vanguards of Marshals Marmont and Mortier and, when Parisians gathered, it was no longer to sew on their needlepoint but to make bandages for the wounded who were being rushed into the capital's hospitals. Joseph Bonaparte opened an emergency meeting of the Regency Council, which was called to decide whether the empress should leave the threatened city. A letter he read them from the emperor declared that there was no more miserable fate than that of Astyanax, who had been taken prisoner by the Greeks in the Trojan War. Napoleon preferred his son at the bottom of the Seine rather than in the hands of France's enemies. When the opinion of each member of the council was polled on what course of action to pursue Talleyrand, who knew that Joseph mistrusted him and that he only had to recommend one course of action to be sure that the opposite would be adopted, stated with Machiavellian intent that the empress should remain. Because Talleyrand felt that the flight of Marie-Louise and the acting government would almost automatically entail the capitulation of Paris, he wanted her to go. And so it was decided. Hobbling out afterwards, Talleyrand turned to a colleague: "What an historic catastrophe! To bequeath one's name to a series of adventures rather than to one's century! Not everyone wants to be engulfed in the collapse of this edifice!" [12]

Snow was turning into a dreary drizzle which only magnified the lugubrious mood, the following morning, as high imperial officials gathered for the obligatory farewell ceremony, when the empress and l'Aiglon set off for Blois by way of Rambouillet. Joseph was to follow in a few hours after arranging for the imminent departure of the various other grand dignitaries whom the emperor had carefully enumerated—including Talleyrand—who were to follow. That evening there was the usual large number of guests at dinner at the Hôtel Saint-Florentin and, even before the meal was over, the great salon upstairs was filled with anxious visitors who had learned of the empress's departure and wanted to chart a personal course of action. When was Talleyrand leaving to follow her to Blois? Should they depart too?

By dawn the roar of the distant cannon was clearly audible from Talleyrand's bedroom as desperate fighting erupted to the northeast of Paris between the Russians and the French, who were fighting with their backs to the city's walls. Yet there was not a word about the struggle on the front page of the official *Moniteur* where the most prominent story concerned the queen of England's cold. Spectators were filling the chairs that lined the main boulevards to watch the columns of men march forth to join the embattled army—mere youths for the most part. Some of Talleyrand's friends who did not plan to flee had already hired masons and carpenters to build special hiding places for their valuables; others were having diamonds sewed into clothes linings. In the late afternoon, by the time a truce was declared, the allies had already encircled three-quarters of the capital but the west of Paris and the road to Rambouillet were still clear, and Talleyrand should have been on his way. But so many things could happen in the next twenty-four hours that Talleyrand was convinced that he had nothing to gain and everything to lose by leaving now—before the allies arrived. Ever the consummate gambler, he kept postponing his departure.

It was of paramount importance that by staying he not be accused of treason. At 5:00 p.m. a Cease Fire was signed, and Talleyrand went to see Rovigo, whom he tried, unsuccessfully, to convince that at least one high government official must remain in the capital to treat with the allies.

He next changed into traveling clothes and, accompanied by his secretary, appeared at the Porte de la Conference, an exit from Paris on the Chaillot side, where he managed to be refused permission to depart on the grounds that this was not the moment to abandon the city. Claiming indignantly that he was being prevented from doing his duty and joining the empress, he hurried home and hastened to write Her Imperial Highness. "Imagine! He had been refused authorization to depart!" Then he learned, with relief, that Marmont, as commander of the imperial forces in the capital, had begun parleys for an armistice to save Paris the horrors of an assault.

Talleyrand's immediate concern was how to advise the allies that he remained in the city, without flirting with possible treason charges. Around midnight, he went to the Hôtel Pérégueux, the marshal's home on the rue Paradis, ostensibly to inquire whether his chances of rejoining the empress had improved. Although filled with government officials and the military, the atmosphere there was distinctly anti-Bonaparte; few, including Marmont himself, his uniform torn, his hands and face blackened from gunpowder, wanted the fight to continue. Talleyrand created a sensation as he dragged himself through one crowded salon after another, advertising the fact that he was still in Paris and not at Rambouillet. The tsar's two commissioners who had come to sign the French capitulation were dumbfounded. He, in turn, feigned surprise at finding them there and, in a voice loud enough to be heard by all present, begged Count Orloff, whom he knew by sight: "Be so good as to convey to the feet of the Tsar of All the Russians, the profound respect of the Prince de Bénévent." [13] Turning, with a bow, to the assembled guests, he then limped out.

The following morning—"the most important day of my life," according to his *Mémoires*—he scheduled his levée for the unheard-of hour of 6:30 a.m. Courtiade removed the twelve nightcaps wound around his master's head as protection should he fall out of his high, canopied bed, and was busy supervising the two valets powdering his hair when Nesselrode, the Russian foreign minister, was announced. Taken by surprise, Talleyrand leapt to his feet, snatched the towel from around his neck and stumbled eagerly towards the great central staircase. Spewing rice powder, the normally self-controlled man embraced his unexpected visitor so enthusiastically that the latter was white from head to foot in an amber-scented cloud. Nesselrode came with word that Alexander wanted to announce to the Parisians the allies' immediate plans and that the tsar would see Talleyrand following their official entry into the city. Then Caulaincourt arrived from Fontainebleau, where Napoleon had appeared with his remaining troops after two days of forced marches, to ask for support for the Emperor. But, from the little he overheard of the conversation in a corner of the room, Caulaincourt realized there was little hope for Napoleon here.

The war was far from finished and, if several days were lost in futile negotiations, the allies might occupy all France. Up to then Talleyrand had moved prudently and with characteristic slowness. Now, conversely, he would prove himself prompt and audacious, for he was aware that the ensuing twenty-four hours were critical.

At 11:00 a.m., for the first time in four centuries an enemy army entered the French capital, and no Parisian wanted to miss the sight. The weather cleared, lending itself to the occasion, and trumpets heralded their entry as the allied troops—there were thirty-five thousand cavalry alone—followed the boulevards, lined with an immense, cheering crowd, and clattered down the cobblestones of the still unfinished rue de Rivoli. On they came, in red, white, blue, and green uniforms, plumes and tassels waving, burnished helmets gleaming, from all over Europe and included, as well, kamluks from Mongolia, tungus from Siberia, even Circassian chiefs from the Caucasus. At their head, with the King of Prussia on his left and Schwarzenberg on his right, rode Alexander, bowing, smiling, waving, dressed, as usual, all in white, his far from lean waist girdled by a vast black belt, and his narrow shoulders padded out, coquettishly, by glittering gold epaulettes. Surrounded by the giant, red-uniformed Cossacks of his Imperial Guard, trailed by hundreds of officers, that day the tsar seemed the arbiter of Europe. The sovereign whose people had suffered the most, he took the unending parade past in the great square, which bordered on one side the terraces of the Tuileries, and which the Hôtel Saint-Florentin abutted. The grand duchess, who was on a balcony there to watch, recognized Alexander's grey mare as the one Napoleon had given him in happier days at the Erfurt conference. However, Talleyrand was not alongside her to witness the spectacle. He and Nesselrode, who were inside, barely had time to finish drafting the proclamation to the French, in the name of the allies, on which they had been working all morning, when Alexander dismounted and strode across to Talleyrand's hotel as his troops started to disperse.

With Prussia his subservient satellite, the Austrian emperor and Metternich stranded by a troop bottleneck near Dijon, Wellington still in the south, and Castlereagh called home to give an accounting, Alexander had, at the moment the final voice of authority. So it was a stroke of what might be euphemistically called "Talleyrand luck" when, several hours earlier, Count Tolstoi, the tsar's grand marshal, received a supposedly anonymous warning that the Elysée Palace where His Imperial Majesty intended to lodge, was mined. Nothing could have been more providential, for Alexander accepted Talleyrand's timely offer to stay at the Saint-Florentin instead. "Monsieur de Talleyrand . . . you have my confidence and that of my allies. We do not wish to settle anything before we have heard your views. You know France, its needs and desires. Say what we ought to do and we will do it." [14] Since it was imperative to now sell the tsar on a Bourbon restoration, Talleyrand was in an enviable position not only to control those who saw Alexander, but also to guarantee that he would have the last word with his distinguished houseguest—two important factors when dealing with anyone so volatile. France's fate was to be decided in the Hôtel Saint-Florentin, where the tsar occupied center stage and Talleyrand worked behind the scenes for the

Bourbons. As Napoleon's star fell, he emerged from disfavor to be the dominant figure in France.

As soon as the Prussian king and Prince Schwarzenberg appeared, a conference was held which included Dalberg, Nesselrode, and Pozzo di Borgo, a Corsican diplomat who was Alexander's right-hand man of the moment and a bitter enemy of Napoleon. They were there to make a lasting peace but who could speak for France? The emperor had broken away from the peace table at Châtillon; as for Talleyrand, he was only a private individual. When the autocratic Alexander, his ears still ringing from his tumultuous Parisian reception and avid to please the crowds, claimed that he himself had little preference for the regime to be established, provided it spoke for the entire country, Talleyrand pointed out that only a legitimate power could make a permanent and honorable peace. Everyone would accept a Bourbon restoration because of the legitimacy of Louis XVIII's claim. The immediate need was to put the French people in a position to make themselves heard. In a Senate deliberation which he could convoke, the senators had the power to pronounce the fall of Napoleon and to name a provisional government which would, in turn, call for the Bourbons. Talleyrand's program triumphed.

Nesselrode and Dalberg disappeared into an adjacent room to draft such a public declaration. Talleyrand and Nesselrode had already been working on such a document that morning. The tsar glanced at it, changed a word here and there, initialed it, and Talleyrand had it rushed to Michaud, a young royalist printer whom he had taken the precaution of alerting earlier. To create the impression that this proclamation was a spontaneous gesture from Alexander in response to his heart-warming Parisian reception, its publication time was purposely printed on it and falsely given as immediately following the gigantic parade and show of force—"March 31, 3:00 p.m., 1814."

That evening, the crowds already milling around the hundred prime street locations where sign hangers had just finished posting the tsar's "Address to the French Nation" were so huge that the crowned heads, with their mandatory military escort, were forced to detour en route to the Academy of Music in the rue Richelieu. The opera originally scheduled, *Le Triomphe de Trajan*, had been hastily canceled, showcasing as it did the triumphal march that had been composed in honor of Napoleon at the time of his great Prussian victories. Despite such short notice, Spontini's masterpiece, *La Vestale*, was successfully substituted. Word had leaked out that the allied sovereigns planned to attend, and the packed house was a sea of Bourbon blue and white. Every royalist who could beg, borrow, or steal a ticket appeared. The hall was fragrant with lilies, the Bourbon flower—in the women's hair, in their bonnets, in garlands around their neck—while the men sported white cockades, resurrected from some hidden cache and slightly yellowed with age. The Grand Duchess Anna-Dorothea and the Princess Tyszkiewicz were privileged guests, and Alexander and King Friedrich-Wilhelm III appeared after the second curtain. Talleyrand, who sat directly behind the two sovereigns, could have seen very little of the performance, for the tsar was whispering in his ear every other second and he would then dispatch another of the numerous aides who were standing rigidly at attention in the back of the loge and were continuously being replaced as fast as they disappeared. At the spectacle's end, several enthusiastic young Royalists shinnied up the columns on one side of the stage and sent the massive Napoleonic insignias on top of the heavy velvet curtains crashing down with a reverberating thud.

By the time they returned home, an unexpected torrential downpour with grumbling thunder and flashing lightning illuminated Talleyrand's mansion, which was ablaze from cellar to garret with twinkling candles and filled with a multilingual swarm, heavily bemedaled and dripping diamonds and feathers. Cossacks were curled up asleep on bales of straw in the courtyard and the magnificent ceremonial staircase, with its delicately spiraled, wrought-iron balustrade and landings filled with sculpture and paintings now boasted giant Russian Imperial guards, two to a riser. On the second floor, every nook and cranny, every window bay of the pale-grey and crystal *Salon de l'Aigle*, with its life-size, gold leaf eagles supporting gold medallions in each corner of the ceiling, was filled with gesticulating arguing diplomats, both allied and French.

Since Napoleon was considered the main obstacle to peace—the paramount issue of the moment—the vote to provide France with an interim provisional government must be taken without delay. So Talleyrand was closeted with Dalberg and several others deciding which senators should be notified that "Le Prince de Bénévent has been invited by His Majesty the Tsar Alexander to present the proposals of the allied powers to the Senate. . . . Your presence is requested . . ." Convoking that body in this fashion was strictly illegal and dawn was already streaking the eastern sky as messengers fanned out across the capital to summon those so chosen. Just as the kingmaker was about to step into his carriage to be driven to the Luxembourg Palace to deliver the *coup de grâce* to the man to whom he owed so much, Caulaincourt, who was still trying to elicit support for the emperor cornered him once more. Talleyrand answered briefly and evasively. And the tsar told him tersely, "Too late."

This was not the moment to improvise, and Talleyrand came to the Senate with his speech in his pocket. All proceeded according to plan. Of the one hundred and forty legislators constituting that body, the thirty who were present, out of the seventy or more still somewhere in the capital, obediently demanded the ouster of Napoleon. They then created an interim government charged with attending to the immediate needs of the nation and elected a five-man slate to administer it. This, too, had been drawn up the night before, largely by Talleyrand, now the quintet's official head. Chateaubriand, his perpetual gadfly, might qualify three of the four—the senator Beurnonville, the senator Jaucourt, the ubiquitous Dalberg—as the prince's "table of whist" which, indeed, they were, but each constituted an important link with a different pivotal group with whom Talleyrand must now work. The fifth member, the Abbé de Montesquiou, an active agent of Louis XVIII, was included to supply a royalist connection. Throughout the entire session, Talleyrand's emissaries were still scurrying about Paris rounding up additional, absentee votes so that, ultimately, by 9:00 p.m., sixty-four senators had finally acquiesced. The unanimity with which those present conducted the business at hand greatly impressed the tsar who accepted these results from a rump senate as the voice of the people's government. In less than forty-eight hours Talleyrand had become officially, as well as actually, the most powerful man in the country, the one Frenchman to whom the allies looked for guidance, and whose home was now the nerve center of Europe.

To flatter Alexander's self-esteem and self-image as the magnanimous dispenser of all good things to the French—which was more than he ever was for his own Russians—Talleyrand arranged for the tsar to receive and congratulate the Senate on its wise decisions at a reception later at his hotel. When patriotic qualms caused a goodly number of the lawgivers to decline, Talleyrand substituted a number of actors so that this solemn audience with His Majesty would appear to be well attended. In their borrowed senatorial finery, with their velvet suits and cloaks embroidered in gold and lined with yellow silk, lace cravat, white culottes and fancily decorated black felt hats, it was impossible to distinguish them from the genuine article. Talleyrand turned the entire second floor of the Saint-Florentin over to the tsar and kept the six rooms on the entresol for himself. Of these, the three on the court were given over to the public. In the first was a crowd of would-be helpers; beyond was a second room for more important collaborators. In the third, Roux de Laborie gave private audiences when he could fight his way through the crowd of favor-seekers. Similar disorder was apparent in the remaining three, so-called private, rooms which overlooked the rue de Rivoli and the Tuileries gardens. Talleyrand's bedroom became his working headquarters; the other four members of the Provisional Government were largely figureheads. A small adjoining salon was filled with secretaries, ministers, and men awaiting orders or making reports; and, at the end of the hall was a miniscule library where Talleyrand met a privileged few. It was a comical sight to see him navigate with his difficult walking style from his bedroom to the library where someone whom he had promised to see might have been waiting patiently for hours. As he shuffled across the room, he was stopped every few feet by a harried man who had a question, seized by the coattails by another who wanted a favor, found his way barred by a third who absolutely had to talk to him that very instant.

The nomination of a Provisional Government implied the Emperor's removal and, when the Senate met Saturday morning, it docilely voted for his ouster. However, Napoleon still held a trump card—the army, which was his glory and strength. If it remained loyal, anyone trying to overturn the imperial regime might set off a civil war. So, in an effort to detach the military from him, a proclamation went out to the armed forces: "You are no longer Napoleon's soldiers. The Senate and all France releases you from your oaths of allegiance to him." [15] Meanwhile, the allies kept their armed forces on the alert, ready to fight at a moment's notice, for they were not blind to the formidable fighting power Napoleon still commanded. Most of this was still far away in eastern France, but various imperial units were hurrying, hour after hour, to nearby Fontainebleau. Everything indicated that an attack was being planned. France was by no means exhausted and most of the country remained loyal to the Emperor. In the farthest reaches of the empire, not one of Napoleon's numerous strongholds from Paris to the Rhine had yet surrendered. But, closer at hand, the war was going very badly.

The Austrians had taken France's second city, Lyons; Wellington was approaching Toulouse.

A reassuring normalcy was cultivated in the capital and welcomed by the man-in-the-street. The official occupation ran smoothly, suppressing any manifestation that might arouse allied resentment or lead to violence. Cafés and restaurants were filled, with lines forming outside the popular theaters along the boulevards. Caricatures of Talleyrand's "whist table" were popular. Large crowds gawked brazenly at the Cossack bivouacs scattered in the Champs Élysées amid the market gardens and woods stretching from the mansions on the Right Bank to the Seine. Here, in low-pitched tents, sturdy fighters from the Russian steppes were mending their bizarre clothing, boots, and harnesses, and singing exotic songs amid strange, tantalizing cooking odors while their tiny horses, tied to nearby trees, were busy eating off all the bark underneath the branches from which were hung their strange-looking equipment.

When Anna-Dorothea received her first billet from Talleyrand since the allies' arrival, with it was a request for Dorothea to come into the city. She must come by way of Aubergenville, and a detachment of Cossacks would meet her at the relay post of Saint-Germain to escort her through the various roadblocks. Dorothea would be an additional adornment to the Hôtel Saint-Florentin. *L'oncle* did not want to overlook any detail that might keep the temperamental Alexander happy.

While the Legislative Corps, with fewer than eighty of its three hundred and eighty members present, was voting, as had the Senate before, for the deposition of Napoleon, Talleyrand continued his efforts to tie Napoleon's hands, militarily-speaking, by winning the support of the most influential imperial officers for the Provisional Government. Marmont was the key. Not only did he command the strongest unit close at hand, some twelve thousand men who, under the terms of the armistice, were now stationed in Essonne, a vital position covering Napoleon, like a shield, at Fontainebleau. But he was also known for his loyalty to the Emperor ever since the Egyptian campaign; therefore he would be the ideal bellwether. Talleyrand's carefully chosen emissary, a former Marmont aide, the fervent royalist, Charles de Montessuis, disguised as a Cossack, complete with baggy trousers and a knout, did his job well. The night of April 4, while Marmont was leading his entire corps out of the imperial fold into the allied camp at Versailles, Caulaincourt and several other marshals raced to Alexander with

Napoleon's written abdication, conditional on the establishment of a regency for his son, l'Aiglon, with Marie-Louise as regent. Candles burned around-the-clock and no one slept, as Talleyrand and the vacillating Alexander discussed the pros and cons of the imperial proposal, and Talleyrand warned that "Napoleon would always be listening at the door." His opinion prevailed and Napoleon II was irretrievably doomed.

Napoleon's subsequent suicide attempt failed and his now unconditional abdication, he was barely forty-four, was in allied hands. That same day, the senators and deputies, united in a joint session to save time, passed unanimously a new constitution, largely inspired by Talleyrand, who promptly christened it "the Charter." This instituted a constitutional monarchy and was based to a considerable degree on the constitution of 1791, which Talleyrand had advocated at that time, but with the important substitution of two chambers for one. While the Charter summoned Louis-Stanislaus-Xavier, the brother of the last king, to the throne, the re-establishment of the hereditary monarchy was subordinated to his acceptance of the Charter—that is to say, to the will of the people.

Talleyrand being Talleyrand, it was too much to imagine that that complex man did not have other things on his mind of a more personal nature in addition to affairs of state. Despite the confusion around him, the military coming and going with their clinking swords, the foreign diplomats scurrying to and fro, consulting in hurried whispers, he was never one to overlook a financial opportunity. Because the maintenance of his newest country estate, at Saint-Brice, was proving exorbitant even by his standards, Talleyrand found the banker who held the government concession controlling all Paris gambling an unenthusiastic, albeit willing, buyer who was anxious to accommodate him.

Another personal matter needed even more immediate attention. Since Talleyrand aspired to as important a position in the Bourbon regime as any he had held heretofore, it was imperative to lay his hands on any compromising documents dealing with his role in certain sensitive past issues. Unfortunately, the rue du Bac archives housed only material dealing with Talleyrand's various tenures as foreign affairs minister when his role had been, essentially, to transmit Napoleon's orders and see that they were carried out. What were vital were his notes to Napoleon as First Consul and, later, as Emperor, giving him needed information and advice on those affairs which were particularly sensitive from a Bourbon point of view—the Enghien affair, various dealings with the Holy See, and the sorry

Spanish imbroglio. As such, they were filed in the imperial secretariat located on the Place du Carrousel, under the galleries of the Louvre. As soon as he was president of the Provisional Government, Talleyrand had sent a trusted colleague to inventory these holdings. With Napoleon's abdication finally in hand, and under cover of the heavy fog blanketing the capital for several days, dossiers singled out by Talleyrand, as well as any written memoranda which could conceivably establish his responsibility in these matters, were removed, despite the protests of M. Bary, the archivist. All evidence was then destroyed in an *auto-da-fé*, under Talleyrand's personal supervision, and with his secretary Perrey's assistance, in the library at his hotel. If a letter inculpating him in the Enghien affair ever actually existed and which Talleyrand's *bête noire*, Chateaubriand, claimed, many years later, to have seen it now either slipped accidentally behind a drawer and escaped his attention or was stolen by Perrey when Talleyrand was briefly absent.

This year the Greek and Roman Catholic Easter coincided and, on Sunday, Talleyrand had a ringside view of the service that was performed on an altar that had been especially constructed in the great square below his balcony at the tsar's command. The day was cool, with the brilliance of a polished diamond, and a few cottonball clouds hovered lazily overhead. There is no indication whether Talleyrand felt a sense of pride in his role in ending the carnage as he watched the overflowing crowd of people of every faith kneeling there to celebrate the end of bloodshed.

The transportation bottleneck around Dijon was broken at last and, upon his arrival in Paris this same morning, Metternich hastened to the Hôtel Saint-Florentin. Here he found that his absence had handed Alexander what the Austrian chancellor had until then successfully denied him—effective control of the allied leadership. With Alexander's Lenten fast at an end, the three sovereigns and assorted dignitaries were guests later at what Talleyrand chose to label "a family dinner—not a political one." Talleyrand had requested that his brother Archambaud also be present so that the latter's daughter-in-law, as a Talleyrand, might do the family honors which etiquette demanded. And Dorothea did, sitting slender and poised, facing *l'oncle* across the fabulous vermeil dinner service while the wind instruments, tucked in a corner, played only melodies from Gluek's "Iphigenia." For the host's instructions to his resident music director had been: "Nothing serious should be heard tonight, mind you. I suggest something soothing that will not require concentration or take my guests' minds from the conversation." [16]

Monday, the treaty of abdication was signed, finalizing Napoleon's abdication and exiling him to Elba, although Talleyrand—and England—had wanted him sent farther away, at least as far as the Azores. It was bad enough for the king's brother, the Comte d'Artois, to arrive and find France's Provisional Government housed in the home of a married priest—the former Bishop d'Autun—of revolutionary fame. It was even worse to find it located on the floor underneath that of a foreign ruler. So, after dining once more with his host, Anna-Dorothea, and Dorothea, Alexander moved over to the Elysée. He was accompanied by Carême, now unanimously considered the number one chef in Paris, on loan from Talleyrand on the theory that the way to the tsar's heart lay through his stomach.

The following noon Talleyrand, together with the Municipal Council of Paris, rode out in a gala procession to the Barrière de Bondy to greet Artois. He had not seen him since their interview at Marly in 1789, and he would serve as proxy for his brother, Louis XVIII, until the latter's gout permitted him to cross the Channel. Handing the government of France over to him as lieutenant-governor completed for Talleyrand the substitution of a monarchy for the dying empire. It was a remarkable operation, which had been accomplished with the help of foreign arms and without complications.

13

L'Ambassadeur Extraordinaire

"... Talleyrand is behaving as though he were the Minister of Louis XIV."
—Tsar Alexander I [1]

AFTER A TRADITION-LADEN, ceremonial greeting Talleyrand and Artois, surrounded by their attendant cortèges, proceeded to Notre Dame for a *Te Deum*. That night the king's brother slept soundly in the bed recently vacated by Marie-Louise in the Tuileries, where workmen were already starting to remove imperial eagles and bees from every ceiling and corner, and replacing them with the Bourbon fleur-de-lys. Meanwhile, at supper at the Hôtel Saint-Florentin Napoleon's proposed place of exile was being heatedly discussed. Talleyrand felt the island of Elba in the Mediterranean was dangerously close to the mainland he had troubled for so long, and someone else suggested America. Metternich, who was seated next to Anna-Dorothea, raised his shoulders with an expression of resignation and glanced significantly at Alexander, who was adamantly opposed to this. Giving the tinkling laugh the Austrian chancellor remembered so well, the grand duchess retorted, "Wouldn't James and Dolly Madison have a fit!" [2]

Not surprisingly, when Artois set up a pro tempore Grand Council of State, two days later, to assist him in governing until his brother, Louis XVIII, returned, its core was the previous Provisional Government, and Talleyrand's role remained as predominant as ever. Only two royalist members were added. With the Bourbons now on the scene, it was time for an armistice to replace the Cease Fire which had been in effect ever since Marmont laid down arms, but which applied only to Paris. Then the final step, a peace treaty, could follow once Louis XVIII arrived and established his own regular government. Accordingly, on the nineteenth, Metternich submitted a proposal to begin negotiations for the official end of hostilities, and it was with Talleyrand that the allies wanted to treat. They did not know Artois.

This was a delicate task no diplomat would envy but, if Talleyrand wanted to continue to play a prominent role in the future regime, here was a god-given opportunity to prove he was indispensable. Fortunately, through his past functions at Napoleon's elbow, he had unequalled prestige as well as personal relations with the foreign sovereigns and ministers with whom he must now deal. But he came to the table with a poor hand for France was exhausted, whereas the allies were in a position to dictate. For the most part their armies were composed not of mercenaries but of soldiers full of hatred and revenge, anxious to treat France as Napoleon had treated their respective fatherlands. The country had been at war since 1792; men, money, and resources lacked. After Napoleon's fall Russia was the most redoubtable power on the continent. The tsar's troops not only blanketed Paris but, together with divisions from the various German states, occupied France's northern and eastern provinces. Spanish and English armies stretched from the Pyrénées to Bordeaux, and the remainder of the French countryside was still controlled by imperial forces.

To conserve his credibility with the foreign sovereigns, Talleyrand must show himself accommodating; it was also essential to obtain Europe's confidence and good will for the nascent Bourbon regime. However, if Talleyrand was in no position to resist the enemies' demands, he held one trump. Their significant role in Louis XVIII's return imposed upon the Big Four—England, Austria, Russia, Prussia—an obligation to help maintain France's legitimate dynasty lest another revolution topple it and once more spread over Europe or, even worse, lead to a resurgence of bonapartism. While some later-day critics might disagree, in the light of future events, and label the armistice a capitulation, Talleyrand gambled that such an agreement, quickly reached, was the surest way to overcome

Europe's ingrained distrust of France. He was right. His contemporaries, anxious to have France evacuated as promptly as possible, went along with him for, if the occupation army was on its good behavior in the capital, this was not the case in the provinces. After four days of intensive, round-the-clock negotiations, Talleyrand initialed the convention and advised Anna-Dorothea: "I have finished my armistice. It is a good thing." [3]

Meanwhile, when his gout eased sufficiently, the stocky fifty-nine-year-old monarch, who could not walk unassisted, set forth across the Channel in antiquated garb featuring light blue velvet gaiters that looked as if they must still reek of mothballs. With an inordinate fondness for etiquette that was often ludicrous, given his physical condition, and ill-fitted by temperament and experience for the crushing task ahead, Louis XVIII was returning home after a twenty-five-year absence. The minute he landed, before His Majesty had time to finish designating the royal household—Talleyrand's uncle, the old Archbishop of Reims, was reconfirmed as royal chaplain—His Majesty received Talleyrand's request that his nephew, Edmond, be selected as one of the royal aides-de-camp. He also asked that Dorothea serve as a lady-in-waiting to the Duchess d'Angoulême. The wife of the king's nephew and the daughter of Louis XVI and Marie-Antoinette, the duchess, as Madame Royale, would serve as the childless widower's official hostess. By return courier Edmond was elevated, instead, to brigadier-general, but no mention was ever made concerning Dorothea, probably because His Majesty did not want anyone in the new Bourbon court who had served in the imperial one. For whatever reason, Louis XVIII would never even acknowledge that he had met "ma petite italienne," as the monarch used to call Dorothea when he dandled her on his knee during his brief stay, as an exile, in Mitau, where he had been lodged in one of the former Courland palaces.

Because of the importance of having a Talleyrand-Périgord present among the distinguished throng of courtiers awaiting the returning sovereign at the pier Talleyrand, whose duties winding up the armistice prevented his own appearance, delegated Archambaud to represent the family. But Talleyrand was at Compiègne, a few days later, when Louis XVIII finally arrived there. Instead of being ushered into the august presence immediately, as he had every right to expect, in the light of his services to the house of Bourbon, Talleyrand was kept sitting interminably in an antechamber bulging with royalists, who all took obvious delight at his discomfort. This deliberate, three-hour wait made it abundantly clear that, in the king's eyes he was still the Bishop d'Autun, married, and an apostate.

His Most Christian Majesty had made his point and, since no one else was on hand when Talleyrand was finally ushered into the royal presence, who can gainsay the only account of their interview as it subsequently appeared in Talleyrand's notoriously biased *Mémoires*? If Talleyrand was disappointed by his reception, he did not admit it. As though he had set a stage for their meeting, Louis XVIII, one year his junior, was seated at a desk in the far corner of the large salon when Talleyrand entered. Despite his cumbersome appearance, His Majesty exuded a dignity which was enhanced by his unquestioning acceptance of the sanctity of his claims as, cordially extending his hand and speaking slowly, in his deep voice, he bade his visitor take a seat. He had already made his point; neither suffered any illusions about the true nature of their reciprocal feelings. Whether or not Louis XVIII evoked the past and the ancient lineage of both their families, as Talleyrand would claim, His Majesty significantly passed over his years of exile and thanked him for his recent efforts on the royal behalf. However, instead of manifesting gratitude, Louis XVIII made it painfully clear that this was no more than his due as the legitimate and undisputed Bourbon successor to the throne. This same impression was reinforced later when Talleyrand bowed low in greeting to the king's niece, the sour-faced Duchess d'Angoulême. That indifferently dressed, unpleasant young woman barely replied to the man who, in her eyes, had played a prominent part, years before, in Napoleon's execution of the unfortunate Duc d'Enghien.

Alexander was similarly displeased. Still considering himself the man of the hour, the tsar rushed out from Paris full of advice for the sovereign on whose behalf he had spilled untold quantities of Russian blood. After a pleasant welcome the French monarch, who considered the Romanovs parvenus—the Bourbons had been established on the French throne for eight centuries before the advent of Alexander's family—and was old enough to be Alexander's father, adopted a paternal attitude. After listening attentively, His Majesty, with a skillful mixture of affection and superiority, gave the tsar to understand that he had already decided on his course of action. Furious, Alexander cut the interview short and demanded to retire at once to his own quarters. Nor did it help matters when His Imperial Majesty discovered that he had been assigned to the unimpressive apartments of the governor of the château. When dinner was announced the king, not the tsar, led the way, requested Alexander to follow and—in keeping with protocol—to escort his niece, the Duchess d'Angoulême. The startled Talleyrand, who was already seated farther down the long table, could hardly believe his eyes when the trio entered and then Louis XVIII plumped down into the one and only armchair. So he was scarcely surprised, the minute the meal was over, to see Alexander call for his carriage and leave for Paris, boiling with rage. The king held court for several days at Compiègne and, following Sunday mass, Talleyrand presented his wife, Catherine, to His Majesty before the royal cortège set out for Saint-Ouen. There, as his last official act, Talleyrand introduced the members of the Senate to Louis XVIII. On Tuesday, the same day Napoleon set foot on Elba—traveling alone because Emperor Francis forbade his daughter, Marie-Louise, or her son, l'Aiglon, to accompany him, and refusing Flahaut's offer, as an imperial aide-de-camp, to go along—the monarch made his formal entry into his capital.

All Paris had been awakened early by the sound of drums summoning the national guard to arms. Security was so heavy that flowerpots on windowsills and carriages, other than those in the official procession, were forbidden along the royal route, which was tastefully decorated with white standards ornamented with blue tassels covered with fleurs-de-lys. Pealing church bells and roaring cannon heralded the arrival of the royal carriage, drawn by eight white horses with white plumes nodding in their harnesses and, inside, a smiling Louis XVIII with his solemn niece, Mme Royal. To highlight this historic moment, the famed aeronaut, intrepid Mme Blanchard, ascended in her balloon, which got caught for one breathtaking moment on the statue of Henry IV on the Pont Neuf. Once freed and soaring higher, she released a flock of doves to wing their way across the skies as a symbol of the longed-for peace. The following afternoon the allied forces paraded along the quais, led by the tsar's brother, Grand Duke Constantine. Out of deference to their ailing guest-of-honor, Louis XVIII, the allied sovereigns did not march with their troops but appeared together at an open window of the Louvre. The unwieldy Bourbon bulk was stuffed into a sturdy armchair in front of the Austrian emperor and the Prussian king while the vain tsar, standing conspicuously in the foreground and playing to the crowd below, did the honors. But Wellington stole the show.

After winding up a most successful Peninsular campaign, he surprised the high command by arriving in time to ride with the British contingent, and even the sovereigns craned their necks for a first glimpse of this fresh allied hero. In the evening, society shuttled between Talleyrand's, the grand duchess's, and the British Embassy. At the Hôtel Saint-Florentin Catherine de Talleyrand, more voluminous and less voluble than ever, received at the end of the customary two long rows of chairs, seated with her feet resting upon a gigantic cushion on which she herself had embroidered the Périgord arms, to remind those present that she was Talleyrand's wife. There was a cosmopolitan scene at Anna-Dorothea's, while Wellington starred at the small ball hosted by the English ambassador for *tout Paris*, dance division. Guests were still queued up, in the wee hours, to shake Milord's hand and congratulate him on his elevation, several hours earlier, to dukedom.

Only with the greatest reluctance did Louis XVIII accept the Charter—France's new constitution—according to which His Majesty was recalled to France by the sovereignty of the people and not, automatically, because of his lineage. His first act as ruler was to replace the Provisional Government with a Bourbon ministry and, for services rendered, Talleyrand had every right to expect to be named its president. When Louis XVIII preferred to assume that post himself, Talleyrand cynically quipped, "King by the grace of God is the protocol of ingratitude." [4] Although handicapped by knowing neither available personnel nor details of the most pertinent current affairs, the monarch retained just a pair of the previous ministers: Talleyrand, as foreign affairs minister; and Montesquiou, at Interior, the two portfolios with the heaviest responsibilities. While Talleyrand henceforth had no say about domestic matters, he remained the most important man on the scene, largely because of the obscurity and political insignificance of the others.

Louis XVIII was not as liberal as Talleyrand felt the situation demanded. The freedom of the press, which Napoleon had repressed was not restored, and His Majesty also ignored Napoleon's advice from afar— "to only change the sheets on the beds." Nine times out of ten, the king yielded to the never-ending pressure of the returned royalists who lived on their resentments. They had learned nothing and forgotten nothing, and were endlessly complicating Talleyrand's Herculean task. Although he did not care for the Duc de Blacas, one of Louis XVIII's companions in exile and the only person who had any influence with His Majesty,

Talleyrand felt it expedient to be seen frequently in his company at the *à la mode* Tivoli Gardens and even at the popular Café Tortoni, eating an ice like *tout Paris*. Small wonder his normally pale face was drawn from lack of sleep, and he confessed to the grand duchess: "You scolded me a little yesterday. I didn't merit it, but your scolding gave me pleasure. I like to see the person I love have spirit. . . . You must let me berate you occasionally, to work off the small irritations I endure during the day." [5]

In the midst of all this frenzied activity, little Dorothea-Charlotte, the second of Dorothea's children, came down with a severe case of measles. Busy though he was Talleyrand, as head of the family, felt duty-bound to stop by the rue Grange-Batelière daily to see how his tiny god-daughter was progressing. When the little girl took a turn for the worst, Talleyrand dispatched his personal physician to keep an around-the-clock vigil and report to him directly. That good man so alarmed Talleyrand about the health of Dorothea herself that, the following morning, he awakened the grand duchess with an earlier billet than usual, because the doctor warned that the young mother had still not regained sufficient strength after her last difficult pregnancy to withstand the shock of seeing her offspring so ill. Anna-Dorothea must keep Dorothea with her and not let her go home. "If Dorothea could accomplish anything by being at her bedside" Talleyrand concluded, "I wouldn't say a word." That same evening the small patient died. And Dorothea retreated into a shell, inconsolable. Even when her sister, Wilhelmina, the one great love of the philandering Austrian Metternich's life, arrived in Paris in time to celebrate his forty-first birthday, Dorothea could not be roused to join in a family reunion. Her other two sisters, Joanna and Paulina, also appeared and, although Metternich grumbled that Talleyrand was "monopolizing the Courland princesses," *l'oncle* somehow found time to continue routinely to the rue Grande-Batelière to console his niece.

Now that France had a permanent government Talleyrand, as foreign affairs minister, was charged with making the definitive peace treaty, based on the armistice terms, regularizing Bourbon France's new boundaries and relations with the triumphant allies. When one considers that the allies for most of the past twenty years had been at war with France, it can hardly be claimed that its terms were unjustly harsh. In a memo to the king Talleyrand maintained that the prompt renunciation of the present frontiers and a retreat to the pre-revolutionary limits was the one way to overcome European distrust of France. By relinquishing all

French holdings on the left bank of the Rhine—the one barrier capable of protecting Paris from afar—in addition to handing over the empire's countless fortified places east of that river, together with their material and combined garrisons of over one hundred thousand men, he allayed the allies' spirit of bitterness and desire for revenge. To bolster the nascent regime, no indemnities were demanded despite the enormous war-related damages. At Talleyrand's request, France was also allowed to retain the myriad pieces of pilfered art—especially from Italy—when Talleyrand pointed out that to do otherwise would make the restored Bourbons highly unpopular. So the allies settled for those objects not on public display everywhere but tucked away, for lack of adequate space, in innumerable museum reserves and storerooms. Talleyrand's pleasure in his handiwork was evident when he advised Anna-Dorothea that the treaty he initialed on May 30 was "by equals to equals" and not one imposed by a conqueror on the vanquished. His counterparts were likewise in a more relaxed mood. At the last of the remaining official entertainments, Wellington danced the polonaise. Prussia's leading field marshal performed a country allemande, and his elderly Russian counterpart, not to be outdone, leaped to his feet and contributed a Cossack number, nodding, whinnying, and stomping like a horse.

Article XXXII of the Treaty of Paris convoked a congress to be held in Vienna in the fall to settle the fate of the vast land mass Napoleon had regurgitated and, as a condition of signing the document, France was invited to be present—but only as a spectator. From the start, the Big Four never intended the rank and file in attendance to have a voice in the decisions to be resolved there. So the British plenipotentiary invited his other three colleagues to London to thrash out some preliminary agreements on the forthcoming conclave's two main issues—the related Polish and Saxon real estate questions—before presenting such an emotionally charged matter to the three-hundred-odd delegates.

Preceding the rest, mercurial Alexander, in another huff, stormed across the Channel alone, without even granting Talleyrand the customary, anticipated farewell. Despite the fact that the temperamental tsar had more than a million slaves of his own, he did not feel the Charter in its final form was sufficiently liberal and blamed Talleyrand, although the latter—who actually agreed with the Russian ruler—did not even sit on the committee drawing it up. The Austrian emperor, anxious to get home to oversee preparations for the coming event, did not cross the Channel.

Whether, before he left, Emperor Francis showed his pleasure by presenting Talleyrand with the customary lucrative rewards to a diplomat for a job well done, His Apostolic Majesty did bestow on him his country's highest honor, the *Toison d'Or*—the Golden Fleece—a distinction heretofore reserved only for members of his Hapsburg family.

The London junket turned into a fiasco. Through a series of unheard-of diplomatic and social faux-pas, the unpredictable tsar soon lost the goodwill of the Tory cabinet and the Prince Regent. The situation was further aggravated by the erratic behavior of his favorite sister, Cathou, the recently widowed, scatter-brained Grand Duchess of Oldenburg, who had tagged along on an unsuccessful, husband-searching foray. While no consensus could be reached on the Big Four's primary concerns, Metternich did, however, succeed in wresting control of the coalition back from Alexander. And the fact that the forthcoming congress was to be held in the Austrian capital, which had been chosen because it was the most centrally located for the countries involved, automatically made him its president—another advantage. As the chancellor passed through Paris, homeward-bound, he picked up his head chef whom he had left in tutelage at the Hôtel Saint-Florentin to learn a few new gastronomical feats from Talleyrand's famed Carême with which to dazzle congressional visitors that fall.

By the first week in June, the occupation troops began slowly moving out, concrete evidence to the man-in-the-street that the country's long travail was ending. The war was over at last. This summer was one of the very few when Talleyrand did not take his annual cure at Bourbon-l'Archambault nor go to the country, but devoted himself, instead, to preparations for his role as head of France's delegation to Vienna. Only one matter of a personal nature was allowed to intrude. He took time to arrange for the marriage of his adopted daughter, Charlotte, who was now sixteen, to his nephew, the Baron Alexander de Talleyrand-Périgord, Boson's son. The marriage contract assured the girl legally of a name that was probably her birthright, and cannily kept her substantial dowry in the family. Then he gave the traditional engagement dinner in her honor. He rarely went to the Tuileries, where he was poorly received, although he was flattered when Louis XVIII named him "the Prince de Talleyrand" and elevated his new distinction to an hereditary one. Whether the French sovereign did so as a mark of approval or whether it was to save France any future embarrassment in Vienna is hard to say. It was bad enough that His Most Christian Majesty's foreign affairs minister should be a married bishop. It was something else again if, as the result of action taken there, France's plenipotentiary should have to return to the Holy See the land whence came his erstwhile imperial title, the Prince de Bénévent.

The Congress of Vienna was the most important European conclave to date, and Talleyrand's role there would crown his career. For a man who was eternally concerned with what posterity might think of him, it would be his most challenging undertaking and, certainly, the key to continuing royal favor. Talleyrand's underlying thought was to renegotiate regicide France's rightful place in the circle of great European powers and give her back her say in continental affairs. Unfortunately, the Treaty of Paris, which authorized his presence there, specifically denied him a vote. Although of the eleven nations to be represented—both Italy and Germany were mere geographical expressions—France with its twenty-nine million inhabitants, the double of that of England, was the most populated, the most homogeneous, and compact on the continent.

Long hours were spent with Louis XVIII, working out the details of his mission. Talleyrand had a lot of character failings but common sense was not one, and it speaks volumes for his tact that, despite their inherent lack of sympathy, he gained the monarch's trust. The two were in complete accord on what had to be accomplished and how to proceed and, because of the slowness of communications, Talleyrand was given *carte blanche* to take decisions on the spot, without referral to His Majesty.

French interests presupposed European equilibrium, yet the continent at the moment was in a state of chaos. The congress must dispose of all of Napoleon's real estate, but many of the countries involved were without legitimate rulers; some were occupied by the military. Relying on his firsthand acquaintance with the European crowned heads and their diplomats—a distinct advantage—Talleyrand must convince them that Bourbon France had repudiated the Napoleonic heritage of conquest and was no longer casting covetous eyes elsewhere.

In the past, while his opinions had carried weight with the belligerent Directoire and, subsequently, with the imperial adventurer, Talleyrand executed other people's wishes, though he was often in disagreement with them. Now, for the first time, he could finally apply the doctrine of moderation he had formulated years before: Europe as a system of states which must coexist in harmony, with France as the cornerstone, supported by England and—or—Austria. This followed along the lines set out by Richelieu and Mazarin, two great statesmen of the past, and would have been approved by Vergennes, Louis XIV's great foreign minister. It was very similar to that held by His Majesty, who had had ample time to meditate on such matters during his long years of wandering exile, and both agreed that Russia should not get the whole of Poland, nor Prussia, the whole of Saxony.

All aristocratic Europe, that is to say, everyone who was anyone or who pretended to be, was already packing. They were coming to Vienna to celebrate peace and forget *la grande peur*, the terror they had been living under since July 14, 1789, and which had taken its toll from almost every family. The gathering promised to be especially brilliant, for Metternich and his emperor were determined to show that the Hapsburgs had not sunk in a sea of debt and had survived the ignominy of the ill-fated weddings of the Archduchess Marie-Antoinette and the Archduchess Marie-Louise to two Frenchmen. With diplomacy the prerogative of the privileged class, European power rested in the hands of a relative few with whom Talleyrand was completely at home. They spoke the same language—French—had the same scale of values and similar educations. No frontiers existed for them. The "fatherland" was where one's family castle was located. The Austrian emperor was Italian; Metternich, his chancellor, came from the Rhineland; the Russian delegation consisted of three Germans, a Pole, a Greek, one Frenchman, and a single Russian.

Known as the "faubourg Saint-Germain of Europe," Vienna was the quintessence of aristocratic Paris prior to the revolution—only more so—and, to restore, in that bastion of blue bloods, the prestige of regicide France who had been Europe's problem child for twenty-five years, was not going to be easy. Yet, to be effective on France's behalf, the French embassy there must be the focal point of that elite, even if it took a near miracle. Since France's dominant European role in the past had been based on its cultural contributions and the power of its wealth, these were the aspects Talleyrand planned to emphasize in his campaign to woo the Viennese and the congress leaders.

Because he was anxious to remove the bad taste still in the mouths of the Viennese *crème*, whose reputation as formidable power-brokers was often decried by frustrated diplomats stationed there,

Talleyrand was determined that the embassy's salons must be more *ancien régime* than any in Vienna. As in Paris, no one must dispute the exquisite taste of his establishment, the luxury of his receptions, and the refinement of his table. Talleyrand had already chosen the principal members of his staff. His number two man was to be his long-time associate, Dalberg. The baron, with his relationship to the handful of great families who owned half of Europe, had enough centuries of blue blood to look down his nose at anyone. In addition, with his mother-in-law at Schönbrun palace as Marie-Louise's mistress-of-the-robes, he should have ready access to whatever news came from Elba. Talleyrand was also taking along the Comte Alexis de Noailles, one of the principal aides-de-camp of the Comte d'Artois, the king's brother. Since the Ultras—the overly reactionary, returning Royalists—did not trust Talleyrand, it was a given that Artois would insist the French plenipotentiary be watched abroad to make sure he toed the accepted line. "If one must be spied on," Talleyrand explained to Anna-Dorothea, *à propos* of his appointment of the Comte de Noailles, "at least it is better to choose the spy oneself." This select group was rounded out by an aristocrat of distinguished lineage and social graces, who was so handsome that the ladies would love him. Young La Tour du Pin's lack of brains was immaterial; he would do very nicely for signing passports. One regular from the rue du Bac, La Besnardière, went along to do the essential work. He was expected to act as a link with Paris, not only to keep Talleyrand informed of the intrigues going on there behind his back but also, together with the other three—especially in the case of Noailles—to report to his enemies what Talleyrand wished them to learn.

This was an open-ended game, which two could play. Unbeknown to his plenipotentiary, Louis XVIII subsequently had some of his own instructions to Talleyrand countermanded by a royal "end-play" through Count de Bombelles, the Austrian minister in Paris.

To further batten down the hatches and preconditioned by years of living under the shadow of Napoleon's secret police, Talleyrand also planned to bring along his entire household, including an army of pastry chefs and sauce chefs. When he was alerted that Baron Hager's *Oberste und Censu Hofstelle* was already planning to place a spy among his vegetable peelers, he took the necessary precautions and, temperamental sulks notwithstanding, his "cher maître"—Carême—would have to find a replacement before leaving home. Talleyrand would not tolerate any local

Viennese domestics. He did not want his wastebaskets searched, the ashes from each porcelain stove sifted. As it was, Dalberg would leave enough love letters scattered around for a dozen major scandals. He always did. That should suffice to keep the baron's men busy. And, Talleyrand's efforts notwithstanding, they did eventually succeed in placing on their payroll three Kaunitz doorkeepers and chambermaids, as well as a minor legation official. Talleyrand also ordered that informants be placed in most of the foreign embassies in Vienna. He instructed his staff, in advance, to warmly welcome the countless dissatisfied Saxons and Wurtembourgeois, not to mention the dispossessed natives of Nassau and other small German states, who would doubtless appear to volunteer information.

A single position in the French contingent still remained to be filled and this was the most important one of all, for most of the decisions at the congress would be made in Vienna's salons and ballrooms rather than around a green, baize-covered table. Talleyrand's hostess must not only help restore France's reputation in those circles where it had suffered most; she must also hold her own, through looks, breeding, and intelligence, in the web of political intrigue that would underlie the event. Talleyrand remained impeccably correct towards Catherine, who continued to preside at the Saint-Florentin, and custom decreed that he take the princess to Vienna but political expediency said no. A married bishop and his wife in that Catholic stronghold, the former seat of the Holy Roman empire of German states? Especially Catherine with her pretentious airs? By now, Mme Malàprop's absurdities and affectations were so well known that nothing less than total disaster might be expected if she was suddenly thrust into the midst of the snobbish Viennese. Throwing Catherine to the wolves would be more merciful than placing her in the middle of that arrogant clan, where everyone was related to everyone else and for whom only bloodlines mattered. Another insurmountable hurdle was Catherine's earlier, widely publicized affair with the Duc de San Carlos, the equerry of the two Spanish princes when they had been held prisoners at Valençay. With the elder of the pair now ruling as Alphonse VII of Spain, the Duc de San Carlos had become an important figure in the Madrid government and was frequently in Paris—and still with Catherine. Consequently, the Princess de Talleyrand's presence at Talleyrand's side could make the French plenipotentiary a Viennese laughingstock as a cuckolded husband. Not that Talleyrand personally prized marital constancy, but the irregularities of

Talleyrand's past life—political, religious, and social—provided enough handicaps to overcome in Vienna. Her presence there would scream of Talleyrand's deplorable *mésalliance* and the inextricable situation in which, as a result, he still found himself with the Church. Yet a rupture at this late date was out of the question because it would spotlight his nuptial predicament and, while he might be inclined to shrug off the imprecations of the religious community, the burst of widespread laughter which would greet such a revelation was something else again. Certain things were better left unsaid. Furthermore, even if Louis XVIII had been willing to shut his eyes—which was wishful thinking—Emperor Francis was a family man and never would have. Certain customs of polite society had to be observed, at least superficially, by His Most Christian Majesty's envoy.

It was equally out of the question for Talleyrand to take as hostess the grand duchess who was tailor-made for this role, and dying to so serve. But she knew this was an impossibility, and to appear in anything but the number-one spot was beneath her. However, another lady in Talleyrand's family, the grand duchess's youngest daughter, twenty-one-year-old Dorothea was as well equipped to go as Catherine was not. In looks she compared favorably with anyone she would meet; her intellect was the equal of statesmen with whom the French embassy would have to deal. Furthermore, by education and training, as the originally intended fiancée of the important Polish diplomat, Prince Czartoryski, Dorothea was well qualified to hold her own with them. By birth she was entitled to a place of honor in the most exalted circles, and a vast number of the people designated to represent their countries at Vienna were her blood relatives. She counted the Prussian royal family among her oldest friends; Alexander was an intimate of her mother. Her oldest sister, Wilhelmina, the Duchess de Sagan, was in a position to be extremely helpful as Metternich's mistress. So, too, to a lesser degree, were her other two sisters who were now, also, living in Vienna. Paulina's husband, Friedrich-Hermann-Otto von Hohenzollern-Hechingen, would be one of several south German princes attending, and the field marshal who was her present lover was slated for a leading part in the forthcoming negotiations. The third sister, Joanna, was playing the field but, like each of the Courland princesses, was well placed in the Austrian capital for the transmittal of information.

Since Dorothea was Talleyrand's niece by marriage, society would countenance his taking her, and her very youth silenced wagging tongues.

Talleyrand had been worried about her ever since the death of her little girl. Grudgingly, she had moved at *l'oncle's* insistence—and at Catherine's outspoken displeasure—to the rue Saint-Florentin. He felt a change of atmosphere would do her good and had hoped the continuous activity in the great mansion might distract her. But Dorothea rarely set foot outside her ground-floor apartments; something else was needed to draw her out of herself. The change and excitement in Vienna would help her assuage her grief, and it was time that Dorothea, who had already done her duty and assured the continuance of the Talleyrand line by producing two sons, had some compensation for her unhappy marriage. Dorothea herself had nothing to lose. Her original indifference to Edmond, who had only recently been released as a prisoner-of-war and promptly returned to his former profligate life, had deepened into aversion and signaled to the world the break-up of their union in all but the most formal terms. Drastic decision though it was, she accepted without a backward glance, the opportunity to escape that *l'oncle* offered. For Talleyrand to take Dorothea without her husband was a serious matter. But he, too, was heartily tired of his nephew's follies and extravagances, and he was serving notice that, as head of the Talleyrand-Périgord family, he was on Dorothea's side, not Edmond's.

A past master at using the opposite sex to his own advantage, what undoubtedly tipped the scales most heavily in his decision was Wilhelmina's public liaison with Metternich which, translated into power politics, meant that the Duchess de Sagan's outstanding Viennese salon would be at his disposal. This promised to be an enormous asset for a man in Talleyrand's delicate situation at the forthcoming meetings. For, no matter how often the spoiled, handsome Austrian chancellor might roam, the duchess remained the one great love of his life. Tiny, like all the Courland women, Wilhelmina, the oldest, was a ravishing blonde. The prettiest of Anna-Dorothea's daughters she was, at twenty-eight, one of the loveliest in that city of beauties and had already disposed of two husbands. She possessed a thorough understanding of the complex history of the ruling courts of Central Europe from firsthand acquaintance with many of the leading actors and was kept better informed than most contemporary statesmen through her far-flung network of family and friends. Reinforced by her prominent social position and unlimited wealth, her sharp mind and her fluent knowledge of five languages—like her mother—the Duchess de Sagan was a behind-the-scenes figure to be reckoned with in Vienna. News was hard to come by, and since much could be gleaned at drawing-room gatherings from the guests' private letters, ministers, and their aides regularly went the circuit to supplement their mail pouches. More top-level government matters were resolved in the drawing rooms of the *crème* than within the austere walls of the Foreign Office on the Ballhausplatz. Naturally, Wilhelmina would want to see Dorothea frequently. This, translated into power politics, meant that the two sisters—and Talleyrand and Metternich—could have their private meetings in the duchess's spacious, rented apartment in the Palm Palace at 54 Schenkenstrasse, without undue public suspicion.

There is no indication that the proud Talleyrand and His Most Christian Majesty ever discussed the former's marital situation and the problem it posed in regard to the Vienna Congress, but there must have been some unspoken understanding about it. His old friend Jaucourt was recruited to serve as acting minister at the rue du Bac in his absence, where he could be trusted to carry out Talleyrand's policies, as well as keep him informed of developments in the French capital. Jaucourt could also be relied upon to see that the Paris diplomatic corps and Talleyrand's intimates continued to surround Catherine with attention.

Surely one of the more disgraceful incidents in Talleyrand's long life was the ignominious manner in which he set forth in September on the most historically important task of his entire career. Rather than risk an unpleasant public scene with his unpredictable wife, who had never liked the arrogant Courland princess, he did not disclose his intentions. Leaving Paris clandestinely, in mid-September, his great, luxuriously appointed, traveling coach had barely passed the city limits when it pulled up alongside Dorothea's carriage discreetly parked at a small crossing awaiting him. By the time that Catherine learned from an officious friend that his niece was accompanying him, their berlin was rolling eastward at top speed, Talleyrand's congress instructions—forty printed pages in octavo, signed by Louis XVIII—tucked in the portfolio at his feet. The tsar and the King of Prussia, traveling together, were already on their way, and Talleyrand was determined to precede them. He was concerned about any undisclosed understandings that might have been reached between the Big Four when they were in London and was anxious to marshal his forces—particularly among the smaller powers—before their arrival. With straining horses pushed to the limit by the postillions' cracking whips and loud hallos, and chasseurs on fleet-footed horses racing ahead to assure that the time spent in each relay post was kept to a minimum, they made only two stops en route, in Strasbourg and in Munich, and covered the six hundred miles in a record-breaking seven days.

Talleyrand had selected the Kaunitz palace, the home of Metternich's father-in-law and predecessor, the great Austrian chancellor of Empress Maria-Theresa, Prince von Kaunitz, whose only grandchild was Metternich's wife, as a fitting cadre for his delegation because that Italianate residence with its three vast wings was one of Vienna's handsomest. It stood at 1029 Johannesgasse, a narrow street in the section known as "the old city," almost in the shadow of the Cathedral of Saint Stephen, two steps from the Church of Saint Etienne, a short walk from the Hofburg—the imperial palace—the Ballhausplatz, and busy, central Kartnerstrasse. Unfortunately, the Kaunitz had rarely been occupied for several decades and required more attention than anticipated. Its mattresses were ruined by maggots and there were moth-eaten rugs, bedding, and drapes, but these were housekeeping details. The interior was exuberant Viennese rococo—sheer fantasy; frolicking cherubini abounded in sharp contrast to its forbidding, gray-stone exterior.

September 23, the day they arrived, was to be a working day, like all the days to come. After a brief rest and taking only time to change their clothes, uncle and niece were once more in their carriage, their horses trotting smartly along the Leopoldstrasse. The torches of the running footmen, preceding them, illuminated the theatrical livery of the doormen with their mighty staffs and bandoliers in front of the great palaces lining the way. Tomorrow the pair would begin the round of calls prescribed by protocol, which would normally require eight to ten days, since the entire imperial family as well as the diplomatic corps must be visited. Meantime, no one could question the propriety of Dorothea's wish to see Wilhelmina immediately. Although Dorothea had always been intimidated by her older sister and had never felt close to her, she knew it was imperative for *l'oncle* that she immediately establish the pattern of informal, daily access to the Duchess de Sagan.

Wilhelmina's elegant apartment was located on the second floor of the cavernous Palm Palace, an enormous Schenkenstrasse mansion, which was large enough to accommodate three to four families without their ever meeting each other. Here she provided the chancellor with an indispensable locale for discreet, informal discussions with many important visitors and delegates with whom the duchess had family or personal connections. Her establishment, on the left, was labeled by the secret police the "Austrian camp," as opposed to the one on the right, occupied by her great rival, the Russian Princess Bagration, whose quarters were the center of the important local Russian colony and an invaluable source of information regarding the Romanoff court. The great-niece of Catherine the Great, Katya had been born on the steps of the Russian throne and was a cousin of Alexander. Known as the "Naked Princess" because of the daring décolletages she affected, the young blonde widow of General Bagration, the elderly Russian war hero, shared the coveted distinction, together with Wilhelmina, of being one of the Austrian capital's leading political hostesses. She had also shared Metternich—until the chancellor abandoned her for the Duchess de Sagan, some years before—and their twelve-year-old daughter, brazenly called Clementine after her father, was being raised on the Schenkenstrasse's top floor.

Talleyrand, entering Wilhelmina's salon with Dorothea on his arm, caused a considerable stir, which the ubiquitous *Oberste und Censu Hofstelle* were quick to note in their daily report, presented to titillate the gossip-loving, Austrian emperor while drinking his morning *caffee mit schläg*. Everything about Talleyrand excited curiosity, and the initial impression *l'oncle* and his niece made as they walked, slowly—because of his bad right foot—the length of the salon to greet Wilhelmina was the one Vienna would always retain of them. Both emanated elegance: he so old and so tall; she so young and so small. Dorothea, though she had the delicate, overly long Medem nose, was far too exotic a bird for the Courland aviary, with her striking black hair and huge dark eyes—a paternal heritage which bespoke her illegitimacy. She was still not conventionally pretty, even with her pale oval face now filled out. But a small, delicate head set on a long slim neck enhanced her distinguished carriage, and her innate dignity added inches to Dorothea's height. Her slight stutter when she was excited would never desert her, but her deportment and gestures now formed an enchanting ensemble.

—"Leave it to that old scoundrel to bring that pretty young thing along as a decoy," somebody muttered. "As a Courland princess she will force doors that would not otherwise open to the ex-Bishop of Autun." When the brother of the Prussian ambassador to Vienna entered, Wilhelmina gestured towards Dorothea, and the distinguished scientist hastened over to kiss her delightedly on both cheeks.

—"Why shouldn't the baron be pleased to see her?" another guest remarked. "He knew her as a child when she was growing up in Berlin."

—"That's true, but see, he's talking to Talleyrand, too. One of the foremost leaders of Prussian resistance to French tyranny, talking to Napoleon's former right-hand man! I never thought I'd live to see the day."

Talleyrand had hardly set foot in the Austrian capital before he heard disquieting news that confirmed his worst fears. The Big Four had already been conferring. Taking up where the abortive London talks had left off, they hoped to resolve the Prussian-Russian conundrum to their own satisfaction and intended to present their decisions as a *fait accompli*, ready for ratification, once the conclave itself was called into session. Originally scheduled for the tiny spa of Baden at Vienna's gates, where the *crème* always gathered to enjoy the last of the season, these preliminary conferences were currently being held, instead, in Metternich's completely refurbished chancellery offices on the Ballhausplatz. The very pregnant wife of the Russian ambassador wanted to be near her doctor in the capital, and her husband did not want to leave her. Naturally the little powers now arriving for the forthcoming congress were concerned that they were being bypassed. The meetings had been called to make decisions as a group, with each country having an equal voice, not to be dictated to by the Great Sanhedrin. Resentful of their treatment, they shared a common interest with France in preventing the quartet's dictatorship of the assemblage and formed a natural constituency for the wily French plenipotentiary who was determined to call a halt to the Big Four's game. Winning their confidence was essential to assure Talleyrand of their support.

Like an old war horse smelling gunpowder, he lost no time cultivating their dissatisfaction and went to work to transform France into the unlikely protector of these smaller nations who, for the better part of the past quarter of a century, had lived in fear and trembling of insatiable Napoleon. The fact that France, with its boundaries already settled by the recent Treaty of Paris, was the only country present that wanted nothing for itself helped him become these disgruntled delegates' patron saint. The Big Four might ignore voteless, defeated France, but they could not readily turn their backs on a France that was the champion of the rest of Europe. He immediately invited the Spanish plenipotentiary and various other representatives of the smaller countries for dinner. To round out the party Talleyrand also included the Prince de Ligne, the patriarch of European society. A living legend and the quintessence of the eighteenth century at its best, his presence would dispel the unpleasant rumor that none of the Austrian *crème* would set foot in the Kaunitz after the way that France had treated a Hapsburg archduchess. Imagine beheading Marie-Antoinette! The prince could be counted on to discuss the superlative menu in mouth-watering detail and to spread the guest list, sowing apprehension in the allied camp, making them wonder what the wily statesman was up to.

His battle plan, parlaying France's weakness into strength, quickly paid off. Bavaria was the first to respond. Flattered to have on their side the man whom everyone considered the foremost diplomat of the day and who shared, with Alexander, the limelight due the most prominent personalities gathered there, Sweden, Spain, Denmark, Portugal and the other small Germanic states soon followed suit. Not only did each conveniently manage to put a veil over Talleyrand's past history as the minister who had played such a prominent role in some of the same imperial acquisitions which Europe was now gathered to disentangle. So skillfully did he play his hand that they also did not find it strange that today he had switched, like a chameleon and, as the plenipotentiary of France's legitimate sovereign, he was, paradoxically, wrapping himself in that same cloak of legitimacy.

On September 25 a blast of cannon announced that Alexander had left the border town of Nikolsburg, two and a half hours away. The Austrian emperor had gone only as far as Schönbrun to greet the other sovereigns but, today, he was going farther, to the left bank of the Danube, at the end of the Tabor Bridge. The Tsar of All the Russias was the hero of the day to the Viennese for his participation in the continental crusade against Napoleon, and His Apostolic Imperial Majesty was prepared to give him his due. Vienna's many church bells were pealing when the imperial cortège swung into the somber, weather-beaten Hofburg palace grounds, where the visiting royalty—four kings, one queen, two emperors and empresses, two hereditary princes, three grand duchesses, and three princes of the blood—were already housed and now waiting in the main, inner courtyard. Drums rolled and soldiers presented arms as the masters of the north, Alexander and King Friedrich-Wilhelm III, who was accompanying him, trotted in together. This heavy-handed emphasis of their political solidarity did not bode well for Metternich if Alexander remained as capricious as he had been in London. That night the highlight of the gala at the Kärntnertor Theater was the ballet *Zephyr and Flora*, starring the great French ballerina, la Bigottini, whose presence in Vienna was part of Talleyrand's campaign to tout French culture. A supper followed, as the congress's overload of festivities now got under way in earnest with the Austrian emperor as host. Not a day would pass without some similar special entertainment, and he was emulated on a lesser scale by the other princes of the imperial house. His guests would have thought that the Hapsburg court was lowering itself if it did not receive with a magnificence worthy of its position and the occasion, even though the rank and file of Europe, taken as a whole, was hungry, afraid, and without hope regarding the future.

Most of the reigning princes accompanied their diplomats. Like the majority of the nobility converging there, who disdained work, these crowned heads had never concerned themselves with affairs of state and did not intend to start now. A certain amount of unusual freedom existed, as the various sovereigns whirled around in little carriages with an almost nonexistent retinue or, often, even alone, and walked together through the narrow Viennese streets amid crowds of the natives out gawking at their emperor's distinguished guests. Taking advantage of the golden autumn, the visitors strolled through the famous Prater Park, sweet with the odor of decaying leaves and noisy with waltzes, the current dance rage, played by countless little bands. In the salons and ballrooms, where *tout* Europe flirted, gossiped, ate, and danced, the strict formality of the *ancien régime* was also being relaxed. Balls were good locales to continue negotiations started in conference rooms earlier. Here, amid the potted palms, the rustling of satin and taffeta, the coquettish flutter of fans, the plenipotentiaries might forego the formality of asking a crowned head for an audience. The art of accosting a sovereign on his way through a crowded salon and engaging his attention, became an important new factor in diplomacy.

A week to the day after his arrival, Talleyrand received a personal note from the Austrian chancellor inviting him, informally, to be briefed at a meeting of the Big Four that afternoon. He quickly ascertained that Don Pedro Labrador, the Spanish plenipotentiary, was likewise asked. Why the Portuguese and Swedish representatives who were the only other signers of the Treaty of Paris were not included has never been made clear. However, every other detail of this reunion has been scrupulously recorded, not only in Talleyrand's *Mémoires* and in his letters to Louis XVIII but also, word for word, in the report of the chevalier

Friedrich von Gentz. Known as Metternich's "spare brain," the little redheaded Jew, who had helped himself to the "von," and would be the most important second-string man of the forthcoming congress—he was its secretary—would never forget Talleyrand's *tour de force* that afternoon. Had the French plenipotentiary ever needed to earn a living as an actor, he could certainly have qualified on the strength of his performance there.

According to Gentz, the purpose of the meeting was to make the French and Spanish representatives accept the Big Four's resolution which would leave in the latter's hands the settlement of all the important matters to be raised later. When Talleyrand arrived, punctually, at 2:00 p.m., he found the meeting already in progress with Lord Castlereagh, who was seated at the head of the table, apparently presiding. With that haughty ease he used when with lesser mortals, Talleyrand took an empty chair, between the Russian representative, Nesselrode, and the Prussian Prince von Hardenberg, then glanced in feigned amazement at Humboldt and Gentz. Metternich explained that Gentz, with his sheaves of paper and battery of quills, was in charge of the minutes of today's meeting and that Humboldt was there to assist the stone-deaf Prince von Hardenberg. "We all have our infirmities—to be exploited when need be." [6] Talleyrand replied coldly, as Humboldt poked his sharply creased face towards von Hardenberg and repeated each word, enunciating carefully in order that his handicapped colleague might read his lips, while the prince, with the helpless expression of the hard-of-hearing, cupped his hearing horn to his ear and kept demanding "Why? . . . What?" Accordingly it was suggested that, next time, Talleyrand should be accompanied by his colleague, Dalberg, so he might lean on his arm. The French plenipotentiary had made his point, a small one but, as one prominent diplomat and historian has pointed out, details are important in the art of diplomacy and, taken all together as a whole, can work wonders.

Metternich handed Talleyrand the *procès-verbal* signed by the Big Four. He started to read it. Almost immediately, he laid it down, shaking his head and saying, with a tone of bewilderment, "I don't understand." Then, picking it up again, he pretended to be making a great effort to follow the sense of the document, stopping from time to time to look up and demand an explanation of one phrase after another. Talleyrand put the dumbfounded Metternich on the defensive from the start with his frequent interruptions, his embarrassing questions and biting remarks, and hopelessly scuttled the Austrian's plans. "He protested against the procedures we had adopted and soundly reprimanded us for two hours," Gentz concluded. "It was a scene I shall never forget." [7] Most important from Talleyrand's point of view was his discovery that the coalition was inherently fragile. The Big Four were speechless at his performance and buckled under, saying that they attached little importance to the protocol in question, and agreed to withdraw it and to start afresh another day—with Talleyrand and Labrador, of course.

Talleyrand at once took the offensive. Instead of waiting for that meeting to be called, he sent a note to those ministers who had been present, establishing his position that the congress alone had the sole right to make decisions. The powers who had signed the Paris Treaty were only qualified to prepare the questions for the congress to act upon. Talleyrand's subsequent moves were to ferret out the coalition's differences on how to reconstruct Europe, exploit them, and harvest the results. Austria was automatically against any disturbance of the European status quo, while England remained faithful to her traditional policy of a balance of power. However, Prussia and Russia, unlike at Paris earlier, were now nakedly greedy for land acquisitions, thereby handing Talleyrand the necessary wedge he sought. Self-interest created fertile soil for a battle royal over the principle that conquest does not create sovereignty; legitimacy does.

Two days later, Talleyrand had a stormy session with the tsar who dreamt of making an enormous leap into the heart of central Europe. To achieve this he intended to reassemble the presently fragmented kingdom of Poland, make himself its new king and incorporate the restored kingdom, with a pretense of autonomy, into the Russian empire. Consequently, he needed the Polish territory which Prussia had previously gobbled up during Warsaw's years of travail and, to recompense the Prussian king, Alexander proposed Saxony, which had belonged to the Saxon king's family since the tenth century and whose two and a half million natives Prussia coveted.

"I have two hundred thousand men in the duchy of Warsaw and . . . no one is going to chase me out!" the temperamental Alexander shouted, losing his sangfroid. "If the Saxon king does not abdicate, he will be taken to Russia and he will die there. One King of Poland [Stanislaus Poniatowski] has already died there. Why not a King of Saxony? . . . I prefer to go to war rather than give up what I already possess."

Talleyrand turned to the white and gold wall paneling "closest to me," as he later described the dramatic scene to Louis XVIII, "and, putting my head against it, I struck it with my forehead, exclaiming 'Europe, O Europe! Unhappy Europe! Will it be said that you have lost it?' " [8]

Rationalizing the outrageous steal he was proposing as punishment for the rotund Frederick-Augustus III, who had made the mistake of remaining loyal to Napoleon until the bitter end, the tsar persisted in referring to the hapless Saxon king as "the one who has betrayed the cause of Europe." "That, sire, is a question of dates." [9] Was Talleyrand's famous retort intended as a reminder that, seven years before on the barge at Tilsit, Alexander himself had embraced Napoleon? Or was it a subconscious, Freudian slip—Talleyrand's personal excuse for his own shifting of sides as the occasion might warrant?

On the sixth there was a fête; the day following a hunt was scheduled. In the midst of these and similar social activities there had been ample occasions for *sub rosa* meetings *à deux* and *à trois*, in a curtained alcove or in the Hofburg corridors, to a lilting waltz or to a stately minuet. On the eighth, Talleyrand and Labrador met once more with the Big Four. Afterwards, as proof that Talleyrand had won an important victory, he sent the Grand Duchess Anna-Dorothea the announcement of the postponement of the congress opening until November 1, a delay which should allow ample time to iron out all difficulties. He added, perhaps as an afterthought: "Our child [Dorothea] is enjoying a great success here. She is popular with all ages . . . I am delighted." [10]

By early November the delegates were still in an uproar over the Saxon king's predicament. Cardinal Consalvi, the papal representative, kept referring, in his dispatches destined for the Holy See, to Talleyrand's "vigorous campaign" to arouse opposition to the scandalous Russian proposal. Unfortunately, at the moment, the Austrian chancellor was not much help. Metternich had other personal matters on his mind, fueled by the gossip mongering in the salons and fanned by Princess Bagration's harebrained jealousy of Wilhelmina. Whether or not the Duchess de Sagan was actually seeing a former lover, as Baron Hager's secret police reported, Metternich was so upset at the possibility of losing Wilhelmina that he was paying more attention to her than to the Prussian-Russian imbroglio. The other evening when Talleyrand tried to discuss the latest complications, the chancellor was completely engrossed in showing Wilhelmina some engravings she had requested him to bring in order to help her choose a costume for a forthcoming Metternich masked ball.

November 23 was the date set for the famous carrousel which all Vienna—natives as well as distinguished guests—was impatiently awaiting. Weeks of preparation were required and its participants came from the elite of Hungary, Bohemia, and Austria with the single exception of the two Courland sisters. Tallyrand wrote Anna-Dorothea what a great coup it was for the French embassy to have Dorothea among those chosen and asked her to be sure that the official Paris *Moniteur* carried an account of this brilliant affair. The night of the spectacle, the regular Hungarian palace guards, resplendent with their tiger skin calpacs, were reinforced by special squadrons of mounted police to help hold back the curious Viennese who gathered, well ahead of time and in spite of the cold, to catch a glimpse of the titled guests as they were handed out of their carriages in front of the Spanish Riding School. The mirrored galleries of this immense baroque parallelogram, built by Fischer von Erlach for Charles V, were a rippling river of light, reflecting thousands of shimmering candles. Promptly at 8:00 p.m., amid a rustle of anticipation and the murmur of fans, heralds-at-arms sounded a fanfare of trumpets, and the orchestra, which contained every musician of note in Vienna, burst into festive seventeenth-century music. Fine horsemanship was still among the most admired of skills, and the grand finale was an exhibition of dressage, the medieval army maneuvers for which the imperial Lippizaner horses were famous.

But congress matters were never far from the statesmen's minds. After the banquet and much talked about, much rehearsed quadrille that followed—once again featuring Wilhelmina and Dorothea—Alexander encountered Metternich talking with Talleyrand and several ministers: "You diplomats make decisions and then we soldiers have to let ourselves be shot into cripples for you!" [11] His Imperial Majesty fired at the startled chancellor. Then he steered Prince von Hardenberg, the Prussian plenipotentiary, into a nearby back room for still another private conversation. The carrousel's resounding success—it would be repeated twice to overflow audiences—was another triumph in Talleyrand's campaign to sell France as the cultural center of the universe and amply justified his insistence that the well-known Paris artist, Isabey, accompany him to Vienna. For Talleyrand had succeeded in having the famous painter appointed the carrousel's artistic coordinator.

As winter tightened its grip, Vienna was a hotbed of rumors, and the sniping between Austria and England on one side, and Prussia and Russia on the other, intensified, with the lines between them more clearly defined daily as each intrigued to strengthen its position in the ultimate settlement of the Polish-Saxon quandary. By Talleyrand's ceaseless, skillful stoking, the discord provoked by the exorbitant claims of the two masters of the north and his insistence that legitimate owners be given back their rightful possessions, France, the country all Europe had united to bring to its knees, now became the determining factor holding the balance. One day Talleyrand and Metternich thought they had won over the King of Prussia; the next, Alexander asked Friedrich-Wilhelm III to dinner and their work was undone. Another time, His Imperial Majesty publicly vented his spleen on the French plenipotentiary. Snarling, "Talleyrand is behaving as though he were the minister of Louis XIV," [12] he unwittingly handed Talleyrand the ultimate compliment by equating the amount of influence that he now wielded at Vienna with that of a minister of the all-powerful Sun King. Everyone was reading political significance into the principals' most negligible acts, even when the tsar danced several polonaises with Lady Castlereagh and a *grand-père* with Lady Mathilda at an affair at the British embassy.

In the eyes of the *crème*, France's position as an outcast was considerably ameliorated by Talleyrand's strong stand on behalf of the old Saxon monarch. The best indication that the corner of Viennese acceptance had been turned was when the snobbish Gentz admitted publicly to having eaten two meals on the same evening. He received the French invitation too late to decline another one but, since Talleyrand dined earlier than most in Vienna, the tiny chevalier was able to accept both—with the help of one of his purple digestive powders. For where else in the Austrian capital could one eat like a god and have the best conversation this side of Paris?

As the number and importance of the guests at the Kaunitz table improved, the disposition of Talleyrand's chef, Carême, brightened proportionately. But he had not yet had any crowned heads to taste the gastronomical miracles he was performing with the fresh Danube fish, hard firm apples, and other seasonal delicacies available, or to immortalize with a special dish or sauce. Anyone overhearing Talleyrand and his "cher Maître" daily analyze the evening's forthcoming repast might be excused for thinking the famous cook had missed a second calling. He was a born diplomat. The popularity of the delegates, and the progress of the congress's negotiations, could be measured—from Carême's point of view—by the absence or presence, and relative position, on the dinner menu of the culinary *chef-d'oeuvre* honoring each one. Carême would no longer consider serving "Nesselrode Pudding," which had been dedicated to the aforesaid Russian foreign minister, or "Charlotte Russe," with its molded exterior of lady fingers—two sublime concoctions that the great master had created when the tsar was a guest at the Hôtel Saint-Florentin and the French-Russian honeymoon was in full bloom. Here in Vienna, the dish might be the same with perhaps a subtle variation of the sauce, but it would bear a good Austrian name, like "Bombe à la Metternich," or "Clam-Martinitz Torte." For Carême was also not above playing cupid and, like the rest of the legation household, he knew of Dorothea's blossoming love for the dashing young Count Karl Clam-Martinitz.

Because Alexander was laid low for almost two weeks—too much night life and running after women was the *Oberste und Censu Hofstelle* diagnosis—the Saxon-Polish question hung suspended, frozen in mid-air, like the delegates' breath those crisp, early December mornings. But once His Imperial Majesty was back in circulation, his relationship with the chancellor hit a new low. After Metternich as good as called the tsar a liar and Alexander declared his intention to challenge the former to a duel, Emperor Francis had to step in. Now, whenever their paths crossed, Alexander looked straight through the Austrian as if he did not exist, and Princess Bagration and others in the Russian camp were instructed to entertain on Mondays, the evening of the Metternichs' weekly reception, so the tsar would have an excuse not to appear at the Chancellery. At the same time Alexander, after baring his teeth early on, was now trying to woo Talleyrand and, when he next met him, His Imperial Highness pressed his hand and begged that he call on him informally—"*en frac.*"

The coming of Advent put a noticeable damper on the excessive entertainment and the more serious-minded delegates hoped that the congress would finally buckle down to business. Since custom now dictated a more subdued form of entertainment Maria-Ludovici inaugurated her favorite "Living Pictures." While Dorothea had only a small supporting role in the first series, which depicted paintings by contemporary artists then on exhibition in the Austrian capital, *l'oncle* proudly advised the grand duchess: "Dorothea is proving herself an actress. She plays as well as Mlle Mars in one of her best nights at the Comédie. . . . In fact, Dorothea does well anything she tries."

The *London Morning Chronicle* was telling the truth when its Austrian correspondent reported:

> "We learn from high sources a project is made, how Vienna's grand congress the Christmas will spend, since public affairs have so long been delayed, they may very well wait til the holidays end."

This was the first year Vienna had ever seen Christmas trees, and Dorothea had her Count Clam take her in a sleigh out into the countryside to the foot of the Köhlenberg to find one that she judged to be the right size and shape to place under the curving ceremonial staircase in the Kaunitz's spacious main hall. She then supervised festooning it with multicolored garlands and lighted candles. When it was time for Wilhelmina to give her annual servants' ball, the Courland sisters and their friends peeked from behind a curtained gallery on their maids, seamstresses, and lackeys frolicking below. Dorothea suggested to *l'oncle* that they celebrate the festive days ahead as she had when growing up in Berlin. Several long consultations were held with the major-domo, and soon the smell of marzipan and butter cookies mingled with the heady fragrance of pine emanating from the public rooms which were gaily decorated with boughs, swags, and bow-tied wreaths. On Christmas Eve Talleyrand and his niece gave a large party for the embassy and household staffs that concluded with singing merrymakers gathering under the great fir, where Dorothea handed each one a brightly wrapped package from its spreading branches. Continuing to celebrate in the German fashion—in France, gifts were exchanged on New Year's Day instead—Talleyrand and Dorothea gave each other their presents later that same evening.

At the Hofburg's traditional Saint Sylvester's Eve ball, when the orchestra stopped tuning up and was ready to start playing, the tsar, as usual, led off the opening polonaise. The long line behind him was soon undulating through the various palace drawing rooms and halls into the distant cardroom where Talleyrand was. He looked up, annoyed at the disturbance. The whist players were tucked too far away for the music to be audible, and only mischievousness could cause His Imperial Highness to snake through there. Or imperial displeasure at the increasing rapprochement between Talleyrand and Metternich and at the way the former continued to successfully thwart Alexander's Polish plans. Talleyrand finally got up from the card table, collected his niece and dragged himself slowly into the large salon where the buffets and tables with seats for the ladies were located; the men stood at these affairs. When he observed Castlereagh, he excused himself to confer with His Lordship about a meeting the tsar had called of the Big Four—without France—the previous day, to urge acceptance of the desired Russian solution. Milord angrily complained that Alexander was trying to lay down the law for all Europe and added, ominously, that England would not be dictated to. Talleyrand, who had always favored a British as well as an Austrian alliance and had been patiently awaiting this moment for a long time, soothingly suggested a defensive pact between France, Austria, and Britain. "Why not," the British diplomat replied, "since we three agree on the rights of the Saxon king." While a secret, tripartite agreement was being drawn up, with each party to field an army to come to the aid of the other if attacked, Castlereagh received word that the United States and England had signed the peace ending the War of 1812 and thereby, fortuitously, releasing all England's armed forces.

The next morning Talleyrand was able to write Louis XVIII: "Sire, France is no longer isolated in Europe." [13]

14

President of the First Ministry of the Second Restoration

"She [Dorothea] is charming and very intelligent. There's nothing young about her except her freedom from affectation."
—Talleyrand [1]

AS DAWN WAS BREAKING a few days later, Talleyrand was awakened by the alarm drum of Vienna's fire squad. The superb Landstrasse Palace of Count Andreas Razumovsky, the Russian ambassador, which was one of the capital's most sumptuous and had taken twenty years to complete, was ablaze and raging out of control. Because of the unusual cold, caution had been thrown to the winds, and the fire had started in the overheated pipes laid in the floors and walls, a modern heating system that was the wonder and the short-lived envy of Vienna. No fire buff, unlike His Apostolic Imperial Majesty, who was already hastening to the scene, Talleyrand rolled over and went back to sleep.

The natives chose to interpret the heavy snowfall, that first week in 1815, as an omen indicating that the new year was to start with a clean slate, like the fresh snow. Carriages swept along the narrow streets to the swishing accompaniment of the runners that had replaced their wheels. The days were cold and clear, and the Graben and other public squares were crowded with visitors and delegates who were out, like the natives, for a breath of fresh air.

The French embassy had become one of the focal points of life in Vienna—concrete evidence, as Talleyrand intended it to be, that France was now more rich and powerful than ever, as a result of his recent political masterpiece, the breakup of the alliance of the four great powers and the substitution of France in a new tripartite union. The Kaunitz's *ancien régime* atmosphere, carrying with it the ultimate felicities of life, created an ambiance that neither the magnificence of Emperor Francis's Hofburg nor the oriental splendor of the Razumovsky Palace, where Alexander had done his official entertaining before the fire, managed to convey. Talleyrand and his niece had become the most famous couple in Vienna. A certain *parfum de scandale* helped, and the fact that he was so old and she so young made the whispers more titillating. The secret police intimated "With those scandalous Courland Princesses, anything goes." And in Gentz's journal these days, the four sisters were referred to on every other page as the "Courland whores," for Joanna, the youngest, had just jilted him.

The delegates' extracurricular activities continued in an atmosphere of increasing boredom and satiety. The inventiveness of the empress's festival committee was by now as strained as the imperial exchequer, and the man in the street was worried that he would soon be taxed to raise the fifty thousand guldens per diem the congress's board alone was costing. Since Vienna was the music capital of the world, with many talented composers and more generous patrons than elsewhere on the continent, musical events were on an exceptional scale including a concert of one hundred pianos in a joint recital under the baton of Antonio Salieri, the first kappelmeister of the Austrian court. Dr. Justice Bollman, a German-born American doctor and the sole overseas visitor to attend the congress, was much in demand for his ghost stories. Tombolas and mascarades continued to prove popular, and the august Prince de Ligne thoughtfully provided the congress with one spectacle that jaded group had not yet witnessed—the pomp and ceremony of a grand field marshal's funeral.

On January 21, the twenty-second anniversary of Louis XVI's death on the guillotine, both his body and Marie-Antoinette's, which had lately been discovered in an unmarked common grave in Paris, were to be reburied ceremoniously in the Bourbon family crypt at Saint Denis, outside of the French capital. Seizing this as a splendid opportunity to consecrate the principle of legitimacy—and the need for it to prevail in the resolution of the fates of Saxony and Poland—Talleyrand held a requiem mass in the martyred rulers' memory in Vienna on the same day. As a gesture of sympathy, Emperor Francis volunteered to foot the expenses and forbade any entertainment in the city for twenty-four hours. Nothing was spared to make the solemn occasion reflect the grandeur of the French crown. The painter Isabey was again in charge of the overall artistic effect and, with the help of Empress Maria-Ludovica's interior decorator, the entire nave of Saint Stephan's Cathedral was hung with black drapery richly embroidered in silver. Talleyrand's personal music director, Sigismund von Neukomm, composed special orchestral music and a requiem without instrumentation for a choir of two hundred and fifty voices. To guarantee there would be room for those he most wanted to impress, Talleyrand made the service invitational and took pains to assure the Prussian king and the tsar and tsarina prominent places. Talleyrand did not want them to miss the point he was making or to forget that the Saxon king they were trying to despoil was a cousin of the late Louis XVI—and, consequently, of his brother, Louis XVIII. For reasons of his own, unpredictable Alexander refused to accept.

In an abrupt change of mood, the imperial sleigh ride was scheduled for the next day, after numerous postponements due to recurrent thaws. Thirty-two sleighs, elaborately decorated in emerald green velvet, embroidered and fringed in gold, with more gold on the axles, were lined up on the Josephsplatz awaiting the guests, while their impatient steeds, caparisoned in tiger skins and other rich furs, with ribbons and bows braided in their manes and nodding ostrich plumes on their heads, champed at the bit and pawed the air. Around 2:00 p.m., after the usual confusion, a large detachment of cavalry set off to lead the way, followed by a six-horse sledge of trumpeters and drummers. The sovereigns followed, then twenty-four pages in medieval costume, a squadron of the imperial guards, and the rest of the party, including *l'oncle* and his niece. Bringing up the rear was another sledge with a group of court musicians in Turkish garb.

The cavalcade proceeded at a walk through the winding streets so the crowds waiting on the ramparts might enjoy the show. Once they crossed the Danube, the horses were given their heads, and they dashed along the country lanes, the myriad bells in their elaborate harnesses tinkling. After circling through Schönbrun's elaborate grounds—with a brief, distant glimpse of l'Aiglon out sliding—and a long stop for a figure-skating exhibition on the main lake, the group entered the palace for a banquet. Later, the imperial opera troupe presented a German version of *Cinderella*, which Marie-Louise also witnessed, sight unseen, from a specially prepared, concealed cubbyhole. As they reentered Vienna, their way illuminated by the thousands of new, pear-shaped glass lanterns that were the emperor's pride and joy—even though they were filled with a foul-smelling mixture of linseed oil and pork drippings—the wind shifted and the thermometer dropped. Everyone got thoroughly chilled and, the minute the pair reached the Kaunitz, they hastened to the ground-floor study, the warmest room there, where Dorothea casually raised the back of her elaborate skirt and layers of lace petticoats to warm her *derrière* in front of the porcelain stove. Only lackeys were present. They did not count as men, and Talleyrand was, well, *l'oncle*.

Since there was little way to readily exert pressure on congress affairs, Wilhelmina's apartments remained crowded. Distinguished men who enjoyed her superior mind and respected her opinion swarmed round; so did her usual circle of admiring swains—one holding her fan, another her shawl, a third fetching her a glass of lemonade to sip. The rulers of the small principalities, not to mention important foreigners who needed recommendations and contacts, also flocked to the Schenkenstrasse to seek her widespread influence. Even here, congress affairs were never long absent from the statesmen's thoughts. As a result of the secret tripartite treaty, the Big Four had become a committee of five. Talleyrand was admitted at the insistence of Metternich and the British foreign secretary, and the trio frequently met in the left wing of the Palm to discuss plans before joining the two masters of the north, difficult Alexander and King Friedrich-Wilhelm III.

Due to the strengthened resistance to his wishes, Alexander was becoming suspicious of some secret agreement but, since the others were in harmony, the impasse disappeared like snow in June. Despite the tsar's smouldering anger, Castlereagh succeeded in hammering out the fine print of a settlement before he left to defend his Tory government's foreign policy when Parliament sat. Alexander resigned himself to retaining the bulk of the duchy of Warsaw and little more. The Prussian king, who had wanted all of Saxony to strengthen his predominance among the other small, independent German states, was to get only a little more than half of the hapless Saxon monarch's territory. He also received most of the rich but poorly organized Rhineland, an addition which placed Prussia in direct contact with France on the left bank of the Rhine. What appeared to be practical sense at the time—albeit catastrophic, with hindsight, in the light of three future westbound invasions—dictated the abandonment of the Rhineland and the maintenance of a shrunken Saxony with a loose confederacy of German-speaking states, a static, compact German mass, set in the middle of Europe. Since it was England who was so insistant about this rearrangement Talleyrand, who could ill afford to alienate his closest ally, went along, as did his contemporaries.

Although he confessed in a letter to a seraglio stalwart that he was "tired occasionally," such a compromise for the marathon Polish-Saxon controversy was worth it, from Talleyrand's point of view. For it represented a continuation of the same moderate policy for which he had long tried to work an alliance with England, or Austria, or both, for the maintenance of European peace. It also had the added advantage of pleasing Louis XVIII who was adamant about not completely despoiling Frederick Augustus III, a close relative through his mother, a Saxon princess.

Wellington, who was presently his country's ambassador in Paris, was Castlereagh's replacement, and his arrival breathed fresh life into the social season. Not unexpectedly Talleyrand, whose prestige in the diplomatic world was at an all-time high because of the resolution of the Russian-Prussian Gordian knot, snared the plum of introducing the famous general to the Austrian capital. Sitting between the two imperial consorts—the Austrian empress on one side, her frail, consumptive body weighed down by the awesome Hapsburg jewels; the ash-blonde, sad-faced tsarina, over-rouged by all but Saint Petersburg standards, on the other—Talleyrand, in his elegant, long-tailed, plum velvet suit, aglitter with the beribboned, diamond-and-enamel stars and orders of the sovereigns who were his guests, personified power. Across from him, gowned in Leroy's stiff white brocade with ropes of the famous Courland pearls—part of the jewels she had borrowed from Mama for the Vienna visit—wound around her neck and arms and in her ink black hair, Dorothea presented an enchanting picture as she leaned over the top of her great white ostrich-feather fan to address the tsar in his good ear. *L'oncle's* small chamber ensemble under von Neukomm lulled the ear with music by Haydn, then Mozart. That of Beethoven, who had recently conducted the premiere of his Seventh Symphony in the Kärntnertor Theater, was too controversial for such an evening. And a succession of white-wigged footmen in the aubergine Talleyrand livery passed an endless procession of epicurean delights, although Maître Carême regretted it was no longer January, a month the great chef preferred because of the variety and quality of foodstuffs to be had then in Vienna's markets.

Talleyrand seldom allowed dinner to last more than an hour, and tonight was no exception. In the Kaunitz's great salons, which opened one onto the next and had been transformed into a solid mass of white carnations and azaleas, stars of the diplomatic world and the *crème* awaited the sixty dinner guests. The painter Isabey wandered about doing sketches—Wellington, who was conscious that his hatchet nose was a cartoonist's delight, egotistically stipulated he must be drawn face on—and later, a trio of French ballerinas, whom Talleyrand had insisted appear in the Austrian capital during the congress, performed. A ball followed as the evening's finale.

Never had the forty days of abstinence before Easter seemed so essential to salvation as after the festivities that year during Fashing, the six traditionally merry weeks preceding Lent. With the subdued social activities dictated by Lent and the burning question of the day now out of the way, Wellington cranked the congress's creaking machinery into action, and the end was in sight. The delegates, each with a pet project to push, settled down with scissors and paste for the tidying-up process.

Talleyrand's letters to the grand duchess were full of "our girl's" triumphs and Anna-Dorothea's, to him, of the rising unrest in France, where Louis XVIII was looking less and less like a Sun King and more like a paper lantern carried around by a foreigner. Meanwhile, the French consul in Leghorn kept forwarding countless rumors about the former emperor's suspicious activities on Elba. Aroused by these continuing reports, Talleyrand was not the only person in Vienna who continued to worry about Napoleon's uncomfortably close proximity to the mainland. Finally the congress met in a secret session in which they overrode Alexander's continuing objections and determined to ship the former ruler farther off. But before they had to time to do so Napoleon, who undoubtedly had spies—and sympathizers—in the Austrian capital, realized his time was running out and took matters in his own hands.

On Tuesday morning, March 7, Dorothea was perched on a corner of Talleyrand's great canopied bed, sipping her morning *café au lait* and chatting with *l'oncle,* who was propped up there, still wearing his nightcap. The pair were discussing a final dress rehearsal of Kötzebue's *Old Love Affair,* in which she had a prominent role, when their conversation was interrupted by a knock at the door, and a valet entered with a note that had just been delivered by a Metternich footman. "It's probably to advise me of the time of our meeting to day," Talleyrand commented, handing the envelope to Dorothea to open.

—"Napoleon has escaped from Elba!" she cried, reading it at a glance. "Oh, *mon oncle,* what about my rehearsal?"

—"It will be held on schedule, of course," he blandly reassured her.

—"And the performance this evening?" Would all her work be wasted?

—"Life goes on, even if the heavens fall in."

Something in *l'oncle's* voice caught Dorothea up short. Suddenly the enormity of the news penetrated—and the childish selfishness of her reaction. Anxiously she demanded, "What is going to happen now?" Talleyrand shook his head. How he wished he knew. He had been caught unawares, a cardinal sin, and was disconcerted, for there had been plenty of warnings but he had not believed the accumulating evidence. "What audacity!" he concluded admiringly.

Foregoing his *levée,* which had become more of a ceremony here than in Paris—possibly to further emphasize the *ancien régime* aspect of everything he did—Talleyrand was the first of the ministers to arrive at the chancellery. Metternich handed him the six-line dispatch from the Austrian consul-general at Genoa advising that the former French emperor, together with a thousand men, had disappeared on board the brig, *The Inconstant,* and on seven smaller craft.

The Austrian had already notified his emperor, met with the Prussian king and, then, with the tsar—his personal difficulties with the latter forgotten in the urgency of the moment. Once the others assembled, it was quickly agreed to resume military operations. Special couriers were sent scurrying to the commander-in-chief of the coalition forces and the scattered allied commands, but the sensational news was temporarily withheld from everyone else. Even Gentz, although he was the secretary of the congress and made it a point to be the first to know everything, was not informed and spent the morning leisurely soaking—he was afflicted with rheumatism—in the Diana Baths' thermal waters.

That evening, the harp and the flute were playing the overture, and the sovereigns were assembled in the Hofburg's great ballroom, where a temporary stage had been set up, surrounded by sweet-smelling, boxed orange trees in bloom, when an aide-de-camp of the tsar appeared and whispered in his good ear. Alexander immediately arose and followed him out. The candles in the massive silver torchères were being extinguished and the stage curtains slowly pulled open by the time he was back. His Imperial Majesty murmured a few words of apology to the countess on his left. She turned and said something to her neighbor, who turned and said something to hers. The news spread like the sails of the barque taking Napoleon from Elba. Spring was early this year, and the Eagle was returning—as he himself had predicted—with the violets. The tsarina clutched her pearls convulsively. The superb collar broke and the guests, who were glad to have something to do to relieve the tension, stooped under their chairs to retrieve the marble-sized beads. "Don't trouble yourselves," Her Imperial Majesty pleaded. "They're not worth the effort."

The play was beginning. The young stars, Dorothea and Metternich's seventeen-year-old daughter, Marie—his favorite child and the debutante of the season—sensed that they had lost their audience and made a valiant effort to recapture their attention, but no one was interested in the play, or in the *tableaux vivants* or in the ballet that followed. Afterwards, those present crowded around to commiserate with Talleyrand. Napoleon's flight was not conceived as a threat, but they concurred that this time, when the former emperor was seized, he must be sent farther away, so he could never again disturb Europe's peace. A consummate card player, Talleyrand acted as if he held a full flush and bluffed his way through the evening with customary aplomb.

But where was Napoleon? While rumors flooded in as to his whereabouts, the wind-up of the congress's business continued. So Talleyrand, Metternich, and Wellington set forth, forty-eight hours later, for Pressburg, nearby on the Danube, where Frederick Augustus I was being held as a prisoner of war while Russian troops blanketed his land. As a triumph for Talleyrand's principle of legitimacy—that legitimate sovereignty could only be acquired by cession—it was essential to procure the consent of the old Saxon king for his immolation on behalf of the general peace. While there Talleyrand took time to see a former mistress,

Mme de Brionne, who was critically ill and had sent word that she would like to see him before she died. When Talleyrand had passed through, the previous time, he was in the entourage of Napoleon. The countess being a devout royalist had left town rather than receive him. One of the earliest members of his seraglio who, eons before, tried to get him a cardinal's biretta, she had emigrated at the beginning of the Revolution. Because she still maintained the customs and mode of an earlier day, she must have covered her shoulders with a small fichu. Perhaps she still had the coquetry to have her hair arranged in a high coiffure with long curls to remind him of the woman he loved thirty-five years before. In a rare display of emotion Talleyrand admits, in his selective *Mémoires*: "I flung myself at her feet ... I couldn't say a word." She would be dead three weeks later.

He was hardly back in Vienna and at the Metternichs' weekly Monday supper when a courier from the King of Sardinia arrived, travel-stained and weary, after crossing the Alps by forced marches. His message, "Napoleon has landed outside Cannes!" transformed the astounded Talleyrand once more into a pariah before the eyes of the speechless gathering. The orchestra tried to coax somebody back onto the floor, but no one felt like dancing. Until this moment the congress and the Viennese, with no news other than that of the fugitive's disappearance, had been making book on Napoleon's capture and death within a fortnight. Suddenly the still-fresh memories of the past twenty-five years—the capitals invaded, the industries paralyzed, the battlefields piled high with corpses—came flooding back and everyone huddled in worried little groups, talking.

The Prussian king motioned to the Duke of Wellington, and both left, with the tsar and Emperor Francis hard on their heels. Their precipitate departure made the rest of the company uneasy and, one by one, others followed suit. As he watched the spacious salons emptying prematurely, Talleyrand commented to Metternich, "Napoleon, not wishing to finish by a tragedy, will finish by a farce." Shortly afterwards, the chancellor, in turn, excused himself to follow his master for any further instructions occasioned by this unexpected turn of events, leaving Dorothea and Tallyrand standing there alone. Not a muscle of the latter's face betrayed any emotion. *Sic transit gloria mundi*. Trite but how true.

Couriers arrived daily, each with still more surprising news as the former emperor continued his triumphal march north, and the French army, dissatisfied with its treatment at Bourbon hands and seething at unpaid pensions, flocked in droves to his side, instead of stopping him. Town after town, displeased with Louis XVIII's ineptitude and the returned royalists' vindictiveness, was swinging to the eagle-headed standards as Napoleon passed through. Rumors poured in. And all bad. Recent visitors to Elba might describe him as a middle-aged man with a too-tight waistcoat, a bloated, yellowish face, and sparse hair, but to the enthusiastic Frenchmen who were clearing his passage, he was surrounded with the aura of a superman and appeared seven feet tall, young, and handsome. Now the chief concern of the congress was no longer Saxony but Napoleon's Paris-bound progress, as the news flashed like lightning throughout the continent that Lyons, France's second city, accorded him a liberator's welcome.

Talleyrand had a profound love for France and to save his country from dismemberment—once Napoleon was again defeated, as he was convinced the little Corsican would be—Talleyrand worked desperately to put his daring escape and victorious return into proper perspective. It was imperative that the congress brand Napoleon an outlaw, subject to public vengeance, and to label France, under the lawful government of Louis XVIII, his first victim. It was against the former emperor and not against France that the wrath of Europe and its armies must be directed. As he set off for the Ballhausplatz, the proposed manifesto, on which he had been feverishly working, was tucked in the attaché case underneath his arm.

"Wait here for me, Madame," *l'oncle* urged as Dorothea and the entire legation staff anxiously accompanied him to the door of the Kaunitz to wish him luck. "Watch for my return. If I triumph, you will see me, through the carriage window, wave the treaty on which will depend the fate of France—and of Europe." Hours later, he returned, brandishing the proclamation impressively plastered with black and red seals. "I don't believe another such document has ever been written," he exulted. "History furnishes no example of a similar rejection by all mankind." At a subsequent meeting at the Austrian chancellery, the original Big Four declared war against Napoleon, and were joined, two days later, by Talleyrand, representing Louis XVIII.

When Napoleon issued an edict of amnesty en route, Talleyrand was one of the few omitted but, once back in the Tuileries—without a shot being fired—he immediately tried to re-enlist the services of the man whose vast holdings he had lately sequestered. For, as Napoleon explained to one of his ministers: "Talleyrand is still the man who knows the most about this country, the cabinets, and the people." First, Napoleon sent Talleyrand's son, General Flahaut, to rally his father to the imperial cause. When Charles was turned back at Stuttgart and not allowed to pass through Wurtemburg, a Talleyrand intimate, Montrond, was dispatched, tempted by the offer of an enormous lifetime pension if he was successful. Then others. To no avail. Although Napoleon offered the sun, the moon, and the stars, there is no evidence that during this period Talleyrand wavered in his allegiance to the Bourbon cause. Or whether he was surprised at the speed and completeness of the imperial takeover. However, as a realist and given the size of the forces being arrayed against the former emperor—almost a million men were soon to be in the field—Talleyrand must have known it was not in the cards for Napoleon to retain his regained empire for long.

Before setting forth to take command of the allied forces in the west, Wellington's last night in Vienna was spent in the left wing of the Palm palace with Talleyrand and Metternich. Wilhelmina's youngest foster daughter could not take her eyes off the resplendent red uniform that she had never seen the duke wear before. Creeping up behind him, the girl gently stroked the magnificent gold epaulets of her erstwhile playmate, but this was not the night for their usual romp on the floor. Kissing each lady present good-bye and arranging a rendezvous in Paris with one and all, Wellington was the first to leave.

The grand duchess, who was not one to panic, stayed in Paris until gouty Louis XVIII fled at midnight in his bedroom slippers. Then she streaked like a homing pigeon to Vienna. Talleyrand had been writing her on the average of twice a week so she naturally elected to stay at the Kaunitz rather than at Wilhelmina's on the Schenkenstrasse. If she soon overheard any of the ongoing Viennese gossip intimating that the sexagenarian was now more attentive to Dorothea than the situation warranted or if, by chance, she caught Wilhelmina's idle quip, "At least the great man's kept in the family," she chose to ignore it. Anna-Dorothea was too old a hand at the delicate shadings of love not to soon detect a subtle change in Talleyrand's attitude towards her youngest daughter. Well, "men would be men," as the old adage went, and Talleyrand had long since bettered Don Giovanni's *mille et tre*. Small wonder Dorothea had stirred the old Adam in him. If, indeed, she had. The grand duchess herself hardly recognized the girl. For, in Vienna, with the Kaunitz her fief and surrounded by admirers—and lovers, starting with Prince Trauttmansdorff, Master of the Horse for Emperor Franz—the twenty-two-year-old was unfurling like a blossom in the noon-day sun. At the moment, however, no matter how interested Talleyrand might have become in his niece, she continued to have eyes for only the young Austrian major, Count Karl Clam-Martinitz, who had been her partner, some months earlier, in the fabled carrousel. Since it took two to waltz and Anna-Dorothea's relationship with Talleyrand was the most precious thing in the autumn of her life, she was well able to turn a blind eye to anything she did not wish to see. And, as his fabled seraglio bore witness, Talleyrand managed, throughout a long life, to keep his discarded mistresses' undying affection. Whether, at this point, Talleyrand's personal feelings about her daughter had actually altered is the enigma one would expect of a sphinx.

On the other hand, his public life was an open book. The French statesman was now isolated on an island of mistrust that grew increasingly desolate each time the newfangled, semaphor-telegraph's arm waggled with additional news from Paris—provided the weather was clear enough to see the signal. The government Talleyrand continued to represent existed solely in the person of Louis XVIII who, his divine right notwithstanding, had not felt safe until he shambled across the frontier and settled down in Ghent. Here, at the Hôtel d'Hane-Steenhuys, the home of the Governor of East Flanders, he was waiting to see what might happen and could easily flee back across the Channel once more, should the need arise. Meanwhile, His Majesty went out, each afternoon, in a six-horse carriage, accompanied by his First Gentleman of the Bedchamber and, escorted by his guards, made the rounds of the town, just as in Paris.

Finances soon presented another problem for His Majesty's luxury-loving ambassador because, now, Viennese bankers refused to extend him credit. Ultimately Britain came to his rescue with a subsidy sufficiently adequate for him to remain at the Kaunitz, provided expenses were drastically trimmed. Therefore, Maître Carême and the entire legation staff were shipped home, except for one secretary, two clerks, and his faithful Courtiade, and local domestics filled in the gaps.

Dorothea helped out by writing letters for—and with—*l'oncle*. To better insure secrecy the young woman had originally started copying certain pages for him but, what started as an occasional exercise became routine, because Talleyrand hated writing lengthy letters personally. Now he carried out his entire correspondence to Louis XVIII with his niece, and he relied on these frequent sessions with her to turn the rough draft, prepared for him from his notes, into a finished report. Since His Most Christian Majesty prided himself on being a man of letters, *l'oncle* took pains to prove himself a master of the French language. Warmly wrapped in a purple velvet dressing gown lined in sable, he limped slowly to and fro, dragging his bad right foot across the Aubusson rug and the parquet, across the parquet and the Aubusson, reading, then rereading the amended, amplified version. The only other sound was the clock ticking away in the belly of a small bronze Venus atop the desk's elaborate, mahogany-and-ormolu *cartonnier*. Not until they had "fought the battle of words"—as he expressed it—after each sentence was weighed, rejected, replaced, each phrase and nuance carefully adjusted, was his niece able to lay down her quill, snap the inkwell shut, and rush off to join her major.

The great shadow of the little Corsican haunted everyone and dominated every conversation. While Napoleon's amazing adventure hastened the congress's closing, it had little actual effect on the business at hand, and the delegates were winding down various committees on secondary problems, including slavery and the policing of rivers and streams. These did not concern Talleyrand who had more important questions on his mind: Would Napoleon's second reign soon burst and disappear like a meteor? Would his pacific declarations and efforts to restructure France's constitution into a liberal document convince Europe he was now a man of peace? Would his efforts to divide the allies fail? When a copy was found of the secret tripartite agreement of January, uniting England, France, and Austria, which had inadvertently been left behind when the king fled, Napoleon dispatched the incriminating document posthaste to the tsar. But wisely, for once, tempestuous Alexander chose to ignore it—momentarily.

A show of force was in the offing. As processions of young Viennese boys and girls from the working class marched daily with banners and flags to the city's different churches to pray for victory, the allies' armies were on the way west in a giant crescent from the Alps to the North Sea, preparatory to converging on France. And Dorothea's Count Clam left to rejoin Schwarzenberg's general staff.

In vain, Louis XVIII continued writing Talleyrand to come to Ghent. Finally, His Majesty formally demanded that his ambassador join him immediately. Talleyrand's reply required courage. It is never easy to tell someone outright that his troubles are largely of his own making, especially when addressing one's sovereign, so he adopted the strategy of claiming his personal criticisms were direct quotes of the tsar. Talleyrand also included sound personal advice about remedying the situation in the future. And he did not budge from Vienna. Back came the curt royal response, "Come at once."

Louis XVIII's minister had several personal reasons for not wanting to leave Vienna at that precise moment. The congress had decided to return the principality of Bénévento, a small enclave about fifty kilometers northwest of Naples, to the Papal State, from which Napoleon had stripped it before bestowing the land on Talleyrand. Recently discovered documents also seem to indicate that an annual rent from the Holy See was now under negotiation, payable, of course, to the erstwhile Prince de Bénévent. Another dynastic matter, the Sicilian one, which was an even more complicated affair and was close to His Most Christian Majesty's heart, was also approaching a solution. When the throne was subsequently returned to its rightful owner, Louis XVIII's cousin, Ferdinand IV, Talleyrand wasted no time in dispatching a trusted minion, Perrey, to Naples to collect his *pourboire* for purported services rendered.

Last, but not least—or maybe first and foremost—among Talleyrand's motives for staying on was Dorothea's determination to remain in the Austrian capital until her major returned. This was not *l'oncle's* view. He had brought her there, and he had no intention of returning home without her. Then the headstrong young woman emotionally changed her mind and decided she had a better chance of a rendezvous with her paramour if she went north. Such a trip Talleyrand deemed madness. When he failed to dissuade her from following her lover, like a run-of-the-mill camp follower, *l'oncle*, to salvage what face he could for his niece, spread the story that business matters concerning her vast Silesian estates required her presence. One thing was certain. Dorothea, whom Talleyrand had brought to Vienna to pamper, amuse, and make use of, was leaving the city as his trusted friend, a counselor with an intuitive understanding of the personalities she was in contact with, and on whose judgment he had come to depend increasingly. Early in June she was off after being delayed by a final sitting for her newest portrait. When Anna-Dorothea departed, in turn, for Karlsbad and her annual cure, Wilhelmina heaved a sigh of relief. She was tired of hearing Maman discuss "nothing but that old cripple who is taking it into his head to play the fool at sixty-one!"

At 10:00 p.m., on Friday, June 9, after a great court gala, Talleyrand and the other negotiators initialed the General Act of the Vienna

Congress at its first, last, and only plenary session. This took place on a round table in a room that had been especially modified to provide a separate door for each sovereign present, to circumvent the always troublesome question of precedence.

The next morning he departed at dawn. Of course, Talleyrand made the prerequisite stop to take the waters en route; after a congress, a statesman's first obligation was to his liver. He also wanted to collect some money due him for "services rendered," especially from the King of The Two Sicilies—Ferdinand. Furthermore, never one to hurry, he was not anxious to enter the hornets' nest awaiting him at Ghent, where some three thousand fleeing royalists were now congregated and where, as a result, he feared he might no longer have the king's ear. This could be catastrophic. For with little serious native opposition manifested to Napoleon's dramatic reappearance—although many factors other than Bourbon ineptitude shared responsibility for France's present internal woes—the French people could no longer be considered the outlawed emperor's first victims. While the turncoat army played the lead in his comeback by laying down its arms before him, the military would not have gone over to their former commander-in-chief so completely—and so quickly—had it not been supported by fickle popular opinion. Consequently, the allies once again faced France, the nation, and its ruler of choice.

Napoleon, meanwhile, had been devoting himself to two major problems: reorganizing his government along more liberal lines and preparing for the inevitable war. Merging the bulk of the men still under his command into a single striking force, he soon led a lightning attack into Belgium before the rest of the enemy troops coming from the east had time to arrive. He was anxious to defeat Wellington and Blücher, the most famous and feared of the allied commanders, who had already joined forces there, and he was well aware of the psychological effect of such a victory. Talleyrand was still en route when he learned that the armies were engaged and fighting at Quatre Bras. He reached Aix-la-Chapelle before he heard of the bloody battle at Waterloo, on June 18, which the French, despite their inferior numbers, almost won three times. Here Napoleon expended his last reserves. Only later did Talleyrand learn that Charles was the imperial aide-de-camp who had been sent to order up the massed cavalry which made the last charge of the empire and who, after that long, disastrous fight, supported his exhausted emperor on the sad road home. "He [Napoleon] was so overcome by fatigue and the exertion of the preceding days, that several times he was unable to resist the sleepiness which overcame him and, had I not been there to uphold him, he would have fallen from his horse," [2] he later related.

With Waterloo, the wars that had devastated Europe for so long were finally at an end. When Talleyrand learned that Louis XVIII, impatient to return to his capital, was already following the allied rear-guard there and approaching Mons, he, too, headed that way.

The misunderstanding that arose at Mons between the king and the diplomat had all the elements of a farce. Not unexpectedly, the account in Talleyrand's *Mémoires* differs widely from that of the only other eyewitness present, Chateaubriand, who realized the gravity of the situation and tried to act as a go-between. Louis XVIII was in a foul mood because he was being forced, by a vicious Ultra cabal, largely fueled by jealousy, to finally oust the Duc de Blacas, and His Majesty knew Talleyrand was of the same mind. The latter felt the royal favorite, an ardent proponent of Louis XVIII's "divine rights," presented an impossible stumbling block to any future, mandatory accord between the monarch and the French liberals.

Undisputed details are hard to come by but, when Talleyrand arrived at Mons, around 6:00 p.m., almost two weeks after leaving Vienna—approximately fourteen days for a trip that normally took seven—instead of rushing immediately to his liege lord, as custom dictated, he chose to postpone paying his respects until the morrow. "I am never in a hurry," he haughtily informed the crowd of sycophants who quickly clustered round. When troublemakers hastened to repeat such *lèse majesté* to Louis XVIII, His Majesty, who was impatiently awaiting the malingerer, curtly informed them that, nevertheless, he intended to resume his journey at 3:00 a.m. Talleyrand was asleep in the handsome hotel of M. Fontaine-Spitaels, a wealthy local citizen, when he was awakened, several hours later, with word that the king was about to leave as planned. For a man whose morning ritual always required a minimum of two hours, Talleyrand dressed in record-breaking time and was soon dragging himself, on the arm of a friend, across the tiny town's dimly lit, cobblestone square. The pair arrived just as the lead horses of the monarch's berlin emerged from the porte-cochère of the mayor's home. Upon learning that M. de Talleyrand was outside Louis XVIII, though thoroughly aggravated, consented to go back and accord his dilatory official an audience. Instead of the royal accolades, which he had every reason to expect for services rendered at Vienna, Talleyrand found himself having to justify yesterday's conduct. His Majesty listened coolly to what Talleyrand had to say before calmly dismissing him. "Prince, you are leaving us. The baths will do you good. You will write and give us news of yourself." [3] He nodded in an imperious and unmistakable sign that the interview was over, leaving Talleyrand no alternative but to follow him silently to the courtyard where His Majesty's great traveling coach quickly resumed its journey. Turning to the little group of fawning courtiers who had gathered to say a respectful farewell, a disgruntled Talleyrand spat out: "Go and tell all Europe how I have been treated by the king—I, who set the crown of France upon his head!" [4] Later, at supper, he was in the best of spirits, so full of amusing stories and witty sayings that Count Beugnot, another guest, reported that "one would never have taken him for a minister who had been disgraced a few hours before." [5]

This unfortunate encounter did not bode well for their future relationship, especially at a time when the sovereign and Talleyrand must work closely together, because the end of the military campaign had given rise to countless problems. Wellington, whose Waterloo victory made him the *pro tem* arbiter of the coalition, was worried at this break between the sovereign recognized by the Big Four and the official who had their confidence. As king makers the allies had been responsible for Louis XVIII's first restoration, and they felt that, partly due to royal incapacity, their previous efforts and the subsequent bloody battlefields had all been in vain. Under no circumstances was His Majesty free to dismiss Talleyrand because they considered him the sole person capable of reconciling Europe with France and, thus assuring the continent's tranquility. His Most Christian Majesty was not the master in his own palace. Swallowing with difficulty the royal pride, Louis XVIII recalled the man he had just dismissed. And, forty-eight hours later Talleyrand, encouraged by his uncle, the aged cardinal, who was still in the royal entourage, rejoined the king at Cambrai where the British temporarily established their general headquarters.

Since the Bourbon cause hardly commanded unanimous support within France, who knew how His Majesty would be received there now? Louis XVIII had made too many errors, committed too many mistakes, especially by his cavalier treatment of the French military, for Parisians to throw themselves into his arms enthusiastically. To facilitate the royal homecoming, Talleyrand was entrusted with preparing a declaration that would reassure all those whom the king's previous policies had alienated.

The proclamation was printed up exactly as Talleyrand worded it, including those instances, which he carefully spelled out, where the sovereign had ignored his advice; then, it was scattered broadside to the French people. Louis XVIII was no fool. While His Majesty did not consider Talleyrand indispensable, though the allies did, the king knew he was not afraid to stand up to his royal brother, the Comte d'Artois, and to the latter's troublemaking, reactionary coterie of Ultras. So the monarch also acquiesced, grudgingly, to Wellington's decision that Talleyrand assume the leadership of the new royal council, which the prince on the strength of the Englishman's backing, agreed to set up. Events were moving rapidly, and certain decisions must be made as the royal entourage continued slowly Paris-bound, behind the British troops.

Talleyrand's reaction can only be imagined when he first learned that his former colleague, Fouché, with whom he had enjoyed a love-hate relationship over the years, had been recalled by Napoleon to serve again as minister of general police. In control of the police machinery of France—a post which he held originally during the Directoire and, then, headed throughout the empire—Fouché now, once again, switched allegiance and forced Napoleon to abdicate in favor of his son, the three-year-old l'Aiglon. A Provisional Government of five was set up and, with a handful of faithful adherents, including Flahaut, the defeated man retired to Malmaison, Josephine's former home and the scene of happier days.

The same day that Napoleon left for the Channel ports and ultimate exile, Wellington began negotiating for an armistice. Out of consideration for French self-respect, the appearance was maintained that the nation was free to regulate its own internal political questions, and the capitulation was signed. Talleyrand, who remained at the British General Headquarters, wrote Anna-Dorothea, four days later: "In one hour I shall be leaving . . . for Paris. . . . I will keep an eye on your home. . . . Bonaparte is about to embark. . . . He is winding up as his character deserves."

The fear of the natives rioting and of street fighting was so real that, as the king slowly advanced, emissaries of every political hue appeared, each emphasizing that His Majesty was exposing himself to the gravest danger if he did not make Fouché a member of his new government. Even the Ultras pushed for the acknowledgment of the former Jacobean deputy and regicide, whom they once called "the butcher of Lyon" because of his ruthless revolutionary role in France's second largest city. "Without Fouché, no security!" was the universal clamor.

On the evening of July 5 Talleyrand went to Neuilly to meet with Fouché in the presence of Wellington. They talked until dawn but could not agree on anything other than to meet again. When Talleyrand reported to the king, His Majesty agreed that the responsibility of maintaining order in Bourbon France be given him. Armed with these instructions, Talleyrand returned to Neuilly to dine with Wellington and Fouché and relayed to the latter Louis XVIII's offer of the minister of police in the new ministry being assembled. Fouché accepted. At the Château d'Arnouville, near the great Benedictine Abbey of Saint Denis, Talleyrand escorted him in to be formally presented to the king. Watching from an alcove the ubiquitous Chateaubriand commented, "There goes Vice leaning on the arm of Crime," [6] while, in the distance, could be heard the Prussian military bands, composed entirely of wind instruments, heralding the allied march into Paris.

The next afternoon Talleyrand, who had recommended that His Majesty return surrounded only by Frenchmen, preferred not to participate when Louis XVIII, escorted by the British, re-entered his capital by the traditional route of France's kings. Instead, he arrived inconspicuously and went directly to 2, rue Saint-Florentin. The seals Napoleon had ordered placed on his residence had only been raised once during his absence, at the request of sieur Bouissette, the *valet de chambre* in charge of the hotel's upholstery and rugs, who had been worried about moths as the weather turned warm. Everything was as Talleyrand had left it, except for a heavy coat of dust. Even the great malachite bowls for burning the amber he loved were still in place—and filled with ash.

The following morning, July 9, a royal ordinance announced the makeup of the first ministry of the second Restoration with Talleyrand, as president and foreign affairs minister, a two-fold, backbreaking assignment. The savage political passions that were released were much more violent than those during the first and were further aggravated by Ultra intrigues and by a vicious reaction, known as "the White Terror," which soon shook the Midi. The chaotic scene was compounded by the need to rid the country as fast as possible of the allied occupation forces, which were costing France a million francs a day and, underlying everything, was the necessity to achieve peace conditions that did not affect the country's integrity and honor. Unfortunately, Talleyrand himself was on shaky ground, his great Viennese success swept into oblivion by the tidal wave of the "Hundred Days," as Napoleon's foiled coup d'état had come to be known. The king reappointed him without enthusiasm; the royalists regarded him with suspicion. Feelings waxed strong in the elegant Salon de l'Aigle at the Saint-Florentin, and Talleyrand was forever interceding:

—"But, Messieurs, you want to bring back the *ancien régime*, and that is not possible."

—"Monseigneur," an Ultra riposted, "Who would dream of making you once more the Bishop d'Autun? What foolishness!"

Talleyrand's personal situation was no less complicated than France's. For a man aspiring to continued high office under His Most Christian Majesty, no time must be lost to resolve his marital relationship with the princess as quickly and discreetly as possible. Pretentious Catherine, now plump and blousy, whose pet dormices's cage was a golden duplicate of Valençay's donjon and towers, and whose lady's maid, a down-at-the-heels countess, was required to show proper respect by walking sedately six feet behind her mistress, was still in London, whither she had fled during the "Hundred Days."

As beset as he was with problems, Talleyrand was not one to neglect this god-given opportunity to resolve the anomaly of his marital status as a married bishop in a France once more royalist and predominantly Catholic. There is no way of knowing how long Talleyrand had been contemplating such a step but the timing was right, for exceptional circumstances continued to make him indispensable to Louis XVIII. Simultaneously, the confusion and attendant difficulties of everyday life also supplied Parisians with sufficient problems of their own and with few spare moments in which to try to unravel the private life of "Monsieur the president of the council." Very shortly after Talleyrand assumed office, his personal solicitor, Roux-Laborie, was dispatched across the Channel with this agenda. He returned almost immediately with a letter from Catherine to initiate an eventually successful dialogue concerning a proposed "separation of domiciles due to the pressing demands of urgent government business."

As if this was not sufficient distaff distraction, suddenly Dorothea reappeared because her Major Clam was ordered to join the Austrian General Staff now being stationed in Paris. Since the young woman had no intention of returning to her husband, she once more installed herself—and her two small sons—at the Hôtel Saint-Florentin. Her husband came out a poor second when measured alongside the dashing Austrian officer in the flesh, and Dorothea was determined to cut herself free from her unhappy marriage, although divorce was impossible for Catholics and a legal separation hard for a woman to procure. Not surprisingly Edmond took a dim view of the situation. In Vienna, his wife's liaison was only another of those glamorous Courland sisters' affairs, but it created a furor in Paris because of Talleyrand's prominence. Edmond felt honor bound to challenge Clam and, soon, *tout Paris* was whispering about an early morning duel in the Bois de Boulogne. Clam received only a scratch, while Edmond made the rounds with an awkward bandage accentuating a great slash extending from one nostril to an ear. As might be expected where anything that might cast aspersions on the family name was concerned, no mention of the matter appeared on the Paris police blotter—*l'oncle* would have seen to that. But the scandal was quickly whispered into amused Hapsburg ears, vouchsafed by no less an authority than Baron Hager's impeccable *Oberste und Censu*.

Meanwhile the victorious allied armies continued to swarm into the northern and eastern regions of the country and were behaving badly, especially the Prussians, who were still smarting over their treatment in the past at the former emperor's hand. Wellington himself had to intervene more than once to keep Blücher under control. When that officer threatened to blow up the new Iéna Bridge over the Seine because its name commemorated one of Prussia's bloodiest defeats by the French, Talleyrand seized the opportunity to build some goodwill on behalf of His Majesty. Like a first-class press agent, he spread the rumor that Louis "Dix-Huîtres"—as the irreverent natives now referred to their plump sovereign because of his fondness for oysters[1]—was prepared to sit on the bridge and be blown up with it, if Blücher persisted. Fortunately, a providential name change to the "École Militaire"—France's West Point was nearby—diplomatically saved the day.

As a preliminary to beginning peace negotiations, the allies insisted that the French troops be disbanded and that those responsible for the "Hundred Days" be punished, a nasty job which Fouché tackled. Two lists were drawn up, on the first of which were those guilty of military treason, including Flahaut, until his father succeeded in having his son's name erased.

---
[1] 18 = dix-huit = dix-huîtres = 10 oysters

Talleyrand drew up the roster constituting the new, ninety-two-member, upper legislative assembly before sending it to the king to sign, thereby creating another hereditary peerage almost as casually as if he were making out a guest list for a ball. The Chamber of Deputies had also been dissolved, and Talleyrand made every effort to assure that its successor be monarchist. He succeeded beyond his wildest dreams, which was unfortunate because the new deputies—elected by a restricted franchise which gave the vote largely to the rich bourgeoisie—showed such an ultra-royalist cast that the lower House was soon nicknamed "la Chambre Introuvable"—whose like would never be duplicated. It quickly proved itself on a par with the antagonistic Ultra clique which was once more headquartered in the suite of its ringleader, the Comte d'Artois, in the Tuileries's Pavillon Marsan. For Talleyrand this meant one more cloud on the horizon. With such a political *mise-en-scène* and the final terms of the peace treaty still to be resolved, how could his cabinet, already divided on many issues and in which he and Fouché sat uneasily side by side, hope to function? And for how long? He confided his discouragement to Anna-Dorothea: "Everything is going so badly, so painfully, that one has to believe that things cannot continue as they are . . ." [7]

At the beginning of September, the Duc d'Angoulême, Artois's oldest son, and his wife made a trip of state to the southwest of France in an effort to calm tempers there and, on their return, the cabinet, in accordance with protocol, requested an audience to officially welcome them back. The duchess replied that she could not stand the sight of the man who had sent her father to the scaffold and refused to receive Fouché. This rebuff and similar recent instances involving the police minister gave Talleyrand the opening he had been seeking to finally rid himself of his *bête noire*. Perhaps the disappearance from the scene of such a controversial official might smooth over some of the increasing splits within his cabinet and, likewise, serve as a sop to the contentious Ultras. Since the king was delighted to get rid of the minister whom he had been forced to accept earlier, there was no difficulty persuading His Majesty to appoint him ambassador to the Court of Saxony and, shortly afterwards, Fouché left for gilded exile in Dresden.

Metternich was now openly sympathetic to Prussian interests, and Alexander did not hide his hostility to French ones, not only because Talleyrand had thwarted his plans at Vienna, but also because he was the prime mover behind January's secret tripartite treaty. Even the grand duchess, who hastened back to be of what help she could where Alexander was concerned, rarely saw the obdurate tsar. It did not help that His Imperial Highness had discovered religion—and the Baltic seer, Baroness Julie de Krudener. He rarely left the Elysée, which had been assigned to him but, when he did, it was to see her. The pietist's vague mysticism and mixture of sincere exaltation and charlatism enthralled susceptible Alexander, and she convinced him that he was the "Elect of God," destined to regenerate the world. This new title as Europe's moral leader was a timely one, for Alexander was jealous of Wellington's social success and military laurels.

Although his work as master of the country should have required far more hours than there were in a day, Talleyrand did not change his personal routine and rarely turned his attention to affairs of state until mid-afternoon. He was not now, and never had been, a detail man, and the innumerable, additional ledgers that required his attention as president of the council literally piled up, unattended, on the floor. Not surprisingly, His Majesty was annoyed. Only the Foreign Affairs Ministry was functioning properly because it still had the same competent staff that had served so faithfully over the years. It also helped that Wellington, Metternich, and the Russian foreign minister dined regularly at the Saint-Florentin. In addition, Talleyrand re-established his personal relationships with the sovereigns and other ministers present in the capital and, several times a week, his salons were open to them at 11:00 p.m. for a soirée followed by a dinner for sixty or so. But genuine cordiality was a thing of the past. While the campaign of 1814 had not left any hatred, even on a public level, now scarcely a day passed without violence, somewhere in the capital or in the countryside.

To compound the problems, stupefied associates found the prince a changed man. "Is it age?" some asked. One prominent diplomat hinted at the cause both in letters and a memoir, but only the minister of justice, Pasquier, an old friend who saw Talleyrand almost daily, dared make the obvious comment that the latter's mind was elsewhere. Another shrewd observer, Count Molé, the minister of transportation, and a more reliable witness, arrived independently at the same conclusion. Both were flabbergasted by Talleyrand's strange indifference to public affairs, so foreign to his nature. At a time when his mind should be free of all but his country's travail, he was absorbed by other personal concerns, which by a process of elimination, they could only attribute to late-blooming, unrequited love. His associates might have difficulty interpreting the available evidence but, in such a case where the imponderables of the human heart are concerned, conjectures are just that—conjectures. Whatever the causes, the results seemed obvious. Talleyrand might be suffering the pangs of jealousy while Clam was under foot. But his niece's idyll ended abruptly, when her lover was transferred to Milan to help with arrangements to celebrate his emperor's restoration of power in northern Italy, and now Talleyrand, fearful for her health, watched helpless as she took to her *chaise longue*, indulging in the fashionable melancholia of the day. Restless and miserable, the young woman lay stretched out with her vinaigrette, a little articulated fish filled with rosemary and rue, never far from her nose for days on end.

Marie-Thérèse, the Princess Tyszkiewicz, the grand duchess's long-standing Polish friend who was now, perhaps, the most devoted of Talleyrand's seraglio, kept running across the rue Saint-Florentin from her apartment, at number 7, to smother him with attention, and bore the brunt of his present peevishness. One day, when she asked him for the tenth time, "How are your legs?" Talleyrand, who was thoroughly annoyed, stopped twirling his gold-and-ivory lorgnon, stared pointedly at her glass eye, and snapped, "As you see, Madame."

The prince was in this frame of mind when the peace treaty negotiations, which had been prolonged because of allied demands, were terminated. So harsh and humiliating were its conditions that Talleyrand balked. He was well aware of the precarious situation of his cabinet and menaced, as it was, by both the hostile Chamber of Deputies and the Ultras. He may also have felt that no one else could, or would, replace him and saw little reason to saddle his administration with the stigma of signing a difficult peace treaty that was bound to be unpopular unless he could be sure of his gouty sovereign's unequivocal backing.

The afternoon of September 24, Talleyrand went to the Tuileries, flanked by Baron de Dalberg and another cabinet member, to ask His Majesty to guarantee them his formal support. "Should he not be of such a mind, we ask the king this very day to choose new counselors."

Louis XVIII heard him out. Then, pursing his lips, the heavyset sovereign stared up at the ceiling for a long time in silence before replying, with an air of complete indifference that would have done Talleyrand himself proud: "Eh bien! I suppose I shall have to find another cabinet." [8]

15

Grand Chamberlain 1815

"It is so rare to have someone all to oneself, without a secret, without a separate interest."—TALLEYRAND [1]

IF TALLEYRAND WAS AMAZED, his sangfroid and legendary impassivity stood him in good stead. En route home, he stopped to give his version of this startling turn of events to Princess de Vaudémont so it could be quickly spread abroad by his faithful seraglio before all Paris heard the news. This was of paramount importance. Then, the moment he reached his hotel he instructed the footman to have the carriage wait to deliver a short note which he immediately scribbled to alert the grand duchess, ending "Ingratitude is the protocol of divine rights." How could a family for whose restoration he had twice been largely responsible do this to him? But, he added, he did not expect to be out of circulation very long. That night the Hôtel Saint-Florentin was ablaze as Parisians of every persuasion, not to mention the many foreign dignitaries thronging the capital, stopped off to hear the story from the prince himself. The candles were burning low when Talleyrand finally sent for a footman to escort Dorothea to her own apartment.

Promptly at 11:00 a.m., the next morning, it was time for the prince's sacrosanct levée, that hand-me-down from the feudal era, which was to become one of the curiosities of the day. The prince's heavy embroidered bed curtains were pulled back by Courtiade who, in powdered wig and white silk stockings, helped him sit upright. Then Talleyrand emerged, padded like an infant in swaddling clothes with multiple wool bonnets on his head from a morbid fear of falling out of bed. Wrapped in a pleated, smocked peignoir, he had a waxed toile serviette tucked around his neck, as another lackey held a huge silver bowl under the prince's chin. While his doctor and familiars respectfully watched, Talleyrand inhaled several large glassfuls of slightly salted, warm water, gargled and then ejected the liquid as noisily as an elephant through his trunk. This performance was a recent Indian addition from his Vienna sojourn, copied from Metternich's father-in-law, the late great prime minister, Prince von Kaunitz, because of its reputed medicinal qualities to cleanse the larynx and throat.

One by one favored friends, anxious to hear the shocking latest developments, dropped in, and Talleyrand acknowledged their appearance with a nod. His ablutions finished, he bathed his feet in a pail of foul-smelling Barrèges water, exhibiting, with a cynical indifference that always surprised, the distorted claw that served as his right foot. Simultaneously, two hairdressers, their gray uniforms covered by large aprons, bustled from side to side, like mechanical dolls, dressing his abundant hair with curling irons, then blew a powder, lightly perfumed with amber, over the finished product which must last all day. Next came his shoes, and the right one with its cruel brace was buckled securely under that knee. Simultaneously, Talleyrand signed papers, dictated, and, last but not least, settled various matters of prime importance for the evening's meal with Carême, his famous chef. Nearby at a large table a secretary leafed through journals, cutting out articles, speeches, and opinions that might interest the prince. Finally he stood up to dress—a series of elaborate, choreographed maneuvers, assisted by numerous lackies, that lasted another hour, during which he faced his audience and continued to converse unperturbed and uninterruptedly. The procedure was so elegantly performed, under cover of so many robes, that there was nothing to make any lady—and there were always several present—blush. A good two hours later, he was ready to face his world.

That his ouster from the government was not intended as a disgrace became clear, four days later, when His Majesty sent him a hand-written note informing him of his appointment as grand chamberlain. Although, with the evolution of custom, this charge, one of the six highest offices of the Crown, had evolved into a largely honorary post, it assured him entry to the court at any time, and an opportunity to see—and hear—what was going on, although the general atmosphere there was not helped by internal dissension within the royal family. And it was now accompanied by a huge salary. Since Talleyrand was already a hereditary member of the Chamber of Peers, he could also participate in their sessions in the Luxembourg Palace, although such actions there amounted largely to pinpricks. In a move to placate Alexander, who was the main stumbling block to the current peace negotiations, Louis XVIII appointed as Talleyrand's replacement the Duc de Richelieu, who had given up his post as governor of the large south Russian province of the Crimea, which he had held ever since fleeing the French revolution, in order to return to France with his friend, the tsar. In a note to Anna-Dorothea, who was living, since her return from Vienna, in a mansion on the corner of the Esplanades des Invalides with a full-length portrait of the prince in every room, Talleyrand sarcastically approved: "He is the one Frenchman who knows the most about Odessa." [2] With the tsar's behind-the-scenes assistance, a new Treaty of Paris, signed in late November of this year—1815—brought France back, roughly speaking, to her boundaries of 1789, but not to those of 1792 which France had regained in the earlier Treaty of Paris.

As if Talleyrand did not have enough on his mind, after an exchange of five letters, at year's end, there was an inexplicable break in the on-going, discreet dialogue about the Princess de Talleyrand's future which had been initiated almost at once after he assumed the presidency of the council by Roux-Laborie, his personal secretary. Jean-Baptiste Billecoq represented Catherine's interests. So, the prince called on the Marquis d'Osmond for help. The new French Ambassador to the Court of Saint James, Osmond was obligated to him for this prestigious new appointment, and soon these delicate negotiations resumed.

By then wan, moping Dorothea, with *l'oncle's* grudging acquiescence, had returned to Vienna where she soon announced that she was divorcing her husband to marry Major Clam. Talleyrand, horrified, appealed to her conscience and sense of accountability for her two small sons in Paris and, also, enlisted Gentz's assistance to forestall such a move. The minute that persuasive gentleman returned in Metternich's entourage from the Paris meetings, he started a campaign urging the young woman to reconsider. Her mother, Anna-Dorothea, was also untiring in her efforts to get her daughter back home and implored Wilhelmina to convince her not to ruin her life by any ill-advised decision. Finally, the worldly grand duchess assumed Dorothea must have "the nine-months sickness" and, in desperation, she offered to come to Vienna to help her youngest child over "this difficult period" and to find some way to make her long absence from her family plausible. Speaking, no doubt, from her own experience, the grand duchess then added: "to frequent someone as spiritual as *l'oncle* can easily replace actual sensual pleasures."

Some months later Dorothea, slim and svelte once more, was back in the Hôtel Saint-Florentin for good. *L'oncle*, well aware of the importance of appearances, knew that if a patina of respectability was observed, there would be no public scandal, even though she and Edmond did not have an official separation—either ecclesiastical or civil—a point of some significance in royalist France of the day. Moreover living quarters in the expansive Hôtel Saint-Florentin lent themselves to such an arrangement. *L'oncle's* suite of six rooms on the right-wing mezzanine opened on the rue de Rivoli. On the opposite side of the courtyard, as far away as possible, was the rest of his household, composed of various family groups, with one suite always reserved for Charlotte, who was married now, and for her family whenever any of them happened to be in Paris. Another suite was occupied by Perrey, still another factotum whose wife had formerly been Charlotte's governess. There were even living quarters for Neukomm, the in-house musician and his family. And, now, too, for Dorothea. But Talleyrand could be niggardly in some respects like Frederick the Great of Prussia, his recent contemporary, who used to count the pits of the greenhouse cherries he had just eaten at dinner and also how many he left untouched on his plate to be returned for another meal.

With spring in the air Talleyrand and Dorothea, followed shortly by Anna-Dorothea and the Princess Tyszkiewicz, set out by way of Sèvres and Versailles to Valençay, about 240 kilometers away, where he had not set foot since 1808 when Napoleon billeted there, as his war prisoners, the captive Spanish princes. One of the jewels of the Loire valley, Valençay, was more habitable than Chambord and more imposing than Chenonceaux, and other favorite residences, and its huge parks were some of the most beautiful in all France, but it was far from any stagecoach or post horse route. Almost feudal relations still existed between the lord of the manor and his surroundings, and Talleyrand considered himself a country squire, but he lived here on as elaborate a scale as in Paris, choosing for himself a room on the main floor which gave onto the park and which the *Infante* had occupied. In the guise of decoration that royal young man had nailed onto its walls some fifty self-made wolf traps and added tiers of steps all around on which to raise, in sandstone pots, the Spanish vegetables His Royal Highness preferred. These he had watered daily by means of a so-called water pump with which he also managed to inundate drapes, furniture and the handsome parquet floor.

One of the first places to be restored—Valençay needed a lot of renovation—was the apartment assigned to Anna-Dorothea and which Talleyrand assured her he would oversee himself, even changing the carpets and curtains, and seeing that everything was washed and cleaned. Then she was off east to check on her own vast estates and visit with the rest of her family. As he tucked her in the great traveling coach, he had a basket filled with jars of her favorite pâté, made at Valençay, packed alongside, together with a farewell billet: "I hope, my dearest friend, we may spend our lives in the same place and in the same manner as we have in the past. I can think of nothing comparable to the happiness of passing my life with you." [3] Even allowing for the extravagant euphemisms so typical of the period, it is hard to explain away, as window dressing, all the sentiments Talleyrand expressed in similar notes awaiting her at the first relay stop and at all the subsequent ones along her route.

Unfortunately, the prince could not stay long at Valençay. As grand chamberlain he was obliged to be at Fontainebleau to greet Marie-Caroline of Naples who was coming to wed the king's nephew, the Duc de Berry, and he was to ride out in the royal coach from Paris to greet her. The special treatment that Talleyrand was receiving was exceptional, but he had pushed for this marriage over that of another contender, a sister of Tsar Alexander, so the selection of Marie-Caroline represented a personal triumph. The royal group met the bride-to-be at Héren, the same crossroad where Talleyrand had stood alongside Napoleon, years before, to greet Pius VII and, today, he was just behind the king as the trumpets sounded and the drums beat, and the seventeen-year-old princess stepped down. A grave question at once divided the court: "Was she, or wasn't she, *oui ou non*, squint-eyed?" A sight to behold in his new red velvet costume trimmed with gold and his white culottes, Talleyrand did not miss an event, making every effort to amuse the king, being as charming as only he knew how to be, but he was still old-fashioned enough to find the magnificent ball that first evening spoilt because the newly imported waltz prevailed. At the nuptial ceremonies later, at the Tuileries, his uncle, the royal chaplain, Monseigneur Alexandre-Angélique, presided.

Dorothea, who had not been included, remained at Valençay and, in another bow to convention, the plump Countess Tyszkiewicz, who now had her own room in the west tower there, assumed what would henceforth be her role as chaperon—"soi-disant"—in Talleyrand's entourage. With age, the countess was dressing even more bizarrely, with more and more ornaments in her coiffure, no doubt to draw attention from her false eye, and since she was only eight years younger than the prince himself, there was no cause for jealousy on Dorothea's part. The "Princess," as Talleyrand always called her, had also learned the game of whist, and stayed for hours at his side, silently playing for high stakes.

During *l'oncle's* absence the young woman received a letter from Major Clam definitely ending their relationship. Concurrently, she also learned that Catherine, bored with life in England, had crossed over and installed herself at Pont-de-Sains, a country property near the Belgian border, which Talleyrand had given her by contract. Dorothea was aware that Cathy had never forgiven her assumption of the role of Talleyrand's hostess in Vienna, and now Dorothea wanted no further part of her at the Hôtel Saint-Florentin. If Cathy had become dissatisfied with life in London, it wasn't hard, a furious Dorothea wrote the prince, to imagine that she would soon feel the same way about Pont-de-Sains. Then, one fine day she would hasten on to Paris. "There she would begin by telling you that she would only stay a couple of hours but she wanted to have a talk with you—in the hope of getting more money. The only sensible course for her and for you is to make her stay in England. As money is the true motive underlying all the actions of Madame de T [sic], one must never forget this when dealing with her. I am taking the liberty of giving you some advice which will spare you a painful, distasteful conversation. . . . Arm M. Perrey"—his trusted secretary—"with a letter of credit and tell him to advise Madame de T that she will not be able to touch a cent of the income that you are going to give her until she is once again in England. Have M. Perrey accompany her as far as Calais or Ostende and not come back until he sees her boat embark." [4]

When the king teased Talleyrand about Cathy's proposed plans, the latter icily retorted: "Sire, I, too, must have my March 20." At this pointed reference to His Majesty's ignominious, headlong flight north, up the road to Ghent, the day of Napoleon's triumphant reoccupation of the Tuileries, the monarch paled with anger. Then he blushed with shame but he could not think of a suitable reply, while the courtiers edged away from Talleyrand, who stood in their midst, his face as expressionless as always.

The prince, famed though he was for political prudence, was considered by most Parisians to be the leader of the *mécontents* because he did not bother to hide his categorical opposition to Decazes, the police minister. The climax came at a dinner party in November of 1816 at the British Embassy, the former home of Pauline Bonaparte, on the rue faubourg Saint-Honoré. Talleyrand was presently on a bizarre diet and fasted until evening when he ate little and drank more than was proper. Consequently, by the end of the meal he was often overly and indiscriminately loquacious, and this evening was no exception. After getting up from the table and leading the wife of his host into the salon, he began inveighing against the government, pinpointing Decazes, whom he claimed looked like an Italian hairdresser and called a *maquereau*—a pimp—against whom he bore a grudge for keeping him under police surveillance. The guests were flabbergasted and crowded around not to miss a word. So Talleyrand raised his voice, which always carried well. He next directed a tirade at Pasquier, a former colleague who, in his eyes, had committed a form of treason—to him—by accepting the presidency of the Chambre des Deputés. Realizing that gentleman did not want to listen to such comments, Talleyrand was hastening towards him as fast as possible, dragging his lame foot, when a footman appeared to announce that Pasquier's carriage was now at the door, and that gentleman hastened out.

The party was quickly over as everyone scattered to repeat the scandal of how he had insulted a minister of the king. Imagine! And under the roof of a foreign ambassador! For a man who normally placed propriety above all else, Talleyrand now realized he had acted foolishly and knew that his enemies would quickly take advantage of his lapse in judgment. So he rushed to see Madame de Laval to be sure his faithful seraglio dutifully spread abroad his personal version of the incident. To no avail. There had been too many witnesses, so the Council of Ministers had no choice but to take corrective action. Because a high dignitary could not be allowed to insult the king's ministers with impunity, it was decided to banish the offender from the Tuileries for an indefinite period.

The prince's disgrace gave his salon an even greater animation, and more and more discontented souls swarmed there. As if to offset this blow to his pride, Talleyrand received the tiny Mediterranean island of Dino, supposedly in payment for help in restoring his crown to Ferdinand I of the Two Sicilies. There was nothing much on this dot in the Calabrian Sea except for a lot of sardines. However, the title of duc went to its possessor, which by some discreet finagling Talleyrand was able to pass on to his nephew Edmond, whose wife, snobbish Dorothea, was ecstatic. As the Duchess de Dino, she was henceforth entitled to remain seated in the royal presence while less fortunate females must stand.

Did she also know that *l'oncle's* marriage was now a thing of the past? Talleyrand's dignity and peace of mind demanded an honorable solution to assure Catherine's departure from his life, and he had been determined to avoid giving her any chance to complain of underhanded proceedings or of resorting to financial pressure such as Dorothea had earlier recommended.

Belated evidence documents the efforts of the prince for a conciliatory dialogue. His secretary's first letter was sent while Talleyrand was still the head of the government; five others followed before the end of the year. Then silence. When the Marquis d'Osmond was appointed ambassador to the Court of Saint James in London, largely due to Talleyrand, the prince prevailed upon him to intercede, and an amicable settlement was achieved. Cathy was set up with a "more than honorable" lifestyle, and he would never see her again.

Shortly after the first of the following January an elaborate expiatory service was ordered at Saint Denis to celebrate the anniversary of the death of Louis XVI. Since only the Tuileries had been forbidden him, Talleyrand, outfitted in formal attire as grand chamberlain—only the Austrian emperor and the tsar could ever boast more sumptuous garb—presented himself together with the other grand officers of the crown in the choir of the basilica. Imagine his surprise when M. de Dreux-Brézé, the Grand Mâitre de Ceremonies, invited him, in the king's name, to sit more modestly among the Peers. This he did and remained there throughout the entire ceremony without showing any outward trace of such an affront. He had endured much worse.

Worried that by ostracizing him the opposition would claim him as their leader, Wellington soon intervened and, together with Richelieu, had him recalled to the court where Louis XVIII made it a point to greet him. His Majesty clasped both Talleyrand's hands as if he had just seen him and asked how he was. Then, after a brief conversation, the king made sure the two were observed together in the crowded Tuileries salons. This return to favor was announced in the official *Moniteur* the next day, and their relationship resumed its former guarded civility.

Was it spite over his continued political inactivity that made Talleyrand now stoop, ignobly, to try to sell Napoleon's letters to Austria? This is one of the most contemptible affairs in which the prince ever indulged and Metternich would beat him at his own game. Did Talleyrand actually need money? The asking price was stiff—half-a-million francs— but so, too, were the risks involved and, in a letter about now to Anna-Dorothea he mentions "outrageous expenses" without being more specific. He had lately sold his library and, that July, his famous painting gallery, which passed as one of the best in Europe for its Dutch and Flemish masterpieces—and, especially, for his Wouwerman—would shortly go under the gavel at the hall on the rue de la Grange-Batelière.

Claiming he was afraid that with Russian influence then so prevalent in Paris, Napoleon's correspondence might fall into the tsar's hands, the prince confided some eight hundred and thirty-two of these documents to a Vienna-bound Portuguese courier furnished by a former mistress, Adèle de Flahaut de Souza, whose husband was the recent Portuguese ambassador to France. It was one thing for the prince to have kept his own papers from the Foreign Office, but to possess those of other past administrators was hardly distinguishable from theft and to offer such documents to a foreign power might easily be construed as treason, for included were letters of Champagny, the Duc de Cadore; and of Maret, the Duc de Bassano. Talleyrand was asking a half million francs, a high price but so, too, were the risks involved. If he were apprehended he might be prosecuted and disgraced, and one of the conditions of the proposed sale was that the Austrian emperor must grant him asylum, should the need arise. Metternich got the better of him, returning the documents—but not every one—fifteen months later with the bland assurance that they had been properly examined, although he failed to admit that he had had copies made of them. Taking advantage of Talleyrand's delicate position, the Austrian refused payment on the grounds that the documents were less important than Talleyrand claimed. Of the eight hundred and thirty-two pieces sent, only seventy-three were the "originals," signed by Napoleon, that had been promised, and not all of these were returned.

Meanwhile Talleyrand's nephew had resumed his playboy existence, running through his own inheritance and starting to invade his wife's until *l'oncle*, as head of the family, prudently arranged a legal separation of their finances and also assumed the living expenses of the young couple's two sons. However, the prince could be niggardly in certain unexpected aspects, and there is no way of knowing what he did for Dorothea herself, although he charged Charlotte, who was now married, for even the candles she used as well as for her horses' fodder, whenever she was in residence.

This same late spring of 1817 Talleyrand, Dorothea, and the Princess Tyszkiewicz were back at Valençay but, instead of proceeding on, as usual, to Bourbon-l'Archambault for his thermal baths they went further south to Cauterets, in the Pyrénées, because Dorothea was complaining of bronchitis and of not feeling well. According to persistent reports which would dog her more than once, his niece gave birth here to a child of unknown parentage. Nor was this to be the only time the young Duchess de Dino would succumb to another stallion's call. Talleyrand's reactions can only be surmised.

The trio always traveled in the midst of three separate convoys of coaches and baggage wagons, with maids, groom, footmen, and Dr. Andral; there was also a repair wagon with a blacksmith and a farrier. Generally the two women went ahead to make certain proper accommodations were ready for the arrival of the grand chamberlain to the Most Christian King of France. The presence of Madame Tyszkiewicz, and the separate travel arrangements, were all part of the patina of respectability which Talleyrand was determined to impart to his entourage, for he was now as careful of appearances as he had been lax earlier. The cavalcade never failed to be in residence at Valençay to celebrate each of Talleyrand's two saints' days—those of Saint Charles and Saint Maurice—with suitable pomp, and a table was wheeled in with presents from his faithful seraglio. There was also a *Te Deum*, fireworks—weather permitting—and even a bonfire for the feasting Valençay villagers. Guests arriving at Valençay usually stayed a month because of the long trip down from Paris. Then life became gay with promenades in calèches, hunts, balls, even plays, like

Voltaire used to present at Ferney and in which Dorothea enjoyed acting. When her two sons were in residence, each with his own tutors and entourages, the great château was transformed even further. The arrival of the mail was treated as an event, with each letter read aloud and savored by all. The meal in the late afternoon was the main event of the day and was as fine as at the Saint-Florentin. So far as outdoor pleasures were concerned, the prince's were limited by his crippled right foot. Wherever he went he was shadowed by his great dog, whom he had named Carlos, with typical humor, after the Princess de Talleyrand's lover, the Duc de San Carlos, whose tenure dated from the days of the Spanish princes' imprisonment here. Reading out loud, especially from the great masters of the seventeenth century, was popular and, of course, there was the inevitable whist game lasting far into the night.

During the winter season, in Paris, the Saint-Florentin was one of the few remaining establishments where a visitor could be sure to find a crowd and a good supper after the theater, just as during the empire. Talleyrand chose Monday for his weekly at-home primarily because it was also Decazes's and he hoped to siphon off a goodly portion of the latter's guests. France's leading gourmet did not feel food should be swallowed in one gulp, as a distinguished British visitor, Lady Shelley, discovered: "During the whole repast the general conversation revolved around eating.... Food was to be savored by means of analysis and debate. Each dish was discussed, and the antiquity of the wine supplied the most eloquent annotations.... [The host] himself analyzed the dinner with as much interest and seriousness as if he had been discussing some political question of importance." And if an inflammatory subject came up, the prince escaped to the whist table. Talleyrand had been careful to keep up relations which his long presence at Napoleon's side had enabled him to make with the princes and statesmen of Europe. They assured him of a unique position in France and constituted the basis of his own prestige, permitting him not only to impose himself on his indifferent sovereign but also to conserve his influence. At the rue Saint-Florentin he received all the most important dignitaries passing through Paris. In a day when travel was too difficult to be indulged in by many, the chance to meet these people visiting the capital was a greatly appreciated favor that Talleyrand reserved for his friends.

But the prince never failed to appear when duty called him to the Tuileries. He might resent the cold courtesy with which he was greeted there, but what irritated him even more was the court's stodginess and lack of congenial company, and he caused a sensation when he was seen with increasing frequency at the home of the king's cousin, the Duc d'Orléans, the head of the junior branch of the royal family and with whose father Talleyrand had been on friendly terms. The wealthiest man in France, his home, the Palais Royal, long the magnet for the smartest and gayest Parisians, was slowly being transformed into a meeting place for those displeased with the present government. The Grand Duchess Amélie, the duke's wife, made it a point to always receive Talleyrand and Dorothea together, with no questions asked, whereas the hidebound Tuileries considered Talleyrand's niece a fallen woman. Although she had no more affairs than others of noble rank, Dorothea needed but to be seen with a man before he was labeled her latest lover, and she was invited to the Bourbon court only when not to have been included would have been an intolerable insult. Meanwhile, Mademoiselle Adélaïde, the duke's spinster sister, who was the political mind of the present-day family, had lately renewed long dormant ties with Talleyrand dating back to revolutionary times when the Orléans, like Talleyrand, were refugees in London.

Talleyrand experienced a latent unhappiness at being relegated to the sidelines of public affairs and never failed to appear in Paris when his duties so demanded. After the Duc de Berry, the heir to the throne, was assassinated in front of the Opéra House, it was Talleyrand in his role as grand chamberlain who bent over the royal cradle to authenticate Berry's posthumous son's birth.

Age and increasing ill health were banking the remaining smouldering coals of Anna-Dorothea's love for the prince, and the tedious trip to and from Paris loomed ever more formidable for her. However, she realized the importance of respecting convention and came west for her daughter's next happy event and, incidentally, in time to order her new winter wardrobe from Madame Germont, the oracle of fashion. Meanwhile, from the sidelines, the sharp tongue of one of the prince's earlier loves—Adèle de Flahaut de Souza—had a field day announcing to all and sundry: "Perhaps she [Dorothea] herself does not know who the father is. . . . Her husband . . . sees their minds so inclined to believe in miracles that for all he knows he may be forced to suckle the infant." However, gossip would feel vindicated when, six months to the day after the birth of his reputed daughter, Pauline, Edmond would move out of the Saint-Florentin for good.

While twentieth century descendants of the young woman steadfastly maintain that Edmond was, indeed, the father, this was not the view of most contemporaries who claimed the sixty-six-year-old prince was still notoriously attractive to women. "Minette," as the child was quickly nicknamed, was Talleyrand's favorite of the entire clan. Neither he nor Dorothea would do anything to stop the chatter about her parentage, and he would remember her in his will with far more generosity than the rest of his family.

Decazes was ultimately washed out of office, but it was Villèle, with a cabinet exclusively from the Right, who replaced him, to Talleyrand's outspoken disappointment. By the slamming of the door on constitutional government, this triumph of the Ultras constituted a turning point in the history of the Restoration and was followed by a wave of reactionary sentiment with the liberalism of the bourgeoisie and the reactionary, antagonistic convictions of the upper class in direct conflict. Well might Talleyrand have quoted his late English contemporary, Charles Fox: "Of all revolutions, the worst is a restoration."

Villèle and his followers, confident that the birth of the late Duc de Berry's son, had secured the throne from the danger of a revolution, now wished to place it beyond attack by forcing the government to sponsor a censorship bill drastically curtailing the liberty of the press. Talleyrand, who could still voice his views albeit in a limited fashion in the Chamber of Peers, which sat at the Luxembourg Palace, declared this proposal "was so silly that it can not possibly be French." Nor did he deign to reply when he was viciously attacked for his stand. "I am an old umbrella on whom it has been raining for more than forty years. What difference does one more drop make?" [5]

So outspoken was Talleyrand in his opposition that the king advised him to leave Paris. "Aren't you planning to return to the country?" His Majesty demanded one day.

—"Non, Sire, unless Your Majesty is going to Fontainebleau. Then I shall have the honor to accompany him to carry out the duties of my office," the prince replied in the third person, like a polished courtier.

—"Non, non, that is not what I mean. What I want to know is whether you are not returning home."

—"Non, Sire."

—"Ah! Tell me, how far is Valençay from Paris?"

—"Sire, I don't know exactly." Then, catching the drift of His

Majesty's remark, Talleyrand added: "It must be about the same distance as from Paris to Ghent." [6]

This was a pointed reference to Louis XVIII's earlier, ignominious midnight flight from the Tuileries when Napoleon escaped from captivity and returned triumphantly home.

The following summer Talleyrand was dining in Paris when news was received of Napoleon's death on Saint Helena. His hostess broke the stunned silence: "Oh, good God! What an event!" "Non, Madame," Talleyrand's deep voice responded. "It is no longer an event. It is only a bit of news." That evening he spoke at great length about the late emperor to Lord Holland. "His genius was inconceivable. He was certainly a great man—an extraordinary man by virtue of his talents and by his fortune. He encountered three capital stumbling blocks—Spain, Russia, and the pope. These were responsible for his downfall, which was scarcely less surprising than his elevation." [7]

Now death touched Talleyrand more intimately. Since returning east, the grand duchess had not been well, and he wrote her that mid-June bemoaning that he was not present to shower her with his tenderest affection. "Perhaps I have never before realized how deeply I am attached to you." [8] A short time later, Anna-Dorothea died at Löbikau at sixty. This loss was a painful one for the prince. Looking with Dorothea at a portrait of her mother, he burst into tears, murmuring: "I do not believe there was ever a woman on earth more worthy of being adored." [9]

Valençay now had an interesting new neighbor, Pierre-Paul Royer-Collard. A provincial bourgeois, who held the chair of philosophy at the Faculty of Letters in Paris, he had lately inherited and moved into Châteauvieux, a gloomy ancestral dwelling only four to five leagues distant as the crow flies from Valençay. Nine years the prince's junior, Royer-Collard was also the titular head of the Doctrinaires, a political party which was so small that one wit quipped that all its members could be seated together on a single divan. Composed of a handful of distinguished citizens who offered constitutional opposition to His Majesty's policies, they had little else in common with Talleyrand. But newcomers were rare in that corner of France and prompted, probably, by a desire, as always, for good conversation, Talleyrand made the first advances. Traveling to Royer-Collard's home to meet him, he announced, "Monsieur, you are very hard to approach." For Châteauvieux was perched on an inhospitable, rocky outcropping which gave it a somber

In 1803, Napoleon ordered Talleyrand to purchase Château de Valençay as a place to receive foreign dignitaries. Ferdinand VII of Spain and his brother would spend six pleasurable years in captivity at Valençay and were released in 1813. Gouache, 1.16 x 1.77 ft. Artist: Louis Gabriel the Elder Moreau (1740–1806). Photo: J.G. Berizzi. Location: Louvre, Paris, France. Réunion des Musées Nationaux / Art Resource, NY.

Princess de Courland, Dorothea, Duchess de Dino (1792–1862) was a Baltic German noblewoman and the youngest daughter of one of the wealthiest families in Europe. She was married to Talleyrand's nephew Edmond de Talleyrand. Artist: Catherine-Caroline Thevenin (1813–92). Pastel, 1.9 x 1.63 ft. Photo: Gerard Blot. Location: Châteaux de Versailles et de Trianon, Versailles, France. Réunion des Musées Nationaux / Art Resource, NY.

OPPOSITE PAGE: Edmond de Talleyrand, Duc de Talleyrand-Périgord (1787–1872) was a French general of the Napoleonic Wars. He was the son of Archambaud de Talleyrand-Périgord and Madeleine Olivier de Senozan de Viriville, and the nephew of Charles-Maurice de Talleyrand. He married Princess de Courland, Duchess de Dino. Artist: François Joseph Kinson (1770–1839). Oil on canvas. Photo: Daniel Arnaudet. Location: Châteaux de Versailles et de Trianon, Versailles, France. Photo Credit: Réunion des Musées Nationaux / Art Resource, NY.

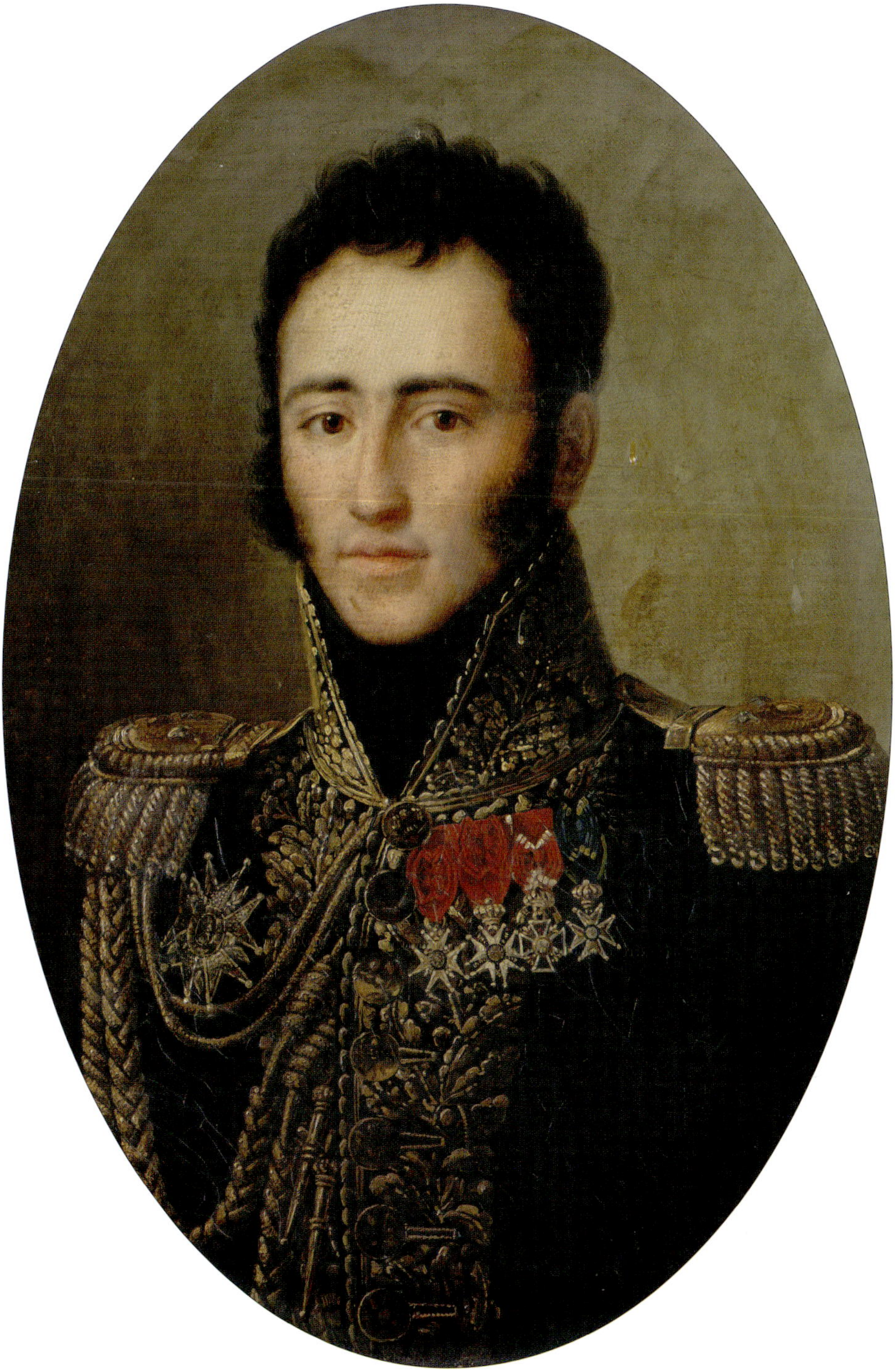

TOP RIGHT: Countess Marie-Thérèse Tyszkiewicz was the niece of Stanislaus-Augustus, the last king of Poland, and a mistress of Talleyrand.

BOTTOM RIGHT: Count Charles-Robert Nesselrode (1780–1862) was a Russian diplomat who became state secretary in 1814 and was the head of Russia's official delegation to the Congress of Vienna. In 1816, he became a Russian foreign minister. Collection: Hulton Archive. Photographer: Illustrated London News. Getty Images.

OPPOSITE PAGE: Clemens-Lothar Wenzel, Chancellor Prince Metternich (1773–1859) was an Austrian politician and had the distinction of being one of the two greatest statesmen in western Europe in the first half of the nineteenth century (Talleyrand being the other). Metternich chaired the Congress of Vienna that was held from November 1814 to June 1815. Artist: Thomas Lawrence (1769–1830). Oil on canvas. Photo: René-Gabriel Ojéda. Location: Châteaux de Versailles et de Trianon, Versailles, France. Photo Credit: Réunion des Musées Nationaux / Art Resource, NY.

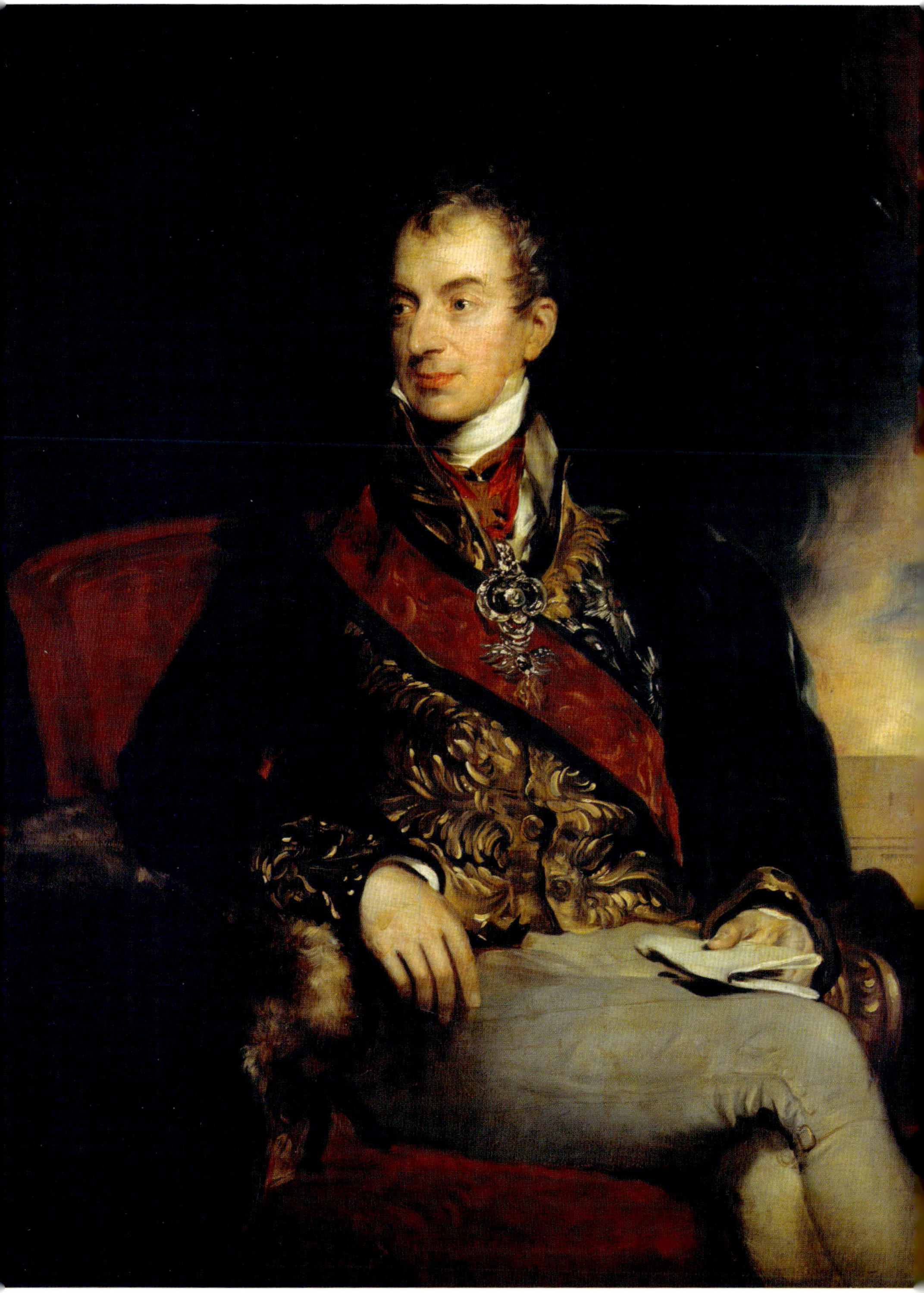

Central Europe in 1763.

Central Europe in 1812.

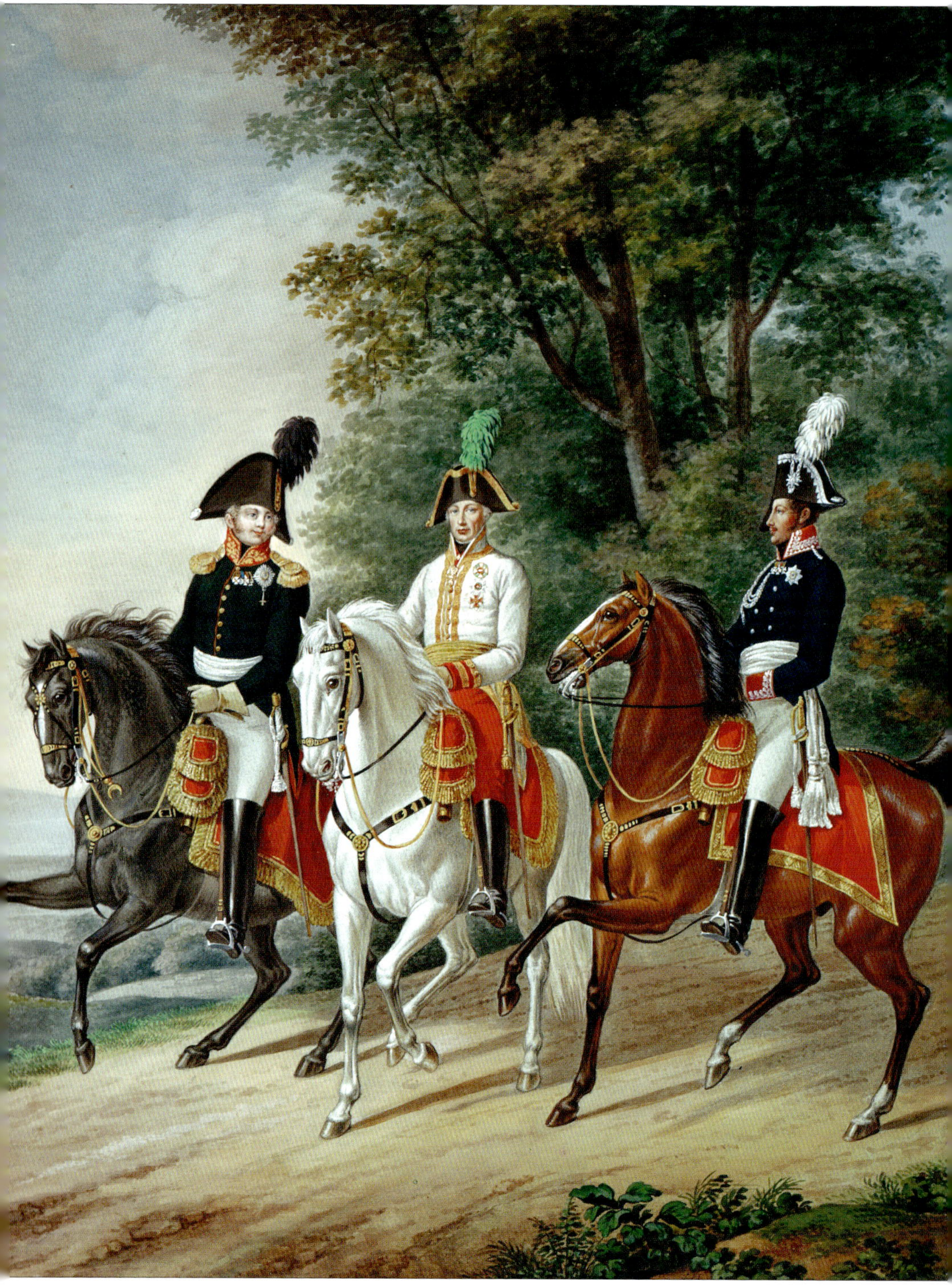

The triumphant Tsar Alexander leads the Allied armies into Paris, March 31, 1814. Above the Arc de Triomphe are the horses of St. Mark's that Napoleon had forcibly removed from the basilica and carried off to Paris in 1797, which Metternich returned to Venice in 1815. On the skyline center appears the figure of Napoleon on the column in the Place Vendôme. Contemporary engraving.

OPPOSITE PAGE: The three monarchs on horseback: Emperor Franz I, Tsar Alexander I, and King Friedrich-Wilhelm III. Artists: J. G. Mansfeld and Johann Adam Klein, 1816. Watercolor and white wash, 22.3 x 18.7 in. Location: Graphische Sammlung Albertina, Vienna, Austria. Photo Credit: Erich Lessing / Art Resource, NY.

Napoleon signed his abdication at Fontainebleau Castle on April 4, 1814. Artist: Gaetano Ferri (1822–96). Oil on canvas, 53.9 x 63.4 in. Photo: Gérard Blot. Location: Châteaux de Versailles et de Trianon, Versailles, France. Photo Credit: Réunion des Musées Nationaux / Art Resource, NY.

OPPOSITE PAGE: Alexander I of Russia (1777–1825) was raised by his grandmother Catherine the Great. He became emperor of Russia after his father's assassination in 1801, became the ruler of Poland in 1815, and ruled until his mysterious death in 1825. Artist: François Gérard (1770–1837). Location: Chateaux de Malmaison et Bois-Preau, Rueil-Malmaison, France. Photo Credit: Erich Lessing / Art Resource, NY.

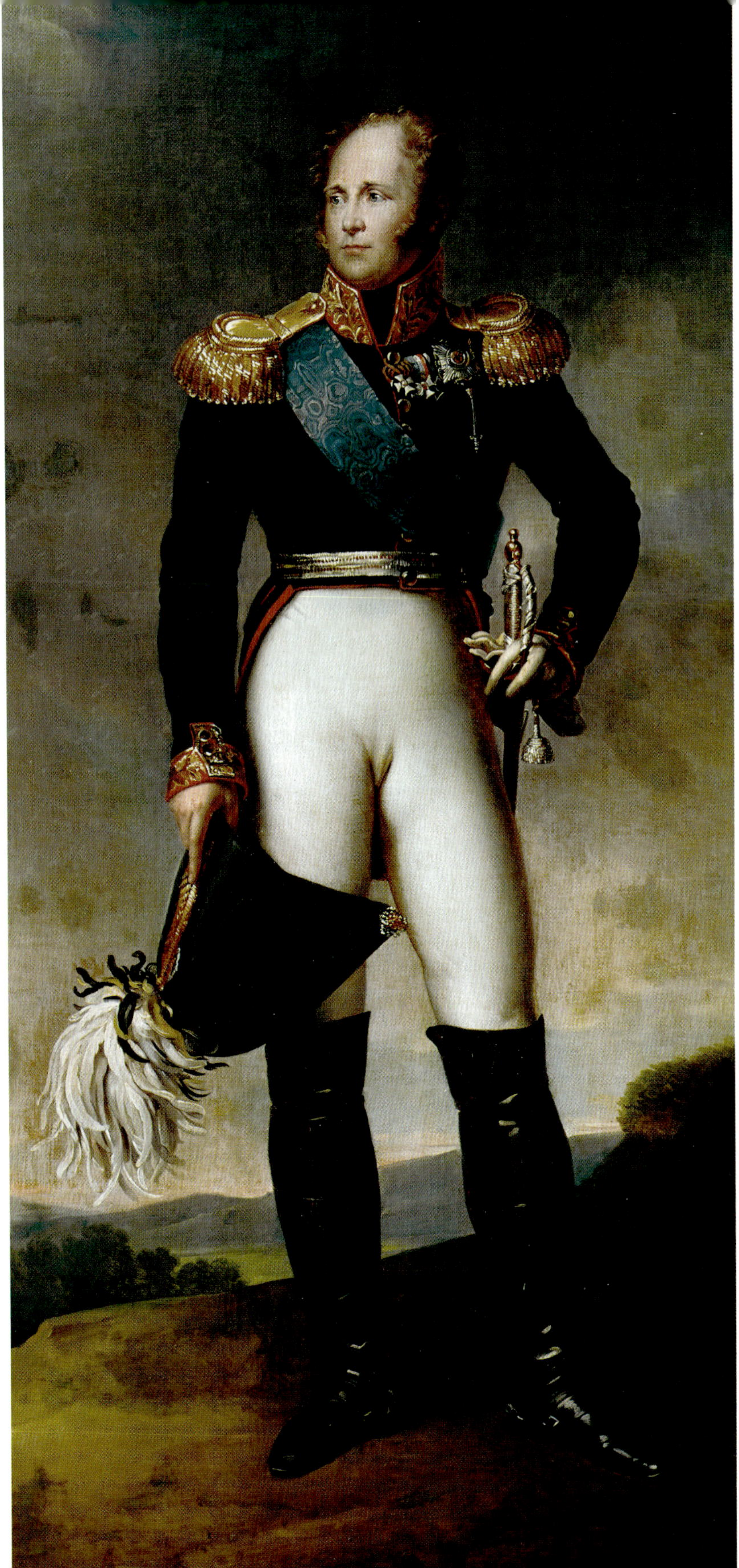

Josephine Pauline de Talleyrand-Périgord (1820–90) was a French noblewoman and the daughter of Dorothea Courland. She was thought to be fathered by Talleyrand and grew up in his *hôtel particulier*. She was nicknamed "Minette" by Talleyrand and was extremely fond of him. She married Henri de Castellane in 1839 and was widowed in 1847. She lived the rest of her life at the Château de Rochecotte, which was given to her by her mother.

OPPOSITE PAGE: Louis XVIII (1755–1824) was king of France from 1814 to 1824, except for the Hundred Days in 1815 when he was exiled. He had been previously exiled from 1791 to 1814 due to the French Revolution. Artist: François Gérard (1770–1837). Oil on canvas. Photo: Gérard Blot. Location: Chateaux de Versailles et de Trianon, Versailles, France. Photo Credit: Réunion des Musées Nationaux / Art Resource, NY.

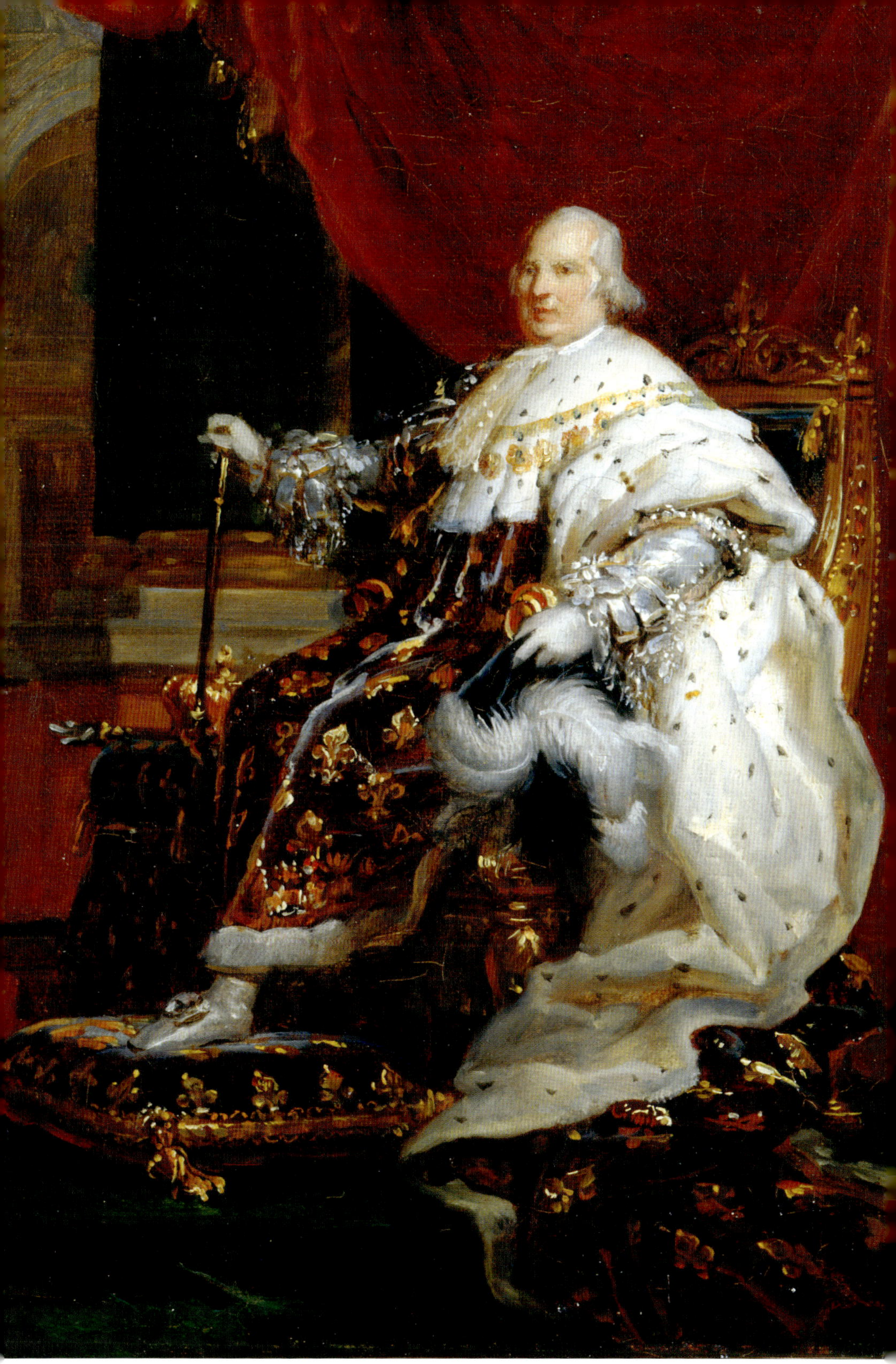

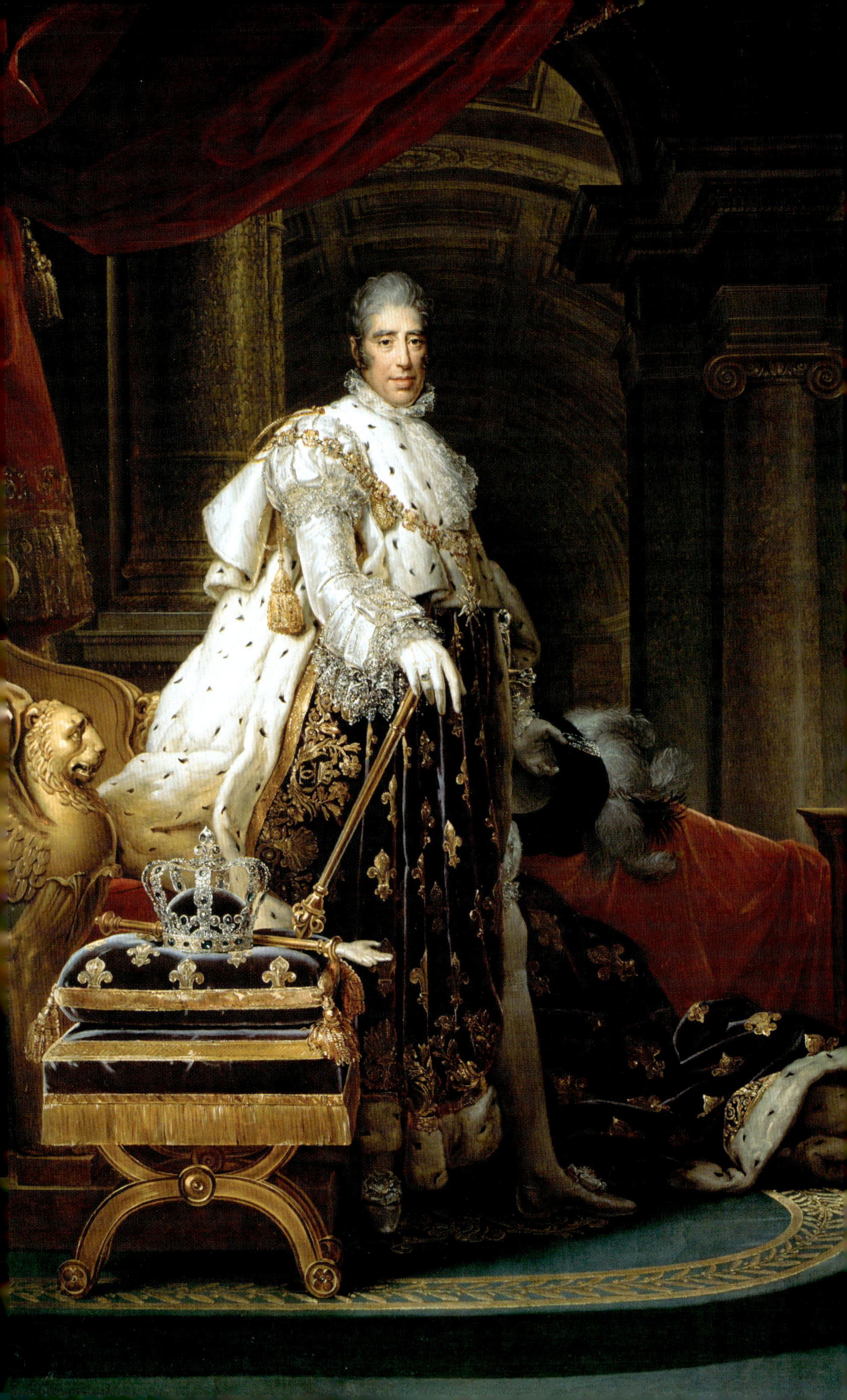

Louis-Philippe I (1773–1850) was king of the French from 1830 to 1848 in what was known as the July Monarchy. He was the fifth cousin of Louis XVI, Louis XVIII, and Charles X. Artist: Franz Xaver Winterhalter (1805–73). Oil on canvas, 1839. Musée national du Château de Versailles.

OPPOSITE PAGE: Charles X, Comte d'Artois, (1757–1836) was king of France from 1824 to 1830. He was the younger brother of Kings Louis XVI and Louis XVIII. His rule ended due to the July Revolution when Louis-Philippe, Duc d'Orléans, was elected king of the French. Charles X was exiled and died in Gorizia, Austria. Artist: François Gérard (1770–1837). Oil on canvas. Location: Musée du Palais du Tau, Reims, France. Photo Credit: Réunion des Musées Nationaux / Art Resource, NY.

Charles-Maurice de Talleyrand-Périgord (1754–1838) is known as one of the most influential diplomats in western European history. Collection: Time & Life Pictures. Getty Images.

feudal aspect in a countryside so full of ravines and wild undergrowth that it took several hours to arrive there from Valençay. The two men did not lack for subject matter as they were both violently opposed to an expedition the Tuileries was currently contemplating not only to help the embattled Bourbon king, formerly Napoleon's prisoner at Valençay, reclaim his Spanish throne, but also to simultaneously distract the unhappy French.

Talleyrand knew little about conditions in Spain and when he was back again in Paris he made a special effort to meet Adolph Thiers. Barely five feet tall, this ambitious, young Marseillais had come to Paris to make a name for himself on the strength of his brilliant, two-volume *History of the Revolution*, which had just been published. Since then Thiers had made a special trip through the northern part of that country to the south to learn more of the situation there firsthand and now returned to write about it for the great left-wing journal *The Constitutional*. Though he was not an art critic, he also subsequently covered the Salon of Art that year, enthusiastically acclaiming *Dante and Virgil in Hell*, the romantic masterpiece of Eugène Delacroix, and qualified the young artist, Talleyrand's reputed bastard, as "a painter of genius." The older man's interest aroused, as Thiers had intended, he arranged to meet Thiers in the salon of the banker Laffitte where the principal adversaries of the government were now to be seen. The prince appreciated intelligence wherever he found it and showed great tolerance for the ideas of this brash, young newcomer who often dared to contradict him in his thick Marseillais accent. Declaring "he's a gamin who has *le feu sacré*," Thiers represented for Talleyrand a future which belonged not to the aristocracy but to the bourgeoisie, and he showered him with advice. Without scruples, lacking some of the more elementary social graces necessary for success in Paris of that day—how to present himself in a salon, how to handle himself at a dinner table—Thiers was never one to waste an opportunity, especially one he had created for himself. Soon he was a "regular" in Talleyrand's great "Salon des Aigles" on the rue Saint-Florentin.

Thiers might represent the future, but now another voice rose up from France's recent past to trouble the prince. For Savary, the Duc de Rovigo, published an article consisting largely of extracts from his personal memoirs, in which, while absolving himself of any blame in the tragic death of the Bourbon Duc d'Enghien, some years before, he accused Talleyrand of having proposed and urged Napoleon to arrest the duke and, then, insisted on his execution. Talleyrand met this storm head on. For Rovigo's disclosures, if not refuted immediately, might well discredit Talleyrand personally and ruin him politically. Therefore he appealed to Louis XVIII for an inquiry and judgment by the Chamber of Peers. The last thing the king wanted at this juncture was a rehashing of a twenty-year-old controversy; there was enough tumult already in the streets. So His Majesty forbade Rovigo to set foot inside the Tuileries and personally wrote Talleyrand: "Let the past remain forgotten." The prince was always welcome at court. "You will not find anyone here who displeases you." [10] And Talleyrand emerged from this contretemps "as white as snow," Dorothea wrote a mutual friend.

Did Talleyrand ever learn that Napoleon personally absolved him of any blame in Enghien's death? The former emperor wrote in the margin of a book found on his bedside table which he had been reading on Saint Helena before he died: "Le Prince de Talleyrand behaved on this occasion as such a faithful minister that the emperor never reproached him about this affair." [11]

The summer of 1824 Louis XVIII lay dying, so Talleyrand cut short his annual stay at Bourbon-l'Archambault to be present at his death. He was not in good health himself, but protocol required that he remain standing in the king's chamber for many hours each day, rendering services which, as Dorothea noted, were "the most painful and disgusting ones possible for a man of the age and infirmities of M. de T. [sic]" Louis XVIII passed away in August and his brother, the Comte d'Artois, succeeded him as Charles X.

The new king, a deeply religious man, may have felt uncomfortable in the presence of a prelate, only three years his senior, who had denied his religion. However, he reconfirmed Talleyrand in his court functions and the prince participated in the royal coronation procession to Reims in a magnificent new berlin covered with his numerous coats-of-arms. On Trinity Sunday, 1825, salvoes of artillery were fired where Jeanne d'Arc had participated some four hundred years before in identical ceremonials and where, a scant fifty years ago, Talleyrand had been in this same cathedral for the sacre of Louis XV. During the following two weeks of Charles X's inaugural festivities, Talleyrand, seated in the royal box in Paris, observed, as an augury of things to come, that the ballerinas' tutus had already been lengthened to below the knees. Nor was any time wasted in passing a number of unpopular measures setting a course to the Right and designed to deprive the peasants and bourgeoisie of advantages they had gained during the Revolution and empire.

Incidents and demonstrations against the new regime were beginning in the streets but, when Talleyrand pointed this out, His Majesty naively replied that the Ultras would save the kingdom. "Sire," retorted Talleyrand, whose tongue was as sharp as ever, "I never believed that the Capitole was saved by a gaggle of squawking geese." [12] He saw no good for the country and especially for himself with the change in sovereigns. A true Bourbon, Charles X was forever going hunting and delighted in the sport. "What do you have to say about the king's hunts?" Talleyrand wrote his friend Royer-Collard. "In one, he shot down 1,793 pieces of game, which no king of France has ever done before. What progress in civilization!"

However, His Majesty did come home to greet the newest addition to the royal menagerie, one of Mohammed Ali Pacha's favorite giraffes, sent by the Viceroy of Egypt in an effort to improve his country's strained relations with France. Little Pauline was at the seashore with her mother to get saltwater baths to ward off some fancied illness—the *à la mode* cure of the moment—and Talleyrand's charming letters, just right for a child of her age, were keeping Minette posted on this exciting newcomer to Paris. After a triumphant, forty-one-day march from the Mediterranean, with countless welcoming receptions en route, she arrived with a miniature Koran draped around her neck to ward off diseases, two antelopes to keep her company, and three Sudanese natives as attendants. The entire royal family turned out to welcome her at Saint-Cloud in a colorful shower of rose petals before she was transferred to a heated apartment in the rotunda of the Jardin des Plantes where Talleyrand promised to take Minette to see her. Meanwhile, the capital was inundated with giraffe-decorated items—snuff boxes, bracelets, pins, and materials.

Now, whenever the prince and Dorothea went South, they spent more and more time at "Rochecotte," a charming property in Touraine, overlooking the Loire, that she had recently acquired and furnished with an elegant luxury—vases à la Medici, Boule armoires, Chinese porcelains. While she had her personal suite in the Saint-Florentin, the young woman had never been in her own home until she acquired this property which, according to rumor, was chosen because it was near the estate of her current paramour, Theobald Piscatory, seven years younger than she and whose child she had reputedly borne. And *l'oncle* would write a friend that the reason he now preferred Rochecotte to any other place was because "here I am not only with Madame de Dino but staying in her home, which is for me an added attraction." [13]

Her apartments at the Saint-Florentin were also at *l'oncle's* disposal to meet with those people with whom he did not want to be seen in public. As the Duchess de Dino, Dorothea was free to invite whomever she pleased to dine—now mainly the leaders of the liberal opposition. Talleyrand would appear later. He himself did not think France was ready for a republic; he certainly was not. Without seeming to have anything to do with public affairs, he was now determined to encourage the idea, already in the air, of giving the throne to the Orléans, the younger branch of the ruling Bourbons. For Charles X was heading towards disaster by looking more and more to the past and tightening the bonds between altar and throne. When the incumbent Villèle produced a law by which nothing could be printed that had not been submitted to the proper authorities five days beforehand, the prince tersely commented: "It is not French because it is silly." [14]

The prince was standing alongside a row of royal carriages outside a ceremony at Saint Denis, early in 1827, waiting for the royal cavalcade to leave, when a tall, disheveled man, dressed all in black, pushed his way through the usual crowd of gawkers. Throwing himself upon the startled, seventy-three-year-old Talleyrand, the stranger slapped him in the face and sent him sprawling to the snow, then gave his prostrate victim several kicks. Shouting, "That old rascal!" he claimed that Talleyrand was the cause of his ruin, and made no effort to escape. The intruder really did slap him, according to an eyewitness from one of the adjacent coaches, and a slap was much more of an insult than a mere blow. The prince's assailant, Count de Guerry-Maubreuil, a member of the petty country nobility, possessed an unsavory reputation and had already caused one scandal by dragging his Légion d'Honneur medal through the streets of Paris attached to his horse's tail. Now he maintained that, earlier, Talleyrand had hired him to assassinate Napoleon and his son, a claim that no one took seriously—considering the source. Rushed home, the prince was bled three times and leeches were applied. Concerned visitors found him, later, bundled up in fur robes, on a settee in the main salon of his hotel, repeating to all and sundry his version of the day's events, each time clenching his fist to demonstrate the blow. For several days, he would send a footman downstairs every hour to consult the visitors' book at the entrance and report back with the names of those who had stopped by to inquire after him. The resulting court trials would last two years, and Guerry-Maubreuil eventually received a watered-down sentence for assault.

By now the prince was seen more frequently with other likeminded friends, especially Royer-Collard, Thiers, and Montrond, at the Palais Royal where increasing numbers of malcontents thronged its spacious salons. The Duc d'Orléans, himself, was playing his cards close to his chest. Both he and his old-maid sister, Madame Adélaïde, listened to Talleyrand as to an oracle but, in order to allay suspicions, the prince did not ostensibly visit them more frequently. Since it was important to have a source of information close to the Palais and the duke had no mistress, Talleyrand tightened his ties with his sister instead, as the gulf dividing him from the Bourbons steadily widened. Unprepossessing but intelligent, Madame Adélaïde, who had known Talleyrand briefly when they were émigrés in London during the Revolution, had all the boldness her brother lacked. Sitting by the fireplace in her personal quarters, the *de rigueur* at-home bonnet perched squarely on top of her coiffure, a large shawl draped over her shoulders, and surrounded by her mélange of dogs, she exulted in intrigue and was never happier than when presiding over the deliberations of some secret committee.

In August, 1829, when Charles X selected another cabinet, his choice of Jules de Polignac as its guiding force moved him one step closer to despotism. The leader of the extreme Ultra faction, whose mother's head had been paraded around Paris on a pole at the height of the Revolution— as befitting an intimate of Marie-Antoinette—Polignac stood in the minds of most of the French for all the vices and errors of the *ancien régime*. Since the duke believed that if he relied on divine guidance he could not fail because the Virgin Mary would tell him what to do, Talleyrand could no longer fool himself. The day of reckoning was near. Rumblings were to be heard everywhere, for Charles X and his new minister made no secret of their desire to restore the *ancien régime* in all its glory—and misery. Talleyrand, on the other hand, felt that what was needed was another king, a liberal one who could appease the republicans and thereby avoid a republic. In the months to follow many newspapers discussed this possibility openly.

Adolph Thiers, now thirty-two; Armand Carrel, twenty-nine, a brilliant writer and politician; and thirty-four-year-old Mignot, the historian, were determined to fight the government but could only do so through the press, which was beginning to show the effects of the king's policy of intimidation. No editors were bold enough to suit their tastes. To resolve this problem, that December, at Talleyrand's request, Dorothea invited these three young men to Rochecotte. There they eagerly talked over various plans, while their hostess, bent over her tapestry, listened. All agreed that the press would play a decisive role in the political crisis that was looming, and it was decided to form a new journal. Money was forthcoming from Jacques Lafitte, the banker, and others, including Talleyrand, anonymously, and a daily, *The National*, was born. As its name indicated, it represented all of France, not any special group. Inaugurating a series of polemics against the Polignac ministry, the first issue under Thiers's aegis appeared on the streets in January 1830, and was quickly snatched up by the liberal bourgeoisie.

As an auger of things to come, that March, when His Majesty mounted the steps of the throne at the opening of the Chambers, he stumbled. His toque fell off and rolled down to the floor where the Duc d'Orléans picked it up—an omen, for those so inclined. But His Majesty still refused to dismiss the unpopular Polignac. Instead, he dissolved the recently elected Chamber of Deputies because of the last election's unsatisfactory results and set new polls for the end of June.

Spring was especially warm this year. Flowering lilacs and chestnuts perfumed the Paris air with a profusion of flowers and bouquets for sale at every corner, while on the boulevards young French blades were heatedly discussing the government's new North African campaign before setting off to participate, the end of May. For Charles X, following an old French tradition, was sending a military expedition to Algiers, supposedly to extract vengeance for an insult to the French consul stationed there but, actually, to present Parisians with something to take their minds off internal affairs. On June 10 a telegraph, that new-fangled marvel of the day, crackled out the news that the French troops had been successful and the way was now open to establish a colony in North Africa. But Talleyrand saw nothing to celebrate, advising a friend that it was too late for such "distractions" and that it would have been far wiser for the administration, "rather than to squander money for conquest, to reduce taxes at home.... Nothing can now prevent disaster." And, on the fourteenth of June, the day before he left for his annual cure, he wrote Baron de Barante: "We are marching towards an unknown world without a pilot and without a compass. Only one thing is certain; all this will end up with a shipwreck." [15]

The dissatisfaction in the nation—a low, barely perceptible rumble—was caught increasingly by Talleyrand's finely attuned ear. When the July 19 elections indicated an outright defeat for Polignac and the Ultras, the alarmed sovereign reacted quickly with a series of four ordinances, which appeared in the official *Moniteur* on Monday, July 26. These suspended the freedom of the press, dissolved the just elected Chamber of Deputies, narrowed the franchise, reduced the number of deputies, and, calling for still another vote, convoked that body for later in the same month. Alerted by a Tuileries connection, Talleyrand hurriedly returned to Paris and ordered his broker to sell his government bonds.

That same Monday afternoon agitated journalists, after seeing texts of the ordinances, streamed excitedly into *The National* offices which Thiers's vigorous, anti-government campaign had designated as a rallying point. Tuesday morning, *The National* carried a direct challenge to the government, dictated by Thiers and signed by forty-five of these men, representing twelve of the country's most influential papers. In retaliation, Charles X, who was at Saint-Cloud, ordered the minister of police to smash the printing presses of those who had defied him. As word of such destruction spread, people began pouring into the streets marching up and down, and shaking clenched fists. Order was restored when darkness fell—the city's first gaslights had only recently begun to be installed—and exhaustion drove everyone home. Meanwhile couriers came and went from different parts of the city to keep the Hôtel Saint-Florentin abreast of the latest developments.

Wednesday, the twenty eighth, the second of the "Three Glorious Days" as they came to be called, dawned bright and hot. Two government arsenals were looted, and the streets were filling with angry Parisians, many of whom were now armed. Barricades were quickly multiplying, with an overturned cart here, felled trees there and, in some places, with furniture tossed down from second story windows. Marshal Marmont, who had just been appointed commandant of Paris, declared the city in a state of siege and stationed his men roundabout. These were already considerably reduced in number because of the drain of the African campaign and the loss of still other troops who were now permanently on the agitated Belgian border. Talleyrand prudently ordered the inscription "l'Hôtel de Talleyrand" on top of his porte-cochère taken down as the boom of the cannon, the sinister toll of the tocsin from Notre Dame, the rumble of the drums calling citizens to arms filled the air.

By 11:00 a.m., Thursday, the twenty-ninth, the heat of the day was already beginning to be felt. Talleyrand, who was dictating his *Mémoires*, hidden behind the long windows of his salon facing the rue de Rivoli and the Place de la Concorde, looked out in time to see Marmont's disorganized troops evacuate the Tuileries and flee up the Champs Élysées. A few minutes later "the Suisses," who had been left behind as a rear guard, did likewise, pursued through the Gardens by a pack of yelling citizens. The British ambassador, who was walking cautiously along the rue de Rivoli, trying to see how the situation was unfolding, caught the prince's eye, and the latter motioned him to come upstairs where a group of prominent liberals were gathering. Apparently no one there noticed two heavily veiled women—courageous, curious, Madame Adélaïde d'Orléans and a friend, each clutching the arm of a uniformed footman—out on the street to judge the scene for themselves. That evening, while Charles X calmly played cards in the "Salon de la Vérité" at Saint-Cloud, there was no longer any question of what was happening in Paris. The insurrection was victorious, and the tricolor was flying from the Hôtel de Ville.

Without losing any more time, Talleyrand sent Comanche, his secretary, to Neuilly with a brief note to Madame Adélaïde. Encouraged by her, Orléans, who had moved still farther out for greater security, hurried back to Paris. There he found that the city, now completely deserted by Marshal Marmont, was engaged in a tug of war between the republicans and the Orléanists, and that the walls of many buildings were already being plastered with giant Orléans posters. Early Saturday morning, the thirty-first, Thiers and a group of deputies arrived at the Palais Royal to ask Orléans to accept the title of lieutenant-general of the kingdom. The duke requested an hour to make up his mind and dispatched General Sebastiani galloping down the rue de Rivoli to ask Talleyrand for advice. Back came the answer: "Let him accept." Meanwhile word reached the city that a worried Charles X and his family were already en route to England—and safety.

"You see," Talleyrand declared at the news. "It is not I who have abandoned the king. It is the king who has abandoned us." [16] A short time later, Orléans proceeded on horseback to the Hôtel de Ville. There he appeared on the balcony, one hand holding the tricolor, the other resting on the shoulder of the octogenarian Marquis de Lafayette, one of the most popular figures in France and the head of the just reconstituted National Guard. To avoid coalescing all Europe against France, it was necessary to push aside the dynasty to save the institution of monarchy, and Orléans was in the best position to accomplish this. Power was now up for grabs. From Talleyrand's point of view the sole immoveable principle of the monarchy was to encourage simultaneously the certainty and the suppleness of an uninterrupted evolution in the spirit of 1789. And the Duc d'Orléans did just that.

16

Ambassador to England

> "*My equilibrium is as difficult to maintain as that of Europe.*"—TALLEYRAND [1]

ON AUGUST 7 THE DUKE was officially summoned to the throne as Louis-Philippe I. One of his first visitors as sovereign was Talleyrand, who arrived at the Palais Royal, that same night, to discuss what now lay ahead for "The Usurper" as His Majesty was already referred to by his disgruntled opponents. From Talleyrand's long-range point of view the July Revolution represented the final victory of the bourgeoisie in France—a fight begun with the storming of the Bastille in 1789. And the Duc d'Orléans conciliated the monarchic principles and those of 1789. However, not everyone was willing to accept the "Barricades King." This was especially true of the conservative regimes of the continent—Russia, Prussia, Austria—who were fearful of another French revolution, despite the fact that the principle of a monarchy was saved. Even the British cabinet received the news with disquieting coldness. However, Talleyrand reasoned that if London were to recognize the Orléans regime, the rest of Europe would surely follow. So it was of overwhelming importance that France be assured of English support, a basic fact that placed the prince at seventy-six once again in the foreground of France's foreign affairs.

The first subject Talleyrand and Louis-Philippe talked over was how to obtain recognition of the principles of this revolution by foreign powers and get, if not their good will, at least their non-interference in internal French affairs. The British cabinet reluctantly granted recognition, and his acceptance of the London Embassy with unlimited powers was in itself a great service as well as a guarantee for the duration of the new regime. For it was well known that the prince never sided with an uncertain or a compromised cause. Talleyrand considered it imperative to reach an understanding with Britain as it was the only chance to avoid the formation of a new coalition. "Revolution" was hardly the password to popularity among the governments of Europe in 1830 but, of all the courts of Europe the outlook for England to lead the way for Louis-Philippe's acceptance was the most promising. If recognition was accorded by England, the newly crowned French monarch could feel confident that other powers would soon follow suit. How could a power which such a *grand seigneur* consented to serve be treated as vulgar and revolutionary?

As the quintessence of a *grand seigneur* of the *ancien régime*, one asset Talleyrand possessed, in addition to vast experience and great prestige, was an aristocratic heritage so authentic that even the most conservative Tories then in power in England must regard him as one of themselves. This was a great advantage, together with the fact that others wanted peace or he could not, perhaps, have succeeded. Throughout his life Talleyrand had always felt that England should remain the pivot of French foreign policy and so expressed himself to Louis-Philippe at their first meeting after he ascended the throne. But for this policy to be successful much depended on the personality of the French representative in London. There was needed a man of great political experience and of consummate diplomatic skill, who combined liberal opinions and aristocratic manners, for an ambassador who was not a gentleman would be at a disadvantage in London whether Tories or Whigs were in office. The prince's age was only a minor objection.

Talleyrand would speak French there, although his English was adequate from his time spent in America as well as in England when a young man. He also had his own way of conducting business which was not in accord with diplomatic usage. He always preferred the services of women as intermediaries, and before leaving he made arrangements not only with the French king's old-maid sister, Mme Adélaïde, who had so much influence over her brother, but also with Talleyrand's close intimate, the Princess de Vaudémont, to correspond with the pair regularly and therefore by-pass the French foreign minister. Thus Talleyrand could be sure that all his correspondence of political importance should reach His Majesty with whom both women were intimate. Talleyrand knew that they would support whatever he suggested and that the king's sister had more influence over him than anyone else.

A few days before leaving Paris, Talleyrand paid his farewell visit to the king who was still living in the Palais Royal while the Tuileries was being adapted for his large family. Talleyrand loved ceremony and appeared like a reliquary, laden down with his decorations. Nonetheless, Paris saluted his departure with caricatures like Daumier's famous vicious one, which portrayed him coiffed with a weathercock and labeled "M. Bien-au-Vent." On the Channel, before embarking he met by chance Ouvrard, the banker, one of his business associates, who informed him that Belgium, the former Austrian Netherlands, which had been given to the Dutch kingdom of the Low Countries when the spoils at the recent Congress of Vienna were allocated, was revolting and hoping for French assistance.

Seven hours of continuous wind made for a poor crossing, but the cannon of Dover's fortress saluted him on his arrival as if he were a sovereign, and Wellington's son was there with his regiment to accompany him to London as an honor guard. The English, like their government, were not hostile to the new regime in France, but they were uneasy. So Talleyrand was determined from the start to do what he could to assure himself—and, therefore, France—of public favor. Accordingly, he made his entry into London in a carriage that was decked out with tricolor streamers and his grooms were adorned with gigantic matching cockades in their hats. The crowds were pleased and applauded wildly for the message was clear to the lowliest Britisher: the Prince de Talleyrand was in London as the representative of a popular and even a revolutionary government. At last Talleyrand was to get a chance for the alliance with England that he had always wanted and that he considered as "the most stable guarantee of the happiness of these two nations and of the peace of the world." [2]

Wellington, who had come in from his country seat to decide how to react to what was happening in Belgium, entertained Talleyrand at dinner that night. What would the man in the street have thought had he seen this ambassador of the people decked out in silks, covered with diamonds and jeweled orders, his hair scrupulously powdered in the style of the *ancien régime*? Nothing less than the *grand seigneur*, Talleyrand was a visual representative of the most ancient, aristocratic traditions of Europe who, to vast experience and great prestige, added a personal heritage so authentic that even conservative Tories must regard him as one of themselves.

Several months before, George IV had died and, in presenting his credentials to his simple-minded brother, William IV, shortly after his arrival, Talleyrand purposely referred to His Majesty as "a descendant of the illustrious house of Brunswick," thereby emphasizing his Germanic forebears. Actually, the current royal family had already ruled in England for over one hundred years but, by so doing, Talleyrand cleverly recalled to the king that he, too, was of a revolutionary origin.

Dorothea had pushed to accept the London post, and she followed him over within a week. She was haughty enough to suit the British, and society accepted the relationship of the legendary Talleyrand and his niece at face value. Devoured with ambition, she had always coveted a high post and was pleased when protocol decided to accord her the rank of ambassadress. Although her reputation was not of the best, Lady Grey, the local arbiter of society, spoke up for her: "I like Mme de Dino a great deal. She is always good-natured and very good company." [3] By her intelligence and charm and her perfect usage of the world, she quickly won the good will of the British aristocracy, so well known for its exclusiveness, and they flocked to 50 Portland Place, the Georgian mansion which had been leased to serve as the French embassy by Chateaubriand, *l'oncle's* predecessor there.

The Belgian revolution placed a serious obstacle in the way of a better understanding with England and was the subject of Talleyrand's first conversations with the British government. For the Belgians, who had been under Dutch domination since the Congress of Vienna, had within a few days driven the Dutch troops out of all their towns with the exception of Antwerp. Talleyrand at once reaffirmed the principle of non-intervention; France was not going to interfere in internal Belgian affairs. In accord with Louis-Philippe, he held out for an international conference to resolve the problem and, together with Wellington's behind-the-scenes assistance, arranged to have the meetings take place in London rather than in Paris. This meant that Talleyrand, not the French foreign minister, would be in the driver's seat.

Before long Dorothea wrote Paris with delight that the newspapers were full, each morning, of the galas and fêtes at their embassy and that the prince was delighted with the publicity. "Our dinners are most successful but they are ruinously expensive and M. de Talleyrand is greatly alarmed at the cost." [4] She added that the English, who were famous for their fondness of eccentrics, were mad about "old Talleyrand," and many a man lifted his wife up in his arms so she could see the prince better when he stepped out of his carriage.

The English, like their government, were not hostile to Louis-Philippe, but they were uneasy, and Talleyrand did all possible to reassure the new French regime's favor in the public eye. Dorothea did likewise. Though dissatisfied with the present embassy building—and its surroundings—she quickly transformed it into the kind of establishment that would simultaneously attract the English and enhance France's prestige, while the inexhaustible wit of the host and her own personal charm soon made their receptions the most brilliant and eagerly attended in London. In no time the pair succeeded in establishing themselves as the leaders of everything that was most fashionable at the moment. Behaving like an actor who had missed his calling, Talleyrand neglected no opportunity to make his presence felt, and English high society soon adjusted to one of his most bizarre habits. Instead of rinsing his mouth at the table at the end of each evening meal, as was done in polite society, his dinner guests arose and remained standing in dead silence alongside their seats while Talleyrand stepped to an adjacent sideboard to perform his customary ablutions of inhaling and gargling salted warm water. His dinner partner, almost always Lady Jersey, one of the proudest and wittiest women in all England, waited patiently alongside to proffer a large white damask napkin with which he wiped his mouth when he had finished. "That is a very good habit, mon prince," she would comment as Talleyrand, after keeping everyone waiting at least five minutes, would then take her by the arm, and lead the way into the adjacent salon. "Oh, a very dirty one, a very dirty one!" was his invariable reply. Talleyrand's every word and action were commented upon and, if possible, imitated. As befitting the star of the season, his portrait by Ary Scheffer soon hung in a window in solitary splendor at Colmaghi's, the well-known art dealer.

For the opening of Parliament, November 2, His Majesty had a special tribune set up for Talleyrand who chose, instead, to remain standing throughout the lengthy ceremony together with the other foreign diplomats. He was loudly applauded later as he drove home through the streets crowded with Londoners who were as anxious as he to avoid a war over the still simmering Belgian upheaval. Talleyrand had successfully convinced Wellington of the need for an international conference to be held in London to resolve this impasse, and it was scheduled to start forty-eight hours later at the Foreign Office. That day the Tory cabinet fell ushering in the Whigs under Lord Grey, and the Foreign Office was given to Palmerston, whom Talleyrand would describe in his *Mémoires* as one of the cleverest men with whom he ever had to deal, and who, within twenty-four hours, was able to announce that both the Netherlands and Belgium formally accepted a proposed armistice.

It was not until General Sebastiani, an old friend and collaborator, took over as French foreign minister that Talleyrand was able to work seriously for a solution of the Belgian quagmire, which was the most critical of the issues presently facing him. Charles de Flahaut, his reputed son, now came over on what Talleyrand termed "a somewhat complicated mission"—ostensibly another plan regarding a new frontier. The prince quickly realized that Charles was there primarily to stake out for himself a claim to the French Embassy post in London, which Talleyrand's great age should surely oblige him to soon resign. Nor was this plan so absurd, for everyone considered Charles to be Talleyrand's son and his large, heavyset wife, Meg, was related to many of the great Whig and Tory families. Who was better qualified to replace Talleyrand than Charles? This seemed reasonable to everyone but Talleyrand and, especially, to Dorothea, whose objections were personal rather than professional. Her sentiments were predictably reciprocated by Meg, five years her senior, who, in her calmer moments, referred to Dorothea as a "lying little devil" and a "horrid little serpent." Lady Granville, an amused spectator, reported that the "pair meet and dine each other but it is like meetings in cock-and-bull fights." [5] Ultimately nothing came of the Flahauts' behind-the-scenes maneuvering, and this unfortunate family situation would soon be remedied by Charles's appointment as ambassador to Berlin, a post he only held briefly before settling down in Paris, where he was ultimately assigned as head equerry to the heir to the British throne.

Talleyrand succeeded in having Belgium declared an independent, neutral state, in perpetuity, thereby assuring the protection of France's northeastern frontier. This document was signed by the five powers present—France, England, Prussia, Russia, and Austria—in early January. And Talleyrand triumphantly wrote the Princess Adélaïde, his almost daily correspondent: "I will dare say to Mlle, who permits me to report to her all my impressions, even that of vanity, that yesterday was one of those days which seems to me must hold a good place in my life." These articles of the London Conference were accepted by the newly appointed Belgian National Conference which then, early that summer, with French and British approval, elected Prince Leopold of Saxe-Coburg-Gotha, as their king. After further trouble with the Dutch which necessitated the intervention of French troops, the King of Holland withdrew from Belgium proper and, in the "Treaty of 24 Articles," signed at London, November 15, 1831, the frontiers of the new Belgian state were definitely established. The Lord Mayor of London celebrated this victory of intelligence and peace—the kind that Talleyrand preferred—at a great dinner where all the guests were English, except Talleyrand, the guest of honor. In the meantime, to better accommodate their needs, the couple moved to larger, more elegant quarters at 21 Hanover Square, at the corner of Brooks Street, a handsome eighteenth century hotel which belonged to the Duke of Devonshire.

Early summer of 1832 Talleyrand had such a lingering cold that Dorothea insisted he demand a holiday and go home. As Talleyrand assured the British sovereign, "I need to catch my breath. I have to think of my legs, of my eyes, and I have to look after my affairs." [6] And he wrote the Princess de Vaudémont that he expected to avoid speaking a "single word that might be of interest to anyone." This was the first time Talleyrand was back in Paris since Louis-Philippe had finished with the remodeling needed in the Tuileries to accommodate his large family. As he proceeded from the royal presence, he noted, however, that he still had to traverse the Gallery of Diana which now served as a dining room, and that the odors of preparations for the next meal perfumed the air. Everyone at court received him with great reverence and when his cane was heard tapping from afar on the magnificent parquet floors, a pregnant silence fell and a whisper rustled along the corridors: "The Prince! The Prince!" His court dress was hopelessly outdated, but the esteem in which Louis-Philippe continued to hold Talleyrand was an acknowledged fact of

French political life. After a cure at Bourbon-l'Archambault and time spent at Valençay and at Rochecotte, the pair returned to London in the fall.

Lingering problems remained with the Dutch king who was stubbornly hanging on to Antwerp. So Talleyrand reached an agreement with Palmerston and, in a joint operation, a British Naval squadron blocked that port while the French army corps besieged the city proper and, by the end of the year, Antwerp finally capitulated. The creation of this new, independent state of Belgium on France's northeast frontier, with its perpetual neutrality guaranteed by the five participating powers, was followed by the dismantling of the thirteen citadels along the French-Belgium frontier which had been erected after the Congress of Vienna and were a menace to the French flanks. So doing partially annulled the consequences of Waterloo and permitted France to resume her place in the concert of great nations. This political masterstroke was the corollary of Talleyrand's personal success; nor did he neglect to invest successfully on the exchange.

However, Talleyrand's energy was expended by the prolonged, late night sessions, and he fell seriously ill. Even though bedridden, he continued to participate in the negotiations "now assembled at my bedside," he advised Paris. Meanwhile, a young career diplomat, Adolphe de Bacourt, was dispatched from Paris to help with the workload. In short order, Bacourt and Dorothea, more than twelve years his senior, showed signs of a strong mutual attachment. This did not escape Talleyrand's attention, nor did it particularly disturb him. But while *l'oncle* had winked at her discreet affairs in the past, this was harder to do now with Bacourt housed under the same embassy roof.

The English politicians lived mainly in the countryside even when their party was in power, and Talleyrand resolved many a delicate matter on one of their vast estates away from London. When the London season with its assemblies and balls began, Talleyrand and Dorothea were automatically included. Such a program soon exhausted Dorothea who would flee to nearby Richmond to rest, and the prince then came out to dine with her there. Likewise, when Talleyrand was too busy to leave the city, Dorothea often went into the country alone to visit. As a couple they spent time with Warwick at Warwick Castle, which was filled with historical documents, including the saddle and harness of Queen Elizabeth I and, when English society followed the court to Brighton for the baths, so did Talleyrand and Dorothea. Here dinner was set nightly for forty and in the evening they all sat together at a great round table while the king snoozed and the queen did needlework.

But the London diplomatic scene was changing. The Esterházys, their Hungarian friends from the Congress of Vienna days, were recalled and suddenly, at the very end of 1832, that long-standing favorite of Talleyrand, the Princess de Vaudémont, passed away. Life lost some of its charm and, for the first time in his life, he became ill tempered and short with his staff. When her furnishings were sold, he left orders to buy "the silver coffee pot which she used when she entertained five or six, as well as two dozen place settings." His spirit of economy made him be precise. He wanted to keep a souvenir of his old friend but not at the risk of raising the price.

Now seemed an auspicious time to underscore the prestige of the new French dynasty, so Louis-Philippe decided to send his son and heir to the Court of Saint James on a state visit. Flahaut was part of the entourage which was to accompany the prince, but Talleyrand was not getting along with Charles and his wife at the moment and had their names crossed off the list. Young Orléans pleased everyone and was very well received, but it helped that Talleyrand knew how to entertain and did not spare any expense. He also made it a point to accompany the royal guest everywhere, although his schedule was a very demanding one for a man of the prince's years.

By the end of September, Talleyrand asked for another leave of absence. He was worried about the continuing ill health of his brother Archambaud and was seriously thinking of retiring, although he realized that at his age a resignation meant the end of an active life. However, when he was back in Paris in December, a series of long talks with the king determined him to return to London because there were still some minor problems to resolve regarding Belgium.

Relations between Talleyrand and Palmerston were now very poor. In the latter's eyes the doyen of European diplomacy was merely "old Talley" whom he did not scruple to leave in his waiting room for an hour or two, and he no longer accepted an invitation to dine at the French embassy. Talleyrand, who could remember the court of Louis XV, must have found it difficult to brook the behavior of this flamboyant Harrovian with his dyed whiskers and striped pantaloons. However, he never allowed his personal irritation to interfere with his political agenda, which was more than Palmerston could do. The latter had a typical, mid-nineteenth century

Englishman's regard for foreigners and was especially distrustful of the French. Whatever the cause of his conduct towards Talleyrand, it kept Dorothea in a state of constant rage, and the prince came to despise him.

The five great powers who had understood one another in 1830 regarding the Belgian question were now, in 1834, divided into two groups. On one side were France and England, who together had been responsible for resolving the conflict between Brussels and the Dutch. On the other were Austria, Prussia, and Russia, who remained faithful to the spirit of the Sainte Alliance and were opposed to anything slightly liberal. The best way to circumvent them was to tighten the bonds between England and France, and this was now accomplished by a Quadruple Alliance between England, France, Spain, and Portugal, which established a new equilibrium and was finally signed in London at the end of April. A few months later Talleyrand initialed a codicil to this treaty. The independence of Belgium, the safeguard of the northern frontier of France, was now officially recognized. The reconciliation of France and England, the dream of his youth, fifty years earlier when he and Mirabeau discussed the future, became a reality, and he was back in Paris on August 22.

Dorothea had preceded him to Valençay because she had some housekeeping matters she wanted to attend to in order to make him more comfortable there, should he now retire, as she hoped. London diplomatic society as they had known it was disintegrating, and the Russian Ambassador, the Prince Lieven, was being recalled. The past few years had provided the princess with the kind of rivalry that she enjoyed and one well-known memorialist of the day described "the female Lieven and the Dino" as furnishing the principle entertainment at more than one large house party in the English countryside.

Talleyrand had not yet finally decided what to do, but Dorothea had. She now set forth her argument in a long letter: "I irritate you sometimes by talking and then I stop before I have said all that I think . . . so let me write to you. . . . Declare yourself old, lest people should find that you have aged . . . say nobly, simply to the world: The hour has struck." [7] Throughout autumn at Rochecotte and, later, at Valençay, Talleyrand and Dorothea meditated what course to take. The prince knew that at his age a resignation must necessarily mean an end to an active life. By now, his limping was so pronounced that at each step his body oscillated from right to left as if he were about to tumble, and he wrote Bacourt: "I must not fall. My equilibrium is as difficult to maintain as that of Europe." [8]

The end of October, as autumn fog mounted the valley of the Nahon towards Valençay, the young Duc d'Orléans, the heir to the throne, was due to arrive on a three-day visit. When Montrond, who was a permanent guest there, for once overplayed his hand, Dorothea, tired of his criticizing everything and everybody, showed him the door, and he missed the royal visit. No one seems to have known the exact reason for the prince's trip or whether he came with some personal message from his father, the king, but he arrived an hour ahead of schedule which greatly upset Dorothea. Since the Grande Mademoiselle's visit in 1653, no member of the royal house had been in Bercy. So all the chatelaines from neighboring Tours and Blois, in addition to the prefect of the department and the other authorities of the region, were invited to a great dinner and ball in his honor.

Orléans had barely left when the Princess Tyszkiewicz, who had had her own room in the west tower for so many years, died. This was a shock for Talleyrand. As Dorothea pointed out: "What makes it all the worst, at Monsieur de Talleyrand's age it is not only an affliction to endure, it is a warning to receive." [9] Following the princess's wishes, Talleyrand arranged for her funeral in the small chapel which bears his name that he had had built on the main street in Valençay, and which now held the gold and lapis lazuli chalice given by Pius VI to her brother, Prince Poniatowski, the Archbishop of Cracow and Prince of Poland. He also made sure that his entire household staff was given fresh black clothing so that they would be suitably attired to attend her services, as was customary for someone of her rank.

Their minds were now finally made up, and Dorothea wrote the first draft of Talleyrand's letter of resignation. Then Talleyrand went over it himself several times, and Royer-Collard added a word and a phrase, here and there, before it was sent off to the Foreign Office in Paris. The prince felt his task had been accomplished and, before the year was out, he also so informed His Majesty. Mme Adélaïde was so upset at the thought of his stepping down that she refused to have the matter discussed within her hearing, and Louis-Philippe offered him the Vienna embassy, not once but twice, as an alternative. Meanwhile, Palmerston was now out of office and Wellington, who replaced him, was very anxious for the prince to return to London. But Talleyrand did not change his mind.

Life in Paris was more formal and demanding than at Valençay, but the prince was not created for solitude. With his sight and hearing unimpaired, he continued to enjoy the pleasures of conversation, and as the revered elder statesman of Europe, his hotel remained the rendezvous of France's parliamentary and diplomatic world. He received them one and all, seated in a huge armchair, his long, white hair powdered in the old style, his bad leg propped up on an ottoman. Visitors commented on his mask of indifference and on his half-closed eyes, which would suddenly open wide to greet a friend.

Talleyrand's situation in the political life of France was now that of a man of great influence; this he used cautiously. He retained the ear of Mme Adélaïde, and he made use of that position mainly to support Thiers. Royer-Collard was almost continuously with him and, when Talleyrand evoked his souvenirs, he would say: "M. de Talleyrand is not making anything up. He is talking about himself." [10] It became an unspoken rule that the conversation at his dinner table should be of a general nature. If a potentially inflammatory subject was broached, the prince would arise and go over to the whist table where his silence spoke louder than any words. Seized again, however, by his fondness of political intrigue, he appeared on the arm of his grand-nephew, Napoléon-Louis, Dorothea's older son, and an escort of the most elegant women in his seraglio surrounded him to affirm his protection publicly when Thiers was received into the Académie Française.

Talleyrand's longer stays at Valençay pleased him, provided he was never there alone. Thiers came with a caravan consisting of his teenage wife, her sister, and her mother, Mme Dosne; but, unlike most of the other guests, he did not stay a month. The Princess Lieven, whose diplomat husband was now back in Russia, arrived accompanied by a niece who was condemned to mount guard over her aunt's jewels whenever the latter went for a walk. But the weather was bad and the princess was soon bored to distraction. Her irrepressible yawns were awe-inspiring and, although she was older than Dorothea, the latter treated her like a spoiled child. No other guests were there at the moment and, since Mme Lieven could not, as was her want, either flirt or hatch intrigues, she manufactured complaints. After having occupied the room on the first floor of the New Tower, which had recently been furnished with the bed of Talleyrand's old friend, Mme de Staël, that Talleyrand had lately purchased, Mme Lieven decided her room smelled of paint—

although it had not been repainted in the last thirteen years—so she moved. The new room's walls were too thick and gave her the "spleen." Once more she moved; then, again. Eventually she ended up back in her original room where the odor of paint had now vanished as mysteriously as it had come.

Talleyrand had a bad fall on the cobblestone courtyard. But he loved careening down the sheltered alleys of the great park with Richard, the valet, pushing him in the wheelchair designed originally to carry around the obese Louis XVIII and which Louis-Philippe had sent down to Valençay. Montrond, frail and suffering from gout, was back in Dorothea's good graces because she knew how fond Talleyrand was of him, and he generally accompanied the prince, propelled in a similar vehicle. One day, when the pair returned, Talleyrand asked Mme Lieven:

—"Do you know, Princesse, why I like Montrond so much?"
—"No. Not really."
—"Eh bien, it is because he is not overly scrupulous."
—At this Montrond chimed in: "Do you know, Princesse, why I am so fond of the Prince de Talleyrand?"
—"I would be curious to know why."
—"Eh bien, Princesse, the reason I am so fond of the Prince de Talleyrand is because he is not at all scrupulous." [11]

To wind up his day, the prince would go out once again, alone, at 9:00 p.m., for a brief drive. There was no sound except that of an occasional screech owl rising from the nearby woods as he returned to play whist until 11:00 p.m., when the Paris post, if any, was due to arrive. This they all shared together.

Talleyrand and his wife Cathy had not seen each other since their separation, years before, and he was in very poor health when Dorothea received word, the end of the following year, that she was dying. This was a reminder that death was also around the prince's own corner, so she broke the news gently. "That simplifies my position," was his sole comment. Feigning indifference, he must have felt only relief. His marriage had been the one scandal he had never been able to live down and, now, he would no longer be a married bishop. The prince saw to it that Cathy had a decent funeral and was buried in a plot he purchased for her in the cemetery at Montparnasse, but he did not appear at either service, pretexting heart problems.

Talleyrand still enjoyed going out for dinner and he did so frequently, now, when Wilhelmina came from Vienna for a visit. If he had renounced active politics for himself he was still pushing Thiers from behind the scenes, especially when the little man formed a new government, but it only lasted for several months. Talleyrand also wrote "A Declaration" or, as he called it, "A Manifesto," which was a follow-up to his Will, which he had made two years before, and was to be read to his heirs after his death. The prince, who all his life never cared what people said about him, was beginning to feel some anxiety as to what might be thought once he was gone. So here, following a brief justification of some of his actions, he stipulated that Dorothea, to whom he left all his papers that he had been reworking for so long, must not publish any of them until thirty years after his death. By then all those in a position to contest their contents should be dead, and it would be Talleyrand who would have the final say.[1]

The prince, Dorothea, and Pauline were invited to Fontainebleau for the Duc d'Orléan's wedding the following June, and, as a special sign of favor, Talleyrand was lodged in what had originally been Mme de Maintenon's suite. Some months later, when word reached him that Dorothea, who was attending to some family matters alone at Rochecotte, had become ill enough to call for the village priest, Talleyrand rushed to her. She had not been as sick as he had been led to believe. Why, then, he queried, had she sent for that rascally fellow?

——"To set an example.... *Que voulez-vous.* It is a good thing to set an example for the villagers every now and then..." Talleyrand interrupted her: "In truth there is nothing less aristocratic than skepticism." But nothing more pertinent was recorded to indicate that he had been thinking along these lines.

---

[1] Because of matters beyond his control, they did not appear until fifty-three years later, not thirty.

17

Death of a Bishop

*"M. de Talleyrand has died like a man
who knows how to live."—1838*
—Mme de Girardin, une dame de la Vieille Cour [1]

TALLEYRAND WAS FOND OF GOING for long drives through Paris with Pauline, just as the pair had done in London, and she spoke with increasing frequency about the Abbé Dupanloup, a protégé of Monseigneur de Quélen, the Archbishop of Paris. Upon the family's return to France Dorothea had enrolled her in a class of religious instruction taught by this popular abbé who was now her "directeur de conscience." Talleyrand's interest was aroused, and he told her he would like to meet this abbé about whom he had been hearing so much. Ambitious and of imposing appearance, Dupanloup was one of the most talked about young priests in the capital. Endowed with a great distinction of manner, he had lately been chosen as the confessor of the young Duc de Bordeaux, "l'enfant du miracle," the supreme hope of the Bourbon dynasty since the murder of his father who had been the heir to the throne. So Talleyrand invited him to dine February 6, the day of the Sainte Dorothéa.

This invitation came as such a flattering surprise that the abbé accepted, but he soon had second thoughts and declined, claiming the demands of his ministry. Talleyrand was vexed and Pauline disappointed, so Dorothea managed to get him reinvited on Sunday, the fifteenth of February, along with some twenty other guests. Talleyrand asked that he sit alongside him at the table, and Dupanloup would later write a full account of this, their first meeting: "He only lacked a cross upon his chest to convince me that I was talking to one of the most venerable bishops in France." [2] Some time later Dupanloup came to call on the prince with a copy of the book he had written on Fénélon. This meeting was followed by two more, equally private but, apparently, no record was kept of any of their conversations.

Talleyrand was now a legendary figure. He had always despised the opinions of his contemporaries, but he was not equally indifferent to the verdict of posterity. Because he was beginning to feel the need for a wide audience for a formal justification of his life, he decided to deliver a funeral oration at the Academy of Moral and Political Science in memory of his friend, Count Charles Reinhard, who had recently died. Dorothea, anxious for his health, tried in vain to dissuade him, and his physician stated flatly that he would not answer for the consequences. "Who asked you to?" was Talleyrand's tart reply.

Strangers were admitted to the séances of this academy, but no women, and it was here, forty years earlier, that he had made his debut in the world of affairs. Saturday, March 3, was cold with an unpleasant rain, but the hall was packed with the elite of business and finance and also with many politicians. Because Talleyrand was now unable to climb the stairs, he was carried up by two servants in livery and, when the gentleman usher announced the prince, the academy's perpetual secretary went out to meet him. Everyone stood up as Talleyrand entered the hall, leaning on M. Mignot's arm and dragging himself along with a cane. His eulogy of his friend, which he read without glasses and in a firm voice from a carefully prepared text, contained his final words to the people of Europe. It was at once clear that Talleyrand was not talking about Reinhard, but about Talleyrand himself and that he was using this occasion to present some of the conclusions he had reached during his long life; he also included a description of the perfect minister of Foreign Affairs. The whole speech lasted a scant half hour and was quickly the talk of the capital. More and more concerned about his personal affairs, two weeks later, Talleyrand added a codicil to his Will, confirming Dorothea as his sole legatee with the proviso that she was to dispose of all his papers which, he stipulated again, could not appear until thirty years after his death. Also, a sum of money was designated to Bacourt to publish Talleyrand's *Mémoires*.

The end of April when his long-suffering brother, Archambaud, died, Dupanloup again called on the prince. For Talleyrand had now said goodbye to the world, and it was time to consider his reception in the next. The prince was above all an aristocrat and, as such, he must not die like the scum of the earth. The blessing of the Church was as essential to the worthy end of a nobleman as armorial bearings on his tomb, an obligation imposed on him as his birthright. Furthermore, Talleyrand was not just a simple sinner for he had been ordained as a priest and consecrated as a bishop and never freed from his vows. Monseigneur de Quélen, when questioned about Talleyrand's situation, informed Dorothea that he must solemnly abjure not only the oath he had taken to the Civil Constitution of the Clergy, but also his consecration of the constitutional bishops, as well as his marriage, and return to the "*ordre commun*," which he had unfortunately left. And she so repeated to *l'oncle*.

Without a word to anyone, in early May, Talleyrand handed Dorothea a sheet of paper covered on both sides with writing—and a number of erasures—which he asked her to give to the archbishop when next she visited him. It was the first draft of his "submission" to Rome—his treaty with heaven. Upon her return home after so doing, she told him that Monseigneur de Quélen deeply appreciated the paper but it must be rewritten in a fitting style, and he would send her the proper ecclesiastical one. Talleyrand replied that he also intended to write a letter of explanation to the pope, but what he wrote must be dated the same week as his talk to the academy: "I do not want people to say that I wrote it in my second childhood." [3]

A few days later on Thursday, May 10, Talleyrand's health, which had been troublesome, sufficiently improved so that he went for a drive through the Parc Monceau. These magnificent English gardens, designed by Carmontelle in 1785 for the future Philippe Égalité, always reminded him of his youth when he had strolled in them as a young abbé. Saturday, he had dinner guests. On Sunday, when he got up in the afternoon he suffered a violent attack of suffocation, which Dr. Cruveilhier diagnosed as caused by a gangrenous carbuncle in the lumbar region, and advised surgery. Professor Marjolin operated the next day. Anesthetics were unknown but, once the professor was finished, Talleyrand was carried back into the salon where he received, as usual, seven or eight guests, including Bacourt. Although he was feverish, Talleyrand insisted that tea be served and delighted in talking of the difficulty that Marjolin had had to make Carlos, his dog, behave and not jump on him while the cupping glasses were placed over his wounds. The lancing did not stop the infection and, Tuesday, Dupanloup was hastily called. "Il est bien mal! Bien mal!" That night Talleyrand was miserable. He could not rest lying down because of the enormous wound he now had on his back. Under the silken canopy of his majestic bed, he was leaning on a large cushion suspended from the ceiling by cords and pulleys, and was propped up by one pillow and supported by a pair of liveried lackeys who were rotated every two hours. The pain was too excruciating to permit him any other position.

On Wednesday the sixteenth, the archbishop rewrote and sent Dupanloup, as promised, Talleyrand's retraction and a letter intended for the pope—originally a single document—which Quélen, following the prince's specific wishes, now made into two. Although Dupanloup offered to read these to him, Talleyrand shook his head. He wanted to go over them with Dorothea. Meanwhile the adjacent parlors were overflowing with curious visitors anxious to be among the first to spread the news of the prince's waning hours. When Dupanloup reappeared at 8:00 p.m., the two sheets had not yet been signed. Talleyrand was making it a matter of pride not to seem forced or influenced. "It will be done," he informed the worried abbé.

—"But when will that be, my dear uncle?" Pauline asked anxiously.

—"Tomorrow, between five and six in the morning," a time when Talleyrand, still the negotiator who did not want to be hurried, knew there would be no strangers about.

That night he suffered from renewed attacks of suffocation, and his family and friends were frantic. Dupanloup reappeared on Thursday, the seventeenth, as dawn was breaking. "Is it six o'clock?" someone asked. It was only 5:00 a.m., but carriages were soon dispatched through the dark, silent streets to fetch the witnesses of impeccable integrity designated by Quélen for the signing of the documents intended for Rome.

These were the Prince de Poix, representing the aristocracy of the *ancien régime*; Saint-Aulaire, ambassador to Vienna; and Barante, ambassador to Saint Petersburg, standing in for the diplomatic service; Molé, president of the council, representing the government; and his friend, Royer-Collard. Upon arrival they were stationed, partially hidden, alongside a door from the bedchamber into the adjacent suites, so they could see but not be seen. When the clock struck 6:00 a.m. at the neighboring church of the Madeleine, an hour when Talleyrand knew his salons would be empty, Duc de Valençay, Dorothea's older son, and M. de Bacourt approached to support Talleyrand upright on the edge of his bed. There were eight in all in the room—Dupanloup, Dorothea, her daughter Pauline, Dr. Cruveilhier, Duc de Valençay, Bacourt, and Hélie, whom Talleyrand had chosen to represent his household staff.

The dying man listened with the greatest attention while Dorothea then read the papers intended for Rome, now divided, as Talleyrand wished, into two distinct documents in which an excuse was expressed rather than a confession. One was an explanation destined for Pope Gregory XVI, which announced that his *Mémoires* would justify his conduct during the revolution; the other was a declaration of regret and entire submission to the Church. Both were couched in language equally vague. There was no admission of specific error nor had the prince ever ceased to regard himself as a son of the Church. Shaking his head to keep his dangling white locks out of his eyes, the dying man asked the date of his speech at the academy.

—"March 3."
—"Well, date this the tenth, so it will be the same week."

Then, without a moment's hesitation, he asked for a pen and scrawled in large letters "Charles-Maurice, Prince de Talleyrand"—as he had done for his great diplomatic treaties. The two documents were at once carried to the waiting Quélen, who dispatched them to Rome by special courier.

Talleyrand dozed off and, at 8:00 a.m., when the king and Mme Adélaïde were unexpectedly announced, there was some trouble awakening him. Once fully aware of what was happening, Talleyrand rallied. As grand chamberlain, he still remembered court etiquette and, raising himself slightly, he presented those who surrounded him to His Majesty. Louis-Philippe was withdrawn and silent and seemed more affected than

Talleyrand. After a few brief moments, as the royal pair were about to leave, the old courtier ended his farewell to His Majesty with a compliment: "Sire, our home has today received an honor worthy of being inscribed in our annals and that my ancestors will recall with pride and gratitude." [4] Mme Adélaïde lingered behind briefly, pressing the prince's hand as he murmured: "Je vous aime bien—I like you." She followed her brother out and everyone else then left the room. But the prince was so exhausted he could not confess until he rested once more.

Wearing the robes of his office, Dupanloup heard Talleyrand's confession—his first since January, 1789—in which an excuse was expressed rather than an avowal. When Dupanloup pronounced, "Ego te absoudre," and it came to the sprinkling of the holy oil, the prince held out his hands closed, palms down, stammering: "Do not forget I am a bishop." These were his last words. Half a century before he had received the Episcopal unction on his palms. Dupanloup began the prayers for the dying as the family knelt around the bed. Brusquely at 3:25 p.m.—May 17, 1838—Talleyrand's head fell down on his chest. He died as he had lived—in public. By sunset all Paris had heard the news: "The prince is dead."

Disregarding *l'oncle's* wishes for a simple funeral, Dorothea felt Talleyrand must have a ceremony worthy of his career and of his family. So his body was embalmed the way the Egyptians did and exposed on a bed of state to receive final homage. In the afternoon of May 22, an elaborate funeral procession transported him to the Church of the Assumption for the burial services. The imposing hearse, decorated with ostrich feathers, silver tears, and numerous family coats of arms, was drawn by horses covered with black saddlecloths down to the ground. These were likewise trimmed with silver and on them could be read the proud family device "Ré que Dieu—No king but God." Next came the various attending delegations: first those of the *Chambre des Paires*, then those from the Institute, the diplomatic corps, the civil and military authorities, *le tout Paris*—worldly, political, and intellectual—followed by six carriages with the personnel from the royal households.

The crypt under the chapel, Saint-Maurice de Valençay, where Talleyrand wanted to be buried was not quite ready. On September 2, a long convoy set forth from Paris containing Talleyrand's casket as well as that of his brother Archambaud and that of still another family member, little three-year-old Yolande de Périgord, who had died two years before.

The somber procession arrived at Valençay two days later, and the next morning the prince was put to rest in the discreet chapel, which formed one of the three main buildings of the Maison de Charité which the prince had founded. Here the Princess Tyszkiewicz had preceded him.

Talleyrand left Dorothea, his sole legatee, the Hôtel Saint-Florentin in Paris, which she sold less than two months later. She eventually married Pauline's daughter into the Prussian royal family and returned to spend the rest of her life in Berlin and in her various inherited family properties in eastern Europe.

Bibliography

UNPUBLISHED

Letters of Adelaide de Flahaut belong to M. de Heurtaumont, Manche, France: Château de Beauvrigny.

PUBLISHED

Abrantès, la duchesse [Laure Junot]. *Histoire des Salons de Paris*. [6 vol.] Paris: Ladvocat, 1836-1838. [Chapter on Talleyrand's salon.]
Mémoires. [Re: Talleyrand's ball for Josephine.]

Albany, la comtesse d'. *Portefeuille de la comtesse d'Albany: 1806–24*. Paris: Pelissier, 1902.

Almeras, Henri d'. *Vie Parisienne sous le Consulat et l'empire*.
Vie Parisienne sous la Revolut et la Directoire.
Vie sous L. Philippe.

Anonymous. *Album Perdu*. Paris: 1829.

Apponyi, comte Rodolphe. *Mémoires*. [4 vol.] 1913–26, Paris: Plon.

Arrigon, Louis Jules. *Une Amie de Talleyrand, la Duchesse de Courlande*. Paris: Flammarion, 1945.

Aujay, Edouard. *Talleyrand*. Paris: J. Tallandrier, 1945.

Aulard. *Paris sous la convention thermidorienne.
Paris sous le Consulat.
Paris sous le Directoire.
Paris sous le 1er Empire*. [3 vol.]

Beau, André. *Talleyrand: Chronique Indiscrète*. Paris: Royer, 1992.

Bernard, Jack. *Talleyrand*. Putnam, 1973.

Bernardy, Françoise de. *Le Dernier Amour de Talleyrand, la Duchesse de Dino*. Paris: Hachette, 1956.

Bertaut, Jules. *Les belles émigrées*. Hachette, 1947.

Beugnot, comte Claude. *Mémoires*. [2 vol.] Paris: Dentu, 1866.

Bibliothèque Nationale. Talleyrand Exposition, Catalogue. 1965.

Billecoq, André. *La Separation Aimable du prince et de la princesse de Talleyrand*. Paris: Clavreuil, 1987.

Bizardel, Yvon. *Les Améicains à Paris pendant la Révolution*. Paris: Calmann-Lèvy, 1972.

Blei, Franz. *Talleyrand, Homme d'État*. Payot, 1935 [Reissued, 1980, Payot].

Bonneau, François. *Talleyrand à Table*. Châteauviex, 1988.

Bordonove, Georges. *Talleyrand: Les Grandes Heures de l'Histoire de France*. Pygmalion, 1999.

Brinton, Crane. *The Lives of Talleyrand*. London: G. Allen and Unwin, printed in USA, 1937; apparently reprinted in London, 1963.

Bruce, Evangeline. *Napoleon and Josephine: The Improbable Marriage*. Scribner, 1995.

Burney, Fanny. Diary and Letters. [7 vol.] London: 1752–1840.

Carrère, Casimir. *Talleyrand Amoureux*. 1975.

Castellot, André. *Talleyrand*. Librarie Académique, Perrin, 1980.

Clary et Aldringen. *Souvenirs de Prince Charles de Clary: Trois mois à Paris lors du marriage de L'Empereur et Marie-Louise*. Paris: 1914.

Colmache, Edward M. *Reminiscences of Prince Talleyrand*. [French edition, 2 vol.] London: 1843.

Cooper, Duff. *Talleyrand*. 1932 [re-issued 1986, Fromm, International Publishing].

Couchod, Paul-Louis et Jean-Paul. *Talleyrand: Mémoires*. Introduction, notes et etblsmt de texte. [2 vol.] Paris: Plon, 1957.

Créquy, marquise de. *Souvenirs*. [5 vol.] Paris: De Fournier Jeane, 1834.

Dard, Emile. *Napoleon et Talleyrand*. Plon, 1935.

DeVoghel, Franz. *Financiers d'Autrefois*. [1989 or 1990.]

Dino, la Duchesse de. *Chronique de 1831 à 1862*. 1909.

Dodd, Anna Bowman. *Talleyrand*. Putnam's. 1927.

Dufresne, Claud. *Morny*. Paris: Perrin, 1983.

Dupuy, Micheline. *La Duchesse de Dino. Princesse de Courland Egerie du Prince de* Talleyrand. Perrin, 2002.

Dwyer, Philip G. *Talleyrand—Profiles in Power*. Great Britain: Longman, 2002.

Fabre-Luce, Alfred. *Talleyrand*. ["Histoire Vérité", 11.] Paris: Dargaud, 1969 [Pseudonym for Jacques Sindral.]

Ferrero, G. *La Reconstruction: Talleyrand et le Congrès de Vienne*. Plon, 1940.

Flahaut, Ch. De la Billarderie. [See also Thouvenel.] *The First Napoleon*: Some unpublished documents from the Bowood Papers. Edited by the Earl of Kerry, covers years, 1809–29. Constable.

Fleury, Serge. *Talleyrand, Maître Souverain de la Diplomatie*. Montreal: 1942. Edit. Variêês.

Garde-Chambonas, comte August-L-Ch de la. *Souvenirs du Congrès de Vienne*. [2 vol.] Paris: Appert, 1843.

Greville, Henry. *Diary*. [3 vol.] Edited by Reeve. Longman's, 1874.

Hastier, Louis. *Vieilles Histoires, Etranges Enigmes: La Fille Adoptive de Talleyrand*. 1954 [or 1955?].

Hobhouse, John Cam [became Lord Broughtom]. *Recollections of a Long Life*. 1865.
The Last Reign of Napoleon from April 8, 1815-July, 1820: Recollections of an Englishman resident in Paris. [Published in London anonymously.] [2 vol.] Ridgeways, 1816.

Hortense, la Reine. *Mémoires*. [3 vol.] Edited by J. Hanoteau. Paris: 1927.

Hubert, Emmanuelle. *Les Cent Jours*. Paris: Juillard, 1966.

Huth, Hans and Pugh, Wilma J. *Talley- in America as a financial Promoter, Unpublished Letters and Memoirs, 1794–96*. WDC, 1942. Publication of copy of Talleyrand manuscript found at Sagan and given to Library of Congress, MS division. Copied verbatim by Dr. Huth. [Published in toto, in a Bulletin of the American Historical Association's Annual Report, vol. 2 for 1941 [also published in an unabridged republ by the Da Capo Press, N.Y. [s.d.]]

Joelson, Annette. *Catherine Grand, Princesse de Talleyrand*. London: A. Redman, 1966.

Jones, Proctor P. *Napoleon, an Intimate Account of the Years of Supremacy — 1800–14*. 1992.

Kerry, sixth marquis of Lansdowne. [See Flahaut.]

Kolb, Ernest. *Talleyrand Intime* [d'après sa correspondence Inédite]. 1891.

Lachoque, Henry and Anne S. K. Brown. *The Anatomy of Glory*. Brown University Press, 1961.

Lacombe. *L'Evêque d'Autun*. 1903.
La Vie Privée de Talleyrand. 1910.

Lacour-Gayet, Georges. *Talleyrand*. [4 vol.] Paris: Payot, 1928–34.

Lacretelle, Pierre. *Secrets et Malheurs de la Reine Hortense*. Paris: 1936.

La Garde-Chambonas. See under "G", depends on correct spelling.

Lansdowne. See Kerry.

Lettres de Sismondi, Bonstetten, Mme de Staël et de Mme de Souza à la comtesse d'Albany. Paris: Saint René-Taillandier, 1863.

Lieven, la princesse de [Dorothée Benkendorff, dite Daria Christoforovna]. *Correspondence of the Princess de Lieven and Lord Grey: 1824–41*. [3 vol.] London: Bentley & Sons, 1890. [Vol. 2, beginning 1830.]
Letters [written during her residence in London, 1812–34]. London: Longmans, 1902.

Loliée, Frédéric. *Talleyrand et la Sociêté Européene*. Paris: Emile Paul.
Talleyrand et la Société Française. Paris: Emile Paul, 1910.

Madelin, L. *Talleyrand*. Paris: Flammarion, 1944.

Maille, la Duchesse de. *Souveniers des 2 Restaurations*. Paris: Perrin, 1985.

Makanawitskuy. See Norman.

Malo, Henri. *Le Beau Montrond*. Paris: 1926.

Manceron, Henri. *Twilight of the Old Order*. Knopf, 1977.

Maricourt, baron André de. *Mme de Souza et sa Famille*. Paris: Emile Paul, 1907.

Marie-Amalie, la Reine. *Journal Inédit*. Perrin, 1980.

Mirabeau, comtesse de. *Le Prince de Talleyrand et la Maison d'Orléans*. Calmann-Lèvy, 1890.

Missoffe, Michel. *Le Coeur Secret de Talleyrand*. Paris, Perrin, 1956.

Morlot, Georges-Albert. *Talleyrand. Une Mystification Historique*. Verier et Kronos, 1991.

Morris, Gouverneur. *A Diary of the French Revolution* [1783–92]. Edited by Beatris Cary Davenport. Houghton: Mifflin, 1939. [2 vol., unexpurgated.]

Nicholson, Sir Harold. *The Congress of Vienna*. New York: Harcourt/Brace & Co., 1946.

Noël, Léon. *Enigmatique Talleyrand*. Fayard, 1975.

Norman, Barbara. *Napoleon and Talleyrand: The Last Two Weeks*. Stein and Day, 1975.

Orieux, Jean. *Talleyrand*. Flammarion, 1970.

Pflaum, Rosalynd. *By Influence and Desire: The True Story of Three Extraordinary Women — the Grand Duchess of Courland and her Daughters*. New York: M. Evans and Co., 1984.
Mme de Staël. Paris: Fischbacher, 1969.

Pichot, Amédée. *Souveniers Intimes sur M. de Talleyrand*. 1870.

Poniatowski, prince Michel. *Talleyrand aux États Unis*. Paris: Presses de la Cité, 1967.
Talleyrand et le Directoire. Perrin, 1982.
Talleyrand et le Consulat. Perrin, 1986.
Talleyrand et l'Ancienne Régime. Perrin, 1988.
Talleyrand: Les Années Occultées, 1789–92. Perrin, 1995.

Potocka, comtesse de. *Mémoires*. Edited by Stryiewski. Paris: Plon, 1897.

Rémusat, Mme Claire de. *Mémoires*. [1780–1821.] [3 vol.] Paris: C. Levy, 1893. [Published by Grandson Paul, Paris, 1957.]

Saint-Aulaire, comte de. *Talleyrand*. Paris: Dunod, 1936.

Sainte-Beuve. *Portraits des Femmes* [Adèle de Flahaut]. Paris, 1882.
"Monsieur de Talleyrand." An essay from his *Nouveaux Lundis*, vol. 12.

Schuma. *Citizens!* Knopf, 1989.

Schumann, Maurice. *Talleyrand, Prophet of the Entente Cordial.* Oxford-Clarendon Press, 1977.

Sellier, Gérard. *Humeurs et humour de M. de Talleyrand.* Paris: J. Grancher, 1992.

Sneyers, Jr. *Belles Demeures d'Autrefois.* Paris: Horay, 1957.

Sorel, Albert. *L'Europe et la Revolution française. Talleyrand au Congrès de Vienne.* "Europe et la Revolution: Essais d'hist et de Critique" 8 (1895):55–84. [382 pgs.]

Souza. See Flahaut, Adèlaide.

Swiggett, Howard. *The Extraordinary Gouverneur Morris.* Doubleday, 1952.

Talleyrand. *Mémoires.* Edited by the duc de Broglie. [5 vol.] Paris: C. Lévy, 1891–92. [Also see Couchod above.] *Miroir de Talleyrand.* Lettres Inedites à la Duchesse de Courlande pendant le Congres de Vienne. Paris: Librairie Academique Perrin, 1926 or 1976?

Vigée-Le Brun, Elizabeth. *Souvenirs.* [3 vol.] Paris: Fournier, 1835.

Vincent, Jacques. *Dames et Seigneurs du Château de Neuilly.* Paris: Tours, Arrault, 1940, 231 pgs.

Vivent, Jacques. "Vie Privée de Talleyrand." 1940 Hachette, Collections *Les Vies Privées.*

Waresquiel, Emmanuel de. *Talleyrand, le Prince Immobile.* Librairie Arthème Fayard, 2003.

Weil, H [Commandant]. *Les Dessous du Congres de Vienne.* Paris: Payot, 1917 (2 vol.).

Wright, Constance. *Daughter to Napoleon.* Holt, Rinehart and Winston, 1961.

Ziegler, Philip. *The Duchess of Dino.* New York: John Day, 1963.

EXHIBITION

Exposition du 6e Arrondissement, Paris: *Talleyrand* – Text par M. Poniatowski. Présenté par la Délégation à L'Action Artistique de la Ville de Paris, 1989.

MAGAZINES

American Historical Association. 1941 annual Bulletin. Unpublished letters and memoirs of Talleyrand while in U.S., 1794–96.

Amis de l'Histoire. Michael, Bernard. "Les Grands Enigmes du Temps Jadis," 1968; "Talleyrand et le Congres de Vienne," 1969.

Aux Carrefours de l'Histoire. Bonmariage, Sylvain. "La Princesse de Bénévent." January 1959, #17.

Bulletin de la Soc des Antiquaires de la Morinie. Coolen. "Mme Grand et Talleyrand." Mars, 1950, t. 17: 320–30.

Le Correspondant, 1893. Corresp de Talleyrand et de Bacourt. "Les 100 Days et le ministère Talleyrand-Fouché." 1905, #184.

Feuilles d'Histoire. Guyot, R. "Mme Grand à Paris." Mai, 1909.

Gazette des Beaux Arts. "Charlotte de Talleyrand." Juillet, 1922: 38–44.

Heraldique et Généalogique. Gaudart, Michel. "La Duchesse de Talleyrand-Périgord, Princess de Bénévent." Juin-Aout, 1969.

HISTORIA:

Herriot, Edouard. "Talleyrand ou le Diable Boiteux." #59.

Rieset, le vicomte de. "Le Roman de la princesse de Talleyrand." #78.

Reynaud, Paul. "Talleyrand à la Conquete du pouvoir." #86.

Gaxotte, Pierre. "La France de la Restoration." #104. Madelin. "Il y a 150 ans, Talleyrand trahit son maître." #143.

Miroir de l'Histoire:

Nabonne, Bernard de. "M. de Talleyrand et sa fiancée." #1.

Pronunciation du nom de Talleyrand." #19.

De La Gorce, Pierre. "Le mysterieux voyage de la Duchesse de Dino à Luchon." #117.

Revue Bleue. "A Propos du Mariage de Talleyrand." 1926.

Revue de France. Dard, E. "Les salons de M. de Talleyrand." 15 Nov., 1935.

Revue de Paris. Kosimian, Andre. "Le carnet d'un Mondain sous la Restauration." Janv.-Fev., 1900.

Welschinger, Henri. "L'Ami de M. de Talleyrand." [Malo] Feb. 1, 1895.

Revue des Deux Mondes. "Les Deux Mariages de Talleyrand." 15 Oct. ler Nov., 1935.

Noël. "Enigmatique Talleyrand." Oct. 1975.

Revue des Etudes Napoléoniennes. Ledos. "Talleyrand et son entourage à la suite de la Grande Armée." 1919.

Revue Hebdomadaire. Reiset, vicomte de. "Catherine Worlé, Princesse de Talleyrand." 1910.

Quotes

Quotes from self-evident sources, and source for quotes of ten words, more or less, not always given.

PROLOGUE

[1] "...remarkable women...whose friendship never ceased to add enchantment to my life." Talleyrand [*Mémoires*]

CHAPTER 1: A CRIPPLED CHILDHOOD

[1] "I want people to talk about me for centuries, to discuss what I have been, what I thought and what I wanted." Talleyrand [Morlot, *Talleyrand*, 980]

[2] "...You are always talking to me about women...But what are politics, if not women." [Cooper, 298]

[3] "I know what I owe to God and to mankind..." Talleyrand [Morlot, 884]

[4] "Who made you a count?" "Who made you a king?"" [Orieux, 68]

[5] "I am sorry to be so long without him." The Comtesse de Talleyrand [Poniatowski: *Ancien Regime*, 49]

[6] "...because I think this made me feel closer to her." Talleyrand [*Mémoires* via Bernard, 22]

[7] "Do as the abbé tells you, my son." The Comte de Talleyrand [Loliée, S, 11]

[8] "... one of our ancestors, Henri de Talleyrand, Comte de Chalais, became the favorite of Louis XIII..." The Comte de Talleyrand [Dodd, circa 14]

[9] "My oldest son seems very happy, which pleases me." The Comtesse de Talleyrand [Poniatowski, *Ancien Regime*, 63, n.]

[10] "They are forcing me to be a priest...They'll be sorry." Talleyrand [Lacombe, *Vie Privée*]

[11] "Anyone who has not lived in the years prior to 1789 cannot appreciate the sweetness of living." Talleyrand [Noel, 42]

[12] "If they're any good, they won't last long. M. l'Abbé is very generous and will want to treat all his friends." A family retainer [Poniatowski, n. 122]

[13] "There are three kinds of knowledge: *le savoir*—knowledge itself; *le savoir vivre*—to know how to live (good breeding); and *le savoir faire*—to know what to do. And possession of the last two dispenses with any need for the first!" Talleyrand [Sellier, 22]

[14] "No one ever...possessed such fascinating conversation." Talleyrand [Bernard, s.p.]

[15] "It's too late. There's no turning back now." Talleyrand [Lacombe, Vie Priveé]

CHAPTER 2: AN ABBÉ A LA MODE

[1] "The Abbé de Périgord would sell his soul for money; and he would be right for he would be exchanging dung for gold." Mirabeau [Cooper, 28]

[2] "...let oneself learn the things he already knows from those people who do not know it." [Historia: Herriot, 243]

[3] "Society is divided into two classes: the shearers and the shorn. One must always be with the former against the latter." [Poniatowski, 371] or [Talleyrand's *Mémoires*, via Leon Introduction, 45–46]

[4] "Le Saint Esprit serait seulement l'esprit tout court." [Noel, circa 30]

[5] *See* [1].

[6] "...the only man who knew how to make the chicken with the golden eggs lay eggs without gutting it." [Poniatowski, 295]

[7] "Mon cousin, now that you are going to become a shopkeeper ..." [Encyclopedia, rues de Paris, see Palais Royal]

CHAPTER 3: THE BISHOP

Morris quotes from journal not listed herein, as with other quotes which have with equally obvious sources.

[1] "People are always saying either too many good or too many bad things about me. I enjoy the honors of exaggeration." Talleyrand [Lacour-Gayet I, 5]

[2] "...we have formed a solid and equitable constitution as our constituents have asked us to do." Bailly [Schama, 359]

[3] "deployed more skill than vigor" [Swiggett] [Famous Latin quote: "*suaviter in modo* if not *fortiter in Re*." [Missoffe, 69b]

[4] "...one of those halfway minds which see just far enough to bewilder themselves." [Swiggett]

[5] *See* [1].

[6] "In France when all other expedients have been exhausted..." [Castelot, 63]

[7] "If reason refuses to accept the means which I propose, necessity will do so." [Poniatowski, 108]

[8] "Should you not add that such a man should be strongly marked by the smallpox?" [Cooper, 36]

[9] "If [his] conversation could be purchased, I would gladly go into bankruptcy." [Bernard, 104]

CHAPTER 4: THE DEPUTY

[1] "Laissez-passer Maurice Talleyrand, allant à Londres par nos ordres" Danton [Morlot, 185]

[2] "indescribable beauty... A fine moonshine, a dead Silence..." [Morris]

[3] "...calling on European sovereigns..." [From well-known Pillnitz Declaration signed by Austrian Emperor and Prussian King]

[4] "I will shortly be able to place their money most advantageously." [Poniatowski, 426]

[5] "...as much for the people's own good as for His Majesty's personal security." [Poniatowski, 457]

CHAPTER 5: THE EXILE

[1] "America has thirty-two religions and a single entrée." Talleyrand [Poniatowski aux États-Unis, 171] [It is a paraphrase of Voltaire's via a newspaper: "We have sixty religions and one sauce."]

[2] "I can pardon . . . [them] for not sharing my opinions but I cannot pardon them for theirs." [Talleyrand's *Mémoires*, Joval Publ., 1953]

[3] "I shall always lack something essential until I am able to prove to you my gratitude." [Poniatowski, 470]

[4] "...in order to avoid the scandal of coquetry, she always yielded easily." [Talleyrand's *Mémoires*]

[5] "I promise not to look too surprised." [Cooper, 69]

[6] "...one of the finest members and one of the most charming of this exquisite set..." [Cooper, 63]

[7] "Oh, but he will be unhappy to miss anything." [Cooper, 63]

[8] "...two prim little figures straight out of the sedate drawing rooms..." [Cooper, 64]

[9] "She seems equally attached to M. de Talleyrand…" [Cooper, 64]

[10] "…after four months snatched from life's wreckage…" [Lacour-Gayet, 172]

[11] "See that we are not apart for more than a year…" [Poniatowski aux États-Unis, 66]

[12] "No, no. No! You cannot go alone and unattended…" [Poniatowski aux États-Unis, 67]

[13] *See* [1]

[14] "…if some of the friends of Monsieur, your father…" [Bernard, 155]

[15] "…less than fifty leagues from the nation's capital …" [Talleyrand's *Mémoires*]

[16] "Alas, yes, Monseigneur, I am." [Talleyrand's *Mémoires*] [Noël, 37]

[17] "It is impossible to thrust a spit through a leg of mutton with a greater air of majesty." [Dodd, 339]

[18] "If I have to stay here a year, I shall die." [Missoffe, 85]

[19] "…she slept every night with her husband, which is very commendable here. They only have one bedroom. Warn . . . Narbonne about that and be sure to emphasize that this is an essential if one wants a good reputation over here." [Poniatowski aux États-Unis, 101]

[20] "What are politics if not women?" [Poniatowski, Direct, 96] [Fleury, 103]

[21] "Money is the one universal cult …" [Morlot, 266] ["He found money worshipped with a devotion that astounds and even shocks him" [Bernard] and said to a friend: "Don't speak to me about a country where I found no one who was not ready to sell me his dog." [Brinton, s.p.]

[22] "To such an extent that if it were not for her intrigues…" [Cooper, 72]

[23] "…the rest of my life I will spend wherever you are. Will M. de Staël give me a small room?" [LacVie, after 203] or [Poniatowski, 307]

CHAPTER 6: MINISTER OF THE DIRECTOIRE

[1] "He has all the vices of the *ancient regime* as well as those of the new one. He will always keep a foot in both camps." Mme de Staël [Orieux, 259] [Castelot, 126]

[2] "On ne pouvait pas être plus richement déshabillé!" (One could not be more richly undressed!) [Poniatowski, n., 77]

[3] "…the former Bishop d'Autun is moving heaven and earth to be employed by the Directoire." [Poniatowski, 92]

[4] "…the well-being and glory of the French Republic." [Poniatowski, 107]

[5] "…at my disposal and even at my feet for me to do with as I wished." [Barras, Memoirs]

[6] *See* [1]

[7] "in important circumstances, one should put women to work." [Saint-Aulaire, Part B, 118]

[8] "[Talleyrand] signed events; he did not make them happen." Chateaubriand [Madelin, 79]

[9] "I swear on my word of honor that is not true." – "Don't raise your hand," countered Barras. "It will drip blood all over." [Talleyrand's *Mémoires*, Vol. I, s.p.]

[10] "I gain confidence from the knowledge that your glory cannot fail to facilitate any negotiations that I may be required to undertake." [Bernard, 48]

[11] "I will be flattered to exchange letters with you often so as to keep you fully informed." Napoleon ["L'Europe Nouvelle" 7 mars. 1925] [via Poniatowski]

[12] "That's because it takes four Turkish women to equal one French one." [Poniatowski, n., 199]

[13] "We had to ignore the Constitution for just one second, but never again, I hope." [Dard, s.p.]

[14] "Adieu, General. Adieu. Friendship, admiration, respect, gratitude; I could continue indefinitely…" [Saint-Aulaire, 130]

[15] "Destiny's choice…Twenty victories are so becoming to a pale young hero with fine eyes and a look of exhaustion…" [Talleyrand's *Mémoires*, s.p.]

[16] "…what we should fear is his ambition…that we may be unable to tear him away from a studious life in retreat." [Norman, s.p.]

[17] "When the happiness of the French is based on better organic laws, all Europe will become free."

[Schom *or* Bourienne's Memoirs, 5 vol. Garnier, 1899–1900, Vol. 2, 26–27] [Poniatowski, 414, n]

CHAPTER 7: A CO-CONSPIRATOR

[1] "One must put women to work." Talleyrand [Saint-Aulaire, Part B, 118]

[2] *Ibid.*

[3] "Who is the greatest woman alive or dead?…She who has produced the most children." [Herold, 182]

[4] "Vile émigré! Thy reasoning is as distorted as thy foot!" [Pichot, 26]

[5] "When M. de Talleyrand is not plotting, he's trafficking." Chateaubriand [Lacour-Gayet, vol. II, 399]

[6] "Piedcourt importunes me from morning til evening…" [Poniatowski, 329]

[7] "Mme Grand has just been arrested as conspirator…" [Carrère, 262] [Poniatowski, 746]

[8] "Charlotte will be fourteen in October." [Poniatowski, Consulat, 450]

[9] "I can pardon people for not being of the same opinion…" [Sellier, 58]

[10] "He possesses a lot of what is necessary for negotiations…" Napoleon [Lacour-Gayet]

[11] "That is very simple. I bought government bonds…" [Kerry, *Napoleon*, 362] [Sainte-Beuve, 54]

[12] "Be assured that I will be killed or else I will justify your choice." [Bernardy, Flahaut, 32]

CHAPTER 8: FOREIGN AFFAIRS MINISTER

[1] "Any miscalculation can be denied." Talleyrand [Sainte-Beuve, circa 50]

[2] "What good is a senate if it is never used?" Talleyrand [Orieux, 381]

[3] "No doubt, Madame, you have nursed your children yourself?" [Herold, 228]

[4] "My forthcoming absence will create for me the most painful of privations…I am distraught at going…my devotion will only end with my life." [Castelot, 185]

[5] "It was a time of general disorder…Nothing was of any real importance." [Castelot, 676]

Lacour-Gayet III, 33]

[6] "Because if I had, we would never have been able to get anything else accomplished. When you are happy, you can think of nothing else." [Morlot, 415]

[7] "...the request for secularization by citizen Talleyrand is personally agreeable to me." [Poniatowski, s.p.]

[8] "I will arrive late, after your guests are seated, so everyone will look around to see who is causing so much commotion. Then, when I have their attention,..." [said by Sainte-Foy] [Poniatowski, 420]

[9] "If you're in mud up to your neck, what difference does it make if you have it over your head?" [Lacour-Gayet, IIz, 102]

[10] "To think that we have come to this, after having enjoyed the favors of..." Courtiade [Castelot, 205]

[11] "Power and marriage make so great a difference here that not paying a visit [there]...would be reckoned a ridicule." [Cooper, 132]

[12] "...good conduct of the citizeness Talleyrand would make everyone forget the past indiscretions of Mme Grand...I only have to be inspired by the example of Mme Bonaparte." First Consul [Pichot, 6] [Aujay, circa 154]

[13] "She has disguised both herself and me as women." [Herold, 93] [Orieux, 411]

[14] "It was worse than a crime; it was a blunder." [Bernard,]

[15] "Come, come...Are you mad? What is there to make such a fuss about? A conspirator is captured near the frontier, he is brought to Paris and shot. What is so extraordinary about that? [Cooper, 141]

[16] "If, as you say, Bonaparte has been guilty of committing a crime, there is no reason for me to do something foolish." [Sainte-Beuve, 52]

CHAPTER 9: IMPERIAL GRAND CHAMBERLAIN, 1804

[1] "You are one of the principal interests in my life..." Talleyrand [Castelot, 269]

[2] "Madam, can you tell me what a charlotte is?..." Mme Duroc [Poniatowski, 433]

[3] "The price was not exorbitant... Do you think I married the pope?" Catherine [Lacour-Gayet

II, circa 107]

[4] "A horrible place with some four thousand wounded...dying in quantities each day." Talleyrand [Castelot, 245]

[5] "You can see for yourself what I have just done for you." Napoleon [Note to Talleyrand]

[6] "How shall I address Your Excellency now? Will His Serene Highness wear the same suit His Excellency wore yesterday?" Courtiade [Bernardy, 265]

[7] "She's the one to congratulate ..." Talleyrand [Carrère, 266] [Aujay 2, 180]

[8] "...to oppose with all his strength and influence, the destructive projects of the Emperor." Metternich [Bernard, 264]

[9] "The attentions of a man who rarely confers them are always effective..." Hortense [Talleyrand Memoirs, ed. 1927, vol. I, 269] [Cooper, 156]

[10] "His (i.e. Talleyrand's) aristocratic hauteur never leaves him, whatever he does." A guest [Potocka Memoirs, s.p.]

[11] "Today I have written...to repeat my request that he recall you to his side..." Talleyrand to Murat [Castelot, 269]

[12] "Why have I given you a writing master..." Talleyrand [Poniatowski, 433, n.5]

[13] "She is a Peruvian gold mine." Batowski [Pflaum, Courland]

[14] "Scoundrel! How dare you sleep in the presence of the Emperor!" Napoleon [Castelot, 270]

[15] "...exposing himself to new perils...Your Majesty disdains them." Talleyrand to Napoleon [Morlot, 521]

[16] "And what, pray tell, will he be doing on the other side?" Talleyrand [Schom, 449]

CHAPTER 10: VICE-GRAND ELECTOR

[1] "The only vice he lacks..." Fouché [Saint-Aulaire, 197] or [Orieux, 469]

[2] "I do not want to become the executioner of Europe." Talleyrand [Bernard, 280]

[3] See [1]

[4] "I will not permit a single

English envoy in Europe!..." Napoleon [Castelot, 288]

[5] "If the prince...should become attached to some pretty woman ..." Napoleon [Lacour-Gayet, 228] or [Morlot, 548]

[6] "...Mon dieu! It's very simple and I will give you an example..." Talleyrand [*Mémoires*]

[7] "Sire, it is for you to save Europe ..." Talleyrand [*Mémoires*] or [Cooper, 176]

[8] "When I was a lieutenant in the French artillery..." Napoleon [Madelin, *Historia*, 389]

[9] "One can conceive of his having such a face..." Goethe [Madelin, 157]

[10] "He who laughs last, gets the best laugh." Alexander [Dard listed as source]

[11] "You deserve to be broken like a glass. I have the power to do so, but you're not worth the trouble ...You would sell your own father..." Napoleon [Castelot, *Napoleon*, 345]

[12] "What a pity that such a great man should have such bad manners." Talleyrand [Castelot, "Napoleon" 345]

[13] "There are some things one can never pardon." Talleyrand [Castelot, "Napoleon" 345]

[14] "I do not think M. de Talleyrand ever drafted the most important diplomatic note with greater care than he gave this letter." Dorothea [P. Ziegler, "The Duchess of Dino" 62]

CHAPTER 11: A TRAITOR OR LOYAL OPPOSITION

[1] "[Talleyrand was] in their arms and at their feet but never in their hands." The Comte de Saint Aulaire [Castelot, 36]

[2] "You have stipulated one hundred million francs as indemnity for France, every sou of which will go to the Treasury, I know ...Settle this affair at once." Napoleon [Blei, Franz, Talleyrand Homme d'État-Payot, 178]

[3] "We shall do everything to make your stay a pleasant and a long one." Napoleon [Pflaum, 110]

[4] "It would have been possible to bare more and show less!..." Talleyrand [Castelot, 36]

[5] "Black as the devil, Hot as hell, Pure as an angel, Sweet like love."

[poem] [Poniatowski, *Talleyrand aux États Unis*, 171]

[6] "…with his limping gait, his heavy body, his flashing eyes, his snake-like mouth and jaw, his paralyzing smile, and his affected flatteries." Comtesse Kiemannsegge [Cooper, 205]

[7] "…Ney, Oudinot, and so many others never began or finished a battle without demanding such gifts from me…" Napoleon [Missoffe: *Le Coeur Secret*] or [Orieux, 543]

CHAPTER 12: PRESIDENT OF THE PROVISIONAL GOVERNMENT

[1] "Even his civilities are usurious investments which must be paid for before the day's end." Pozzo di Borgo [Madelin, 231]

[2] "…Bonaparte must be near his end…If you answer him tell him that I accept the augury of his good memory." The future Louis XVIII to the Archbishop of Reims [Aujay or Saint-Aulaire, 233+] [12/508]

[3] "Today you still have some chips …" Talleyrand to Napoleon [Bernard, 313]

[4] "I confess that I have no wish to expose myself…" Talleyrand to Aimée de Coigny [her memoirs]

[5] "What opinion do you think posterity will have of me…" Talleyrand to the Comtesse Kielmannssegge [Orieux, 527]

[6] "…I love you…in harsh times as well as in gentler ones." Talleyrand [Pflaum, *By Influence and Desire*, 173]

[7] "One would have to be without an ounce of French blood…" Talleyrand [Pflaum, *By Influence and Desire*, 174]

[8] "The lion isn't dead yet…too early to piss on him." Napoleon [Pflaum, *By Influence and Desire*, 173]

[9] "Ah ma Chère…tenderest interest of my love…" Talleyrand [Pflaum, *By Influence and Desire*, 174]

[10] "…You are walking on crutches …" Talleyrand dictated while Dalberg wrote [Pflaum, *By Influence and Desire*, 176]

[11] "…The proverbial Austrian slowness never deserved its reputation more." Talleyrand to Dorothea [Norman, 169]

[12] "What an historic catastrophe! …" Talleyrand [Norman, circa 168]

[13] "Be so good as to convey… the respect of the Prince de Bénévent." Talleyrand [Pflaum, 124]

[14] "Monsieur de Talleyrand…you have my confidence…You know France, its needs…" Alexander [Castelot, 449]

[15] "You are no longer Napoleon's soldiers. The Senate and all France releases you from your oaths of allegiance to him." [Castelot, 458]

[16] "Nothing serious should be heard tonight…soothing, that will not require concentration…" Talleyrand [Morlot, #12 circa 558]

CHAPTER 13: L'AMBASSADEUR EXTRAORDINAIRE

[1] "Talleyrand is behaving as though he were the Minister of Louis XIV." Tsar Alexander [Sorel, 86/3]

[2] "Wouldn't James and Dolly Madison have a fit!" the Grand Duchess [Pflaum, *By Influence and Desire* 187]

[3] "I have finished my armistice. It is a good thing." Talleyrand [Morlot, 726]

[4] "King by the grace of God is the protocol of ingratitude." Talleyrand [Lacour-Gayet, 126]

[5] "You scolded me…" Talleyrand to the Grand Duchess [Pflaum, *By Influence and Desire* 187]

[6] "We all have our infirmities—to be exploited when need be." Talleyrand [Cooper, 249]

[7] "It was a scene I shall never forget." Gentz [Cooper, 252]

[8] "Europe! O Europe!" Talleyrand scene with Tsar [Saint-Aulaire, 5, part D, circa 314]

[9] "…that, sire, is a question of dates." Talleyrand [Saint-Aulaire, circa 314; Bernard, 375 or 387; Cooper, 252]

[10] "…our child is enjoying a great success here…" Talleyrand [Castelot, 521] [13/596]

[11] "…you diplomats make decisions…" Alexander… [Pflaum, 230]

[12] *See* [1].

[13] "Sire, France is no longer isolated in Europe." Talleyrand [Castelot, 534]

CHAPTER 14: PRESIDENT OF THE FIRST MINISTRY OF THE SECOND RESTORATION

[1] "She [Dorothea] is charming and very intelligent…" Talleyrand

[2] "He [Napoleon] was so overcome by fatigue…" Flahaut [Kerry: The First Napoleon]

[3] "…You will write and give us news…" Louis XVIII [Bernard, 426]

[4] "…I, who set the crown of France upon his head!" Talleyrand [Bernard, 426]

[5] "…one would never have taken him [Talleyrand] for a minister who had been disgraced…" Count Beugnot [Cooper, 269]

[6] "There goes Vice leaning on the arm of Crime." Chateaubriand [Cole, 292]

[7] "Everything is going so badly…that one has to believe…" Talleyrand [Orieux, 640]

[8] "…I suppose I shall have to find another cabinet." His Majesty [Orieux, 648]

CHAPTER 15: GRAND CHAMBERLAIN, 1815

[1] "It is so rare to have someone all to oneself, without a secret, without a separate interest" Talleyrand [*Mémoires*]

[2] "He is the one Frenchman who knows the most about Odessa." Talleyrand [Orieux, 648]

[3] "…I can think of nothing comparable to the happiness…" Talleyrand [Mirabeau, 656 or 465]

[4] "…Arm M. Perry with a letter of credit…and not come back until he sees her boat embark." Dorothea [Orieux, 659]

[5] "…could not possibly be French…I am an old umbrella…" Talleyrand [Bourdonove, 325]

[6] "No, sire…to accompany him to carry out the duties of my office…same distance as from Paris to Ghent." Talleyrand [Bernard, 476]

[7] "It is no longer an event. It is only a bit of news…less surprising than his elevation…" Talleyrand [Bernard, 476]

[8] "Perhaps I have never before realized how deeply I am attached to you." Talleyrand [Pflaum, *By Influence and Desire*, 279]

[9] "I do not believe...a woman... more worthy of being adored." Talleyrand [Pflaum, *By Influence and Desire*, 279]

[10] "Let the past remain forgotten...You will not find any one here who displeases you..." Sa Majesté, Louis XVIII [Castelot, 150]

[11] "Le Prince de Talleyrand behaved on this occasion as such a faithful minister that the emperor never reproached him about this affair." Napoleon [Castelot, 615]

[12] "I never believed that the Capitole was saved by a gaggle of squawking geese." Talleyrand [Castelot, 585]

[13] "...here I am not only with Madame de Dino but staying in her home, which is an added attraction" Talleyrand [Lacour-Gayet, 316]

[14] "It is not French because it is silly." Talleyrand [Cooper, 314]

[15] "We are marching towards an unknown world without a pilot and without a compass. Only one thing is certain; all this will end up with a shipwreck." Talleyrand [Bernard, 515]

[16] "It is not I who have abandoned the king. It is the king who has abandoned us." Talleyrand [Madelin, circa 290 or 210?]

CHAPTER 16: AMBASSADOR TO ENGLAND

[1] "My equilibrium is as difficult to maintain as that of Europe." Talleyrand [Lacour-Gayet, fall, 1834]

[2] "...the most stable guarantee of the happiness of these two nations and of the peace of the world.." Talleyrand [Orieux, 745]

[3] "I like Mme de Dino a great deal. She is always good-natured and very good company." Lady Grey [Orieux, 745]

[4] "Our dinners are most successful but they are ruinously expensive and M. de Talleyrand is greatly alarmed at the cost." Mme de Dino [Orieux, 746]

[5] "...pair meet and dine each other but it is like meetings in cock-and-bull fights." Lady Granville [Bourdonove, 345]

[6] "I need to catch my breath. I have to think of my legs, of my eyes, and I have to look after my affairs." Talleyrand [Madeline, 298]

[7] "I irritate you sometimes by talking and then I stop before I have said all that I think...so let me write to you...Declare yourself old, lest people should find that you have aged...say nobly, simply to the world: The hour has struck." Mme de Dino [Cooper, 343]

[8] "I must not fall. My equilibrium is as difficult to maintain as that of Europe." [Lacour-Gayet, 1834]

[9] "What makes it all the worst, at Monsieur de Talleyrand's age it is not only an affliction to endure, it is a warning to receive." Mme de Dino [Orieux, 778]

[10] "M. de Talleyrand is not making anything up. He is talking about himself." Royer-Collard [Orieux, 781]

[11] "Do you know, Princesse, why I like Montrond so much?...No. Not really...I would be curious to know why...Eh bien, Princesse, the reason I am so fond of the Prince de Talleyrand because he is not at all scrupulous." Montrond [Castelot, 655]

CHAPTER 17: DEATH OF A BISHOP

[1] "M. de Talleyrand has died like a man who knows how to live." Mme de Girardin [Orieux, 818]

[2] "He only lacked a cross upon his chest to convince me that I was talking to one of the most venerable bishops in France." Dupanloup [Orieux, 803]

[3] "I do not want people to say that I wrote it in my second childhood" Talleyrand [Bernardy, circa 315]

[4] "Sire, our home has today received an honor worthy of being inscribed in our annals and that my ancestors will recall with pride and gratitude." Talleyrand [Cooper, 374]

Index

Abbaye de Saint-Rémy, 13–14, 34
   Grand Prieur of the Abbaye, 13
Académie Française, 422
Adams, President John, 171, 183, 200
Adet, French minister, 137
Age of Enlightenment, 38–39, 83
Aix, archbishop of, 43, 47
Alexander I, 207, 226, 237, 251, 260, 262–68, 271, 277–79, 285, 290, 294–95, 297, 299, 302, 306, 310, 316, 319, 322–26, 328–31, 333, 336–37, 340–41, 343, 346, 348, 352, 355–56, 358–60, 363, 366–67, 370, 375, 384–85, 389, 395
Alien Bill, 124–26
Allonville, Comte d', 156
Alphonse VII of Spain, 345, 401
American Continental Congress, 76, 183
American Philosophical Society, 130
American War for Independence, 35, 42, 50–51, 73, 82, 105–06, 115, 126, 135
   American Revolution, 38, 172, 212
   Declaration of Independence, 38
Amiens, 211, 213, 216, 218–19, 233, 258, 310–11
ancien régime, 18, 24, 28, 31–32, 37–38, 61, 68, 82, 86, 95, 142, 144, 147, 152, 161, 163, 167, 173, 197, 236, 343, 353, 364, 369, 382, 405, 412, 414, 428
Angiviller, Comte d'
   Academies of Painting and Sculpture, director of, 54
   Royal Buildings, director of, 54
Angiviller, Comtesse d', 55–56
Angoulême, Duchess d', Mme Royal, 311, 335–37, 384
Angoulême, Duc d', 384
Antigny, Marquise d', 22, 37
Arblay, General d', 122–23
Artois, Comte d', Charles X, 49, 78, 104, 316, 331, 333–34, 344, 380, 384, 402–08
Assembly of Notables, 58–60, 69
Augereau, Charles Pierre François, 166, 169–70
Austrian emperor, 104, 205, 226, 292, 316, 323, 337, 340, 343, 350, 352, 394–95

Bacourt, Adolphe de, 418, 421, 427–29
Bagration, Princess, Katya, 350, 356, 359
Bailly, Sylvain, 74
Barante, Baron de, Amable Guillaume Prosper Brugière, 406, 429
Barras, Paul François Jean Nicolas, Vicomte de, 138, 141, 149–52, 155–57, 160–66, 168–69, 171–72, 174, 178, 182, 185–86, 188–92
Barry, Mme du, 19, 31, 49, 56
Bastille, 76–77, 79, 88, 93, 209, 411
Batowski, Count Alexander, 248, 267–68, 277–79
Beaugeard, Mme, 255
Beauharnais, Alexander de, 132

Beauharnais, Eugène de, Viceroy of Italy, 195, 239, 259, 273
   married, Princess Augusta, 239
Beauharnais, Hortense de, Queen of Holland, 178, 195, 211, 242, 258, 294–95, 307
Beaumarchais, *The Barber of Seville*, author of, 51, 319–20
Beaumetz, Baron Albert Briois de, 126, 128–30, 132, 137–39, 141
Beaumont, 43
Beauvau, Prince de, 34
Belgian National Conference, 417
Belgian revolution, 414, 416
Bellamy, 183
Bellanger, 178
Bellechasse, 37–38, 48–50, 54, 57, 63, 128
Benedictine Abbaye de Hautvilliers, 29
Berry, Duc de, Charles Ferdinand d'Artois, 391, 398
Berry, Marie-Caroline, Princess Maria Carolina Ferdinanda Luisa of Naples and Sicily, 391
Berthier, General, 247–49, 258, 261
Besnardière, Jean-Baptiste de Gouy de la, 164, 344
Bibracte, 64
Big Four, 314, 334, 340–41, 348, 351, 353–56, 361, 366, 372, 379
Billecoq, Jean–Baptiste, 389
Bingham, Mrs. William, 130
Biron, Maréchal de, 62
Blacas, Duc de, 338, 378
Blücher, Gebhard Leberecht von, 377, 383
Boisgelin, Abbé de, 47, 57
Boisgelin, Count Bruno de, 302, 308
Bollman, Dr. Justice, 364
Bonaparte, Caroline, 245, 254, 259, 273, 313
Bonaparte, Charles Joseph, "l'Aiglon" [the Eaglet], 295–96, 301, 308, 312, 316, 320, 329, 337, 366, 380
Bonaparte, Jérôme, King of Westphalia, 255, 259, 262
Bonaparte, Joseph, 65, 185, 201, 239, 254, 259–60, 273, 315, 320
Bonaparte, Louis, 211, 239, 259
Bonaparte, Louis-Napoleon, Napoleon III, 258
Bonaparte, Lucien, 172, 185, 188–90, 193, 210
Bonaparte, Napoleon, 17–18, 28, 65, 120, 124, 140–41, 149, 156, 159, 165–68, 170, 172–75, 177–204, 206–15, 217–26, 229–40, 242–54, 256–68, 270–77, 279, 284–97, 300–03, 305–14, 319–20, 324–31, 333, 337, 340, 342, 351–52, 356, 365, 368–69, 372, 375, 377–78, 380, 382–83, 393, 395–96, 400–02
Bordeaux, Duc de, 425
Bouchardie, Eugénie, Countess de la, 140, 150
Boufflers, Mme de, 147
Bougainville, Louis-Antoine, Comte de, 173

Bourachot, superior-general, M., 33
Bourbon-Condé, Louis Antoine Henri de, *see* Enghien, Duc d'
Bourbon dynasty, 19–20, 127, 152, 155, 188, 199, 222, 225, 227, 243, 271, 273, 302, 306, 308, 315–16, 318, 323–25, 329, 333–34, 336, 338–40, 342, 373, 425
Bourse, 49 52, 82, 163, 204
Brancas, Duchess de, 156
Brionne, Comtesse de, 53, 236, 262, 370–71
   granddaughter, Comtesse Adrienne de Canisy, 262
British East India Co., 136
Brummel, Beau, 151
Brunswick, Duke of, 110, 114, 215
Bruix, Admiral, 187–89, 191–93, 216
Buffon, 67
Bulletin des Lois, 215
Burney, Dr. Charles, 121–23
Burney, Fanny, 121, 123
Burr, Aaron, 139
Buzot, 83

Cabarrus, 67
   Thérèse, daughter, Notre Dame de Thermidor, 67
Cacault, François, 214
Cadore, Duc de, 395
Cadoudal, Georges, 222–26
Cagliostro, 52
Caisse d'Escompte, 52
Calonne, General Controller of Finances, 51–52, 57–59, 127
Cambacérès, Jean-Jacques de, 196, 215, 226, 254
Campo Formio treaty, 170–71, 175
Capet, Hugues, Count of Paris, 20
Caprara, Monseigneur, 209, 229
Carême, Antoine, 270–71, 282, 298, 331, 341, 344, 358–59, 368, 374, 388
Carnot, Lazare, 164–65
Carrel, Armand, 405–06
Castlereagh, Lord, 323, 354, 358, 361, 366–67
Catherine the Great of Russia, 42, 101, 106, 267
Caulaincourt, General, 250, 262–63, 268, 277, 296, 303, 306–07, 311, 313–14, 317, 322, 326, 328
Cazenove, Théophile, 128, 130, 132, 145
Cent Gardes, 70
Cercle Constitutionel, 155, 162
Chalais, Princess de, 23–25, 28
Chamillart, 21
Champ de Mars, 93–95
Champagny, Nompère de, 284, 395
Charlemagne, 14, 205, 229–30, 234, 254, 284
Charles I, 121
Charles IV, King, 256, 258
   Queen Maria-Louisa, 256
Charles X, *See* Artois, Comte d'
Chateaubriand, François-René de, 134, 164, 181, 186, 225, 257, 326, 330, 378, 381, 414
Châtre, Countess de la, 117, 121
Chauvelin, marquis de, the Keeper

of His Majesty's Wardrobe, 107, 112
Chenier, André, 140
Chenier, Marie-José, 140, 150
Choiseul-Gouffier, Auguste de, 37, 44, 51, 158, 180, 200, 221
Church of Notre Dame, 70, 213, 231, 250, 254, 296, 302, 333
Church of Sainte-Marguerite, 84
Church of Saint-Louis, 70
Civil Constitution of the Clergy, 93, 97, 99–101
Clam-Martinitz, Count Karl, 359–60, 374–75, 382–83, 386, 389, 392
Clovis, 13–14
Club de Clichy, 155
Cobenzl, Count Louis de, 200, 209, 226
Coigny, Marquise Aimée de, 302, 308, 315, 318
Colbert, Minister, 21, 23
Comédie-Française, 32, 38, 41, 43, 50, 92, 200, 249, 255, 265, 319
Committee of Public Safety, 135
Commune, the, 110–11, 113–15
Compiègne, 29
Compte Rendu, 51
Concordat, 209, 213–15
Concorde, Place de la, 30
Confederation of the Rhine, 240–42
Congress of Vienna, 19, 342, 345–76, 413–14
General Act of the Vienna Congress, 376–77
Consalvi, Cardinal Hector, 208, 216, 356
Constant, Albertine, 154
Constant, Benjamin, 150, 154–55, 162
Constitution of the Year III, 148, 160
Council of Ancients, 148, 152, 159–60, 165, 168, 189–90, 193–94
Council of Five Hundred, 148, 152, 159–60, 165, 168, 189–90, 193–94
Constitutional Committee, 81
Constitutional Convention, 76
Consulate, 164, 204, 206, 222
Continental Blockade, 243, 256, 270, 284, 293–94
convent of the Grands Augustins, 35, 47
convent of Saint-Joseph, 39
Coppet, on Lake Geneva, 97, 102, 121, 124–25, 138, 150, 153
Cornwallis, Lord Charles, 212–13
Cosway, Maria, 119
Council of State, 215–16
coup du 18 brumaire, 18, 190–94
coup du 18 fructidor, 18, 169
Courland, Anna Charlotte Dorothea von Medem, Grand Duchess de, 267–68, 277–79, 281–88, 290, 292, 295–99, 301–03, 306–07, 313–14, 316–19, 323, 325, 328, 331, 333, 335, 338–40, 344, 346, 356, 368, 373–74, 376, 380, 384–87, 389–91, 395, 398, 400
Courland, Dorothea, Duchess de Dino, 248, 267, 277–79, 281–83, 292–93, 296–97, 301–03, 305, 310, 318, 328, 330–31, 335, 339, 346–50, 356–57, 359–60, 364, 366–74, 376, 382, 386–87, 389–90, 392, 394, 396–400, 402–04, 406, 414–16, 418, 420–21, 423–30
children, Alexander–Edmond, 313, 422, 429; Dorothea-Charlotte, 313, 339, 396; Napoléon-Louis, 295, 313, 422, 429; Pauline, "Minette," 399, 403, 424–26, 428–29, 431
Courland, Joanna, Katharina, Duchess de Acerenza, 339, 346, 364
Courland, Paulina, Duchess de Sagan, 339, 364
husband, Friedrich-Hermann-Otto von Hohenzollern-Hechingen, 346
Courland, Wilhelmina, Duchess de Sagan, 339, 346–47, 349–50, 356–57, 364, 366, 373, 376, 390, 424
Courtiade, 117, 127, 133–34, 137–38, 173, 191, 216, 238, 240, 244, 287, 298, 303, 322, 374, 388
Court of Saint James, 93, 106, 389, 395, 419
Creusot, 66
Cruveilhier, Dr., 427, 429
Curtis, Martha, 134
Czartoryski, Prince Adam, 277–79, 346

Dalberg, Baron Emmerich de, 240, 242, 246, 316–17, 324–26, 344–45, 354, 386
Dalberg, Baron Karl-Theodor, Archbishop Charles, Prince-Primate, 240–42, 277, 279
Danton, 27, 102–03, 111–15, 120, 135, 137
Cordelier club, 102–03
Dauphin of France, Louis, 25, 30
Dauphine of France, Marie Josephe de Saxe, 25, 30
Dauphin and Marie-Louise, marriage of, 30
Dauphiné, 61, 73
David, Jacques-Louis, 231–32
Decazes, 393, 397, 399
Declaration of the Rights of Man, 81, 141, 181
Declaration of Pillnitz, 104
Deffand, Mme du, 39–41
Delacroix, Charles-François, 157
Delacroix, Eugène, 157, 401
Delacroix, Mme, 157
Denon, Baron Vivant, 197, 270
Department of Paris, 98, 100, 103, 110–11
Department of the Seine, Executive Committee of, 109
Desaix, General, 180
Desrenaudes, Abbé Martial Borye, 63, 138–40, 164, 192
Dillon, Count Arthur, 135
Directoire, 18, 141, 145, 148–50, 152–54, 160, 162, 164–65, 167–70, 174, 177, 179–81, 183–85, 187, 192, 222, 232, 238, 256, 293, 306, 322, 380
The Five, 148–49, 153, 155, 160, 164–65, 168, 170–71, 174, 177, 180–83, 185–88
Dorinville, Dorothée Luzy, 32

Doudou, 136–37
Dreux-Brézé, M. de, 394
Ducos, Roger, 193
Dumouriez, 119, 224
Dupanloup, Abbé, 425–30
Dupont de Nemours, 52, 59–60, 206
Dupont, Victor, 184

École Militaire, 93
Effendi, Esseid Ali, 167–68
Emperor Joseph II of Austria, 51, 83
Enghien, Duc d', Bourbon-Condé, Louis Antoine Henri de, 104, 223–26, 256, 263, 308, 329–30, 336, 402
England, 35, 38
commercial treaty, 57
Espagnac, l'Abbé, 52
Executive Committee of the Department of Paris, 103
Executive Council, 111–12, 114–15, 118, 137
Expilly, Abbé, 100

Fauchet, Joseph, 129
Ferdinand I, King of The Two Sicilies, Ferdinand IV of Naples, 376–77, 394
Ferdinand, the Prince of Asturias, 256, 258–60
Fesch, Cardinal, 241
Fête de la Fédération, 133, 138
Finistère, 100
Fitzjames, Duchess de, 96
Flahaut, Charles de, 55–56, 81, 90, 98, 100, 110, 115, 118, 143, 169, 186, 198, 218, 245–47, 250, 258, 261, 294–95, 297, 307–08, 373, 377–78, 380, 383, 416, 419
Flahaut, de la Billarderie, Comte de, 54–55, 110–11
Flahaut de Souza, Adélaïde de Filleul de, Comtesse de, 53–55, 66–68, 70, 75, 79–81, 83–85, 88, 90, 92, 98, 100, 103, 107–10, 112, 115–16, 118, 121, 124–26, 142–44, 158, 169, 246–47, 294, 307, 395, 398
Flahaut, Emilie de, 107
Fleury, Cardinal, 31
Foreign Affairs, 153, 161–62, 168
Foreign Office, 106, 157, 161, 181, 196
Forest, Count Antoine de la, 139
Forges-les-Eaux, 23
Fouché, Joseph, 158, 186, 189–90, 203, 222, 254, 272–74, 298, 380–81, 383–84
Fox, Charles James, 107, 242, 399
Fox, Henry, 163
Fragonard, 54, 92
Francis II, Hapsburg, 237–38
becomes Francis I, emperor of Austria, 241, 316, 340–41, 346, 348, 359, 364–65, 371
François I, 57, 232, 262
François II, 226, 266, 271
Franconi's circus, 79, 283, 319
Franklin, Benjamin, 41–42, 60, 66, 130
Frederick Augustus I, King of Saxony, Elector Frederick Augustus III, Duke Frederick

Augustus I of Warsaw, 289, 356, 367, 370
Frederick the Great of Prussia, 57, 83, 166, 242, 265, 390
Freemasons, 60
Friedrich-Wilhelm II, 58
Friedrich-Wilhelm III, 110, 205, 236, 251, 309–10, 323–25, 337, 352, 358, 366, 371
French Republic, 117, 120, 137–38, 155, 164, 169, 171, 179, 184–85, 188, 190, 193, 224
French Revolution, 18, 20, 25, 45, 49, 67, 78, 86, 101, 108–09, 114, 148, 151, 158–59, 162, 173, 204, 206, 214, 221, 231, 233, 271, 289, 317, 371

Gagern, Baron de, Prince de Nassau-Siegen, 205, 216
General Assembly of the Clergy, 35, 40, 43, 47–48, 56
General Estates, 60–61, 63, 65–66, 69–74, 77, 79
Genlis, Comtesse de, 115, 143–45
Genlis, Comtesse de, Mme, 119
Gentz, Friedrich von, 354, 358, 364, 369, 389
George III, 106, 108, 168, 207
George IV, 414
Gérard, François, 270
Germany, 149
Gerry, Elbridge, 171 –72, 183
Gibbons, Edward, 40
Girondists, 107, 109
Gluck, Christoph Willibald, 39
Godoy, Spanish prime minister, 256, 258
Goethe, 265
Grand, Catherine-Noël Worlée, 119, 158–60, 168–69, 172, 182–84, 186, 190, 193, 197, 204, 209–11, 214–17, 220–22, 226–27, 230, 233–34, 240, 246, 258–59, 261, 285, 297–98, 307, 337–38, 345–46, 348, 382, 389, 392–94, 423
Grand, George François, 183, 216
Gregory XVI, Pope, 429
Grenville, Lord, 106, 118, 126
Greuze, 54, 97
Grey, Lord, 416
Grimaldi, Monseigneur, the Bishop of Noyon, 62
Guerry-Maubreuil, Count de, 404
Guillotin, Dr. Joseph-Ignace, 74
Gustave III of Sweden, 53

Hager, Baron, 344, 356
Hamilton, Alexander, 128–29, 135–36, 138, 154
Hanseatic League, 145
Harcourt, Collège d', 26–30, 34, 37, 42, 200
l'Abbé Hardi, 26
Lehoc, M., 27
Lerond, Mme, 27
Lycée Saint-Louis, 26
Hardenberg, Prince von, 354, 357
Harris, James, Lord Malmesbury, 159, 172
Hauterive, Alexandre Blanc de la Nautte d', 164
Hauteval, 183
Helvétius, Claude Adrien, 42
Helvétius, Minette, 42
Henry IV, 62, 71, 150, 296

Henry VIII, 262
Herculaneum, 151
Higginson, Stephen, 133
Hoche, General, 165
Holland Land Company, 128
Holy Roman Empire, 205
Hostages of the Holy Ampulla, 13
Holy Ampulla, 14
Hôtel Galliffet, 162, 164–69, 173, 180, 182, 185, 194, 196–97, 200, 210, 217, 227, 253, 256, 269
Galliffet, Marquis de, 162
Legrand, Jacques-Guillaume, architect, 162
Hôtel de Guerchy, 37
Hôtel de Sarin, 63
Hôtel de Ville, 78–79, 111
Hottinguer, 183
Houdon, 67, 172
Huidecoper, Harm, Jan, 132, 134
Hope and Company, 132
Hundred Days, 382–83

Imperial Diet in Ratisbonne, 205
Indian (American), 134
Invalides, 77, 198, 206, 211, 213, 239, 296, 305
Isabey, Jean-Baptiste, 231–32, 357, 365, 368
Italian Republic, 213, 234

Jacobins, 145, 149, 179, 182, 186, 188, 191, 203–04, 223, 273
Jaucourt, François de, 118, 121, 326, 348
Jay, John, 129, 133
Jefferson, Thomas, 66, 72, 81, 109, 119, 219
Jesuits, 26
Johnson, Dr. Samuel, 122
Josephine, Empress, Comtesse de Beauharnais, Madame la Générale Bonaparte, 132, 141, 151, 160, 165, 175, 177–79, 182, 187–88, 190–91, 194–95, 197, 203, 210–11, 215, 229, 231–32, 234–35, 238–39, 242, 255, 258–59, 262–63, 266, 273–74, 283–84, 287–91, 294, 296, 312, 380
July Revolution, 411
Juniper Hall, 120–21, 123
Junot, 258, 260

Kaunitz Palace, Vienna, 345, 349, 352, 358, 360, 364, 366, 368, 372–74
Kaunitz, Prince von, 349, 388
Kielmannsegge, Comtesse, 298–99, 309
King, Rufus, 183
Knox, General Henry, 132, 142
Krudener, Baroness Julie de, 385

Labrador, Don Pedro, 353, 355–56
Laclos, Choderlos de
Les Liasons Dangereuses, 108
Lafayette, Marquis de, General, 60, 73, 78–81, 95, 100–01, 118, 122, 130–31, 408
Lameth, Charles de, 115
Lameth, Théodore de, 115, 118
Landry, M., 32
Lansdowne, Marquis of, 98, 107, 128–29, 138

LaPorte, M. de, 120
Latouche-Tréville, Admiral Louis-René Levassor de, 230
Lauzun, Duc de Biron, 106–08
Laval, Vicomtesse de, 96, 299–300, 393
Law, Thomas, 134, 136, 139
married Curtis, Martha, 134
Lebrun, Charles
Adoration of the Virgin, 31
Descent of the Holy Ghost, 31
Lebrun, Charles-François, 158, 196, 254
Legislative Assembly, 103–04, 108, 111, 115, 117
Legislative Corps, 204, 328
Lekain, 32
L'Enfant, Pierre, 142
Leopold I, Prince, of Saxe-Coburg-Gotha, 417–18
Leopold II of Austria, 104, 107
les Italiens, 50
Lessart, Valdec de, 159
Lieven, Prince, 420, 422
Lieven, Princess, 422–23
Ligne, Prince de, 351, 364
Lomez, Bishop de, 34
London Conference, 19
London Gazette, 184
Louis Joseph Xavier François of France, Dauphin of France, 51, 71, 74
Louis-Philippe I, *see* Orléans, Duc
Louis XIII, 27
Louis XIV, The Sun King, 21, 23–24, 38, 54, 74, 83, 213, 239, 255, 284, 358
Louis XV, 13, 19, 31–32, 37–38, 49, 54, 56, 87, 255, 402, 420
Louis XVI, 13–15, 20, 36, 38, 44, 48, 50, 57–58, 60–61, 70–74, 76–78, 80, 84, 86, 92–97, 100–03, 107–08, 112, 121, 137, 148, 220, 226, 232, 289, 306, 364–65, 394
coronation of, 13–15, 34
"Laying–on–of–Hands" ceremony, 34
Royal Council, 48
Royal family flees to Paris, 84
Louis XVIII, Louis-Stanislaus-Xavier, 44, 155, 204, 223, 306, 308, 315, 318, 324, 326, 329, 331, 334–38, 341–42, 344, 346, 348, 353, 355, 361, 367–68, 371–76, 378–79, 381–82, 386, 388–89, 393, 395, 399–400, 402, 423
Louisiana Purchase, 199, 201, 219
Louvre, 54–55, 63, 75, 79–80, 83–84, 88, 90, 92, 98, 102, 110, 197, 290, 319, 337; Hall of the Caryatides, 153–54, 157
Low Countries, 99, 110, 145, 205, 413
Batavian Republic, 145
Luçon, Bishop of, 63
Lunéville, 200–01, 203–05, 211, 213, 218
Luynes, Duchess de, 96
Luxembourg Palace, 150, 159, 188, 191, 194, 315, 326, 389

Madison, James and Dolly, 333
Malmaison, 194, 197, 200, 206–07, 211, 219–20, 242, 284, 291, 312, 380

Manège, 87, 91–93, 97, 102, 110, 115
Maret, Hugues-Bernard, Duc de Bassano, 395, 395
  wife, Duchess de Bassano, 301
Mareuil, Durand de, 205
Marie-Antoinette, 14, 38–39, 44, 50, 56–57, 66, 71, 80, 83, 102, 104, 109–10, 119, 125, 148, 159, 289, 343, 352, 364
Marie-Louise of France, Empress, Archduchess of Austria, 289–92, 301, 307, 310, 312–13, 318–20, 329, 333, 337, 343, 366
  birth of François Charles Joseph Bonaparte, "l'Aiglon" [the Eaglet], 295–96
Marigny, Marquis de, 54–55
  wife, Julie, 54–56
  sister, Mme de Pompadour, 54
  sister–in–law, Adèle Flahaut, 54
Marini, Monseigneur, 214
Marjolin, Professor, 427–28
Marmont, Marshal Auguste de, 318, 320–21, 328, 334, 407–08
Marmontel, 54
Marolles, Abbé de, 100
Marshall, Brigadier-General John, 171–72, 183, 200
Médicis, Marie de, 150
Melito, Comte Miot de, 166
Metropolitan Museum of Art, 159
Metternich, Chancellor Prince, 15, 20, 105, 241–42, 254, 261–63, 271, 273, 276, 290, 309–10, 316, 323, 330, 333–34, 341, 343, 346–48, 351–54, 356–60, 366, 369–71, 373, 384–85, 389, 395
Mignot, 405–06, 426
Ministry of Justice, 114
Mirabeau, Honoré Gabriel de Riquetti, Comte de, 27, 58–60, 70, 73–74, 80, 85–88, 92, 94, 98, 101–03, 120, 420
Molé, Count, 385, 429
Molière, 24
Moniteur, 102, 120, 184, 240, 271, 275, 321, 357, 395, 407
  Bulletin XXIX, 303
Monroe, James, 219
Montespan, Marquise de, 21
Montesquiou, Abbé de, 204, 326, 338
Montgolfier, Etienne, 51
Montmorin, 80
Montrond, Comte Casimir de, 151, 164, 192–93, 151, 207, 268, 295, 373, 405, 421, 423
  his mistress, Fortunée Hamelin, 151, 193
Morris, Gouverneur, 66–68, 70, 72, 75–76, 79–81, 83–85, 87–90, 92, 98, 102–03, 109–10, 114–16, 119, 126, 143–44
Morris, Robert, 145
Motte, Mme de La, 56
Mount Montjeu, 64
Mozart
  The Magic Flute, 60, 241
Murat, Joachim, 193, 212, 218, 223, 242, 245–47, 259, 273

Narbonne, Comte de, 37, 89, 92, 98, 104–05, 107, 111, 120,
122–24, 126, 136
Nassau-Seigen, Prince de, 205
National Assembly, 18, 73, 81–82, 85–88, 91, 98
National Constituent Assembly, 74, 82, 86, 103, 150, 153, 155
National Convention, 117, 120, 137, 140
National Guard, 78
Necker, Germaine, *see* Staël
Necker, Jacques, 50–51, 60, 72, 76–77, 83, 88, 97, 124, 131
Necker, Mme, 50, 77
Nelson, Admiral Horatio, 184, 207, 236
Nesselrode, Count Charles-Robert, 277, 294, 299, 317–18, 322–24, 354
Neukomm, Sigismund von, 269, 365, 390
Noailles, Comte Alexis de, 344
Noailles, Vicomte de, 81, 131
Noel, Jean–François, 113

Olive, M., 139
Opéra, 50, 53, 92, 102, 200–01, 274, 283
Oratorian Church, 100
Oratorian College, 65
Orléans dynasty, 19, 75, 144–45
Orléans, Duc d', Louis-Philippe I, King of the French, 19, 21, 119, 143, 308, 398, 404–23, 429
Orléans, Duc d', Louis-Philippe II, Philippe Égalité, 59–61, 71, 75, 108, 119, 124, 284, 427
Orléans, Grand Duchess Amélie, 398
Orléans, Prince Ferdinand-Philippe d', 419, 421
Orléans, Princess Adélaïde d', 119, 143, 398, 405, 408, 413, 417, 421–22, 429–30
Osmond, Marquis d', 389, 394
Ottoman empire, 180–81

Palais Royal, 59, 61, 75, 96, 101, 190, 217, 398, 405, 408, 411, 413
Palatinate of Bavaria, elector, 205
Palmerston, Lord, 416, 418–22
Palm Palace, 54 Schenkenstrasse, Vienna, 348–50, 366, 373
Panchaud, Isaac, 49, 51–52, 57–60, 127–28
Paris, 19
Parlement, 26
Parliament, 59, 106, 121
Pasquier, Étienne-Denis, 385, 393
Paul I of Russia, 204, 207
Penn, William, 136
Périgord, Adelbert de, 20
Perregaux, Frédéric, 52, 151–53, 168, 189
Phillips, Mrs. Susanna, 121, 123
Piccinni, Niccolò, 39
Pinckney, Charles, 171, 183
Piscatory, Theobald, 403
Pitt, William, 91, 105–06, 108, 126, 156, 168, 207, 242
Pius VI, Pope, 53, 101–02, 421
Pius VII, Pope, 199, 208–09, 213–14, 229–32, 258, 284, 391
Poix, Prince de, 429
Polignac, Armand de, 225

Polignac, Jules de, 405–07
Poniatowski, Prince Josef, 249, 421
Portalis, 215
Praslin, Duc de, 196
Pressburg treaty, 239
Prince of Wales, 108

Queen Charlotte, 121
Quélen, Monseigneur de, Archbishop of Paris, 425, 427–29

Radcliffe, Ann, 125
Razumovsky, Count Andreas, 363
Recamier, Mme de, 206
Reign of Terror, 135, 148, 217
Reims, 15, 29–30, 40
  diocese of, 33
  cathedral of Saint–Lazare, 13
  Archbishop of Reims, 13, 14, 29–30, 33, 105
Reinhard, Count Charles-Frederick, 145, 185, 426
Remusat, Comtesse Claire de, 257
Remusat, François-Marie-Charles de, 235
Retz, Cardinal de, 29
Réveillière, La, 160
Rewbell, Jean-François, 156, 160, 180
Rhenish-Palatinate, 104
Ricci, M. de, 142
Richelieu, Cardinal de, 29, 36, 59, 63, 201, 205, 343
Richelieu, Duc de, 389, 395
Riquette, 179
Robespierre, Maximilien, 27, 103, 135–36, 139, 150
Rochecotte, 403, 406, 418, 421, 424
Roederer, Antoine, 191, 194, 215–16
Roederer, Pierre-Louis, 187–88, 191–92
Rohan, Prince de, Cardinal Archbishop of Strasbourg, 55–56
Rosny, Château de, 283, 313, 318
Rousseau, Jean-Jacques, 22, 26, 43, 315
  Émile, 22
Roux-Laborie, 382, 389
Rovigo, Duc de, 298–99, 314, 321, 401–02
Royal Council, 48
Royal Garden, 67
Royal Military College of Brionne, 65
Royer-Collard, Pierre-Paul, 400, 403, 405, 421–22, 429

Sahib, Tipu, 108
Saint-Aulaire, Comte de, 429
Saint-Cloud, 101, 190, 192–93, 220, 226, 242, 254, 290, 301, 309–10, 403, 407–08
Saint-Denis in Reims, abbaye de, 36
Sainte-Agnes-hors-les-Murs, 63
Sainte-Foy, Radix de, 49, 78, 100, 108, 131, 151–52, 161, 164, 168, 206, 216
Saint-Eustache, 101
Saint-Germain-de-Pré, abbey of, 35
Saint James, court of, 93
Saint-Lazare, cathedral of, 13–14, 64

Saint-Méry, General Moreau de, 130, 222
Saint-Méry, Mme Moreau de, 130
Saint-Nicolas-du-Chardonnet, chapel of, 34
Saint-Rémy, Abbey de, 14, 34
Saint-Saveur, 62
Saint-Sulpice, 36, 42, 62, 100, 112
  church of, 21–22, 32
  consecrated, 33
  departure from, 33
  Grand Seminary of, 31
  seminary of, 30
Saint-Thierry, 40
  Abbey de, 51
Salieri, Antonio, 364
Salle des Menus Plaisirs, 59, 72–74, 77, 83–84
San Carlos, Duc de, 285, 297, 345, 397
Sandoz-Rollin, Wilhelm, 181
Sardinia, King of, 212, 371
Savary, General, 250
Scheffer, Ary, 416
Schuyler, General, 135–36, 139
Schwarzenberg, Prince, 309, 318, 323–24, 375
Sebastiani, General, 408, 416
Seiffert, M. André, 186
Sémonville, M. de, 110
Senate, 204, 226, 291, 294, 309, 324, 326–28, 337
Seven Years War, 51
Shelley, Lady, 270, 397
Sheridan, 107
Sidmouth, Henry Addington, 207
Sieyès, Abbé Emmanuel Joseph, 73, 155, 185–86, 188–89, 191, 193–94
Simons, Michel, 152, 193, 205, 210, 294
Smith, Colonel W. S., 134
Solitude d'Issy, 62
Sorbonne, 26, 31, 33, 36, 43, 60, 112
  Bachelor of Sacred Theology, 33
  Bishop of Paris, 43
  Faculty of Theology, 33
Souza-Botelho Mourão e Vasco cellos, José Maria de, 144, 395
Spina, Monseigneur, 202, 207
Spinola, Marquis Cristofero, 159–60, 168
Stadion, Count, 271
Staël, Germaine Necker, Mme de, 19, 88–89, 97, 102, 104, 109, 111, 118, 120–26, 128, 131, 136, 138–40, 145, 153–56, 160–62, 168, 173, 179, 184, 206–07, 218, 222, 423
Stanislaus-Augustus, King, 249, 277, 355
Sulpicien seminary, 65
Sutherland, Lady, 98
Suze, Chamillart de la, 26
  Château de La Suze in Maine, 27

Talleyrand, Alexander-François-Jacques, 23
Talleyrand, Alexandre-Angélique de, Monsignor, 13, 29–30, 33–35, 40–41, 43, 47, 51, 78, 86, 97, 105, 204, 306, 335, 379, 392
Talleyrand, Archambaud, 27–28, 44, 136, 149, 268, 279, 282, 330, 335, 419, 427, 430
Talleyrand, Boson, 27–28, 50, 126, 149, 222; son, Baron Alexander de Talleyrand-Périgord, 341
Talleyrand, Catherine de, see Grand, Catherine-Noël Worlée
Talleyrand, Charles-Daniel de, Comte de, 13, 21–22, 25–30, 34, 40–41, 45, 61–62, 215
Talleyrand, Charles-Maurice de
  American Philosophical Society, 130
  ancestry, 20–21, 24
  banking houses, Baring in London, 49, 189; Hope in Amsterdam, 49; Baring Bank, 52
  birthright, 28, 30, 44, 53, 82, 427
  career, army or the church, 28
  children, see Flahaut, Charles de; and Talleyrand, Charlotte
  Civil Constitution of the Clergy, 93–95, 99–101, 103, 427
  Club des Valois, 61
  club foot/crippled/handicap, 20, 22, 32, 40, 50, 53, 71, 75, 88, 123, 128, 132, 173, 211, 235, 244, 246
  Congress of Vienna, 19, 342, 345–76, 413–14
  Constituent Assembly, 103–05, 130
  Constitutional Church, founder of, 18, 98–99
  Constitutional Club, 60
  coronation of Louis XVI, 13, 15
  death, 19, 426–30
  dispensations, 33–34, 36, 41
  early life, 20, 22, 23–28, 37
  education, 26–27, 30–31, 33, 36–37, 41; "the Triumvirate" 37–38, 44, 51
  England, 105–07, 117–20, 124–26
  Executive Committee of the Department of Paris, 103
  Executive Council, 111–12, 114–15, 118
  Finance Ministry, 59
  foreign affairs minister, 147, 153, 159, 161–62, 164–69, 171–72, 174, 180–89, 193–96, 199–203, 207–15, 219–20, 223–26, 229–30, 233–45, 247–53, 306–07, 338–48, 381–85
  General Act of the Vienna Congress, 376–77
  general agent, 43–44, 47–49, 51–52, 56–58, 85
  General Assembly of the clergy, 35, 40, 43, 47
  General Estates, 70–80
  grand chamberlain, 227, 229–32, 234, 247, 254, 262–63, 275, 389–404, 429
  homes, château at Saint-Brice-la-Forêt, 300, 309, 313, 329; Château de la Tuilerie, 152; d'Anjou-Saint-Honoré, 196, 200, 211, 258; Hôtel de Guerchy, 37; Hôtel de Sarin, 63; Hôtel Matignon, 268–72, 275–77, 282–83, 287, 293–94, 298–99; townhouse of the Marquis d'Hervas, at 2, rue Saint-Florentin, 300, 312, 320, 323, 330, 333, 338, 341, 345–46
  illness, smallpox, 27
  income, 87; Abbey de Celles-en-Poitou, 62; as chaplain in his own diocese of Reims, 33, 40; foreign affairs minister, 163; Portugal's peace treaty, 163; Saint-Denis in Reims, abbaye de, 36
  Institut de France, 149, 153–54, 157, 167, 180; Napoleon's interest in, 175, 200
  Louis-Philippe I becomes King of the French, 411
  Louis XVI, services to, 102
  marriage to Catherine Grand, 215–16, 382
  Mémoires, 15, 17, 20, 23, 25–26, 45, 51, 55, 57, 78, 86, 99, 101, 113, 124, 143, 162, 165, 168, 172, 190, 225, 243, 253, 256, 266, 322, 336, 353, 371, 378, 408, 416, 427, 429
  Memoir on Commercial Relations of the United States with England, 153
  minister of the first consul, 66
  Monseigneur the Bishop of Autun, 20, 61, 63–66, 94–97, 113, 382; resigned, 99
  National Assembly, 18, 73, 81–82, 85–88
  National Constituent Assembly, 74, 82, 86, 92–93, 98, 103, 150
  ordained, 13; bishop, monseigneur, 62–63; chaplain, 33, 43; deacon, 43; priest, 45; subdeacon, 34
  order for his arrest, 120
  parents marriage, 21
  personal interests/social life/salons, 31, 38–40, 49–50, 55, 75–76, 79–81, 83, 88–89, 92, 96, 100, 107, 114, 119, 122–23, 130, 151–52, 156, 177–79, 190, 192, 197, 200, 206, 219–20, 258, 282, 286–88, 312–14, 318–19, 338
  personal library, book collection, 37, 75, 116–17, 124, 242, 268, 294, 395
  prince, 15
  Prince de Bénévent, 240, 342
  Prince de Talleyrand, 341
  Provisional Government, president of, 327–31, 333–38
  resignation, 420–21
  retirement, 421–23
  sale of Napoleon's letters to Austria, 395–96
  school reform, 103; Report on Public Education, 150
  the Charter, 329
  travel, 23, 29, 64, 106, 117, 126–40, 142, 245; Amsterdam, 145; Batavian Republic, 145; Brussels, 145; Chalais château in Périgord, 23–25; England, 117, 413–20; Hamburg, 144–45, 149; Paris, return to, 146;

United States, 126–42, 157; Vienna, 345; Warsaw, 244, 248–49
vice–grand elector, 254, 256–59, 261–67, 271–77, 289, 292–95, 297–303, 305–06, 309–15, 317–20, 322–29
XYZ affair, 183, 185, 198, 219
Talleyrand, Charlotte, Élisa Alix Sara, 186, 210–11, 220, 230, 234, 247, 255–56, 269, 282–83, 297–98, 302, 309, 341, 390
Talleyrand, Edmond de, 262, 267–68, 277–79, 283, 301, 310, 335, 347, 382–83, 390, 394, 396, 399
Talleyrand, Henri de, Comte de Chalais, 27
Talleyrand, Louis de, 247, 262
Talleyrand, Marie-Victoire-Éléonore de Damas d'Antigny, Comtesse de, 14, 21–22, 25–30, 40–41, 45, 86, 97, 149, 215, 222, 283
Tallien, Jean-Lambert, 67, 139
Tallien, Thérèse, Notre Dame de Thermidor, 139, 150
her home La Chaumière, 151, 169, 182, 201
Talma, Julie, 175
Talon, Omer, 131
Temple, 111
The Conservateur, 157
The National, 406–07
Thiers, Adolph, 19, 401, 405–08, 422, 424
Third French Republic, 19
Touche, Méhée de la, 112
Tour du Pin, Madame de la, Lucy, 134–36, 139, 158, 167, 310–11

Tour du Pin, Monsieur de la, 134–36, 139, 344
Tour-et-Taxis, Princess de, 263, 265
Tours, Archbishop of, 43
Trauttmansdorff, Prince, 373
Treaty of Paris, 340, 342, 351, 353, 355
new Treaty of Paris, 389
Treaty of 24 Articles, 417
Treilhard, Jean Baptiste, 83
Tuileries, 18, 84, 87, 102, 109–12, 114, 120, 151, 169, 190, 198, 200, 208, 212–13, 217, 219, 232–33, 254–55, 257, 261, 270, 283, 285–86, 288, 291, 295–96, 300, 303, 307, 312, 323, 333, 372, 386, 392–95, 397, 401–02, 407–08, 413, 417
Turgot, 92
Tyszkiewicz, Countess Marie-Thérèse, 249, 286–87, 290, 301–02, 325, 386, 390, 392, 396, 421, 430

Valençay, 221–22, 259–61, 268–70, 294, 300, 345, 390, 392, 396, 399–401, 418, 420–22, 430
Valence, General de, 115
Valence, Mme de, 115, 154
Valois, Marguerite de, 62
Van der Goes, 217
Varennes, 102
Variétés, 92
Vatican, 20, 41, 83, 93, 97, 99, 199, 202, 209, 214–15, 229–30, 284
Vatican states, 207
Vaudémont, Princess de, 272, 387, 413, 417, 419
Versailles, 21–23, 25, 36, 38, 49–50, 54–55, 59, 67, 74–77, 81, 84, 86, 95, 109, 156, 284, 307
Hall of Mirrors, 56
Salle des Menus Plaisirs, 69, 73, 81
Salon d'Hercule, 69
Vigée-Le Brun, Mme, 50, 54, 119, 159–60, 270
Villèle, Comte de, 399, 404
Villette, Marquise Reine-Philibert de, 172
Vitrolles, Baron de, 316–19
Voltaire, 41–43, 60, 83, 166, 172, 205, 396
Irène, 41
Oedipe, 265
Tancrède, 32
Volunteer Polish Corps, 249

Walewska, Countess Marie de, 246, 249, 287
Walkiers, Vicomte Edouard de, 248
War of 1812, end of, 361
Washington, President George, 35, 67, 85, 92, 127, 129, 171
Waterloo, 377–79, 418
Wellesley, Duke of Wellington, 260, 302, 317, 323, 328, 337–38, 340, 367–68, 370–71, 373, 377, 379–81, 383, 385, 395, 413–16, 422
White Terror, 381
Whitworth, Sir Charles, 219
William IV, 414
Wurtemberg, Catherine de, 255
Wycombe, Lord, 98, 103, 107, 116, 118, 125, 144

*This book was designed
with care by*

Mary Susan Oleson
NASHVILLE, TENNESSEE